Intelligence Activities and the Rights of Americans
1976 US Senate Report on Illegal Wiretaps and Domestic Spying by the FBI, CIA and NSA

Church Committee (US Senate Select Committee on Intelligence Activities Within the United States)

Red and Black Publishers, St Petersburg, Florida   2007

Publishers Cataloging in Publication Data –

Church Committee (US Senate Select Committee on Intelligence Activities Within the United States)
Intelligence Activities and the rights of Americans: 1976 US Senate Report on Illegal Wiretaps and Domestic Spying by the FBI, CIA and NSA/ Church Committee (US Senate Select Committee on Intelligence Activities Within the United States)
p. cm.

ISBN: XXXXXXXXXXXXXXXXXXXXXXXXXXXXXX
1. United States – Central Intelligence Agency. 2. United States – Federal Bureau of Investigation. 3. United States – National Security Agency.
I. Title
KF31.5 .G7 2007
364.1   LCCN: XXXXXXXXXXXX

Red and Black Publishers, PO Box 7542, St Petersburg, Florida, 33734
Contact us at: info@RedandBlackPublishers.com

Printed and manufactured in the United States of America

Preface to Red and Black Edition

It is almost a cliché to say that "those who cannot remember the past, are condemned to repeat it". Yet, in the history of the United States, we continuously blunder into the same mistakes, over and over again. Gore Vidal once famously called us the "United States of Amnesia". Americans never learn from our history because we don't *have* any history. America's collective memory has the lifespan of a fruit fly.

When it was first revealed that the George W Bush administration had implemented a secret program of warrantless wiretaps and domestic spying on US citizens, including infiltration of antiwar groups, few Americans knew that all of this had happened before, repeatedly. Indeed, the United States has a long history of restricting civil rights during periods of political and military crisis.

In the early 1970's, in the wake of the Watergate scandal, it was revealed that United States government agencies, including the FBI, CIA, NSA and IRS, were being used as part of a deliberate plan to infiltrate and disrupt political opponents, that this plan had continued for 20 years under four different Presidents, both Democratic and Republican, and that it included illegal wiretaps, mail interception, and "dirty tricks". The Senate Select Committee on Intelligence Activities Within the United States, chaired by Idaho Senator Frank Church, was formed to investigate. This is the Church Committee's report.

Among their discoveries: the US government had engaged in several conspiracies to assassinate foreign leaders that it didn't like, including a partnership with the Mafia to attempt to kill Cuban President Fidel Castro; the CIA had illegally tested several mind-altering chemicals on unsuspecting American citizens; the FBI and US military had carried out a systematic program called COINTELPRO to infiltrate and disrupt political dissent, including Martin Luther King, Cesar Chavez, and opponents of the Vietnam War; the FBI had carried out illegal burglaries ("black bag jobs") in an effort to obtain information on dissidents and other political targets, and the CIA, FBI and NSA had all illegally tapped the phones and intercepted the mail of targeted individuals and organizations.

As a result of this investigation, a number of legal changes were made. Laws were passed making it illegal for US intelligence agencies to attempt to kill foreign leaders. And Congress passed the Foreign Intelligence Surveillance Act (FISA), which made it illegal to carry out any wiretap or mail interception without a court order from a special "FISA Court" that was specifically set up for the purpose.

In the wake of the 9-11 attacks, however, President George W Bush ordered the National Security Agency to begin a series of warrantless wiretaps on Americans without a court order. Bush's justification, ironically, was the same one used by President Nixon to defend himself against the Church Committee – the President, he argued, has the inherent authority to ignore American laws in the name of "national security". "When the President of the United States does it," Nixon declared, "it's not illegal".

Thirty years after Nixon, Bush not only began warrantless wiretaps by the NSA, but also introduced a policy of suspending habeus corpus rights for certain people, and imprisoning those people indefinitely, without charges, based on "secret evidence" obtained through torture. There have also been reports of antiwar groups and other political opponents of the Bush Administration being infiltrated by Federal law enforcement officers.

The entire secret history of the Bush Administration's curtailment of civil liberties will probably not be written for several years. But when it is, there is a high likelihood that it will look a lot like the Church Committee Report.

Editor, Red and Black Publishers
January 2008

Contents

Supplementary Reports On Intelligence Activities And The Rights Of Americans

I. Introduction And Summary

The resolution creating this Committee placed greatest emphasis on whether intelligence activities threaten the "rights of American citizens."

The critical question before the Committee was to determine how the fundamental liberties of the people can be maintained in the course of the Government's effort to protect their security. The delicate balance between these basic goals of our system of government is often difficult to strike, but it can, and must, be achieved. We reject the view that the traditional American principles of justice and fair play have no place in our struggle against the enemies of freedom. Moreover, our investigation has established that the targets of intelligence activity have ranged far beyond persons who could properly be characterized as enemies of freedom and have extended to a wide array of citizens engaging in lawful activity.

Americans have rightfully been concerned since before World War II about the dangers of hostile foreign agents likely to commit acts of espionage. Similarly, the violent acts of political terrorists can seriously endanger the rights of Americans. Carefully focused intelligence investigations can help prevent such acts. But too often intelligence has lost this focus and domestic intelligence activities have invaded individual privacy and violated the rights of lawful assembly and political expression. Unless new and tighter controls are established by legislation, domestic intelligence activities threaten to undermine our democratic society and fundamentally alter its nature.

We have examined three types of "intelligence" activities affecting the rights of American citizens. The first is intelligence collection—such as infiltrating groups with informants, wiretapping, or opening letters. The second is dissemination of material which has been collected. The third is covert action designed to disrupt and discredit the activities of groups and individuals deemed a threat to the social order. These three types of "intelligence" activity are closely related in the practical world. Information which is disseminated by the intelligence community or used in disruptive programs has usually been obtained through surveillance. Nevertheless, a division between collection, dissemination and covert action is analytically useful both in understanding why excesses have occurred in the past and in devising remedies to prevent those excesses from recurring.

A. Intelligence Activity: A New Form of Governmental Power to Impair Citizens' Rights

A tension between order and liberty is inevitable in any society. A Government must protect its citizens from those bent on engaging in violence and criminal behavior, or in espionage and other hostile foreign intelligence activity. Many of the intelligence programs reviewed in this report were established for those purposes. Intelligence work has, at times, successfully prevented dangerous and abhorrent acts, such as bombings and foreign spying, and aided in the prosecution of those responsible for such acts.

But, intelligence activity in the past decades has, all too often, exceeded the restraints on the exercise of governmental power which are imposed by our country's Constitution, laws, and traditions.

Excesses in the name of protecting security are not a recent development in our nation's history. In 1798, for example, shortly after the Bill of Rights was added to the Constitution, the Allen and Sedition Acts were passed. These Acts, passed in response to fear of proFrench "subversion", made it a crime to criticize the Government. During the Civil War, President Abraham Lincoln suspended the writ of habeas corpus. Hundreds of American citizens were prosecuted for anti-war statements during World War I, and thousands of "radical" aliens were seized for deportation during the 1920 Palmer Raids. During the Second World War, over the opposition of J. Edgar Hoover and military intelligence, 120,000 Japanese-Americans were apprehended and incarcerated in detention camps.

Those actions, however, were fundamentally different from the intelligence activities examined by this Committee. They were generally executed overtly under the authority of a statute or a public executive order. The victims knew what was being done to them and could challenge the Government in the courts and other forums. Intelligence activity, on the other hand, is generally covert. It is concealed from its victims and is seldom described in statutes or explicit executive orders. The victim may never suspect that his misfortunes are the intended result of activities undertaken by his government, and accordingly may have no opportunity to challenge the actions taken against him.

It is, of course, proper in many circumstances — such as developing a criminal prosecution — for the Government to gather information about a citizen and use it to achieve legitimate ends, some of which might be detrimental to the citizen. But in criminal prosecutions, the courts have struck a balance between protecting the rights of the accused citizen and protecting the society which suffers the consequences of crime. Essential to the balancing process are the rules of criminal law which circumscribe the techniques for gathering evidence 6 the kinds of evidence that may be collected, and the uses to which that evidence may be put. In addition, the criminal defendant is given an opportunity to discover and then challenge the legality of how the Government collected information about him and the use which the Government intends to make of that information.

This Committee has examined a realm of governmental information collection which has not been governed by restraints comparable to those in criminal proceedings. We have examined the collection of intelligence about the political advocacy and actions and the private lives of American citizens. That information has been used covertly to discredit the ideas advocated and to "neutralize" the actions of their proponents. As Attorney General Harlan Fiske Stone warned in 1924, when he sought to keep federal agencies from investigating "political or other opinions" as opposed to "conduct . . . forbidden by the laws":

> When a police system passes beyond these limits, it is dangerous to the proper administration of justice and to human liberty, which it should be our first concern to cherish.

> There is always a possibility that a secret police may become a menace to free government and free institutions because it carries with it the possibility of abuses of power which are not always quickly apprehended or understood.

Our investigation has confirmed that warning. We have seen segments of our Government, in their attitudes and action, adopt tactics unworthy of a democracy, and occasionally reminiscent of the tactics of totalitarian regimes. We have seen a consistent pattern in which programs initiated with limited goals, such as preventing criminal violence or identifying foreign spies, were expanded to what witnesses characterized as "vacuum cleaners"," sweeping in information about lawful activities of American citizens.

The tendency of intelligence activities to expand beyond their initial scope is a theme which runs through every aspect of our investigative findings. Intelligence collection programs naturally generate ever-increasing demands for new data. And once intelligence has been collected, there are strong pressures to use it against the target.

The pattern of intelligence agencies expanding the scope of their activities was well described by one witness, who in 1970 had coordinated an effort by most of the intelligence community to obtain authority to undertake more illegal domestic activity:

> The risk was that you would get people who would be susceptible to political considerations as opposed to national security considerations, or would construe political considerations to be national security considerations, to move from the, kid with a bomb to the kid with a picket sign, and from the kid with the picket sign to the kid with the bumper sticker of the opposing candidate. And you just keep going down the line.

In 1940, Attorney General Robert Jackson saw the same risk. He recognized that using broad labels like "national security" or "subversion" to invoke the vast power of the government is dangerous because there are "no definite standards to determine what constitutes a 'subversive activity, such as we have for murder or larceny." Jackson added:

> Activities which seem benevolent or helpful to wage earners, persons on relief, or those who are disadvantaged in the struggle for existence may be regarded as 'subversive' by those whose property interests might be burdened thereby. Those who are in office are apt to regard as 'subversive'

the activities of any of those who would bring about a change of administration. Some of our soundest constitutional doctrines were once punished as subversive. We must not forget that it was not so long ago that both the term 'Republican' and the term 'Democrat' were epithets with sinister meaning to denote persons of radical tendencies that were 'subversive' of the order of things then dominant.

This wise warning was not heeded in the conduct of intelligence activity, where the "eternal vigilance" which is the "price of liberty" has been forgotten.

B. The Questions
We have directed our investigation toward answering the, following questions:
Which governmental agencies have engaged in domestic spying?
How many citizens have been targets of Governmental intelligence activity?
What standards have governed the opening of intelligence investigations and when have intelligence investigations been terminated?
Where have the targets fit on the spectrum between those who commit violent criminal acts and those who seek only to dissent peacefully from Government policy?
To what extent has the information collected included intimate details of the targets' personal lives or their political views, and has such information been disseminated and used to injure individuals?
What actions beyond surveillance have intelligence agencies taken, such as attempting to disrupt, discredit, or destroy persons or groups who have been the targets of surveillance?
Have intelligence agencies been used to serve the political aims of Presidents, other high officials, or the agencies themselves?
How have the agencies responded either to proper orders or to excessive pressures from their superiors? To what extent have intelligence agencies disclosed, or concealed them from, outside bodies charged with overseeing them?
Have intelligence agencies acted outside the law? What has been the attitude of the intelligence community toward the rule of law?
To what extent has the Executive branch and the Congress controlled intelligence agencies and held them accountable?
Generally, how well has the Federal system of checks and balances between the branches worked to control intelligence activity?

C. Summary of the Main Problems
The answer to each of these questions is disturbing. Too many people have been spied upon by too many Government agencies and to much information has been collected. The Government has often undertaken the secret surveillance of citizens on the basis of their political beliefs, even when those beliefs posed no threat of violence or illegal acts on behalf of a hostile foreign power. The Government, operating primarily through secret informants, but also using other intrusive techniques such as wiretaps, microphone "bugs", surreptitious mail opening, and break-ins, has swept in vast amounts of information about the personal lives, views, and associations of American citizens. Investigations of groups deemed potentially dangerous — and even of groups suspected of associating with potentially dangerous organizations — have continued for decades, despite the fact that those groups did not engage in unlawful activity. Groups and individuals have been harassed and disrupted because of their

political views and their lifestyles. Investigations have been based upon vague standards whose breadth made excessive collection inevitable. Unsavory and vicious tactics have been employed—including anonymous attempts to break up marriages, disrupt meetings, ostracize persons from their professions, and provoke target groups into rivalries that might result in deaths. Intelligence agencies have served the political and personal objectives of presidents and other high officials. While the agencies often committed excesses in response to pressure from high officials in the Executive branch and Congress, they also occasionally initiated improper activities and then concealed them from officials whom they had a duty to inform.

Governmental officials—including those whose principal duty is to enforce the law—have violated or ignored the law over long periods of time and have advocated and defended their right to break the law.

The Constitutional system of checks and balances has not adequately controlled intelligence activities. Until recently the Executive branch has neither delineated the scope of permissible activities nor established procedures for supervising intelligence agencies. Congress has failed to exercise sufficient oversight, seldom questioning the use to which its apropriations were being put. Most domestic intelligence issues have not reached the courts, and in those cases when they have reached the courts, the judiciary has been reluctant to grapple with them.

Each of these points is briefly illustrated below, and covered in substantially greater detail in the following sections of the report.

1. The Number of People Affected by Domestic Intelligence Activity

United States intelligence agencies have investigated a vast number of American citizens and domestic organizations. FBI headquarters alone has developed over 500,000 domestic intelligence files, and these have been augmented by additional files at FBI Field Offices. The FBI opened 65,000 of these domestic intelligence files in 1972 alone. In fact, substantially more individuals and groups are subject to intelligence scrutiny than the number of files would appear to indicate, since typically, each domestic intelligence file contains information on more than one individual or group, and this information is readily retrievable through the FBI General Name Index.

The number of Americans and domestic groups caught in the domestic intelligence net is further illustrated by the following statistics:

-- Nearly a quarter of a million first class letters were opened and photographed in the United States by the CIA between 1953-1973, producing a CIA computerized index of nearly one and one-half million names.

-- At least 130,000 first class letters were opened and photographed by the FBI between 1940-1966 in eight U.S. cities.

-- Some 300,000 individuals were indexed in a CIA computer system and separate files were created on approximately 7,200 Americans and over 100 domestic groups during the course of CIA's Operation CHAOS (1967-1973).

-- Millions of private telegrams sent from, to, or through the United States were obtained by the National Security Agency from 1947 to 1975 under a secret arrangement with three United States telegraph companies.

-- An estimated 100,000 Americans were the subjects of United States Army intelligence files created between the mid 1960's and 1971.

-- Intelligence files on more than 11,000 individuals and groups were created by the Internal Revenue Service between 1969 and 1973 and tax investigations were started on the basis of political rather than tax criteria.

-- At least 26,000 individuals were at one point catalogued on an FBI list of persons to be rounded up in the event of a "national emergency".

2. Too Much Information Is Collected For Too Long

Intelligence agencies have collected vast amounts of information about the intimate details of citizens' lives and about their participation in legal and peaceful political activities. The targets of intelligence activity have included political adherents of the right and the left, ranging from activitist to casual supporters. Investigations have been directed against proponents of racial causes and women's rights, outspoken apostles of nonviolence and racial harmony; establishment politicians; religious groups; and advocates of new life styles. The widespread targeting of citizens and domestic groups, and the excessive scope of the collection of information, is illustrated by the following examples:

(a) The "Women's Liberation Movement" was infiltrated by informants who collected material about the movement's policies, leaders, and individual members. One report included the name of every woman who attended meetings, and another stated that each woman at a meeting bad described "how she felt oppressed, sexually or otherwise". Another report concluded that the movement's purpose was to "free women from the humdrum existence of being only a wife and mother", but still recommended that the intelligence investigation should be continued.

(b) A prominent civil rights leader and advisor to Dr. Martin Luther King, Jr., was investigated on the suspicion that he might be a Communist " sympathizer". The FBI field office concluded he was not. Bureau headquarters directed that the investigation continue using a theory of "guilty until proven innocent:"

> The Bureau does not agree with the expressed belief of the field office that - - - - - - - - - - - - - - - - - is not sympathetic to the Party cause. While there may not be any evidence that - - - - - - - - - - - - - - - - - is a Communist neither is there any substantial evidence that he is anti-Communist.

(c.) FBI sources reported on the formation of the Conservative American Christian Action Council in 1971. In the 1950's, the Bureau collected information about the John Birch Society and passed it to the White House because of the Society's "scurrillous attack" on President Eisenhower and other high Government officials.

(d) Some investigations of the lawful activities of peaceful groups have continued for decades. For example, the NAACP was investigated to determine whether it "had connections with" the Communist Party. The investigation lasted for over twenty-five years, although nothing was found to rebut a report during the first year of the investigation that the NAACP had a "strong tendency" to "steer clear of Communist activities." Similarly, the FBI has admitted that the Socialist Workers Party has committed no criminal acts. Yet the Bureau has investigated the Socialist Workers Party for more than three decades on the basis of its revolutionary rhetoric- which the FBI concedes falls short of incitement to violence-and its claimed international links. The Bureau is currently using its informants to collect information about SWP members' political views, including those on "U.S. involvement in Angola," "food prices," "racial matters," the "Vietnam War," and about any of their efforts to support non-SWP candidates for political office.

(e) National political leaders fell within the broad reach of intelligence investigations. For example, Army Intelligence maintained files on Senator Adlai

Stevenson and Congressman Abner Mikva because of their participation in peaceful political meetings under surveillance by Army agents. A letter to Richard Nixon, while he was a candidate for President in 1968, was intercepted under CIA's mail opening program. In the 1960's President Johnson asked the FBI to compare various Senators' statements on Vietnam with the Communist Party line and to conduct name checks on leading antiwar Senators.

(f) As part of their effort to collect information which "related even remotely" to people or groups "active" in communities which had "the potential" for civil disorder, Army intelligence agencies took such steps as: sending agents to a Halloween party for elementary school children in Washington, D.C., because they suspected a local "dissident" might be present; monitoring protests of welfare mothers' organizations in Milwaukee; infiltrating a coalition of church youth groups in Colorado; and sending agents to a priests' conference in Washington, D.C., held to discuss birth control measures.

(g) In the, late 1960's and early 1970s, student groups were subjected to intense scrutiny. In 1970 the FBI ordered investigations of every member of the Students for a Democratic Society and of "every Black Student Union and similar group regardless of their past or present involvement in disorders." Files were opened on thousands of young men and women so that, as the former head of FBI intelligence explained , the information could be used if they ever applied for a government job.

In the 1960's Bureau agents were instructed to increase their efforts to discredit "New Left" student demonstrators by tactics including publishing photographs ("naturally the most obnoxious picture should be used"), using "misinformation" to falsely notify members events had been cancelled and writing "tell-tale" letters to students' parents.

(h) The FBI Intelligence Division commonly investigated any indication that "subversive" groups already under investigation were seeking to influence or control other groups. One example of the extreme breadth of this "infiltration" theory was an FBI instruction in the mid-1960's to all Field Offices to investigate every "free university" because some of them had come under "subversive influence. "

(i) Each administration from Franklin D. Roosevelt's to Richard Nixon's permitted, and sometimes encouraged, government agencies to handle essentially political intelligence. For example:

-- President Roosevelt asked the FBI to put in its files the names of citizens sending telegrams to the White House opposing his "national defense" policy and supporting Col. Charles Lindbergh.

-- President Truman received inside information on a former Roosevelt aide's efforts to influence his appointments, labor union negotiating plans, 44 and the publishing plans of journalists.

-- President Eisenhower received reports on purely political and social contacts with foreign officials by Bernard Baruch, Mrs. Eleanor Roosevelt, and Supreme Court Justice William 0. Douglas.

-- The Kennedy Administration had the FBI wiretap a Congressional staff member , 48 three executive officials, a lobbyist, and a, Washington law firm. Attorney General Robert F. Kennedy received the fruits of a FBI "tap" on Martin Luther King, Jr. and a "bug" on a Congressman both of which yielded information of a political nature.

-- President Johnson asked the FBI to conduct "name checks" of his critics and of members of the staff of his 1964 opponent, Senator Barry Goldwater. He also requested purely political intelligence on his critics in the Senate, and received extensive intelligence reports on political activity at the 1964 Democratic Convention from FBI electronic surveillance.

-- President Nixon authorized a program of wiretaps which produced for the White House purely political or personal information unrelated to national security, including information about a Supreme Court justice.

3. Covert Action and the Use of Illegal or Improper Means

(a) Covert Action.—Apart from uncovering excesses in the collection of intelligence, our investigation has disclosed covert actions directed against Americans, and the use of illegal and improper surveillance techniques to gather information. For example:

(i) The FBI's COINTELPRO—counterintelligence program—was designed to "disrupt" groups and "neutralize" individuals deemed to be threats to domestic security. The FBI resorted to counterintelligence tactics in part because its chief officials believed that the existing law could not control the activities of certain dissident groups, and that court decisions had tied the hands of the intelligence community. Whatever opinion one holds about the policies of the targeted groups, many of the tactics employed by the FBI were indisputably degrading to a free society. COINTELPRO tactics included:

-- Anonymously attacking the political beliefs of targets in order to induce their employers to fire them;

-- Anonymously mailing letters to the spouses of intelligence targets for the purpose of destroying their marriages;

-- Obtaining from IRS the tax returns of a target and then attempting to provoke an IRS investigation for the express purpose of deterring a protest leader from attending the Democratic National Convention;

-- Falsely and anonymously labeling as Government informants members of groups known to be violent, thereby exposing the falsely labelled member to expulsion or physical attack;

-- Pursuant to instructions to use "misinformation" to disrupt demonstrations, employing such means as broadcasting fake orders on the same citizens band radio frequency used by demonstration marshalls to attempt to control demonstrations, 60 and duplicating and falsely filling out forms soliciting housing for persons coming to a demonstration, thereby causing "long and useless journeys to locate these addresses";

-- Sending an anonymous letter to the leader of a Chicago street gang (described as "violence-prone") stating that the Black Panthers were supposed to have "a hit out for you". The letter was suggested because it "may intensify . . . animosity" and cause the street gang leader to "take retaliatory action".

(ii) From "late 1963" until his death in 1968, Martin Luther King, Jr., was the target of an intensive campaign by the Federal Bureau of Investigation to "neutralize" him as an effective civil rights leader. In the words of the man in charge of the FBI's "war" against Dr. King, "No holds were barred."

The FBI gathered information about Dr. King's plans and activities through an extensive surveillance program, employing nearly every intelligence-gathering technique at the Bureau's disposal in order to obtain information about the "private activities of Dr. King and his advisors" to use to "completely discredit" them.

The program to destroy Dr. King as the leader of the civil rights movement included efforts to discredit him with Executive branch officials, Congressional leaders, foreign heads of state, American ambassadors, churches. universities, and the press.

The FBI mailed Dr. King a tape recording made from microphones hidden in his hotel rooms which one agent testified was an attempt to destroy Dr. King's marriage. The tape recording was accompanied by a note which Dr. King and his advisors interpreted as threatening to release the tape recording unless Dr. King committed suicide.

The extraordinary nature of the campaign to discredit Dr. King is evident from two documents:

-- At the August 1963 March on Washington, Dr. King told the country of his "dream" that:

> all of God's children, black men and white men, Jews and Gentiles, Protestants and Catholics, will be able to join hands and sing in the words of the old Negro spiritual, "Free at last, free at last, thank God Almighty, I'm free at last."

The Bureau's Domestic Intelligence Division concluded that this "demagogic speech" established Dr. King as the "most dangerous and effective Negro leader in the country." Shortly afterwards, and within days after Dr. King was named "Man of the Year" by Time magazine, the FBI decided to "take him off his pedestal," reduce him completely in influence," and select and promote its own candidate to "assume the role of the leadership of the Negro people."

-- In early 1968, Bureau headquarters explained to the field that Dr. King must be destroyed because he was seen as a potential "messiah" who could "unify and electrify" the "black nationalist movement". Indeed, to the FBI he was a potential threat because he might "abandon his supposed 'obedience' to white liberal doctrines (non-violence)." In short, a non-violent man was to be secretly attacked and destroyed as insurance against his abandoning non-violence.

(b) Illegal or Improper Means — The surveillance which we investigated was not only vastly excessive in breadth and a basis for degrading counterintelligence actions, but was also often conducted by illegal or improper means. For example:

(1) For approximately 20 years the CIA carried out a program of indiscriminately opening citizens' first class mail. The Bureau also had a mail opening program, but cancelled it in 1966. The Bureau continued, however, to receive the illegal fruits of CIA's program. In 1970, the heads of both agencies signed a document for President Nixon, which correctly stated that mail opening was illegal, falsely stated that it had been discontinued, and proposed that the illegal opening of mail should be resumed because it would provide useful results. The President approved the program, but withdrew his approval five days later. The illegal opening continued nonetheless. Throughout this period CIA officials knew that mail opening was illegal, but expressed concern about the "flap potential" of exposure, not about the illegality of their activity.

(2) From 1947 until May 1975, NSA received from international cable companies millions of cables which had been sent by American citizens in the reasonable expectation that they would be kept private.

(3) Since the early 1930's, intelligence agencies have frequently wiretapped and bugged American citizens without the benefit of judicial warrant. Recent court decisions have curtailed the use of these techniques against domestic targets. But past subjects of these surveillances have included a United States Congressman, a Congressional staff member, journalists and newsmen, and numerous individuals and groups who engaged in no criminal activity and who posed no genuine threat to the national security, such as two White House domestic affairs advisers and an anti Vietnam War protest group. While the prior written approval of the Attorney General has been required for all warrantless wiretaps since 1940, the record is replete with instances where this requirement was ignored and the Attorney General gave only after-the-fact authorization.

Until 1965, microphone surveillance by intelligence agencies was wholly unregulated in certain classes of cases. Within weeks after a 1954 Supreme Court decision denouncing the FBI's installation of a microphone in a defendant's bedroom, the Attorney General informed the Bureau that he did not believe the decision applied to national security cases and permitted the FBI to continue to install microphones subject only to its own "intelligent restraint".

(4) In several cases, purely political information (such as the reaction of Congress to an Administration's legislative proposal) and purely personal information (such as coverage of the extra-marital social activities of a high-level Executive official under surveillance) was obtained from electronic surveillance and disseminated to the highest levels of the federal government.

(5) Warrantless break-ins have been conducted by intelligence agencies since World War II. During the 1960's alone, the FBI and CIA conducted hundreds of break-ins, many against American citizens and domestic organizations. In some cases, these break-ins were to install microphones; in other cases, they were to steal such items as membership lists from organizations considered "subversive" by the Bureau.

(6) The most pervasive surveillance technique has been the informant. In a random sample of domestic intelligence cases, 83% involved informants and 5% involved electronic surveillance. Informants have been used against peaceful, law-abiding groups; they have collected information about personal and political views and activities. To maintain their credentials in violence-prone groups, informants have involved themselves in violent activity. This phenomenon is well illustrated by an informant in the Klan. He was present at the murder of a civil rights worker in Mississippi and subsequently helped to solve the crime and convict the perpetrators. Earlier, however, while performing duties paid for by the Government, he had previously "beaten people severely, had boarded buses and kicked people, had [gone] into restaurants and beaten them [blacks] with blackjacks, chains, pistols." Although the FBI requires agents to instruct informants that they cannot be involved in violence, it was understood that in the Klan, "he couldn't be an angel and be a good informant."

4. Ignoring the Law

Officials of the intelligence agencies occasionally recognized that certain activities were illegal, but expressed concern only for "flap Potential." Even more disturbing was the frequent testimony that the law, and the Constitution were simply ignored. For example, the author of the so-called Huston plan testified:

Question. Was there any person who stated that the activity recommended, which you have previously identified as being illegal opening of the mail and breaking and entry or burglary—was there any single person who stated that such activity should not be done because it was unconstitutional?

Answer. No.

Question. Was there any single person who said such activity should not be done because it was illegal?

Answer. No.

Similarly, the man who for ten years headed FBI's Intelligence Division testifed that:

> ... never once did I hear anybody, including myself, raise the question: "Is this course of action which we have agreed upon lawful, is it legal, is it ethical or moral." We never gave any thought to this line of reasoning, because we were just naturally pragmatic.

Although the statutory law and the Constitution were often not "[given] a thought", there was a general attitude that intelligence needs were responsive to a higher law. Thus, as one witness testified in justifying the FBI's mail opening program:

> It was my assumption that what we were doing was justified by what we had to do . . . the greater good, the national security.

5. Deficiencies in Accountability and Control

The overwhelming number of excesses continuing over a prolonged period of time were due in large measure to the fact that the system of checks and balances—created in our Constitution to limit abuse of Governmental power—was seldom applied to the intelligence community. Guidance and regulation from outside the intelligence agencies—where it has been imposed at all—has been vague. Presidents and other senior Executive officials, particularly the Attorneys General, have virtually abdicated their Constitutional responsibility to oversee and set standards for intelligence activity. Senior government officials generally gave the agencies broad, general mandates or pressed for immediate results on pressing problems. In neither case did they provide guidance to prevent excesses and their broad mandates and pressures themselves often resulted in excessive or improper intelligence activity.

Congress has often declined to exercise meaningful oversight, and on occasion has passed laws or made statements which were taken by intelligence agencies as supporting overly-broad investigations.

On the other hand, the record reveals instances when intelligence agencies have concealed improper activities from their superiors in the Executive branch and from the Congress, or have elected to disclose only the less questionable aspects of their activities.

There has been, in short, a, clear and sustained failure by those responsible to control the intelligence community and to ensure its accountability. There has been an equally clear and sustained failure by intelligence agencies to fully inform the proper authorities of their activities and to comply with directives from those authorities.

6. The Adverse Impact of Improper Intelligence Activity

Many of the illegal or improper disruptive efforts directed against American citizens and domestic organizations succeeded in injuring their targets. Although it is sometimes difficult to prove that a target's misfortunes were caused by a counter-intelligence program directed against him, the possibility that an arm of the Untied States Government intended to cause the harm and might have been responsible is itself abhorrent.

The Committee has observed numerous examples of the impact of intelligence operations. Sometimes the harm was readily apparent—destruction of marriages, loss of friends or jobs. Sometimes the attitudes of the public and of Government officials responsible for formulating policy and resolving vital issues were influenced by distorted intelligence. But the most basic harm was to the values of privacy and freedom which our Constitution seeks to protect and which intelligence activity infringed on a broad scale.

(a) General Efforts to Discredit.—Several efforts against individuals and groups appear to have achieved their stated aims. For example:

-- A Bureau Field Office reported that the anonymous letter it had sent to an activist's husband accusing his wife of infidelity "contributed very strongly" to the subsequent breakup of the marriage.

-- Another Field Office reported that a draft counsellor deliberately, and falsely, accused of being an FBI informant was "ostracized" by his friends and associates.

-- Two instructors were reportedly put on probation after the Bureau sent an anonymous letter to a university administrator about their funding of an anti-administration student newspaper.

-- The Bureau evaluated its attempts to "put a stop" to a contribution to the Southern Christian Leadership Conference as "quite successful."

-- An FBI document boasted that a "pretext" phone call to Stokeley Carmichael's mother telling her that members of the Black Panther Party intended to kill her son left her "shocked". The memorandum intimated that the Bureau believed it had been responsible for Carmichael's flight to Africa the following day.

(b) Media Manipulation—The FBI has attempted covertly to influence the public's perception of persons and organizations by dissemminating derogatory information to the press, either anonymously or through "friendly" news contacts. The impact of those articles is generally difficult to measure, although in some cases there are fairly direct connections to injury to the target. The Bureau also attempted to influence media reporting which would have any impact on the public image of the FBI. Examples include:

-- Planting a series of derogatory articles about Martin Luther King, Jr., and the Poor People's Campaign.

For example, in anticipation of the 1968 "poor people's march on Washington, D.C.," Bureau Headquarters granted authority to furnish "cooperative news media sources" an article "designed to curtail success of Martin Luther King's fund raising."

Another memorandum illustrated how "photographs of demonstrators" could be used in discrediting the civil rights movement. Six photographs of participants in the poor people's campaign in Cleveland accompanied the memorandum with the following note attached: "These [photographs] show the militant aggressive appearance of the participants and might be of interest to a cooperative news source." Information on the Poor People's Campaign was provided by the FBI to friendly reporters on the condition that "the Bureau must not be revealed as the source."

-- Soliciting information from Field Offices "on a continuing basis" for "prompt . . . dissemination to the news media . . . to discredit the New Left movement and its adherents." The Headquarters directive requested, among other things, that:

> specific data should be furnished depicting the scurrilous and depraved nature, of many of the characters, activities, habits, and living conditions representative of New Left adherents. Field Offices were to be exhorted that: "Every avenue of possible embarrassment must be vigorously and enthusiastically explored."

-- Ordering Field Offices to gather information which would disprove allegations by the "liberal press, the bleeding hearts, and the forces on the left" that the Chicago police used undue force in dealing with demonstrators at the 1968 Democratic Convention.

-- Taking advantage of a close relationship with the Chairman of the Board— described in an FBI memorandum as "our good friend"—of a magazine with national circulation to influence articles which related to the FBI. For example, through this relationship the Bureau: "squelched" an "unfavorable article against the Bureau" written by a free-lance writer about an FBI investigation; "postponed publication" of an article on another FBI case; "forestalled publication" of an article by Dr. Martin Luther King, Jr.; and received information about proposed editing of King's articles. 96

(c.) Distorting Data to Influence Government Policy and Public Perceptions

Accurate intelligence is a prerequisite to sound government policy. However, as the past head of the FBI's Domestic Intelligence Division reminded the Committee:

> The facts by themselves are not too meaningful. They are something like stones cast into a heap.

On certain crucial subjects the domestic intelligence agencies reported the "facts" in ways that gave rise to misleading impressions.

For example, the FBI's Domestic Intelligence Division initially discounted as an "obvious failure" the alleged attempt's of Communists to influence the civil rights movement. Without any significant change in the factual situation, the Bureau moved from the Division's conclusion to Director Hoover's public congressional testimony characterizing Communist influence on the civil rights movement as "vitally important."

FBI reporting on protests against the Vietnam War provides another example, of the manner in which the information provided to decision-makers can be skewed. In acquiescence with a judgment already expressed by President Johnson, the Bureau's reports on demonstrations against the War in Vietnam emphasized Communist efforts to influence the anti-war movement and underplayed the fact that the vast majority of demonstrators were not Communist controlled.

(d) "Chilling" First Amendment Rights—The First Amendment protects the Rights of American citizens to engage in free and open discussions, and to associate with persons of their choosing. Intelligence agencies have, on occasion, expressly attempted to interfere with those rights. For example, one internal FBI memorandum called for "more interviews" with New Left subjects "to enhance the paranoia endemic in these circles" and "get the point across there is an FBI agent behind every mailbox."

More importantly, the government's surveillance activities in the aggregate— whether or not expressly intended to do so—tends, as the Committee concludes at p. 290 to deter the exercise of First Amended Rights by American citizens who become aware of the government's domestic intelligence program.

(e) Preventing the Free Exchange of Ideas—Speakers, teachers, writers, and publications themselves were targets of the FBI's counterintelligence program. The FBI's efforts to interfere with the free exchange of ideas included:

-- Anonymously attempting to prevent an alleged "Communist-front" group from holding a forum on a midwest campus, and then investigating the judge who ordered that the meeting be allowed to proceed.

-- Using another "confidential source" in a foundation which contributed to a local college to apply pressure on the school to fire an activist professor.

-- Anonymously contacting a university official to urge him to "persuade" two professors to stop funding a student newspaper, in order to "eliminate what voice the New Left has" in the area.

-- Targeting the New Mexico Free University for teaching "confrontation politics" and "draft counseling training".

7. Cost and Value

Domestic intelligence is expensive. We have already indicated the cost of illegal and improper intelligence activities in terms of the harm to victims, the injury to constitutional values, and the damage to the democratic process itself. The cost in dollars is also significant. For example, the FBI has budgeted for fiscal year 1976 over $7 million for its domestic security informant program, more than twice the amount it spends on informants against organized crime. The aggregate budget for FBI domestic security intelligence and foreign counterintelligence is at least $80 million. 104 In the late 1960s and early 1970s, when the Bureau was joined by the CIA, the military, and NSA in collecting information about the anti-war movement and black activists, the cost was substantially greater.

Apart from the excesses described above, the usefulness of many domestic intelligence activities in serving the legitimate goal of protecting society has been questionable. Properly directed intelligence investigations concentrating upon hostile foreign agents and violent terrorists can produce valuable results. The Committee has examined cases where the FBI uncovered "illegal" agents of a foreign power engaged in clandestine intelligence activities in violation of federal law. Information leading to the prevention of serious violence has been acquired by the FBI through its informant penetration of terrorist groups and through the inclusion in Bureau files of the names of persons actively involved with such groups. Nevertheless, the most sweeping domestic intelligence surveillance programs have produced surprisingly few useful returns in view of their extent. For example:

-- Between 1960 and 1974, the FBI conducted over 500,000 separate investigations of persons and groups under the "subversive" category, predicated on the possibility that they might be likely to overthrow the government of the United States. Yet not a single individual or group has been prosecuted since 1957 under the laws which prohibit planning or advocating action to overthrow the government and which are the main alleged statutory basis for such FBI investigations.

-- A recent study by the General Accounting Office has estimated that of some 17,528 FBI domestic intelligence investigations of individuals in 1974, only 1.3 percent resulted in prosecution and conviction, and in only "about 2 percent" of the cases was advance knowledge of any activity — legal or illegal — obtained.

-- One of the main reasons advanced for expanded collection of intelligence about urban unrest and anti-war protest was to help responsible officials cope with possible violence. However, a former White House official with major duties in this area under the Johnson administration has concluded, in retrospect, that "in none of these situations . . . would advance intelligence about dissident groups [have] been of much help," that what was needed was "physical intelligence" about the geography of major cities, and that the attempt to "predict violence" was not a "successful undertaking"

-- Domestic intelligence reports have sometimes even been counterproductive. A local police chief, for example, described FBI reports which led to the positioning of federal troops near his city as:

> . . . almost completely composed of unsorted and unevaluated stories, threats, and rumors that had crossed my desk in New Haven. Many of these had long before been discounted by our Intelligence Division. But they had made their way from New Haven to Washington, had gained completely unwarranted credibility, and had been submitted by the Director of the FBI to the President of the United States. They seemed to present a convincing picture of impending holocaust.

In considering its recommendations, the Committee undertook an evaluation of the FBI's claims that domestic intelligence was necessary to combat terrorism, civil disorders, "subversion," and hostile foreign intelligence activity. The Committee reviewed voluminous materials bearing on this issue and questioned Bureau officials, local police officials, and present and former federal executive officials.

We have found that we are in fundamental agreement with the wisdom of Attorney General Stone's initial warning that intelligence agencies must not be "concerned with political or other opinions of individuals" and must be limited to investigating essentially only "such conduct as is forbidden by the laws of the United States." The Committee's record demonstrates that domestic intelligence which departs from this standard raises grave risks of undermining the democratic process and harming the interests of individual citizens. This danger weighs heavily against the speculative or negligible benefits of the ill-defined and overbroad investigations authorized in the past. Thus, the basic purpose of the recommendations contained in Part IV of this report is to limit the FBI to investigating conduct rather than ideas or associations.

The excesses of the past do not, however, justify depriving the United States of a clearly defined and effectively controlled domestic intelligence capability. The intelligence services of this nation's international adversaries continue to attempt to conduct clandestine espionage operations within the United States. Our recommendations provide for intelligence investigations of hostile foreign intelligence activity.

Moreover, terrorists have engaged in serious acts of violence which have brought death and injury to Americans and threaten further such acts. These acts, not the politics or beliefs of those who would commit them, are the proper focus for investigations to anticipate terrorist violence. Accordingly, the Committee would permit properly controlled intelligence investigations in those narrow circumstances.

Concentration on imminent violence can avoid the wasteful dispersion of resources which has characterized the sweeping (and fruitless) domestic intelligence investigations of the past. But the most important reason for the fundamental change in the domestic intelligence operations which our Recommendations propose is the need to protect the constitutional Rights of Americans.

In light of the record of abuse revealed by our inquiry, the Committee is not satisfied with the position that mere exposure of what has occurred in the past will prevent its recurrence. Clear legal standards and effective oversight and controls are necessary to ensure that domestic intelligence activity does not itself undermine the democratic system it is intended to protect.

II. The Growth Of Domestic Intelligence: 1936 To 1976

A. Summary

1. The Lesson: History Repeats Itself
During and after the First World War, intelligence agencies, including the predecessor of the FBI, engaged in repressive activity.

A new Attorney General, Harlan Fiske Stone, sought to stop the investigation of "political or other opinions." This restraint was embodied only in an executive pronouncement, however. No statutes were passed to prevent the kind of improper activity which had been exposed. Thereafter, as this narrative will show, the abuses returned in a new form. It is now the responsibility of all three branches of government to ensure that the pattern of abuse of domestic intelligence activity does not recur.

2. The Pattern: Broadening Through Time
Since the re-establishment of federal domestic intelligence programs in 1936, there has been a steady increase in the government's capability and willingness to pry into, and even disrupt, the political activities and personal lives of the people. The last forty years have witnessed a relentless expansion of domestic intelligence activity beyond investigation of criminal conduct toward the collection of political intelligence and the launching of secret offensive actions against Americans.

The initial incursions into the realm of ideas and associations were related to concerns about the influence of foreign totalitarian powers.

Ultimately, however, intelligence activity was directed against domestic groups advocating change in America, particularly those who most vigorously opposed the Vietnam war or sought to improve the conditions of racial minorities. Similarly, the targets of intelligence investigations were broadened from groups perceived to be violence prone to include groups of ordinary protesters.

3. Three Periods of Growth for Domestic Intelligence The expansion of domestic intelligence activity can usefully be divided into three broad periods: (a) the pre-war - and World War II period; (b) the Cold War era, and (c) the period of domestic dissent beginning in the mid-sixties. The main developments in each of these stages in the evolution of domestic intelligence may be summarized as follows:

a. 1936-1945

By presidential directive—rather than statute—the FBI and military intelligence agencies were authorized to conduct domestic intelligence investigations. These investigations included a vaguely defined mission to collect intelligence about "subversive activities" which were sometimes unrelated to law enforcement. Wartime exigencies encouraged the unregulated use of intrusive intelligence techniques; and the FBI began to resist supervision by the Attorney General.

b. 1946-1963

Cold War fears and dangers nurtured the domestic intelligence programs of the FBI and military, and they became permanent features of government. Congress deferred to the executive branch in the oversight of these programs. The FBI became increasingly isolated from effective outside control, even from the Attorneys General. The scope of investigations of "subversion" widened greatly. Under the cloak of secrecy, the, FBI instituted its COINTELPRO operations to "disrupt" and "neutralize" "subversives". The National Security Agency, the FBI, and the CIA re-instituted instrusive wartime surveillance techniques in contravention of law.

c. 1964-1976

Intelligence techniques which previously had been concentrated upon foreign threats and domestic groups said to be under Communist influence were applied with increasing intensity to a wide range of domestic activity by American citizens. These techniques were utilized against peaceful civil rights and antiwar protest activity, and thereafter in reaction to civil unrest, often without regard for the consequences to American liberties. The intelligence agencies of the United States—sometimes abetted by public opinion and often in response to pressure from administration officials or the Congress—frequently disregarded the law in their conduct of massive surveillance and aggressive counterintelligence operations against American citizens. In the past few years, some of these activities were curtailed, partly in response to the moderation of the domestic crisis; but all too often improper programs were terminated only in response to exposure, the threat of exposure, or a change in the climate of public opinion, such as that triggered by the Watergate affair.

B. Establishing A Permanent Domestic Intelligence Structure: 1936-1945

1. Background—The Stone Standard

The first substantial domestic intelligence programs of the federal government were established during World War I.

The Justice Department's Bureau of Investigation (as the FBI was then known), military intelligence, other federal investigative agencies, and the volunteer American Protective League were involved in these programs. In the period immediately following World War I, the Bureau of Investigation took part in the notorious Palmer Raids and other activities against persons characterized as "subversive."

Harlan Fiske Stone, who became Attorney General in 1924, described the conduct of Justice Department and the Bureau of Investigation before he took office as "lawless, maintaining many activities which were without any authority in federal statutes, and engaging in many practices which were brutal and tyrannical in the extreme."

Fearing that the investigative activities of the Bureau could invade privacy and inhibit political freedoms, Attorney General Stone announced:

> There is always the posibility that a secret police may become a menace to free government and free institutions, because it carries with it the possibility of abuses of power which are not always quickly apprehended or understood. ... It is important that its activities be strictly limited to the performance of those functions for which it was created and that its agents themselves be not above the law or beyond its reach. ... The Bureau of Investigation is not concerned with political or other opinions of individuals. It is concerned only with their conduct and then only with such conduct -as is forbidden by the laws of the United States. When a police system passes beyond these limits, it is dangerous to the proper administration of justice and to human liberty, which it should be our first concern to cherish.

When Stone appointed J. Edgar Hoover as Acting Director of the Bureau of Investigation, he instructed Hoover to adhere to this standard:

> The activities of the Bureau are to be limited strictly to investigations of violations of law, under my direction or under the direction of an Assistant Attorney General regularly conducting the work of the Department of Justice.

Nevertheless, beginning in the mid-thirties, at White House direction, the FBI reentered the realm of collecting intelligence about ideas and associations.

2. Main Developments of the 1936-1945 Period

In the years preceding World War II, domestic intelligence activities were reinstituted, expanded, and institutionalized. Based upon vague and conflicting orders to investigate the undefined areas of "subversion" and "potential crimes" related to national security, the FBI commenced a broad intelligence program. The FBI was authorized to preempt the field, although the military engaged in some investigation of civilians.

The FBI's domestic intelligence jurisdiction went beyond investigations of crime to include a vague mandate to investigate foreign involvement in American affairs. In the exercise of this jurisdictional authority, the Bureau began to investigate law abiding domestic groups and individuals; its program was also open to misuse for political purposes. The most intrusive intelligence techniques — initially used to meet wartime exigencies—were based on questionable statutory interpretation, or lacked any formal legal authorization.

The executive intentionally kept the issue of domestic intelligence-gathering away from the Congress until 1939, and thereafter the Congress appears to have deliberately declined to confront the issue. The FBI generally complied with the Attorney General's policies, but began to resist Justice Department review of its activities. On one occasion, the Bureau appears to have disregarded an Attorney General's policy directive.

However important these developments were in themselves, the enduring significance of this period is that it opened the institutional door to greater excesses in later years.

3. Domestic Intelligence Authority: Vague and Conflicting Executive Orders

The executive orders upon which the Bureau based its intelligence activity in the decade before World War II were vague and conflicting. By using words like "subversion"—a term which was never defined—and by permitting the investigation of "potential" crimes, and matters "not within the specific provisions of prevailing statutes," the foundation was laid for excessive intelligence gathering about Americans.

a. The Original Roosevelt Orders

In 1934, according to a memorandum by J. Edgar Hoover, President Roosevelt ordered an investigation of "the Nazi movement in this country." In response, the FBI conducted a one-time investigation, described by FBI Director Hoover as "a so-called intelligence investigation." It concentrated on "the Nazi group," with particular reference to "anti-racial" and "anti-American" activities having "any possible connection with official representatives of the German government in the United States."

Two years later, in August 1936, according to a file memorandum of Director Hoover, President Roosevelt asked for a more systematic collection of intelligence about:

subversive activities in the United States, particularly Fascism and Communism.

Hoover indicated further that the President wanted:

a broad picture of the general movement and its activities as [they] may affect the economic and political life of the country as a whole.

The President and the FBI Director discussed the means by which the Bureau might collect "general intelligence information" on this subject. The only record of Attorney General Homer Cummings' knowledge of, or authorization for, this intelligence assignment is found in a memorandum from Director Hoover to his principal assistant.

b. Orders in 1938-39: The Vagueness of "Subversive Activities" and "Potential" Crimes

In October 1938, Director Hoover advised President Roosevelt of the "present purposes and scope" of FBI intelligence investigations, "together with suggestions for expansion." His memorandum stated that the FBI was collecting:

information dealing with various forms of activities of either a subversive or so-called intelligence type.

Despite the references in Director Hoover's 1938 memorandum to "subversive-type" investigations, an accompanying letter to the President from Attorney General Homer Cummings made no mention of "subversion" and cited only the President's interest in "the so-called espionage situation." Cummings' successor, Attorney General Frank Murphy, appears to have abandoned the term "subversive activities." Moreover, when Director Hoover provided Attorney General Frank Murphy a copy of his 1938 plan, he described it, without mentioning "subversion," as a program "intended to ascertain the identity of persons engaged in espionage, counterespionage, and sabotage of a nature *not within the specific provisions of prevailing statutes.*" [Emphasis added.] Murphy thereafter recommended to the President that he issue an order concentrating "investigation of all espionage, counterespionage, and sabotage matters" in the FBI and military intelligence.

President Roosevelt agreed and issued an order which, like Murphy's letter, made no mention of "subversive," or general intelligence:

> It is my desire that the investigation of all espionage, counter espionage, and sabotage matters be controlled and handled by the Federal Bureau of Investigation of the Department of Justice, the Military Intelligence Division of the War Department, and the Office of Naval Intelligence in the Navy Department. The directors of these three agencies are to function as a committee to coordinate their activities.
>
> No investigations should be conducted by any investigative agency of the Government into matters involving actually or potentially any espionage, counterespionage, or sabotage, except by the three agencies mentioned above.

Precisely what the President's reference to "potential" espionage or sabotage was intended to cover was unclear. Whatever it meant, it was apparently intended to be consistent with Director Hoover's earlier description of the FBI program to Attorney General Murphy.

Three months later, after the outbreak of war in Europe, Director Hoover indicated his concern that private citizens might provide information to the "sabotage squads" which local police departments were creating rather than to the FBI. Hoover urged the Attorney General to ask the President to request local officials to give the FBI all information concerning "espionage, counterespionage, sabotage, subversive activities, and neutrality regulations."

The President immediately issued a statement which continued the confusing treatment of the breadth of the FBI's intelligence authority. On the one hand, the statement began by noting that the FBI had been instructed to investigate:

> matters relating to espionage, sabotage, and violations of the neutrality regulations.

On the other hand, the President concluded by adding "subversive activities" to the list of information local law enforcement officials should relay to the FBI.

c. Orders 1940-43: The Confusion Continues

President Roosevelt used the term "subversive activities" in a secret directive to Attorney General Robert Jackson on wiretapping in 1940. Referring to activities of other nations engaged in "propaganda of so-called 'fifth columns'" and "preparation for sabotage." He directed the Attorney General to authorize wiretaps "of persons suspected of subversive activities against the Government of the United States, including suspected spies." The President instructed that such wiretaps be limited "insofar as possible" to aliens. Neither the President nor the Attorney General subsequently clarified the scope of the FBI's authority to investigate "subversive activity."

The confusion as to the breadth of President Roosevelt's authorization reappeared in Attorney General Francis Biddle's description of FBI jurisdiction in 1942 and in a new Presidential statement in 1943.

Biddle issued a lengthy order defining the duties of the various parts of the Justice Department in September 1942. Among other things, the FBI was charged with a duty to "investigate" criminal offenses against the United States. In contrast, the FBI was to function as a "clearing house" with respect to "espionage, sabotage, and other subversive matters."

Four months later, President Roosevelt renewed his public appeal for cooperation by police and other "patriotic organizations" with the FBI. In this statement, he described his September 1939 order as granting "investigative" authority to the FBI for "espionage, sabotage, and violation of the neutrality regulations." The President did not adopt Attorney General Biddle's "clearing-house" characterization, nor did he mention "subversion."

4. The Role of Congress
a. Executive Avoidance of Congress
In 1938, the President, the Attorney General, and the FBI Director explicitly decided not to seek legislative authorization for the expanding domestic intelligence program.

Attorney General Cummings cautioned that the plan for domestic intelligence "should be held in the strictest confidence." Director Hoover contended that no special legislation should be sought "in order to avoid criticism or objections which might be raised to such an expansion by either ill-informed persons or individuals with some ulterior motive." Hoover thought it "undesirable to seek any special legislation which would draw attention to the fact that it was proposed to develop a special counter-espionage drive of any great magnitude" because the FBI's intelligence activity was already "much broader than espionage or counterespionage."

Director Hoover contended that the FBI had authority to engage in intelligence activity beyond investigating crimes at the request of the Attorney General or the Department of State. He relied on an amendment to the FBI Appropriations Act, passed before World War I, authorizing the Attorney General to appoint officials not only to "detect and prosecute" federal crimes but also to:

> conduct such other investigations regarding official matters under the control of the Department of Justice, or the Department of State, as may be directed by the Attorney General.

After conflicts with the State Department in 1939, however, the FBI no longer relied upon this vague statute for its authority to conduct intelligence investigations, instead relying upon the Executive orders.

b. Congress Declines to Confront the Issue
Even though Executive officials originally avoided Congress to prevent criticism or objections, after the President's proclamation of emergency in 1939 they began to

inform Congress of FBI intelligence activities In November 1939, Director Hoover told the House Appropriations Committee that the Bureau had set up a General Intelligence Division, "by authority of the President's proclamation." And in January 1940, he told the same Committee that the FBI had authority, under the President's September 6, 1939 statement to investigate espionage, sabotage, neutrality violations, and "any other subversive activities."

There is no evidence that the Appropriations Committee objected or inquired further into the meaning of that last vague term, although members did seek assurance that FBI intelligence could be curtailed when the wartime emergency ended.

In 1940, a joint resolution was introduced by New York City Congressman Emmanuel Celler which would have given the FBI broad jurisdiction to investigate, by wiretapping or other means, or "frustrate" any "interference with the national defense" due to certain specified crimes (sabotage, treason, seditious conspiracy, espionage, and violations of the neutrality laws) or "in any other manner." Although the resolution failed to reach the House floor, it seems likely that, rather than opposing domestic intelligence investigations, Congress was simply choosing to avoid the issue of defining the FBI's intelligence jurisdiction. This view is supported by Congress' passage in 1940 and 1941 of two new criminal statutes: the Smith Act made it a crime to advocate the violent overthrow of the Government; and the Voorhis Act required "subversive" organizations advocating the Government's violent overthrow and having foreign ties to register or be subject to criminal penalties.

Although, as indicated, the Executive branch disclosed the fact that the FBI was doing intelligence work and Congress generally raised no objection, there was one occasion when an Executive description of the Bureau's work was less than complete. Following Director Hoover's testimony about the establishment of an Intelligence Division and some public furor over the FBI arrest of several Communist Party members in Detroit, Senator George Norris (R. Neb.) asked whether the Bureau was violating Attorney General Stone's assurance in 1924 that it would conduct only criminal investigations. Attorney General Jackson replied:

> Mr. Hoover is in agreement with me that the principles which Attorney General Stone laid down in 1924 when the Federal Bureau of Investigation was reorganized and Mr. Hoover appointed as Director are sound, and that the usefulness of the Bureau depends upon a faithful adherence to these limitations.

> The Federal Bureau of Investigation will confine its activities to the investigation of violation of Federal statutes, the collecting of evidence in cases in which the United States is or may be a party in interest, and the service of process issued by the courts.

The FBI was, in fact, doing much more than that and had informed the Appropriations Committee of its practice in general terms. Attorney General Jackson himself stated later that the FBI was conducting "steady surveillance" of persons beyond those who had violated federal statutes, including persons who were a "likely source" of federal law violation because the were "sympathetic with the systems or designs of foreign dictators."

---

5. Scope of Domestic Intelligence

a. Beyond Criminal Investigations

According to Director Hoover's account of his meeting with President Roosevelt in 1936, the President wanted "a broad picture" of the impact of Communism and Fascism on American life." Similarly, the FBI Director described his 1938 plan as "broader than espionage" and covering "in a true sense real intelligence." Thus it appears that one of the first purposes of FBI domestic intelligence was to perform the "pure intelligence" function of supplying executive officials with information believed of value for making policy decisions. This aspect of the assignment to investigate "subversion" was entirely unrelated to the enforcement of federal criminal laws. The second purpose of FBI domestic intelligence gathering was essentially "preventive," in compliance with the President's June 1939 directive to investigate "potential" espionage or sabotage. As war moved closer, preventive intelligence investigations focused on individuals who might be placed on a Custodial Detention List for possible internment in case of war.

Both pure intelligence about "subversion" and preventive intelligence about "potential" espionage or sabotage involved investigations based on political affiliations and group membership and association. The relationship to law enforcement was often remote and speculative; the Bureau did not focus its intelligence gathering solely on tangible evidence of preparation for crime.

Directives implementing the general preventive intelligence instruction to investigate "potential" espionage or sabotage were vague and sweeping. In 1939, for instance, field offices were told to investigate persons of German, Italian, and Communist "sympathies" and any other persons "whose interests may be directed primarily to the interest of some other nation than the United States." FBI offices were directed to report the names of members of German and Italian societies, "whether they be of a fraternal character or of some other nature," and members of any other groups "which might have pronounced Nationalistic tendencies." The Bureau sought lists of subscribers and officers of German, Italian, and Communist foreign language newspapers, as well as of other newspapers with "notorious Nationalistic sympathies." The FBI also made confidential inquiries regarding "various so-called radical and fascist organizations" to identify their "leading personnel, purposes and aims, and the part they are likely to play at a time of national crisis."

The criteria for investigating persons for inclusion on the Custodial Detention List was similarly vague. In 1939, the FBI said its list included persons with "strong Nazi tendencies" and "strong Communist tendencies." FBI field offices were directed in 1940 to gather information on individuals who would be considered for the list because of their "Communistic, Fascist, Nazi, or other nationalistic background."

b. "Infiltration," Investigations The FBI based its pure intelligence investigations on a theory of subversive "infiltration" which remained an essential part of the rationale for domestic intelligence after the war: anyone who happened to associate with Communists or Fascists or was simply alleged to have such associations became the subject of FBI intelligence reports. Thus, "subversive" investigations produced intelligence about a wide variety of lawful groups and law-abiding citizens. By 1938, the FBI was investigating alleged subversive infiltration of:

> the maritime industry; the steel industry; the coal industry; the clothing, garment, and fur industries; the automobile industry; the newspaper field; educational institutions; organized labor organizations; Negroes; youth groups; Government affairs; and the armed forces.

This kind of intelligence was transmitted to the White House. For example, in 1937 the Attorney General sent the President an FBI report on a proposed pilgrimage to Washington to urge passage of legislation to benefit American youth. The report stated that the American Youth Congress, which sponsored the pilgrimage, was understood to be strongly Communistic. Later reports in 1937 described the Communist Party's role in plans by the Workers Alliance for nationwide demonstrations protesting the plight of the unemployed, as well as the Alliance's plans to lobby Congress in support of the federal relief program.

Some investigations and reports (which went into Justice Department and FBI permanent files) covered entirely legal political activities. For example, one local group checked by the Bureau was called the League for Fair Play, which furnished "speakers to Rotary and Kiwanis Clubs and to schools and colleges." The FBI reported in 1941 that:

> the organization was formed in 1937, apparently by two Ministers and a businessman for the purpose of furthering fair play, tolerance, adherence to the Constitution, democracy, liberty, justice, understanding 'and good will among all creeds, races and classes of the United States. A synopsis of the report stated, "No indications of Communist activities."

In 1944, the FBI prepared an extensive intelligence report on an active political group, the Independent Voters of Illinois, apparently because it was considered a target for Communist "infiltration." The Independent Voters group was reported to have been formed:

> for the purpose of developing neighborhood political units to help in the re-election of President Roosevelt, and the election of progressive congressmen. Apparently, IVI endorsed or aided Democrats for the most part, although it was stated to be "independent." It does not appear that it entered its own candidates or that it endorsed any Communists. IVI sought to help elect those candidates who would favor fighting inflation, oppose race and class discrimination, favor international cooperation, support a "full employment" program, oppose Facism, etc.

Thus, in its search for subversive "influence," the Bureau gathered extensive information about the lawful activities of left-liberal political groups. At the opposite end of the political spectrum, the activities of numerous right-wing groups like the Christian Front and Christian Mobilizers (followers of Father Coughlin), the American Destiny Party, the American Nationalist Party, and even the less extreme "America First" movement were reported by the FBI.

c. Partisan Use

The collection of pure intelligence and preventive intelligence about "subversives" led to the inclusion in FBI files of political intelligence about the President's partisan critics. In May 1940, President Roosevelt's secretary sent the FBI Director hundreds of telegrams received by the White House. The attached letter stated:

> As the telegrams all were more or less in opposition to national defense, the President thought you might like to look them over, noting the names and addresses of the senders.

Additional telegrams expressing approval of a speech by one of the President's leading critics, Colonel Charles Lindbergh, were also referred to the FBI. A domestic intelligence program without clearly defined boundaries almost invited such action.

d. Centralized Authority: FBI and Military Intelligence

The basic policy of President Roosevelt and his four Attorneys General was to centralize civilian authority for domestic intelligence in the FBI. Consolidation of domestic intelligence was viewed as a means of protecting civil liberties. Recalling the hysteria of World War I, Attorney General Frank Murphy declared:

> Twenty years ago, inhuman and cruel things were done in the name of justice; sometimes vigilantes and others took over the work. We do not want such things done today, for the work has now been localized in the FBI.

Centralization of authority for domestic intelligence also served the FBI's bureaucratic interests. Director Hoover complained about attempts by other agencies to "literally chisel into this type of work." He exhorted: "We don't want to let it slip away from us."

Pursuant to President Roosevelt's 1939 directive authorizing the FBI and military intelligence to conduct all investigations of "potential" espionage and sabotage, an interagency Delimitation Agreement in June 1940 assigned most such domestic intelligence work to the FBI. As revised in February 1942, the Agreement covered "investigation of all activities coming under the categories of espionage, subversion and sabotage." The FBI was responsible for all investigations "involving civilians in the United States" and for keeping the military informed of "the names of individuals definitely known to be connected with subversive activities."

The military intelligence agencies were interested in intelligence about civilian activity. In fact, they requested extensive information about civilians from the FBI. In May 1939, for instance, the Army G-2 Military Intelligence Division (MID) transmitted a request for the names and locations of "citizens opposed to our participation in war and conducting anti-war propaganda." Despite the Delimitation Agreement, the MID's Counterintelligence Corps collected intelligence on civilian "subversive activity" as part of a preventive security program using volunteer informers and investigators.

6. Control by the Attorney General: Compliance and Resistance

The basic outlines of the FBI's domestic intelligence program were approved by Attorney General Cummings in 1938 and Attorney General Murphy in 1939. Director Hoover also asked Attorney General Jackson in 1940 for policy guidance concerning the FBI's "suspect list of individuals whose arrest might be considered necessary in the event the United States becomes involved in war."

The FBI Director initially opposed, however, Attorney General Jackson's attempt to require more detailed supervision of the FBI's role in the Custodial Detention Program. To oversee this program and others, Jackson created a Neutrality Laws Unit (later renamed the Special War Policies Unit) in the Justice Department. When the Unit proposed to review FBI intelligence, reports on individuals, Director Hoover protested that turning over the FBI's confidential reports would risk the possibility of "leaks." He argued that if the identity of confidential informants became known, it would endanger their "life and safety" and thus the Department would "abandon" the "subversives field."

After five months of negotiation, the FBI was ordered to transmit its "dossiers" to the Justice Department Unit. To satisfy the FBI's concerns, the Department agreed to take no formal action against an individual if it "might interfere with sound investigative techniques" and not to disclose confidential informants without the Bureau's "prior approval." Thus, from 1941 to 1943, the Justice Department had the machinery to oversee at least this aspect of FBI domestic intelligence.

In 1943, however, Attorney General Biddle ordered that the Custodial Detention List should be abolished as "impractical. unwise, and dangerous." His directive stated that there was "no statutory authority or other present justification" for keeping the list. The Attorney General concluded that the system for classifying "dangerous" persons was "inherently unreliable;" the evidence used was "inadequate;" and the standards applied were "defective." Biddle observed:

> the notion that it is possible to make a valid determination as to how dangerous a person is in the abstract and without reference to time, environment, and other relevant circumstances, is impractical, unwise, and dangerous.

Returning to the basic standard espoused by Attorney General Stone, Attorney General Biddle declared:

> The Department fulfills its proper function by investigating the activities of persons who may have violated the law. It is not aided in this work by classifying persons as to dangerousness.

Upon receipt of this order, the FBI Director did not in fact abolish its list. The FBI continued to maintain an index of persons "who may be dangerous or potentially dangerous to the public safety or internal security of the United States." In response to the Attorney General's order, the FBI merely changed the name of the list from Custodial Detention List to Security Index. Instructions to the field stated that the Security Index should be kept "strictly confidential," and that it should never be mentioned in FBI reports or "discussed with agencies or individuals outside the Bureau" except for military intelligence agencies.

This incident provides an example of the FBI's ability to conduct domestic intelligence operations in opposition to the policies of an Attorney General. Despite Attorney General Biddle's order, the "dangerousness" list continued to be kept, and investigations in support of that list continued to be a significant part of the, Bureau's work.

7. Intrusive Techniques: Questionable Authorization

a. Wiretaps: A Strained Statutory Interpretation

In 1940, President Roosevelt authorized FBI wiretapping against "persons suspected of subversive activities against the United States, including suspected spies," requiring the specific approval of the Attorney General for each tap and directing that they be limited "insofar as possible to aliens. "

This order was issued in the face of the Federal Communications Act of 1934, which had prohibited wiretapping. However, the Attorney General interpreted the Act of 1934 so as to permit government wiretapping. Since the Act made it unlawful to "intercept and divulge" communications, Attorney General Jackson contended that it did not apply if there was no divulgence, outside the Government. Attorney General Jackson's questionable Interpretation was accepted by succeeding Attorneys General (until 1968) but never by the courts.

Jackson informed the Congress of his interpretation. Congress considered enacting an exception to the 1934 Act, and held hearings in which Director Hoover said wiretapping was "of considerable importance" because of the "gravity" to "national safety" of such offenses as espionage and sabotage. Apparently relying upon Jackson's statutory interpretation, Congress then dropped the matter, leaving the authorization of wiretaps to Executive discretion, without either statutory standards or the requirement of a judicial warrant.

The potential for misuse of wiretapping was demonstrated during this period by several FBI wiretaps approved by the, Attorney General or by the White House. In 1941, Attorney General Biddle approved a wiretap on the Los Angeles Chamber of Commerce with the caveat:

> There is no record of espionage at this time; and, unless within a month from today there is some evidence connecting the Chamber of Commerce with espionage, I think the surveillance should be discontinued.

However, in another case Biddle disapproved an FBI request to wiretap a Philadelphia bookstore "engaged in the sale of Communist literature" and frequented by "important Communist leaders" in 1941.

Materials located in Director Hoover's "Official and Confidential" file indicate that President Roosevelt's aide Harry Hopkins asked the FBI to wiretap his own home telephone in 1944. Additional reports from "technical" surveillance of all unidentified target were sent to Hopkins in May and July 1945, when he served as an aide to President Truman.

In 1945 two Truman White House aides, E. D. McKim and General H. H. Vaughn, received reports of electronic surveillance of a high executive official. One of these reports included "transcripts of telephone conversations between [the official] and Justice Felix Frankfurter and between [the official] and Drew Pearson."

From June 1945 until May 1948, General Vaughn received reports from electronic surveillance of a former Roosevelt White House aide. A memorandum by J. Edgar Hoover indicates that Attorney General Tom Clark "authorized the placing of a technical surveillance" on this individual and that, according to Clark, President Truman "was particularly concerned" about the activities of this individual "and his associates" and wanted "a very thorough investigation" so that "steps might be taken, if possible, to see that such activities did not interfere with the proper administration of government." Hoover's memorandum did not indicate what these "activities" were.

b. Bugging, Mail Opening and Surreptitious Entry.

Intrusive techniques such as bugging, mail opening and surreptitious entry were used by the FBI without even the kind of formal Presidential authorization and requirement of Attorney General approval that applied to warrantless wiretapping.

During the war, the FBI began "chamfering" or surreptitious mail opening, to supplement the overt censorship of international mail authorized by statute In Wartime. The practice of surreptitious entry - or breaking-and-entering - was also used by the FBI in wartime intelligence operations. The Bureau continued or resumed the use of these techniques after the war without explicit outside authorization.

Furthermore, the installation of microphone surveillance ("bugs"), either with or without trespass, was exempt from the procedure for Attorney General approval of wiretaps. Justice Department records indicate that no Attorney General formally considered the question of microphone surveillance involving trespass, except on a hypothetical basis, until 1952.

C. Domestic Intelligence In The Cold War Era: 1946-1963

1. Main Developments of the 1946-1963 Period

The domestic intelligence programs of the FBI and the military intelligence agencies, which were established under presidential authority before World War II, did not cease with the end of hostilities. Instead, they set the pattern for decades to come.

Despite Director Hoover's statement that the intelligence structure could be "discontinued or very materially curtailed" with the termination of the national emergency, after the war intelligence operations were neither discontinued nor curtailed. Congressional deference to the executive branch, the broad scope of investigations, the growth of the FBI's power, and the substantial immunity of the Bureau from effective outside supervision became increasingly significant features of domestic intelligence in the United States. New domestic intelligence functions were added to previous responsibilities. No attempt was made to enact a legislative charter replacing the wartime emergency orders, as was done in the foreign intelligence field in 1947.

The main developments during the Cold War era may be summarized as follows:

a. Domestic Intelligence Authority

During this period there was a national consensus regarding the danger to the United States from Communism; little distinction was made between the threats posed by the Soviet Union and by Communists within this country. Domestic intelligence activity was supported by that consensus, although not specifically authorized by the Congress.

Formal authority for FBI investigations of "subversive activity" and for the agreements between the FBI and military intelligence was explicitly granted in executive directives from Presidents Truman and Eisenhower, the National Security Council, and Attorney General Kennedy. These directives provided no guidance, however, for controlling such investigations.

b. Scope of Domestic Intelligence

The breadth of the FBI's investigation of "subversive infiltration" continued to produce intelligence reports and massive files on lawful groups and law-abiding citizens who happened to associate, even unwittingly, with Communists or with socialists unconnected with the Soviet Union who used revolutionary rhetoric. At the same time, the scope of FBI intelligence expanded to cover civil rights protest activity as well as violent "Klan-type" and "hate" groups, vocal anticommunists, and prominent opponents of racial integration. The vagueness of the FBI's investigative mandate and the overbreadth of its collection programs also placed it in position to supply theh White House with numerous items of domestic political intelligence apparently desired by Presidents and their aides.

In response to White House and congressional interest in right-wing organizations, the Internal Revenue Service began comprehensive investigations of right-wing groups in 1961 and later expanded to left-wing organizations. This effort was directed at identifying contributions and ascertaining whether the organizations were entitled to maintain their exempt status.

c. Accountability and Control

Pervasive secrecy enabled the FBI and the Justice Department to disregard as "unworkable" the Emergency Detention Act intended to set standards for aspects of domestic intelligence. The FBI's independent position also allowed it to withhold significant information from a Presidential commission and from every Attorney General, and no Attorney General inquired fully into the Bureau's operations.

During the same period, apprehensions about having a "security police" influenced Congress to prohibit the Central Intelligence Agency from exercising law enforcement powers or performing "internal security functions." Nevertheless, in secret and without effective internal controls, the CIA undertook programs for testing chemical and biological agents on unwitting Americans, sometimes with tragic consequences. The CIA also used American private institutions as "cover" and used intrusive techniques affecting the rights of Americans.

d. Intrusive Techniques

The CIA and the National Security Agency illegally instituted programs for the interception of international communications to and from American citizens, primarily first class mail and cable traffic.

During this period, the FBI also used intrusive intelligence gathering techniques against domestic "subversives" and counterintelligence targets. Sometimes these techniques were covered by a blanket delegation of authority from the Attorney General, as with microphone surveillance; but frequently they were used without outside authorization, as with mail openings and surreptitious entry. Only conventional wiretaps required the Attorney General's approval in each case, but this method was still misused due to the lack of adequate standards and procedural safeguards.

e. Domestic Covert Action

In the mid-fifties, the FBI developed the initial COINTELPRO operations, which used aggressive covert actions to disrupt and discredit Communist Party activities. The FBI subsequently expanded its COINTELPRO activities to discredit peaceful protest groups whom Communists had infiltrated but did not control, as well as groups of socialists who used revolutionary rhetoric but had no connections with a hostile foreign power.

Throughout this period, there was a mixture of secrecy and disclosure. Executive action was often substituted for legislation, sometimes with the full knowledge and consent. of Congress and on other occasions without informing Congress or by advising only a select group of legislators. There is no question that Congress, the courts, and the public expected the FBI to gather domestic intelligence about Communists. But the broad scope of FBI investigations, its specific programs for achieving "pure intelligence" and "preventive intelligence" objectives, and its use of intrusive techniques and disruptive counterintelligence measures against domestic "subversives" were not fully known by anyone outside the Bureau.

2. Domestic Intelligence Authority

a. Anti-Communist Consensus

During the Cold War era, the strong consensus in favor of governmental action against Communists was reflected in decisions of the Supreme Court and acts of Congress. In the Korean War period, for instance, the Supreme Court upheld the conviction of domestic Communist Party leaders under the Smith Act for conspiracy to advocate violent overthrow of the government. The Court pinned its decision upon the conspiratorial nature of the Communist Party of the United States and its ideological links with the Soviet Union at a time of stress in Soviet-American relations.

Several statutes buttressed the FBI's claim of legitimacy for at least some aspects of domestic intelligence. Although Congress never directly authorized Bureau intelligence operations, Congress enacted the Internal Security Act of 1950 over President Truman's veto. Its two main provisions were: the Subversives Activities Control Act, requiring the registration of members of communist and communist "front" groups; and the Emergency Detention Act, providing for the internment in an emergency of persons who might engage in espionage or sabotage. In this Act, Congress made findings that the Communist Party was "a disciplined organization" operating in this nation "under Soviet Union control" with the aim of installing "a Soviet style dictatorship." Going even further in 1954, Congress passed the Communist Control Act, which provided that the Communist Party was "not entitled to any of the rights, privileges, and immunities attendant upon legal bodies created under the jurisdiction of the laws of the United States."

In 1956, the Supreme Court recognized the existence of FBI intelligence aimed at "Communist seditious activities." The basis for Smith Act prosecutions of "subversive activity" was narrowed in 1957, however, when the Court overturned the convictions of second-string Communist leaders, holding that the government must show advocacy "of action and not merely abstract doctrine." In 1961. the Court sustained the constitutionality under the First Amendment of the requirement that the Communist Party register with the Subversive Activities Control Board.

The consensus should not be portrayed as monolithic. President Truman was concerned about risks to constitutional government posed by the zealous anti-Communism in Congress. According to one White House staff member's notes during the debate over the Internal Security Act:

> The President said that the situation . . . was the worst it had been since the Alien and Sedition Laws of 1798, that a lot of people on the Hill should know better but had been stampeded into running with their tails between their legs.

Truman announced that he would veto the Internal Security Act "regardless of how politically unpopular it was—election year or no election year." But President Truman's veto was overridden by an overwhelming margin.

b. The Federal Employee Loyalty-Security Program

(1) Origins of the Program—President Truman established a federal employee loyalty program in 1947. Its basic features were retained in the federal employee security program authorized by President Eisenhower in public Executive Order 10450, which, with some modifications, still applies today.

Although it had a much broader reach, the program originated out of well-founded concern that Soviet intelligence was then using the Communist Party as a vehicle for the recruitment of espionage agents. President Truman appointed a Temporary Commision on Employee Loyalty in 1946 to examine the problem. FBI Director Hoover submitted a memorandum on the types of activities of "subversive or disloyal persons" in government service which would constitute a "threat" to security. As Hoover saw it, however, the danger was not limited to espionage or recruitment for espionage. It extended to "influencing" government policies in favor of "the foreign country of their ideological choice." Consequently, he urged that attention be given to the associations of government employees with "front" organizations, including "temporary organizations, 'spontaneous' campaigns, and pressure movements so frequently used by subversive groups."

The President's Commission accepted Director Hoover's broad view of the threat, along with the view endorsed by a Presidential Commission on Civil Rights that there also was a danger from "those who would subvert our democracy by ... destroying the civil rights of some groups." Consequently, the Executive Order included, as an indication of disloyalty, membership in or association with groups designated on an "Attorney General's list" as:

> totalitarian, fascist, communist, or subversive, or as having adopted a policy of advocating or approving the commission of acts of force, or violence to deny others their rights under the Constitution of the United States, or as seeking to alter the form of government of the United States by unconstitutional means."

The Executive Order was used to provide a legal basis for the FBI's investigation of allegedly "subversive" organizations which might fall within these categories. 94 Such investigations supplied a body of intelligence data against winch to check the names of prospective federal employees.

(2) Breadth of the Investigations — By the mid-1950s, the Bureau believed that the Communist Party was no longer used for Soviet espionage; it represented only a "potential" recruiting ground for spies. Thereafter, FBI investigations of Communist organizations and other groups unconnected to espionage but falling within the standards of the Attorney General's list frequently became a means for monitoring the political background of prospective federal employees by means of the "name check" of Bureau files. These investigations also served the "pure intelligence" function of informing the Attorney General of the influence and organizational affiliations of socalled "subversives."

No organizations were formally added to the Attorney General's list after 1955. However, the FBI's "name check" reports on prospective employees were never limited to information about listed organizations. The broad standards for placing a group on the Attorney General's list were used to evaluate an employee's background, regardless of whether or not lie was a member of a group on the list. If a "name check" uncovered information about a prospective employee's association with a group which might come within those standards, the FBI would report the data and attach a "characterization" of the organization relating tothe standards.

(3) FBI Control of Loyalty-Security Investigations — President Eisenhower's 1953 order specifically designated the FBI as responsible for "a full field investigation" whenever a "name check" or a background investigation by the Civil Service Commission or any other agency uncovered information indicating a potential security risk. President Truman had refused to give the Bureau this exclusive power initially, but he fought a losing battle.

Director Hoover had objected that President Truman's order did not give the FBI exclusive power and threatened "to withdraw from this field of investigation rather than to engage in a tug of war with the Civil Service Commission." President Truman was apprehensive about the FBI's growing power. The notes of one presidential aide on a meeting with the President reflect that Truman felt "very strongly anti-FBI" on the issue and wanted "to be sure and hold FBI down, afraid of 'Gestapo.' "

Presidential assistant Clark Clifford reviewed the situation and came down on the side of the FBI as "better qualified" than the Civil Service Commission. But the President insisted on a compromise which gave Civil Service "discretion" to call on the FBI "if it wishes." Director Hoover protested this "confusion" about the FBI's jurisdiction. When Justice Department officials warned that Congress would "find flaws" with the compromise, President Truman noted on a memorandum from Clifford:

> J. Edgar will in all probability get this backward looking Congress to give him what he wants. It's dangerous.

President's Truman's prediction was correct. His budget request of $16 million for Civil Service and $8.7 million for the FBI to conduct loyalty investigations was revised by Congress to allocate $7.4 million to the FBI and only $3 million to Civil Service. The issue was finally resolved to the FBI's satisfaction when the President issued a statement declaring that there were "to be no exceptions" to the rule that the FBI would make all loyalty investigations."

c. Executive Directives: Lack of Guidance and Controls

Two public presidential statements on FBI domestic intelligence authority — by President Truman in 1950 and by President Eisenhower in 1953 -- specifically declared that the FBI was authorized to investigate "subversive activity," electing the broader interpretation of the directive of conflicting Roosevelt directives. Moreover, a confidential directive of the National Security Council in 1949 granted authority to the FBI and military intelligence for investigation of "subversive activities." In 1962 President Kennedy issued a confidential order shifting supervision of these investigations from the NSC to the Attorney General, and the NSC's 1949 authorizations were reissued by Attorney General Kennedy in 1964.

As with the earlier Roosevelt directives, these statements, orders and authorizations failed to provide guidance on conducting or controlling "subversive" investigations.

Under President Truman, the Interdepartmental Intelligence Conference (IIC) was formally authorized in 1949 to supervise coordination between the FBI and the military of "all investigation of domestic espionage, counterespionage, sabotage, subversion, and other related intelligence matters affecting internal security."

The confidential Delimitations Agreement between the FBI and the military intelligence agencies was also revised in 1949 to require greater exchange of "information of mutual interest" and to require the FBI to advise military intelligence of developments concerning "subversive" groups who were "potential" dangers to the security of the United States.

In 1950, after the outbreak of the Korean war and in the midst of Congressional consideration of new internal security legislation, Director Hoover recommended that Attorney General J. Howard McGrath and the NSC draft a statement which President Truman issued in July 1950 providing that the FBI:

should take charge of investigative work in matters relating to espionage, sabotage, subversive activities and related matters."'

Despite concern among his assistants, President Truman's statement clearly placed him on the record as endorsing FBI investigations of "subversive activities." The statement said that such investigations had been authorized initially by President Roosevelt's "directives" of September 1939 and January 1943. However, those particular directives had not used this precise language.

Shortly after President Eisenhower took office in 1953, the FBI advised the White House that its "internal security responsibility" went beyond "statutory" authority. The Bureau attached a copy of the Truman statement, but not the Roosevelt directive. The FBI again broadly interpreted the Roosevelt directive by saving that it had authorized "investigative work" related to "subversive activities."

In December 1953 President Eisenhower issued a statement reiterating President Truman's "directive" and extending the FBI's mandate to investigations under the Atomic Energy Act.

President Kennedy issued no public statement comparable to the Roosevelt, Truman, and Eisenhower "directives." However, in 962 he did transfer the Interdepartmental Intelligence Conference to "the supervision of the Attorney General;" and in 1964 Attorney General Robert Kennedy reissued the IIC charter, citing as authority the President's 1962 order and retaining the term "subversion." The 'charter added that it did not "modify" or "affect" the previous "Presidential Directives" relating to the duties of the FBI, and that the Delimitations Agreement between the FBI and military intelligence "shall remain in full force and effect."

None of the directives, orders, or charters provided any definition of the broad and loose terms "subversion" or "subversive activities;" and none of the administrations provided effective controls over the FBI's investigations in this area.

3. Scope of Domestic Intelligence
a. "Subversive Activities"
The breadth of the FBI's investigations of "subversive activity" led to massive collection of information on law abiding citizens. FBI domestic intelligence investigations extended beyond known or suspected Communist Party members. They included other individuals who regarded the Soviet Union as the "champion of a superior way of life" and "persons holding important positions who have shown sympathy for Communist objectives and policies." Members of "non-Stalinist" revolutionary socialist groups were investigated because, even though they opposed the Soviet regime, the FBI viewed them as regarding the Soviet Union "as the center for world revolution." Moreover, the FBI's concept of "subversive Infiltration" was so broad that it permitted the investigation for decades of peaceful protest groups such as the NAACP.

(1) The Number of Investigations—By 1960 the FBI had opened approximately 432,000 files at headquarters on individuals and groups in the "subversive" intelligence field. Bet Between 1960 and 1963 an additional 9,000 such files were opened. An even larger number of investigative files were maintained at FBI field offices. Under the Bureau's filing system, a single file on a group could include references to hundreds or thousands of group members or other persons associated with the group in any way; and such names were indexed so that the information was readily retrievable.

(2) Vague and Sweeping Standards—The FBI conducted continuing investigations of persons whose membership in the Communist Party or in "a revolutionary group" had "not been proven," but who had "anarchistic or revolutionary beliefs" and had "committed past acts of violence during strikes, riots. or demonstrations." Persons not currently engaged in "activity of a subversive nature" were still investigated if they had engaged in such activity "several years ago"' and there was no "positive indication of disaffection."

The FBI Manual stated that it was "not possible to formulate any hard-and-fast standards for measuring "the dangerousness of individual members or affiliates of revolutionary organizations." Persons could be investigated if they were "espousing the line" of "revolutionary movements". Anonymous allegations could start an investigation if they were "sufficiently specific and of sufficient weight." The Manual added,

> Where there is doubt an individual may be a current threat to the internal security of the nation, the question should be resolved in the interest of security and investigation conducted.

The FBI Manual did not define "subversive" groups in terms of their links to a foreign government. Instead, they were "Marxist revolutionary-type" organizations "seeking the overthrow of the U. S. Government." One purpose of investigation was possible prosecution under the Smith Act. But no prosecutions were initiated under the Act after 1957. The Justice Department advised the FBI in 1956 that such a prosecution required "an actual plan for a violent revolution." The Department's position in 1960 was that "incitement to action in the foreseeable future" was needed. Despite the strict requirements for prosecution, the FBI continued to investigate "subversive" organizations "from an intelligence viewpoint" to appraise their "strength" and "dangerousness."

(3) COMINFIL—The FBI's broadest program for collecting intelligence was carried out under the heading COMINFIL, or Communist infiltration. The FBI collected intelligence about Communist "influence" under the following categories:

> Political activities Legislative activities Domestic administration issues
> Negro question Youth matters Women's matters Farmers' Matters
> Cultural activities Veterans' matters Religion Education Industry

FBI investigations covered "the entire spectrum of the social and labor movement in the country." The purpose—as publicly disclosed in the Attorney General's Annual Reports—was pure intelligence: to "fortify" the Government against "subversive pressures," or to "strengthen" the Government against "subversive campaigns."

In other words, the COMINFIL program supplied the Attorney General and the President with intelligence about a wide range of groups seeking to influence national policy under the rationale of determining whether Communists were involved. The FBI said it was not concerned with the "legitimate activities" of "nonsubversive groups," but only with whether Communists were "gaining a dominant role." Nevertheless, COMINFIL reports inevitably described "legitimate activities" totally unrelated to the alleged "subversive activity." This is vividly demonstrated by the COMINFIL reports on American's leading civil rights group in this period, the NAACP. The investigation continued for at least twenty-five years in cities throughout the nation, although no evidence was ever found to rebut the observation that the NAACP had a "strong tendency" to "steer clear of Communist activities."

(4) Exaggeration of Communist Influence—The FBI and the Justice D partment justified the continuation of COMINFIL investigations, despite the Communist Party's steady decline in the fifties and early sixties, on the theory that the Party was "seeking to repair its losses" with the "hope" of being able to "move in" on movements with "laudable objectives."

The FBI reported to the White House in 1961 that the Communist Party had "attempted" to take advantage of "racial disturbances" in the South and had "endeavored" to bring "pressure to bear" on government officials "through the press, labor unions, and student groups." At that time the FBI was investigating "two hundred known or suspected communist front and communist-infiltrated organizations. "By not stating how effective the "attempts" and "endeavors" of the Communists were, and by not indicating whether they were becoming more or less successful, the FBI offered a deficient rationale for its sweeping intelligence collection policy.

William C. Sullivan, a former head of the FBI Intelligence Division, has testified that such language was deliberately used to exaggerate the threat of Communist influence. "Attempts" and "influence" were "very significant words" in FBI reports, he said. These terms obscured what he felt to be the more significant criterion - the degree of Communist success. The Bureau "did not discuss this because we would have to say that they did not hit the target, hardly any."

A distorted picture of Communist "infiltration" later served to justify the FBI's intensive investigations of the groups involved in protests against the Vietnam War and the civil rights movement, including Dr. Martin Luther King, Jr., and the Southern Christian Leadership Conference.

b. "Racial Matters" and "Hate Groups"

In the 1950s, the FBI also developed intelligence programs to investigate "Racial Matters" and "hate organizations" unrelated to "revolutionary-type" subversives. "Hate organizations" were investigated if they had "allegedly adopted a policy of advocating, condoning, or inciting the use of force or violence to deny others their rights under the Constitution." Like the COMINFIL program, however, the Bureau used its "established sources" to monitor the activities of "hate groups" which did not "qualify" under the "advocacy of violence" standard.

In 1963, FBI field offices were instructed to report "the formation and identities" of "rightist or extremist groups" in the "anticommunist field." Headquarters approval was needed for investigating "groups in this field whose activities are not in violation of any statutes."

Under these, programs, the FBI collected and disseminated intelligence about the John Birch Society and its founder, Robert Welch, in 1959. The activities of another right-wing spokesman, Gerald L. K. Smith, who headed the Christian Nationalist Crusade, were the subject of FBI reports even after the Justice Department had concluded that the group had not violated federal law and that there was no basis for including the group on the "Attorney General's list."

The FBI program for collecting intelligence on "General Racial Matters" was even broader. It went beyond "race riots" to include "civil demonstrations" and "similar developments." These "developments" included:

> proposed or actual activities of individuals, officials, committees, legislatures, organizations, etc., in the racial field.

The FBI's "intelligence function" was to advise "appropriate" federal and local officials of "pertinent information" about "racial incidents."

A briefing of the Cabinet by Director Hoover in 1956 illustrates the breadth of collection and dissemination under the racial matters program. The briefing covered not only incidents of violence and the "efforts" and "plans" of Communists to "influence'" the civil rights movement, but also the legislative strategy of the NAACP and the activities of Southern Governors and Congressmen on behalf of groups opposing integration peacefully.

C. FBI Political Intelligence for the White House

Numerous items of political intelligence were supplied by the FBI to the White House in each of the three administrations during the Cold War era, apparently satisfying the desires of Presidents and their staffs.

President Truman and his aides received regular letters from Director Hoover labeled "Personal and Confidential" containing tidbits of political intelligence. The letters reported on such subjects as: inside information about the negotiating position of a non-Communist labor union; the activities of a former Roosevelt aide who was trying to influence the Truman administration's appointments; a report from a "confidential source" that a "scandal" was brewing which would be "very embarrassing" to the Democratic administration; a report from a "very confidential source" about a meeting of newspaper representatives in Chicago to plan publication of stories exposing organized crime and corrupt politicians; the contents of an in-house communication from Newsweek magazine reporters to their editors about a story they had obtained from the State Department, and criticism of the government's internal security programs by a former Assistant to the Attorney General.

Letters discussing Communist "influence" provided a considerable amount of extraneous information about the legislative process, including lobbying activities in support of civil rights legislation and the political activities of Senators and Congressmen.

President Eisenhower and his aides received similar tid-bits of political intelligence, including an advance text of a speech to be delivered by a prominent labor leader, reports from Bureau "sources" on the meetings of an NAACP delegation with Senators Paul Douglas and Everett Dirksen of Illinois; the report of an "informant" on the role of the United Auto Workers Union at an NAACP conference, summaries of data in FBI files on thirteen persons (including Norman Thomas, Linus Pauling, and Bertrand Russell) who had filed suit to stop nuclear testing, a report of a "confidential source" on plans of Mrs. Eleanor Roosevelt to hold a reception for the head of a civil rights group, and reports on the activities of Robert Welch and the John Birch Society.

The FBI also volunteered to the White House information from its most "reliable sources" on purely political or social contacts with foreign government officials by a Deputy Assistant to the President, Bernard Baruch, Supreme Court Justice William 0. Douglas, and Mrs. Eleanor Roosevelt.

Director Hoover sent to the White House a report from a "confidential informant" on the lobbying activities of a California group called Women for Legislative Action because its positions "paralleled" the Communist line.

As in the prior administrations, requests also flowed from the Eisenhower White House to the FBI. For example, a presidential aide asked the FBI to check its files on Rev. Carl McIntyre of the International Council of Christian Churches.

The pattern continued during the Kennedy administration. A summary of material in FBI files on a prominent entertainer was volunteered to Attorney General Kennedy because Hoover thought it "may be of interest." Attorney General Kennedy sent to the President an FBI memorandum on the purely personal life of Dr. Martin Luther King, Jr. Director Hoover supplied Attorney General Kennedy with background information on a woman who told an Italian newspaper that she had once been engaged to marry President Kennedy and on the husband of a woman who was reported in the press to have stated that the President's daughter would enroll in a cooperative nursery with which she was connected. The FBI Director also passed on information from a Bureau "source" r egarding plans of a group to publish allegations about the President's personal life.

In 1962 the FBI complied unquestioningly with a request from Attorney General Kennedy to interview a Steel Company executive and several reporters who had written stories about the Steel executive. The interviews were conducted late at night and early in the morning because, according to the responsible FBI official, the Attorney General indicated the information was needed for a White House meeting the next day.

Throughout the period, the Bureau also disseminated reports to high executive officials to discredit its critics. The FBI's Inside information on plans of the Lawyers Guild to denounce Bureau surveillance in 1949 gave the Attorney General the opportunity to prepare a rebuttal well in advance of the expected criticism. When the Knoxville Area Human Relations Council charged in 1960 that the FBI was practicing racial discrimination, the FBI did "name checks" on members the Council's board of directors and sent the results to the Attorney General. The name checks dredged up derogatory allegations from as far back as the late thirties and early forties.

d. IRS Investigations of Political Organizations

The IRS program that came to be used against the domestic dissidents of the 1960s was first used against Communists in the 1950s. As part of its COINTELPRO against the Communist Party, the FBI arranged for IRS investigations of Party members, and obtained their tax returns. In its efforts against the Communist Party, the FBI had unlimited access to tax returns: it never told the IRS why it wanted them, and IRS never attempted to find out.

In 1961, responding to White House and congressional interest in right-wing organizations, the IRS began comprehensive investigation of right-wing groups to identify contributors and ascertain whether or not some of them were entitled to their tax exempt status. Left-wing groups were later added, in an effort to avoid charges that such IRS activities were all aimed at one part of the political spectrum. Both right- and left-wing groups were selected for review and investigation because of their political activity and not because of any information that they had violated the tax laws.

While the IRS efforts begun in 1961 to investigate the political activities of tax exempt organizations were not as extensive as later programs in 1969-1973, they were a significant departure by the IRS from normal enforcement criteria for investigating persons or groups on the basis of information indicating noncompliance. By directing tax audits at individuals and groups solely because of their political beliefs, the

Ideological Organizations Audit Project (as the 1961 program was known) established a precedent for a far more elaborate program of targeting "dissidents."

During the Cold War period, there were serious weaknesses in the system of accountability and control of domestic intelligence activity. On occasion the executive chose not to comply with the will of Congress with respect to internal security policy, and the Congressiona attempt to exclude U.S. foreign intelligence agencies from domestic activities was evaded. Intelligence agencies also conducted covert programs in violation of laws protecting the rights of Americans. Problems of accountability were compounded by the lack of effective congressional oversight and the vagueness of executive orders, which allowed intelligence agencies to escape outside scrutiny.

a. The Emergency Detention Act

In 1946, four years before the Emergency Detention Act of 1950 was passed, the FBI advised Attorney General Clark that it had secretly compiled a security index of "potentially dangerous" persons. The Justice Department then made tentative plans for emergency detention based on suspension of the privilege of the writ of habeas corpus. Department officials deliberately avoided going to Congress, advising the FBI in a "blind memorandum:"

> The present is no time to seek legislation. To ask for it would only bring on a loud and acrimonious discussion.

In 1950, however, Congress passed the Emergency Detention Act which established standards and procedures for the detention, in the event of war, invasion or insurrection "in aid of a foreign enemy," of any person:

> as to whom there is reasonable ffround to believe that such person probably will engage in, or probably will conspire with others to engage in, acts of espionage or sabotage.

The Act did not authorize the suspension of the privilege of the writ of habeas corpus, and it provided that detained persons could appeal to a review board and to the courts.

Shortly after passage of the Detention Act, according to a Bureau document, Attorney General J. Howard McGrath told the FBI to disregard it and to "Proceed with the program as previously outlined." Department officials stated that the Act was "in conflict with" their plans, and was "unworkable." FBI officials agreed that the statutory procedures - such as "recourse to the courts" instead of suspension of habeas corpus - would "destroy" their program. Moreover, the Security Index used broader standards to determine "potential dangerousness" than those prescribed in the statute; and, unlike the Act, Department plans provided for issuing a Master Search Warrant and a Master Arrest Warrant. Two subsequent Attorneys General endorsed the decision to ignore the Emergency Detention Act.

b. Withholding Information

Not only did the FBI and the Justice Department jointly keep their noncompliance with the Detention Act secret from Congress, but the FBI withheld important aspects of its program from the Attorney General. FBI personnel had been instructed in 1949 that :

> no mention must be made in any investigative report relating to the classifications of top functionaries and key figures, nor to the Detcom and Comsab Programs, nor to the Security Index or the Communist Index.

These investigative procedures and administrative aides are confidential and should not be known to any outside agency.

FBI documents indicate that only the Security Index was made known to the Justice Department.

In 1955, the FBI tightened formal standards for the Security Index, reducing its size from 26,174 to 12,870 by 1958. However, there is no indication that the FBI told the Department that it kept the names of persons taken off the Security Index on a Communist, Index, because the Bureau believed such persons remained "potential threats." The secret Communist Index was renamed the Reserve Index in 1960 and expanded to include "influential" persons deemed likely to "aid subversive elements" in an emergency because of their "subversive associations and ideology." Such individuals fell under the following categories:

> Professors, teachers, and educators, labor union organizers and leaders; writers, lecturers, newsmen and others in the mass media field; lawyers, doctors, and scientists; other potentially influential persons on a local or national level; individuals who could potentially furnish financial or material aid.

Persons on the Reserve Index would receive "priority consideration" for "action" after detention of Security Index subjects. The breadth of this list is illustrated by the inclusion of the names of author Norman Mailer and a professor who merely praised the Soviet Union to his class.

In addition to keeping these programs secret, the FBI withheld information about espionage from the Justice Department on at least two occasions. In 1946 the FBI had "identified over 100 persons" whom it "suspected of being in the Government Communist Underground." Neither this number nor any names from this list were given to the Department because Director Hoover feared "leaks," and because the Bureau conceded in its internal documents that it did "not have evidence, whether admissible or otherwise, reflecting actual membership in the Communist Party." 196 Thus the Bureau's "suspicions" were not tested by outside review by the Justice Department and the investigations could continue. In 1951 the FBI again withheld from the Department names of certain espionage subjects "for security reasons," since disclosure "would destroy chances of penetration and control."

Even the President's Temporary Commission on Employee Loyalty could not get highly relevant information from the Bureau. FBI Assistant Director D.M. Ladd told the Commission in 1946 that there was a "substantial" amount of Communist "infiltration of the government." But Ladd declined to answer when Commission members asked for more details of FBI intelligence operations and the information which served as the basis for his characterization of the extent of infiltration. The Commission prepared a list of questions for the FBI and asked that Director Hoover appear in person. Instead, Attorney General Clark made an "informal" appearance and supplied a memorandum stating that the number of "subversives" in government had "not yet reached serious proportions," but that the possibility of "even one disloyal person" in government service constituted a "serious threat." Thus, the President's Commission chose not to insist upon making a serious evaluation of FBI intelligence operations or the extent of the danger.

The record suggests that executive officials were forced to make decisions regarding security policy without full knowledge. They had to depend on the FBI's estimate of the problem, rather than being able to make their own assessment on the basis of complete information. It is also apparent that by this time outside officials were sometimes unwilling to oppose Director Hoover or to inquire fully into FBI operations.

c. CIA Domestic Activity

(1) Vague Controls on CIA.—The vagueness of Congress's prohibitions of "internal security functions" by the CIA left room for the Agency's subsequent domestic activity. A restriction against "police, law enforcement or internal security functions" first appeared in President Truman's order establishing the Central Intelligence Group in 1946.

General Vandenburg, then Director of Central Intelligence, testified in 1947 that this restriction was intended to "draw the lines very sharply between the CIG and the FBI" and to "assure that the Central Intelligence Group can never become a Gestapo or security police." 202 Secretary of the Navy James Forrestal testified that the CIA would be "limited definitely to purposes outside of this country, except the collection of information gathered by other government agencies." The FBI would be relied upon "for domestic activities."

In the House floor debate Congressman Holifield stressed that the work of the CIA:

is strictly in the field of secret foreign intelligence—what is known as clandestine intelligence. They have no right in the domestic field to collect information of a clandestine military nature. They can evaluate it; yes.

Consequently, the National Security Act of 1947 provided specifically that the CIA

shall have no police, subpoena, law-enforcement powers, or internal security functions.

However, the 1947 Act also contained a vague and undefined duty to protect intelligence "sources and methods" which later was used to justify domestic activities ranging from electronic surveillance and break-ins to penetration of protest groups.

(2) Drug Testing and Cover Programs.—In the early 1950s, the CIA began a program of surreptitiously testing, chemical and biological materials, which included drug testing on unwitting Americans. The existence of such a program was kept secret because, as the CIA's Inspector General wrote 1957, it, was necessary to "protect operations from exposure" to "the American public" as well as "enemy forces." Public knowledge of the CIA's "unethical and illicit activities" was thought likely to have serious "political repercussions." CIA drug experimentors disregarded instructions of their superiors within the Agency and failed to take "reasonable precautions" when they undertook the test which resulted in the death of Dr. Frank Olsen.

The CIA made extensive use of the Bureau of Narcotics and Dangerous Drugs in conducting its program of drug testing on unwitting subjects.

Military intelligence also administered drugs to volunteer subjects who were unaware of the purpose or nature of the tests in which they were participating.

The CIA's drug research was conducted in part through arrangements with universities, hospitals, and "private research organizations" in a manner which concealed "from the institution the interests of the CIA," although "key individuals" were made witting of Agency sponsorship. There were similar covert relationships with American private institutions in other CIA intelligence activities. 211

5. Intrusive Techniques

Throughout the cold war period, the intelligence agencies used covert techniques which invaded personal privacy to execute their vague, uncontrolled, and overly broad mandate to collect intelligence. Intelligence techniques were not properly controlled by responsible authorities; some of the techniques were misused by senior administration officials. On the other hand, the nature of the programs—and, in some cases, their very existence—was often concealed from those authorities.

a. Communications Interception: CIA and NSA

During the 1950s the Central Intelligence Agency instituted a major program for opening mail between the United States and the Soviet Union as it passed through postal facilities in New York City. Two other short-term CIA projects in the fifties also involved the opening of international mail within the United States, through access to Customs Service facilities. Moreover, in the late 1940s the Department of Defense made arrangements with several communications companies to receive international cable traffic, reinstating a relationship that had existed during World War II. These programs violated not only the ban on internal security functions by foreign intelligence agencies in the 1947 Act, but also specific statutes protecting the privacy of the mails and forbidding the interception of communications.

While their original purpose was to obtain foreign intelligence, the programs frequently did not distinguish between the messages of foreigners and of Americans. Furthermore, by the late fifties and early sixties, the CIA and NSA were sharing the "take" with the FBI for domestic intelligence purposes.

In this period, the CIA opened mail to and from the Soviet Union largely at random, intercepting letters of Americans unrelated to foreign intelligence or counterintelligence. After the FBI learned of the CIA program, it levied requests in certain categories. Apart from foreign counterintelligence criteria, the Bureau expressed interest in letters from citizens professing "pro-Communist sympathies" and "data re U.S. peace groups going to Russia."

The secret arrangements with cable companies to obtain copies of international traffic were initially authorized by Secretary of Defense James Forrestal and Attorney General Tom Clark, although it is not clear that they knew of the interception of American as well as foreign messages. They developed no formal legal rationale, and their later successors were never consulted to renew the authorization.

The CIA sought no outside authorization before instituting its mail opening program. Several Post Office officials were misled into believing that the CIA's request for access to the mail only involved examining the exterior of the envelopes. President Kennedy's Postmaster General, J. Edward Day, testified that he told CIA Director Allen Dulles he did not want to "know anything about" what the CIA was doing. Beyond undocumented assumptions by CIA officials, there is no evidence that the President or the Attorney General was ever informed about any aspect of CIA mail-opening operations in this period.

b. FBI Covert Techniques

(1) Electronic Surveillance.

(a) The Question of Authority: In 1946 Attorney General Toni Clark asked President Truman to renew the authorization for warrantless wiretapping issued by President Roosevelt in 1940. Clark's memorandum, however, did not refer to the portion of the Roosevelt directive which said wiretaps should be limited "insofar as possible to aliens." It stressed the danger from "subversive activity here at home," and requested authority to wiretap "in cases vitally affecting the domestic security."

The President gave his approval. Truman's aides later discovered Attorney General Clark's omission and the President considered, but decided against, returning to the terms of Roosevelt's authorization.

In 1954 the Supreme Court denounced the Fourth Amendment violation by police who placed a microphone in a bedroom in a local gambling case.

Soon thereafter, despite this decision — and despite his predecessor's ruling that trespassory installation of bugs was in the "area" of the Fourth Amendment — Attorney General Herbert Brownell authorized the "unrestricted use" in the "national interest" of "trespass in the installation of microphones."

From 1954 until 1965, when Attorney General Nicholas Katzenbach reconsidered the policy and imposed stricter regulations, the FBI had unsupervised discretion to use microphone surveillance and to conduct surreptitious entries to install microphones. Thus, the safeguard of approval by the Attorney General for each wiretap had been undercut by the FBI's ability to intrude into other, often more intimate conversations by microphone "bugging."

(b) Extensive Bugging: In May 1961, Director Hoover advised Deputy Attorney General Byron White that the FBI was using "microphone surveillances" involving "trespass" for "intelligence purposes" in the "internal security field." He called White's attention to the 1954 Brownell memorandum, although he said microphones were used "on a restricted basis" and cited as examples only "Soviet intelligence agents and Communist Party leaders."

In fact, the FBI had already used microphone surveillance for broader coverage than Communists or spies. Indeed, it had "bugged" a hotel room occupied by a Congressman in February 1961. There is no evidence that Attorney General Kennedy or Deputy Attorney General White were specifically informed of this surveillance. But the Attorney General received information which came from the "bug" and authorized a wiretap of the Congressman's secretary.

Furthermore, FBI records disclose that the FBI conducted warrantless microphone surveillances in 1960-1963 directed at a "black separatist group," "black separatist group functionaries" and a "(white) racist organization." There may have been others for purely domestic intelligence purposes.

The FBI maintained no "central file or index" to record all microphone surveillances in this period, and FBI records did not distinguish "bugs" involving trespass.

(2) "Black Bag Jobs." — There is no indication that any Attorney General was informed of FBI "black bag" jobs, and a "Do Not File" procedure was designed to preclude outside discovery of the FBI's use of the technique.

No permanent records were kept for approvals of "black bag jobs," or surreptitious entries conducted for purposes other than installing a "bug". The FBI has described the procedure for authorization of surreptitious entries as requiring the approval of Director Hoover or his Assistant Clyde Tolson. The authorizing memorandum was filed in the Director's office under a "Do Not File" procedure, and thereafter destroyed. In the field office, the Special Agent in Charge maintained a record of approval in his office safe. At the next yearly field office inspection, an Inspector would review these records to ensure that the SAC had secured FBI headquarters approval in conducting surreptitious entries. Upon completion of the review, these records were destroyed.

The only internal FBI memorandum found discussing the policy for surreptitious entries confirms that this was the procedure and states that "we do not obtain authorization from outside the Bureau" because the technique was "clearly illegal." The memorandum indicates that "black bag jobs" were used not only "in the espionage field" but also against "subversive elements" not directly connected to espionage activity. It added that the techniques resulted "on numerous occasions" in obtaining the "highly secret and closely guarded" membership and mailing lists of "subversive" groups.

(3) Mail Opening — The FBI did not seek outside authorization when it reinstituted mail opening programs in the fifties and early sixties. Eight programs were conducted for foreign intelligence and counterespionage purposes, and Bureau officials who supervised these programs have testified that legal considerations were simply not raised at the time.

Beyond their original purpose, the FBI mail opening programs produced some information of an essentially domestic nature. For example, during this period one program supplied "considerable data" about American citizens who expressed pro-Communist sympathies or made "anti-U.S. statements." Some of the mail-opening by-product regarding Americans was disseminated to other agencies for law enforcement purposes, with the source disguised.

c. Use of FBI Wiretaps

The authorization for wiretapping issued by President Truman in 1946 allowed the Attorney General to approve wiretaps in the investigation of "subversive activity" to protect the "domestic security."

A wiretap on an official of the Nation of Islam, originally authorized by Attorney General Herbert Brownell in 1957, continued thereafter without re-authorization until 1965. Attorney General Robert Kennedy approved FBI requests for wiretaps on an Alabama Klan leader in 1963 and on black separatist group leader Malcolm X in 1964. Kennedy also authorized wiretap coverage requested by the Warren Commission in 1964. Kennedy's approval of FBI requests for wiretaps on Dr. Martin Luther King and several of his associates are discussed in greater detail elsewhere in the Committee's report.

In addition, Attorney General Kennedy approved wiretaps on four American citizens during investigations of "classified information leaks." The taps failed to discover the sources of the alleged "leaks" and involved procedural irregularities. In 1961 Attorney General Kennedy told Director Hoover that the President wanted the FBI to determine who was responsible for an apparent "leak" to Newsweek reporter Lloyd Norman, author of an article about American military plans in Germany. But the Attorney General was not asked to approve a wiretap on Norman's residence until after it was installed.

According to contemporaneous Bureau memoranda, wiretaps in 1962 on the residence of New York Times reporter Hanson Baldwin and his secretary to determine the source of an article about Soviet missile sites were also instituted without prior written approval of the Attorney General; and one of them - the tap on the secretary - was instituted without the Attorney General's prior knowledge. Kennedy's written approval was obtained, however, three days after the Baldwin tap was installed and four days after the tap on the secretary was installed.

The pattern, including ex post facto approval, was repeated for wiretaps of a former FBI agent who disclosed "confidential" Bureau information in a public forum. The first tap lasted for eight days in 1962, and it was reinstituted in 1963 for an undetermined period. Attorney General Kennedy was advised that the FBI desired to place the initial coverage; but he was not informed that it had been effected the day before, and he did not grant written approval until the day it was terminated. It appears that only oral authorization was obtained for reinstituting the tap in 1963.

In February 1961, Attorney General Kennedy requested the FBI to initiate an investigation for the purpose of developing:

> intelligence data which would provide President Kennedy a picture of what was behind pressures exerted on behalf of [a foreign country] regarding sugar quota deliberations in Congress . . . in connection with pending sugar legislation.

This investigation lasted approximately nine weeks, and was reinstituted for a three-month period in mid-1962.

According to an FBI memorandum, the Attorney General authorized the wiretaps in 1961 on the theory that "the administration has to act if money or gifts are being passed by the [representatives of a foreign country]." Specifically, he approved wiretaps on several American citizens: three officials of the Agriculture Department (residences only); the clerk of the House Committee on Agriculture who was also secretary to the chairman (residence only) ; and a registered agent of the foreign country (both residence and business telephones). After passage of the Administration's own sugar bill in April 1961, these wiretaps were discontinued.

The investigation was reinstituted in June 1962, when the Bureau learned that representatives of the same foreign country again might be influencing congressional deliberations concerning an amendment to the sugar quota legislation. Attorney General Kennedy approved wiretaps on the office telephone of an attorney believed to be an agent of the foreign country and, again, on the residence telephone of the Clerk of the House, Agriculture Committee. The latter tap continued for one month, but the former apparently lasted for three months.

These wiretaps in 1961 and 1962 were arguably related to "foreign intelligence" — but not to "subversive activity" unless that term is interpreted beyond its conventional meaning. More important, they generated information which was potentially useful to the Kennedy administration for purely political purposes relating to the legislative process.

The wiretap authorized by Attorney General Kennedy on another high executive official in this period did not relate to political considerations, but to concern about possible disclosure of classified information to a foreign government. There is no indication that the wiretap authorized by Attorney General Katzenbach in 1965 on the editor of an anti-communist newsletter was related in any way to the book he had written in 1964 alleging personal impropriety by Attorney General Kennedy.

6. Domestic Covert Action

In its COINTELPRO operation, the FBI went beyond excessive information-gathering and dissemination to the use of secret tactics designed to "disrupt" and "neutralize" domestic intelligence targets. At the outset, the target was the Communist Party, U.S.A. But, consistent with the pattern revealed in other domestic intelligence activities, the program widened to other targets, increasingly concentrating on domestic dissenters. The expansion of COINTELPRO began in the Cold War period and accelerated in the latter part of the 1960s.

a. COINTELPRO: Communist Party

The COINTELPRO program, authorized by Director Hoover against the Communist Party in 1956, had its roots in two lines of Bureau policy going back to the 1940s. The first was the accepted FBI practice of attempting to disrupt "subversive" organizations. A former head of the FBI Intelligence Division has testified:

> We were engaged in COINTELPRO tactics, to divide, confuse, weaken, in diverse ways, an organization. We were engaged in that when I entered the Bureau in 1941.

The memorandum recommending the institution of COINTELPRO stated that the Bureau was already seeking to "foster factionalism" and "cause confusion" within the Communist Party.

The second line of pre-existing Bureau policy involved propaganda to discredit the Communist Party publicly. For example, in 1946, an earlier head of the FBI Intelligence Division proposed that efforts be made to release "educational material" through "available channels" to influence "public opinion." The "educational" purpose was to undermine Communist support among "labor unions," "persons prominent in religious circles," and "the Liberal elements," and to show "the basically Russian nature of the Communist Party in this country." By 1956, a propaganda effort was underway to bring the Party and its leaders "into disrepute before the American public."

The evidence indicates that the FBI did not believe that the Communist Party, when the COINTELPRO program was formalized in 1956, constituted as serious a threat in terms of actual espionage as it had in the 1940s. Nevertheless, the FBI systematized its covert action program against the Communist Party in part because the surfacing of informants in legal proceedings had somewhat limited the Bureau's coverage of Party activities, and also to take advantage of internal conflicts within the Party. Covert "disruption" was also designed to make sure that the Party would not reorganize under a new label and thus would remain an easier target for prosecution.

In the years after 1956, the purpose of the Communist Party COINTELPRO changed somewhat. Supreme Court decisions substantially curbed criminal prosecution of Communists. Subsequently, the FBI "rationale" for COINTELPRO was that it had become "impossible to prosecute Communist Party members" and some alternative was needed "to contain the threat."

b. Early Expansion of COINTELPRO

From 1956 until 1960, the COINTELPRO program was primarily aimed at the Communist Party organization. But, in March 1960, participating FBI field offices were directed to make efforts to prevent Communist "infiltration" of "legitimate mass organizations, such as Parent-Teacher Associations, civil organizations, and racial and religious groups." The initial technique was to notify a leader of the organization, often by "anonymous communications," about the alleged Communist in its midst. In some cases, both the Communist and the "infiltrated" organization were targeted.

This marked the beginning of the progression from targeting Communist Party members, to those allegedly under Communist "influence," to persons taking positions supported by the Communists. For example, in 1964 targets under the Communist Party COINTELPRO label included a group with some Communist participants urging increased employment of minorities and a non-Communist group in opposition to the House Committee on Un-American Activities.

In 1961, a COINTELPRO operation was initiated against the Socialist Workers Party. The originating memorandum said it was not a "crash" program; and it was never given high priority. The SWP's support for "such causes as Castro's Cuba and integration problems arising in the South" were noted as factors in the FBI's decision to target the organization. The Bureau also relied upon its assessment that the SWP was "not just another socialist group but follows the revolutionary principles of Marx, Lenin, and Engels as interpreted by Leon Trotsky" and that it was "in frequent contact with international Trotskyite groups stopping short of open and direct contact with these groups. The SWP had been designated as "subversive" on the "Attorney General's list" since the 1940s.

D. Intelligence And Domestic Dissent: 1964-1976

1. Main Developments of the 1964-1976 Period

Beginning in the mid-sixties, the United States experienced a period of domestic unrest and protest unparalleled in this century. Violence erupted in the poverty-stricken urban ghettos, and opposition to American intervention in Vietnam produced massive demonstrations.

A small minority deliberately used violence as a method for achieving political goals — ranging from the brutal murder and intimidation of black Americans in parts of the South to the terrorist bombing of office buildings and government-supported university facilities. But three Presidential commissions found that the larger outbreaks of violence in the ghettos and on the campuses were most often spontaneous reactions to events in a climate of social tension and upheaval.

During this period, thousands of young Americans and members of racial minorities came to believe in civil disobedience as a vehicle for protest and dissent.

The government could have set an example for the nation's citizens and prevented spiraling lawlessness by respecting the law as it took steps, to predict or prevent violence. But agencies of the United States, sometimes abetted by public opinion and government officials, all too often disregarded the Constitutional rights of American in their conduct of domestic intelligence operations.

The most significant developments in domestic intelligence activity during this period may be summarized as follows:

a. Scope of Domestic Intelligence

FBI intelligence reports on protest activity and domestic dissent accumulated massive information on lawful activity and law-abiding citizens for vaguely defined "pure intelligence" and "preventive intelligence" purposes related only remotely or not at all to law enforcement or the prevention of violence. The FBI exaggerated the extent of domestic Communist influence, and COMINFIL investigations improperly included groups with no significant connections to Communists.

The FBI expanded its use of informers for gathering intelligence about domestic political groups, sometimes upon the urging of the Attorney General. No significant limits were placed on the kind of political or personal information collected by informers, recorded in FBI files, and often disseminated outside the Bureau.

Army intelligence developed programs for the massive collection of information about, and surveillance of, civilian political activity in the United States and sometimes abroad.

In contrast to previous policies for centralizing domestic intelligence investigations, the Federal Government encouraged local police to establish intelligence programs both for their own use and to feed into the Federal intelligence-gathering process. This greatly expanded the domestic intelligence apparatus, making it harder to control.

The Justice Department established a unit for storing and evaluating intelligence about civil disorders which was designed to use non-intelligence agencies as regular sources of information, which, in fact, drew on military intelligence as well as the FBI, and which transmitted its computer list of citizens to the CIA and the IRS.

b. Domestic Intelligence Authority Intelligence gathering related to protest activity was generally increased in response to vague requests by Attorneys General or other officials outside the intelligence agencies; such increases were sometimes ratified retroactively by such officials.

The FBIs exclusive control over civilian domestic intelligence at the Federal level was consolidated by formal agreements with the Secret Service regarding protective intelligence and with the Bureau of Alcohol, Tobacco, and Firearms regarding terrorist bombings.

c. Domestic Covert Action

The FBI developed new covert programs for disrupting and discrediting domestic political groups, using the techniques originally applied to Communists. The most intensive domestic intelligence investigations, and frequently COINTELPRO operations, were targeted against persons identified not as criminals or criminal suspects, but as "rabble rousers," "agitators," "key activists," or "key black extremists" because of their militant rhetoric and group leadership. The Security Index was revised to include such persons.

Without imposing adequate safeguards against misuse, the Internal Revenue Service passed tax information to the FBI and CIA, in some cases in violation of tax regulations. At the urging of the White House and a Congressional Committee, the IRS established a program for investigating politically active groups and individuals, which included auditing their tax returns.

d. Foreign Intelligence and Domestic Dissent

A 1966 agreement concerning "coordination" between the CIA and the FBI permitted CIA involvement in internal security functions. Under pressure from the Johnson and Nixon White Houses to determine whether there was "foreign influence" behind anti-war protests and black militant activity, the CIA began collecting intelligence about domestic political groups.

The CIA also conducted operations within the United States under overly broad interpretations of responsibility to protect the physical security of its facilities and to protect intelligence "sources" and "methods." These operations included surreptitious entry, recruitment of informers in domestic political groups, and at least one instance of warrantless wiretapping approved by the Attorney General.

In the same period, the National Security Agency monitored international communications of Americans involved in domestic dissent despite the fact that its mission was supposed to be restricted to collecting foreign intelligence and monitoring only foreign communications.

e. Intrusive Techniques

As domestic intelligence operations broadened and focused upon dissenters, the Government increased the use of many of its most intrusive surveillance techniques. During the period from 1964 to 1972, the standards and procedures for warrantless electronic surveillance were tightened, but actual practice was sometimes at odds with the articulated policy. Also during these years, CIA mail opening expanded at the Bureau's request, and NSA monitoring expanded to target domestic dissenters. However, the FBI cut back use of certain techniques under the pressure of Congressional probes and changing public opinion.

f. Accountability and Control

During this period several sustained domestic intelligence efforts illustrated deficiencies in the system for controlling intelligence agencies and holding them accountable for their actions.

In 1970, presidential approval was temporarily granted for a plan for interagency coordination of domestic intelligence activities which included several illegal programs. Although the approval was subsequently revoked, some of the programs were implemented separately by various agencies.

Throughout the administrations of Presidents Johnson and Nixon, the investigative process was misused as a means of acquiring political intelligence for the White House. At the same time, the Justice Department's Internal Security Division, which should have been a check against the excesses of domestic intelligence, generally failed to restrain such activities. For example, as late as 1971-1973, the FBI continued to evade the will of Congress, partly with Justice Department approval, by maintaining a secret "Administrative Index" of suspects for round-up in case of national emergency.

g. Reconsideration of FBI Authority

Partly in reaction to congressional inquiries, the FBI in the early 1970s began to reconsider the extent of its authority to conduct domestic intelligence activities and requested clarification from the Attorney General and an executive mandate for intelligence investigations of "terrorists" and "revolutionaries".

In the absence of any new standards imposed by statute, or by the Attorney General, the FBI continued to collect domestic intelligence under sweeping authorizations issued by the Justice Department in 1974 for investigations of "subversives," potential civil disturbances, and "potential crimes". These authorizations were explicitly based on broad theories of inherent executive power. Attorney General Edward H. Levi recently promulgated guidelines which represent the first significant attempt by the Justice Department to set standards and limits for FBI domestic intelligence investigations.

2. Scope of Domestic Intelligence

During this period the FBI continued the same broad investigations of the lawful activities of Americans that were based on the Bureau's vague mandate to collect intelligence about "subversion."

In addition, the Bureau—joined by CIA, NSA, and military intelligence agencies—took on new and equally broad assignments to investigate "racial matters," the "New Left," "student agitation," and alleged "foreign influence" on the antiwar movement.

a. Domestic Protest and Dissent: FBI

"We are an intelligence agency," stated a policy directive to all FBI offices in 1966, "and as such are expected to know what is going on or is likely to happen." Written in the context of demonstrations over the Vietnam war and civil rights, this order illustrates the general attitude among Bureau officials and high administration officials who established intelligence policy: in a country in ferment, the FBI could, and should, know everything that might someday be useful in some undefined manner.

(1) Racial Intelligence—During the 1960s, the FBI, partly on its own and partly in response to outside requests, developed sweeping programs for collecting domestic intelligence concerning racial matters. These programs had roots in the late 1950s. 284 By the early 1960s, they had grown to the point that the Bureau was gathering intelligence about proposed "civil demonstrations" and the related activities of "officials, committees, legislatures, organizations, etc.," in the "racial field."

In 1965, FBI field offices were directed to supply "complete," information (including "postponement or cancellation") :

> regarding planned racial activity, such as demonstrations, rallies, marches, or threatened opposition to activity of this kind.

Field offices reported their full "coverage" of "meetings" and "any other pertinent information concerning racial activities."

In late 1966, field offices were instructed to begin preparing semi monthly summaries of "existing racial conditions in major urban areas," relying upon "established sources," and "racial," "criminal," and security informants." These reports were to describe the "general programs" of all "civil rights organizations" and "black nationalist organizations" as well as subversive or "hate-type" groups. The information to be gathered was to include: "readily available personal background data" on "leaders and individuals in the civil rights movement" and other "leaders and individuals involved," as well as any data in Bureau files on "subversive associations" they might have; the "objectives sought by the minority community;" the community reaction to "minority demands;" and "the number, character, and intensity of the techniques used by the minority community, such as picketing or sit-in demonstrations, to enforce their demands."

Thus, the FBI was mobilized to used all its available resources to discover everything it could about "general racial conditions." While the stated objective was to arrive at an "evaluation" of potential for violence, the broad sweep of the directives issued to the field resulted in the collection and filing of vast amounts of information unrelated to violence.

Some programs concerning "general racial matters" were directed to concentrate on groups with a "propensity for violence and civil disorder." But even these programs were so overbroad in their application as to include Dr. Martin Luther King, Jr. and his non-violent Southern Christian Leadership Conference in the "radical and violence-prone" "hate group" category. The stated justification, unsupported by any facts, was that Dr. King might "abandon his supposed 'obedience' to 'white, liberal doctrines' (nonviolence) and embrace black nationalism."

Another leading civil rights group, the Congress of Racial Equality (CORE), was investigated under the "Racial Matters" Program because the Bureau concluded that it was moving "away from a legitimate civil rights organization" and "assuming a militant black nationalist posture." The FBI reached this conclusion on the grounds that "some leaders in their public statements" had condoned "violence as a means of attaining Negro rights." The investigation was intensified, even though it was recognized there was no information that its members "advocate violence" or "participate in actual violence."

The same overbreadth characterized the FBI's collection of intelligence about "white militant groups." Among the groups investigated were those "known to sponsor demonstrations against integration and against the busing of Negro students to white schools." As soon as a new organization of this sort was formed, the Bureau used its informants and "established sources" to determine "the aims and purposes of the organization, its leaders, approximate membership," and other "background data" bearing upon "the militancy" of the group.

(2) "New Left" Intelligence.—The FBI collected intelligence under its VIDEM (Vietnam Demonstration) and STAG (Student Agitation) Programs on "anti-Government demonstrations and protest rallies" which the Bureau considered "disruptive." Field offices were warned against "incomplete and nonspecific reporting" which neglected such details as "number of protesters present, identities of organizations, and identities of speakers and leading activists."

The FBI attempted to define the "New Left," but with little success. The Bureau agent who was in charge of New Left intelligence conceded that:

> It has never been strictly defined, as far as I know.... It's more or less an attitude, I would think.

He also stated that the definition was expanded continually.

Field offices were told that the New Left was a "subversive force" dedicated to destroying our "traditional values." Although it had "no definable ideology," it was seen as having "strong Marxist, existentialist, nihilist and anarchist overtones." Field offices were instructed that "proper areas of inquiry" regarding the subjects of "New Left" investigations were "public statements, the writings and the leadership activities" which might establish their "rejection of law and order" and thus their "potential" threat to security. Such persons would also be placed on the Security Index (for detention in a time of emergency) because of these "anarchistic tendencies," even if the Bureau could not prove "membership in a subversive organization."

A Bureau memorandum which recommended the use of disruptive techniques against the "New Left" paid particular attention to one of its "anarchistic tendencies":

> the New Left has on many occasions viciously and scurrilously attacked the Director and the Bureau in an attempt to hamper our investigations and drive us off the college campuses.

Later instructions to the field stated that the term "New Left" did not refer to "a definite organization," but to a "loosely bound, freewheeling, college-oriented movement" and to the "more extreme and militant anti-Vietnam war and antidraft protest organizations." These instructions directed a "comprehensive study of the whole movement" for the purpose of assessing its "dangerousness." Quarterly reports were to be prepared, and "subfiles" opened, under the following headings:

> Organizations ("when organized, objectives, locality which active, whether part of a national organization") Membership (and "sympathizers" — use "best available informants and sources") Finances (including identity of "angels" and funds from "foreign sources") Comunist Influence Publications ("describe publications, show circulation and principal members of editorial staff"] Violence Religion ("support of movement by religious groups or individuals") Race Relations Political Activities ("details relating to position taken on political matters including efforts to influence public opinion, the electorate and Government bodies") Ideology Education ("courses given together with any educational outlines and assigned or suggested reading") Reform ("demonstrations aimed at social reform") Labor ("all activity in the labor field") Public Appearances of

Leaders ("on radio and television" and "before groups, such as labor, church and minority groups," including "summary of subject matter discussed") Factionalism Security Measures International Relations ("travel in foreign countries," "attacks on United States foreign policy") Mass Media ("indications of support of New Left by mass media")

Through these massive reports, the FBI hoped to discover "the true nature of the New Left movement." Few Bureau programs better reflect "pure intelligence" objectives which extended far beyond even the most generous definition of "preventive intelligence."

Apart from the massive general reports required on the "New Left," examples of particular investigations included: a stockholders group planning to protest their corporation's war production at the annual stockholders meeting; a university professor who was "an active participant in New Left demonstrations," publicly surrendered his draft card, and had been arrested in antiwar demonstrations, but not convicted; and two university instructors who helped support a student "underground" newspaper whose editorial policy was described as "left-of-center, anti-establishment, and opposed [to] the University administration."

The FBI also investigated emerging "New Left" groups, such as "Free Universities" attached to various college campuses, to determine whether they were connected "in any way" with "subversive groups." For example, when an article appeared in a newspaper stating that one "Free University" was being formed and that it was "anti-institutional," the FBI sought to determine its "origin," the persons responsible for its "formation," and whether they had "subversive backgrounds." The resulting report described in detail the formation, curriculum content, and associates of the group. It was disseminated to military intelligence and Secret Service field offices and headquarters in Washington as well as to the State Department and the Justice Department.

b. FBI Informants

The FBI Manual has never significantly limited informant reporting about the lawful political activities or personal lives of American citizens, except for prohibiting reports about legal defense "plans or strategy," "employer-employee relationships" connected with labor unions, and "legitimate campus activities." In practice, FBI agents imposed no other limitations on the informants they handled and, on occasion, disregarded the prohibitions of the Manual.

(1) Infiltration of the Klan—In mid-1964, Justice Department officials became increasingly concerned about the spread of Ku Klux Klan activity and violence in the Deep South. Attorney General Kennedy advised President Johnson that, because of the "unique difficulty" presented by a situation where "lawless activities" had the "sanction of local law enforcement agencies," the FBI should apply to the Klan the same "techniques" used previously "in the infiltration of Communist groups."

Former Attorney General Katzenbach, under whose tenure FBI activities against the Klan expanded, vigorously defended this decision as necessary to "deter violence" by sowing "deep mistrust among Klan members" and making them aware that they were "under constant observation." The FBI Manual did, in fact, advise Bureau agents against "wholesale investigations" of persons who "merely attend meetings on a regular basis. "But FBI intelligence officials chafed under this restriction and sought expanded informant coverage. Subsequently, the Manual was revised in 1967 to require the field to furnish the "details" of Klan "rallies" and "demonstrations." By 1971, the Special Agents in Charge of field offices had the discretion to investigate not only persons with "a potential for violence," but also anyone else who in the SAC's "judgment" was an "extremist."

(2) "Listening Posts" in the Black Community — Two special informant programs illustrate the breadth of the Bureau's infiltration of the black community. In 1970, the FBI used its "established informants" to determine the "background, aims and purposes, leaders and Key Activists" in every black student group in the country, "regardless of [the group's] past or present involvement in disorders." Field offices were instructed to "target informants" against these groups and to "develop such coverage" where informants were not already available."

In response to Attorney General Clark's instructions regarding civil disorders intelligence in 1967, the Bureau launched a "ghetto informant program" which lasted until 1973. The number of ghetto informants expanded rapidly: 4,067 in 1969 and 7,402 by 1972. The original concept was to establish a "listening post" by recruiting a person "who lives or works in a ghetto area" to provide information regarding the "racial situation" and "racial activities." Such information could include "the proprietor of a candy store or barber shop." As the program developed, however, ghetto informants were:

> utilized to attend public meetings held by extremists, to identify extremists passing through or locating in the ghetto area, to identify purveyors of extremist literature as well as given specific assignments where appropriate.

Material to be furnished by ghetto informants included names of "Afro-American type book stores" and their "owners, operators and clientele."

(3) Infiltration of the "New Left". — The FBI used its "security" informant program to report extensively on all activities relating to opposition to the Vietnam war. Moreover, informants already in groups considered "subversive" by the FBI also reported on the activities of other organizations and their members, if the latter were being "infiltrated" by the former groups.

The agent who handled one informant in an antiwar group believed to be infiltrated by "subversive groups and/or violent elements" testified that the informant told him "everything she knew" about the chapter she joined. Summaries of her reports indicate that she reported extensively about personal matters and lawful political activity. 320 This informant estimated that her reports identified as many as 1,000 people to the FBI over an 18-month period. The vast majority of these persons were members of peaceful and law-abiding groups, including the United Church for Christ, which were engaged in joint social welfare projects with the antiwar group which the informant had infiltrated.

Other FBI informants reported, for example, on the Women's Liberation 'Movement, identifying its members at several mid-western universities and reporting statements made by women concerning their personal reasons for participating in the women's movement.

Moreover, as in the case of informants in the black community, efforts were made to greatly increase the number of informants who could report on antiwar and related groups. In 1969, the Justice Department specifically asked the FBI to use not only "existing sources," but also "any other sources you may be able to develop" to collect information about "serious campus disorders." 324 The Bureau ordered its field offices in 1970 to "make every effort" to obtain "informant coverage" of every "New Left commune." Later that year, after Director Hoover lifted restrictions against recruiting 18 to 21-year-old informants, field offices were urged to take advantage of this "tremendous opportunity" to expand coverage of New Left "collectives, communes, and staffs of their underground newspapers."

c. Army Surveillance of Civilian Political Activity

In the early 1960s, after several commitments of troops to control racial disturbances and enforce court orders in the South, Army intelligence began collecting information on civilian political activity in all areas where it believed civil disorders might occur. The growth of the Army's domestic intelligence program typifies, once again, the general tendency of information-gathering operations to continually broaden their coverage.

Shortly after the Army was called upon to quell civil disorders in Detroit and to cope with an antiwar demonstration at the Pentagon in 1967, the Army Chief of Staff approved a recommendation for "continuous counterintelligence investigations" to obtain information on "subversive personalities, groups or organizations" and their "influence on urban populations" in promoting civil disturbances. The Army's "collection plan" for civil disturbances specifically targeted as "dissident elements" (without further definition) the "civil rights movement" and the "anti-Vietnam/anti-draft movements." As revised later, Army intelligence-gathering extended beyond "subversion" and "dissident groups" to "prominent persons" who were "friendly" with the "leaders of the disturbance" or "sympathetic with their plans."

d. Federal Encouragement of Local Police Intelligence

In reaction to civil disorders in 1965-1966, Attorney General Katzenbach turned for advice to the newly created President's Commission on Law Enforcement and Administration of Justice. After holding a conference with police and National Guard officials, the President's Commission urged police not to react with too much force to disorder "in the course of demonstrations," but to make advance plans for "a true riot situation." This meant that police should establish "procedures for the acquisition and channeling of intelligence" for the use of "those who need it." Former Assistant Attorney General Vinson recalled the Justice Department's concern that local police did not have "any useful intelligence or knowledge about ghettos, about black communities in the big cities."

During the winter of 1967-1968, the Justice Department and the National Advisory Commission on Civil Disorders reiterated the message that local police should establish "intelligence units" to gather and disseminate information on "potential" civil disorders. These units would use "undercover police personnel and informants" and draw on "community leaders, agencies, and organizations in the ghetto." The Commission also urged that these local units be linked to "a national center and clearinghouse" in the Justice Department. One consequence of these recommendations was that the FBI, because of regular liaison with local police, became a channel and repository for much of this intelligence data.

Local police intelligence provided a convenient manner for the FBI to acquire information it wanted while avoiding criticism for using covert techniques such as developing campus informants. For example, in 1969, Director Hoover decided "that additional student informants cannot be developed" by the Bureau. Field offices were instructed, however, that one way to continue obtaining intelligence on "situations having a potential for violence" was to develop "in-depth liaison with local law enforcement agencies. "Instead of recruiting student informants itself, the FBI would rely on local police to do so.

These Federal policies contributed to the proliferation of local police intelligence activities, often without adequate controls. One result was that still more persons were subjected to investigation who neither engaged in unlawful activity, nor belonged to groups which might be violent. For example, a recent state grand jury report on the Chicago Police Department's "Security Section" described its "close working relationship" with Federal intelligence agencies, including Army intelligence and the FBI. The report found that the police intelligence system produced "inherently inaccurate, and distortive data" which contaminated Federal intelligence. One police officer testified that he listed "any person" who attended two "public meetings" of a group as a "member." This conclusion was forwarded "as a fact" to the FBI. Subsequently, an agency seeking, "background information" on that person from the Bureau in an employment investigation or for other purposes would be told that the individual was "a member." The grand jury stated:

> Since federal agencies accepted data from the Security Section without questioning the procedures followed, or methods used to gain information, the federal government cannot escape responsibility for the harm done to untold numbers of innocent persons.

e. The Justice Department's Interdivision Information Unit (IDIU)

Joseph Califano, President Johnson's assistant in 1967, testified that the Newark and Detroit riots were a "shattering experience" for Justice Department officials and "for us in the White House." They were concerned about the "lack of intelligence" about "black groups." Consequently, "there was a desire to have the Justice Department have better intelligence, for lack of a better term, about dissident groups." This desire "precipitated the intelligence unit" established by Attorney General Ramsey Clark in late 1967. According to Califano, the President and the White House staff were insisting: "There must be a way to predict violence. We've got to know more about this."

In September 1967 Attorney Genera l Clark asked Assistant Attorney General John Doar to review the Department's "facilities" for civil disorders intelligence. Doar recommended creating a Departmental "intelligence unit" to analyze FBI information about "certain persons and groups" (without further definition) in the urban ghettos. He proposed that its "scope be very broad initially" so as to "measure the influence of particular groups." Doar recommended that, in addition to the FBI, agencies who should "funnel information" to the unit should include:

Community Relations Service Poverty Programs Neighborhood Legal Services Program Labor Department Programs Intelligence Unit of the Internal Revenue Service Alcohol, Tobacco, and Firearms Division of the Treasury Department Narcotics Bureau (then in the Treasury Department) Post Office Department

Doar recognized that the Justice Department's Community Relations Service, designed to conciliate racial conflicts, risked losing its "credibility" and thereby its ability to help prevent riots, but he assured the Attorney General that the "confidentiality" of its information could be protected.

A later study for Attorney General Clark -added the following agencies to Doar's list:

President's Commission on Civil Disorders New Jersey Blue Ribbon Commission (and similar state-agencies) State Department Army Intelligence Office of Economic Opportunity Department of Housing and

Urban Development (surveys and Model City applications) Central Intelligence Agency National Security Agency

This study recommended that FBI reports relating "to the civil disturbance problem" under the headings "black power, new left, pacifist, pro-Red Chinese, anti-Vietnam war, pro-Castro, etc." be used to develop "a master index on individuals, or organizations, and by cities."

Attorney General Clark approved these recommendations and established the Interdivision Information Unit (IDIU) for:

reviewing and reducing to quickly retrievable form all information that may come to this Department relating to organizations and individuals who may play a role, whether purposefully or not, either in instigating or spreading civil disorders, or in preventing or checking them.

In early instructions, Clark had stated that the Department must "endeavor to increase" such intelligence from "external sources."

In fact, according to its first head, the IDIU did use intelligence from the Army, the Internal Revenue Service, and "other investigative agencies." Sometimes IDIU information was used to "determine whether or not" the Community Relations Service should "mediate" a dispute. The Unit developed a computer system which could generate lists of all "members or affiliates" of an organization, their location and travel, "all incidents" relating to "specific issues", and "all information" on a "planned specific demonstration."

By 1970, the IDIU computer was receiving over 42,000 "intelligence reports" a year relating to "civil disorders and campus disturbances" from:

the FBI, the U.S. Attorneys, Bureau of Narcotics, Alcohol, Tobacco, and Firearms Division of the Treasury Department and other intelligence gathering bodies within the Executive Branch.

IDIU computer tapes, which included 10-12,000 entries on "numerous anti-war activists and other dissidents," were provided to the Central Intelligence Agency in 1970 by Assistant Attorney General Jerris Leonard, then the Attorney General's Chief of Staff for Civil Disturbance and head of the Civil Rights Division. This list of persons was sent to the Internal Revenue Service where the Special Services staff opened intelligence files on all persons and organizations listed. Many of them were later investigated or audited, in some cases merely because they were on the list.

In 1971, the IDIU computer included data on such prominent persons as Rev. Ralph Abernathy, Caesar Chavez, Bosley Crowther (former New York Times film critic), Sammy Davis, Jr., Charles Evers, James Farmer, Seymour Hersh, and Coretta King. Organizations on which information had been collected included the NAACP, the Congress of Racial Equality, the Institute for Policy Studies, VISTA, United Farm Workers of California, and the Urban League. Ordinary private citizens who were not nationally prominent were also included. One was described as "a local civil rights worker," another as a "student at Merritt College and a member of the Peace and Freedom Party as of mid-68," and another as "a bearded militant who writes and recites poetry."

Thus, beginning in 1967-1968, the IDIU was the focal point of a massive domestic intelligence apparatus established in response to ghetto riots, militant black rhetoric, antiwar protest, and campus disruptions. Through IDIU, the Attorney General received the benefits of information gathered by numerous agencies, without setting limits to intelligence reporting or providing clear policy guidance. Each component of the structure FBI, Army, IDIU, local police, and many others — set its own generalized standards and priorities, resulting in excessive collection of information about law abiding citizens.

   f. COMINFIL Investigations: Overbreadth

In the late 1960's the Communist infiltration or association concept continued to be used as a central basis for FBI intelligence investigations. In many cases it led to the collection of information on the same groups and persons who were swept into the investigative net by the vague missions to investigatie such subjects as "racial matters" or the "New Left." As it had from its beginning, theCOMINFIL concept produced investigations of individuals and groups who were not Communists. Dr. Martin Luther King, Jr. is the best known example. 348 But the lawful activities of many other persons were recorded in FBI files and reports, because they associated in some wholly innocent way with Communists, a term which the Bureau required its agents to "interpret in its broad sense" to include "splinter" and "offshoot" groups.

During this period, when millions of Americans demonstrated in favor of civil rights and against the Vietnam war, many law-abiding citizens and groups came under the scrutiny of intelligence agencies. Under the COMINFIL program, for example, the Bureau compiled extensive reports on moderate groups, like the NAACP.

The FBI significantly impaired the democratic decisionmaking process by its distorted intelligence reporting on Communist infiltration of and influence on domestic political activity. In private remarks to Presidents and in public statements, the Bureau seriously exaggerated the extent of Communist influence in both the civil rights and anti- Vietnam war movements.

   3. Domestic Intelligence Authority

During this period there were no formal executive directives outlining the scope of authority for domestic intelligence activity of the sort previously issued by Presidents Roosevelt, Truman, Eisenhower, and Kennedy. 352 However, there was a series of high-level requests for intelligence concerning racial and urban unrest directed to the FBI and military intelligence agencies. As with the earlier formal Presidential directives on subjects like "subversion," these instructions provided no significant guidelines or controls.

   a. FBI Intelligence

Since the early 1960s, the Justice Department had been making sporadic requests for intelligence related to specific racial events. For example, the FBI was requested to provide a tape recording of a speech by Governor-elect George Wallace of Alabama in late 1962 and for "photographic coverage" of a civil rights demonstration on the 100th anniversary of the Emancipation Proclamation. On its own initiative, the FBI supplied the Civil Rights Division with information from a "confidential source" about plans for a demonstration in Virginia, including background data on its "sponsor" and the intention to make "a test case." The Civil Rights Division prepared regular summaries of information from the Bureau on "demonstrations and other racial matters."

A formal directive, for a similar purpose, was sent by Attorney General Kennedy to U.S. Attorneys throughout the South in May 1963. It instructed them to "make a survey" to ascertain "any places where racial demonstrations are expected within the next 30 days" and to make "assessments of situations" in their districts. The FBI was "asked to cooperate. "

President Johnson ordered the FBI to investigate and report on the origins and extent of the first small-scale Northern ghetto disturbances in the summer of 1964. After the FBI submitted a report on the Watts riot in Los Angeles in 1965, however, Attorney General Katzenbach advised President Johnson that the FBI should investigate "directly" only the possible "subversive involvement." Katzenbach did not believe that the FBI should conduct a "general investigation" of "other aspects of the riot," since these were local law enforcement matters. The President approved this "limited investigation." Nonetheless, internal Bureau instructions in 1965 and 1966 went far beyond this limitation. By 1967 new Attorney General Ramsey Clark reversed the Department's position on such limitations.

After the riots in Newark and Detroit in the summer of 1967, President Johnson announced that the FBI had "standing instructions" for investigating riots "to search for evidence on conspiracy." This announcement accompanied the creation of a National Advisory Commission on Civil Disorders to investigate the "basic factors and causes leading to" the riots, including the "influence" of groups or persons "dedicated to the incitement or encouragement of violence." The President ordered the FBI in particular to "provide investigative information and assistance" to the Commission. Director Hoover also agreed to investigate "allegations of subversive influence, involvement of out-of-state influences, and the like. "

In September 1967, Attorney General Clark directed the FBI to:

> use the maximum resources, investigative and intelligence, to collect and report all facts bearing upon the question as to whether there has been or is a scheme or conspiracy by any group of whatever size, effectiveness or affiliation, to plan, promote or aggravate riot activity.

Justice Department executives were generally aware of, and in some cases sought to widen, the scope of FBI intelligence collection. In a lengthy review of Bureau reports, John Doar, Assistant Attorney General for the Civil Rights Division, expressed concern that the FBI had not "taken a broad spectrum approach" to intelligence collection, since it had "focused narrowly" on "traditional subversive groups" and on persons suspected of "specific statutory violations."

Reiterating this viewpoint, Attorney General Clark told Director Hoover that "existing intelligence sources" may not have "regularly monitored" possible riot conspirators in "the urban ghetto." He added that it was necessary to conduct a "broad investigation" and that

> sources or informants in black nationalist organizations, SNCC (Student Nonviolent Coordinating Committee) and other less publicized groups should be developed and expanded to determine the size and purpose of these groups and their relationship to other groups . . .

Clark described his directive as setting forth "a relatively new area of investigation and intelligence reporting for the FBI."

In response to the Attorney General's instructions, the FBI advised its field offices of the immediate "need to develop additional penetrative coverage of the militant black nationalist groups and the ghetto areas."

b. Army Intelligence

On January 10, 1968, a meeting took place at the White House for the purpose of "advance planning for summer riots." The White House memorandum of the meeting reported:

The Army has undertaken its own intelligence study, and has rated various cities as to their riot potential. They are making contingency plans for troop movements, landing sites, facilities, etc.

It added that the Attorney General and the Deputy Secretary of Defense "had agreed to coordinate their efforts." The Army General Counsel's memorandum of the meeting stated that Attorney General Clark had "stressed the difficulty of the intelligence effort," especially because there were "only 40 Negro FBI agents" out of the total of about 6,300. Clark added that "every resource" was needed in "the intelligence collection effort," although he asked the Defense Department to "screen" its "incoming intelligence" and send "only key items" to the Justice Department.

There is no record that at this or any other similar meeting in this period the Attorney General or White House aides explicitly ordered the Army to conduct intelligence investigations using infiltration or other covert surveillance techniques. However, even though Army collection plans which were circulated to the Justice Department and the FBI did not mention techniques of collection, the information they described could only be obtained by covert surveillance. No objections were voiced by the Justice Department.

Not until 1969 was there a formal civilian decision specifically authorizing Army surveillance of civilian political activity. At that time, Attorney General John Mitchell and Secretary of Defense Melvin Laird considered the matter and over the objections of the Army General Counsel, decided that the Army would participate in intelligence collection concerning civil disturbances. The Army's collection plan was not rescinded until June 1970, after public exposure and congressional criticism.

c. FBI Interagency Agreements

After the assassination of President Kennedy, the FBI and the rot Service negotiated an -agreement which recognized that the Bureau had "general jurisdiction" over "subversion." The term was more narrowly than it had been defined by practice in the past, knowingly or wilfully advocat[ing]" overthrow of the Government by "force or violence" or by "assassination." Except for "temporary" action to "neutralize" -a threat to the President, the Secret Service agreed to "conduct no investigation" of "members of subversive WU without notifying the FBI. The Bureau, on the other hand, would not investigate individuals "solely" to determine their "dangerousness to the President."

After Congress enacted antibombing legislation in 1970, the FBI was assigned primary responsibility for investigating "offenses perpetrated by terrorist/revolutionary groups." When these guidelines were developed, the FBI shifted supervision of bombing cases from its General Investigative Division to the Intelligence Division because, as one official put it, the specific criminal investigations were "so interrelated with the gathering of intelligence in the racial and security fields that overlap constantly occurs."

The agreement with Secret Service and the "guidelines" covering bombing investigations did not give the FBI any additional domestic intelligence-gathering authority. They simply provided for dissemination of information to Secret Service and allocated criminal investigative jurisdiction between the FBI and the Alcohol, Firearms, and Tobacco Division. Nevertheless, both presupposed that the FBI had broad authority to investigate "subversives" or "terrorist/revolutionary groups."

4. Domestic Covert Action

a. COINTELPRO

The FBI's initiation of COINTELPRO operations against the Ku Klux Klan, "Black Nationalists" and the "New Left" brought to bear upon a wide range of domestic groups the techniques previously developed to combat Communists and persons who happened to associate with them.

The start of each program coincided with significant national events. The Klan program followed the widely-publicized disappearance in 1964 of three civil rights workers in Mississippi. The "Black Nationalist" program was authorized in the aftermath of the Newark and Detroit riots in 1967. The "New Left" program developed shortly after student disruption of the Columbia University campus in the spring of 1968. While the initiating memoranda approved by Director Hoover do not refer to these specific events, it is clear that they shaped the context for the Bureau's decisions.

These programs were not directed at obtaining evidence for use in possible criminal prosecutions arising out of those events. Rather, they were secret programs—"under no circumstances" to be "made known outside the Bureau"—which used unlawful or improper acts to "disrupt" or "neutralize" the activities of groups and individuals targeted on the basis of imprecise criteria.

(1) Klan and "White Hate" COINTELPRO—The expansion of Klan investigations, in response to pressure from President Johnson and Attorney General Kennedy, was accompanied by an internal Bureau decision to shift their supervision from the General Investigative Division to the Domestic Intelligence Division. One internal FBI argument for the transfer was that the Intelligence Division was "in a position to launch a disruptive counterintelligence program" against the Klan with the "same effectiveness" it had against the Communist Party.

Accordingly, in September 1964 a directive was sent to seventeen field offices instituting a COINTELPRO against the Klan and what considered to be other "White Hate" organizations (e.g., American Nazi Party, National States Rights Party) "to expose, disrupt, and otherwise neutralize" the activities of the groups, "their leaders, and adherents."

During the 1964-1971 period, when the program was in operation, 287 proposals for COINTELPRO actions against Klan and "White Hate" groups were authorized by FBI headquarters. Covert techniques used in this COINTELPRO included creating new Klan chapters to be controlled by Bureau informants and sending an anonymous letter designed to break up a marriage.

(2) "Black Nationalist" COINTELPRO—The stated strategy of the "Black Nationalist" COINTELPRO instituted in 1967 was "to expose, disrupt, misdirect, discredit, or otherwise neutralize" such groups and their "leadership, spokesmen, members, and supporters." The larger objectives were to "counter" their "propensity for violence" and to "frustrate" their efforts to "consolidate their forces" or to "recruit new or youthful adherents." Field offices were instructed to exploit conflicts within and between groups; to use news media contacts ridicule and otherwise discredit groups; to prevent "rabble rousers" from spreading their "philosophy" publicly; and to gather information on the "unsavory backgrounds" of group leaders.

In March 1968, the program was expanded from twenty-three to forty-one field offices and the following long-range goals were set forth:

(1) prevent the "coalition of militant black nationalist groups;" (2) prevent the rise of a "messiah" who could "unify and electrify" the movement, naming specifically Dr. Martin Luther King, Jr., Stokely Carmichael, and Elijah Muhammed; (3) prevent violence by pinpointing "potential troublemakers" and "neutralizing" them before they "exercise their potential for violence;" (4) prevent groups and leaders from gaining "respectabily by discrediting them to the "responsible" Negro community, the "responsible" white community, "liberals" with "vestiges of sympathy" for militant black nationalists, and "Negro radicals;" and (5) "prevent these groups from recruiting young people."

After the Black Panther Party emerged as a group of national stature, FBI field offices were instructed to develop "imaginative and hard-hitting counterintelligence measures aimed at crippling the BPP." Particular attention was to be given to aggravating conflicts between the Black Panthers and rival groups in a number of cities where such conflict had already taken on the character of "gang warfare with attendant threats of murder and reprisals."

During 1967-1971, FBI headquarters approved 379 proposals for COINTELPRO actions against "black nationalists." These operations utilized dangerous and unsavory techniques which gave rise to the risk of death and often disregarded the personal rights and dignity of the victims.

(3) "New Left" COINTELPRO—The most vaguely defined and haphazard of the COINTELPRO operations was that initiated against the "New Left" in May 1968. It was justified to the FBI Director by his subordinates on the basis of the following considerations:

The nation was "undergoing an era of disruption and violence" which was "caused to a large extent" by individuals "generally connected with the New Left."

Some of these, "activists" were urging "revolution" and calling for "the defeat of the United States in Vietnam."

The problem was not just that they committed "unlawful acts," but also that they "falsely" alleged police brutality, and that they "scurrilously attacked the Director and the Bureau" in an attempt to "hamper" FBI investigations and to "drive us off the college campuses."

Consequently, the COINTELPRO was intended to "expose, disrupt, and otherwise neutralize" the activities of "this group" and "persons connected with it." The lack of any clear definition of "New Left" meant, as an FBI supervisor testified, that "legitimate" and nonviolent antiwar groups were targeted because they were "lending aid and comfort" to more disruptive groups.

Further directives issued soon after initiation of the program urged field offices to "vigorously and enthusiastically" explore "every avenue of possible embarrassment" of New Left adherents. Agents were instructed to gather information on the "immorality" and the "scurrilous and depraved" behavior, "habits, and living conditions" of the members of targeted groups. This message was reiterated several months later, when the offices were taken to task for their failure to remain alert for and seek specific data depicting the "depraved nature and moral looseness of the New Left" and to "use this Material in a vigorous and enthusiastic approach to neutralizing them."

In July 1968, the field offices were further prodded by FBI headquarters to:

(1) prepare leaflets using "the most obnoxious pictures" of New Left leaders at various universities;

(2) instigate "personal conflicts or animosities" between New Left leaders;

(3) create the impression that leaders are "informants for the Bureau or other law enforcement agencies" (the "snitch jacket" technique) ;

(4) send articles from student or "underground" newspapers which show "depravity" ("use of narcotics and free sex") of New Left leaders to university officials, donors, legislators, and parents;

(5) have members arrested on marijuana charges;

(6) send anonymous letters about a student's activities to parents, neighbors, and the parents' employers;

(7) send anonymous letters about New Left faculty members (signed "A Concerned Alumni" or "A Concerned Taxpayer") to university officials, legislators, Board of Regents, and the press;

(8) use "cooperative press contacts;"

(9) exploit the "hostility" between New Left and Old Left groups;

(10) disrupt New Left coffee houses near military bases which are attempting to "influence members of the Armed forces;"

(11) use cartoons, photographs, and anonymous letters to "ridicule" the New Left;

(12) use "misinformation" to "confuse and disrupt" New Left activities, such as by notifying members that events have been cancelled.

During the period 1968-1971, 291 COINTELPRO actions against the "New Left" were, approved by headquarters. Particular emphasis was placed upon preventing the targeted individuals from public speaking or teaching and providing "misinformation" to confuse demonstrators.

b. FBI Target Lists

The FBI's most intensive domestic intelligence investigations and COINTELPRO operations were directed against persons identified, not as criminals or criminal suspects, but in vague terms such as "rabble rouser," "agitators," "key activists," or "key black extremists." The Security Index for detention in time of national emergency was revised to include such persons.

(1) "Rabble Rouser/Agitator" Index—Following a meeting with the National Advisory Commission on Civil Disorders in August 1967, Director Hoover ordered his subordinates to intensify collection of intelligence about "vociferous rabble-rousers." He also directed a "Key Black Extremist" "that an index be compiled of racial agitators and individuals who have demonstrated a potential for fomenting racial discord."

The already vague standards for the Rabble Rouser Index were broadened in November 1967 to cover persons with a "propensity for fomenting" any disorders affecting the "internal security" — as opposed to only racial disorders — and to include persons of local as well as national interest. This included "black nationalists, white supremacists, Puerto Rican nationalists, anti-Vietnam demonstration leaders, and other extremists." A rabble rouser was defined as:

a person who tries to arouse people to violent action by appealing to their emotions, prejudices, etcetera; a demagogue.

In March 1968, the Rabble Rouser Index was renamed the Agitator Index and field offices were ordered to obtain a photograph of each person on the Index. However, expanding the size of the Agitator Index lessened its value as an efficient target list for FBI intelligence operations. Consequently, the Bureau developed a more refined tool for this purpose-the Key Activist Program.

(2) "Key Activist" Program. — Instructions were issued to ten major field offices in January 1968 to designate certain persons as "Key Activists," who were defined as

> individuals in the Students for Democratic Society and the anti-Vietnam war groups [who] are extremely active and most vocal in their statements denouncing the United States and calling for civil disobedience and other forms of unlawful and disruptive acts.

There was to be an "intensive investigation" of each Key Activist, which might include "high-level informant coverage" and "technical surveillances and physical surveillances."

The "New Left" COINTELPRO was designed in part to "neutralize" the Key Activists, who were "the moving forces behind the New Left. One of the first techniques employed in this program was to obtain the Federal income tax returns of Key Activists for use in disrupting their activities. In October 1968, the Key Activist Program was expanded to virtually all field offices. The field agents were instructed to recommend additional persons for the program and to "consider if the individual was rendered ineffective would it curtail [disruptive] activity in his area of influence." While the FBI considered Federal prosecution a "logical" result of these investigations and "the best deterrent," Key Activists were not selected because they were suspected of committing or planning to commit any specific Federal crime.

(3) "Key Black Extremist" Program. — A "Key Black Extremist" target list for concentrated investigation and COINTELPRO actions was instituted in 1970. Key Black Extremists were defined as

> leaders or activists [who] are particularly extreme, agitative, anti-Government, and vocal in their calls for terrorism and violence.

Field offices were instructed to place all Key Black Extremists in the to priority category of the Security Index and in the Black Nationalist Photograph Album, which concentrated on "militant black nationalists" who traveled extensively. In addition, the following steps were to be taken:

(1) All aspects of the finances of a KBE must be determined. Bank accounts must be monitored. . . .

(2) Continuing consideration must be given by each office to develop means to neutralize the effectiveness of each KBE. . . .

(3) Obtain suitable handwriting specimens. . . .

(4) Particular efforts should be made to obtain records of and/or reliable witnesses to, inflammatory statements. . . .

(5) Where there appears to be a possible violation of a statute within the investigative jurisdiction of the Bureau, [it should be] vigorously investigated. . . .

(6) Particular attention must be paid to travel by a KBE and every effort made to determine financial arrangements for such travel. . . .

(7) The Federal income tax returns of all KBEs must be checked annually. . . .

Reports on all Key Black Extremists were to be submitted every ninety days, and the field was urged to use "initiative and imagination" to achieve "the desired results." Once again, the "result" was not limited to prosecution of crimes and the targets were not chosen because they were suspected of committing crimes.

(4) Security Index — The Agitator Index was abolished in 1971 because "extremist subjects" were "adequately followed" through the Security Index. In contrast to the other indices, the Security Index was not reviewed by the FBI alone. It had, from the

late 1940's, been largely a joint FBI-Justice Department program based on the Department's plans for emergency detention. According to FBI memoranda, moreover, President Johnson was directly involved in the updating of emergency detention plans.

After a large-scale march on the Pentagon against the Vietnam War in October 1967, President Johnson ordered a comprehensive review of the government's emergency plans. Attorney General Clark was appointed chairman of a committee to review the Presidential Emergency Action Documents (PEADs) prepared under the Emergency Detention Program. One result of this review, in which the FBI took Part, was a decision to bring the Detention Program into line with the Emergency Detention Act of 1950, reversing the previous decision to "disregard" as "unworkable" the procedural requirements of the Act, which were tighter than the standards which had been applied by FBI and Justice.

The Bureau also had to revise its criteria for inclusion of names on the Security Index, which since 1950 had disregarded the statutory standards. However, the definition chosen of a "dangerous individual" was so broad that it enabled the Bureau to add persons not previously eligible. A "dangerous individual" was defined as a

> person as to whom there is reasonable ground to believe that such person probably will engage in, or probably will conspire with others to engage in, acts of espionage and sabotage, including acts of terrorism or assassination and any interference with or threat to the survival of and effective operation of the national, state, and local governments and of the national defense effort.

The emphasized language greatly broadened the Security Index standards. It gave FBI intelligence officials the opportunity to include on the Security Index "racial militants", "black nationalists", and individuals associated with the "New Left" who were not affiliated with the "basic revolutionary organizations" as the Bureau characterized the Communist Party, which had previously been the focus of the Security Index. Once again, the limitations which a statute was intended to impose were effectively circumvented by the use of elastic language in a Presidential directive.

Moreover, the Bureau adopted a new "priority" ranking for apprehension in case of an emergency. Top priority was now given not only to leaders of "basic subversive organizations," but also to "leaders of anarchistic groups." 410 It was said to be the "anarchistic tendencies" of New Left and racial militants that made them a "threat to the internal security. "

Initially, the Justice Department approved informally these changes in the criteria for "the persons listed for apprehension." After several months of "study," the Justice Department's Office of Legal Counsel formally approved the new Security Index criteria. This was the first time since 1955 that the Department had fully considered the matter, and the previous policy of disregarding the procedures of the Emergency Detention Act of 1950 was formally abandoned. If an emergency occurred, the Attorney General would abide by "the requirement that any person actually detained will be entitled to a hearing at which time the evidence will have to satisfy the standards of [the Act]." However, the Office of Legal Counsel declared that the Security Index criteria themselves could be - as they were - less precise than those of the Act because of the "needed flexibility and discretion at the operating level in order to carry on an effective surveillance program." Thus while the plan to ignore Congress' procedural limitations was abandoned, Congress' substantive standards were disregarded as insufficiently "flexible."

c. Internal Revenue Service Program

(1) Misuse by FBI and CIA.—IRS information was used as an instrument of domestic intelligence mainly by the FBI. For example, in 1965, the Bureau obtained the tax returns of Ku Klux Klan members in order to develop "discrediting or embarrassing" information as part of the Bureau's COINTELPRO against the Klan. The procedure by which FBI obtained access to tax returns and related information held by IRS was deemed "illegal" when it was discovered by the Chief of the IRS Disclosure Branch in 1968. The FBI had not followed the procedures for obtaining returns which required written application to the IRS Disclosure Branch. Instead the Bureau had arranged to obtain the returns and information surreptitiously through contacts inside the IRS Intelligence Division. The procedure for FBI access was regularized by the IRS after 1968: a formal request on behalf of the Bureau was made to the IRS Disclosure Branch, by the internal Security Division of the Justice Department.

During this same period, the CIA was obtaining tax returns in a similar manner to the FBI, although in much smaller numbers. Yet even after procedures were changed for the FBI's access to tax information in 1968, the IRS did not re-examine the CIA's practices. Therefore, CIA continued to receive tax return information without filing requests as required by the regulations.

Between 1968 and 1974, either directly or through the Internal Security Division of the Justice Department, the FBI requested at least 130 tax returns for domestic intelligence purposes. This included the returns of 46 "New Left activists" and 74 "black extremists," as part of Bureau COINTELPRO operations to "neutralize" these individuals. These requests were not predicated upon any specific information suggesting delinquency in fulfilling tax obligations.

Even after a formal request was required before supplying the FBI with tax returns, the IRS accepted the Justice Department's undocumented assertions that tax information was "necessary" in connection with an "official matter" involving "internal security." Yet in making such assertions, the Justice Department's Internal Security Division relied entirely on the Bureau's judgment. Thus, while the IRS is required by the statute to release tax information only where necessary, it in effect delegated its responsibility to the Internal Security Division which in turn delegated the decision to the FBI. Although most FBI requests for tax information were for targets of various COINTELPRO operations, the Justice Department official who made the requests on behalf of the Bureau said he was never informed of the existence of COINTELPRO.

Even after 1968, the Bureau sometimes used tax information in improper or unlawful ways. For example, the Bureau attempted to use such information to cause IRS to audit a mid-western college professor associated with "new left" activities at the time he was planning to attend the 1968 Democratic Party National Convention in Chicago. The FBI agent in charge of the operation against the professor explained its purpose in a memorandum:

> if IRS contact with [the Professor] can be arranged within the next two weeks their demands upon him may be a source of distraction during the critical period when he is engaged in meetings and plans for disruption of the Democratic National Convention. Any drain upon the time and

concentration which [the Professor], a leading figure in Demcon planning, can bring to bear upon this activity can only accrue to the benefit of the Government and general public.

Among the tax returns which the CIA obtained informally from IRS in an informal and illegal manner were those of the author of a book, the publication of which the CIA sought to prevent, and of Ramparts magazine which had exposed the CIA's covert use of the National Student Association. In the latter case, CIA memoranda indicate that its officials were unwilling to risk a formal request for tax information without first learning through informal disclosure whether the tax returns contained any information that would be helpful in their effort to deter this "attack on the CIA" and on "the administration in general ."

(2) The Special Service Staff. — IRS Targeting of Ideological Groups. — In 1969, the IRS established a Special Service Staff to gather intelligence on a category of taxpayers defined essentially by political criteria. The SSS attempted to develop tax cases against the targeted taxpayers and initiated tax fraud investigations against some who would otherwise never have been investigated.

The SSS originated as a result of pressure from the permanent Subcommittee on Investigations of the Senate Committee on Government Operations and from President Nixon, acting through White House assistants Tom Charles Huston and Dr-Arthur Burns. According to the IRS Commissioner's memorandum, Dr. Burns expressed to him the President's concern

> over the fact that tax-exempt funds may be supporting activist groups engaged in stimulating riots both on the campus and within our inner cities.

The administration did not supply any facts to support the assertion that such groups were violating tax laws.

After the SSS was established, the FBI and the Justice Department's Interdivisional Information Unit (IDIU) became its largest sources of names. An Assistant IRS Commissioner requested the FBI to provide information regarding "various organizations of predominantly dissident or extremist nature and/or people prominently identified within those organizations." The FBI agreed, believing, as one intelligence official put it, that SSS would "deal a blow" to "dissident elements."

Among the material received by SSS from the FBI was a list of 2,300 organizations categorized as "Old Left," "New Left," and "Right Wing." The SSS also received about 10,000 names on IDIU computer printouts. SSS opened files on all these taxpayers, many of whom were later subjected to tax audits and some to tax fraud investigations. There is no reason to believe that the names listed by the FBI or the IDIU were selected on the basis of any probable noncompliance with the tax laws. Rather, these groups and individuals were targeted because of their political and ideological beliefs and activities.

The SSS, by the time it was disbanded in 1973, had gone over approximately half of the IDIU index and established files on those individuals on whom it had no file. Names on the SSS list included Nobel Prize winner Linus Pauling, Senators Charles Goodell and Ernest Gruening, Congressman Charles Diggs, journalists Joseph Alsop and Jimmy Breslin. and attorney Mitchell Rogovin. Organizations on the SSS list included: political groups ranging from the John Birch Society to Common Cause; religious organizations such as the B'nai Brith Antidefamation League and the Associated Catholic Charities; professional associations such as the American Law

Institute and the Legal Aid Society; private foundations such as the Carnegie Foundation; publications ranging from "Playboy" to "Commonwealth;" and government institutions including the United States Civil Rights Commission.

SSS officials have conceded that some cases referred to the field for tax investigations would not have qualified for referral but for the ideological category in which they fell. While IRS field offices closed out many cases because, of the lack of tax grounds upon which legal action could be taken, referral from the SSS probably resulted in the examination of some cases despite the lack of adequate grounds. Interviews with IRS field personnel confirm that this did occur in several instances.

Upon discovering that its functions were not tax-related, new IRS Commissioner Alexander ordered the Special Service Staff abolished. He testified:

> Mr. ALEXANDER. I ordered the Special Service staff abolished. That order was given on August the 9th, 1973. It was implemented by manual supplements issued on August the 13th, 1973. We held the files. I ordered the files be held intact—I'm not going to give any negative assurances to this Committee—in order that this Committee and other Committees could review these files to see what, was in them, and see, what sort of information was supplied to us on this more than 11,000 individuals and organizations as to whom and which files were maintained.

> I suggested, Mr. Chairman, that at the end of all of these inquiries, I would like to take those files to the Ellipse and have the biggest bonfire since 1814.

> The CHAIRMAN. Well, I concur in that judgment. I would only say this to you; in a way, it might be a more important bonfire than the Boston Tea Party when it comes to protecting individual rights of American citizens. I am glad you feel that way. I am glad you took that action.

5. Foreign Intelligence and Domestic Dissent

In the late 1960's, CIA and NSA, acting in response to presidential pressure, turned their technological capacity and great resources toward spying on certain Americans. The initial impetus was to determine whether the antiwar movement—and to a lesser extent the "black power" movement—were controlled by foreigners. Despite evidence that there was no significant foreign influence, the intelligence gathering which culminated in CIA's "Operation CHAOS" followed the general pattern of broadening in scope and intensity. The procedure for one aspect of these programs was established by an informal agreement between the CIA and FBI in 1966, which permitted CIA to engage in "internal security" activities in the United States.

a. Origins of CIA Involvement in "Internal Security Functions"

The National Security Act of 1947 explicitly prohibited the CIA from exercising "police, subpoena, or law-enforcement powers, or internal security functions." But the Act did not address the question of the CIA's authority to conduct clandestine intelligence activity within the United States for what Secretary Forrestal called "purposes outside of this country."

Under Director Hoover, the FBI interpreted the term "internal security functions" broadly to encompass almost "anything that CIA might be doing in the

United States." Throughout the 1950's and into the early 1960's, Director Hoover's position led to jurisdictional conflicts between the CIA and the FBI.

The Bureau insisted on being informed of the CIA's activity in the United States so that it could be coordinated with the Bureau. As the FBI liaison with the CIA in that period recalled, "CIA would take action, it would come to our attention and we would have a flap."

In 1966 the FBI and CIA negotiated an informal agreement to regularize their coordination. This agreement was said to have "led to a great improvement" and almost eliminated the "flaps."

Under the agreement, the CIA would "seek concurrence and coordination of the FBI" before engaging in clandestine activity in the United States and the FBI would "concur and coordinate if the proposed action does not conflict with any operation, current or planned, including active investigation of the FBI." When an operative recruited by the CIA abroad arrived in the United States, the FBI would "be advised" and the two agencies would "confer regarding the handling of the agent in the United States." The CIA would continue its "handling" of the agent for "foreign intelligence" purposes. The FBI would also become involved where there were "internal security factors," although it was recognized that the CIA might continue to "handle" the agent in the United States and provide the Bureau with "information" bearing on "internal security matters."

As part of their handling of "internal security factors," CIA operatives were used after 1966 to report on domestic "dissidents" for the FBI. There were infrequent instances in which, according to the former FBI liaison with CIA:

> CIA had penetrations abroad in radical, revolutionary organizations and the individual was coming here to attend a conference, a meeting, and would be associating with leading dissidents, and the question came up, can he be of any use to us, can we have access to him during that period.

In most instances, because he was here for a relatively short period, we would levy the requirement or the request upon the CIA to find out what was taking place at the meetings to get his assessment of the individuals that he was meeting, and any other general intelligence that he could collect from his associations with the people who were of interest to us.

The policies embodied in the 1966 agreement and the practice under 'it clearly involved the CIA in the performance of "internal security functions." At no time did the Executive branch ask Congress to amend the 1947 act to modify its ban against CIA exercising "internal security functions." Nor was Congress asked to clarify the ambiguity of the 1947 act about the CIA's authority to conduct clandestine foreign intelligence and counterintelligence activities within the United States, a matter dealt with even today by Executive Order.

Moreover, National Security Council Intelligence Directive 5 provided authority within the Executive Branch for the Director of Central Intelligence to coordinate, and for the CIA to conduct, counterintelligence activities abroad to protect the United States against not only espionage and sabotage, but also "subversion." However, NSCID 5 did not purport to give the CIA authority for counterintelligence activities in the United States, as provided in the FBI-CIA agreement of 1966.

b. CIA Intelligence About Domestic Political Groups

In the late 1960s, the CIA increasingly was drawn into collecting intelligence about domestic political groups, particularly the anti-war movement, in response to

FBI requests and to pressure from Presidents Johnson and Nixon. A principal assistant to President Johnson testified that high governmental officials could not believe that

> a cause that is so clearly right for the country, as they perceive it, would be so widely attacked if there were not some [foreign] force behind it.

The same pressures and beliefs led to CIA investigations of "militant black nationalists" and radical students.

(1) CIA Response to FBI Requests. — The FBI was the main channel for mobilizing foreign intelligence resources and techniques against domestic targets. The FBI regularly notified the CIA that it wished coverage of Americans overseas. Indeed, the CIA regarded the mention of a name in any of the thousands of reports sent to it by the FBI as a standing requirement from the FBI for information about those persons. FBI reports flowed to the CIA at a rate of over 1,000 a month. From 1967 to 1974, the CIA responded with over 5,000 reports to the FBI. These CIA disseminations included some reports of information acquired by the CIA in the course of its own operations, not sought in response to a specific FBI request.

The FBI's broad approach to the investigations of foreign influence which it coordinated with the CIA is shown by a memorandum prepared in the Intelligence Division early in 1969 summarizing its "Coverage of the New Left:"

> Foreign influence of the New Left movement offers us a fertile field to develop valuable intelligence data. To date there is no real cohesiveness between international New Left groups, but ... despite the factionalism and confusion now so prevalent, there is great potential for the development of an international student revolutionary movement.

The memorandum expressed concern that "old line" leftist groups were

> ... making a determined effort to move into the New Left movement ... [and were] influencing the thinking of the against the police in general and the FBI in particular, to drive us off the campuses; as well as attacks against the new administration to degrade President Nixon.

There was no mention of, or apparent concern for, direct influence or control of the "New Left" by agents of hostile foreign powers. Instead, the stress was almost entirely upon ideological links and similarities, and the threat of ideas considered dangerous by the FBI.

The enlistment of both CIA and NSA resources in domestic intelligence is illustrated by the "Black Nationalist" investigations. In 1967, FBI Headquarters instructed field offices that:

> . . . penetrative investigations should be initiated at this time looking toward developing any information regarding contacts on the part of these individuals with foreign elements and looking toward developing any additional information having a bearing upon whether the individual involved is currently subjected to foreign influence or direction. . . .

> During your investigative coverage of all militant black nationalists, be most alert to any foreign travel. Advise the Bureau promptly of such in order that appropriate overseas investigations may be conducted to establish activities and contacts abroad.

The FBI passed such information to the CIA, which in turn began to place individual black nationalists on a "watch list" for the interception of international communications by the National Security Agency. After 1969, the FBI began submitting names of citizens engaged in domestic protest and violence to the CIA not only for investigation abroad, but also for placement on the "watch list" of the CIA's mail opening project. Similar lists of names went from the FBI to the National Security Agency, for use on a "watch list" for monitoring other channels of international communication.

(2) Operation CHAOS—The CIA did not restrict itself to servicing the FBI's requests. Under White House pressure, the CIA developed its own program—Operation CHAOS—as an adjunct to the CIA's foreign counterintelligence activities, although CIA officials recognized from the outset that it bad "definite domestic counterintelligence aspects."

Former CIA Director Richard Helms testified that he established the program in response to President Johnson's persistent interest in the extent of foreign influence on domestic dissidents. According to Helms, the President would repeatedly ask, "How are you getting along with your examination?" and "Have you picked up any more information on this subject?"

The first CHAOS instructions to CIA station chiefs in August 1967 described the need for "keeping tabs on radical students and U.S. Negro expatriates as well as travelers passing through certain select areas abroad." The originally stated objective was "to find out [the] extent to which Soviets, Chicoms (Chinese Communists) and Cubans are exploiting our domestic problems in terms of espionage and subversion."

Following the consistent pattern of intelligence activities, those original instructions gradually broadened without any precision in the kind of foreign contacts which were to be targeted by CIA operations. For example:

--President Johnson asked the CIA to conduct a study of "International Connections of the U.S. Peace Movement" following the October 1967 demonstration at the Pentagon. In response, CIA headquarters sent a directive to CIA stations seeking information on "illegal and subversive" connections between U.S. activists and "communist, communist front, or other anti-American and foreign elements abroad. Such connections might range from casual contacts based merely on mutual interest to closely controlled channels for party directives."

--In mid-1968, the DDP described CHAOS to CIA stations as a "high priority program" concerning foreign "contacts" with the "Radical Left," which was defined as: "radical students, antiwar activists, draft resisters and deserters, black nationalists, anarchists, and assorted 'New Leftists.'"

--In 1969, President Nixon's White House required the CIA to study foreign communist support of American protest groups and stressed that "support" should be "liberally construed" to include "encouragement" by Communist countries.

--In the fall of 1969, CIA stations were asked to report on any foreign support, guidance, or "inspiration" to protest activities in the United States.

Thus, this attempt to ascertain and evaluate "foreign links', was so broadly defined that it required much more than background information or investigation of a few individuals suspected of being agents directed by a hostile power. Instead, at a time when there was considerable international communication and travel by Americans engaged in protest and dissent, a substantial segment by American protest groups was encompassed by CIA collection requirements to investigate foreign "encouragement," "inspiration," "casual contacts" or "mutual interest." Once again, the use of elastic words in mandates for intelligence activity resulted in overbroad coverage and collection.

In addition to their intelligence activity directed at Americans abroad, CHAOS undercover agents, while in the United States in preparation for overseas assignment or between assignments, provided substantial information about lawful domestic activities of dissident American groups, as well as providing leads about possible foreign activities. In a few instances, the CIA agents appear to have been encouraged to participate in specific protest activity or to obtain particular domestic information. The CHAOS program also involved obtain information about Americans from the CIA mail opening project other domestic CIA components and from a National Security Agency international communications intercept program.

CIA officials recognized that the CIA's examination of domestic groups violated the Agency's mandate and thus accorded it a high degree of sensitivity. As CIA Director Richard Helms wrote in 1969, when he transmitted to the White House the CIA's study of "Restless Youth:"

> In an effort to round out our discussion of this subject, we have included a section on American students. This is an area not within the charter of this Agency, so I need not emphasize how extremely sensitive this makes the paper. Should anyone learn of its existence, it would prove most embarrassing for all concerned.

The reaction to such admissions of illegality was neither an instruction to stop the program or an attempt to change the law. Rather, the White House continued to ask for more information and continued to urge the CIA to confirm the theory that American dissidents were under foreign control.

Director Richard Helms testified that the only manner in which the CIA could support its conclusion that there was no significant foreign influence on the domestic dissent, in the face of incredulity at the White House, was to continually expand the coverage of CHAOS. Only by being able to demonstrate that it had investigated all anti-war persons and all contacts between them and any foreign person could CIA "prove the negative" that none were under foreign domination.

In 1972, the CIA Inspector General found "general concern" among the overseas stations "over what appeared to constitute a monitoring of the political views and activities of Americans not known to be, or suspected of, being involved in espionage." Several stations had "doubts as to the nature and legitimacy of the program" because requests for reports on "prominent persons" were based on "nebulous" allegations of "subversion." This led to "a reduction in the intensity of attention to political dissidents," although the program was not terminated until March 1974.

By the end of the CHAOS program, 13,000 different files were accumulated, including more than 7,200 on American citizens. Documents in these files included the names of more than 300,000 persons and groups indexed by computer. 468 In addition to collecting information on an excessive number of persons, some of the kinds of information were wholly irrelevant to the legitimate interests of the CIA or any other government agency. For example, one CIA agent supplying information on domestic activities to Operation CHAOS submitted detailed accounts of the activities of women who were interested in "women's liberation."

c. CIA Security Operations Within the United States: Protecting "Sources" and "Methods"

The National Security Act of 1947 granted the Director of Central Intelligence a vaguely-worded responsibility for "protecting intelligence sources and methods from unauthorized disclosure." The legislative history of this provision suggests that it was initially intended to allay concerns of the military services that the new CIA would not operate with adequate safeguards to protect the military intelligence secrets which would be shared with the CIA. However, this authority was later read by the CIA to authorize infiltration of domestic groups in order to protect CIA personnel and facilities from possibly violent public demonstrations. It was also read to permit electronic surveillance and surreptitious entry to protect sensitive information.

The CIA undertook a series of specific security investigations within the United States, in some cases to find the, source of news leaks and in others to determine whether government employees were involved in espionage or otherwise constituted "security risks." These investigations were directed at former CIA employees, employees of other government agencies, newsmen and other private, citizens in this country. Among the techniques used were physical surveillance, mail and tax information coverage, electronic surveillance, and surreptitious entry. Attorney General Robert Kennedy appears to have authorized CIA wiretapping in one of these investigations. With this exception, however, there is no suggestion that the CIA's security investigations were specifically approved by the Attorney General.

The CIA Office of Security established two programs directed at protest demonstrations which involved the CIA in domestic affairs on the theory that doing so was necessary to safeguard CIA facilities in the United States. Project MERRIMACK (1967 to 1973) involved the infiltration by CIA agents of Washington-based peace groups and Black activist groups. The stated purpose of the program was to obtain early warning of demonstrations and other physical threats to the CIA. However, the collection requirements were broadened to include general information about the leadership, funding, activities, and policies of the targeted groups.

Project RESISTANCE (1967 to 1973) was a broad effort to obtain general background information about radical groups across the country, particularly on campuses. The CIA justified this program as a means of predicting violence which might threaten CIA installations, recruiters, or contractors, and gathering information with which to evaluate applicants for CIA employment. Much of the reporting by CIA field offices to headquarters was from open sources such as newspapers. But additional information was obtained from cooperating police departments, campus officials, and other local authorities, some of whom in turn were using collection techniques such as informants.

These programs illustrated fundamental weaknesses and contradictions in the statutory definition of CIA authority in the 1947 Act. While the Director of Central Intelligence is charged with responsibility to protect intelligence "sources and methods," the CIA is forbidden from exercising law enforcement and police powers and "internal security functions." The CIA never went to Congress for a clarification of this ambiguity, nor did it seek interpretation from the chief legal officer of the United States — the Attorney General — except on the rarest of occasions.

d. NSA Monitoring

The National Security Agency was created by Executive Order in 1952 to conduct "signals intelligence," including the interception and analysis of messages transmitted by electronic means, such as telephone calls and telegrams. In contrast to the CIA, there has never been a statutory "charter" for NSA.

The executive directives which authorize NSA's activities prohibit the agency from monitoring communication between persons within the United States and communication concerning purely domestic affairs. The current NSA Director testified:

[The] mission of NSA is directed to foreign intelligence obtained from foreign electrical communications . . . .

However, NSA has interpreted "foreign communications" to include communication where one terminal is outside the United States. Under this interpretation, NSA has, for many years, intercepted communications between the United States and a foreign country even though the sender or receiver was an American. During the past decade, NSA increasingly broadened its interpretation of "foreign intelligence" to include economic and financial matters and "international terrorism."

The overall consequence, as in the case of CIA activities such as Project CHAOS, was to break down the distinction between "foreign" and "domestic" intelligence. For example, in the 1960s, NSA began adding to its "watch lists," at the request of various intelligence agencies, the names of Americans suspected of involvement in civil disturbance or drug activity which had some foreign aspects. Second, Operation Shamrock, which began as an effort to acquire the telegrams of certain foreign targets, expanded so that NSA obtained from at least two cable companies essentially all cables to or from the United States, including millions of the private communications of Americans.

6. Intrusive Techniques

As domestic intelligence activity increasingly broadened to cover domestic dissenters under many different programs, the government intensified the use of covert techniques which intruded upon individual privacy.

Informants were used to gather more information about more Americans, often targeting an individual because of his political views and "regardless of past or present involvement in disorders." The CIA's mail opening program increasingly focused upon domestic groups, including "protest and peace organizations" which were covered at the FBI's request. Similarly, NSA-largely in response to Army, CIA, and FBI pressures—expanded its international interception program to include "information on U.S. organizations or individuals who are engaged in activities which may result in civil disturbances or otherwise subvert the national security of the United States."

During this period, Director Hoover ordered cutbacks on the FBI's use of a number of intrusive techniques. Frustration with Hoover's cutbacks was a substantial contributing factor to the effort in 1970 -- coordinated by White House Aide Tom Charles Huston and strongly supported by CIA Director Helms, NSA Director Gaylor and Hoover's Intelligence Division subordinates—to obtain Presidential authorization for numerous illegal or questionable intelligence techniques.

a. Warrantless Electronic Surveillance

(1) Executive Branch Restrictions on Electronic Surveillance: 1965-1968 -- In March 1965, Attorney General Nicholas deB. Katzenbach established a new requirement for the FBI's intelligence operations: the Bureau had to obtain the written approval of the Attorney General prior to the implementation of an microphone

surveillance. He also imposed a six month limitation on both wiretaps and microphone surveillances, after which time new requests had to be submitted for the Attorney General's re-authorization.

Upon Katzenbach's recommendation, President Johnson issued a directive in June 1965 forbidding all federal government wiretapping "except in conjunction with investigations related to national security." This standard was reiterated by Attorney General Katzenbach, for both wiretapping and microphone surveillances three months later, and again in July 1966.

While the procedures were tightened, the broad "national security" standard still allowed for questionable authorizations of electronic surveillance. In fact, Katzenbach told Director Hoover that he would "continue to approve all such requests in the future as I have in the past." He saw "no need to curtail any such activities in the national security field."

In line with that policy, Katzenbach approved FBI requests for wiretaps on the Student Non-Violent Coordinating Committee, Students for a Democratic Society, the editor of an anti-communist newsletter, a Washington attorney with whom the editor was in frequent contact, a Klan official, and a leader of the black Revolutionary Action Movement. According to FBI records, Katzenbach also initialed three memoranda informing him of microphone surveillances of Dr. Martin Luther King, Jr.

There were no similar electronic surveillance authorizations by Attorney General Ramsey Clark in cases involving purely domestic "national security" considerations. Clark has stated that his policy was "to confine the area of approval to international activities directly related to the military security of the United States.

(2) Omnibus Crime Control Act of 1968—In response to a 1967 Supreme Court decision that required judicial warrants for the use of electronic surveillance in criminal cases, Congress enacted the Omnibus Crime Control Act of 1968. This Act established warrant procedures for wiretapping and microphone surveillances, but it included a provision that neither it nor the Federal Communications Act of 1934 "shall limit the constitutional power of the President." Although Congress did not purport to define the President's power, the Act suggested five broad categories in which warrantless electronic surveillance might be permitted. The first three categories related to foreign intelligence and counterintelligence matters:

(1) to protect the nation against actual or potential attack or other hostile acts of a foreign power;

(2) to obtain foreign intelligence information deemed essential to the security of the United States; and

(3) to protect national security information against foreign intelligence activities.

The last two categories dealt with domestic intelligence interests:

(4) to protect the United States against overthrow of the government by force or other unlawful means, or

(5) against any other clear and present danger to the structure or existence of the government.

Thus, although Congress suggested criteria for warrantless electronic surveillance for intelligence purposes, it left to the courts the task of defining the scope of the national security exception, if any, to the warrant requirement.

Between 1969 and 1972, the Nixon administration used these criteria to justify a number of questionable wiretaps. One New Left organization was tapped because, among other factors, its members desired to "take the radical politics they learned on campus and spread them among factory workers." Four newsmen were wiretapped or bugged during this period, as were sixteen executive branch officials, one former executive official, and a relative of an executive official." There were numerous wiretaps and some microphones used against the Black Panther Party and similar domestic groups. Attorney Gen John Mitchell approved FBI requests for wiretaps on organizations involved in planning the November 1969 antiwar "March on Washington" including the moderate Vietnam Moratorium Committee.

(a) Supreme Court Restrictions on National Security Electronic Surveillance: 1972 — The issue of national security electronic surveillance was not addressed by the Supreme Court until 1972, when it held in the so-called Keith case that the President did not have the "constitutional power" to authorize warrantless electronic surveillance to protect the security of the nation from "domestic" threats. The Court remained silent, however, on the legality of warrantless electronic surveillance where there was a 'significant connection with a foreign power, its agents or agencies." As a result of this decision, the Justice Department eliminated as criteria for the use of warrantless electronic surveillance the two categories, described by Congress in the 1968 Act, dealing with domestic intelligence interests.

b. CIA Mail Opening

Although Director Hoover terminated the FBI's own mail opening programs in 1966, the Bureau's use of the CIA program continued. In 1969, uopn the recommendation of the official in charge of the CIA's CHAOS program, the FBI began submitting names of domestic political radicals and black militants to the CIA for inclusion on its mail opening "Watch List." By 1972, the FBIs list of targets for CIA mail opening included:

New Left activists, extremists, and other subversives.

Extremist and New Left organizations.

Protest and peace organizations, such as People's Coalition for Peace and Justice National Peace Action Committee, and Women's Strike for Peace.

Subversive and extremist groups, such as the Black Panthers, White Panthers, Black Nationalists and Liberation Groups, Students for a Democratic Society, Resist, Revolutionary Union, and other New Left Groups.

Traffic to and from Puerto Rico and the Virgin Islands showing anti-U.S. or subversive sympathies."'

Thus, the mail opening program that began fourteen years earlier as a means of discovering hostile intelligence efforts in the United States had expanded to encompass communications of domestic dissidents of all types.

c. Expansion of NSA Monitoring

Although NSA began to intercept and disseminate the communications of selected Americans in the early 1960s, the systematic inclusion of a wide range of American names on the "Watch List" did not occur until 1967.

The Army Chief of Staff for Intelligence requested "any information on a continuing basis" that NSA might intercept concerning:

A. Indications that foreign governments or individuals or organizations acting as agents of foreign governments are controlling or attempting to control or influence the activities of U.S. "peace" groups and "Black Power" organizations.

B. Identities of foreign agencies exerting control or influence on U.S. organizations.

C. Identities of individuals and organizations in U.S. in contact with agents of foreign governments.

D. Instructions or advice being given to U.S. groups by agents of foreign governments.

Two years later, NSA issued an internal instruction intended to ensure the secrecy of the fact that it was monitoring and disseminating communications to and from Americans. This memorandum described the "Watch List" program in terms which indicated that it had widened beyond its originally broad mandate. In addition to describing the program as covering foreigners who "are attempting" to "influence, coordinate or control" U.S. groups or individuals who "may foment civil disturbance or otherwise undermine the national security of the U.S.," the memorandum indicated that the program intercepted communications dealing with:

> Information on U.S. organizations or individuals who are engaged in activities which may result in civil disturbances or otherwise subvert the national security of the U.S.

This standard, which was clearly outside the foreign intelligence mandate of NSA, resulted in sweeping coverage. Communications such as the following were intercepted, disseminated. and stored in Government files: discussion of a peace concert, the interest of the wife of a U.S. Senator in peace causes; a correspondent's report from Southeast Asia to his magazine in New York; an anti-war activist's request for a speaker in New York.

According to testimony before the Committee, the material which resulted from the "Watch List" was of little intelligence value; most intercepted communications were of a private or personal nature or involved rallies and demonstrations that werepublic knowledge.

d. FBI Cutbacks

The reasons for J. Edgar Hoover's cutback in 1966 on FBI use of several covert techniques are not clear. Hoover's former assistants have cited widely divergent factors.

Certainly by the mid-1960s, Hoover was highly sensitive to the possibility of damage to the FBI from public exposure of its most intrusive intelligence techniques. This sensitivity was reflected in a memorandum to Attorney General Katzenbach in September 1965, where Hoover referred to "the present atmosphere" of "Congressional and public alarm and opposition to any activity which could in any way be termed an invasion of privacy." The FBI Director was particularly concerned about an inquiry by the Subcommittee on Administrative Practice and Procedure of the Senate Judiciary Committee chaired by Senator Edward Long.

(1) The Long Subcommittee Investigation—The Senate Subcommittee was primarily investigating electronic surveillance and mail cover. The Bureau was seen as a major subject of the inquiry, although the Internal Revenue Service and other Executive agencies also included.

In February 1965, President Johnson asked Attorney General Katzenbach to coordinate all matters relating to the investigation, and Katzenbach then met with senior FBI officials to discuss the problems it raised. According to a memorandum by A. H. Belmont, one of the FBI Director's principal assistants, Katzenbach stated that he planned to see Senator Edward Long, the Subcommittee chairman, for the purpose of "impressing on him that the committee would not want to stumble by mistake into an area of extreme interest to the national security." According to Belmont, the Attorney General added that he "might have to resort to pressure from the President" and that he did not want the Subcommittee to "undermine the restricted and tightly controlled operations of the Bureau." FBI officials had assured Katzenbach that their activities were, indeed "tightly controlled" and restricted to "important security matters."

The following note on the memorandum of this meeting provides a sign of Director Hoover's attitude at that time:

> I don't see what all the excitement is about. I would have no hesitancy in discontinuing all techniques — technical coverage, microphones, trash covers, mail covers, etc. While it might handicap us I doubt they are as valuable as some believe and none warrant the FBI being used to justify them.

Several days later, according to a memorandum of the FBI Director, the Attorney General "advised that he had talked to Senator Long," and that the Senator "said he did not want to get into any national security area." Katzenbach has confirmed that he "would have been concerned" in these circumstances about the Subcommittee's demands for information about "matters of a national security nature" and that he was "declining to provide such information" to Long. Again in 1966, the FBI took steps to, in the words of Bureau official Cartha DeLoach, "neutralize" the "threat of being embarrassed by the Long Subcommittee." This time the issue involved warrantless electronic surveillance by the FBI, particularly in organized crime matters. DeLoach and another ranking Bureau official visited Senator Long to urge that he issue a statement that "the FBI had never participated in uncontrolled usage of wiretaps or microphones and that FBI usage of such devices had been completely justified in all instances." The Bureau prepared such a statement for Senator Long to release as his own, which apparently was not used. At another meeting with DeLoach, Senator Long agreed to make "a commitment that he would in no way embarrass the FBI." When the Subcommittee's Chief Counsel asked if a Bureau spokesman could appear and "make a simple statement," DeLoach replied that this would "open a Pandora's box, in so far as our enemies in the press were concerned." Senator Long then stated that he would call no FBI witnesses.

(2) Director Hoover's Restriction — The Director subsequently issued instructions that the number of warrantless wiretaps installed at any one time be cut in half. One of his subordinates speculated that this was done out of a concern that the Subcommittee's "inquiry might get into the use of that technique by the FBI."

In July 1966, after hundreds of FBI "black bag job" operations had been approved over many years, Director Hoover decided to eliminate warrantless surreptitious entries for purposes other than microphone installations. In response to an Intelligence Division analysis that such break-ins were an "invaluable technique," although "clearly illegal," Hoover stated that "no more such techniques must be used." 526 Bureau subordinates took Hoover's "no more such techniques" language as an injunction against the Bureau's mail opening program as well. Apparently, a termination order was issued to field offices by telephone. FBI mail-opening was suspended, although the Bureau continued to seek information from CIA's illegal mail-opening program until its suspension in 1973.

A year and a half before Hoover's cutbacks on wire-tapping, "black bag jobs," and mail-opening, he prohibited the FBI's use of other covert techniques such as mail covers and trash covers.

FBI intelligence officials persisted in requesting authority for "black bag" techniques. In 1967 Director Hoover ordered that "no such recommendations should be submitted." At about this time, Attorney General Ramsey Clark was asked to approve a "breaking and entering" operation and declined to do so. There was an apparently unauthorized surreptitious entry directed at a "domestic subversive target as late as April, 1968. A proposal from the field to resume mail opening for foreign counterintelligence purposes was turned down by FBI officials in 1970.

7. Accountability and Control

a. The Huston Plan: A Domestic Intelligence Network

In 1970, pressures from the White House and from within the intelligence community led to the formulation of a plan for coordination and expansion of domestic intelligence activity. The so-called "Huston Plan" called for Presidential authorization of illegal intelligence techniques, expanded domestic intelligence collection, and centralized evaluation of domestic intelligence. President Nixon approved the plan and then, five days later, revoked his approval. Despite the revocation of official approval, many major aspects of the plan were implemented, and some techniques which the intelligence community asked for permission to implement had already been underway.

In 1970, there was an intensification of the social tension in America that had provided the impetus in the 1960s for ever-widening domestic intelligence operations. The spring invasion of Cambodia by United States forces triggered the most extensive campus demonstrations and student "strikes" in the history of the war in Southeast Asia. Domestic strife heightened even further when four students were killed by National Guardsmen at Kent State University. Within one twenty-four hour period, there were 400 bomb threats in New York City alone. To respond, White House Chief of Staff, H. R. Haldeman, assigned principal responsibility for domestic intelligence planning to staff assistant Tom Charles Huston.

Since June 1969, Huston had been in touch with the head of the FBI Domestic Intelligence Division, Assistant Director William C. Sullivan. Huston initially contacted Sullivan on President Nixon's behalf to request "all information possibly relating to foreign influences and financing of the New Left." Huston also made similar requests to CIA, NSA, and the Defense Intelligence Agency. The quality of the data provided by these agencies, especially the FBI, had failed to satisfy Huston and Presidential assistant John Ehrlichman. Thereafter, Huston's continued discussions with Assistant Director Sullivan convinced him that the restraints imposed upon domestic intelligence techniques by Director Hoover impeded the collection of important information about dissident activity.

(1) Intelligence Community Pressures—The interest of the White House in better intelligence about domestic protest activity coincided with growing dissatisfaction among the foreign intelligence agencies with the FBI Director's restrictions on their performance of foreign intelligence functions in America.

The CIA's concerns crystallized in March 1970 when—as a result of a "flap" over the CIA's refusal to disclose information to the FBI—Hoover issued an order that "direct liaison" at FBI headquarters with CIA "be terminated" and that "any contact with CIA in the future" was to take place "by letter only." This order did not bar interagency communication; secure telephones were installed and working-level contacts continued. But the position of FBI "liaison agent" with CIA was eliminated.

CIA Director Helms subsequently attempted to reopen the question of FBI cooperation with CIA requests for installing electronic surveillances and covering mail. Hoover replied that he agreed with Helms that there should be, expanded "exchange of information between our agencies concerning New Left and racial extremist matters." However, he refused the request for aid with electronic surveillance and mail coverage. Hoover cited the "widespread concern by the American public regarding the possible misuse of this type of coverage." Their use, in "domestic investigations" posed legal problems not encountered "in similar operations abroad." Hoover added, "The FBI's effectiveness has always depended in large measure on our capacity to retain the full confidence of the American people."

(2) The Interagency Committee Report.—In the following months, Tom Charles Huston arranged a meeting between President Nixon and the directors of the FBI, CIA, NSA, and DIA on June 5, 1970. The President's emphasis was upon improved coordination among the agencies to strengthen their capabilities to collect intelligence about "revolutionary activism" and "the support—ideological and otherwise—of foreign powers" for these activities. The talking paper prepared by Huston for the President to read at the meeting declared, "We are now confronted with a new and grave crisis in our country—which we know too little about."

From this meeting emanated the Special Report of the Interagency Committee on Intelligence (Ad Hoc), prepared jointly by representatives of the FBI, CIA, NSA, and DIA, and submitted to the President a month later. The report presented the President a series of options, and Huston recommended that the President approve the following:

(1) "coverage by NSA of the communications of U.S. citizens using international facilities;"

(2) "intensification" of "electronic surveillances and penetrations" directed at individuals and groups "who pose a major threat to the internal security" and at "foreign nationals" in the United States "of interest to the intelligence community;"

(3) removal of restrictions on "legal" mail coverage and relaxation of "restrictions on covert coverage" [mail opening] on "selected targets of priority foreign intelligence and internal security interest;"

(4) modification of "present restrictions" on "surreptitious entry" to allow "procurement of vitally needed foreign cryptographic material" and "to permit selective use" against "high priority internal security targets;"

(5) relaxation of "present restrictions" on the "development of campus sources" to permit "expanded coverage of violence-prone and student-related groups;'

(6) "increased" coverage by CIA "of American students (and others) traveling or living abroad;"

(7) appointment of a "permanent committee consisting of the FBI, CIA, NSA, DIA, and the military counterintelligence agencies" to evaluate "domestic intelligence" and to carry out the other objectives specified in the report."

Huston also raised and dismissed questions about the legality of two collection techniques in particular. "Covert [mail opening] coverage is illegal, and there are serious risks involved," he wrote. "However, the advantages to be derived from its use outweigh the risks." As for surreptitious entry, Huston advised:

> Use of this technique is clearly illegal: it amounts to burglary. It is also highly risky and could result in great embarrassment if exposed. However, it is also the most fruitful tool and can produce the type of intelligence which cannot be obtained in any other fashion."

Huston testified that his recommendations "reflected what I understood to be the consensus of the working group" of intelligence officials on the interagency committee.

Just over a week later, the FBI, CIA, NSA, and DIA were advised by Huston that "the President has ... made the following decisions"to adopt all of Huston's recommendations. Henceforth, with Presidential authority, the intelligence community could intercept the international communications of Americans; eavesdrop electronically on anyone deemed a "threat to the internal security;" read the mail of American citizens; break into the homes of anyone regarded as a security threat; and monitor the activities of student political groups at home and abroad.

There is no indication that the President was informed at this time that NSA was already covering the international communications of Americans and had been doing so for domestic intelligence purposes since at least 1967. Nor is there any indication that he was told that the CIA was opening the mail of Americans and sharing the contents with the FBI and the military for domestic intelligence purposes. In effect, the "Huston plan" supplied Presidential authority for operations previously undertaken in secret without such authorization. For instance, the plan gave FBI Assistant Director Sullivan the "support" from "responsible quarters" which he had believed necessary to resume the "black bag jobs" and mail-opening programs Director Hoover had terminated in 1966.

Nevertheless, the FBI Director was not satisfied with Huston's memorandum concerning the authorization of the plan. Hoover went immediately to Attorney General Mitchell, who had not known of the prior deliberations or the President's "decisions." In a memorandum, Director Hoover said he would implement the plan, but only with the explicit approval of the Attorney General or the President:

Despite my clear-cut and specific opposition to the lifting of the various investigative restraints referred to above and to the creation of a permanent interagency committee on domestic intelligence, the FBI is prepared to implement the instructions of the White House at your direction. Of course, we would continue to seek your specific authorization, where appropriate, to utilize the various sensitive investigative techniques involved in individual cases.

CIA Director Helms shortly thereafter indicated his support for the to the Attorney General, telling him "we had put our backs into exercise." Nonetheless, Mitchell advised the President to withdraw his approval. Huston was told to rescind his memorandum, and the White House Situation Room dispatched a message requesting its return.

(3) Implementation—The President's withdrawal of approval for the "Huston plan" did not, in fact, result in the termination of either the NSA program for covering the communications of Americans or the CIA mail-opening program. These programs continued without formal authorization which had been hoped for. The directors of the CIA and NSA also continued to explore means of expanding their involvement in, and access to, domestic intelligence. A new group, the Intelligence Evaluation Committee (IEC), was created by Attorney General Mitchell within the Justice Department to consider such expansion. NSA, CIA, Army counterintelligence, and the FBI each sent representatives to the IEC. NSA Director Gayler provided the IEC with a statement of NSA's capabilities and procedures for supplying domestic intelligence. Although the IEC merely evaluated raw intelligence data, over 90 percent of which came to it through the FBI, it had access to domestic intelligence

from NSA coverage and the CIA's mail-opening and CHAOS programs, which was channeled to the FBI.

Two of the specific recommendations in the "Huston Plan" were thereafter implemented by the FBI — the lowering of the age limit for campus informants from 21 to 18 and the resumption of "legal mail covers." Two men who had participated in developing the "Huston Plan" were promoted to positions of greater influence within the Bureau. More important the Bureau greatly intensified its domestic intelligence investigations in the fall of 1970 without using "clearly illegal" techniques. The Key Black Extremist Program was inaugurated and field offices were instructed to open approximately 10,500 new investigations, including investigations of all black student groups "regardless of their present or past involvement in disorders." All members of "militant New Left campus organizations" were also to be investigated even if they were not "known to be violence prone." The objective of these investigations was "to identify potential" as well as "actual extremists."

The chief of the Domestic Intelligence Division in 1970 said the "Huston Plan" had "nothing to do" with the FBI's expanded intelligence activities. Rather, both the "Huston Plan" and the Bureau intensification represented the same effort by FBI intelligence officials "to recommend the types of action and programs which they thought necessary to cope with the problem." Brennan admits that "the FBI was getting a tremendous amount of pressure from the White House," although he attributes this pressure to demands from "a vast majority of the American people" who wanted to know "why something wasn't being done" about violence and disruption in the country.

b. Political Intelligence

The FBI practice of supplying political information to the White House and, on occasion, responding to White House requests for such information was established before 1964. However, under the administrations of President Lyndon Johnson and Richard Nixon, this practice grew to unprecedented dimensions.

(1) Name Check Requests — White House aides serving under Presidents Johnson and Nixon made numerous requests for "name checks" of FBI files to elicit all Bureau information on particular critics of each administration. Johnson aides requested such reports on critics of the escalating war in Vietnam. 568 President Johnson's assistants also requested name checks on members of the Senate staff of Presidential candidate Barry Goldwater in 1964, on Justice and Treasury Department officials responsible for a phase of the criminal investigation of Johnson's former aide Bobby Baker, on the authors of books critical of the Warren Commission report, a nd on prominent newsmen. President Nixon's aides asked for similar name checks on another newsman, the Chairman of Americans for Democratic Action, and the producer of a film critical of the President.

According to a memorandum by Director Hoover, Vice President Spiro Agnew received ammunition from Bureau files that could be used in "destroying [the] credibility" of Southern Christian Leadership Conference leader Reverend Ralph Abernathy.

(2) Democratic National Convention, Atlantic City, 1964 — On August 22, 1964, at the request of the White House, the FBI sent a "special squad" to the Democratic National Convention site in Atlantic City, New Jersey. The squad was assigned to assist the Secret Service in protecting President Lyndon Johnson and to ensure that the convention itself would not be marred by civil disruption.

But it went beyond these functions to report political intelligence to the White House. Approximately 30 Special Agents, headed by Assistant Director Cartha DeLoach, "were able to keep the White House fully apprised of all major developments during the Conventions' course" by means of "informant coverage, by use of various confidential techniques, by infiltration of key groups through use of undercover agents, and through utilization of agents using appropriate cover as reporters." Among these "confidential techniques" were: a wiretap on the hotel room occupied by Dr. Martin Luther King, Jr., and microphone surveillance of a storefront serving as headquarters for the Student Nonviolent Coordinating Committee and another civil rights organization.

Neither of the electronic surveillances at Atlantic City were specifically authorized by the Attorney General. At that time, Justice Department procedures did not require the written approval of the Attorney General for bugs such as the one directed against SNCC in Atlantic City. Bureau officials apparently believed that the wiretap on King was justified as an extension of Robert Kennedy's October 10, 1963, approval for surveillance of King at his then-current address in Atlanta, Georgia, or at any future address to which he might move. The only recorded reason for instituting the wiretap on Dr. King in Atlantic City, however, was set forth in an internal memorandum prepared shortly before the Convention:

> Martin Luther King, Jr., head of the Southern Christian Leadership Conference (SCLC), an organization set up to promote integration which we are investigating to determine the extent of Communist Party (CP) influence on King and the SCLC, plans to attend and possibly may indulge in a hunger fast as a means of protest.

Walter Jenkins, an Administrative Assistant to President Johnson who was the recipient of information developed by the Bureau, stated that he was unaware that any of the intelligence was obtained by wiretapping or bugging. DeLoach, moreover, has testified that he is uncertain whether he ever informed Jenkins of these sources.

Walter Jenkins, and presumably President Johnson, received a significant volume of information from the electronic surveillance at Atlantic City, much of it purely political and only tangentially related to possible civil disturbances. The most important single issue for President Johnson at the Atlantic City Convention was the seating challenge of the Mississippi Freedom Democratic Party to the regular Mississippi delegation. From the electronic surveillances of King and SNCC, the White House was able to obtain the most intimate details of the plans of individuals supporting the MFDP's challenge unrelated to the possibility of violent demonstrations.

Jenkins received a steady stream of reports on political strategy in the struggle to seat the MFDP delegation and other political plans and discussions by the civil rights groups under surveillance. Moreover, the 1975 Inspection Report stated that "several Congressmen, Senators, and Governors of States" were overheard on the King tap."

According to both Cartha DeLoach and Walter Jenkins, the Bureau's coverage in Atlantic City was not designed to serve political ends. DeLoach testified:

> I was sent there to provide information . . . which could reflect on the orderly progress of the convention and the danger to distinguished individuals, and particularly the danger to the President of the United States, as exemplified by the many, many references [to possible civil disturbances] in the memoranda furnished Mr. Jenkins . . . .

Jenkins has stated that the mandate of the FBI's special unit did not encompass the gathering of political intelligence and speculated that the dissemination of any such intelligence was due to the inability of Bureau agents to distinguish dissident activities which represented a genuine potential for violence. Jenkins did not believe the White House ever used the incidental political intelligence that was received. However, a document located at the Lyndon B. Johnson Presidential Library suggests that at least one political use was made of Mr. DeLoach's reports.

Thus, although it may have been implemented to prevent violence at the Convention site, the Bureau's coverage in Atlantic City—which included two electronic surveillances—undeniably provided useful political intelligence to the President as well.

(3) By-Product of Foreign Intelligence Coverage—Through the FBI's coverage of certain foreign officials in Washington, D.C., the Bureau was able to comply with President Johnson's request for reports of the contacts between members of Congress and foreign officials opposed to his Vietnam policy. According to a summary memorandum prepared by the FBI:

On March 14, 1966, then President Lyndon B. Johnson informed Mr. DeLoach [Cartha DeLoach, Assistant Director of the FBI] ... that the FBI should constantly keep abreast of the actions of [certain foreign officials] in making contact with Senators and Congressmen and any citizen of a prominent nature. The President stated he strongly felt that much of the protest concerning his Vietnam policy, particularly the hearings in the Senate, had been generated by [certain foreign officials].

As a result of the President's request, the FBI prepared a chronological summary—apparently based in part on existing electronic surveillances of the contacts of each Senator, Representative, or legislative staff member who communicated with selected foreign officials during the period July 1, 1964, to March 17, 1966. This 67-page summary was transmitted to the White House on March 21, 1966, with a note that certain foreign officials were "making more contacts" with four named Senators "than with other United States legislators." A second summary, prepared on further contacts between Congressmen and foreign officials, was transmitted to the White House on May 13, 1966. From then until the end of the Johnson Administration in January 1969, biweekly additions to the second summary were regularly disseminated to the White House.

This practice was reinstituted during the Nixon Administration. On July 27, 1970, Larry Higby, Assistant to H. R. Haldeman, informed the Bureau that Haldeman "wanted any information possessed by the FBI relating to contacts between [certain foreign officials] and Members of Congress and its staff." Two days later, the Bureau provided the White House with a statistical compilation of such contacts from January 1, 1967, to the present. Unlike the case of the information provided to the Johnson White House, however, there is no indication in related Bureau records that President Nixon or his aides were concerned about critics of the President's policy. The Bureau's reports did not identify individual Senators; they provided overall statistics and two examples of foreign recruitment attempts (with names removed.

In at least one instance the FBI, at the request of the President and with the approval of the Attorney General, instituted an electronic surveillance of a foreign target for the express purpose of intercepting telephone conversations of an American citizen. An FBI memorandum states that shortly before the 1968 Presidential election, President Johnson became suspicious that the South Vietnamese were trying to sabotage his peace negotiations in the hope that Presidential candidate Nixon would win the election and then take a harder line toward North Vietnam. To determine the validity of this suspicion, the White House instructed the FBI to institute physical surveillance of Mrs. Anna Chennault, a prominent Republican, as well as electronic surveillance directed against a South Vietnamese target.

The electronic surveillance was authorized by Attorney General Ramsey Clark on October 29, 1968, installed the same day, and continued until January 6, 1969. Thus, a "foreign" electronic surveillance was instituted to target indirectly an American citizen who could not be legitimately surveilled directly. Also as part of this investigation, President Johnson personally ordered a check of the long distance toll call records of Vice Presidential candidate Spiro Agnew.

(4) The Surveillance of Joseph Kraft (1969) — There is no substantial indication of any genuine national security rationale for the electronic surveillance overseas of columnist Joseph Kraft in 1969. John Erlichman testified before the Senate Watergate Committee that the national security was involved, but did not elaborate further.

Beyond this general claim, however, there is little evidence that any national security issue was involved in the case. Former Deputy Attorney General and Acting FBI Director William Ruckelshaus testified that after reviewing the matter he "could never see any national security justification" for the surveillance of Kraft. Ruckelshaus stated that the Administration's "justification" for bugging Kraft's hotel room was that he was "asking questions of some members of the North Vietnamese Government." Ruckelshaus believed that this was not an adequate national security justification for placing "any kind of surveillance on an American citizen or newsman." Mr. Kraft agreed he was in contact with North Vietnamese officials while he was abroad in 1969, but noted that this was a common practice among journalists and that "at the time" he never knowingly published any classified information.

The documentary record also reveals no national security justification for the FBI's electronic surveillance of Mr. Kraft overseas. The one memorandum which referred to "Possible Leaks of Information" by Kraft does not indicate that there clearly was a leak of national security significance or that Mr. Kraft was responsible for such a leak if it occurred. Furthermore, the hotel room bug did not produce any evidence that Kraft received or published any classified information.

Similarly, there is no evidence of a national security justification for the physical surveillance and proposed electronic surveillance of Kraft in the fall of 1969. A Bureau memorandum suggests that the Attorney General requested some type of coverage of Kraft, but the record reveals no purpose for this coverage. The physical surveillance was discontinued after five weeks because it had "not been productive." Apparently, the Attorney General himself was unconvinced that a genuine national security justification supported the Kraft surveillance: he refused to authorize the requested wiretap, and it was consequently never implemented.

(5) The "17" Wiretaps — The relative ease with which high administration officials could select improper intelligence targets was demonstrated by the "17" wiretaps on Executive officials and newsmen installed between 1969-1971 under the rationale of determining the source of leaks of sensitive information. In three cases no national security claim was even advanced. While national security issues were at least arguably involved in the initiation of the other taps, the program continued in two instances against persons who left the government and took positions as advisors to Senator Edmund Muskie, then the leading Democratic Presidential prospect.

The records of these wiretaps were kept separate from the FBI's regular electronic surveillance files; their duration in many cases went beyond the period then required for re-authorization by the Attorney General; and in some cases the Attorney General did not authorize the tap until after it had begun. In 1971, the records were removed from the FBI's possession and sent to the White House.

Thus, misuse of the FBI had progressed by 1971 from the regular receipt by the White House of political "tid-bits" and occasional requests for name checks of Bureau files to the use of a full array of intelligence operations to serve the political interests of the administration. The final irony was that the Nixon administration came to distrust Director Hoover's reliability and, consequently, to develop a White House-based covert intelligence operation.

c. The Justice Department's Internal Security Division

FBI intelligence reports flowed consistently to the Justice Department, especially to the IDIU established by Attorney General Clark in 1967 and to the Internal Security Division. Before 1971, the Justice Department provided little guidance to the FBI on the proper scope of domestic intelligence investigations. For example, in response to a Bureau inquiry in 1964 about whether a group's activities came "within the criteria" of the employee security program or were "in violation of any other federal statute," the Internal Security Division replied that there was "insufficient evidence" for prosecution and that the group's leaders were "becoming more cautious in their utterances." Nevertheless, the FBI continued for years to investigate the group with the knowledge and approval of the Division.

(1) The "New" Internal Security Division — When Robert Mardian was appointed Assistant Attorney General in late 1970, the Internal Security Division assumed a more active posture. In fact, one of the alternatives to implementation of the "Huston Plan" suggested to Attorney General John Mitchell by White House aide John Dean was the invigoration of the Division. This included Mardian's establishment of the IEC to prepare domestic intelligence estimates. Equally significant, however, was Mardian's preparation of a new Executive Order on federal employee security. The new order assigned to the moribund Subversive Activities Control Board the function of designating groups for what had been the "Attorney General's list". This attempt to assign broad new functions by Executive fiat to a Board with limited statutory responsibilities clearly disregarded the desires of the Congress.

According to Mardian, there was a "problem" because the list had "not been updated for 17 years." He expected that the revitalized SACB would "deal specifically with the revolutionary/terrorist organizations which have recently become a part of our history."

Assistant Attorney General Mardian's views coincided with those of FBI Assistant Director Brennan, who had seen a need to compile massive data on the "New Left" for future employee security purposes. Since FBI intelligence investigations were based in part on standards for the "Attorney General's list," the new Executive Order substantially redefined and expanded FBI authority. The new order included groups who advocated the use of force to deny individual rights under the "laws of any State" or to overthrow the government of "any State or subdivision thereof." The new order also continued to use the term "subversive," although it was theoretically more restrictive than the previous standard for the Attorney General's list because it required "unlawful" advocacy.

Mardian made it clear that, under the order, the FBI was to provide intelligence to the Subversive Activities Control Board:

> We have a new brand of radical in this country and we are trying to address ourselves to the new situation. With the investigative effort of the

FBI, we hope to present petitions to the Board in accordance with requirement of the Executive Order.

FBI intelligence officials learned that the Internal Security Division intended to "initiate proceedings against the Black Panther Party, Progressive Labor Party, Young Socialist Alliance, and Ku Klux Klan." They also noted: "The language of Executive Order 11605 is very broad and generally coincides with the basis for our investigation of extremist groups." Mardian had, in effect, provided a new and wider "charter" for FBI domestic intelligence.

(2) The Sullivan-Mardian Relationship — In 1971, Director Hoover expressed growing concern over the close relationship developing between his FBI subordinates in the Domestic Intelligence Division and the Internal Security Division under Mardian. For example, when FBI intelligence officials met with Mardian's principal deputy, A. William Olsen, to discuss "proposed changes in procedure" for the Attorney General's authorization of electronic surveillance, Hoover reiterated instructions that Bureau officials be "very careful in our dealings" with Mardian. Moreover, to have a source of legal advice independent of the Justice Department, the FBI Director created a new position of Assistant Director for Legal Counsel and required that he attend "at any time officials of the Department are being contacted on any policy consideration which affects the Bureau."

In the summer of 1971, William C. Sullivan openly challenged FBI Director Hoover, possibly counting on Mardian and Attorney General Mitchell to back him up and oust Hoover. Sullivan charged in one memorandum to Hoover that other Bureau officials lacked "objectivity" and "independent thinking" and that "they said what they did because they thought this was what the Director wanted them to say."

Shortly thereafter, Director Hoover appointed W. Mark Felt, formerly Assistant Director for the Inspection Division, to a newly created position as Sullivan's superior. Apparently realizing that he was on his way out, Sullivan gave Assistant Attorney General Mardian the FBI's documents recording the authorization for, and dissemination of, information from the "17" wiretaps placed on Exccutive officials and newsmen in 1969-1971. The absence of these materials was not discovered by other FBI officials until after Sullivan was forced to resign in September 1971. Mardian eventually took part in the transfer of these records to the White House.

Thus, the Attorney General's principal assistant for internal security collaborated with a ranking FBI official to conceal vital records, ultimately to be secreted away in the White House. This provides a striking example of the manner in which channels of legitimate authority within the Executive Branch can be abused.

d. The FBI's Secret "Administrative Index"

In the fall of 1971, the FBI confronted the prospect of the first serious Congressional curtailment of domestic intelligence investigations — repeal of the Emergency Detention Act of 1950 -- and set a course of evasion of the will of Congress which continued, partly with Justice Department approval, until 1973.

An FBI Inspection Report viewed the prospect of the repeal without great alarm. In the event the Act was repealed, the FBI intended to continue as before under "the Government's inherent right to protect itself internally." After the repeal took place, Bureau officials elaborated the following rationale for keeping the Security Index of "potentially dangerous subversives:"

Should this country come under attack from hostile forces, foreign or domestic, there is nothing to preclude the President from going before a joint session of Congress and requesting necessary authority to apprehend and detain those who would constitute a menace to national defense. At this point, it would be absolutely essential to have an immediate list, such as the SI, for use in making such apprehensions.

Thus, FBI officials hoped there would be a way to circumvent the repeal "in which the essence of the Security Index and emergency detention of dangerous individuals could be utilized under Presidential powers."

Assistant Director Dwight Dalbey, the FBI's Legal Counsel, recommended writing to the Attorney General for "a reassessment" in order to "protect" the Bureau in case "some spokesman of the extreme left" claimed that repeal of the Detention Act eliminated FBI authority for domestic intelligence activity. Dalbey agreed that, since the Act "could easily be put back in force should an emergency convince Congress of its need," the Bureau should "have on hand the necessary action information pertaining to individuals." Thereupon, a letter was sent to Attorney General Mitchell proposing that the Bureau be allowed to "maintain an administrative index" of individuals who "pose a threat to the internal security of the country." Such an index would be an aid to the Bureau in discharging its "investigative responsibility." However, the letter made no reference to the theory prevailing within the FBI that the new "administrative index" would serve as the basis for a revived detention program in some future emergency.

Thus, when the Attorney General replied that the repeal of the Act did not prohibit the FBI from compiling an "administrative index" to make "readily retrievable" the "results of its investigations," he did not deal with the question of whether the index would also serve as a round-up list for a future emergency. The Attorney General also stated that the Department did not "desire a copy" of the new index, abdicating even the minimal supervisory role performed previously by the Internal Security Division in its review of the names on the Security Index. FBI officials realized that they were "now in a position to make a sole determination as to which individuals should be included in an index of subversive individuals."

There were two major consequences of the new system. First, the new "administrative index" (ADEX) was expanded to include an elastic category: "the new breed of subversive." Second, the previous Reserve Index, which had never been disclosed to the Justice Department, was incorporated into the ADEX. It included "teachers, writers, lawyers, etc." who did not actively participate in subversive activity "but who were nevertheless influential in espousing their respective philosophies." It was estimated that the total case load under the ADEX would be "in excess of 23,000."

One of the FBI standards for placing someone on the ADEX list demonstrates the vast breadth of the list and the assumption that it could be used as the basis for detention in an emergency:

An individual who, although not a member of or participant in activities of revolutionary organizations or considered an activist in affiliated fronts, has exhibited a revolutionary ideology and is likely to seize upon the opportunity presented by national emergency to commit acts of espionage or sabotage, including acts of terrorism, assassination or any interference with or threat to the survival and effective operation of the national, state, and local governments and of the defense efforts.

These criteria were supplied to the Justice Department in 1972, and the Attorney General did not question the fact that the ADEX was more than an administrative aid for conducting investigations, as he had previously been told.

A Bureau memorandum indicates that "representatives of the Department" in fact agreed with the view that there might be "circumstances" where it would be necessary "to quickly identify persons who were a threat to the national security" and that the President could then go to Congress "for emergency legislation permitting apprehension and detention."

Thus, although the Attorney General did not formally authorize the ADEX as a continuation of the previous detention list, there was informal Departmental knowledge that the FBI would proceed on that basis. One FBI official later recognized that the ADEX could be "interpreted as a means to circumvent repeal of the Emergency Detention Act."

8. Reconsideration of FBI Authority

In February 1971, the Subcommittee on Constitutional Rights of the Senate Judiciary Committee began a series of hearings on federal data banks and the Bill of Rights which marked a crucial turning point in the development of domestic intelligence policy. The Subcommittee, chaired by Senator Sam J. Ervin of North Carolina, reflected growing concern among Americans for the protection of "the privacy of the individual against the 'information power' of government."

Largely in response to this first serious Congressional inquiry into domestic intelligence policy, the Army curtailed its extensive surveillance of civilian political activity. The Senate inquiry also led, after Director Hoover's death in 1972, to reconsideration by the FBI of the legal basis for its domestic intelligence activities and eventually to a request to the Attorney General for clarification of its authority.

a. Developments in 1972-1974

There is no indication that FBI "guidelines" material or the FBI Manual provisions themselves were submitted to, or requested by, the Justice Department prior to 1972. Indeed, when Deputy Attorney General Richard Kleindienst testified in February 1972 at the hearings on his nomination to be Attorney General, he stated that be was "not sure" what guidelines were used by the FBI. Kleindienst also stated that he believed FBI investigations were "restricted to criminal conduct or the likelihood of criminal conduct." Director Hoover noted on a newspaper report of the testimony, "Prepare succinct memo to him on our guidelines."

After Hoover's death in 1912, a sharp split developed within the Domestic Intelligence Division over whether or not the Bureau should continue to rely on the various Executive Orders as a basis for its authority.

Acting Director Gray postponed making any formal decisions on this matter; he did not formally request advice from the Attorney General. Meanwhile, the Domestic Intelligence Division proceeded on its own to revise the pertinent Manual sections and the ADEX standards. The list was to be trimmed to those who were "an actual danger now," reducing the number of persons on the ADEX by two-thirds.

A revision of the FBI Manual was completed by May 1973. It was described as "a major step" away from "heavy reliance upon Presidential Directives" to an approach "based on existing Federal statutes. Although field offices were instructed to "close" investigations not meeting the new criteria, headquarters did not want "a massive review on crash basis" of all existing cases.

After a series of regional conferences with field office supervisors, the standards were revised to allow greater flexibility. For the first time in FBI history, a copy of the

Manual section for "domestic subversive investigations" was sent to the Attorney General.

After Clarence M. Kelley was confirmed as FBI Director, he authorized a request for guidance from Attorney General Elliot Richardson. 647 Kelley advised that it "would be folly" to limit the Bureau to investigations only when a crime "has been committed," since the government had to "defend itself against revolutionary and terrorist efforts to destroy it." Consequently, he urged that the President exercise his "inherent Executive power to expand by further defining the FBI's investigative authority to enable it to develop advance information" about the plans of "terrorists and revolutionaries who seek to overthrow or destroy the Government."

Director Kelley's request initiated a process of reconsideration of FBI intelligence authority by the Attorney General.

The general study of FBI authority was superceded in December 1973 when Acting Attorney General Robert Bork, in consultation with Attorney General-designate William Saxbe, gave higher priority to a Departmental inquiry into the FBI's COINTELPRO practices. Responsibility for this inquiry was assigned to a committee headed by Assistant Attorney General Henry Peterson.

Even at this stage, the Bureau resisted efforts by the Department to look too deeply into its operations. Director Kelley advised the Acting Attorney General that the Department should exclude from its review the FBI's "extremely sensitive foreign intelligence collection techniques."

As a result, the Petersen committee's review of COINTELPRO did not consider anything more than a brief FBI prepared summary of foreign counterintelligence operations. Moreover, the inquiry into domestic COINTELPRO cases was based mainly on short summaries of each incident compiled by FBI agents, with Department attorneys making only spot-checks of the underlying files to assure the accuracy of the summaries. Thus, the inquiry was unable to consider the complete story of COINTELPRO as reflected in the actual memoranda discussing the reasons for adopting particular tactics and the means by which they were implemented.

Thus, at the same time that the Bureau was seeking guidance and clarification of its authority, vestiges remained of its past resistance to outside scrutiny and its desire to rely on Executive authority, rather than statute, for the definition of its intelligence activities.

b. Recent Domestic Intelligence Authority

In the absence of any new standards imposed by statute, or by the Attorney General, the FBI continued to collect domestic intelligence under sweeping authorizations issued by the Justice Department in 1974 for investigations of "subversives," potential civil disturbances, and "potential crimes." These authorizations were explicitly based on conceptions of inherent Executive power, broader in theory than the FBI's own claim in 1973 that its authority could be found in the criminal statues. Attorney General Levi has recently promulgated guidelines which stand as the first significant attempt by the Justice Department to set standards and limits for FBI domestic intelligence investigations.

(1) Executive Order 10450, As Amended—The Federal employee security program continued to serve as a basis for FBI domestic intelligence investigations. An internal Bureau memorandum stated that the Justice Department's instruction regarding the program:

> specifically requires the FBI to check the names of all civil applicants and
> incumbents of the Executive Branch against our records. In order to meet

this responsibility FBIHQ records must contain identities of all persons connected with subversive or extremist activities, together with necessary identifying information.

FBI field offices were instructed in mid-1974 to report to Bureau headquarters such data as the following:

Identities of subversive and/or extremist groups or movements (including front groups) with which subject has been identified, period of membership, positions held, and a summary of the type and extent of subversive or extremist activities engaged in by subject (e.g., attendance at meetings or other functions, fundraising or recruiting activities on behalf of the organization, contributions, etc.).

In June 1974, President Nixon formally abolished the "Attorney General's list" upon the recommendation of Attorney General Saxbe. However, the President's order retained a revised definition of the types of organizations, association [with] which would still be considered in evaluating prospective federal employees. The Justice Department instructed the FBI that it should "detect organizations with a potential" for falling within the terms of the order and investigate "individuals who are active either as members of or as affiliates of" such organizations. The Department instructions added:

It is not necessary that a crime occur before the investigation is initiated, but only that a reasonable evaluation of the available information suggests that the activities of the organization may fall within the prescription of the Order....

It is not possible to set definite parameters covering the initiation of investigations of potential organizations falling within the Order but once the investigation reaches a stage that offers a basis for determining that the activities are legal in nature, then the investigation should cease, but if the investigation suggests a determination that the organization is engaged in illegal activities or potentially illegal activities it should continue.

The Department applied "the same yardstick" to investigations of individuals "when information is received suggesting their involvement."

(2) Civil Disorders Intelligence — The Justice Department also instructed the FBI in 1974 that it should not, as the Bureau had suggested, limit its civil disturbance reporting "to those particular situations which are of such a serious nature that Federal military personnel may be called upon for assistance." The Department advised that this suggested "guideline" was "not practical" since, it "would place the burden on the Bureau" to make an initial decision as to "whether military personnel may ultimately be needed," and this responsibility rested "legally" with the President. Instead, the FBI was ordered to "continue" to report on

all significant incidents of civil unrest and should not be restricted to situations where, in the judgment of the Bureau, military personnel eventually may be used.

Moreover, under this authority the Bureau was also ordered to "continue" reporting on

all disturbances where there are indications that extremist organizations such as the Communist Party, Ku Klux Klan, or Black Panther Party are believed to be involved in efforts to instigate or exploit them.

The instructions specifically declared that the Bureau "should make timely reports of significant disturbances, even when no specific violation of Federal law is indicated." This was to be done, at least in part, through "liaison" with local law enforcement agencies.

Even after the Justice Department's IDIU dismantled its computerized data bank, its basic functions continued to be, performed by a Civil Disturbance Unit in the office of the Deputy Attorney General, and the FBI was under instructions to disseminate its civil disturbance reports to that Unit.

FBI officials considered these instructions "significant" because they gave it "an official, written mandate from the Department." The Department's desires were viewed as "consistent with what we have already been doing for the past several years," although the Bureau Manual was rewritten to "incorporate into it excerpts from the Department's letter."

(3) "Potential" Crimes. — The FBI recently abolished completely the administrative index (ADEX) of persons considered "dangerous now." However, the Justice Department has advanced a theory to support broad power for the Executive Branch in investigating groups which represent a "potential threat to the public safety" or which have a "potential" for violating specific statutes. For example, the Department advised the FBI that the General Crimes Section of the Criminal Division had "recommended continued investigation" of one group on the basis of "potential violations" of the antiriot statutes. These same instructions added that there need not be a "potential" for violation of any specific statute.

(4) Claim of Inherent Executive Power — The Department's theory of executive power was set forth in 1974 testimony before the House Internal Security Committee. According to Deputy Assistant Attorney General Kevin Maroney, "the primary basis" for FBI domestic intelligence authority rests in "the constitutional powers and responsibilities vested in the President under Article II of the Constitution." These powers were specified as: the President's duty undertaken in his oath of office to "preserve, protect, and defend the Constitution of the United States;" the Chief Executive's duty to "take care that the laws be faithfully executed:" the President's responsibilities as Commander-in-Chief of the military; and his "power to conduct our foreign relations."

The chairman of the Internal Security Committee, Rep. Richard H. Ichord, stated at that time that, except in limited areas, the Congress "has not directly imposed upon the FBI clearly defined duties in the acquisition, use, or dissemination of domestic or internal security intelligence."

Subsequently, the FBI Intelligence Division revised its 1972-1973 position on its legal authority, and in a paper completed in 1975 it returned to the view "that the intelligence-gathering activities of the FBI have had as their basis the intention of the President to delegate his Constitutional authority," as well as the statutes "pertaining to the national security."

The Attorney General has continued to assert the claim of inherent executive power to conduct warrantless electronic surveillance of American citizens, although this power has been exercised sparingly. The Justice Department has also claimed that this inherent executive power permits warrantless surreptitious entries. However, the Executive Branch has recently joined a bipartisan group of Senators and Representatives in sponsoring a legislative proposal requiring judicial warrants for all electronic surveillance by the FBI.

(5) Attorney General Levi's Guidelines—During 1975, the Congress and the Executive Branch began major efforts to review the field of domestic intelligence. A Presidential commission headed by Vice President Rockefeller inquired into the CIA's improper surveillance of Americans. Attorney General Edward H. Levi established a committee in the Justice Department to develop "guidelines" for the FBI, and the Justice Department began to work on draft legislation to require warrants for national security electronic surveillance.

These efforts have begun to bear fruit in recent months. President Ford has issued an Executive Order regulating foreign intelligence activities; Attorney General Levi has promulgated several sets of "guidelines" for the FBI. And the administration has endorsed a specific bill to establish a warrant procedure for all national security wiretaps and bugs in the United States.

These Executive initiatives are a major step forward in creating safeguards and establishing standards, but they are incomplete without legislation. Among the issues left open by the President's Executive Order, for example, are: (1) the definition of the term "foreign subversion" used to characterize the counter-intelligence responsibilities of the CIA and the FBI; and (2) clarification of the vague provisions in the National Security Act of 1947 relating to the authority of the Director of Central Intelligence to protect "sources" and "methods;" and (3) amplification of the 1947 Act's prohibition against the CIA's exercise of "law enforcement powers" or "internal security functions."

Although they represent only a partial answer to the need for permanent restraints, the initiatives of the Executive Branch demonstrate a willingness to seriously consider the need for legislative action. The Attorney General has recognized that Executive "guidelines" are not enough to regulate, and authorize FBI intelligence activities. The Committee's conclusions and recommendations in Part IV of this report indicate the areas most in need of legislative attention.

III. Findings

The Committee makes seven major findings. Each finding is accompanied by subfindings and by an elaboration which draws upon the evidentiary record set forth in our historical narrative (Part II herein) and in the thirteen detailed reports which will be published as supplements to this volume. We have sought to analyze in our findings characteristics shared by intelligence programs, practices which involved abuses, and general problems in the system which led to those abuses.

The findings treat the following themes that run through the facts revealed by our investigation of domestic intelligence activity: (A) Violating and Ignoring the Law; (B) Overbreadth of Domestic Intelligence Activity; (C) Excessive Use of Intrusive Techniques; (D) Using Covert Action to Disrupt and Discredit Domestic Groups; (E) Political Abuse of Intelligence Information; (F) Inadequate Controls on Dissemination and Retention; (G) Deficiencies in Control and Accountability.

Viewed separately, each finding demonstrates a serious problem in the conduct and control of domestic intelligence operations. Taken together, they make a compelling case for the necessity of change. Our recommendations (in Part IV) flow from this analysis and propose changes which the Committee believes to be appropriate in light of the record.

(A) Violating and Ignoring the Law

(B) Overbreadth of Domestic Intelligence Activity

© Excessive Use of Intrusive Techniques

(D) Using Covert Action to Disrupt and Discredit Domestic Groups

(E) Political Abuse of Intelligence Information

(F) Inadequate Controls on Dissemination and Retention

(G) Deficiencies in Control and Accountability

A. Violating And Ignoring The Law

Major Finding

The Committee finds that the domestic activities of the intelligence community at times violated specific statutory prohibitions and infringed the constitutional rights of American citizens. The legal questions involved in intelligence programs were often not considered. On other occasions, they were intentionally disregarded in the belief that because the programs served the "national security" the law did not apply. While intelligence officers on occasion failed to disclose to their superiors programs which were illegal or of questionable legality, the Committee finds that the most serious breaches of duty were those of senior officials, who were responsible for controlling intelligence activities and generally failed to assure compliance with the law.

Subfindings

(a) In its attempt to implement instructions to protect the security of the United States, the intelligence community engaged in some activities which violated statutory law and the constitutional rights of American citizens.

(b) Legal issues were often overlooked by many of the intelligence officers who directed these operations. Some held a pragmatic view of intelligence activities that did not regularly attach sufficient significance to questions of legality. The question raised was usually not whether a particular program was legal or ethical, but whether it worked.

(c.) On some occasions when agency officials did assume, or were told, that a program was illegal, they still permitted it to continue. They justified their conduct in some cases on the ground that the failure of "the enemy" to play by the rules granted them the right to do likewise, and in other cases on the ground that the "national security" permitted programs that would otherwise be illegal.

(d) Internal recognition of the illegality or the questionable legality of many of these activities frequently led to a tightening of security rather than to their termination. Partly to avoid exposure and a public "flap," knowledge of these programs was tightly held within the agencies, special filing procedures were used, and "cover stories" were devised.

(e) On occasion, intelligence agencies failed to disclose candidly their programs and practices to their own General Counsels, and to Attorneys General, Presidents, and Congress.

(f) The internal inspection mechanisms of the CIA and the FBI did not keep—and, in the case of the FBI, were not designed to keep—the activities of those agencies within legal bounds. Their primary concern was efficiency, not legality or propriety.

(g) When senior administration officials with a duty to control domestic intelligence activities knew, or had a basis for suspecting, that questionable activities had occurred, they often responded with silence or approval. In certain cases, they were presented with a partial description of a program but did not ask for details, thereby abdicating their responsibility. In other cases, they were fully aware of the nature of the practice and implicitly or explicitly approved it.

Elaboration of findings

The elaboration which follows details the general finding of the Committee that inattention to—and disregard of—legal issues was an all too common occurrence in the intelligence community. While this section focuses on the actions and attitudes of intelligence officials and certain high policy officials, the Committee recognizes that a pattern of lawless activity does not result from the deeds of a single stratum of the government or of a few individuals alone. The implementation and continuation of illegal and questionable programs would not have been possible without the cooperation or tacit approval of people at all levels within and above the intelligence community, through many successive administrations.

The agents in the field, for their part, rarely questioned the orders they received. Their often uncertain knowledge of the law, coupled with the natural desire to please one's superiors and with simple bureaucratic momentum, clearly contributed to their willingness to participate in illegal and questionable programs. The absence of any prosecutions for law violations by intelligence agents inevitably affected their attitudes as well. Under pressure from above to accomplish their assigned tasks, and without the realistic threat of prosecution to remind them of their legal obligations, it is understandable that these agents frequently acted without concern for issues of law and at times assumed that normal legal restraints and prohibitions did not apply to their activities.

Significantly, those officials at the highest levels of government, who had a duty to control the activities of the intelligence community, sometimes set in motion the very forces that permitted lawlessness to occur—even if every act committed by intelligence agencies was not known to them. By demanding results without carefully limiting the means by which the results were achieved; by over-emphasizing the threats to national security without ensuring sensitivity to the rights of American citizens; and by propounding concepts such as the right of the "sovereign" to break the law, ultimate responsibility for the consequent climate of permissiveness should be placed at their door.

Subfinding (a)

In its attempt to implement instructions to protect the security of the United States, the intelligence community engaged in some activities which violated statutory law and the constitutional rights of American citizens.

From 1940 to 1973, the CIA and the FBI engaged in twelve covert mail opening programs in violation of Sections 1701-1703 of Title 18 of the United States Code which prohibit the obstruction, interception, or opening of mail. Both of these agencies also engaged in warrantless "surreptitious entries"—break-ins—against American citizens within the United States in apparent violation of state laws prohibiting trespass and burglary. Section 605 of the Federal Communications Act of 1934 was violated by NSA's program for obtaining millions of telegrams of Americans unrelated to foreign targets and by the Army Security Agency's interception of domestic radio communications.

All of these activities, as well as the FBI's use of electronic surveillance without a substantial national security predicate, also infringed the rights of countless Americans under the Fourth Amendment protection "against unreasonable searches and seizures."

The abusive techniques used by the FBI in COINTELPRO from 1956 to 1971 included violations of both federal and state statutes prohibiting mail fraud, wire fraud, incitement to violence, sending obscene material through the mail, and extortion. More fundamentally, the harassment of innocent citizens engaged in lawful forms of political expression did serious injury to the First Amendment guarantee of freedom of speech and the right of the people to assemble peaceably and to petition the government for a redress of grievances. The Bureau's maintenance of the Security Index, which targeted thousands of American citizens for detention in the event of national emergency, clearly overstepped the permissible bounds established by Congress in the Emergency Detention Act of 1950 and represented, in contravention of the Act, a potential general suspension of the privilege of the writ of habeas corpus secured by Article 1, Section 9, of the Constitution.

A distressing number of the programs and techniques developed by the intelligence community involved transgressions against human decency that were no less serious than any technical violations of law. Some of the most fundamental values of this society were threatened by activities such as the smear campaign against Dr. Martin Luther King, Jr., the testing of dangerous drugs on unsuspecting American citizens, the dissemination of information about the sex lives, drinking habits, and marital problems of electronic surveillance targets, and the COINTELPRO attempts to turn dissident organizations against one another and to destroy marriages.

Subfinding (b)

Legal issues were often overlooked by many of the intelligence officers who directed these operations. Some held a pragmatic view of intelligence activities that did not regularly attach sufficient significance to questions of legality. The question raised was usually not whether a particular program was legal or ethical, but whether it worked.

Legal issues were clearly not a primary consideration—if they were a consideration at all—in many of the programs and techniques of the intelligence community. When the former head of the FBI's Racial Intelligence Section was asked whether anybody in the FBI at any time during the 15-year course of COINTELPRO discussed its constitutionality or legal authority for example, he replied: "No, we never gave it a thought." This attitude is echoed by other Bureau officials in connection with other programs. The former Section Chief of one of the FBI's Counterintelligence sections, and the former Assistant Director of the Bureau's Domestic Intelligence Division both testified that legal considerations were simply not raised in policy decisions concerning the FBI's mail opening programs. Similarly, when the FBI was presented with the opportunity to assume responsibility for the CIA's New York mail opening operation, legal factors played no role in the Bureau's refusal; rather, the opportunity was declined simply because of the attendant expense, manpower requirements, and security problems.

One of the most abusive of all FBI programs was its attempt to discredit Dr. Martin Luther King, Jr. Yet former FBI Assistant Director William C. Sullivan testified that he "never heard anyone raise the question of legality or constitutionality, never."

Former Director of Central Intelligence Richard Helms testified publicly that he never seriously questioned the legal status of the twenty-year CIA New York mail opening project because he assumed his predecessor, Allen Dulles, had "made his legal peace with [it]."

"... [F]rom time to time," he said, "the Agency got useful information out of it," so he permitted it to continue throughout his sevenyear tenure as Director.

The Huston Plan that was prepared for President Richard Nixon in June 1970 constituted a virtual charter for the use of intrusive and illegal techniques against American dissidents as well as foreign agents. Its principal author has testified, however, that during the drafting sessions with representatives of the FBI, CIA, NSA, and Defense Intelligence Agency, no one ever objected to any of the recommendations on the grounds that they involved illegal acts, nor was the legality or constitutionality of any of the recommendations ever discussed.

William C. Sullivan, who participated in the drafting of the Huston Plan and served on the United States Intelligence Board and as FBI Assistant Director for Intelligence for 10 years, stated that in his entire experience in the intelligence community he never heard legal issues raised at all:

We never gave any thought to this realm of reasoning, because we were just naturally pragmatists. The one thing we were concerned about was this: Will this course of action work, will it get us what we want, will we reach the objective that we desire to reach? As far as legality is concerned, morals, or ethics, [it] was never raised by myself or anybody else ... I think this suggests really in government that we are amoral. In government—I am not speaking for everybody—the general atmosphere is one of amorality.

Subfinding (c.)

On some occasions when agency officials did assume, or were told, that a program was illegal, they still permitted it to continue. They justified their conduct in some cases on the ground that the failure of "the enemy" to play by the rules granted them the right to do likewise, and in other cases on the ground that the "national security" permitted programs that would otherwise be illegal.

Even when agency officials recognized certain programs or techniques to be illegal, they sometimes advocated their implementation or permitted them to continue nonetheless.

This point is illustrated by a passage in a 1954 memorandum from an FBI Assistant Director to J. Edgar Hoover, which recommended that an electronic listening device be planted in the hotel room of a suspected Communist sympathizer: "Although such an installation will not be legal, it is believed that the intelligence information to be obtained will make such an installation necessary and desirable." Hoover approved the installation.

More than a decade later, a memorandum was sent to Director Hoover which described the current FBI policy and procedures for "black bag jobs" (warrantless break-ins for purposes other than microphone installation). This memorandum read in part:

Such a technique involves trespass and is clearly illegal; therefore, it would be impossible to obtain any legal sanction for it. Despite this, "black bag" jobs have been used because they represent an invaluable technique in combatting subversive activities . . . aimed directly at undermining and destroying our nation.

In other words, breaking the law was seen as useful in combating those who threatened the legal fabric of society. Although Hoover terminated the general use of "black bag jobs" in July 1966, they were employed on a large scale before that time and have been used in isolated instances since then.

Another example of disregard for the law is found in a 1969 memorandum from William C. Sullivan to Director Hoover. In June of that year, Sullivan was requested by the Director, apparently at the urging of White House officials to travel to France for the purpose of electronically monitoring the conversations of journalist Joseph Kraft. With the cooperation of local authorities, Sullivan was able to have a microphone installed in Kraft's hotel room, and informed Hoover of his success. "Parenthetically," he wrote in his letter to the Director, "I might add that such a cover is regarded as illegal."

The attitude that legal standards and issues of privacy can be overridden by other factors is further reflected in a memorandum written by Richard Helms in connection with the testing of dangerous drugs on unsuspecting American citizens in 1963. Mr. Helms wrote the Deputy Director of Central Intelligence:

While I share your uneasiness and distaste for any program which tends to intrude on an individual's private and legal prerogatives, I believe it is necessary that the Agency maintain a central role in this activity, keep current on enemy capabilities in the manipulation of human behavior, and maintain an offensive capability. I, therefore, recommend your approval for continuation of this testimony program . . .

The history of the CIA's New York mail opening program is replete with examples of conscious contravention of the law. The original proposal for large-scale mail opening in 1955, for instance, explicitly recognized that "[t]here is no overt, authorized or legal censorship or monitoring of first class mails which enter, depart or transit the United States at the present time." A 1962 memorandum on the project noted that its exposure could "give rise to grave charges of criminal misuse of the mails by Government agencies" and that "existing Federal statutes preclude the concoction of any legal excuse for the violation . . . And again in 1963, a CIA officer wrote: "There is no legal basis for monitoring postal communications in the United States except during time of war or national emergency . . ."

Both the former Chief of the Counterintelligence Staff and the former Director of Security — who were in charge of the New York project — testified that they believed it to be illegal. One Inspector General who reviewed the project in 1969 also flatly stated: "[O]f course, we knew that this was illegal. [E]verybody knew that it was [illegal] ..."

In spite of the general recognition of its illegality, the New York mail opening project continued for a total of 20 years and was not terminated until 1973, when the Watergate-created political climate had increased the risks of exposure.

With the full knowledge of J. Edgar Hoover, moreover, the FBI continued to receive the fruits of this project for three years after the FBI Director informed the President of the United States that "the FBI is opposed to implementing any covert mail coverage because it is clearly illegal ..." The Bureau's own mail opening programs had been terminated in 1966, but it continued intentionally and knowingly to benefit from the illegal acts of the CIA until 1973.

The Huston Plan is another disturbing reminder of the fact that intelligence programs and techniques may be advocated and authorized with the knowledge that they are illegal. At least two of the options that were presented to President Nixon were described as unlawful on the face of the Report. Of "covert mail coverage" (mail opening) it was written that "[t]his coverage, not having the sanction of law, runs the risk of any illicit act magnified by the involvement of a Government agency." The Report also noted that surreptitious entry "involves illegal entry and trespass." Thus, the intelligence community presented the nation's highest executive official with the option of approving courses of action described as illegal. The fact that President Nixon did authorize them, even if only for five days, is more disquieting still.

When President Nixon eventually revoked his approval of the Huston Plan, the intelligence community nevertheless proceded to initiate some programs suggested in the Plan. Intelligence agencies also continued to employ techniques recommended in the Plan, such as mail opening which had been used previously without presidential approval.

The recent history of Army intelligence provides an additional example of continuing an activity described as illegal. Beginning in 1967, the Army Security Agency monitored the radio communications of amateur radio operators in this country to determine if dissident elements planned disruptive activity at particular demonstrations and events. Because Army officials questioned whether such monitoring was legal under Section 605 of the Federal Communications Act of 1934, they requested a legal opinion from the Federal Communications Commission. At a meeting held in August 1968, the FCC advised the Army that such monitoring was illegal under the Act. FCC representatives also stated that the matter had been raised with Attorney General Ramsey Clark and that he had disapproved the program. The FCC agreed, however, to submit a written reply to the Army, stating only that it could not "Provide a positive answer to the Army's proposal."

Despite having been told that their monitoring activity was illegal, and that the Attorney General himself disapproved it, the Army Security Agency continued to monitor the radio communications of American citizens for another two years.

Several factors may explain the intelligence community's frequent disregard of legal issues.

Some intelligence officials expressed the view that the legal and ethical restraints that applied to the rest of society simply did not apply to intelligence activities. This concept is reflected in a 1959 memorandum on the Army's covert drug testing program: "In intelligence, the stakes involved and the interest of national security may permit a more tolerant interpretation of moral-ethical values . . ."

As William C. Sullivan also pointed out, many intelligence officers had been imbued with a "war psychology." "Legality was not questioned," he said. "it was not an issue." In war, one simply did what was "expected to do as a soldier." "It was my assumption," said one FBI official connected with the Bureau's mail opening programs, "that what we were doing was justified by what we had to do." Since the "enemy" did not play by the rules, moreover, intelligence officials often believed they could not afford to do so either.

One FBI intelligence officer appeared to attribute the disregard of the law in the Bureau's COINTELPRO operations to simple restlessness on the part of "action-oriented" FBI agents. George C. Moore, the Racial Intelligence Section Chief, testified that:

> ... the FBI's counterintelligence program came up because if you have anything in the FBI, you have an action oriented group of people who see something happening and want to do something to take its place.

Others in the intelligence community have contended that questionable and illegal acts were justified by a law higher than the United States Code or the Constitution. An FBI Counterintelligence Section Chief, for example, stated the following reason for believing in the necessity of techniques such as mail opening:

> The greater good, the national security, this is correct. This is what I believed in. Why I thought these programs were good, it was that the national security required this, this is correct.

Similarly, when intelligence officials secured the cooperation of telegraph company executives for Project SHAMROCK, in which NSA received millions of copies of international telegraph messages without the sender's knowledge, they assured the executives that they would not be subjected to criminal liability because the project was "in the highest interests of the nation."

Perhaps the most novel reason for advocating illegal action was proffered by Tom Charles Huston. Huston explained that he believed the real threat to internal security was potential repression by right-wing forces within the United States. He argued that the "New Left" was capable of producing a climate of fear that would bring forth every repressive demagogue in the country. Huston believed that the intelligence professionals, if given the chance, could protect the people from the latent forces of repression by monitoring the New Left, including by illegal means. Illegal action directed against the New Left, in other words, should be used by the Government to forestall potential repression by the Right.

In attempting to explain why illegal activities were advocated and defended, the impact of the attitudes and actions of government officials in supervisory positions — Presidents, Cabinet officers, and Congressmen — should not be discounted. Their occasional endorsement of such activities, as well as the atmosphere of permissiveness created by their emphasis on national security and their demands for results, clearly contributed to the notion that strict adherence to the law was unimportant. So, too, did the concept, propounded by some senior officials, that a "sovereign" president may authorize violations of the law.

Whatever the reasons, however, it is clear that a number of intelligence officers acted in knowing contravention of the law.

Subfinding (d)

Internal recognition of the illegality or questionable legality of many of these activities frequently led to a tightening of security rather than to their termination. Partly to avoid exposure and a public "flap," knowledge of these programs was tightly held within the agencies, special filing procedures were used, and "cover stories" were devised.

When intelligence agencies realized that certain programs and techniques were of questionable legality, they frequently took special security precautions to avoid public exposure, criticism, and embarrassment. The CIA's study of student unrest throughout the world in the late 1960s, for example, included a section on student dissent in the United States, an area that was clearly outside the Agency's statutory charter. DCI's Richard Helms urged the President's national security advisor, Henry Kissinger, to treat it with extreme sensivity in light of the acknowledged jurisdictional violation:

"Herewith is a survey of student dissidence world-wide as requested by the President. In an effort to round out our discussion of this subject, we have included a section on American students. This is an area not within the charter of this Agency, so I need not emphasize how extremely sensitive this makes the paper. Should anyone learn of its existence, it would prove most embarrassing for all concerned."

Concern for the FBI's public image prompted security measures which Protected numerous questionable activities. For example, in approving or denying COINTELPRO proposals, many of which were clearly illegal, a main consideration was preventing "embarrassment to the Bureau.

A characteristic caution to FBI agents appears in the letter which initiated the COINTELPRO against "Black Nationalists":

You are also cautioned that the nature of this new endeavor is such that under no circumstances should the existence of the program be made known outside the Bureau and appropriate within-office security should be afforded to sensitive operations and techniques considered under the program.

Examples of attention to such security are that anonymous letters had to be written on commercially purchased stationery; newsmen had to be so completely trustworthy that they were guaranteed not to reveal the Bureau's interest; and inquiries of law enforcement officials had to be made under the pretext of a criminal investigation. A similar preoccupation with security measures for improper activities affected both the NSA and the Army Security Agency.

NSA's guidelines for its watch list activity provided that NSA's name should not be on any of the disseminated watch list material involving Americans. The aim was to "restrict the knowledge that such information is being collected and processed" by NSA.

The Army Security Agency's radio monitoring activity, which continued even after the Army was told that the FCC and the Attorney General regarded it as illegal, also had to be conducted in secrecy if a public outcry was to be avoided. When Army officials decided to permit radio monitoring in connection with the military's Civil Disturbance Collection Plan, their instruction provided that all ASA personnel had to be "disguised" either in civilian clothes or as members of regular military Units.

The perceived illegality—and consequent "flap potential"—of the CIA's New York mail opening project led Agency officials to formulate a drastic strategy to follow in the event of public exposure. A review of the project by the Inspector General's Office in the early 1960s concluded that it would be desirable to fabricate a "cover story." A formal recommendation was therefore made that "[a]n emergency plan and cover story be prepared for the possibility that the operation might be blown." In response to this recommendation, the Deputy Chief of the Counterintelligence Staff agreed that "a 'flap' will put us 'out of business' immediately and may give rise to grave charges of criminal misuse of the mails by government agencies," but he argued:

Since no good purpose can be served by an official admission of the violation, and existing Federal statutes preclude the concoction of any legal excuse for the violation, it must be recognized that no cover story is available to any Government Agency. Therefore, it is important that all Federal law enforcement and US Intelligence Agencies vigorously deny any association, direct or indirect, with any such activity as charged.... Unless the charge is supported by the presentation of interior items from the Project, it should be relatively easy to "hush up" the entire affair, or to explain that it consists of legal mail cover activities conducted by the Post Office at the request of authorized Federal agencies. Under the most unfavorable circumstances ... it might be necessary after the matter has cooled off during an extended period of investigation, to find a scapegoat to blame for unauthorized tampering with the mails. Such cases by their very nature do not have much appeal to the imagination of the public, and this would he an effective way to resolve the initial charge of censorship of the mails.

This strategy of complete denial and transferring blame to a scapegoat was approved by the Director of Security in February 1962.

Another extreme example of a security measure that was adopted because of the threat that illegal activity might be exposed was the outright destruction of files.

The FBI developed a special filing system—or, more accurately, a destruction system—for memoranda written about illegal techniques, such as break-ins, 48 and highly questionable operations, such as the microphone surveillance of Joseph Kraft. 49 Under this system—which was referred to as the "DO NOT FILE" procedure— authorizing documents and other memoranda were filed in special safes at headquarters and field offices until the next annual inspection by the Inspection Division, at which time they were to be systematically destroyed.

Subfinding (e)

On occasion, intelligence agencies failed to disclose candidly programs and practices to their own General Counsels, and to Attorney Generals, Presidents, and Congress.

(i) Concealment from Executive Branch Officials

Intelligence officers frequently concealed or misrepresented illegal activities to their own General Counsel and superiors within and outside the agencies in order to protect these activities from exposure.

For example, during the entire 20-year history of the CIA's mail opening project, the Agency's General Counsel was never informed of its existence. According to one Agency official, this knowledge was purposefully kept from him. Former Inspector General Gordon Stewart testified:

Well, I am sure that it was held back from [the General Counsel] on purpose. An operation of this sort in the CIA is run—if it is closely held, it is run by those people immediately concerned, and to the extent that it is really possible, according to the practices that we had in the fifties and sixties, those persons not immediately concerned were supposed to be ignorant of it.

The evidence also indicates that two Directors of Central Intelligence under whom the New York mail operations continued—John McCone and Admiral Raborn—were never informed of its existence. In 1954, Postmaster General Arthur Summerfield was informed that the CIA operated a mail cover project in New York, but be was not told that the Agency opened or intended to open any mail. In 1965, the CIA briefly considered informing Postmaster General John A. Gronouski about the project when its existence was felt to be jeopardized by a congressional subcommittee that was investigating the use of mail covers and other investigative techniques by federal agencies. According to an internal memorandum, however, the idea was quickly rejected "in view of various statements by Gronouski before this subcommittee." Since Gronouski had agreed with the subcommittee that tighter administrative controls on mail covers were necessary and generally supported the principle of the sanctity of the mail, it is reasonable to infer that CIA officials assumed he would not be sympathetic to the technique of mail opening.

The only claim that any President may have known about the project was made by Richard Helms, who testified that "there was a possibility" that he "mentioned" it to President Lyndon Johnson in 1967 or 1968. No documentary evidence is available that either supports or refutes this statement. During the preparation of the Huston Plan, neither CIA nor FBI representatives informed Tom Charles Huston, President Nixon's representative, that the mail opening project existed. The final interagency report on the Huston Plan signed by Richard Helms and J. Edgar Hoover, was sent to the President with the statement, contrary to fact, that all mail opening programs by federal agencies had been discontinued.

In connection with another CIA mail opening Project, middle-level Agency officials apparently did not even tell their own superiors within the CIA that they intended to open mail, as opposed to merely inspecting envelope exteriors. The ranking officials testified that they approved the project believing it to be a mail cover program only. No Cabinet officials or President knew of this project and the approval of the Deputy Chief Postal Inspector (for what he also believed to be a mail cover operation) was secured through conscious deception.

A pattern of concealment was repeated by the FBI in their mail opening programs. There is no claim by the Bureau that any Postmaster General, Attorney General, or President was ever advised of the true nature and scope of its mail projects. One FBI official testified that it was an unofficial Bureau policy not to inform postal officials with whom they dealt of the actual intention of FBI agents in receiving the mail, and there is no indication that this policy was ever violated. 60 At one point in 1965, Assistant Director Alan Belmont and Inspector Donald Moore apparently informed Attorney General Nicholas deB. Katzenbach that FBI agents received custody of the mail in connection with espionage cases on some occasions. 61 But Moore testified that the Attorney General was not told that mail was actually opened. When asked if he felt any need to hold back from Katzenbach the fact of mail openings as opposed to the fact that Bureau agents received direct access to the mail, Moore replied:

> It is perhaps difficult to answer. Perhaps I could liken it to ... a defector in place in the KGB. You don't want to tell anybody his name, the location, the title, or anything like that. Not that you don't trust them completely, but the fact is that any time one additional person becomes aware of it, there is a potential for the information to . . . go further.

Another Bureau agent speculated that the Attorney General was not told because, mail opening "was not legal, as far as I knew."

Similarly, there is no indication that the FBI ever informed any Attorney General about its use of "black bag jobs" (illegal break-ins for purposes other than microphone installations) ; the full scope of its activities in COINTELPRO ; or its submission of names for inclusion on either the CIA's "Watch List" for mail opening or, before 1973, on the NSA's "Watch List" for electronic monitoring of international communications.

After J. Edgar Hoover disregarded Attorney General Biddle's 1943 order to terminate the Custodial Detention List by merely changing its name to the Security Index moreover, Bureau headquarters instructed the field officers that the new list should be kept "strictly confidential" and that it should never be mentioned in FBI reports or "discussed with agencies or individuals outside the Bureau" except for military intelligence agencies. For several years thereafter, the Attorney General and the Justice Department were not informed of the FBI's decision.

An incident which occurred in 1967 in connection with the Bureau's COINTELPRO operations is particularly illustrative of the lengths to which intelligence agencies would go to protect illegal programs from scrutiny by executive branch officers outside the intelligence community. As one phase of its disruption of the United Klans of America, the Bureau sent a letter to Klan officers purportedly prepared by the highly secret "National Intelligence Committee" (NIC) of the Klan. The fake letter purported to fire the North Carolina Grand Dragon for personal misconduct and misfeasance in office, and to suspend Imperial Wizard Robert Shelton for his failure to remove the Grand Dragon. Shelton complained to the FBI and the Post Office about this apparent violation of the mail fraud statutes—without realizing that the Bureau had in fact sent the letter. The Bureau, after solemnly assuring Shelton that his complaint was not within the FBI's jurisdiction, approached the Chief Postal Inspector's office in Washington to determine what action the Post Office planned to take regarding Shelton's allegation. The FBI was advised that the matter had been referred to the Justice Department's Criminal Division. At no time did the Bureau inform either the Post Office or the Justice Department that FBI agents had authored the letter. When no investigation was deemed to be warranted by the Criminal Division, FBI Headquarters directed the Bureau's Charlotte, North Carolina office to prepare a second phony NIC letter to send to Klan officials. This letter was not mailed, however, because, the Charlotte office proposed and implemented a different idea—the formation of an FBI-controlled alternative Klan organization, which eventually attracted 250 members.

The Huston Plan itself was prepared without the knowledge of the Attorney General. Neither the Attorney General nor anyone in his office was invited to the drafting sessions at Langley or consulted during the proceedings. Huston testified that it never occurred to him to confer with the Attorney General before making the recommendations in the Report, in part because the plan was seen as an intelligence matter to be handled by the intelligence agency directors.

Similarly, the CIA's General Counsel was not included or consulted in the formulation of the Huston Plan. As James Angleton testified, "the custom and usage was not to deal with the General Counsel, as a rule, until there were some troubles. He was not a part of the process of project approval."

(ii) Concealment from Congress

At times, knowledge of illegal programs and techniques has been concealed from Congress as well as executive branch officials. On two occasions, for example, officials of the Army Security Agency ordered its units—in apparent violation of that Agency's jurisdiction—to conduct general searches of the radio spectrum without regard to the source or subject matter of the transmissions. ASA did not report these incidents to ranking Army officials, even when specifically asked to do so as part of the Army's preparation for the hearings of the Senate Subcommittee on Constitutional Rights in 1971.

Events surrounding the 1965 and 1966 investigation by Senator Edward Long of Missouri into federal agencies' use of mail covers and other investigative techniques clearly showed the desire on the part of CIA and FBI officials to protect their programs from congressional review. Fearing that the New York mail opening program might be discovered by this subcommittee, the CIA considered suspending the, operation until the investigation had been completed. An internal CIA memorandum dated April 23, 1965, reads in part:

Mr. Karamessines [Assistant Deputy Director for Plans] felt that the dangers inherent in Long's subcommittee activities to the security of the Project's operations in New York should be thoroughly studied in order that a determination can be made as to whether these operations should be partially or fully suspended until the subcommittee's investigations are completed.

When it was learned that Chief Postal Inspector Henry Montague had been contacted about the Long investigation and believed that it would "soon cool off", however, it was decided to continue the operation without suspension.

The FBI was also concerned that the subcommittee might expose its mail opening programs. Bureau memoranda indicate that the FBI intended to "warn the Long Committee away from those areas which would be injurious to the national defense." J. Edgar Hoover personally contacted the Chairman of the Senate Judiciary Committee, and urged him "to see Long not later than Wednesday morning to caution him that [the Chief Counsel] must not go into the kind of question he made of Chief Inspector Montague of the Post Office Department" — questioning that had threatened to reveal the FBI's mail project the Previous week.

When the Long subcommittee began to investigate electronic surveillance practices several months later, Bureau officials convinced Senator Edward Long that there was no need to pursue such an investigation since, they said, the FBI's operations were tightly controlled and properly implemented. According to Bureau documents, FBI agents wrote a press release for the Senator from Missouri, with his approval, that stated his subcommittee had

conducted exhaustive research into the activities, procedures, and techniques of this agency [and] based upon careful study ... we are fully satisfied that the FBI has not participated in highhanded or uncontrolled usage of wiretaps, microphones, or other electronic equipment.

Not only was this release written by the FBI itself, it was misleading. The "exhaustive research" apparently consisted of a ninety-minute briefing by FBI officials describing their electronic surveillance practices; neither the Senator nor the public learned of the instances of improper electronic surveillances that had been conducted by the FBI. When Senator Edward Long later asked certain FBI officials to testify about the Bureau's electronic surveillance policy before the Subcommittee, they refused, arguing: ". . . to put an FBI witness on the stand would be an attempt to open a Pandora's box, insofar as our enemies in the press were concerned ...."

After the press release had been delivered to Senator Long and the refusal to testify had been accepted, one FBI official wrote to the Associate Director that while some problems still existed, "we have neutralized the threat of being embarrassed by the Long Subcommittee ..."

Subfinding (f)

The internal inspection mechanisms of the CIA and the FBI did not keep — and, in the case of the FBI, were not designed to keep — the activities of those agencies within legal bounds. Their primary concern was efficiency, not legality or propriety.

The internal inspection mechanisms of the CIA and the FBI were ineffective in ensuring that the activities of these agencies were kept within legal bounds. This failure was sometimes due to structural deficiencies which kept knowledge of questionable programs tightly compartmented and shielded from those who could evaluate their legality.

As noted above, for example, the CIA's General Counsel was not informed about either the New York mail opening project or CIA's participation in the Huston Plan deliberations. The role of the CIA's General Counsel was essentially a passive one; he did not initiate inquiries but responded to requests from other Agency components. As James Angleton stated, the General Counsel was not a part of the normal project approval process and generally was not consulted until "something was going wrong."

When the General Counsel was consulted, he often exerted a positive influence on the conduct of CIA activities. For example, the CIA stopped monitoring telephone calls to and from Latin America after the General Counsel issued an opinion describing the telephone intercepts as illegal. But internal CIA regulations have never required employees who know of illegal, improper, or questionable activities to report them to the General Counsel; rather, employes with such knowledge are instructed to inform either the Director of Central Intelligence or, the Inspector General. The Director and the Inspector General may refer the matter to the General Counsel but until recently they were not obligated to do so. 88a As Richard Helms stated, "Somtimes we did [consult the General Counsel]; sometimes we did not. I think the record on that is rather spotty, quite frankly."

Indeed, the record suggests that those programs that were most questionable — such as the New York mail opening project and Project CHAOS — were not referred to the General Counsel because they were considered extremely sensitive. Even when questionable activities re called to the attention of the General Counsel, moreover, the internal Agency regulations did not guarantee him unrestricted access all relevant information. Thus, the General Counsel was not in a position to conduct a complete evaluation of the propriety of particular programs.

Part of the failure of internal inspection to terminate improper programs and practices may be attributed to the fact that the primary focus of the CIA's Office of the Inspector General and the FBI's Inspection Division has been on efficiency and effectiveness rather than on propriety.

The CIA's Inspector General is charged with the responsibility, among other matters, of investigating activities which might be construed as "illegal, improper, and outside the CIA's legislative charter." In at least one case, the Inspector General did force the suspension of a suspect activity: the surreptitious administration of LSD to unwitting, non-volunteer, human subjects which was suspended in 1963. An earlier Inspector General's review of the larger, more general program for the testing of behavorial control agents, however, had labeled that program "unethical and illegal" and it nonetheless continued for another seven years. In general, as the Rockefeller Commission pointed out, "the focus of the Inspector General component reviews was on operational effectiveness. Examination of the legality or propriety of CIA activities was not normally a primary concern." Two separate reviews of the New York mail opening projects by the Inspector General's office, for example, considered issues of administration and security at length but did riot even mention legal considerations.

Internal inspection at the FBI has traditionally not encompassed legal or ethical questions at all. According to W. Mark Felt, the Assistant FBI Director in charge of the Inspection Division from 1964 to 1971, his job was to ensure that Bureau programs were being operated efficiently, not constitutionally: "There was no instruction to me," he stated, "nor do I believe there is any instruction in the Inspector's manuals, that inspectors should be on the alert to see that constitutional values are being protected." He could not recall any program which was terminated because it might have been violating someone's civil rights.

A number of questionable FBI programs were apparently never inspected. Felt could recall no inspection, for instance, of either the FBI mail opening programs or the Bureau's participation in the CIA's New York mail opening project. Even when improper programs were inspected, the Inspection Division did not attempt to exercise oversight in the sense of looking for wrongdoing. Its responsibility was simply to ensure that FBI policy, as defined by J. Edgar Hoover was effectively implemented and not to question the propriety of the policy. Thus, Felt testified that if, in the course of an inspection of a field office, he discovered a microphone surveillance on Martin Luther King, Jr., the only questions he would ask were whether it had been approved by the Director and whether the procedures had been properly followed.

When Felt was asked whether the Inspection Division conducted any investigation into the propriety of COINTELPRO, the following exchange ensued:

Mr. FELT. Not into the propriety.

Q. So in the case of COINTELPRO, as in the case of NSA interceptions, your job as Inspector was to determine whether the program was being pursued effectively as opposed to whether it was proper?

Mr. FELT. Right, with this exception, that in any of these situations, Counterintelligence Program or whatever, it very frequently happened that the inspectors, in reviewing the files, would direct that a certain investigation be discontinued, that it was not productive, or that there was some reason that it be discontinued.

But I don't recall any cases being discontinued in the Counterintelligence program.

As a result of this role definition, the Inspection Division became an active participant in some of the most questionable FBI programs For example, it was responsible for reviewing on an annual basis all memoranda relating to illegal break-ins prior to their destruction under the "DO NOT FILE" procedure.

Improper programs and techniques in the FBI were protected not only by the Inspection Division's perception of its function, but also by the maxim that FBI agents should never "embarrass the Bureau." This standard, which served as a shield to outside scrutiny, was explicitly reflected in the FBI Manual:

Any investigation necessary to develop complete essential facts regarding any allegation against Bureau employees must be instituted promptly, and every logical lead which will establish the true facts should be completely run out unless such action would embarrass the Bureau ... in which event the Bureau will weigh the facts, along with the recommendations of the division head.

Such an instruction, coupled with the Inspection Division's inattention to the law, could only inhibit or prevent the termination and exposure of illegal practices.

Subfinding (g)

When senior administration officials with a duty to control domestic intelligence activities knew, or had a basis for suspecting, that questionable activities had occurred, they often responded with silence or approval. In certain cases, they were presented with a partial description of a program but did not ask for details, thereby abdicating their responsibility. In other cases, they were fully aware of the nature of the practice and implicitly or explicitly approved it.

On several occasions, senior administration officials with a duty to control domestic intelligence activities were supplied with partial details about questionable or illegal programs but they did not ask for additional information and the programs continued.

Sometimes the failure to probe further stemmed from the administration official's assumption that an intelligence agency would not engage in lawless conduct. Former Chief Postal Inspector Henry Montague, for example, was aware that the FBI received custody of the mail in connection with several of its mail opening programs—indeed, he had approved such custody in one case—but he testified that he believed these were mail cover operations only. Montague stated that he did not ask FBI officials if the Bureau opened mail because he

> never thought that would be necessary .... I trusted them the same as I would another [Postal] Inspector. I would never feel that I would have to tell a Postal person that you cannot open mail. By the same token, I would not consider it necessary to emphasize it to any great degree with the FBI.

A former FBI official has also testified, as noted above, that he informed Attorney General Katzenbach about selected aspects of the FBI mail opening programs. This official did not tell Katzenbach that mail was actually opened, but he testified that he "pointed out [to the Attorney General] that we do receive mail from the Post Office in certain sensitive areas." While Katzenbach stated that he never knew mail was opened or that the FBI gained access to mail on a regular basis in large-scale operations, the former Attorney General acknowledged that he did learn that "in some cases the outside of mail might have been examined or even photographed by persons other than Post Office employees". However, neither at this time nor at any other time did the Justice Department make any inquiry to determine the full scope of the FBI mail operations.

Similarly, former Attorneys General Nicholas Katzenbach and Ramsey Clark testified that they were familiar with the FBI's efforts to disrupt the Ku Klux Klan through regular investigative techniques but said they were unaware of the offensive tactics that occurred in COINTELPRO. Katzenbach said he did not believe it necessary to explore possible irregularities since "[i]t never occurred to me that the Bureau would engage in the sort of sustained improper activity which it apparently did."

Both Robert Kennedy and Nicholas Katzenbach were also aware of some aspects of the FBI's investigation of Dr. Martin Luther King, Jr., yet neither ascertained the full details of the Bureau's campaign to discredit the civil rights leader. Kennedy intensified the original "communist influence" investigation in October 1963 by authorizing wiretaps on King's home and office telephones. Kennedy requested that an evaluation of the results be submitted to him in thirty days in order to determine whether or not to maintain the taps, but the evaluation was never delivered to him and he did not insist on it. Since he never ordered the termination of the wiretap, the Bureau could, and did, install additional wiretaps on King by invoking the original authorization. According to Bureau memoranda apparently initialled by Attorney General Katzenbach, Katzenbach received after the fact notification in 1965 that three bugs had been planted in Dr. King's hotel rooms. A transmittal memorandum written by Katzenbach also indicates that he may have instructed the FBI to be "very cautious" in conducting these surveillances. There is no indication, however, that, he requested further details about any of them or prohibited the FBI from future use of this technique against Dr. King.

While there is no evidence that the full extent of the FBI's campaign to discredit Dr. King was authorized by or known to anyone outside of the Bureau, there is evidence that officials responsible for supervising the FBI received indications that some such efforts were being undertaken. For example, former Attorney General Katzenbach and former Assistant Attorney General Burke Marshall both testified that in late 1964 they learned that the Bureau had offered tape recordings of Dr. King to certain newsmen in Washington, D.C. They further stated that they informed President Johnson of the FBI's offers. The Committee has discovered no evidence, however, that the President or Justice Department officials made any further effort to halt the discrediting campaign at this time or at any other time; indeed, the Bureau's campaign continued for several years after this incident.

On some occasions, administration officials did not request further details about intelligence programs because they simply did not want to know. Former Postmaster General J. Edward Day testified that when Allen Dulles and Richard Helms spoke to him about a CIA project in 1961, he interrupted them before they could tell him the purpose of their visit (which Helms said was to say mail was being opened). Day stated:

... Mr. Dulles, after some preliminary visiting and so on, said that he wanted to tell me something very secret, and I said, "Do I have to know about it?" And he said, "No."

I said, "My experience is that where there is something that is very secret, it is likely to leak out, and anybody that knew about it is likely to be suspected of having been part of leaking it out, so I would rather not know anything about it."

What additional things were said in connection with him building up to that, I don't know. But I am sure ... that I was not told anything about opening mail."

By his own account, therefore, Mr. Day did not learn the true nature of this project because he "would rather not know anything about it." Although rarely expressed in such unequivocal terms, this attitude appears to have been all too common among senior government officials.

Even when administration officials were fully apprised of the illegal or questionable nature of certain programs and techniques, they sometimes permitted them to continue. An example of acquiescence is presented in the case of William Cotter, a former Chief Postal Inspector who knew that the CIA opened mail in connection with its New York project but took no direct action to terminate the project for a period of four years. Cotter had learned of this project in his capacity as a CIA official in the mid-1950's and he knew that it was continuing when he was sworn in as Chief Postal Inspector in April 1969. Because the primary responsibility of his position was to insure the sanctity of the mails, he was understandably "very, very uncomfortable with [knowledge of the New York] project," but he felt constrained by the letter and spirit of the secrecy oath which he had signed when he left the CIA in 1969 "attesting to the fact that I would not divulge secret information that came into my possession during the time that I was with the CIA." Cotter stated: "After coming from eighteen years in the CIA, I was hypersensitive, perhaps, to the protection of what I believed to be a most sensitive project . . ." For several years, he placed the dictate of the secrecy oath above that of the law he was charged with enforcing.

Former White House adviser John Ehrlichman also stated that he learned of a program of intercepting mail between the United States and Communist countries "because I had seen reports that cited those kinds of sources in connection with this, the bombings, the dissident activities." Yet he cannot recall any White House inquiry that was made into such a program nor can he recall raising the matter with the President.

When President Nixon learned of the illegal techniques that were recommended in the Huston Plan, he initially endorsed, rather than disavowed them. The former President stated that "[t]o the extent that I reviewed the Special Report of Interagency Committee on Intelligence, I would have been informed that certain recommendations or decisions set forth in that report were, or might be construed to be, illegal." He nonetheless approved them, in part because they represented an efficient method of intelligence collection. As President Nixon explained, "[M]y approval was based largely on the fact that the procedures were consistent with those employed by prior administrations and had been found to be effective by the intelligence agencies."

Mr. Nixon also apparently relied on the theory that a "sovereign" President can authorize the violation of criminal laws in the name of "national security" when the President, in his sole discretion, deems it appropriate. He recently stated:

> It is quite obvious that there are certain inherently governmental actions which if undertaken by the sovereign in protection of the interest of the nation's security are lawful but which if undertaken by private persons are not. . . .

> ... [I]t is naive to attempt to categorize activities a President might authorize as "legal" or "illegal" without reference to the circumstances under which he concludes that the activity is necessary. . . .

> In short, there have been—and will be in the future—circumstances in which Presidents may lawfully authorize actions in the interests of the security of this country, which if undertaken by other persons, or even by the President under different circumstances, would be illegal.

As the former President described this doctrine, it could apply not only to actions taken openly, which are subject to later challenge by Congress and the courts, but also to actions such as those recommended in the Huston Plan, which are covertly endorsed and implemented. The dangers inherent in this theory are clear, for it permits a President to create exceptions to normal legal restraints and prohibitions, without review by a neutral authority and without objective standards to guide him. The Huston Plan itself serves as a reminder of these dangers.

Significantly, President Nixon's revocation of approval for the Huston Plan was based on the possibility of "media criticism" if the use of these techniques was revealed. The former President stated:

> Mr. Mitchell informed me that it was Director Hoover's opinion that initiating a program which would permit several government intelligence agencies to utilize the investigative techniques outlined in the Committee's report would significantly increase the possibility of their public disclosure. Mr. Mitchell explained to me that Mr. Hoover believed that although each of the intelligence gathering methods outlined in the Committee's recommendations had been utilized by one or more previous Administrations, their sensitivity would likely generate media criticism if they were employed. Mr. Mitchell further informed me that it was his opinion that the risk of disclosure of the possible illegal actions, such as unauthorized entry into foreign embassies to install a microphone transmitter, was greater than the possible benefit to be derived. Based upon this conversation with Attorney General Mitchell, I decided to revoke the approval originally extended to the Committee's recommendations.

In more than one instance, administration officials outside the intelligence community have specifically requested intelligence agencies to undertake questionable actions. NSA's program of monitoring telephonic communications between New York City and a city in South America, for example, was undertaken at the specific request of the Bureau of Narcotics and Dangerous Drugs, a law enforcement agency.

BNDD officials had been concerned about drug deals that were apparently arranged in calls from public telephones in New York to South America, but they felt that they could not legally wiretap these telephone booths. In order to avoid tapping a limited number of phones in New York, BNDD submitted the names of 450 American citizens for inclusion in NSA's Watch List, and requested NSA to monitor a communications link between New York and South America which necessitated the interception of thousands of international telephone calls.

The legal limitations on domestic wiretapping apparently did not concern certain officials in the White House or Attorneys General who requested the FBI to do their bidding. In some instances, they specifically requested the FBI to institute wiretaps on American citizens with no substantial national security predicate for doing so.

On occasion, Attorneys General have also encouraged the FBI to circumvent the will of both Congress and the Supreme Court. As noted above, after Congress passed the Emergency Detention Act of 1950 to regulate the FBI program for listing people to be detained in case of war or other emergency, Justice Department officials concluded that its procedural safeguards and substantive standards were "unworkable". Attorney General J. Howard McGrath instructed the FBI to disregard the statute and "proceed with the [Security Index] program as previously outlined." Two subsequent Attorneys General — James McGranery and Herbert Brownell endorsed the decision to ignore the Emergency Detention Act.

In 1954, the Supreme Court denounced the use of microphone surveillances by local police in criminal cases; the fact that a microphone had been installed in a defendant's bedroom particularly outraged the court. Within weeks of this decision, however, Attorney General Herbert Brownell reversed the existing Justice Department policy prohibiting trespassory microphone installations by the FBI, and gave the Bureau sweeping new authority to engage in bugging for intelligence purposes — even when it meant planting microphones in bedrooms. Brownell wrote J. Edgar Hoover:

> Obviously, the installation of a microphone in a bedroom or in some comparably intimate location should be avoided whenever possible. It may appear, however, that important intelligence or evidence relating to matters connected with the national security can only be obtained by the installation of a microphone in such a location. . . .
>
> ... I recognize that for the FBI to fulfill its important intelligence function, considerations of internal security and the national safety are paramount and, therefore, may compel the unrestricted use of this technique in the national interest.

Brownell did not even require the Bureau to seek the Attorney General's prior approval for microphone installations in particular cases. 136 In the face of the Irvine decision, therefore, he gave the FBI authority to bug whomever it wished wherever it wished in cases that the Bureau — and not the Attorney General — determined were "in the national interest."

In short, disregard of the law by intelligence officers was seldom corrected, and sometimes encouraged or facilitated, by officials outside the agencies. Whether by inaction or direct participation, these administration officials contributed to the perception that legal restraints did not apply to intelligence activities.

B. The Overbreadth Of Domestic Intelligence Activity

Major Finding
The Committee finds that domestic intelligence activity has been overbroad in that (1) many Americans and domestic groups have been subjected to investigation who were not suspected of criminal activity and (2) the intelligence agencies have regularly collected information about personal and political activities irrelevant to any legitimate governmental interest.

Subfindings
(a) Large numbers of law-abiding Americans and lawful domestic groups have been subjected to extensive intelligence investigation and surveillance.

(b) The absence of precise standards for intelligence, investigations of Americans contributed to overbreadth. Congress did not enact statutes precisely delineating the authority of the intelligence agencies or defining the purpose and scope of domestic intelligence activity. The executive branch abandoned the standard set by Attorney General Stone — that the government's concern was not with political opinions but with "such conduct as is forbidden by the laws of the United States." Intelligence agencies' superiors issued over-inclusive directives to investigate "subversion" (a term that was never defined in presidential directives) and "potential" rather than actual or likely criminal conduct, as well as to collect general intelligence on lawful political and social dissent.

(c.) The intelligence agencies themselves used imprecise and overinclusive criteria in their conduct of intelligence investigations. Intelligence investigations extended beyond "subversive" or violent targets to additional groups and individuals subject to minimal "subversive influence" or having little or no "potential" for violence.

(d) Intelligence agencies pursued a "vacuum cleaner" approach to intelligence collection — drawing in all available information about groups and individuals, including their lawful political activity and details of their personal lives.

(e) Intelligence investigations in many cases continued for excessively long periods of time, resulting in sustained governmental monitoring of political activity in the absence of any indication of criminal conduct or "subversion."

Elaboration of Findings

The central problem posed by domestic intelligence activity has been its departure from the standards of the law. This departure from law has meant not only the violation of constitutional prohibitions and explicit statutes, but also the adoption of criteria unrelated to the law as the basis for extensive investigations of Americans.

In 1917-1924, the federal government, often assisted by the private vigilante American Protective League, conducted sweeping investigations of dissenters, war protesters, labor organizers, and alleged "anarchists" and "revolutionaries." These investigations led to mass-arrests of thousands of persons in the 1920 "Palmer raids." Reacting to these and other abuses of investigative power, Attorney General Harlan Fiske Stone in 1924 confined the Bureau of Investigation in the Justice Department to the investigation of federal crimes. Attorney General Stone articulated a clear and workable standard:

> The Bureau of Investigation is not concerned with political or other opinions of individuals. It is concerned only with their conduct and then only such conduct as is forbidden by the laws of the United States.

Nevertheless, his restriction lasted for little more than a decade.

In the mid-1930s the FBI resumed domestic intelligence functions, carrying out President Roosevelt's vague order to investigate "subversive activities." The President and the Attorney General authorized FBI and military intelligence investigations of conduct explicitly recognized as "not within the specific provisions of prevailing statutes." As a result, ideas and associations, rather than suspicion of criminal offenses, once again became the focus of federal investigations.

The scope of domestic intelligence investigations consistently widened in the decades after the 1930s, reaching its greatest extent in the late 1960s and early 1970s.

Domestic intelligence investigations were permitted under criteria which more nearly resembled political or social labels than standards for governmental action. Rather than Attorney General Stone's standard of investigating "only such conduct as is forbidden by the laws of the United States," domestic intelligence used such labels as the following to target intelligence investigations:

--"rightist" or "extremist" groups in the "anticommunist field

--persons with "anarchistic or revolutionary beliefs" or who were "espousing the line of revolutionary movements"

--"general racial matters"

--"hate organizations"

--"rabblerousers"

--"key activists"

--"black nationalists"

--"white supremacists"

--"agitators"

--"key black extremists"

These broad and imprecise labels reflect the ill-defined mission of domestic intelligence, which resulted from recurring demands for progressively wider investigations of Americans. Without the firm guidance provided by law, intelligence activities intruded into areas of American life which are protected from governmental inquiry by the constitutional guarantees of personal privacy and free speech and assembly.

Subfinding (a)

Large numbers of law-abiding Americans and lawful domestic groups have been subjected to extensive intelligence investigation and surveillance.

Some domestic intelligence activity has focused on specific illegal conduct or on instances where there was tangible evidence that illegal conduct was likely to occur. But domestic intelligence has gone far beyond such matters in collecting massive amounts of data on Americans. For example:

FBI Domestic Intelligence.—The FBI has compiled at its headquarters over 480,000 files on its "subversion" investigations and over 33,000 files on its "extremism" investigations. During the twenty years from 1955 to 1975, the FBI conducted 740,000 investigations of "subversive matters" and 190,000 investigations of "extremist matters."

The targets for FBI intelligence collection have included:

--the Women's Liberation Movement

--the conservative Christian Front and Christian Mobilizers of Father Coughlin;

--the conservative American Christian Action Council of Rev. Carl McIntyre;

--a wide variety of university, church and political groups opposed to the Vietnam war;

--those in the non-violent civil rights movement, such as Martin Luther King's Southern Christian Leadership Council, the National Association for the Advancement of Colored People (NAACP), and the Council on Racial Equality (CORE).

Army Surveillance of Civilians.—The Army's nationwide intelligence surveillance program created files on some 100,000 Americans and an equally large number of domestic organizations, encompassing virtually every group seeking peaceful change in the United States including:

--the John Birch Society;

--Young Americans for Freedom;

--the National Organization of Women;

--the NAACP;

--the Urban League;

--the Anti-Defamation League of B'nai B'rith; and Business Executives to End the War in Vietnam.

CIA's CHAOS Program—The CIA's extensive CHAOS program—which compiled intelligence on domestic groups and individuals protesting the Vietnam war and racial conditions—amassed some 10,000 intelligence files on American citizens and groups and indexed 300,000 names of Americans in CIA computer records.

IRS Selective Tax Investigations of Dissenters—Between 1969 and 1973, the Internal Revenue Service, through a secret "Special Service Staff" (SSS), targeted more than 10,000 individuals and groups for tax examinations because of their political activity. The FBI and the Internal Security Division of the Justice Department gave SSS lists of taxpayers deemed to be "activists" or "ideological organizations;" the FBI, in providing SSS with a list of over 2,000 groups and individuals classified as "Right Wing," "New Left," and "Old Left," expressed its hope that SSS tax examinations would "deal a blow to dissident elements." A smaller though more intensive selective enforcement program, the "Ideological Organization Project," was established in November 1961 in response to White House criticism of "right-wing extremist" groups. On the basis of such political criteria, 18 organizations were selected for special audit although there was no evidence of tax violation. In 1964, the IRS proosed to expand its program to make "10,000 examinations of tax exempt organizations of all types including the extremist groups." Although this program never fully materialized, the "Ideological Organizations Project" can be viewed as a precursor to SSS.

CIA and FBI Mail Opening.—The 12 mail opening programs conducted by the CIA and FBI between 1940 and 1973 resulted in the illegal opening of hundreds of thousands of first-class letters. In the 1960s and early 1970s, the international correspondence of large numbers of Americans who challenged the condition of racial minorities or who opposed the war in Vietnam was specifically targeted for mail opening by both the CIA and FBI.

The overbreadth of the longest CIA mail opening program—the 20 year (1953-1973) program in New York City—is shown by the fact that of the more than 28 million letters screened by the CIA, the exteriors of 2.7 million were photographed and 214,820 letters were opened. This is further shown by the fact that American groups and individuals placed on the Watch List for the project included:

--The Federation of American Scientists;

--authors such as John Steinbeck and Edward Albee;

--numerous American peace groups such as the American Friends Service Committee and Women's Strike for Peace; and

--businesses, such as Praeger Publishers.

By one CIA estimate, random selection accounted for 75 percent of the 200,000 letters opened, including letters to or from American political figures, such as Richard Nixon, while a presidential candidate in 1968, and Senators Frank Church and Edward Kennedy.

IV NSA's Watch List and SHAMROCK Programs.—The National Security Agency's SHAMROCK program, by which copies of millions of telegrams sent to, from, or through the United States were obtained between 1947 and 1973, involved the use of a Watch List 1967-1973. The watch list included groups and individuals selected by the FBI for its domestic intelligence investigations and by the CIA for its Operation CHAOS program. In addition, the SHAMROCK Program resulted in

NSA's obtaining not only telegrams to an from certain foreign targets, but countless telegrams between Americans in the United States and American or foreign parties abroad.

In short, virtually every element of our society has been subjected to excessive government-ordered intelligence inquiries. Opposition to government policy or the expression of controversial views was frequently onsidered sufficient for collecting data on Americans.

The committee finds that this extreme breadth of intelligence activity is inconsistent with the principles of our Constitution which protact the rights of speech, political activity, and privacy against un"Justified governmental intrusion.

Subfinding (b)

The absence of precise standards for intelligence investigations of Americans contributed to overbreadth. Congress did not enact statutes precisely delineating the authority of the intelligence agencies or defining the purpose and scope of domestic intelligence activity. The Executive branch abandoned the standard set by Attorney General Stone—that the government's concern was not with political opinions but with "such conduct as is forbidden by the laws of the United States." Intelligence agencies' superiors issued overinclusive directives to investigate "subversion" (a term that was never defined in presidential directives) and "potential" rather than actual or likely criminal conduct, as well as to collect general intelligence on lawful political -and social dissent.

Congress has never set out a specific statutory charter for FBI domestic intelligence activity delineating the standards for opening intelligence investigations or defining the purpose and scope of domestic intelligence activity.

Nor have the charters for foreign intelligence agencies—the Central Intelligence Agency and the National Security Agency—articulated adequate standards to insure that those agencies did not become involved in domestic intelligence activity. While the 1947 National Security Act provided that the CIA shall have no "police, subpoena, law enforcement powers or internal security functions," the Act was silent concerning whether the CIA was authorized to target Americans abroad or to gather intelligence in the United States on Americans or foreign nationals in connection with its foreign intelligence responsibilities. By classified presidential directive, the CIA was authorized to conduct counterintelligence operations abroad and to maintain central counterintelligence files for the intelligence community." Counterintelligence activity was defined in the directive to include protection of the nation against "subversion," a term which, as in the directives authorizing FBI domestic intelligence activity, was not defined.

In the absence of specific standards for CIA activity and given the susceptibility of the term "subversion" to broad interpretation, the CIA conducted Operation CHAOS—a large scale intelligence program involving the gathering of data on thousands of Americans and domestic groups to determine if they had "subversive connections"and illegally opened the mail of hundreds of thousands of Americans.

Moreover, the Act does not define the scope of the authority granted to CIA's Director to protect intelligence "sources and methods." This authority has been broadly interpreted to permit surveillance of present and former CIA employees in the United States as well as domestic groups thought to be a threat to CIA installations in the United States.

No statute at all deals with the National Security Agency. That Agency—one of the largest of the intelligence agencies—was created by Executive Order in 1952. Although NSA's mission is to obtain foreign intelligence from "foreign" communications, this has been interpreted to permit NSA to intercept communications where one terminal—the sender or receiver—was in the United States. Consequently when an American has used telephone or telegraph facilities between this country and overseas, his message has been subject to interception by NSA. NSA obtained copies of millions of private telegrams sent from, to or through the United States in its SHAMROCK program and complied with requests to target the international communications of specific Americans through the use of a watch list.

In addition to the failure of Congress to enact precise statutory standards, members of Congress have put pressure on the intelligence agencies for the collection of domestic intelligence without adequate regard to constitutional interests. Moreover, Congress has passed statutes, such as the Smith Act, which, although not directly authorizing domestic intelligence collection, had the effect of contributing to the excessive collection of intelligence about Americans.

Three functional policies, established by the Executive branch and acquiesced in by Congress, were the basis for the overbreadth of intelligence investigations directed at Americans. These policies centered on (1) so-called "subversion investigations" of attempts by hostile foreign governments and their agents in this country to influence the course of American life; (2) the investigation of persons and groups thought to have a "potential" for violating the law or committing violence; and (3) the collection of general intelligence on political and social movements in the interest of predicting and controlling civil disturbances.

Each of these policies grew out of a legitimate concern. Nazi Germany, Japan and the Soviet Union mounted intelligence efforts in this country before World War II; and Soviet operations continued after the war. In the 1960s and early 1970s, racist groups used force to deprive Americans of their civil rights, some American dissidents engaged in violence as a form of political protest, and there were large-scale protest demonstrations and major civil disorders in cities stemming from minority frustrations.

The Committee recognizes that the government had a responsibility to act in the face of the very real dangers presented by these developments. But appropriate restraints, controls, and prohibitions on intelligence collection were not devised; distinctions between legitimate targets of investigations and innocent citizens were forgotten; and the Government's actions were never examined for their effects on the constitutional rights of Americans, either when programs originated or as they continued over the years.

The policies of investigating Americans thought to have a "potential" for violence and the collection of general intelligence on political and social movements inevitably resulted in the surveillance of American citizens and domestic groups engaged in lawful political activity. "Subversive" was never defined in the presidential directives from Presidents Roosevelt to Kennedy authorizing FBI domestic intelligence activity. Consequently, "subversive" investigations did not focus solely on the activities of hostile foreign governments in this country. Rather, they targeted Americans who dissented from administration positions or whose political positions were thought to resemble those of "subversive" groups. An example of the ultimate result of accepting the concept of "subversive" investigations is the Johnson White House, instruction to the FBI to monitor public hearings on Vietnam policy and compare the extent to which Senators' views "followed the Communist Party line."

Similarly, investigations of those thought to have the "potential" for violating laws or committing violence and the collection of general intelligence to prepare for civil disturbances resulted in the surveillance of Americans where there was not reasonable suspicion to believe crime or violence were likely to occur. Broad categories of American society — conservatives, liberals, blacks, women, young people and churches — were targeted for intelligence collection.

Domestic intelligence expanded to cover widespread political protest movements in the late 1960s and early 1970s. For example, in September 1967, Attorney General Ramsey Clark called for a "new area of investigation and intelligence reporting" by the FBI regarding the possibility of "an organized pattern of violence" by groups in the "urban ghetto." He Instructed FBI Director Hoover:

> ... we must make certain that every attempt is being made to get all information bearing upon these problems; to take every step possible to determine whether the rioting is preplanned or organized.... As apart of the broad investigation which must be conducted ... sources or informants in black nationalist organizations, SNCC and other less publicized groups should be developed and expanded to determine the size and purpose of these groups and their relationship to other groups.

Such instructions did not limit investigation to facts pointing to particular criminal or violent activity but called for intensive intelligence surveillance of a broad category of black groups (and their connections with other groups) to determine their "size and purpose."

Similarly, the Army's broad domestic surveillance program reflected administration pressure on the Army for information on groups and individuals involved in domestic dissent. As a former Assistant Secretary of Defense testified, the Army's sweeping collection plan "reflected the all-encompassing and uninhibited demand for information directed at the Department of the Army."

Presidents Johnson and Nixon subjected the CIA to intensive pressure to find foreign influence on the domestic peace movements, resulting in the establishment of Operation CHAOS. When the Nixon Administration called for an intensification of CIA's effort, the CIA was instructed to broaden its targeting criteria and strengthen its collection efforts. CIA was told that "foreign Communist support" should be "liberally construed." The White House stated further that "it appears our present intelligence collection capabilities in this area may be inadequate" and implied that any gaps in CIA"s collection program resulting from "inadequate resources or a low priority of attention" should be corrected.

In short, having abandoned Attorney General Stone's standard that restricted Government investigations to "conduct and then only such conduct as is forbidden by the laws of the United States," the Government's far-reaching domestic intelligence policies inevitably, produced investigations and surveillance of large numbers of lawabiding Americans.

Subfinding (c.)

The intelligence agencies themselves used imprecise and over-inclusive criteria in their conduct of intelligence investigations. Intelligence investigations extended beyond "subversive" or violent targets to additional groups and individuals subject to minimal "subversive influence" or having little or no "potential" for violence.

Having been given vague directions by their superiors and subjected to substantial pressure to report on a broad range of matters, the intelligence agencies themselves often established overinclusive targeting criteria. The criteria followed in the major domestic intelligence programs conducted in the 1960s and 1970s illustrate the breadth of intelligence targeting:

"General Racial Matters" — The FBI gathered intelligence about proposed "civil demonstrations" and related activities of "officials, committees, legislatures, organizations, etc." in the "racial field."

FBI Field Offices were directed to report the "general programs" of all "civil rights organizations" and "readily available personal background data" on leaders and individuals "in the civil rights movement," as well as any "subversive association" that might be recorded in Field Office files. In addition, the FBI reported "the objectives sought by the minority Community."

These broad criteria were also reflected in the FBI's targeting of "white militant groups" in the reporting of racial matters. Those who were "known to sponsor demonstrations against integration and against the busing of Negro students to white schools" were to be investigated.

"New Left" Intelligence. — In conducting a "comprehensive study of the whole New Left movement" (rather than investigating particular violations of law), the FBI defined its intelligence target as a "loosely-bound, free-wheeling, college-oriented movement." Organizations to be investigated were those who fit criteria phrased as the "more extreme and militant anti-Vietnam war and antidraft organizations."

The use of such imprecise criteria resulted in investigations of such matters as (1) two university instructors who helped support a student newspaper whose editorial policy was described by the FBI as "left-of-center, antiestablishment, and opposed to the University Administration"; (2) a dissident stockholder's group planning to protest a large corporation's war production at the annual stockholder's meeting; and (3) "Free Universities" attached to college campuses, whether or not there were facts indicating any actual or potential violation of law.

"Rabble Rouser" Index. — Beginning in August 1967, the FBI conducted intensive intelligence investigations of individuals identified as "rabble rousers."" The program was begun after a member of the National Advisory Commission on Civil Disorders asked the FBI at a meeting of the Commission "to identify the number of militant Negroes and Whites." This vague reference was subsequently used by the FBI as the basis for instructions implementing a broad new program: persons were to be investigated and placed on the "rabble rouser" index who were "racial agitators who have demonstrated a potential for fomenting racial discord."

Ultimately, a "rabble rouser" was defined as:

A person who tries to arouse people to violent action by appealing to their emotions, prejudices, et cetera; a demagogue.

Thus, rather than collecting information on those who had or were likely to commit criminal or violent acts, a major intelligence program was launched to identify "demagogues."

Army Domestic Surveillance of "Dissidents." — Extremely broad criteria were used in the Army's nationwide surveillance program conducted in the late 1960s. Such general terms as "the civil rights movement" and the "anti- Vietnam/anti-draft movements" were used to indicate targets for investigation." In collecting information on these "Movements" and on the "cause of civil disturbances," Army intelligence was to investigate "instigators," "group participants" and "subversive elements" — all undefined.

Under later revisions, the Army collection plan extended even beyond "subversion" and "dissident groups" to "prominent persons" who were "friendly" with the "leaders of the disturbance" or "sympathetic with their plans."

These imprecise criteria led to the creation of intelligence files on nearly 100,000 Americans, including Dr. Martin Luther King, Major General Edwin Walker, Julian Bond, Joan Baez, Dr. Benjamin Spock, Rev. William Sloane Coffin, Congressman Abner Mikva, Senator Adlai Stevenson III, as well as clergymen, teachers, journalists, editors, attorneys, industrialists, a laborer, a construction worker, railroad engineers, a postal clerk, a taxi driver, a chiropractor, a doctor, a chemist, an economist, a historian, a playwright, an accountant, an entertainer, professors, a radio announcer, athletes, business executives and authors — all of whom became subjects of Army files simply because of their participation in political protests or their association with those who were engaged in such political activity.

The IRS Computerized Intelligence Index — In 1973, IRS established a central computer index — the "Intelligence Gathering and Retrieval System" — for general intelligence data, much of it unrelated to tax law enforcement. More than 465,000 Americans were indexed in the IRS computer system, including J. Edgar Hoover and the IRS Commissioner, as well as thousands of others also not suspected of tax violation. Names in newspaper articles and other published sources were indexed wholesale into the IRS computer. Under the system, intelligence gathering preceded any specific allegation of a violation, and possible "future value" was the sole criterion for inclusion of information into the Intelligence Gathering and Retrieval System.

CIA's Operation CHAOS — In seeking to fulfill White House requests for evidence of foreign influence on domestic dissent, the CIA gave broad instructions to its overseas stations. These directives called for reporting on the "Radical Left" which included, according to the CIA, "radical students, antiwar activists, draft resisters and deserters, black nationalists, anarchists, and assorted 'New Leftists'." CIA built its huge CHAOS data base on the assumption that to know whether there was significant foreign involvement in a domestic group "one has to know whether each and every one of these persons has any connection to foreigners." CIA instructed its stations that even "casual contacts based merely on mutual interest" between Americans opposed to the Vietnam war and "foreign elements" were deemed to "casual contacts based merely on mutual interest" between Americans opposed to the Vietnam war and "foreign elements" were deemed to constitute "subversive connections." Similarly, CIA's request to NSA for materials on persons targeted by the NSA Watch List called for all information regardless of how innocuous it may seem."

The Committee's investigation has shown that the absence of precise statutory standards and the use of overbroad criteria for domestic intelligence activity resulted in the extension of intelligence investigations beyond their original "subversive" or violent targets. Intelligence investigations extended to those thought to be subject to "subversive influence." Moreover, those thought to have a "potential" for violence were also targeted and, in some cases, investigations extended even to those engaged in wholly non-violent lawful political expression.

FBI "COMINFIL" Investigations — Under the FBI's COMINFIL ("communist infiltration") program, large numbers of groups and individuals engaged in lawful political activity have been subjected to informant coverage and intelligence scrutiny. Although COMINFIL investigations were supposed to focus on the Communist Party's alleged efforts to penetrate domestic groups, in practice the target often became the domestic groups themselves.

FBI COMINFIL investigations reached into domestic groups in virtually every area of American political life. The FBI conducted COMINFIL investigations in such areas as "religion," "education," "veterans' matters," "women's matters," "Negro question," and "cultural activities." The "entire spectrum of the social and labor movement" was covered. The overbreadth that results from the practice of investigating groups for indications of communist influence, or infiltration is illustrated by the following FBI COMINFIL intelligence investigations:

NAACP — An intensive 25 year long surveillance of the NAACP was conducted, ostensibly to determine whether there was Communist infiltration of the NAACP. This surveillance, however, produced detailed intelligence reports on NAACP activities wholly unrelated to any alleged communist "attempts" to infiltrate the NAACP, and despite the fact that no evidence was ever found to contradict the FBI's initial finding that the NAACP was opposed to communism.

Northern Virginia Citizens Concerned About the ABM — In 1969, the FBI conducted an intelligence investigation and used informants to report on a meeting held in a public high school auditorium at which the merits of the Anti-Ballistic Missile System were debated by, among others, Department of Defense officials. The investigation was apparently opened because a communist newspaper had commented on the fact that the meeting was to be held.

National Conference on Amnesty for Vietnam Veterans — In 1974, FBI informants reported on a national conference sponsored by church and civil liberties groups to support amnesty for Vietnam veterans. The investigation was based on a two-step "infiltration" theory. Other informants had reported that the Vietnam Veterans Against the War (which was itself the subject of an intelligence investigation because it was thought to be subject to communist or foreign influence) might try to "control" the conference. Although the conference was thus twice removed from the original target, it was nevertheless subjected to informant surveillance.

FBI intelligence investigations to find whether groups are subject to communist or "subversive" influence result in the collection of information on groups and individuals engaged in wholly legitimate activity. Reports on the NAACP were not limited to alleged communist infiltration. Similarly, the investigation of the National Amnesty Conference produced reports describing the topics discussed at the conference and the organization of a steering committee which would include families of men killed in Vietnam and congressional staff aides. The reports on the meeting concerning the ABM system covered the past and present residence of the person who applied to rent the high school auditorium, and plans for a future meeting, including the names of prominent political figures who planned to attend.

The trigger for COMINFIL-type investigations — that subversive attempts" to infiltrate groups were a substantial threat — was greatly exaggerated. According to the testimony of FBI officials, the mention in a communist newspaper of the citizens' meeting to debate the ABM was sufficient to produce intelligence coverage of that meeting. A large public teach-in on Vietnam, including representatives of Catholic, Episcopal, Methodist and Unitarian churches, as well as a number of spokesmen for antiwar groups, was investigated because a Communist Party official had "urged" party members to attend and one speaker representing the W. E. B. DuBois Club was identified as a communist. The FBI surveillance of the teach-in resulted in a 41-page intelligence report based on coverage by 13 informants and sources. And the FBI's investigation of all Free Universities near colleges and universities was undertaken because "several" allegedly had been formed by the Communist Party "and other subversive groups."

Similarly, the FBI's broad COMINFIL investigations of the civil rights movement in the South were based on the FBI's conclusion that the Communist Party had "attempted" to take advantage of racial unrest and had "endeavored" to pressure U.S. Government officials "through the press, labor unions and student groups". No mention was made of the general failure of these attempts.

The Committee finds that COMINFIL investigations have been based on an exaggerated notion of the threat posed by "subversives" and foreign influence on American political expression. There has been unjustified belief that Americans need informants and government surveillance to protect them from "subversive" influence in their unions, churches, schools, parties and political efforts.

Investigations of Wholly Non-Violent Political Expression — Domestic intelligence investigations have extended from those who commit or are likely to commit violent acts to those thought to have a "potential" for violence, and then to those engaged in purely peaceful political expression. This characteristic was graphically described by the White House official who coordinated the intelligence agencies' recommendations for "expanded" (and illegal) coverage in 1970. He testified that intelligence investigations risked moving

> from the kid with a bomb to the kid with a picket sign, and from the kid with the picket sign to the kid with the bumper sticker of the opposing candidate. And you just keep going down the line.

Without precise standards to restrict their scope, intelligence investigations did move beyond those who committed or were likely to commit criminal or violent acts. For example:

--Dr. Martin Luther King, Jr., was targeted for the FBI's COINTELPRO operations against "Black Nationalist Hate Groups" on the theory, without factual justification, that Dr. King might "abandon" his adherence to nonviolence.

--The intensive FBI investigation of the Women's Liberation Movement was similarly predicated on the theory that the activities of women in that Movement might lead to demonstrations and violence.

--The FBI investigations of Black Student Unions proceeded from the concern of the FBI and its superiors over violence in the cities. Yet, the FBI opened intelligence investigations on "every Black Student Union and similar group regardless of their past or present involvement in disorders."

--The nationwide Army Intelligence surveillance of civilians was conducted in connection with civil disorders. However, the Army collection plan focused not merely on those likely to commit violence but was "so comprehensive . . . that any category of information related even remotely to people or organizations active in a community in which the potential for violence was present would fall within their scope."

The Committee finds that such intelligence surveillance of groups and individuals has greatly exceeded the legitimate interest of the government in law enforcement and the prevention of violence. Where unsupported determinations as to "potential" behavior are the basis for surveillance of groups and individuals, no one is safe from the inquisitive eye of the intelligence agency.

Subfindings (d)

Intelligence agencies pursued a "vacuum cleaner" approach to intelligence collection—drawing in all available information about groups and individuals, including their lawful political activity and details of their personal lives.

Intelligence agencies collect an excessive amount of information by pursuing a "vacuum cleaner" approach that draws in all available information, including lawful political activity, personal matters, and trivia. Even where the theory of the investigation is that the subject is likely to be engaged in criminal or violent activity, the overbroad approach to intelligence collection intrudes into personal matters unrelated to such criminal or violent activity.

FBI officials conceded to the Committee that in conducting broad intelligence investigations to determine the "real purpose" of an organization, they sometimes gathered "too much information."

The FBI's intelligence investigation of the "New Left," for example, was directed towards a "comprehensive study of the whole movement" and produced intensive monitoring of such subjects as "support of movement by religious groups or individuals," "demonstrations aimed at social reform," "indications of support by mass media," "all activity in the labor field," and "efforts to influence public opinion, the electorate and Government bodies."

Similar overbreadth characterized the FBI's collection of intelligence on "white militant groups." In 1968 FBI field offices were instructed not to gather information solely on actual or potential violations of law or violence, but to use informants to determine the "aims and purposes of the organization, its leaders, approximate membership" and other "background data" relating to the group's "militancy." In 1971 the criteria for investigating individuals were widened. Special Agents in Charge of FBI field offices were instructed to investigate not only persons with "a potential for violence," but also anyone else "who in judgment of SAC should be subject of investigation due to extremist activities."

Even in searching for indications of potential violence in black urban areas or in collecting information about violence prone Ku Klux Klan chapters, there was marked overbreadth. In black urban areas, for example, FBI agents were instructed to have their informants obtain the names of "Afro-American type bookstores" and their "owners, operators and clientele." The activities of civil rights and black groups as well as details of the personal lives of Klan members, were reported on by an FBI intelligence informant in the Ku Klux Klan. Under this approach, the average citizen who merely attends a meeting, signs a petition, is placed on a mailing list, or visits a book store, is subject to being recorded in intelligence files.

A striking example of informant reporting on all they touch was provided by an FBI informant in an antiwar group with only 55 regular members and some 250 persons who gave occasional support. The informant estimated she reported nearly 1,000 names to the FBI in an 18-month period -- 60-70 percent of whom were members of other groups (such as the United Church of Christ and the American Civil Liberties Union) which were engaging in peaceful, lawful political activity together with the antiwar group or who were on the group's mailing list. Similarly in the intelligence investigation of the Women's Liberation Movement, informants reported the identities of individual women attending meetings (as well as reporting such matters as the fact that women at meetings had stated "how they felt oppressed, sexually or otherwise.").

Such collection of "intelligence" unrelated to specific criminal or violent activity constitutes a serious misuse of governmental power. In reaching into the private lives of individuals and monitoring their lawful political activity — matters irrelevant to any proper governmental interest — domestic intelligence collection has been unreasonably broad.

Subfinding (e)

Intelligence investigations in many cases continued for excessively long periods of time, resulting in sustained governmental monitoring of political activity in the absence of any indication of criminal conduct or "subversion."

One of the most disturbing aspects of domestic intelligence investigations found by the Committee was their excessive length. Intelligence investigations often continued, despite the absence of facts indicating an individual or group is violating or is likely to violate the law, resulting in long-term government monitoring of lawful political activity. The following are examples:

(i) The FBI Intelligence Investigation of the NAACP (1941-1966) — The investigation of the NAACP began in 1941 and continued for at least 25 years. Initiated according to one FBI report as an investigation of protests by 15 black mess attendants about racial discrimination in the Navy, the investigation expanded to encompass NAACP chapters in cities across the nation. Although the ostensible purpose of this investigation was to determine if there was "Communist infiltration" of the NAACP, the investigation constituted a long-term monitoring of the NAACP's wholly lawful political activity by FBI informants. Thus:

--The FBI New York Field Office submitted a 137-page report to FBI headquarters describing the national office of the NAACP, its national convention, its growth and membership, its officers and directors, and its stand against Communism.

--An FBI informant in Seattle obtained a list of NAACP branch officers and reported on a meeting where signatures were gathered on a "petition directed to President Eisenhower" and plans for two members to go to Washington, D.C., for a "Prayer Pilgrimage."

--In 1966, the New York Field Office reported the names of all NAACP national officers and board members, and summarized their political associations as far back as the 1940s.

--As late as 1966, the FBI was obtaining NAACP chapter membership figures by "pretext telephone call ... utilizing the pretext of being interested in joining that branch of the NAACP."

--Based on the reports of FBI informants, the FBI submitted a detailed report of a 1956 NAACP-sponsored Leadership Conference on Civil Rights and described plans for a Conference delegation to visit Senators Paul Douglas, Herbert Lehman, Wayne Morse, Hubert Humphrey, and John Bricker. Later reports covered what transpired at several of these meetings with Senators. Most significantly, all these reports were sent to the White House.

(ii) The FBI Intelligence Investigation of the Socialist Workers Party (1940 to date).—The FBI has investigated the Socialist Workers Party (SWP) from 1940 to the present day on the basis of that Party's revolutionary rhetoric and alleged international links. Nevertheless, FBI officials testified that the SWP has not been responsible for any violent acts nor has it urged actions constituting an indictable incitement to violence.

FBI informants have been reporting the political positions taken by the SWP with respect to such issues as the "Vietnam War," "racial matters," "U.S. involvement in Angola," "food prices," and any SWP efforts to support a non-SWP candidate for political office.

Moreover, to enable the FBI to develop "background information" on SWP leaders, informants have been reporting certain personal aspects of their lives, such as marital status. The informants also have been reporting on SWP cooperation with other groups who are not the subject of separate intelligence investigations.

(iii) The Effort to Prove Negatives.—Intelligence investigations and programs have also continued for excessively long periods in efforts to prove negatives. CIA's Operation CHAOS began in 1967. From that year until the program's termination in 1974, the CIA repeatedly reached formal conclusions that there was negligible foreign influence on domestic protest activity. In 1967, the CIA concluded that Communist front groups did not control student organizations and that there were no significant links with foreign radicals; in 1968, the CIA concluded that U.S. student protest was essentially homegrown and not stimulated by an international conspiracy; and in 1971 the CIA found "there is no evidence that foreign governments, organizations, or intelligence services now control U.S. New Left Movements ... the U.S. New Left is basically self-sufficient and moves under its own impetus."

The result of these repeated findings was not the termination of CHAOS's surveillance of Americans, but its redoubling. Presidents Johnson and Nixon pressured the CIA to intensify its intelligence effort, to find evidence of foreign direction of the U.S. peace movement. As Director Helms testified:

> When a President keeps asking if there is any information, "how are you getting along with your examination," "have you picked up any more information on this subject," it isn't a direct order to do something, but it seems to me it behooves the Director of Central Intelligence to find some way to improve his performance, or improve his Agency's performance.

In an effort to prove its negative finding to a skeptical White House—and to test its validity each succeeding year—CIA expanded its program, increasing its coverage of Americans overseas and building an ever larger "data base" on domestic political activity. Intelligence was exchanged with the FBI, NSA, and other agencies and eventually CIA agents who had infiltrated domestic organizations for other purposes supplied general information on the groups' activities. 86 Thus, the intelligence mission became one of continued surveillance to prove a negative, with no thought to terminating the program in the face of the negative findings.

As in the CHAOS operation, FBI intelligence investigations have often continued even in the absence of any evidence of "subversive" activities merely because the subjects of the investigation have not demonstrated their innocence to the FBI's satisfaction. The long term investigations of the NAACP and the Socialist Workers Party described above are typical examples.

A striking illustration of FBI practice is provided by the intelligence investigation of an advisor of Dr. Martin Luther King, Jr. The advisor was investigated on the theory that he might be a communist "sympathizer." The Bureau's New York office concluded he was not. 87 Using a theory of "guilty until proven innocent," FBI headquarters directed that the investigation continue:

> The Bureau does not agree with the expressed belief of the New York office that [-----------] is not sympathetic to the Party cause. While there may not be any evidence that [-----------------] is a Communist neither is there any substantial evidence that he is anti-Communist.

Where citizens must demonstrate not simply that they have no connection with an intelligence target, but must exhibit "substantial evidence" that they are in opposition to the target, intelligence investigations are indeed open ended.

C. Excessive Use Of Intrusive Techniques

Major Finding

The intelligence community has employed surreptitious collection techniques — mail opening, surreptitious entries, informants, and "traditional" and highly sophisticated forms of electronic surveillance — to achieve its overly broad intelligence targeting and collection objectives. Although there are circumstances where these techniques, if properly controlled, are legal and appropriate, the Committee finds that their very nature makes them a threat to the personal privacy and Constitutionally protected activities of both the targets and of persons who communicate with or associate with the targets. The dangers inherent in the use of these techniques have been compounded by the lack of adequate standards limiting their use and by the absence of review by neutral authorities outside the intelligence agencies. As a consequence, these techniques have collected enormous amounts of personal and political information serving no legitimate governmental interest.

Subfindings

(a) Given the highly intrusive nature of these techniques, the legal standards and procedures regulating their use have been insufficient. There have been no statutory controls on the use of informants; there have been gaps and exceptions in the law of electronic surveillance; and the legal prohibitions against warrantless mail opening and surreptitious entries have been ignored.

(b) In addition to providing the means by which the Government can collect too much information about too many people, certain techniques have their own peculiar dangers:

(i) Informants have provoked and participated in violence and other illegal activities in order to maintain their cover, and they have obtained membership lists and other private documents.

(ii) Scientific and technological advances have rendered traditional controls on electronic surveillance obsolete and have made it more difficult to limit intrusions. Because of the nature of wiretaps, microphones and other sophisticated electronic techniques, it has not always been possible to restrict the monitoring of communications to the persons being investigated.

(c.) The imprecision and manipulation of labels such as "national security," "domestic security," "subversive activities," and "foreign intelligence" have led to unjustified use of these techniques.

Elaboration of Findings

The preceding section described how the absence of rigorous standards for opening, controlling, and terminating investigations subjected many diverse elements of this society to scrutiny by intelligence agencies, without their being suspected of violating any law. Once an investigation was opened, almost any item of information about a target's personal behavior or political views was considered worth collecting.

Extremely intrusive techniques—such as those listed above—have often been used to accomplish those overly broad targeting and collection objectives.

The paid and directed informant has been the most extensively used technique in FBI domestic intelligence investigations. Informants were used in 83% of the domestic intelligence investigations analyzed in a recent study by the General Accounting Office. As of June 30, 1975, the FBI was using a total of 1,500 domestic intelligence informants. In 1972 there were over 7,000 informants in the ghetto informant program alone. In fiscal year 1976, the Bureau has budgeted more than $7.4 million for its domestic intelligence informant program, more than twice the amount allocated for its organized crime informant program.

Wiretaps and microphones have also been a significant means of gathering intelligence. Until 1972, the FBI directed these electronic techniques against scores of American citizens and domestic organizations during investigations of such matters as domestic "subversive" activities and leaks of classified information. The Bureau continues to use these techniques against foreign targets in the United States.

The most extensive use of electronic surveillance has been by the National Security Agency. NSA has electronically monitored (without wiretapping in the traditional sense) international communication links since its inception in 1952; because of its sophisticated technology, it is capable of intercepting and recording an enormous number of communications between the United States and foreign countries.

All mail opening programs have now been terminated, but a total of twelve such operations were conducted by the CIA and the FBI in ten American cities between 1940 and 1973. Four of these were operated by the CIA, whose most massive project involved the opening of more than 215,000 letters between the United States and the Soviet Union over a twenty-year period. The FBI conducted eight mail opening programs, three of which included opening mail sent between two points in the United States. The longest FBI mail opening program lasted, with one period of suspension, for approximately twenty-six years.

The FBI has also conducted hundreds of warrantless surreptitious entries—break-ins—during the past twenty-five years. Often these entries were conducted to install electronic listening devices, at other times they involved physical searches for information. The widespread use of warrantless surreptitious entries against both foreign and domestic targets was terminated by the Bureau in 1966 but the FBI has occasionally made such entries against foreign targets in more recent years.

All of these techniques have been turned against American citizens its well as against certain foreign targets. On the theory that the executive's responsibility in the area of "national security" and "foreign intelligence" justified their use without the need of judicial supervision, the intelligence community believed it was free to direct these techniques against individuals and organizations whom it believed threatened the country's security. The standards governing the use of these techniques have been imprecise and susceptible to expansive interpretation and in the absence of any judicial check on the application of these vague standards to particular cases. it was relatively easy for intelligence agencies and their superiors to extend them to many cases where they were clearly inappropriate. Lax internal controls on the use of some of these techniques compounded the problem.

These intrusive techniques by their very nature invaded the private communications and activities both of the individuals they were directed against and of the persons, with whom the targets communicated or associated. Consequently. they provided the means by which all types of information—including personal and political information totally unrelated to any legitimate governmental objective— were collected and in some cases disseminated to the highest levels of the government.

Subfinding (a)

Given the highly intrusive nature of these techniques, the legal standards and procedures regulating their use have been insufficient. There have been no statutory controls on the use of informants; there have been gaps and exceptions in the law of electronic surveillance; and the legal prohibitions against warrantless mail opening and surreptitious entries have been ignored.

1. The Absense of Statutory Restraints on the Use of Information

There are no statutes or published regulations governing the use of informants.,, Consequently, the FBI is free to use informants, guided only by its own internal directives which can be changed at any time by FBI officials without approval from outside the Bureau.

Apart from court decisions precluding the use of informants to entrap persons into criminal activity, there are few judicial opinions dealing with informants and most of those concern criminal rather than intelligence informants. The United States Supreme Court has never ruled on whether the use of intelligence informants in the contexts revealed by the Committee's investigation offend First Amendment rights of freedom of expression and association.

In the absence of regulation through statute, published regulation, or court, decision, the FBI has used informants to report on virtually every aspect of a targeted group or individual's activity, including lawful political expression, political meetings, the identities of group members and their associates, the "thoughts and feelings, intentions and ambitions," of members, and personal matters irrelevant to any legitimate governmental interest. Informants have also been used by the FBI to obtain the confidential records and documents of a group.

Informants could be used in any intelligence investigation. FBI directives have not limited informant reporting to actual or likely violence or other violations of law. Nor has any determination been made concerning whether the substantial intrusion represented by informant coverage is justified by the government's interest in obtaining information, or whether less intrusive means would adequately serve the government's interest. There has also been no requirement that the decisions of FBI officials to use informants be reviewed by anyone outside the FBI. In short, intelligence informant coverage has not been subject to the standards which govern the use of other intrusive techniques such as electronic surveillance, even though informants can produce a far broader range of information.

2. Gaps and Exceptions in the Law of Electronic Surveillance

Congress and the Supreme Court have both addressed the legal issues raised by electronic surveillance, but the law has been riddled with gaps and exceptions. The Executive branch has been able to apply vague standards for the use of this technique to particular cases as it has seen fit, and, in the case of NSA monitoring, the standards and procedures for the use of electronic surveillance were not applied at all.

When the Supreme Court first considered wiretapping, it held that the warrantless use of this technique was constitutional because the Fourth Amendment's warrant requirement applied only to physical trespass and did not extend to the seizure of conversation. This decision, the 1928 case of Olmstead v. United States, involved a criminal prosecution, and left federal agencies free to engage in the unrestricted use of wiretaps in both criminal and intelligence investigations.

Six years later, Congress enacted the Federal Communications Act of 1934, which made it a crime for "any person," without authorization, to intercept and divulge or publish the contents of wire and radio communications. The Supreme Court subsequently construed this section to apply to federal agents as well as to ordinary citizens, and held that evidence obtained directly or indirectly from the interception of wire and radio communications was not admissible in court. But Congress acquiesced in the Justice Department's position that these cases prohibited only the divulgence of contents of wire communications outside the executive branch, and Government wiretapping for intelligence purposes other than prosecution continued.

On the ground that neither the 1934 Act nor the Supreme Court decisions on wiretapping were meant to apply to "grave matters involving the defense of the nation," President Franklin Roosevelt authorized Attorney General Jackson in 1940 to approve wiretaps on "persons suspected of subversive activities against the Government of the United States, including suspected spies." In the absence of any guidance from Congress or the Court for another quarter century, the executive branch first broadened this standard in 1946 to permit wiretapping in "cases vitally affecting the domestic security or where human life is in jeopardy," and then modified it in 1965 to allow wiretapping in "investigations related to the national security." Internal Justice Department policy required the prior approval of the Attorney General before the FBI could institute wiretaps in particular cases, but until the mid-1960's there was no requirement of periodic reapproval by the Attorney General. In the absence of any instruction to terminate, them, some wiretaps remained in effect for years.

In 1967, the Supreme Court reversed its holding in the Olmstead case and decided that the Fourth Amendment's warrant requirement did apply to electronic surveillances. It expressly declined, however, to extend this holding to cases involving the "national security." Congress followed suit the next year in the Omnibus Crime Control Act of 1968, which established a warrant procedure for electronic surveillance in criminal cases but included a provision that neither it nor the Federal Communications Act of 1934 "shall limit the constitutional power of the President." Although Congress did not purport to define the President's power, the Act referred to five broad categories which thereafter served as the Justice Department's criteria for warrantless electronic surveillance. The first three categories related to foreign intelligence and counterintelligence matters:

(1) to protect the Nation against actual or potential attack or other hostile acts of a foreign power;

(2) to obtain foreign intelligence information deemed essential to the security of the United States; and

(3) to protect the national security information against foreign intelligence activities.

The last two categories dealt with domestic intelligence interests:

(4) to protect the United States against overthrow of the government by force or other unlawful means, or

(5) against any other clear and present danger to the structure or existence of the government.

In 1972, the Supreme Court held in United States v. United States District Court, that the President did not have the constitutional power to authorize warrantless electronic surveillances to protect the nation from domestic threats. The Court pointedly refrained, however, from any "judgment on the scope of the Presidents' surveillance power with respect to the activities of foreign powers, within or without this country." Only "the domestic aspects of national security" came within the ambit of the Court's decision.

To conform with the holding in this case, the Justice Department thereafter limited warrantless wiretapping to cases involving a "significant connection with a foreign power, its agents or agencies."

At no time, however, were the Justice Department's standards and procedures ever applied to NSA's electronic monitoring system and its "watch listing" of American citizens. From the early 1960's until 1973, NSA compiled a list of individuals and organizations, including 1200 American citizens and domestic groups, whose communications were segregated from the mass of communications intercepted by the Agency, transcribed, and frequently disseminated to other agencies for intelligence purposes.

The Americans on this list, many of whom were active in the antiwar and civil rights movements, were placed there by the FBI, CIA, Secret Service, Defense Department, and NSA itself without prior judicial warrant or even the prior approval of the Attorney General. In 1970, NSA began to monitor telephone communications links between the United States and South America at the request of the Bureau of Narcotics and Dangerous Drugs (BNDD) to obtain information about international drug trafficking. BNDD subsequently submitted the names of 450 American citizens for inclusion on the Watch List, again without warrant or the approval of the Attorney General.

The legal standards and procedures regulating the use of microphone surveillance have traditionally been even more lax than those regulating the use of wiretapping. The first major Supreme Court decision on microphone surveillance was Goldman v. United States, 316 U.S. 129 (1942), which held that such surveillance in a criminal case was constitutional when the installation did not involve a trespass. Citing this case, Attorney General McGrath prohibited the trespassory use of this technique by the FBI in 1952. But two years later—a few weeks after the Supreme Court denounced the use of a microphone installation in a criminal defendant's bedroom—Attorney General Brownell gave the FBI sweeping authority to engage in bugging for intelligence purposes. ". . . Considerations of internal security and the national safety are paramount," he wrote, "and, therefore, may compel the unrestricted use of this technique in the national interest."

Since Brownell did not require the prior approval of the Attorney General for bugging specific targets, he largely undercut the policy that had developed for wiretapping. The FBI in many cases could obtain equivalent coverage by utilizing bugs rather than taps and would not be burdened with the necessity of a formal request to the Attorney General.

The vague "national interest" standards established by Brownell, and the policy of not requiring the Attorney General's prior approval for microphone installations, continued until 1965, when the Justice Department began to apply the same criteria and procedures to both microphone and telephone surveillance.

3. Ignoring the Prohibitions Against Warrantless Mail Opening and Surreptitious Entries

Warrantless mail opening and surreptitious entries, unlike the use of informants and electronic surveillance, have been clearly prohibited by both statutory and constitutional law. In violation of these prohibitions, the FBI and the CIA decided on their own when and how these techniques should be used.

Sections 1701 through 1973 of Title 18 of the United States Code forbid persons other than employees of the Postal Service "dead letter" office from tampering with or opening mail that is not addressed to them. Violations of these statutes may result in fines of up to $2000 and imprisonment for not more than five years. The Supreme Court has also held that both First Amendment and Fourth Amendment restrictions apply to mail opening.

The Fourth Amendment concerns were articulated as early as 1878, when the Court wrote:

The constitutional guaranty of the right of the people to be secure in their papers against unreasonable searches and seizures extends to their papers, thus closed against inspection, wherever they may be. Whilst in the mail, they can only be opened and examined under like warrant . . . as is required when papers are subjected to search 'it one's own household.

This principle was reaffirmed as recently as 1970 in United States v. Van Leeuwen, 396 U.S. 249 (1970). The infringement of citizens' First Amendment rights resulting from warrantless mail opening was first recognized by Justice Holmes in 1921. "The use of the mails," he wrote in a dissent now embraced by prevailing legal opinion, "is almost as much a part of free speech as the right to use our tongues." This principle, too, has been affirmed in recent years.

Breaking and entering is a common law felony as well as a violation of state and federal statutes. When committed by Government agents, it has long been recognized as "the chief evil against which the wording of the Fourth Amendment is directed."

In the one judicial decision concerning the legality of warrantless "national security" break-ins for physical search purposes, United States District Court Judge Gerhard Gesell held such entries unconstitutional. This case, United States v. Ehrlichman, involved an entry into the office of a Los Angeles psychiatrist, Dr. Lewis Fielding, to obtain the medical records of his client Daniel Ellsberg, who was then under federal indictment for revealing classified documents. The entry was approved by two Presidential assistants, John Ehrlichman and Charles Colson, who argued that it had been justified "in the national interest." Ruling on the defendants' discovery motions, Judge Gesell found that because no search warrant was obtained:

The search of Dr. Fielding's office was clearly illegal under the unambiguous mandate of the Fourth Amendment. . . [T]he Government must comply with the strict constitutional and statutory limitations on trespassory searches and arrests even when known foreign agents are involved.... To hold otherwise, except under the most exigent circumstances, would be to abandon the Fourth Amendment to the whim of the Executive in total disregard of the Amendment's history and purpose.

In the appeal of this decision, the Justice Department has taken the position that a physical search may be authorized by the Attorney General without a warrant for "foreign intelligence" proposes. The warrantless mail opening programs and surreptitious entries by the FBI and CIA did not even conform to the "foreign intelligence" standard, however, nor were they specifically approved in each case by the Attorney General. Domestic "subversives" and "extremists" were targeted for mail opening; and domestic "subversives" and "White Hate groups" were among those targeted for surreptitious entries. Until the Justice Department's recent statement in the Ehrlichman case, moreover, no legal justification had ever been advanced publicly for violating the statutory or constitutional prohibitions against physical searches or opening mail without a judicial warrant, and none has ever been officially advanced by any Administration to justify warrantless mail openings.

Subfinding (b)

In addition to providing the means by which the Government can collect too much information about too many people, certain techniques have their own peculiar dangers:

(i) Informants have provoked and participated in violence and other illegal activities in order to maintain their cover, and they have obtained membership lists and other private documents.

(ii) Scientific and technological advances have rendered obsolete traditional controls on electronic surveillance and have made it more difficult to limit intrusions. Because of the nature of wiretaps, microphones, and other sophisticated electronic techniques, it has not always been possible to restrict the monitoring of communications to the persons being investigated.

a. The Intrusive Nature of the Intelligence Informant Technique

The FBI employs two types of informants: (1) "intelligence informants" who are used to report on groups and individuals in the course of intelligence investigations, and (2) "criminal informants," who are used in connection with investigations of specific criminal activity. FBI intelligence informants are administered by the FBI Intelligence Division at Bureau headquarters through a centralized system that is separate from the administrative system for FBI criminal informants. For example, the FBI's large-scale Ghetto Informant Program was administered by the FBI Intelligence Division. The Committee's investigation centered on the use of FBI intelligence informants. The FBI's criminal informant program fell outside the scope of the Committee's mandate, and accordingly it was not examined.

The Committee recognizes that FBI intelligence informants in violent groups have sometimes played a key role in the enforcement of the criminal law. The Committee examined a number of such cases, and in public hearings on the use of FBI intelligence informants included the testimony of a former informant in the Ku Klux Klan whose reporting and court room testimony was essential to the arrest and conviction of the murderers of Mrs. Viola Liuzzo, a civil rights worker killed in 1965. Former Attorney General Katzenbach testified that informants were vital to the solution of the murders of three civil rights workers killed in Mississippi in 1964.

FBI informant coverage of the Women's Liberation Movement resulted in intensive reporting on the identities and opinions of women who attended WLM meetings. For example, the FBI's New York Field Office summarized one informant's report in a memorandum to FBI Headquarters:

> Informant advised that a WLM meeting was held on _____ Each woman at this meeting stated why she had come to the meeting and how she felt oppressed, sexually or otherwise.

According to this informant, these women are mostly concerned with liberating women from this "oppressive society." They are mostly against marriage, children, and other states of oppression caused by men. Few of them, according to the informant, have had political backgrounds.

> Individual women who attended WLM meetings at midwestern universities were identified by FBI intelligence informants. A report by the Kansas City FBI Field Office stated:

> Informant indicates members of Women's Liberation campus group who are now enrolled as students at University of Missouri, Kansas City, are _____, _____, _____, _____, _____. Informant noted that _____ and _____ not currently students on the UMKC campus are reportedly roommates at _____.

Informants were instructed to report "everything" they knew about a group to the FBI.

> . . . to go to meetings, write up reports . . . on what happened, who was there . . . to try to totally identify the background of every person there, what their relationships were, who they were living with, who they were sleeping with, to try to get some sense of the local structure and the local relationships among the people in the organization.

Another intelligence informant described his mission as "total reporting." Rowe testified that he reported "anything and everything I observed or heard" pertaining to any member of the group he infiltrated.

Even where intelligence informants are used to infiltrate groups where some members are suspected of violent activity, the nature of the intelligence mission results in governmental intrusion into matters irrelevant to that inquiry. The FBI Special Agents who directed an intelligence informant in the Ku Klux Klan testified that the informant

> . . . furnished us information on the meetings and the thoughts and feelings, intentions and ambitions, as best he knew them, of other members of the Klan, both the rank and file and the leadership.

Intelligence informants also report on other groups—not the subject of intelligence investigations—which merely associate with, or are even opposed to, the targeted group. For example, an FBI informant in the VVAW had the following exchange with a member of the Committee:

> Senator HART (Mich.). . . . did you report also on groups and individuals outside the [VVAW], such as other peace groups or individuals who were opposed to the war whom you came in contact with because they were cooperating with the [VVAW] in connection with protest demonstrations and petitions?

> Ms. Cook. . . . I ended up reporting on groups like the United Church of Christ, American Civil Liberties Union, the National Lawyers Guild, liberal church organizations [which] quite often went into coalition with the VVAW.

This informant reported the identities of an estimated 1,000 individuals to the FBI, although the local chapter to which she was assigned had only 55 regular members. Similarly, an FBI informant in the Ku Klux Klan reported on the activities of civil rights and black groups that he observed in the course of his work in the Klan.

In short, the intelligence informant technique is not a precise instrument. By its nature, it extends far beyond the sphere of proper governmental interest and risks governmental monitoring of the private lives and the constitutionally-protected activity of Americans. Nor is the intelligence informant technique used infrequently. As reflected in the statistics described above, FBI intelligence investigations are in large part conducted through the use of informants; and FBI agents are instructed to "develop reliable informants at all levels and in all segments" of groups under investigation.

b. Other Dangers in the Intelligence Informant Technique

In the absence of clear guidelines for informant conduct, FBI paid and directed intelligence informants have participated in violence and other illegal activities and have taken membership lists and other private documents.

1. Participation in Violence and Other Illegal Activity

The Committee's investigation has revealed that there is often a fundamental dilemma in the use of intelligence informants in violent organizations. The Committee recognizes that intelligence informants in such groups have sometimes played essential roles in the enforcement of the criminal law. At the same time, however, the Committee has found that the intelligence informant technique carries with it the substantial danger that informants will participate in, or provoke, violence or illegal activity. Intelligence informants are frequently infiltrated into groups for long-term reporting rather than to collect evidence for use in prosecutions. Consequently, intelligence informants must participate in the activity of the group they penetrate to preserve their cover for extended periods. Where the group is involved in violence or illegal activity, there is a substantial risk that the informant must also become involved in this activity. As an FBI Special Agent who handled an intelligence informant in the Ku Klux Klan testified: "[you] couldn't be an angel and be a good informant."

FBI officials testified that it is Bureau practice to instruct informants that they are not to engage in violence or unlawful activity and, if they do so, they may be prosecuted. FBI Deputy Associate Director Adams testified:

> . . . we have informants who have gotten involved in the violation of the law, and we have immediately converted their status from an informant to

the subject, and have prosecuted, I would say, offhand ... around 20 informants.

The Committee finds, however, that the existing guidelines dealing with informant conduct do not adequately ensure that intelligence informants stay within the law in carrying out their assignments. The FBI Manual of Instructions contain no provisions governing informant conduct. While FBI employee conduct regulations prohibit an FBI agent from directing informants to engage in violent or other illegal activity, informants themselves are not governed by these regulations since the FBI does not consider them as FBI employees.

In the absence of clear and precise written provisions directly applicable to informants, FBI intelligence informants have engaged in violent and other illegal activity. For example, an FBI intelligence informant who penetrated the Ku Klux Klan and reported on its activities for over five years testified that on a number of occasions he and other Klansmen had "beaten people severely, had boarded buses and kicked people off; had went in restaurants and beaten them with blackjacks, chains, pistols." This informant described how he had taken part in Klan attacks on Freedom Riders at the Birmingham, Alabama, bus depot, where "baseball bats, clubs, chains and pistols" were used in beatings.

Although the FBI Special Agents who directed this informant instructed him that he was not to engage in violence, it was recognized that there was a substantial risk that he would become a participant in violent activity.

As one of the Agents testified:

> ... it is kind of difficult to tell him that we would like you to be there on deck, observing, be able to give us information and still keep yourself detached and uninvolved and clean, and that was the problem that we constantly had.

In another example, an FBI intelligence informant penetrated "right wing" groups operating in California under the names "The Minutemen" and "The Secret Army Organization." The informant reported on the activities of these "right wing" paramilitary groups for a period of five years but was also involved in acts of violence or destruction. In addition, the informant actually rose to a position of leadership in the SAO and became an innovator of various harassment actions. For example, he admittedly participated in firebombing of an automobile and was present, conducting a "surveillance" of a professor at San Diego State University, when his associate and subordinate in the SAO took out a gun and fired into the home of the professor, wounding a young woman.

An FBI intelligence informant in a group of antiwar protesters planning to break into a draft board claimed to have provided technical instruction and materials that were essential to the illegal breaktestified to the committee:

> Everything they learned about breaking into a building or climbing a wall or cutting glass or destroying lockers, I taught them. I got sample equipment, the type of windows that we would go through, I picked up off the job and taught them how to cut the glass, how to drill holes in the glass so you cannot bear it and stuff like that, and the FBI supplied me with the equipment needed. The stuff I did not have, the [the FBI] got off their own agents.

The Committee finds that where informants are paid and directed by a government agency, the government has a responsibility to impose clear restrictions on their conduct. Unwritten practice or general provisions aimed at persons other than the informants themselves are not sufficient. In the investigation of violence or illegal activity, it is essential that the government not be implicated in such activity.

2. Membership Lists and Other Private Documents Obtained by the Government Through Intelligence Informants

The Committee finds that there are inadequate guidelines to regulate the conduct of intelligence informants with respect to private and confidential documents, such as membership lists, mailing lists and papers relating to legal matters. The Fourth Amendment provides that citizens shall be "secure in their ... papers and effects, against unreasonable searches and seizures" and requires probable cause to believe there has been a violation of law before a search warrant may issue. Moreover the Supreme Court, in NAACP v. Alabama, held that the First Amendment's protections of speech, assembly and group association did not permit a state to compel the production of the membership list of a group engaged in lawful activity. The Court distinguished the case where a state was able to demonstrate a "controlling justification" for such lists by showing a group's activities involved "acts of unlawful intimidation and violence."

There are no provisions in the FBI Manual which preclude the FBI from obtaining private and confidential documents through intelligence informants. The Manual does prohibit informant reporting of "any information pertaining to defense plans or strategy," but the FBI interprets this as applying only to privileged communications between an attorney and client in connection with a specific court proceeding.

The Committee's investigation has shown that, the FBI, through its intelligence informants and sources, has sought to obtain membership lists and other confidential documents of groups and individuals. For example, one FBI Special Agent testified:

I remember one evening . . . [an informant] called my home and said I will meet you in a half an hour ... I have a complete list of everybody that I have just taken out of the files, but i have to have it back within such a length of time.

Well, naturally I left home and met him and had the list duplicated forthwith, and back in his possession and back in the files with nobody suspecting."

Similarly, the FBI Special Agent who handled an intelligence informant in an antiwar group testified that he obtained confidential papers of the group which related to legal defense matters:

"She brought back several things . . . various position papers taken by various legal defense groups, general statements of . . . the VVAW, legal thoughts on various trials, the Gainesville (Florida) 8 . . . the Camden (New Jersey) 9 . . . various documents from all of these groups."

This informant also testified that she took the confidential mailing list of the group she had penetrated and gave it to the FBI.

She also gave the FBI a legal manual prepared by the group's attorneys to guide lawyers in defending the group's members should they be arrested in connection with antiwar demonstrations or other political activity. Since this document was prepared as a general legal reference manual rather than in connection with a specific trial the FBI considered it outside the attorney-client privilege and not barred by the FBI Manual provision with respect to legal defense and strategy matters.

For the government to obtain membership lists and other private documents pertaining to lawful and protected activities covertly through intelligence informants risks infringing rights guaranteed by the Constitution. The Committee finds that there is a need for new guidelines for informant conduct with-respect to the private papers of groups and individuals.

c. Electronic Surveillance

In the absence of judicial warrant, both the "traditional" forms of electronic surveillance practiced by the FBI wiretapping and bugging—and the highly sophisticated form of electronic monitoring practiced by NSA have been used to collect too much information about too many people.

1. Wiretapping and Bugging

Wiretaps and bugs are considered by FBI officials to be one of the most valuable techniques for the collection of information relevant to the Bureau's legitimate foreign counterintelligence mandate. W. Raymond Wannall, the former Assistant Director in charge of the FBI's Intelligence Division, stated that electronic surveillance assisted Bureau officials in making "decisions" as to operations against foreigners engaged in espionage. "It gives us leads as to persons ... hostile intelligence services are trying to subvert or utilize in the United States, so certainly it is a valuable technique."

Despite its stated value in foreign counterintelligence cases, however, the dangers inherent in its use imply a clear need for rigorous controls. By their nature, wiretaps and bugs are incapable of a surgical precision that would permit intelligence agencies to overhear only the target's conversations. Since wiretaps are placed on particular telephones, anyone who uses a tapped phone—including members of the target's family—can be overheard. So, too, can everyone with whom the target (or anyone else using the target's telephone) communicates. Microphones planted in the target's room or office inevitably intercept all conversations in a particular area: anyone confessing in the room or office, not just the target, is overheard.

The intrusiveness of these techniques has a second aspect as well. It is extremely difficult, if not impossible, to limit the interception to conversations that are relevant to the purposes for which the surveillance is placed. Virtually all conversations are overheard, no matter how trivial, personal, or political they might be. When the electronic surveillance target is a political figure who is likely to discuss political affairs, or a lawyer, who confers with his clients, the possibilities for abuse are obviously heightened.

The dangers of indiscriminate interception are perhaps most acute in the case of microphones planted in locations such as bedrooms. When Attorney General Herbert Brownell gave the FBI sweeping authority to engage in microphone surveillances for intelligence purposes in 1954, he expressly permitted the Bureau to plant microphones in such locations if, in the sole discretion of the FBI, the facts warranted the installation. Acting under this general authority, for example, the Bureau installed no fewer than twelve bugs in hotel rooms occupied by Dr. Martin Luther King, Jr.

The King surveillances which occurred between January 1964 and October 1965, were ostensibly approved within the FBI for internal security reasons, but they produced vast amounts of personal information that were totally unrelated to any legitimate governmental interest; indeed, a single hotel room bug alone yielded twenty reels of tape that subsequently provided the basis for the dissemination of personal information about Dr. King throughout the Federal establishment. 76a Significantly, FBI internal memoranda with respect to some of the installations make clear that they were planted in Dr. King's hotel rooms for the express purpose of obtaining personal information about him.

Extremely personal information about the target, his family, and his friends, is easily obtained from wiretaps as well as microphones. This fact is clearly illustrated by the warrantless electronic surveillance of an American citizen who was suspected of leaking classified data to the press. A wiretap on this individual produced no evidence that he had in fact leaked any stories or documents, but among the items of information that the FBI did obtain from the tap (and delivered in utmost secrecy to the White House) were the following: that "meat was ordered [by the target's family] from a grocer;" that the target's daughter had a toothache; that the target needed grass clippings for a compost heap he was building; and that during a telephone conversation between the target's wife and a friend the "matters discussed were milk bills, hair, soap operas, and church."

The so-called "seventeen" wiretaps on journalists and government employees, which collectively lasted from May 1969 to February 1971, also illustrate the intrusiveness of electronic surveillance. According to former President Nixon, these taps produced "just gobs of material: gossip and bull." FBI summaries of information obtained from the wiretaps and disseminated to the White House suggest that the former President's private evaluation of them was correct. This wiretapping program did not reveal the source of any leaks of classified data, which was its ostensible purpose, but it did generate a wealth of information about the personal lives of the targets — their social contacts, their vacation plans, their employment satisfactions and dissatisfaction, their marital problems, their drinking habits, and even their sex lives.

Among those who were incidentally overheard on one of these wiretaps was a currently sitting Associate Justice of the Supreme Court of the United States, who made plans to review a manuscript written by one of the targets. Vast amounts of political information were also obtained from these wiretaps.

The "seventeen" wiretaps also exemplify the particularly acute problems of wiretapping when the targeted individuals are involved in the domestic political process. These wiretaps produced vast amounts of purely political information, 82 much of which was obtained from the home telephones of two consultants to Senator Edmund Muskie and other Democratic politicians.

The incidental collection of political information from electronic surveillance is also shown by a series of telephone and microphone surveillances conducted during the Kennedy administration. In an investigation of the possibly unlawful attempts of representatives of a foreign country to influence congressional deliberations about sugar quota legislation in the early 1960s, Attorney General Robert Kennedy authorized a total of twelve warrantless wiretaps on foreign and domestic targets. Among the wiretaps of American citizens were two on American lobbyists, three on executive branch officials, and two on a staff member of a House of Representatives' Committee. A bug was also planted in the hotel room of a United States Congressman, the Chairman of the House Agriculture Committee, Harold D. Cooley.

Although this investigation was apparently initiated because of the Government's concern about future relations with the foreign country involved and the possibility of bribery, it is clear that the Kennedy administration was politically interested in the outcome of the sugar quota legislation as well. Given the nature of the techniques used and of the targets they were directed against, it is not surprising that a great deal of potentially useful political information was generated from these "Sugar Lobby" surveillances.

The highly intrusive nature of electronic surveillance also raises special problems when the targets are lawyers and journalists. Over the past two decades there have been a number of wiretaps placed on the office telephones of lawyers. In the Sugar Lobby investigation, for example, Robert Kennedy authorized wiretaps on ten telephone lines of a single law firm. All of these lines were apparently used by the one lawyer who was a target and presumably by other attorneys in the firm as well. Such wiretaps represent a serious threat to the attorney-client privilege, because once they are instituted they are capable of detecting all conversations between a lawyer and his clients, even those relating to pending criminal cases.

Since 1960, at least six American journalists and newsmen have also been the targets of warrantless wiretaps or bugs. These surveillances were all rationalized as necessary to discover the source of leaks of classified information, but, since wiretaps and bugs are indiscriminate in the types of information collected, some of these taps revealed the attitudes of various newsmen toward certain politicians and supplied advance notice of forthcoming newspaper and magazine articles dealing with administration policies. The collection of information such as this, and the precedent set by wiretapping of newsmen, generally, inevitably tends to undermine the constitutional guarantee of a free and independent press.

2. NSA Monitoring

The National Security Agency (NSA) has the capability to monitor almost any electronic communication which travels through the air. This means that NSA is capable of intercepting a telephone call or even a telegram, if such call or telegram is transmitted at least partially through the air. Radio transmissions, a fortiori, are also within NSA's reach.

Since most communications today—to an increasing extent even domestic communications—are, at some point, transmitted through the air, NSA's potential to violate the privacy of American citizens is unmatched by any other intelligence agency. Furthermore, since the interception of electronic signals entails neither the installation of electronic surveillance devices nor the cooperation of private communications companies, the possibility that such interceptions will be undetected is enhanced.

NSA has never turned its monitoring apparatus upon entirely domestic communications, but from the early 1960s until 1973, it did intercept the international communications of American citizens, without a warrant, at the request of other federal agencies.

Under current practice, NSA does not target any American citizen or firm for the purpose of intercepting their foreign communications. As a result of monitoring international links of communication, however, it does acquire an enormous number of communications to, from, or about American citizens and firms.

As a practical matter, most of the communications of American citizens or firms acquired by NSA as incidental to its foreign intelligencegathering process are destroyed upon recognition as a communication to or from an American citizen. But other such communications, which bear upon NSA's foreign intelligence requirements, are processed, and information obtained from them are used in NSA's reports to other intelligence agencies. Current practice precludes NSA from identifying American citizens and firms by name in such reports. Nonetheless, the practice does result in NSA's disseminating information derived from the international communications of American citizens and firms to the intelligence agencies and policymakers in the federal government.

In his dissent in Olmstead v. United States, which held that the Fourth Amendment warrant requirement did not apply to the seizure of conversations by means of wiretapping, Justice Louis D. Brandeis expressed grave concern that new technologies might outstrip the ability of the Constitution to protect American citizens. He wrote:

> Subtler and more far-reaching means of invading privacy have become available to the government ... (and) the progress of science in furnishing the Government with means of espionage is not likely to stop with wiretapping. Ways may some day be developed by which the Government, without removing papers from secret drawers, can reproduce them in court, and by which it will be enabled to expose to a jury the most intimate occurrences of the home .... Can it be that the Constitution affords no protection against such invasions of individual security?

The question posed by Justice Brandeis applies with obvious force to the technological developments that allow NSA to monitor an enormous number of communications each year. His fears were firmly based, for in fact no warrant was ever obtained for the inclusion of 1200 American citizens on NSA's "Watch List" between the early 1960s and 1973, and none is obtained today for the dissemination within the intelligence community of information derived from the international communications of American citizens and firms. In the face of this new technology, it is well to remember the answer Justice Brandeis gave to his own question. Quoting from Boyd v. United States, 116 U.S. 616, he wrote:

> It is not the breaking of his doors, and the rummaging of his drawers that constitutes the essense of the offense; but it is the invasion of his indefeasible right of personal security, personal liberty, and private property . . .

D. Mail Opening

By ignoring the legal prohibitions against warrantless mail opening, the CIA and the FBI were able to obtain access to the written communications of hundreds of thousands of individuals, a large proportion of whom were American citizens. The intercepted letters were presumably sealed with the expectation that they would only be opened by the party to whom they were addressed, but intelligence agents in ten cities throughout the United States surreptitiously opened the seal and photographed the entire contents for inclusion in their intelligence files.

Mail opening is an imprecise technique. In addition to relying on a "Watch List" of names, the CIA opened vast numbers of letters on an entirely random basis; as one agent who opened mail in the CIA's New York project testified, "You never knew what you would hit." Given the imprecision of the technique and the large quantity of correspondence that was opened, it is perhaps not surprising that during the twenty year course of the Agency's New York project, the mail that was randomly opened included that of at least three United States Senators and a Congressman, one Presidential Candidate, and numerous educational, business, and civil rights leaders.

Several of the FBI programs utilized as selection criteria certain "indicators" on the outside of envelopes that suggested that the communication might be to or from a foreign espionage agent. These "indicators" were more refined than the "shotgun approach" which characterized the CIA's New York project, and they did lead to the identification of three foreign spies. But even by the Bureau's own accounting, it is clear that the mail of hundreds of innocent American citizens was opened and read for every successful counterintelligence lead that was obtained by means of "indicators."

Large volumes of mail were also intercepted and opened in other FBI mail programs that were based not on indicators but on far less precise criteria. Two programs that involved the opening of mail to and from an Asian country, for example, used "letters to or from a university, scientific, or technical facility" as one selection criterion. According to FBI memoranda, an average of 50 to 100 letters per day was opened and photographed during the ten years in which one of these two programs operated.

E. Surreptitious Entries

Surreptitious entries, conducted in violation of the law, have also permitted intelligence agencies to gather a wide range of information about American citizens and domestic organization as well as foreign targets. By definition this technique involves a physical entry into the private premises of individuals and groups. Once intelligence agents are inside, no "papers or effects" are secure. As the Huston Plan recommendations stated in 1970, "It amounts to burglary."

The most private documents are rendered vulnerable by the use of surreptitious entries. According to a 1966 internal FBI memorandum, which discusses the use of this technique against domestic. organizations:

[The FBI has] on numerous occasions been able to obtain material held highly secret, and closely guarded by subversive groups and organizations which consisted of membership lists and mailing lists of these organizations.

A specific example cited in this memorandum also reveals the types of information that this technique can collect and the uses to which the information thus collected may be put:

Through a "black bag" job, we obtained the records in the possession of three high-ranking officials of a Klan organization. These records gave us the complete membership and financial information concerning the Klan's operation which we have been using most effectively to disrupt the organization and, in fact, to bring about its near disintegration.

Unlike techniques such as electronic surveillance, government entries into private premises were familiar to the Founding Fathers. "Indeed," Judge Gesell wrote in the Ehrlichman case, "the American Revolution was sparked in part by the complaints of the colonists against the issuance of writs of assistance, pursuant to which the King's revenue officers conducted unrestricted, indiscriminate searches of persons and homes to uncover contraband." Recognition of the intrusiveness of government break-ins was one of the primary reasons for the subsequent adoption of the Fourth Amendment in 1791, and this technique is certainly no less intrusive today.

Subfinding (c.)

The imprecision and manipulation of labels such as "national security," "domestic security," "subversive activities" and "foreign intelligence" have led to unjustified use of these techniques.

Using labels such as "national security" and "foreign intelligence", intelligence agencies have directed these highly intrusive techniques against individuals and organizations who were suspected of no criminal activity and who posed no genuine threat to the national security. In the absence of precise standards and effective outside control, the selection of American citizens as targets has at times been predicated on grounds no more substantial than their lawful protests or their non-conformist philosophies. Almost any connection with any perceived danger to the country has sufficed.

The application of the "national security" rationale to cases lacking a substantial national security basis has been most apparent in the area of warrantless electronic surveillance. Indeed, the unjustified use of wiretaps and bugs under this and related labels has a long history. Among the wiretaps approved by Attorney General Francis Biddle under the standard of "persons suspected of subversive activities," for example, was one on the Los Angeles Chamber of Commerce in 1941. This was approved in spite of his comment to J. Edgar Hoover that the target organization had "no record of espionage at this time." In 1945, Attorney General Tom Clark authorized a wiretap on a former aide to President Roosevelt. According to a memorandum by J. Edgar Hoover, Clark stated that President Truman wanted "a very thorough investigation" of the activities of the former official so that "steps might be taken, if possible, to see that [his] activities did not interfere with the proper administration of government." The memorandum makes no reference to "subversive activities" or any other national security considerations.

The "Sugar Lobby" and Martin Luther King, Jr., wiretaps in the early 1960s both show the elasticity of the "domestic security" standard which supplemented President Roosevelt's "subversive activities" formulation. Among those wiretapped in the Sugar Lobby investigation, as noted above, was a Congressional staff aide. Yet the documentary record of this investigation reveals no evidence indicating that the target herself represented any threat to the "domestic security." Similarly, while the FBI may properly have been concerned with the activities of certain advisors to Dr. King, the direct wiretapping of Dr. King shows that the "domestic security" standard could be stretched to unjustified lengths.

The microphone surveillances of Congressman Cooley and Dr. King under the "national interest" standard established by Attorney General Brownell in 1954 also reveal the relative ease with which electronic bugging devices could be used against American citizens who posed no genuine "national security" threat. Neither of these targets advocated or engaged in any conduct that was damaging to the security of the United States.

In April, 1964, Attorney General Robert Kennedy approved "technical coverage (electronic surveillance)" of a black nationalist leader after the FBI advised Kennedy that he was "forming a new group" which would be "more aggressive" and would "participate in racial demonstrations and civil rights activities." The only indication of possible danger noted in the FBI's request for the wiretaps, however, was that this leader had "recommended the possession of firearms by members for their self-protection.

One year later, Attorney General Nicholas Katzenbach approved a wiretap on the offices of the Student Non-Violent Coordinating Committee on the basis of potential communist infiltration into that organization. The request which was sent to the Attorney General noted that "confidential informants" described SNCC as "the principal target for Communist Party infiltration among the various civil rights organizations" and stated that some of its leaders had "made public appearances with leaders of communist-front organizations" and had "subversive backgrounds." The FBI presented no substantial evidence however, that SNCC was in fact infiltrated by communists — only that the organization was apparently a target for such infiltration in the future.

After the Justice Department adopted new criteria for the institution of warrantless electronic surveillance in 1968, the unjustified use of wiretaps continued. In November 1969, Attorney General John Mitchell approved a series of three wiretaps on organizations involved in planning the antiwar "March on Washington." The FBI's request for coverage of the first group made no claim that its members engaged or were likely to engage in violent activity; the request was simply based on the statement that the anticipated size of the demonstration was cause for "concern should violence of any type break out."

The only additional justification given for the wiretap on one of the other groups, the Vietnam Moratorium Committee, was that it "has recently endorsed fully the activities of the [first group] concerning the upcoming antiwar demonstrations."

In 1970, approval for a wiretap on a "New Left oriented campus group" was granted by Attorney General Mitchell on the basis of an FBI request which included, among other factors deemed relevant to the necessity for the wiretap, evidence that the group was attempting "to develop strong ties with the cafeteria, maintenance and other workers on campus" and wanted to "go into industry and factories and ... take the radical politics they learned on the campus and spread them among factory workers."

This approval was renewed three months later despite the fact that the request for renewal made no mention of violent or illegal activity by the group. The value of the wiretap was shown, according to the FBI, by such results as obtaining "the identities of over 600 persons either in touch with the national headquarters or associated with" it during the preceding three months. Six months after the original authorization the number of persons so identified had increased to 1,428; and approval was granted for a third three-month period."

The "seventeen wiretaps" also show how the term "national security" as a justification for wiretapping can obscure improper use of this technique. Shortly after these wiretaps were revealed publicly, President Nixon stated they had been justified by the need to prevent leaks of classified information harmful to the national security.

Wiretaps for this purpose had, in fact, been authorized under the Kennedy and Johnson administrations. President Nixon learned of these and other prior taps and, at a news conference, sought to justify the taps he had authorized by referring to past precedent. He stated that in the:

> period of 1961 to '63 there were wiretaps on news organizations, on news people, on civil rights leaders and on other people. And I think they were perfectly justified and I'm sure that President Kennedy and his brother, Robert Kennedy, would never have authorized them, unless he thought they were in the national interest. (Presidential News Conference, 8/22/73.)

Thus, questionable electronic surveillances by earlier administrations were put forward as a defense for improper surveillances exposed in 1973. In fact, however, two of these wiretaps were placed on domestic affairs advisers at the White House who had no foreign affairs responsibilities and apparently no access to classified foreign policy materialis. A third target was a White House speech writer who had been overheard on an existing tap agreeing to provide a reporter with background information on a Presidential speech concerning domestic revenue sharing and welfare reform. The reinstatement of another wiretap in this series was requested by H. R. Haldeman simply because "they may have a bad apple and have to get him out of the basket." The last four requests in this series that were sent to the Attorney General (including the requests for a tap on the "bad apple") did not mention any national security justification at all. As former Deputy Attorney General William Ruckelshaus has testified:

> I think some of the individuals who were tapped, at least to the extent I have reviewed the record, had very little, if any, relationship to any claim of national security . . . I think that as the program proceeded and it became clear to those who could sign off on taps how easy it was to institute a wiretap under the present procedure that these kinds of considerations [i.e., genuine national security justifications] were considerably relaxed as the program went on.

None of the "seventeen" wiretaps was ever reauthorized by the Attorney General, although 10 of them remained in operation for periods longer than 90 days and although President Nixon himself stated privately that "[t]he tapping was a very, very unproductive thing ... it's never been useful to any operation I've conducted . . ."

In short, warrantless electronic surveillance has been defended on the ground that it was essential for the national security, but the history of the use of this technique clearly shows that the imprecision and manipulation of this and similar labels, coupled with the absence of any outside scrutiny, has led to its improper use against American citizens who posed no criminal or national security threat to the country.

Similarly, the terms "foreign intelligence" and "counterespionage" were used by the CIA and the FBI to justify their cooperation in the CIA's New York mail opening project, but this project was also used to target entirely innocent American citizens.

As noted above, the CIA compiled a "Watch List" of names of persons and organizations whose mail was to be opened if it passed through the New York facility. In the early days of the project. the names on this list—which then numbered fewer than twenty—might reasonably have been expected to lead to genuine foreign intelligence or counterintelligence information. But as the project developed, the Watch List grew and its focus changed. By the late 1960s there were approximately 600 names on the list, many of them American citizens and organizations who were engaged in purely lawful and constitutionally protected forms of protest against governmental policies. Among the domestic organizations on the Watch List, which was supplemented by submissions from the FBI, were: Clergy and Laymen Concerned about Vietnam, the National Mobilization Committee to End the War in Vietnam, Ramparts, the Student Non-Violent Coordinating Committee, the Center for the Study of Public Policy, and the American Friends Service Committee.

The FBI levied more general requirements on the CIA's project as well. The focus of the original categories of correspondence in which the FBI expressed an interest was clearly foreign counterespionage, but subsequent requirements became progressively more domestic in their focus and progressively broader in their scope. The requirements that were levied by the FBI in 1972, one year before the termination of the project, included the following:

". . . [p]ersons on the Watch List; known communists, New Left activists, extremists, and other subversives . . .

Communist party and front organizations ... extremist and New Left organizations.

Protest and peace organizations, such as People's Coalition for Peace and Justice, National Peace Action Committee, and Women's Strike for Peace.

Communists, Trotskyites and members of other Marxist-Leninist, subversive and extremist groups, such as the Black Nationalists and Liberation groups ... Students for a Democratic Society ... and other New Left groups.

Traffic to and from Puerto Rico and the Virgin Islands showing anti-U.S. or subversive sympathies."

This final set of requirements evidently reflected the domestic turmoil of the late 1960s and early 1970s. The mail opening program that began as a means of collecting foreign intelligence information and discovering Soviet intelligence efforts in the United States had expanded to encompass detection of the activities of domestic dissidents of all types.

In the absence of effective outside control, highly intrusive techniques have been used to gather vast amounts of information about the entirely lawful activities — and privately held beliefs — of large numbers of American citizens. The very intrusiveness of these techniques demands the utmost circumspection in their use. But with vague or non-existent standards to guide them, and with labels such as "national security" and "foreign intelligence" to shield them, executive branch officials have been all too willing to unleash these techniques against American citizens with little or no legitimate justification.

D. Using Covert Action To Disrupt And Discredit Domestic Groups

Major Finding
The Committee finds that covert action programs have been used to disrupt the lawful political activities of individual Americans and groups and to discredit them, using dangerous and degrading tactics which are abhorrent in a free and decent society.

Subfindings
(a) Although the claimed purposes of these action programs were to protect the national security and to prevent violence, many of the victims were concededly

nonviolent, were not controlled by a foreign power, and posed no threat to the national security.

(b) The acts taken interfered with the First Amendment rights of citizens. They were explicitly intended to deter citizens from joining groups, "neutralize" those who were already members, and prevent or inhibit the expression of ideas.

(c.) The tactics used against Americans often risked and sometimes caused serious emotional, economic, or physical damage. Actions were taken which were designed to break up marriages, terminate funding or employment, and encourage gang warfare between violent rival groups. Due process of law forbids the use of such covert tactics, whether the victims are innocent law-abiding citizens or members of groups suspected of involvement in violence.

(d) The sustained use of such tactics by the FBI in an attempt to destroy Dr. Martin Luther King, Jr., violated the law and fundamental human decency.

Elaboration of the Findings

For fifteen years from 1956 until 1971, the FBI carried out a series of covert action programs directed against American citizens. These "counterintelligence programs" (shortened to the acronym COINTELPRO) resulted in part from frustration with Supreme Court rulings limiting the Government's power to proceed overtly against dissident groups.

They ended formally in 1971 with the threat of public exposure. Some of the findings discussed herein are related to the findings on lawlessness, overbreadth, and intrusive techniques previously set forth. Some of the most offensive actions in the FBI's COINTELPRO programs (anonymous letters intended to break up marriages, or efforts to deprive people of their jobs, for example) were based upon the covert use of information obtained through overly-broad investigations and intrusive techniques. Similarly, as noted above, COINTELPRO involved specific violations of law, and the law and the Constitution were "not [given] a thought" under the FBI's policies.

But COINTELPRO was more than simply violating the law or the Constitution. In COINTELPRO the Bureau secretly took the law into its own hands, going beyond the collection of intelligence and beyond its law enforcement function to act outside the legal process altogether and to covertly disrupt, discredit and harass groups and individuals. A law enforcement agency must not secretly usurp the functions of judge and jury, even when the investigation reveals criminal activity. But in COINTELPRO, the Bureau imposed summary punishment, not only on the allegedly violent, but also on the nonviolent advocates of change. Such action is the hallmark of the vigilante and has no place in a democratic society.

Under COINTELPRO, certain techniques the Bureau had used against hostile foreign agents were adoped for use against perceived domestic threats to the established political and social order.

Some of the targets of COINTELPRO were law-abiding citizens merely advocating change in our society. Other targets were members of groups that had been involved in violence, such as the Ku Klux Klan or the Black Panther Party. Some victims did nothing more than associate with targets.

The Committee does not condone acts of violence, but the response of Government to allegations of illegal conduct must comply with the due process of law demanded by the Constitution. Lawlessness by citizens does not justify lawlessness by Government.

The tactics which were employed by the Bureau are therefore unacceptable, even against the alleged criminal. The imprecision of the targeting compounded the abuse. Once the Government decided to take the law into its own hands, those unacceptable tactics came almost inevitably to be used not only against the "kid with the bomb" but also against the "kid with the bumper sticker."

Subfinding (a)

Although the claimed purposes of these action programs were to protect the "national security" and to prevent violence, many of the victims were concededly nonviolent, were not controlled by a foreign power, and posed no threat to the "national security."

The Bureau conducted five "counterintelligence programs" aimed against domestic groups: the "Communist Party, USA" program (1956-71); the "Socialist Workers Party" program (1961-69); the "White Hate" program (1964-1971); the "Black Nationalist-Hate Group" program (1967-71) ; and the "New Left" program (1968-71).

While the declared purposes of these programs were to protect the "national security" or prevent violence, Bureau witnesses admit that many of the targets were nonviolent and most had no connections with a foreign power. Indeed, nonviolent organizations and individuals were targeted because the Bureau believed they represented a "potential" for violence — and nonviolent citizens who were against the war in Vietnam were targeted because they gave "aid and comfort" to violent demonstrators by lending respectability to their cause.

The imprecision of the targeting is demonstrated by the inability of the Bureau to define the subjects of the programs. The Black Nationalist program, according to its supervisor, included "a great number of organizations that you might not today characterize as black nationalist but which were in fact primarily black." Thus, the nonviolent Southern Christian Leadership Conference was labeled as a Black Nationalist "Hate Group."

Furthermore, the actual targets were chosen from a far broader group than the titles of the programs would imply. The CPUSA program targeted not only Communist Party members but also sponsors of the National Committee to Abolish the House Un-American Activities Committee and civil rights leaders allegedly under Communist influence or not deemed to be "anti-Communist". The Socialist Workers Party program included non-SWP sponsors of antiwar demonstrations which were cosponsored by the SWP or the Young Socialist Alliance, its youth group. The Black Nationalist program targeted a range of organizations from the Panthers to SNCC to the peaceful Southern Christian Leadership Conference, and included every Black Student Union and many other black student groups. New Left targets ranged from the SDS to the InterUniversity Committee for Debate on Foreign Policy, from Antioch College ("vanguard of the New Left") to the New Mexico Free University and other "alternate" schools, and from underground newspapers to students protesting university censorship of a student publication by carrying signs with four-letter words on them.

Subfinding (b)

The acts taken interfered with the First Amendment rights of citizens. They were explicitly intended to deter citizens from joining groups, "neutralize" those who were already members, and prevent or inhibit the expression of ideas.

In achieving its purported goals Of protecting the national security and preventing violence, the Bureau attempted to deter membership in the target groups. As the supervisor of the "Black Nationalist" COINTELPRO stated, "Obviously, you are going to prevent violence or a greater amount of violence if you have smaller groups. The chief of the COINTELPRO unit agreed: "We also made an effort . . . to deter recruitment where we could. This was done with the view that if we could curb the organization, we could curb the action or the violence within the organization." As noted above, many of the organizations "curbed" were not violent, and covert attacks on group membership contravened the First Amendment's guarantee of freedom to associate.

Nor was this the only First Amendment right violated by the Bureau. In addition to attempting to prevent people from joining or continuing to be members in target organizations, the Bureau tried to "deter or counteract" what it called "propaganda" — the expression of ideas which it considered dangerous. Thus, the originating document for the "Black Nationalist" COINTELPRO noted that "consideration should be given to techniques to preclude" leaders of the target organizations "from spreading their philosophy publicly or through various mass communication media."

Instructions to "preclude" free speech were not limited to "black nationalists;" they occurred in every program. In the New Left program, for instance, approximately thirty-nine percent of all actions attempted to keep targets from speaking, teaching, writing, or publishing.

The cases included attempts (sometimes successful) to prompt the firing of university and high school teachers; to prevent targets from speaking on campus; to stop chapters of target groups from being formed; to prevent the distribution of books, newspapers, or periodicals; to disrupt or cancel news conferences; to interfere with peaceful demonstrations, including the SCLC's Poor People's Campaign and Washington Spring Project and most of the large anti-war marches; and to deny facilities for meetings or conferences.

As the above cases demonstrate, the FBI was not just "chilling" free speech, but squarely attacking it.

The tactics used against Americans often risked and sometimes caused serious emotional, economic, or physical damage. Actions were taken which were designed to break up marriages, terminate funding or employment, and encourage gang warfare between violent rival groups. Due process of law forbids the use of such covert tactics whether the victims are innocent law-abiding citizens or members of groups suspected of involvement in violence. The former head of the Domestic Intelligence Division described counterintelligence as a "rough, tough, dirty, and dangerous" business. His description was accurate.

One technique used in COINTELPRO involved sending anonymous letters to spouses intended, in the words of one proposal, to "produce ill-feeling and possibly a lasting distrust" between husband and wife, so that "concern over what to do about it" would distract the target from "time spent in the plots and plans" of the organization. The image of an agent of the United States Government scrawling a poison-pen letter to someone's wife in language usually reserved for bathroom walls is not a happy one. Nevertheless, anonymous letters were sent to, among others, a Klansman's wife, informing her that her husband had "taken the flesh of another unto himself," the other person being a woman named Ruby, with her "lust filled eyes and smart aleck figure;" and to a "Black Nationalist's" wife saying that her husband "been maken it here" with other women in his organization "and than he gives us this jive bout their better in bed then you." A husband who was concerned about his wife's activities in a biracial group received a letter which started, "Look man I guess your old lady doesn't get enough at home or she wouldn't be shucking and jiving with our Black Men" in the group. The Field Office reported as a "tangible result" of this letter that the target and her husband separated.

The Bureau also contacted employers and funding organizations in order to cause the firing of the targets or the termination of their support. For example, priests who allowed their churches to be used for the Black Panther breakfast programs were targeted, and anonymous letters were sent to their bishops; a television commentator who expressed admiration for a Black Nationalist leader and criticized heavy defense spending was transferred after the Bureau contacted his employer; and an employee of the Urban League was fired after the FBI approached a "confidential source" in a foundation which funded the League.

The Bureau also encouraged "gang warfare" between violent groups. An FBI memorandum dated November 25, 1968 to certain Field Offices conducting investigations of the Black Panther Party ordered recipient offices to submit "imaginative and hard-hitting counterintelligence measures aimed at crippling the BPP." Proposals were to be received every two weeks. Particular attention was to be given to capitalizing upon differences between the Panthers and US, Inc. (an other "Black Nationalist" group), which had reached such proportions that "it is taking on the aura of gang warfare with attendant threats of murder and reprisals." On May 26, 1970, after U.S. organization members had killed four BPP members and members of each organization had been shot and beaten by members of the other, the Field Office reported:

> Information received from local sources indicate[s] that, in general, the membership of the Los Angeles BPP is physically afraid of US members and take premeditated precautions to avoid confrontations.
>
> In view of their anxieties, it is not presently felt that the Los Angeles BPP can be prompted into what could result in an internecine struggle between the two organizations. . . .
>
> The Los Angeles Division is aware of the mutually hostile feelings harbored between the organizations and the first opportunity to capitalize on the situation will be maximized. It is intended that US Inc. will be appropriately and discreetly advised of the time and location of BPP activities in order that the two organizations might be brought together and thus grant nature the opportunity to take'her due course.

A second Field Office noted:

> Shootings, beatings and a high degree of unrest continues to prevail in the ghetto area of Southeast San Diego. Although no specific counterintelligence action can be credited with contributing to this overall situation, it is felt that a substantial amount of the unrest is directly attributable to this program.

In another case, an anonymous letter was sent to the leader of the Blackstone Rangers (a group, according to the Field Offices' proposal, "to whom violent-type activity, shooting, and the like are second nature") advising him that "the brothers that run the Panthers blame you for blocking their thing and there's supposed to be a hit out for you." The letter was intended to "intensify the degree of animosity between the two groups" and cause "retaliatory action which could disrupt the BPP or lead to reprisals against its leadership."

Another technique which risked serious harm to the target was falsely labeling a target an informant. This technique was used in all five domestic COINTELPROs. When a member of a nonviolent group was successfully mislabeled as an informant, the result was alienation from the group. When the target belonged to a group known to have killed suspected informants, the risk was substantially more serious. On several occasions, the Bureau used this technique against members of the Black Panther Party; it was used at least twice after FBI documents expressed concern over the possible consequences because two members of the BPP had been murdered as suspected informants.

The Bureau recognized that some techniques used in COINTELPRO were more likely than others to cause serious physical, emotional, or economic damage to the targets. Any proposed use of such techniques—for example, encouraging enmity between violent rival groups, falsely labeling group members as informants, and mailing anonymous letters to targets' spouses accusing the target of infidelity—was scrutinized carefully by headquarters supervisory personnel, in an attempt to balance the "greater good" to be achieved by the proposal against the known or risked harm to the target. If the "good" was sufficient, the proposal was approved. For instance, in discussing anonymous letters to spouses, the agent who supervised the New Left COINTELPRO stated:

[Before recommending approval] I would want to know what you want to get out of this, who are these people. If it's somebody, and say they did split up, what would accrue from it as far as disrupting the New Left is concerned? Say they broke up, what then. . . .

[The question would be] is it worth it?

Similarly, with regard to causing false suspicions that an individual was an informant, the chief of the Racial Intelligence Section stated:

You have to be able to make decisions and I am sure that labeling somebody as an informant, that you'd want to make certain that it served a good purpose before you did it and not do it haphazardly.... It is a serious thing ... As far as I am aware, in the black extremist area, by using that technique, no one was killed. I am sure of that.

This official was asked whether the fact that no one was killed was the, result of "luck or planning." He answered: "Oh, it just happened that way, I am sure."

It is intolerable in a free society that an agency of the Government should adopt such tactics, whether or not the targets are involved in criminal activity. The "greater good" of the country is in fact served by adherence to the rule of law mandated by the Constitution.

Subfinding (d)

The sustained use of such tactics by the FBI in an attempt to destroy Dr. Martin Luther King, Jr., violated the law and fundamental human decency.

The Committee devoted substantial attention to the FBI's covert action campaign against Dr. Martin Luther King because it demonstrates just how far the Government could go in a secret war against one citizen. In focusing upon Dr. King, however, it should not be forgotten that the Bureau carried out disruptive activities against hundreds of lesser known American citizens. It should also be borne in mind that positive action on the part of high Government officials outside the FBI might have prevented what occurred in this case.

The FBI's claimed justification for targeting Dr. King—alleged Communist influence on him and the civil rights movement—is examined elsewhere in this report.

The FBI's campaign against Dr. Martin Luther King, Jr. began in December 1963, four months after the famous civil rights March on Washington, when a nine-hour meeting was convened at FBI Headquarters to discuss various "avenues of approach aimed at neutralizing King as an effective Negro leader." Following the meeting, agents in the field were instructed to "continue to gather information concerning King's personal activities ... in order that we may consider using this information at an opportune time in a counterintelligence move to discredit him." 57About two weeks after that conference, FBI agents planted a microphone in Dr. King's bedroom at the Willard Hotel in Washington, D.C. During the next two years, the FBI installed at least fourteen more "bugs" in Dr. King's hotel rooms across the country. Physical and photographic surveillances accompanied some of the microphone, coverage.

The FBI also scrutinized Dr. King's tax returns, monitored his financial affairs, and even tried to determine whether he had a secret foreign bank account.

In late 1964, a "sterilized" tape was prepared in a manner that would prevent attribution to the FBI and was "anonymously" mailed to Dr. King just before he received the Nobel Peace Prize. Enclosed in the package with the tape was an unsigned letter which warned Dr. King, "your end is approaching . . . you are finished." The letter intimated that the tape might be publicly released, and closed with the following message:

> King, there is only one thing left for you to do. You know what it is. You have just 34 days in which to do (this exact number has been selected for a specific reason, it has definite practical significance). You are done. There is but one way out for you . . .

Dr. King's associates have said he interpreted the message as an effort to induce him to commit suicide.

At about the same time that it mailed the "sanitized" tape, the FBI was also apparently offering tapes and transcripts to newsmen. Later when civil rights leaders Roy Wilkins and James Farmer went to Washington to persuade Bureau officials to halt the FBI's discrediting efforts, they were told that "if King want[s] war we [are] prepared to give it to him."

Shortly thereafter, Dr. King went to Europe to receive the Nobel Peace Prize. The Bureau tried to undermine ambassadorial receptions in several of the countries he visited and when he returned to the United States, took steps to diminish support for a banquet and a special "day" being planned in his honor.

The Bureau's actions against Dr. King included attempts to prevent him from meeting with world leaders, receiving honors or favorable publicity, and gaining financial support. When the Bureau learned of a possible meeting between Dr. King and the Pope in August 1964, the FBI asked Cardinal Spellman to try to arrange a cancellation of the audience. Discovering that two schools (Springfield College and Marquette University) were going to honor Dr. King with special degrees in the spring of 1964, Bureau agents tried to convince officials at the schools to rescind their plans. And when the Bureau learned in October 1966 that the Ford Foundation might grant three million dollars to Dr. King's Southern Christian Leadership Conference, they asked a former FBI agent who was a high official at the Ford Motor Company to try to block the award.

A magazine was asked not to publish favorable articles about him. Religious leaders and institutions were contacted to undermine their support of him. Press conference questions were prepared and distributed to "friendly" journalists. And plans were even discussed for sabotaging his political campaign in the event he decided to run for national office. An SCLC employee was "anonymously" informed that the SCLC was trying to get rid of her "so that the Bureau [would be] in a position to capitalize on [her] bitterness." Bureau officials contacted members of Congress, and special "off the record" testimony was prepared for the Director's use before the House Appropriations Committee.

The "neutralization" program continued until Dr. King's death. As late as March 1968, FBI agents were being instructed to neutralize Dr. King because he might become a "messiah" who could "unify, and electrify, the militant black nationalist movement" if he were to "abandon his supposed 'obedience' to 'white liberal doctrines' (nonviolence) and embrace black nationalism." Steps were taken to subvert the "Poor People's Campaign" which Dr. King was planning to lead in the spring of 1968. Even after Dr. King's death, agents in the field were proposing methods for harassing his widow and Bureau officials were trying to prevent his birthday from becoming a national holiday.

The actions taken against Dr. King are indefensible. They represent a sad episode in the dark history of covert actions directed against law abiding citizens by a law enforcement agency.

E. Political Abuse Of Intelligence Information

Major Finding
The Committee finds that information has been collected and disseminated in order to serve the purely political interests of an intelligence agency or the administration, and to influence social policy and political action.

Subfindings
(a) White House officials have requested and obtained politically useful information from the FBI, including information on the activities of political opponents or critics.

(b) In some cases, political or personal information was not specifically requested, but was nevertheless collected and disseminated to administration officials as part of investigations they had requested. Neither the FBI nor the recipients differentiated in these cases between national security or law enforcement information and purely political intelligence.

(c.) The FBI has also volunteered information to Presidents and their staffs, without having been asked for it, sometimes apparently to curry favor with the current administration. Similarly, the FBI has assembled intelligence on its critics and on political figures it believed might influence public attitudes or Congressional support.

(d) The FBI has also used intelligence as a vehicle for covert efforts to influence social policy and political action.

Elaboration of Findings

The FBI's ability to gather information without effective restraints gave it enormous power. That power was inevitably attractive to politicians, who could use information on opponents and critics for their own advantage, and was also an asset to the Bureau, which depended on politicians for support. In the political arena, as in other facets of American life touched by the intelligence community, the existence of unchecked power led to its abuse.

By providing politically useful information to the White House and congressional supporters, sometimes on demand and sometimes gratuitously, the Bureau buttressed its own position in the political structure. At the same time, the widespread—and accurate—belief in Congress and the administration that the Bureau had available to it, derogatory information on politicians and critics created what the late Majority Leader of the House of Representatives, Hale Boggs, called a "fear" of the Bureau:

> Freedom of speech, freedom of thought, freedom of action for men in public life can be compromised quite as effectively by the fear of surveillance as by the fact of surveillance.

Information gathered and disseminated to the White House ranged from purely political intelligence, such as lobbying efforts on bills ail administration opposed and the strategy of a delegate challenge at a national political convention, to "tidbits" about the activities of politicians and public figures which the Bureau believed "of interest" to the recipients.

Such participation in political machinations by an intelligence agency is totally improper. Responsibility for what amounted to a betrayal of the public trust in the integrity of the FBI must be shared between the officials who requested such information and those who provided it.

The Bureau's collection and dissemination of politically useful information was not colored by partisan considerations; rather its effect was to entrench the Bureau's own position in the political structure, regardless of which party was in power at the time. However, the Bureau also used its powers to serve ideological purposes, attempting covertly to influence social policy and and political action.

In its efforts to "protect society," the FBI engaged in activities which necessarily affected the processes by which American citizens make decisions. In doing so, it distorted and exaggerated facts, made use of the mass media, and attacked the leadership of groups which it considered threats to the social order.

Law enforcement officers are, of course, entitled to state their opinions about what choices the people should make on contemporary social and political issues. The First Amendment guarantees their right to enter the marketplace of ideas and persuade their fellow citizens of the correctness of those opinions by making speeches, writing books, and, within certain statutory limits, supporting political candidates. The problem lies not in the open expression of views, but in the covert use of power or position of trust to influence others. This abuse is aggravated by the agency's control over information on which the public and its elected representatives rely to make decisions.

The essence of democracy is the belief that the people must be free to make decisions about matters of public policy. The FBI's actions interfered with the democratic process, because attitudes within the Bureau toward social change led to the belief that such intervention formed a part of its obligation to protect society. When a governmental agency clandestinely tries to impose its views of what is right upon the American people, then the democratic process is undermined.

Subfinding (a)
White House officials have requested and obtained politically useful information from the FBI, including personal life information on the activities of political opponents or critics.

Presidents and White House aides have asked the FBI to provide political or personal information on opponents and critics, including "name checks" of Bureau files. They have also asked the Bureau to conduct electronic surveillance or more limited investigations of such persons. The FBI appears to have complied unquestioningly with these requests, despite occasional internal doubts about their propriety.

Precedents for certain political abuses go back to the very outset of the domestic intelligence program. In 1940 the FBI complied with President Roosevelt's request to file the names of people sending critical telegrams to the White House. There is evidence of improper electronic surveillance for the White House in the 1940s. And an aide to President Eisenhower asked the FBI to conduct a questionable name check. In 1962, the FBI complied unquestioningly with a request from Attorney General Kennedy to interview a steel executive and several reporters who had written stories about a statement by the executive. As part of an investigation of foreign lobbying efforts on sugar quota legislation in 1961 and 1962, Attorney General Kennedy requested wiretaps on a Congressional aide, three executive officials, and two American lobbyists, including a Washington law firm.

Nevertheless, the political misuse of the FBI under the Johnson and Nixon administrations appears to have been more extensive than in previous years.

Under the Johnson administration, the FBI was used to gather and report political intelligence on the, administration's partisan opponents in the last days of the 1964 and 1968 Presidential election campaigns. In the closing days of the 1964 campaign, Presidential aide Bill Moyers asked the Bureau to conduct "name checks" on all persons employed in Senator Goldwater's Senate office, and information on two staff members was reported to the White House. Similarly, in the last two weeks of the 1968 campaign, the Johnson White House requested an investigation (including indirect electronic surveillance and direct physical surveillance) of Mrs. Anna Chennault, a prominent Republican leader, and her relationships with certain South Vietnamese officials. This investigation also included an FBI check of Vice Presidential candidate Spiro Agnew's long distance telephone call records, apparently at the personal request of President Johnson.

Another investigation for the Johnson White House involved executive branch officials who took part in the criminal investigation of former Johnson Senate aide Bobby Baker. When Baker's trial began in 1967, it was revealed that one of the government witnesses had been "wired" to record his conversations with Baker. Presidential aide Marvin Watson told the FBI that Johnson was quite "exercised," and the Bureau was ordered to conduct a discreet "run down" on the former head of the Justice Department's Criminal Division and four Treasury Department officials who had been responsible for "wiring" the witness. The Bureau was specifically insisted to include any associations between those persons and Robert Kennedy.

Several Johnson White House requests were directed at critics of the war in Vietnam, at newsmen, and at other opponents. According a Bureau memorandum, White House aide Marvin Watson attempted to disguise his, and the President's interest in such requests asking the FBI to channel its replies through a lower level White House staff member.

In 1966, Watson asked the FBI to monitor the televised hearings of the Senate Foreign Relations Committee on Vietnam policy and prepare a memorandum comparing statements of the President's Senate critics with "the Communist Party line." Similarly, in 1967 when seven Senators made statements criticizing the bombing of North Vietnam, Watson requested (and the Bureau delivered) a "blind memorandum" setting forth information from FBI files on each of the Senators. Among the data supplied were the following items:

> Senator Clark was quoted in the press as stating that the three major threats to America are the military-industrial complex, the Federal Bureau of Investigation, and the Central Intelligence Agency.

> Senator McGovern spoke at a rally sponsored by the Chicago, Committee for a Sane Nuclear Policy, a pacifist group. Senator McGovern stated that the "United States was making too much of the communist take-over of Cuba."

> [Another Senator now deceased] has, on many occasions, publicly criticized United States policy toward Vietnam. He frequently speaks before groups throughout the United States on this subject. He has been reported as intentionally entering into controversial areas so that his services as a speaker for which he receives a fee, will be in demand.

The Johnson administration also requested information on contacts between members of Congress and certain foreign officials known to oppose the United States presence in Vietnam. According to FBI records, President Johnson believed these foreign officials had generated "much of the protest concerning his Vietnam policy, particularly the hearings in the Senate."

White House requests were not limited to critical Congressmen. Ordinary citizens who sent telegrams protesting the Vietnam war to the White House were also the subject of Watson requests for FBI name check reports. Presidential aide Jake Jacobsen asked for name checks on persons whose names appeared in the Congressional Record as signers of a letter to Senator Wayne Morse expressing support for his criticism of U.S. Vietnam policy. On at least one occasion, a request was channeled through Attorney General Ramsey Clark, who supplied Watson (at the latter's request) with a summary of information on the National Committee for a Sane Nuclear Policy.

Other individuals who were the subject of such name check requests under the Johnson Administration included NBC Commentator David Brinkley, Associated

Press reporter Peter Arnett, columnist Joseph Kraft, Life magazine Washington bureau chief Richard Stolley, Chicago Daily News Washington bureau chief Peter Lisagor, and Ben W. Gilbert of the Washington Post. The Johnson White House also requested (and received) name check reports on the authors of books critical of the Warren Commission report; some of these reports included derogatory information about the personal lives of the individuals.

The Nixon administration continued the practice of using the FBI to produce political information. In 1969 John Ehrlichman, counsel to President Nixon, asked the FBI to conduct a "name check" on Joseph Duffy, chairman of Americans for Democratic Action. Data in Bureau files covered Duffy's "handling arrangements" for an antiwar teach-in in 1965, his position as State Coordinator of the group "Negotiation Now" in 1967, and his activity as chairman of Connecticut Citizens for McCarthy in 1968.

Presidential aide H. R. Haldeman requested a name check on CBS reporter Daniel Schorr. In this instance, the FBI mistakenly considered the request to be for a full background investigation and began to conduct interviews. These interviews made the inquiry public. Subsequently, White House officials stated (falsely) that Schorr was under consideration for an executive appointment. In another case, a Bureau memorandum states that Vice President Agnew asked the FBI for information about Rev. Ralph David Abernathy, then head of the Southern Christian Leadership Conference, for use in "destroying Abernathy's credibility." (Agnew has denied that he made such a request, but agrees that he received the information.)

Several White House requests involved the initiation of electronic surveillance. Apparently on the instructions of President Nixon's aide John Ehrlichman and Director Hoover, FBI Assistant Director William C. Sullivan arranged for the microphone surveillance of the hotel, room of columnist Joseph Kraft while be was visiting a foreign country. Kraft was also the target of physical surveillance by the FBI. There is no record of any specific "national security" rationale for the surveillance.

Similarly, although the "17" wiretaps were authorized ostensibly to investigate national security "leaks," there is no record in three of the cases of any national security claim having been advanced in their support. Two of the targets were domestic affairs advisers at the White House, with no foreign affairs duties and no access to foreign policy materials. A third was a White House speechwriter who had been overheard on an existing tap agreeing to provide a reporter with background on a presidential speech concerning, not foreign policy, but revenue sharing and welfare reform.

Subfinding (b)

In some cases, political or personal information was not specifically requested, but was nevertheless collected and disseminated to administration officials as part of investigations they had requested. Neither the FBI nor the recipients differentiated in these cases between national security or law enforcement information and purely political intelligence.

In some instances, the initial request for or dissemination of information was premised upon law enforcement or national security purposes. However, pursuant to such a request, information was furnished which obviously could serve only partisan or personal interests. As one Bureau official summarized its attitude, the FBI "did not decide what was political or what represented potential strife and violence. We are an investigative agency and we passed on all data."

Examples from the Eisenhower, Kennedy, Johnson, and Nixon administrations illustrate this failure to distinguish between political and nonpolitical intelligence. They include, the FBI's reports to the White House in 1956 on NAACP lobbying activities, the intelligence about the legislative process produced by the "sugar lobby" wiretaps in 1961-1962, the purely political data disseminated to the White House on the credentials challenge in the 1964 Democratic Convention, and dissemination of both political and personal information from the "leak" wiretaps in 1969-1972.

(i) The NAACP

In early 1956 Director Hoover sent the White House a memorandum describing the "potential for violence" in the current "racial situation". Later reports to the White House, however, went far beyond intelligence about possible violence; they included extensive inside information about NAACP lobbying efforts, such as the following:

A report on "meetings held in Chicago" in connection with a planned Leadership Conference on Civil Rights to be held in Washington under the sponsorship of the NAACP.

An extensive report on the Leadership Conference, based on the Bureau's "reliable sources" and describing plans of Conference delegations to visit Senators Paul Douglas, Herbert Lehman, Wayne Morse, Hubert Humphrey, and John Bricker. The report also summarized a speech by Roy Wilkins, other conference proceedings, and the report of "an informant" that the United Auto Workers was a "predominant organization" at the conference.

Another report on the conference included an account of what transpired at meetings between conference delegations and Senators Paul Douglas and Everett Dirksen.

A report including the information that two New Jersey congressmen would sign a petition to the Attorney General.

A presidential aide suggested that Hoover brief the Cabinet on "developments in the South." Director Hoover's Cabinet briefing also included political intelligence. He covered not only the NAACP conference, but also the speeches and political activities of Southern Senators and Governors and the formation of the Federation for Constitutional Government with Southern Congressmen and Governors on its advisory board.

(ii) The Sugar Lobby

The electronic surveillance of persons involved in a foreign country's lobbying activities on sugar quota legislation in 1961-1962, authorized by Attorney General Robert Kennedy for the White House, also produced substantial political intelligence unrelated to the activities of foreign officials. Such information came from wiretaps both on foreign officials and on American citizens, as well as from the microphone surveillance of the chairman of the House Agriculture Committee when he met with foreign officials in a New York hotel room. The following are examples of the purely political (and personal) by-product:

A particular lobbyist "mentioned he is working on the Senate and has the Republicans all lined up."

The same lobbyist said that "he had seen two additional representatives on the House Agriculture Committee, one of whom was 'dead set against us' and who may reconsider, and the other was neutral and 'may vote for us.' "

The Agriculture Committee chairman believed "he had accomplished nothing" and that "he had been fighting over the Rules Committee and this had interfered with his attempt to organize."

The "friend" of a foreign official "was under strong pressure from the present administration, and since the 'friend' is a Democrat, it would be very difficult for him to present a strong front to a Democratic Administration."

A lobbyist stated that Secretary of State Rusk "had received a friendly reception by the Committee and there appeared to be no problem with regard to the sugar bill."

A foreign official was reported to be in contact with two Congressmen's secretaries "for reasons other than business." The official asked one of the secretaries to tell the other that he "would not be able to call her that evening" and that one of his associates "was planning to take [the two secretaries and another Congressional aide] to Bermuda."

The FBI's own evaluation of these wiretaps indicates that they "undoubtedly ... contributed heavily to the Administration's success" in passing the legislation it desired.

(iii) The 1964 Democratic Convention

Political reports were disseminated by the FBI to the White House from the 1964 Democratic convention in Atlantic City. These reports, from the FBI's "special squad" at the convention, apparently resulted from a civil disorders intelligence investigation which got out of hand because no one was willing to shut off the partisan by-product. They centered on the Mississippi Freedom Democratic Party's credentials challenge. Examples of the political intelligence which flowed from FBI surveillance at the 1964 convention include the following:

> Dr. Martin Luther King and an associate "were drafting a telegram to President Johnson . . . to register a mild protest. According to King, the President pledged complete neutrality regarding the selecting of the proper Mississippi delegation to be seated at the convention. King feels that the Credentials Committee will turn down the Mississippi Freedom Party and that they are doing this because the President exerted pressure on the committee along this line."

Another associate of Dr. King contacted a member of the MFDP who "said she thought King should see Governor Endicott Peabody of Massachusetts, Mayor Robert Wagner of New York City, Governor Edmund G. (Pat) Brown of California, Mayor Richard Daley of Chicago, and Governor John W. King of New Hampshire." The purpose was "to urge them to call the White House directly and put pressure on the White House in behalf of the MFDP."

"MFDP leaders have asked Reverend King to call Governor Egan of Alaska and Governor Burns of Hawaii in an attempt to enlist their support. According to the MFDP spokesman, the Negro Mississippi Party needs these two states plus California and New York for the roll call tonight."

An SCLC staff member told a representative of the MFDP: "Off the record, of course, you know we will accept the Green compromise proposed." This referred to "the proposal of Congresswoman Edith Green of Oregon."

In a discussion between Dr. King and another civil rights leader, the question of "a Vice- Presidential nominee came up and King asked what [the other leader] thought of Hugh [sic] Humphrey, and [the other leader] said Hugh Humphrey is not going to get it, that Johnson needs a Catholic ... and therefore the Vice-President will be Muskie of Maine."

An unsigned White House memorandum disclosing Dr. King's strategy in connection with a meeting to be, attended by President Johnson suggests that there was political use of these FBI reports.

(iv) The "17" Wiretaps.

The Nixon White House learned a substantial amount of purely political intelligence from wiretaps to investigate "leaks" of classified information placed on three newsmen and fourteen executive officials during 1969-1971. The following illustrate the range of data supplied:

One of the targets "recently stated that he was to spend an hour with Senator Kennedy's Vietnam man, as Senator Kennedy is giving a speech on the 15th."

Another target said that Senator Fulbright postponed congressional hearings on Vietnam because he did not believe they would be popular at that time.

A well-known television news correspondent "was very distressed over having been 'singled out' by the Vice President."

A friend of one of the targets said the Washington Star planned to do an article critical of Henry Kissinger.

One of the targets helped former Ambassador Sargent Shriver write a press release criticizing a recent speech by President Nixon in which the President "attacked" certain Congressmen.

One of the targets told a friend it "is clear the Administration will win on the ABM by a two-vote margin. He said 'They've got [a Senator] and they've got [another Senator].'."

A friend of one of the targets wanted to see if a Senator would "buy a new amendment" and stated that "they" were "going to meet with" another Senator.

A friend of one of the targets described a Senator as "marginal" on the Cooper-Church Amendment and stated that another Senator might be persuaded to support it.

One of the targets said Senator Mondale was in a "dilemma" over the "trade bill."

A friend of one of the targets said he had spoken to former President Johnson and "Johnson would not back Senator Muskie for the Presidency as he intended to stay out of politics."

There is at least one clear example of the political use of such information. After the FBI Director informed the White House that former Secretary of Defense Clark Clifford planned to write a magazine article criticizing President Nixon's Vietnam policy, White House aide Jeb Stuart Magruder advised John Ehrlichman and H. R. Haldeman that "we are in a position to counteract this article in any number of ways." It is also significant that, after May 1970, the FBI Director's letters summarizing the results of the wiretaps were no longer sent to Henry Kissinger, the President's national security advisor, but to the President's political advisor, H. R. Haldeman.

These four illustrations from administrations of both political parties indicate clearly that direct channels of communication between top FBI officials and the White House, combined with the failure to screen out extraneous information, and coupled with overly broad investigations in the first instance, have been sources of flagrant political abuse of the intelligence process.

Subfinding (c.)

The FBI has also volunteered information to Presidents and their staffs, without having been asked for it, sometimes apparently to curry favor with the current administration. Similarly, the FBI has assembled information on its critics and on political figures it believed might influence public attitudes or Congressional support.

There have been numerous instances over the past three decades where the FBI volunteered to its superiors purely political or personal information believed by the FBI Director to be "of interest" to them.

The following are examples of the information in Director Hoover's letters under the Truman, Eisenhower, Kennedy, and Johnson administrations.

To Major General Harry Vaughn, Military Aide to President Truman, a report on the activities of a former Roosevelt aide who was trying to influence the Truman administration's appointments.

To Matthew J. Connelly, Secretary to President Truman, a report from a "very confidential source" about a meeting of newspaper representatives in Chicago to plan publication of stories exposing organized crime and corrupt politicians.

To Dillon Anderson, Special Assistant to President Eisenhower, the advance text of a speech to be delivered by a prominent labor leader.

To Robert Cutler, Special Assistant to President Eisenhower, a report of a "confidential source" on plans of Mrs. Eleanor Roosevelt to hold a reception for the head of a civil rights group.

To Attorney General Robert Kennedy, information from a Bureau "source" regarding plans of a group to publish allegations about the President's personal life.

To Attorney General Kennedy, a summary of material in FBI files on a prominent entertainer which the FBI Director thought "may be of interest".

To Marvin Watson, Special Assistant to President Johnson, a summary of data in Bureau files on the author of a play satirizing the President.

As these illustrations indicate, the FBI Director provided such data to administrations of both political parties without apparent partisan favoritism.

Additionally, during the Nixon Administration, the FBI's INLET (Intelligence Letter) Program for sending regular short summaries of FBI intelligence to the White House was used on one occasion to provide information on the purely personal relationship between an entertainer and the subject of an FBI domestic intelligence investigation. SACs were instructed under the INLET program to submit to Bureau headquarters items with an "unusual twist" or regarding "prominent" persons.

One reason for the Bureau's volunteering information to the White House was to please the Administration and thus presumably to build high-level political support for the FBI. Thus, a 1975 Bureau report on the Atlantic City episode states:

> One [agent said], "I would like to state that at no time did I ever consider (it) to be a political operation but it was obvious that DeLoach wanted to impress Jenkins and Moyers with the Bureau's ability to develop information which would be of interest to them." Furthermore, in response to a question as to whether the Bureau's services were being utilized for political reasons, [another] answered, "No. I do recall, however, that on one occasion I was present when DeLoach held a lengthy telephone conversation with Walter Jenkins. They appeared to be discussing the President's 'image.' At the end of the conversation DeLoach told us something to the effect, 'that may have sounded a little political to you but this doesn't do the Bureau any harm.'"

In addition to providing information useful to superiors, the Bureau assembled information on its own critics and on political figures it believed might influence public attitudes or congressional support. FBI Director Hoover had massive amounts of information at his fingertips. As indicated above, he could have the Bureau's files checked on anyone of interest to him. He personally received political information and "personal tidbits" from the special agents in charge of FBI field offices. 87 This information, both from the files and Hoover's personal sources, was available to discredit critics.

The following are examples of how the Bureau disseminated information to discredit its opponents:

In 1949 the FBI provided Attorney General J. Howard McGrath and Presidential aide Harry Vaughn inside information on plans of the Lawyers Guild to denounce Bureau surveillance so they would have an opportunity to prepare a rebuttal well in advance of the expected criticism.

In 1960, when the Knoxville Area Human Relations Council in Tennessee charged that the FBI was practicing racial discrimination, the Bureau conducted name checks on members of the Council's board of directors and sent the results to Attorney General William Rogers, including derogatory personal allegations and political affiliations from as far back as the late thirties and early forties.

When a reporter wrote stories critical of the Bureau, he was not only refused any further interviews, but an FBI official in charge of press relations also spread derogatory personal information about him to other newsmen.

The Bureau also maintained a "not to contact list' of "those individuals known to be hostile to the Bureau." Director Hoover specifically ordered that "each name" on the list "should be the subject of memo."

This request for "a memo" on each critic meant that, before someone was placed on the list, the Director received, in effect, a "name check" report summarizing "what we had in our files" on the individual.

In addition to assembling information on critics, name checks were run as a matter of regular Bureau policy on all "newly elected Governors and Congressmen." The Crime Records Division instructed the field offices to submit "summary memoranda" on such officials, covering both "public source information" and "any other information that they had in their files." These "summary memoranda" were provided to Director Hoover and maintained in the Crime Records Division for use in "congressional liason" — which the Division head said included "selling" hostile Congressmen on "liking the FBI."

It has been widely believed among Members of Congress that the Bureau had information on each of them. The impact of that belief led Congressman Boggs to state:

> Our apathy in this Congress, our silence in this House, our very fear of speaking out in other forums has watered the roots and hastened the growth of a vine of tyranny which is ensnaring that Constitution and Bill of Rights which we are each sworn to uphold.
>
> Our society can survive many challenges and many threats.
>
> It cannot survive a planned and programmed fear of its own government bureaus and agencies.

Subfinding (d)

The FBI has also used intelligence as a vehicle for covert efforts to influence social policy and political action.

The FBI's interference with the democratic process was not the result of any overt decision to reshape society in conformance with Bureau-approved norms. Rather, the Bureau's actions were the natural consequence of attitudes within the Bureau toward social change, combined with a strong sense of duty to protect society — even from its own "wrong" choices.

The FBI saw itself as the guardian of the public order, and believed that it had a responsibility to counter threats to that order, using any means available. At the same time, the Bureau's assessment of what constituted a "threat" was influenced by its attitude toward the forces of change. In effect, the Bureau chose sides in the major social movements of the last fifteen years, and then attacked the other side with the unchecked power at its disposal.

The clearest proof of the Bureau's attitude toward change is its own rhetoric. The language used in internal documents which were not intended to be disseminated outside the Bureau is that of the highly charged polemic revealing clear biases.

For example, in one of its annual internal reports on COINTELPRO, the Bureau took pride in having given "the lie" to what it called "the Communist canard" that "the Negro is downtrodden and has no opportunities in America." This was accomplished by placing a story in a newspaper in which a "wealthy Negro industrialist" stated that "the Negro will have to earn respectability and a responsible position in the community before he is accepted as an equal." It is significant that this view was expressed at about the same time as the civil rights movement's March on Washington, which was intended to focus public attention on the denial of opportunities to black Americans, and which rejected the view that inalienable rights have to be "earned."

The rhetoric used in dealing with the Vietnam War and those in opposition to it is even more revealing. The war in Vietnam produced sharply divided opinions in the country; again, the Bureau knew which side it was on. For instance, fifty copies of an article entitled "Rabbi in Vietnam Says Withdrawal Not The Answer" were anonymously mailed by the FBI to members of the Vietnam Day Committee to "convince" the recipients "of the correctness of the U.S. foreign policy in Vietnam." 99

The Bureau also ordered copies of a film called "While Brave Men Die" which depicted "communists, left-wing and pacifist activities associated with the so-called 'peace movement' or student agitational demonstrations in opposition to the United States position in Vietnam." The film was to be used for training Bureau personnel in connection with "increased responsibilities relating to communist inspired student agitational activities."

In the same vein, a directive to the Chicago field office shortly after the 1968 Democratic Convention instructed it to "obtain all possible evidence" that would "disprove" charges that the Chicago police used undue force in dealing with antiwar demonstrations at the Convention:

Once again, the liberal press and the bleeding hearts and the forces on the left are taking advantage of the situation in Chicago surrounding the Democratic National Convention to attack the police and organized law enforcement agencies.... We should be mindful of this situation and develop all possible evidence to expose this activity and to refute these false allegations.

The Bureau also attempted to enforce its view of sexual morality. For example, two students became COINTELPRO targets when they defended the use of a four-letter word, even though the demonstration in which they participated "does not appear to be inspired by the New Left," because it "shows obvious disregard for decency and established morality." An anonymous letter purportedly from an irate parent and an article entitled "Free Love Comes to Austin" were mailed to a state senator and the chairman of the University of Texas Board of Regents to aid in "forcing the University to take action against those administrators who are permitting an atmosphere to build up on campus that will be a fertile field for the New Left." And a field office was outraged at the distribution on campus of a newspaper called SCREW, which was described as "containing a type of filth that could only originate in a depraved mind. It is representative of the type of mentality that is following the New Left theory of immorality on certain college campuses."

As these examples demonstrate, the FBI believed it had a duty to maintain the existing social and political order. Whether or not one agrees with the Bureau's views, it is profoundly disturbing that an agency of the government secretly attempted to impose its views on the American people.

(i) Use of the Media

The FBI attempted to influence public opinion by supplying information or articles to "confidential sources" in the news media. The FBI's Crime Records Division was responsible for covert liaison with the media to advance two main domestic intelligence objectives:

(1) providing derogatory information to the media intended to generally discredit the activities or ideas of targeted groups or individuals; and (2) disseminating unfavorable articles, news releases, and background information in order to disrupt particular activities.

Typically, a local FBI agent would provide information to a "friendly news source" on the condition "that the Bureau's interest in these matters is to be kept in the strictest confidence." Thomas E. Bishop, former Director of the Crime Records Division, testified that he kept a list of the Bureau's "press friends" in his desk. Bishop and one of his predecessors indicated that the FBI sometimes refused to cooperate with reporters critical of the Bureau or its Director.

Bishop stated that as a "general rule," the Bureau disseminated only "public record information" to its media contacts, but this category was viewed by the Bureau to include any information which could conceivably be obtained by close scrutiny of even the most obscure publications.

Within these parameters, background information supplied to reporters "in most cases [could] include everything" in the Bureau files on a targeted individual; the selection of information for publication would be left to the reporter's judgment.

There are numerous examples of authorization for the preparation and dissemination of unfavorable information to discredit generally the activities and ideas of a target;

-- FBI headquarters solicited information from field offices "on a continuing basis" for "prompt ... dissemination to the news media ... to discredit the New Left movement and its adherents." Headquarters requested, among other things, that:

> specific data should be furnished depicting the scurrilous and depraved nature of many of the characters, activities, habits and living conditions representative of New Left adherents.

Field Offices were to be exhorted that "Every avenue of possible embarrassment must be vigorously and enthusiastically explored."

-FBI headquarters authorized a Field Office to furnish a media contact with "background information and any arrest record" on a man affiliated with "a radical New Left element" who had been "active in showing films on the Black Panthers and police in action at various universities during student rioting." The media contact had requested material from the Bureau which "would have a detrimental effect on [the target's] activities."

-- Photographs depicting a radical group's apartment as "a shambles with lewd, obscene and revolutionary slogans displayed on the walls" were furnished to a free-lance writer. The directive from headquarters said: "As this publicity will be derogatory in nature and might serve to neutralize the group, it is being approved."

-- The Boston Field Office was authorized to furnish "derogatory information about the Nation of Islam (NOI) to established source [name excised]":

> Your suggestions concerning material to furnish [name] are good. Emphasize to him that the NOI predilection for violence, preaching of race hatred, and hypocrisy, should be exposed. Material furnished [name] should be either public source or known to enough people as to protect your sources. Insure the Bureau's interest in this matter is completely protected by [name].

One Bureau-inspired documentary on the NOI reached an audience of 200,000. Although the public was to be convinced that the NOI was "violent", the Bureau knew this was not in fact true of the organization as a whole.

-- The Section which supervised the COINTELPRO against the Communist Party intended to discredit a couple "identified with the Communist Party movement" by preparing a news release on the drug arrest of their son, which was to be furnished to "news media contacts and sources on Capitol Hill." A Bureau official observed that the son's "arrest and the Party connections of himself and his parents presents an excellent opportunity for exploitation." The news release noted that "the Russian-born mother is currently under a deportation order" and had a former marriage to the son of a prominent Communist Party member. The release added: "the Red Chinese have long used narcotics to help weaken the youth of target countries."

-- When the wife of a Communist Party leader purchased a new car, the FBI prepared a news item for distribution to "a cooperative news media source" mocking the leader's "prosperity" "as a disruptive tactic." The item commented sarcastically that "comrades of the self-proclaimed leader of the American working class should not allow this example of [the leader's] prosperity to discourage their continued contributions to Party coffers."

-- After a public meeting in New York City, where "the handling of the [JFK assassination] investigation was criticized," the FBI prepared a news item for placement "with a cooperative news media source" to discredit the meeting on the grounds that "a reliable [FBI] source" had reported a "convicted perjurer and identified espionage agent as present in the audience."

-- As part of the New Left COINTELPRO, the FBI sent a letter under a fictitious name to Life magazine to "call attention to the unsavory character" of the editor of an underground magazine, who was characterized as "one of the moving forces behind the Youth International Party, commonly known as the Yippies." To counteract a recent Life "article favorable" to the Yippie editor, the FBI's fictitious letter said that "the cuckoo editor of an unimportant smutty little rag" should be "left in the sewers."

Much of the Bureau's use of the media to influence public opinion was directed at disrupting specific activities or plans of targeted groups or individuals:

-- In March 1968, FBI Headquarters granted authority for furnishing to a "cooperative national news media source" an article "designed to curtail success of Martin Luther King's fund raising" for the poor people's march on Washington, D.C. by asserting that "an embarrassment of riches has befallen King . . . and King doesn't need the money." To further this objective, Headquarters authorized the Miami Office "to furnish data concerning money wasted by the Poor People's Campaign" to a friendly news reporter on the usual condition that "the Bureau must not be revealed as the source."

The Section Chief in charge of the Black Nationalist COINTELPRO also recommended that "photographs of demonstrators" at the march should be furnished; he attached six photographs of Poor People's Campaign participants at a Cleveland rally, accompanied by the note: "These show the militant, aggressive appearance of the participants and might be of interest to a cooperative news source."

--As part of the New Left COINTELPRO, authority was granted to the Atlanta Field Office to furnish a newspaper editor who had "written numerous editorials praising the Bureau" with "information to supplement that already known to him from public sources concerning subversive influences in the Atlanta peace movement. His use of this material in well-timed articles would be used to thwart the [upcoming] demonstrations."

-- An FBI Special Agent in Chicago contacted a reporter for a major newspaper to arrange for the publication of an article which was expected to "greatly encourage factional antagonisms during the SDS Convention" by publicizing the attempt of "an underground communist organization" to take over SDS. This contact resulted in an article headlined "Red Unit Seeks SDS Rule."

-- FBI Director Hoover approved a Field Office plan "to get cooperative news media to cover closed meetings of Students for a Democratic Society (SDS) and other New Left groups" with the aim of "disrupting them."

-- Several months after COINTELPRO operations were supposed to have terminated, the FBI attempted to discredit attorney Leonard Boudin at the time of his defense of Daniel Ellsberg in the Pentagon Papers case. The FBI "called to the attention" of the Washington bureau chief of a major news service information on Boudin's alleged "sympathy" and "legal services" for "communist causes." The reporter placed a detailed news release on the wires which cited Boudin's "identification with Leftist causes" and included references to the arrest of Boudin's daughter, his legal representation of the Cuban government and "Communist sympathizer" Paul Robeson, and the statement that "his name also has been connected with a number of other alleged communist front groups." In a handwritten note, J. Edgar Hoover directed that copies of the news release be sent to "Haldeman, A. G., and Deputy."

The Bureau sometimes used its media contacts to prevent or postpone the publication of articles it considered favorable to its targets or unfavorable to the FBI. For example, to influence articles which related to the FBI, the Bureau took advantage of a close relationship with a high official of a major national magazine, described in an FBI memorandum as "our good friend." Through this relationship, the FBI "squelched" an "unfavorable article against the Bureau" written by a free-lance writer about an FBI investigation; "postponed publication" of an article on another FBI case; "forestalled publication" of an article by Dr. Martin Luther King, Jr.; and received information about proposed editing of King's articles.

The Bureau also attempted to influence public opinion by using news media sources to discredit dissident groups by linking them to the Communist Party:

-- A confidential source who published a "self -described conservative weekly newspaper" was anonymously mailed information on a church's sponsorship of efforts to abolish the House Committee on Un-American activities. This prompted an article entitled "Locals to Aid Red Line," naming the minister, among others, as a local sponsor of what it termed a "Communist dominated plot" to abolish HUAC.

-- The Bureau targeted a professor who had been the president of a local peace center, a "coalition of anti-Vietnam and anti-draft groups." In 1968, he resigned temporarily to become state chairman of Eugene McCarthy's presidential campaign organization. Information on the professor's wife, who had apparently associated with Communist Party members in the early 1950's, was furnished to a newspaper editor to "expose those people at this time when they are receiving considerable publicity in order" to "disrupt the members" of the peace organization.

-- Other instances included an attempt to link a school boycott with the Communists by alerting newsmen to the boycott leader's plans to attend a literary reception at the Soviet mission; furnishing information to the media on the participation of the Communist Party presidential candidate in the United Farm Workers' picket line; "confidentially" informing established sources in three northern California newspapers that the San Francisco County Communist Party Committee had stated that civil rights groups were to "begin working" on the area's large newspapers "in an effort to secure greater employment of Negroes;" and furnishing information to the media on Socialist Workers Party participation in the Spring Mobilization Committee to End the War in Vietnam to "discredit" the antiwar group.

(ii) Attacks on Leaders

Through covert propaganda, the FBI not only attempted to influence public opinion on matters of social policy, but also directly intervened in the people's choice of leadership both through the electoral process and in other, less formal arenas.

For instance, the Bureau made plans to disrupt a possible "Peace Party" ticket in the 1968 elections. One field office noted that "effectively tabbing as communists or as communist-backed the more hysterical opponents of the President on the Vietnam question in the midst of the presidential campaign would be a real boon to Mr. Johnson."

In the FBI's COINTELPRO programs, political candidates were targeted for disruption. The document which originated the Socialist Workers Party COINTELPRO noted that the SWP "has, over the past several years, been openly espousing its line on a local and national basis through running candidates for public office." The Bureau decided to "alert the public to the fact that the SWP is not just another socialist group but follows the revolutionary principles of Marx, Lenin, and Engels as interpreted by Leon Trotsky." Several SWP candidates were targeted, usually by leaking derogatory information about the candidate to the press.

Other COINTELPRO programs also included attempts to disrupt campaigns. For example, a Midwest lawyer running for City Council was targeted because he and his firm had represented "subversives". The Bureau sent an anonymous letter to several community leaders which decried his "communist background" and labelled him a "Charlatan." Under a fictitious name, the Bureau sent a letter to a television on which the candidate was to appear, enclosing a series of questions about his clients and his activities which it believed should be asked. The candidate was defeated. He later ran (successfully, as it happened) for a judgeship. The Bureau attempted to disrupt this subsequent, successful campaign for a judgeship by using an anticommunist group to distribute fliers and write letters opposing his candidacy.

In another instance, the FBI attempted to have a Democratic Party fundraising affair raided by the state Alcoholic Beverage Control Commission. The fund raiser was targeted because of two of the candidates who would be present. One, a state assemblyman running for reelection, was active in the Vietnam Day Committee; the other, the Democratic candidate for Congress, had been a sponsor of the National Committee to Abolish the House Committee on Un-American Activities and had led demonstrations opposing the manufacture of napalm bombs.

Although the disruption of election campaigns is the clearest example, the FBI's interference, with the political process was much broader. For example, all of the COINTELPRO programs were aimed at the leadership of dissident groups.

In one case, the Bureau's plans to discredit a civil rights leader included an attempt to replace him with a candidate chosen by the Bureau. During 1964, the FBI began a massive program to discredit Dr. Martin Luther King, Jr. and to "neutralize" his effectiveness as the leader of the civil rights movement. On January 8, 1964, Assistant Director William C. Sullivan proposed that the FBI select a new "national Negro leader" as Dr. King's successor after the Bureau had taken Dr. King "off his pedestal":

> When this is done, and it can and will be done . . . the Negroes will be left without a national leader of sufficiently compelling personality to steer them in the right direction. This is what could happen, but need not happen if the right kind of Negro leader could at this time be gradually developed so as to overshadow Dr. King and be in the position to assume the role of leadership of the Negro people, when King has been completely discredited.

> I want to make it clear at once that I don't propose that the FBI in any way became involved openly as the sponsor of a Negro leader to overshadow Martin Luther King.... But I do propose that I be given permission to explore further this entire matter....

> If this thing can be set up properly without the Bureau in any way becoming directly involved, I think it would not only be a great help to the FBI but would be a fine thing for the country at large. While I am not specifying at this moment, there are various ways in which the FBI could give this entire matter the proper direction and development. There are highly placed contacts of the FBI who might be very helpful to further such a step . . . .

The Bureau's efforts to discredit Dr. King are discussed more fully elsewhere. It is, however, important to note here that some of the Bureau's efforts coincided with Dr. King's activities and statements concerning major social and political issues.

(iii) Exaggerating The Threat

The Bureau also used its control over the infomiation-gathering process to shape the views of government officials and the public on the threats it perceived to the social order. For example, the FBI exaggerated the strength of the Communist Party and its influence over the civil rights and anti-Vietnam war movements.

Opponents of civil rights legislation in the early 1960s had charged that such legislation was "a part of the world Communist conspiracy to divide and conquer our country from within." The truth or falsity of these charges was a matter of concern to the administration, Congress, and the public. Since the Bureau was assigned to compile intelligence on Communist activity, its estimate was sought and, presumably, relied upon. Accordingly, in 1963, the Domestic Intelligence Division submitted a memorandum to Director Hoover detailing the CPUSA's "efforts" to exploit black Americans, which it concluded were an "obvious failure."

Director Hoover was not pleased with this conclusion. He sent a sharp message back to the Division which, according to the Assistant Director in charge, made it "evident that we had to change our ways or we would all be out on the street." Another memorandum was 'therefore written to give the Director "what Hoover wanted to hear."

The memorandum stated, "The Director is correct;" it called Dr. Martin Luther King, Jr. "the most dangerous Negro of the future in this Nation from the standpoint of communism, the Negro, and national security;" and it concluded that it was "unrealistic" to "limit ourselves" to "legalistic proofs or definitely conclusive evidence" that the Communist Party wields "substantial influence over Negroes which one day could become decisive."

Although the Division still had not said the influence was decisive, by 1964 the Director testified before the House Appropriations Subcommittee that the "Communist influence" in the "Negro movement" was "vitally important." "I Only someone with access to the underlying information would note that the facts could be interpreted quite differently.

A similar exaggeration occurred in some of the Bureau's statements on communist influence on the anti-Vietnam war demonstrations.

In April 1965 President Johnson met with Director Hoover to discuss Johnson's "concern over the anti-Vietnam situation." According to Hoover, Johnson said he had "no doubt" that Communists were "behind the disturbances." Hoover agreed, stating that upcoming demonstrations in eighty-five cities were being planned by the Students for a Democratic Society and that SDS was "largely infiltrated by communists and [it] has been woven into the civil rights situation which we know has large communist influence."

Immediately after the meeting, however, Hoover told his associates that the Bureau might not be able to "technically state" that SDS was "an actual communist organization." The FBI merely knew that there were "communists in it." Hoover instructed, however, "What I want to get to the President is the background with emphasis upon the communist influence therein so that he will know exactly what the picture is." The Director added that he wanted "a good, strong memorandum" pinpointing that the demonstrations had been "largely participated in by communists even though they may not have initiated them;" the Bureau could "at least" say that they had "joined and forced the issue." According to the Director, President Johnson was "quite concerned" and wanted "prompt and quick action."

Once again, the Bureau wrote a report which made Communist "efforts" sound like Communist success. The eight page memorandum detailed all of the Communist Party's attempts to "encourage" domestic dissent by "a crescendo of criticism aimed at negating every effort of the United States to prevent Vietnam from being engulfed by communist aggressors." Twice in the eight pages, for a total of two and a half sentences, it pointed out that most demonstrators were not Party members and their decisions were not initiated or controlled by the communists. Each of these brief statements moreover, was followed by a qualification: (1) "however, the Communist Party, USA ... has vigorously supported these groups and exerted influence;" (2) "While the March [on Washington] was not Communist initiated ... Communist Party members from throughout the nation participated." [Emphasis added.]

The rest of the memorandum is an illustration of what former Assistant Director Sullivan called "interpretive" memo writing in which Communist efforts and desires are emphasized without an evaluation of whether they had been or were likely to be successful.

The exaggeration of Communist participation, both by the FBI and White House staff members relying on FBI reports, could only have had the effect of reinforcing President Johnson's original tendency to discount dissent against the Vietnam War as "Communist inspired"—a belief shared by his successor. It is impossible to measure the full effect of this distorted perception at the very highest policymaking level.

F. Inadequate Controls On Dissemination And Retention

Major Finding
The Committee finds that the product of intelligence investigations has been disseminated without adequate controls. Reports on lawful political activity and law-abiding citizens have been disseminated to agencies having no proper reason to receive them. Information that should have been discarded, purged, or sealed, including the product of illegal techniques and overbroad investigations, has been retained and is available for future use.

Subfindings
(a) Agencies have volunteered massive amounts of irrelevant information to other officials and agencies and have responded unquestioningly in some instances to requests for data without assuring that the information would be used for a lawful purpose.

(b) Excessive dissemination has sometimes contributed to the inefficiency of the intelligence process itself.

(c.) Under the federal employee security program, unnecessary information about, the political beliefs and associations of prospective government employees has been disseminated.

(d) The FBI, which has been the "clearinghouse" for all domestic intelligence data, maintains in readily accessible files sensitive and derogatory personal information not relevant to any investigation, as well as information which was improperly or illegally obtained.

Elaboration of Findings
The adverse effects on privacy of the overbreadth of domestic intelligence collection and of the use of Intrusive Techniques have been magnified many times over by the dissemination practices of the collecting agencies. Information which should not have been gathered in the first place has gone beyond the initial agency to numerous other agencies and officials, thus compounding the original intrusion. The

amount disseminated within the Executive branch has often been so voluminous as to make it difficult to separate useful data from worthless detail.

The Committee's finding on Political Abuse describes dissemination of intelligence for the political advantage of high officials or the self-interest of an agency. The problems of excessive dissemination, however, include more than political use. Dissemination has not been confined to what is appropriate for law enforcement or other proper government purposes. Rather, any information which could have been conceived to be useful was passed on, and doubts were generally resolved in favor of dissemination. Until recently, none of the standards for the exchange of data among agencies has taken privacy interests into account. The same failure to consider privacy interests has characterized the retention of data by the original collecting agency.

Subfinding (a)

Agencies have volunteered massive amounts of irrelevant information to other officials and agencies and have responded unquestioningly in some instances to requests for data without assuring that the information would be used for a lawful purpose.

The following examples illustrate the extent of dissemination:

-- FBI reports on dissident Americans flowed to the CIA at a rate as high as 1,000 a month. CIA officials regarded any names in these reports as a standing requirement from the FBI for information about those persons.

-- In 1967 the Internal Security Division of the Justice Department was receiving 150 reports and memoranda a day from the FBI on "organizations and individuals engaged in agitational activity of one kind or another."

-- Attorney General Ramsey Clark could not "keep up with" the volume of FBI memoranda coming into him and to the Assistant Attorneys General on the 700,000 FBI investigations per year.

-- The Justice Department's IDIU sent its computer list of 10,000 to 12,000 American dissidents to the CIA's Operation CHAOS (which apparently found it useless) and to the Special Service Staff of the Internal Revenue Service which did use it as part of its program of tax investigations).

-- In fiscal year 1974 alone, the FBI, the Civil Service Commission, and military intelligence received over 367,000 requests for "national agency checks," or name checks of their files, on prospective federal government employees.

The information disseminated to other agencies has often been considered useless by the recipients. FBI officials have said they received "very little in the way of good product" from the National Security Agency's interception of the international communications of Americans. FBI officials also considered most of the material on "the domestic scene" sent to them from the CIA mail opening project to be irrelevant "junk." The Secret Service destroyed over ninety percent of the information disseminated to it by the FBI without ever putting it in its own intelligence files. Defense Department directives require the destruction of a great deal of information it receives from the FBI about civilians considered "threatening" to the military, including reports on civilian "subversion."

Sometimes dissemination has become almost an end in itself. The FBI would often anticipate what it considered to be the needs of other "appropriate agencies." The Bureau has disseminated data to military intelligence agencies, regardless of whether or not there was likely to be serious violence requiring the dispatch of troops; the Bureau also disseminated information when there was no connection between the subject of the report and any military personnel or facility. Consequently, the computerized and non-computerized domestic intelligence data banks compiled by the Continental Army Command cited the FBI as "data source" for about 80 percent of the information where a source was identified.

FBI dissemination to the military has shown how information can get into the hands of agencies which have no proper reason to receive it.

The FBI disseminated a large volume of information on domestic political activities to the CIA, thus providing a substantial part of the data for the CHAOS program. Much of this information was also furnished to the State Department." The FBI sometimes disseminated reports to the CIA and the State Department if the subject matter involved public discussion of national security policy and possible "subversive" influence.

The FBI was also the largest source of political targets for tax investigations by the Special Service Staff of the Internal Revenue Service. While still in its formative days, SSS was placed on the FBI's distribution list in response to a request from an Assistant IRS Commissioner for information regarding:

> various organizations of predominantly dissident or extremist nature and/or people prominently identified with those organizations.

The FBI, perceiving that SSS would "deal a blow to dissident elements," decided to supply reports relating to this broad category of individuals and organizations.

The FBI did not select the reports it forwarded on the basis of the presence of a probable tax violation, but on the basis of the political and ideological criteria IRS had supplied- yet the furnishing of the report resulted in establishment of an SSS file and, subject to resource limitations, to a review of possible tax liability. Among the other lists of "extremists," "subversives" and dissidents SSS received was a list of 2,300 organizations the FBI categorized as "Old Left," "New Left," and "Right Wing."

One reason for the Bureau's widespread dissemination of intelligence throughout the Executive branch was recalled by a former FBI official. In the late 1940s a sensitive espionage case involved a high government official. At that time the FBI held such information "very tightly," as it had during World War II. However, one item of information that "became rather significant" had allegedly "not been disseminated to the White House or the Secretary of State."

> Mr. Hoover was criticized for that, and frankly, he never forgot it. From then on, you might say, the policy was disseminate, disseminate, disseminate.

This testimony illustrates the dilemma of an agency which was blamed for inadequate dissemination, but never criticized for too much dissemination. In practice, this dilemma was resolved by passing on any information "which in any way even remotely suggested that there was a responsibility for another agency."

The following are examples of excessive dissemination, drawn from a random sample of materials in FBI headquarters files:

-- In 1969 the FBI disseminated to Army and Air Force intelligence, Secret Service, and the IDIU a report on a Black Student Union; the report which discussed "a tea" sponsored by the group to develop faculty-student "dialogue" as a junior college and the plans of the college to establish a course on "The History of the American Negro." There was no indication of violence whatsoever. Dissemination to the military intelligence agencies and Secret Service took place both at the field level and at headquarters in Washington, D.C. The information came from college officials.

-- In 1970 the FBI disseminated to military intelligence and the Secret Service (both locally and at Headquarters), as well as to the Justice Department (IDIU, Internal Security Division, and Civil Rights Division) a report received from a local police intelligence unit on the picketing of a local Industries of the Blind plant by "blind black workers" who were on strike. The sixteen-page report included a copy of a handbill distributed at a United Church of Christ announcing a meeting at the church to support the strike, as well as copies of "leaflets that had been distributed by the blind workers." The only hint of violence in this report was the opinion of a local police intelligence officer that "young black militants," who supported the strike by urging blacks to boycott white-owned stores in the community, might cause "confrontations that might result in violence."

-- The FBI disseminated a report on Dr. Carl McIntyre's American Christian Action Council to the Secret Service in 1972. The cover memorandum to Secret Service indicated that the group fell within the category of the FBI-Secret Service agreement described as "potentially dangerous because of background, emotional instability or activity in groups engaged in activities inimical to U.S." The report itself reflected no "activities inimical to" the country, but only plans to hold peaceful demonstrations. The report also discussed policies and activities of the group unrelated to demonstrations, including plans to enter lawsuits in "school busing" cases, opposition to "Nixon's China trip" and support for a constitutional amendment for "public school prayer." This data came from a Bureau informant.

-- In 1966 the FBI disseminated to the Army, Navy, and Air Force intelligence divisions, to the Secret Service (locally and at Headquarters), to the Justice Department and to the State Department a ten-page report on a "Free University." The report described in detail the courses offered, including such subjects as "Modern Film," "Workshop on Art and Values," "Contemporary Music," "Poetry Now," and "Autobiography and the Image of Self." Over thirty "associates" were listed by name, although only one was identified as having "subversive connections" (and his course had been "dropped because not enough students had registered.") Others were identified as "involved in Vietnam protest activities" or as being known to officials of a nearby established university as "problem people." The information came from several FBI informants and a confidential source.

-- In 1966 the FBI disseminated to "appropriate federal and local authorities," including military intelligence, Secret Service, the Department of State and Justice, and a campus security officers (who was a former FBI agent) a report on a group formed for "discussion on Vietnam." The "controlling influence" on the organization was said to be "the local Friends Meeting." Only one person characterized as "subversive" was active in the group. The report was devoted to describing a "speak out" demonstration attended by approximately 300 persons on a university campus. The gathering was entirely peaceful and included "speakers who supported U.S. policies in Viet Nam." The data came from two Bureau informants.

-- In 1969 the FBI disseminated reports to the White House, the CIA, the State Department, the three military intelligence agencies, Secret Service, the IDIU, the Attorney General, the Deputy Attorney General, and the Internal Security and Civil Rights Divisions on a meeting sponsored by a coalition of citizens concerned about the Anti Ballistic Missile. The only indication of "subversive" influence was that one woman married to a Communist was assisting in publicity work for the meeting. The reports described (from reliable FBI sources) the speakers, pro and con, including prominent scientists, academics, and a Defense Department spokesman.

-- In 1974 the FBI disseminated to the State Department, the Defense Intelligence Agency, the Secret Service, the Internal Security Division, and the Civil Disturbance Unit (formerly IDIU), extensive reports on a national conference on amnesty for war resisters. One of the participants had "recently organized [a] nonviolent protest demonstration" during a visit by President Ford, two others were identified as draft evaders, and the Vietnam Veterans Against the War were active at the conference. But the report went much further to describe—based on information from FBI informants—the activities of religious, civil liberties, and student groups, as well as "families of men killed in Vietnam" and congressional staff aides.

-- In 1974 the FBI disseminated a report on a peaceful vigil in the vicinity of the Soviet Embassy in support of the rights of Soviet Jews, not just to the Secret Service and the Justice Department's Civil Disturbance Unit, but also to the CIA and the State Department.

-- In 1972 the FBI disseminated a report to the CIA, Army and Navy intelligence, and an un-named "U.S. Government agency which conducts security-type investigations" in West Germany (apparently a military intelligence agency). The latter agency had asked the Bureau for information about an antiwar reservist group and a project to furnish "legal advice to GI's and veterans." The report described not only the reservists group, but also "a group dedicated to giving free legal aid to servicemen" and "an antiwar political group" which endorsed "political candidates for office who have a solid peace position and a favorable chance of being elected." The three groups "planned to share offices." This data came from a Bureau informant.

The FBI does have an obligation to disseminate to local law enforcement agencies information about crimes within their jurisdiction. Nevertheless, there has been improper dissemination to local police under at least two Bureau programs. Such dissemination occurred under COINTELPRO, as part of the FBI's effort to discredit individuals or disrupt groups. Others were in response to local police requests for "public source" information relating to "subversive matters." Experienced police officials confirmed that the term "subversive" is so broad that it inevitably leads to dissemination about political beliefs.

Other executive agencies have also engaged in excessive dissemination. The Justice Department's Inter-Division Information Unit (IDIU) sent its computerized data to the CIA, in order that the CIA could check its records on foreign travel of American dissidents. The IDIU sent the same material to the Internal Revenue Service's Special Service Staff, which used the information as part of its program for initiating tax audits. The Internal Revenue Service itself disseminated tax returns or related tax information to the CIA, the FBI, and the Justice Department's Internal Security Division (which also made requests on behalf of the FBI), without ascertaining whether there was a proper basis for the request or the purpose for which the information would be used.

Subfinding (b)
Excessive dissemination has sometimes contributed to the inefficiency of the intelligence process itself.

The dissemination of large amounts of relatively useless or totally irrelevant information has reduced the efficiency of the intelligence process. It has made it difficult for decision-makers to weigh the importance of reports. Agencies such as the FBI have collected intelligence, not because of its own needs or desires, or because it had been requested to do so, but because the data was assumed to be of value to someone else. Units established to screen and evaluate intelligence have encouraged, rather than reduced, further dissemination.

In some instances the FBI has disseminated information to local police in a manner that was counterproductive to effective law enforcement. One former police chief has described how the Bureau, under "pressure" from the White House to prepare for a specific demonstration, "passed on information in such a way that it was totally useless" because it was not "evaluated" and thus exaggerated the dangers. The need for prior evaluation of the significance of raw intelligence has not been fully recognized in the Bureau's policy for dissemination of data on protest demonstrations.

The impediments to accurate intelligence collection have been augmented by the dissemination practices of some local law enforcement agencies. An example is the report oil the Chicago Police Department's Security Section, which has been described as having passed "inherently inaccurate and distortive data" to federal intelligence agericies. The General Accounting Office has confirmed that this is a general problem. While the Committee has not examined local law enforcement intelligence, the dissemination practices of such agencies require as much careful control as federal agencies.

The assumption that some other agency might need information has not only produced excessive dissemination, but has also served as a specific rationale for collection of intelligence that was not otherwise within an agency's jurisdiction. The best example is the FBI's collection of intelligence on "general racial matters" for the military.

One of the ironies in the recent history of domestic intelligence was that the Justice Department's IDIU, which was set up to collate and evaluate the massive amounts of data flowing to the Justice Department from the FBI, contributed to even more extensive collection and dissemination. The IDIU encouraged numerous federal agencies (including many without regular investigative functions) to disseminate information to it about "organizations and individuals" who might "instigate" or "prevent" civil disorders.

Subfinding (c.)

Under the federal employee security program, unnecessary information about the political beliefs and associations of prospective government employees has been disseminated.

For nearly thirty years the federal employee security program has required a "national agency check" of the files of several government agencies, including the FBI, the Civil Service Commission, and military intelligence, on prospective employees. Although there was often no information to report, federal agencies received "name check" reports on all candidates for employment. This appears to have been the single largest source of regular dissemination of data in intelligence files.

These name check reports have provided information from intelligence files not only about possible criminal activity or personal weaknesses of the individual, but also about lawful political activity and association. Until recently the Executive Order on employee security required reports on any "association" with a person or group supporting "subversive" views. These reports have been required for every federal employee, regardless of whether he or she holds a sensitive position or has access to classified information.

It has been the policy of the FBI, and presumably other agencies as well, to disseminate via name check reports any information in its files — no matter how old or how unreliable — which might relate to the standards of the Executive Order. The current criteria have been substantially narrowed: the basic standards for reporting are group membership and potential criminal conduct. However, the Justice Department has advised the FBI that "it is not possible to set definite parameters" for organizations and that the Bureau should include those with a "potential" for meeting the criteria. The FBI does not determine whether or not the information it furnishes is decisive under these standards. Departmental instructions state:

It is not the Bureau's responsibility to determine whether the information is or is not of importance to the particular agency in the carrying out of its current activities and responsibilities, and whether or not any action is taken by the department or agency is not, of course, a principal concern of the Bureau.

The FBI itself has expressed misgivings about the breadth of its responsibilities under the employee security program. It has continued to seek "clarification" from the Justice Department, and it has pointed out that there have been no "adverse actions" taken against current or prospective Federal employees under the loyalty and security provisions of the Executive Order "for several years." This has been due to the fact "that difficulties of proof imposed by the courts in loyalty and security cases have proved almost insurmountable."

The employee security program has served an essential function in full background investigation and name checks for those having access to classified information. But its extension to vaguely-defined "subversives" in nonsensitive positions has gone beyond the Government's proper need for information on the suitability of persons for employment.

Subfinding (d)

The FBI, which has been the "clearinghouse" for all domestic intelligence data, maintains in readily accessible files sensitive and derogatory personal information not relevant to any investigation, as well as information which was improperly or illegally obtained.

In recent years, the Secret Service, military intelligence, and other agencies have instituted significant programs for the destruction or purging of useless information. However, the FBI has retained its vast general files, accumulated over the years under its duty to serve as a "clearinghouse" for domestic intelligence data. 55 There are over 6,500,000 files at FBI headquarters; and the data is retrievable through a general index consisting of over 58,000,000 index cards. Each Bureau Field Office has substantial additional information in its files. Domestic intelligence information included in the general index is described by the FBI as:

associates and relatives of the subject; members of organizations under investigation or deter-mined to be possible subversive individuals contributing funds to subversive-type activity; subversive or seditious publications; writers of articles in. subversive or seditious publications - bookstores specializing in subversive-type publications and related types of information.

The Committee has found that there are massive amounts of irrelevant and trivial information in these files. The FBI has kept such data in its filing system on the theory that they might he useful someday in the future to solve crimes, for employee background checks, to evaluate the reliability of the source, or to "answer questions or challenges" about the Bureau's conduct.

The FBI has recently issued instructions to its Field Offices to take greater care in recording domestic intelligence information in its files. They are to exercise "judgment" as to whether or not the activity is "pertinent" to the Bureau's "legitimate investigative interest." Nevertheless, current policies still allow the indexing of the names of persons who are not the subject of investigation but just attend meetings of a group under investigation.

Finally, there is Information in FBI files which was collected by illegal or improper means. It ranges from the fruits of warrantless electronic surveillance, mail openings, and surreptitious entries, to the results of sweeping intelligence investigations which collected data about the lawful political activities and personal lives of Americans. Where such intelligence remain in the name-indexed files, it can be retrieved and disseminated along with other information, thus continuing indefinitely the potential for compounding the initial intrusion into constitutionally protected areas.

G. Deficiencies In Control And Accountability

Major Finding

The Committee finds that those responsible for overseeing, supervising, and controlling domestic activities of the intelligence community, although often unaware of details of the excesses described in this report, made those excesses possible by delegating broad authority without establishing adequate guidelines and procedural checks; by failing to monitor and coordinate sufficiently the activities of the agencies under their charge; by failing to inquire further after receiving indications that improper activities may have been occurring; by exhibiting a reluctance to know about secret details of programs; and sometimes by requesting intelligence agencies to engage in questionable practices. On numerous occasions, intelligence agencies have, by concealment, misrepresentation, or partial disclosure, hidden improper activities from those to whom they owed a duty of disclosure. But such deceit and the improper practices which it concealed would not have been possible to such a degree if senior officials of the Executive Branch and Congress had clearly allocated responsibility and imposed requirements for reporting and obtaining prior approval for activities, and had insisted on adherence to those requirements.

Subfindings

(a) Presidents have given intelligence agencies firm orders to collect information concerning "subversive activities" of American citizens, but have failed until recently to define the limits of domestic intelligence, to provide safeguards for the rights of American citizens, or to coordinate and control the ever-expanding intelligence efforts by an increasing number of agencies.

(b) Attorneys General have permitted and even encouraged the FBI to engage in domestic intelligence activities and to use a wide range of intrusive investigative techniques—such as wiretaps, microphones, and informants—but have failed until recently to supervise or establish limits on these activities or techniques by issuing adequate safeguards, guidelines, or procedures for review.

(c.) Presidents, White House officials, and Attorneys General have requested and received domestic political intelligence, thereby contributing to and profiting from the abuses of domestic intelligence and setting a bad example for their subordinates.

(d) Presidents, Attorneys General, and other Cabinet officers have neglected until recently to make inquiries in the face of clear indications that intelligence agencies were engaging in improper domestic activities.

(e) Congress, which has the authority to place restraints on domestic intelligence activities through legislation, appropriations, and oversight committees, has not effectively asserted its responsibilities until recently. It has failed to define the scope of domestic intelligence activities or intelligence collection techniques, to uncover excesses, or to propose legislative solutions. Some of its members have failed to object to improper activities of which they were aware and have prodded agencies into questionable activities.

(f) Intelligence agencies have often undertaken programs without authorization with insufficient authorization, or in disregard of express orders.

(g) The weakness of the system of accountability and control can be seen in the fact that many illegal or abusive domestic intelligence operations were terminated only after they had been exposed or threatened with exposure by Congress or the news media.

Elaboration of Findings

The Committee has found excesses committed by intelligence agencies — lawless and improper behavior, intervention in the democratic process, overbroad intelligence targeting and collection, and the use of covert techniques to discredit and "neutralize" persons and groups defined as enemies by the agencies. But responsibility for those acts does not fall solely on the intelligence agencies which committed them. Systematic excesses would not have occurred if lines of authority had been clearly defined; if procedures for reporting and review had been established; and if those responsible for supervising the intelligence community had properly discharged their duties.

The pressure of events and the widespread confidence in the FBI help to explain the deficiencies in command and authorization discovered by the Committee. Most of the activities examined in this report occurred during periods of foreign or domestic crisis. There was substantial support from the public and all branches of government for some of the central objectives of domestic intelligence policy, including the search for "Fifth Columnists" before World War II; the desire to identify communist "influence" in the Cold War atmosphere of the 1950s; the demand for action against Klan violence in the early 1960s; and the reaction to violent racial disturbances and anti-Vietnam war activities in the late 1960s and early 1970s. It was in this heated environment that President and Attorneys General ordered the FBI to investigate "subversive activities". Further, the Bureau's reputation for effectiveness and professionalism, and Director Hoover's ability to cultivate political support and to inspire apprehension, played a significant role in shaping the relationship between the FBI and the rest of the Government.

With only a few exceptions, the domestic intelligence activities reviewed by the Committee were properly authorized within the intelligence agencies. The FBI epitomizes a smoothly functioning military structure: activities of agents are closedly supervised; programs are authorized only after they have traveled a well-defined bureaucratic circuit; and virtually all activities—ranging from high-level policy considerations to the minutia of daily reports from field agencies—are reduced to writing. These characteristics are commendable. All efficient law enforcement and intelligence-gathering machine, acting consistently with law, can greatly benefit the nation. However, when used for wrongful purposes, this efficiency can pose a grave danger.

It appears that many specific abuses were not known by the Attorney General, the President, or other Cabinet-level officials directly responsible for supervising domestic intelligence activities. But whether or not particular activities were authorized by a President or Attorney General, those individuals must—as the chief executive and the principal law enforcement officer of the United States Government—bear ultimate responsibility for the activities of executive agencies under their command. The President and his Cabinet officers have a duty to determine the nature of activities engaged in by executive agencies and to prevent undesired activities from taking place. This duty is particularly compelling when responsible officials have reason to believe that undesirable activity is occurring, as has often been the case in the context of domestic intelligence.

The Committee's inquiry has revealed a pattern of reckless disregard of activities that threatened our Constitutional system. Intelligence agencies were ordered to investigate "subversive activities," and were then usually left to determine for themselves which activities were "subversive" and how those activities should be investigated. Intelligence agencies were told they could use investigative techniques—wiretaps, microphones, informants—that permitted them to pry into the most valued areas of privacy and were then given in many cases the unregulated authority to determine when to use those techniques and how long to continue them. Intelligence agencies were encouraged to gather "pure intelligence," which was put to political use by public officials outside of those agencies. This was possibly because Congress had failed to pass laws limiting the areas into which intelligence agencies could legally inquire and the information they could disseminate.

Improper acts were often intentionally concealed from the Government officials responsible for supervising the intelligence agencies, or undertaken without express authority. Such behavior is inexcusable. But equally inexcusable is the absence of executive and congressional oversight that engendered an atmosphere in which the heads of those agencies believed they could conceal activities from their superiors. Attorney General Levi's recent guidelines and the recommendations of this Committee are intended to provide the necessary guidance.

Whether or not the responsible Government officials knew about improper intelligence activities, and even if the agency heads failed in their duty of full disclosure, it still follows that Presidents and the appropriate Cabinet officials should have known about those activities. This is a demanding standard, but one that must be imposed. The future of democracy rests upon such accountability.

Subfinding (a)

Presidents have given intelligence agencies firm orders to collect information concerning "subversive activities" of American citizens, but have failed until recently to define the limits of domestic intelligence, to provide safeguards for the rights of

American citizens, or to coordinate and control the ever-expanding intelligence efforts by an increasing number of agencies.

As emphasized throughout this report, domestic intelligence activities have been undertaken pursuant to mandates from the Executive branch, generally issued during times of war or domestic crisis. The directives of Presidents Roosevelt, Truman, and Eisenhower to investigate "subversive activities," or other equally ill-defined targets, were echoed in various orders from Attorneys General, who themselves encouraged the FBI to undertake domestic intelligence activities with vague but vigorous commands.

Neither Presidents nor their chief legal officers, the Attorneys General, have defined the "subversive activities" which may be investigated or provided guidelines to the agencies in determining which individuals or groups were engaging in those activities. No reporting procedures were established to enable Cabinet-level officials or their designees to review the types of targets of domestic investigations and to exercise independent judgment concerning whether such investigations were warranted. No mechanisms were established for monitoring the conduct of domestic investigations or for determining if and when they should be terminated. If Presidents had articulated standards in these areas, or had designated someone to do the job for them, it is possible that many of the abuses described in this report would not have occurred.

Considering the proliferation of agencies engaging in domestic intelligence and the overlapping jurisdictional lines, it is surprising that no President has successfully designated one individual or body to coordinate and supervise the domestic intelligence activities of the various agencies. The half-hearted steps that were taken in that direction appear either to have been abandoned or to have resulted in the concentration of even more power in individual agency heads. For example, in 1949 President Truman attempted to establish a control mechanism—the Interdepartmental Intelligence Conference—to centralize authority for supervising domestic intelligence activities of the FBI and military intelligence agencies in a committee chaired by the Director of the FBI. The Committee reported to the National Security Council, and an NSC staff member was assigned responsibility for internal security. The practical effect of the IIC was apparently to increase the power of the FBI Director and to remove control further from the Cabinet level. In 1962, the functions of the IIC were transferred to the Justice Department, and the Attorney General was put in nominal charge of domestic intelligence. While in theory supervision resided in the Internal Security Division of the Justice Department, that Division deferred in large part to the FBI and provided little oversight. The top two executives of the Internal Security Division were former FBI officials. They appeared sympathetic to the Bureau, and like the Bureau, emphasized threats of Communist "influence" without mentioning actual results.

Another opportunity to coordinate intelligence collection was missed in 1967, when Attorney General Ramsey Clark established the Interdivisional Intelligence Unit (IDIU) to draw on virtually the entire Federal Government's intelligence collecting capability for information concerning groups and individuals "who may play a role, whether purposefully or not, either in instigating or spreading civil disorders, or in preventing or checking them." In the rush to obtain intelligence, no efforts were made to formulate standards or guidelines for controlling how the intelligence would be collected. In the absence of such guidelines and under pressure for results, the agencies undertook some of the most overly broad programs encountered by the Committee. For example, the FBI's "ghetto" informant program was a direct response to the Attorney General's broad requests for intelligence.

The need for centralized control of domestic intelligence was again given serious consideration during the vigorous demonstrations against the war in Vietnam in 1970. The intelligence community's program for dealing with internal dissent—the Huston Plan—envisioned not only relaxing controls on surveillance techniques, but also coordinating intelligence collection efforts. According to Tom Charles Huston's testimony, the President viewed the suggestion of a coordinating body as the most important contribution of the plan. Although the President quickly revoked his approval for the Huston Plan, the idea of a central domestic intelligence body had taken root. Two months later, with the encouragement of Attorney General John Mitchell, the Intelligence Evaluation Committee was established in the Justice Department. That Committee, like its precursor, the IDIU, compiled and evaluated raw intelligence; it did not exercise supervision.

The growing sophistication of intelligence collection techniques underscores the present need for central control and coordination of domestic intelligence activities. Although the Executive Branch has recognized that need in the past, it has not, until recently, faced up to its responsibilities. President Gerald Ford's joint effort with members of Congress to place further restrictions on wiretaps is a welcome step in the right direction. Congress must act expeditiously in this area.

Subfinding (b)

Attorneys General have permitted and even encouraged the FBI to engage in domestic intelligence activities and to use a wide range of intrusive investigative techniques—such as wiretaps, microphones, and informants—but have failed until recently to supervise or establish limits on these activities or techniques by issuing adequate safeguards, guidelines, or procedures for review.

The Attorney General is the chief law enforcement officer of the United States and the Cabinet-level officer formally in charge of the FBI. The Justice Department, until recently, has failed to issue directives to the FBI articulating the grounds for opening domestic intelligence investigations or the standards to be followed in carrying out those investigations. The Justice Department has neglected to establish machinery for monitoring and supervising the conduct of FBI investigations, for requiring approval of major investigative decisions, and for determining when an investigation should be terminated. Indeed, in 1972 the Attorney General said he did not even know whether the FBI itself bad formulated guidelines and standards for domestic intelligence activities, was not aware of the FBI's manual of instructions, and had never reviewed the FBI's internal guidelines.

The Justice Department has frequently levied specific demands on the FBI for domestic intelligence, but has not accompanied these demands with restrictions or guidelines. Examples include the Justice Department's Civil Rights Division's requests for reports on demonstrations in the early 1960's (including coverage of a speech by Governor elect George Wallace and coverage of a civil rights demonstration on the 100th anniversary of the Emancipation Proclamation): Attorney General Kennedy's efforts to expand FBI infiltration of the Ku Klux Klan in 1964; Attorney General Clark's sweeping instructions to collect intelligence about civil disorders in 1967; and the Internal Security Division's request for more extensive investigations of campus demonstrations in 1969. While a limited investigation into some of these areas may have been warranted, the improper acts committed in the course of those investigations were possible because no restraints had been imposed.

The Justice Department also cooperated with the FBI in defying the Emergency Detention Act of 1950 by approving the Bureau's Security Index criteria for the investigation of "potentially dangerous" persons. Even after Congress repealed the Detention Act, the Justice Department allowed the Bureau to continue listing "potentially dangerous" persons on a new Administrative Index. The Department stopped reviewing the names on the FBI's index, and apparently endorsed the FBI's view that the list could, contrary to law, be used for detention purposes in an "emergency."

The FBI's autonomy has been a prominent and long-accepted feature of the Federal bureaucratic terrain. As early as the 1940s the FBI could oppose Justice Department inquiries into its internal affairs by raising the specter of "leaks." The Department acquiesced in the Bureau's claim that it was entitled to withhold its raw files, conceal the identities of informants, and, in a number of cases, refuse to give the Justice Department evidence supporting broad allegations and characterizations. Former Attorney General Katzenbach has pointed out that there were both positive and negative sides to the Bureau's autonomy:

Keeping the Bureau free from political interference was a powerful argument against efforts by politically appointed officials, whatever their motivations, to gain a greater measure of control over operations of the Bureau.... [Director Hoover also] found great value in his formal position as subordinate to the Attorney General and the fact that the FBI was a part of the Department of Justice.... In effect, he was uniquely successful in having it both ways; he was protected from public criticism by having a theoretical superior who took responsibility for his work, and was protected from his superior by his public reputation.

As a consequence of its autonomy, the Bureau could plan and implement many of the abusive operations described in this report. Former Attorneys General have told the Committee that they would never have permitted the more unsavory aspects of the New Left or Racial COINTELPROs if they had been aware of the Bureau's plans. To the extent that Attorneys General were ignorant of the Bureau's activities, it was the consequence not only of the FBI Director's independent political position, but also of the failure of the Attorneys General to establish procedures for finding out what the Bureau was doing and for permitting an atmosphere to evolve in which Bureau officials believed that they had no duty to report their activities to the Justice Department, and that they could conceal those activities with little risk of exposure.

Attorneys General have not only neglected to establish procedures for reviewing FBI programs and activities, but they have at the same time granted the FBI authority to employ highly intrusive investigative techniques with inadequate guidelines and review procedures, and in some instances with no external restraints whatsoever. Before 1965, wiretaps required the approval of the Attorney General in advance, but once the Attorney General had authorized wiretap coverage of a subject, the Bureau could continue the surveillance for as long as it judged necessary.

This permissive policy was current in October 1963 when Attorney General Robert Kennedy authorized the FBI to wiretap the phones of Dr. Martin Luther King, Jr. "at his current address or at any future address to which he may move" and to wiretap the New York and Atlanta SCLC offices. Reading the Attorney General's wiretap authorization broadly, the FBI construed Dr. King's "residence" so as to permit wiretaps on three\, of his hotel rooms and the homes of friends with whom he stayed temporarily. The FBI was still relying on Attorney General Kennedy's initial authorization when it sought reauthorization for the King wiretaps in April 1965 in response to new procedures formulated by Attorney General Katzenbach. Although Attorney General Kennedy's authorizing memorandum in October 1963 said that the FBI should provide him with an evaluation of the wiretaps after 60 days, he failed to complain when the FBI neglected to send him the evaluation. Apparently the Attorney General never mentioned the wiretaps to the FBI again, even though he received FBI reports from the wiretaps until he resigned in September, 1964.

The Justice Department's policy toward the use of microphones has been even more permissive than for wiretaps. Until 1965, the FBI was free to carry out microphone surveillance in national security cases without first seeking the approval of the Attorney General or notifying him afterward. The total absence of supervision enabled the FBI to hide microphones in Dr. Martin Luther King's hotel rooms for nearly two years for the express purpose of not only determining whether he was being influenced by allegedly communist advisers. but to "attempt" to obtain information about the private "activities of Dr. King and his associates" so that Dr. King could be "completely discredited." Attorney General Kennedy was apparently never told about the microphone surveillances of Dr. King, although he did receive reports containing unattributed information from that surveillance from which he might have concluded that microphones were the source.

The Justice Department imposed external control over microphones for the first time in March 1965, when Attorney General Katzenbach applied the same procedures to wiretaps and microphones, requiring not only prior authorization but also formal periodic review. But irregularities were tolerated even with this standard. For example, the FBI has provided the Committee three memoranda from Director Hoover, initialed by Attorney General Katzenbach, as evidence that it informed the Justice Department of its microphone surveillance of Dr. King after the March 1965 policy change. These documents, however, show that Katzenbach was informed about the microphones only after they had already been installed. Such after-the-fact approval was permitted under Katzenbach's procedures. There is no indication that Katzenbach inquired further after receiving the notice.

The Justice Department condoned, and often encouraged, the FBI's use of informants—the investigative technique with the highest potential for abuse. However, the Justice Department imposed no restrictions on informant activity or reporting, and established no procedures for reviewing the Bureau's decision to use informants in a particular case.

In 1954 the Justice Department entered into an agreement with the CIA in which the CIA was permitted to withhold the names of employees whom it had determined were "almost certainly guilty of violations of criminal statutes" when the CIA could "devise no charge" under which they could be prosecuted that would not "require revelation of highly classified information." This practice was terminated by the Justice Department in January, 1975.

Despite the failure of Attorneys General to exercise the supervision that is necessary in the area of domestic intelligence, several Attorneys General have taken steps in the right direction. Of note were Attorney General Nicholas Katzenbach's review procedures for electronic surveillance in 1965; Ramsey Clark's refusal to approve electronic surveillance of domestic intelligence targets and his rejection of repeated requests by the FBI for such surveillance; Acting Deputy Attorney General William Ruckelshaus' inquiries into the Bureau's domestic intelligence program;

Deputy Attorney General Laurence Silberman's inquiry into political abuses of the FBI in early 1975; and Attorney General Saxbe's decision to make the Justice Department's COINTELPRO report public.

During the past year, Attorney General Edward H. Levi has exercised welcome leadership by formulating guidelines for FBI investigations; developing legislative proposals requiring a judicial warrant for national security wiretaps and microphones; establishing the Office of Professional Responsibility to inquire into departmental misconduct; initiating investigations of alleged wrongdoing by the FBI; and cooperating with this Committee's requests for documents on FBI intelligence operations. The Justice Department's concern in recent years is a hopeful sign, but long overdue.

Subfinding (c.)

Presidents, White House officials, and Attorneys General have requested and received domestic political intelligence, thereby contributing to and profiting from the abuses of domestic intelligence and setting a bad example for their subordinates.

The separate finding on "political abuse" sets forth instances in which the FBI was used by White House officials to gather politically useful information, including data on administration opponents and critics. This misuse of the Bureau's powers by its political superiors necessarily contributed to the atmosphere in which abuses flourished.

If the Bureau's superiors were willing to accept the fruits of excessive intelligence gathering, to authorize electronic surveillance, for political purposes, and to receive reports on critics which included intimate details of their personal lives, they could not credibly hold the Bureau to a high ethical standard. If political expediency characterized the decisions of those expected to set limits on the Bureau's conduct, it is not surprising that the FBI considered the principle of expediency endorsed.

Subfinding (d)

Presidents, Attorneys General, and other cabinet officers have neglected, until recently, to make inquiries in the face of clear indications that intelligence agencies were engaging in improper domestic activities.

Executive branch officials contributed to an atmosphere in which excesses were possible by ignoring clear indications of excesses and failing to take corrective measures when directly confronted with improper behavior. The Committee's findings on "Violating and Ignoring the Law" illustrate that several questionable or illegal programs continued after higher officials had learned partial details and failed to ask for additional information, either out of the naive assumption that intelligence agencies would not engage in lawless conduct, or because they preferred not to be informed.

Some of the most disturbing examples of insufficient action in the face of clear danger signals were uncovered in the Committee's investigation of the FBI's program to "neutralize" Dr. Martin Luther King, Jr. as the leader of the civil rights movement. The Bureau informed the Committee that its files contain no evidence that any officials outside of the FBI "were specifically aware of any efforts, steps, or plans or proposals to 'discredit' or 'neutralize' King." The relevant executive branch officials have told the Committee that they were, unaware of a general Bureau program to discredit King. Former Attorney General Katzenbach, however, told the Committee:

Nobody in the Department of Justice connected with Civil Rights could possibly have been unaware of Mr. Hoover's feelings [against Dr. King]. Nobody could have been unaware of the potential for disaster which those feelings embodied. But, given the realities of the situation, I do not believe one could have anticipated the extremes to which it was apparently carried.

The evidence before the Committee confirms that the "potential for disaster" was indeed clear at the time. There is no question that officials in the White House and Justice Department, including President Johnson and Attorney General Katzenbach, knew that the Bureau was taking steps to discredit Dr. King, although they did not know the full extent of the Bureau's efforts.

-- In January 1964 the FBI gave Presidential Assistant Walter Jenkins an FBI report unfavorable to Dr. King. According to a contemporaneous FBI memorandum, Jenkins said that he "was of the opinion that the FBI could perform a good service to the country if this matter could somehow be confidentially given to members of the press." Jenkins, in a staff interview, denied having made such a suggestion.

-- In February 1964 a reporter informed the Justice Department that the FBI had offered to "leak" information unfavorable to Dr. King to the press. The Justice Department's Press Chief, Edwin Guthman, asked Cartha DeLoach, the FBI's liaison with the press, about this allegation and DeLoach denied any involvement. The Justice Department took no further action.

-- Bill Moyers, an Assistant to President Johnson, testified that he learned sometime in early 1964 that an FBI agent twice offered to play a tape recording for Walter Jenkins that would have been personally embarrassing to Dr. King and that Jenkins refused to listen to the tape on both occasions. 36a Moyers testified that he never asked the FBI why it had the tape or was offering to play it in the White House. When asked if he had ever questioned the propriety of the FBI's disseminating information of a personal nature about Dr. King within the Government, he replied, "I never questioned it, no." When he was asked if he could recall anyone in the White House ever questioning the propriety of the FBI disseminating this type of material, Moyers testified. "I think . . . there were comments that tended to ridicule the FBI's doing this, but no."

-- Burke Marshall, Assistant Attorney General in charge of the Civil Rights Division, testified that sometime in 1964 a reporter told him that the Bureau had offered information unfavorable to Dr. King. Marshall testified that he repeated this allegation to a Bureau official and asked for a report. The Bureau official subsequently informed him "The Director wants you to know that you're a . . . damned liar."

-- In November 1964 the Washington Bureau Chief of a national news publication told Attorney General Katzenbach and Assistant Attorney General Marshall that one of his reporters had been approached by the FBI and offered the opportunity to hear some "interesting" tape recordings involving Dr. King. Katzenbach testified that, he had been "shocked," and that he and Marshall had informed President Johnson, who "took the matter very seriously" and promised to contact Director Hoover. Neither Marshall nor Katzenbach knew if the President contacted Hoover. Katzenbach testified that, during this same period, he learned of at least one other reporter who had been offered tape recordings by the Bureau, and that he personally confronted DeLoach, who was reported to have made the offers. DeLoach told Katzenbach that be had never made such offers. The only record of this episode in FBI files is a memorandum by DeLoach stating that Moyers had informed him that the newsman was "telling all over town" that the FBI was making allegations concerning Dr. King, and that Moyers had "stated that the President felt that [the newsman] lacked integrity...." Moyers could not recall this episode, but told the Committee that it would be fair to conclude that the President had been upset by the fact that the newsman revealed the Bureau's conduct rather than by the Bureau's conduct itself.

The response of top White House and Justice Department officials to strong indications of wrongdoing by the FBI was clearly inadequate. The Attorney General went no further than complaining to the President and asking a Bureau official if the charges were true. President Johnson apparently not only failed to order the Bureau to stop, but indeed warned it not to deal with certain reporters because they had complained about the Bureau's improper conduct.

In 1968 Attorney General Ramsey Clark asked Director Hoover if he had "any information as to how" facts about Attorney General Kennedy's authorization of the wiretap on Dr. King had leaked to columnists Drew Pearson and Jack Anderson. Clark requested the FBI Director to "undertake whatever investigation you deem feasible to determine how this happened. Director Hoover's reply, drafted in the office of Cartha DeLoach, expressed "dismay" at the leak and offered no indication of the likely source.

In fact, DeLoach had prepared a memorandum ten days earlier stating that a middle-level Justice Department official with knowledge of the King wiretap met with him and admitted having "discussed this matter with Drew Pearson." According to this memorandum, DeLoach attempted to persuade the official not to allow the story to be printed because "certain Negro groups would still blame the FBI, whether we were ordered to take such action or not." Thus, DeLoach and Hoover deliberately misled Attorney General Clark by withholding their knowledge of the source of the "leak."

Subfinding (e)

Congress, which has the authority to place restraints on domestic intelligence activities through legislation, appropriations, and oversight committees, has not effectively asserted its responsibilities until recently. It has failed to define the scope of domestic intelligence activities or intelligence collection techniques, to uncover excesses, or to propose legislative solutions. Some of its members have failed to object to improper activities of which they were aware and have prodded agencies into questionable activities.

Congress, unlike the Executive branch, does not have the function of supervising the day-to-day activities of agencies engaged in domestic intelligence. Congress does, however, have the ability through legislation to affect almost every aspect of domestic intelligence activity: to erect the framework for coordinating domestic intelligence activities; to define and limit the types of activities in which executive agencies may engage; to establish the standards for conducting investigations; and to promulgate guidelines for controlling the use of wiretaps, microphones, and informants. Congress could also exercise a great influence over domestic intelligence through its power over the appropriations for intelligence agencies' budgets and through the investigative powers of its committees.

Congress has failed to establish precise standards governing domestic intelligence. No congressional statutes deal with the authority of executive agencies to conduct domestic intelligence operations, or instruct the executive in how to structure and supervise those operations. No statutes address when or under what conditions investigations may be conducted. Congress did not attempt to formulate standards for wiretaps or microphones until 1968, and even then avoided the issue of domestic intelligence wiretaps by allowing an exception for an undefined claim of inherent executive power to conduct domestic security surveillance, which was subsequently held unconstitutional. No legislative standards have been enacted to govern the use of informants.

Congress has helped shape the environment in which improper intelligence activities were possible. The FBI claims that sweeping provisions in several vague criminal statutes and regulatory measures enacted by Congress provide a basis for much of its domestic intelligence activity. Congress also added its voice to the strong consensus in favor of governmental action against Communism in the 1950's and domestic dissidents in the 1960's and 1970's.

Congress' failure to define intelligence functions has invited action by the executive. If the top officials of the executive branch are responsible for failing to control the intelligence agencies, that failure is in part due to a lack of guidance from Congress.

During most of the 40-year period covered in this report, congressional committees did not effectively monitor domestic intelligence activities. For example, in 1966, a Senate Judiciary subcommittee undertook an investigation of electronic surveillance and other intrusive techniques by Federal agencies. According to an FBI memorandum, its chairman told a delegation from the FBI that he would make "a commitment that he would in no way embarrass the FBI," and acceded in the FBI's request that the subcommittee refrain from calling FBI witnesses.

Another example of the deficiencies in congressional oversight is seen in the House Appropriations Committee's regular approval of the FBI's requests for appropriations without raising objections to the activities described in the Director's testimony and off-the-record briefings. There is no question that members of a House Appropriations subcommittee were aware not only that the Bureau was engaged in broad domestic intelligence investigations, but that it was also employing disruptive tactics against domestic targets.

In 1958, Director Hoover informed the subcommittee that the Bureau had an "intensive program" to "disorganize and disrupt" the Communist Party, that the program had existed "for years" and that Bureau informants were used "as a disruptive tactic." The next year, the Director informed the subcommittee that informants in 12 field offices

have been carefully briefed to engage in controversial discussions with the Communist Party so as to promote dissention, factionalism and defections from the communist cause. This technique has been extremely successful from a disruptive standpoint.

Under another phase of this program, we have carefully selected 28 items of anticommunist propaganda and have anonymously mailed it to selected communists, carefully concealing the identity of the FBI as its source. More than 2,800 copies of literature have been placed in the hands of active communists.

Hoover described more aggressive "psychological warfare" techniques in 1962:

During the past year we have caused disruption at large Party meetings, rallies and press conferences through various techniques such as causing the last-minute cancellation of the rental of the hall, packing the audience with anticommunists, arranging adverse publicity in the press and making available embarrassing questions for friendly reporters to ask the Communist Party functionaries.

The Appropriations subcommittee was also told during this briefing that the FBI's operations included exposing and discrediting "communists who are secretly operating in legitimate organizations and employments, such as the Young Men's Christian Association, Boy Scouts, civic groups, and the like."

In 1966 Director Hoover informed the Appropriations subcommittee that the disruptive program had been extended to the Ku Klux Klan.

The present Associate Director of the FBI, Nicholas Callahan, who accompanied Director Hoover during several of his appearances before the Appropriations subcommittee, said that members of the subcommittee made "no critical comment" about "the Bureau's efforts to neutralize groups and associations."

Subcommittee Chairman John Rooney's statements in a televised interview in 1971 regarding FBI briefings about Dr. Martin Luther King are indicative of the subcommittee's attitude toward the Bureau:

Representative ROONEY. Now you talk about the F.B.I. leaking something about Martin Luther King. I happen to know all about Martin Luther King, but I have never told anybody.

Interviewer. How do you know everything about Martin Luther King?

Representative ROONEY. From the Federal Bureau of Investigation.

Interviewer. They've told you — gave you information based on taps or other sources about Martin Luther King.

Representative ROONEY. They did.

Interviewer. Is that proper?

Representative ROONEY. Why not?

Former Assistant Attorney General Fred Vinson recalled that in 1967 the Justice Department averaged "fifty letters a week from Congress" demanding that "people like [Stokely] Carmichael be jailed." Vinson said that on one occasion when he was explaining First Amendment limits at a congressional hearing, a Congressman "got so provoked he raised his hand and said, 'to hell with the First Amendment.'" Vinson testified that these incidents fairly characterized "the atmosphere of the time."

The congressional performance has improved, however, in recent years. Subcommittees of the Senate Judiciary Committee have initiated inquiries into Army surveillance of domestic targets and into electronic surveillance by the FBI. House Judiciary Committee subcommittees commissioned a study of the FBI by the General Accounting Office and have inquired into FBI misconduct and surveillance activities. Concurrent with this Committee's investigations, the House Select Committee on Intelligence considered FBI domestic intelligence activities.

Our Constitution envisions Congress as a check on the Executive branch, and gives Congress certain powers for discharging that function. Until recently, Congress has not effectively fulfilled its constitutional role in the area of domestic intelligence. Although the appropriate congressional committees did not always know what intelligence agencies were, doing, they could have asked. The Appropriations subcommittee was aware that the FBI was engaging in activities far beyond the mere collection of intelligence, yet it did not inquire into the details of those programs. If Congress had addressed the issues of domestic intelligence and passed regulatory legislation, and if it had probed into the activities of intelligence agencies and required them to account for their deeds, many of the excesses in this Report might not have occurred.

Subfinding (f)

Intelligence agencies have often undertaken programs without authorization, with insufficient authorization, or in defiance of express orders.

The excesses detailed in this report were due in part to the failure of Congress and the Executive branch to erect a sound framework for domestic intelligence, and in part to the dereliction of responsibility by executive branch officials who were in charge of individual agencies. Yet substantial responsibility lies with officials of the intelligence agencies themselves. They had no justification for initiating major activities without first seeking the express approval of their superiors. The pattern of concealment and partial and misleading disclosures must never again be allowed to occur.

The Committee's investigations have revealed numerous instances in which intelligence agencies have assumed programs or activities were authorized under circumstances where it could not reasonably be inferred that higher officials intended to confer authorization. Sometimes far-reaching domestic programs were initiated without the knowledge or approval of the appropriate official outside of the agencies. Sometimes it was claimed that higher officials had been "notified" of a program after they had been informed only about some aspects of the program, or after the program had been described with vague references and euphemisms, such as "neutralize," that carried different meanings for agency personnel than for uninitiated outsiders. Sometimes notice consisted of references to programs buried in the details of lengthy memoranda; and "authorization" was inferred from the fact that higher officials failed to order the agency to discontinue the program that had been obscurely mentioned.

The Bureau has made no claim of outside authorization for its COINTELPROs against the Socialist Workers Party, Black Nationalists, or New Left adherents. After 1960, its fragile claim for authorization of the COINTELPROs against the Communist Party USA and White Hate Groups was drawn from a series of hints and partial, obscured disclosures to the Attorneys General and the White House.

The first evidence of notification to higher government officials of the FBI's COINTELPRO against the Communist Party USA consists of letters from Director Hoover to President Eisenhower and Attorney General William Rogers in May 1958 informing them that "in August of 1956, this Bureau initiated a program designed to promote disruption within the ranks of the Communist Party (CP) USA." There is no record of any reply to these letters.

Later that same year, Director Hoover told President Eisenhower and his Cabinet:

> To counteract a resurgence of Communist Party influence in the United States, we have a ... program designed to intensify any confusion and dissatisfaction among its members.

> During the past few years, this program has been most effective. Selected informants were briefed and trained to raise controversial issues within

the Party.... The Internal Revenue Service was furnished names and addresses of Party functionaries who had been active in the underground apparatus ... ; Anticommunist literature and simulated Party documents were mailed anonymously to carefully chosen members . . . .

The FBI's only claim to having notified the Kennedy Administration about COINTELPRO rests upon a letter written shortly before the inauguration in January 1961 from Director Hoover to Attorney General-designate Robert Kennedy, Deputy Attorney General-designate Byron R. White, and Secretary of State-designate Dean Rusk. One paragraph in the five-page letter stated that the Bureau had a "carefully planned program of counterattack against the CPUSA which keeps it off balance," and which was "carried on from both inside and outside the party organization." The Bureau claimed to have been "successful in preventing communists from seizing control of legitimate, mass organizations" and to have "discredited others who were secretly operating inside such organizations." Specific techniques were not mentioned, and no additional notice was provided to the Kennedy Administration. Indeed, when the Kennedy White House formally requested of Hoover a report on "Internal Security Programs," the Director described only the FBI's "investigative program," and made no reference to disruptive activities.

The only claimed notice of the COINTELPRO against the Ku Klux Klan was given after the program had begun and consisted of a partial description buried within a discussion of other subjects. In September 1965, copies of a two page letter were sent to President Johnson and Attorney General Katzenbach, describing the Bureau's success in solving a number of cases involving racial violence in the South. That report contained a paragraph stating that the Bureau was "seizing every opportunity to disrupt the activities of Klan organizations," and briefly described the exposure of a Klan member's "kickback" scheme involving insurance company premiums. More questionable tactics, such as sending a letter to a Klansman's wife to destroy their marriage, were not mentioned. The Bureau viewed Katzenbach's reply to its letter—which praises the investigative successes which are the focus of the FBI's letter—as constituting authorization for the White Hate COINTELPRO.

The claimed notification to Attorney General Ramsey Clark of the White Hate COINTELPRO consisted of a ten-page memorandum captioned "Ku Klux Klan Investigations—FBI Accomplishments" with a buried reference to Bureau informants "removing" Klan officers and "provoking scandal" within the Klan organization, Clark told the Committee that he did not recall reading those phrases or interpreting them as notice that the Bureau was engaging in disruptive tactics. Cartha DeLoach, Assistant to the Director during this period, testified that he "distinctly" recalled briefing Attorney General Clark "generally ... concerning COINTELPRO." Clark denied havingbeen briefed.

The letters and briefings described above, which constitute the Bureau's entire claim to notice and authorization for the CPUSA and White Hate COINTELPROs, failed to mention techniques which risked physical, emotional, or economic harm to their targets. In no case was an Attorney General clearly told the nature and extent of the programs and asked for his approval. In no case was approval expressly given.

Former Attorney General Katzenbach cogently described another misleading form of "authorization" relied on by the Bureau and other intelligence agencies:

As far as Mr. Hoover was concerned, it was sufficient for the Bureau if at any time any Attorney General had authorized [a particular] activity in any circumstances. In fact, it was often sufficient if any Attorney General had written something which could be construed to authorize it or had been informed in some one of hundreds of memoranda of some facts from which he could conceivably have inferred the possibility of such an activity. Perhaps to a permanent head of a large bureaucracy this seems a reasonable way of proceeding. However, there is simply no way an incoming Cabinet officer can or should be charged with endorsing every decision of his predecessor . . . .

For example, the CPUSA COINTELPRO was substantially described to the Eisenhower Administration, obliquely to the Kennedy Administration designees, but continued—apparently solely on the strength of those assumed authorizations—through the Johnson Administration and into the Nixon Administration. The idea that authority might continue from one administration to the next and that there is no duty to reaffirm authority inhibits responsible decision making. Circumstances may change and judgments may differ. New officials should be given—and should insist upon—the opportunity to review significant programs.

The CIA's mail opening project illustrates an instance in which an intelligence agency apparently received authorization for a limited program and then expanded that program into significant new areas without seeking further authorization. In May 1954, DCI Allen Dulles and Richard Helms, then Chief of Operations in the CIA's Directorate of Plans, briefed Postmaster General Arthur Summerfield about the CIA's New York mail project, which at that time involved only the examination of envelope exteriors. CIA memoranda indicate that Summerfield's approval was obtained for photographing envelope exteriors, but no mention was made of the possibility of mail opening.

The focus of the CIA's project shifted to mail opening sometime during the ensuing year, but the CIA did not return to inform Summerfield and made no attempt to secure his approval for this illegal operation.

Intelligence officers have sometimes withheld information from their superiors and concealed programs to prevent discovery by their superiors. The Bureau apparently ignored the Attorney General's order to stop classifying persons as "dangerous" in 1943; unilaterally decided not to provide the Justice Department with information about communist espionage on at least two occasions "for security reasons;" and withheld similar information from the Presidential Commission investigating the government's security program in 1947. More recently, CIA and NSA concealed from President Richard Nixon their respective mail opening and communications interception programs.

These incidents are not unique. The FBI also concealed its Reserve Index of prominent persons who were not included on the Security Index reviewed by the Justice Department; its other targeting programs against "Rabble Rousers," "Agitators," "Key Activists," and "Key Extremists;" and its use of intrusive mail opening and surreptitious entry techniques. Indeed, the FBI institutionalized its capability to conceal activities from the Justice Department by establishing a regular "Do Not File" procedure, which assured internal control while frustrating external accountability.

Subfinding (g)

The weakness of the system of accountability and control can be seen in the fact that many illegal or abusive domestic intelligence operations were terminated only after they had been exposed or threatened with exposure by Congress or the news media.

The lack of vigorous oversight and internal controls on domestic intelligence activity frequently left the termination of improper programs to the ad hoc process of public exposure or threat of exposure by Congress, the press, or private citizens. Less frequently, domestic intelligence projects were terminated solely because of an agency's internal review of impropriety.

The Committee is aware that public exposure can jeopardize legitimate, productive, and costly intelligence programs. We do not condone the extralegal activities which led to the exposure of some questionable operations.

Nevertheless two points emerge from an examination of the termination of numerous domestic intelligence activities: (1) major illegal or improper operations thrived in an atmosphere of secrecy and inadequate executive control; and (2) public airing proved to be the most effective means of terminating or reforming those operations.

Some intelligence officers and Executive branch administrators sought the termination of questionable programs as soon as they became aware of the nature of the operation — the Committee praises their actions. However, too often we have seen that the secrecy that protected illegal or improper activities and the insular nature of the agencies involved prevented intelligence officers from questioning their actions or realizing that they were wrong.

There are several noteworthy examples of illegal or abusive domestic intelligence activities which were terminated only after the threat of public exposure:

-- The FBI's widesweeping COINTELPRO operations were terminated on April 27, 1971, in response to disclosures about the program in the press.

-- IRS payments to confidential informants were suspended in March 1975 as a result of journalistic investigation of Operation Leprechaun.

-- The Army's termination of several major domestic intelligence operations, which were clearly overbroad or illegal, came only after the programs were disclosed in the press or were scheduled as the subject of congressional inquiry.

-- On one occasion, FBI Director Hoover insisted that electronic surveillance be discontinued prior to his appearance before the House Appropriations Committee so that he could report a relatively small number of wiretaps in place. Contrary to frequent allegations, however, no general pattern of temporary suspensions or terminations during the Director's appearances before the House Appropriations Committee is revealed by Bureau records.

-- Following the report of a Presidential committee which had been established in response to news reports in 1967, the CIA terminated its covert relationship with a large number of domestically based organizations, such as academic institutions, student groups, private foundations, and media projects aimed at an international audience.

Other examples of curtailment of domestic intelligence activity in response to the prospect of public exposure include: President Nixon's revocation of approval for the Huston Plan out of concern for the risk of disclosure of the possible illegal actions proposed and the fact that "their sensitivity would likely generate media criticism if they were employed;" J. Edgar Hoover's cessation of the bugging of Dr. Martin Luther King, Jr.'s hotel rooms after the initiation of a Senate investigation chaired by

Edward V. Long of Missouri; and the CIA's consideration of suspending mail-opening until the Long inquiry abated and eventual termination of the program "in the Watergate climate." More recently, several questionable domestic intelligence practices have been terminated at least in part as a result of Congressional investigation.

There are several prominent instances of terminations which resulted from an internal review process:

-- In August 1973, shortly after taking office, Internal Revenue Service Commissioner Donald Alexander abolished the Special Service Staff upon learning that it was engaged in political intelligence activities which he considered "antithetical to proper tax administration."

-- An internal legal review in 1973 prompted the termination of the joint effort by NSA and CIA to monitor United States - South American communications by individuals named on a drug traffic "watch list."

-- On May 9, 1973, newly appointed CIA Director James Schlesinger requested from CIA personnel an inventory of all "questionable activities" which the Agency had undertaken. The 694 pages of memoranda received in response to this request—which became known at the CIA as "The Family Jewels"—prompted the termination or limitation of a number of programs which were in violation of the the Agency's mandate, notably the CHAOS project involving intelligence-gathering against American citizens.

-- In the early 1960s, the CIA's MKULTRA testing program, which involved surreptitiously administering drugs to unwitting persons, was "frozen" after the Inspector General questioned the morality and lack of administrative control of the program.

-- Several mail-opening operations were terminated because they lacked sufficient intelligence value, which was often measured in relation to the "flap potential"—or risk of disclosure—of an operation. However, both the CIA and the FBI continued other mail-opening operations after these terminations. 86

The Committee's examination of the circumstances surrounding terminations of a wide range of improper or illegal domestic intelligence activities clearly points to the need for more effective oversight from outside the agencies. In too many cases, the impetus for the termination of programs of obviously questionable propriety came from the press or the Congress rather than from intelligence agency administrators or their superiors in the Executive Branch. Although there were several laudable instances of termination as a responsible outgrowth of an agency's internal review process, the Committee's record indicates that this process alone is insufficient—intelligence agencies cannot be left to police themselves.

IV. Conclusions And Recommendations

A. Conclusions

The findings which have emerged from our investigation convince us that the Government's domestic intelligence policies and practices require fundamental reform. We have attempted to set out the basic facts; now it is time for Congress to turn its attention to legislating restraints upon intelligence activities which may endanger the constitutional rights of Americans.

The Committee's fundamental conclusion is that intelligence activities have undermined the constitutional rights of citizens and that they have done so primarily because checks and balances designed by the framers of the Constitution to assure accountability have not been applied.

Before examining that conclusion, we make the following observations.

-While nearly all of our findings focus on excesses and things that went wrong, we do not question the need for lawful domestic intelligence. We recognize that certain intelligence activities serve perfectly proper and clearly necessary ends of government. Surely, catching spies and stopping crime, including acts of terrorism, is essential to insure "domestic tranquility" and to "provide for the common defense." Therefore, the power of government to conduct proper domestic intelligence activities under effective restraints and controls must be preserved.

-We are aware that the few earlier efforts to limit domestic intelligence activities have proven ineffectual. This pattern reinforces the need for statutory restraints coupled with much more effective oversight from all branches of the Government.

-The crescendo of improper intelligence activity in the latter part of the 1960s and the early 1970s shows what we must watch out for: In time of crisis, the Government will exercise its power to conduct domestic intelligence activities to the fullest extent. The distinction between legal dissent and criminal conduct is easily forgotten. Our job is to recommend means to help ensure that the distinction will always be observed.

-In an era where the technological capability of Government relentlessly increases, we must be wary about the drift toward "big brother government." The potential for abuse is awesome and requires special attention to fashioning restraints which not only cure past problems but anticipate and prevent the future misuse of technology.

-We cannot dismiss what we have found as isolated acts which were limited in time and confined to a few willful men. The failures to obey the law and, in the words of the oath of office, to "preserve, protect, and defend" the Constitution, have occurred repeatedly throughout administrations of both political parties going back four decades.

-We must acknowledge that the assignment which the Government has given to the intelligence community has, in many ways, been impossible to fulfill. It has been expected to predict or prevent every crisis, respond immediately with information on any question, act to meet all threats, and anticipate the special needs of Presidents. And then it is chastised for its zeal. Certainly, a fair assessment must place a major part of the blame upon the failures of senior executive officials and Congress.

In the final analysis, however, the purpose of this Committee's work is not to allocate blame among individuals. Indeed, to focus on personal culpability may divert attention from the underlying institutional causes and thus may become an excuse for inaction.

Before this investigation, domestic intelligence had never been systematically surveyed. For the first time, the Government's domestic surveillance programs, as they have developed over the past forty years, can be measured against the values which our Constitution seeks to preserve and protect. Based upon our full record, and the findings which we have set forth in Part III above, the Committee concludes that:

Domestic intelligence activity has threatened and undermined the constitutional rights of americans to free speech, association and privacy. It has done so primarily became the constitutional system for checking abuse of power has not been applied. Our findings and the detailed reports which supplement this volume set forth a massive record of intelligence abuses over the years. Through a vast network of informants, and through the uncontrolled or illegal use of intrusive techniques — ranging from simple theft to sophisticated electronic surveillance — the Government has collected, and then used improperly, huge amounts of information about the private lives, political beliefs and associations of numerous Americans.

Affect Upon Constitutional Rights — That these abuses have adversely affected the constitutional rights of particular Americans is beyond question. But we believe the harm extends far beyond the citizens directly affected.

Personal privacy is protected because it is essential to liberty and the pursuit of happiness. Our Constitution checks the power of Government for the purpose of protecting the rights of individuals, in order that all our citizens may live in a free and decent society. Unlike totalitarian states, we do not believe that any government has a monopoly on truth.

When Government infringes those rights instead of nurturing and protecting them, the injury spreads far beyond the particular citizens targeted to untold numbers of other Americans who may be intimidated.

Free government depends upon the ability of all its citizens to speak their minds without fear of official sanction. The ability of ordinary people to be heard by their leaders means that they must be free to join in groups in order more effectively to express their grievances. Constitutional safeguards are needed to protect the timid as well as the courageous, the weak as well as the strong. While many Americans have been willing to assert their beliefs in the face of possible governmental reprisals, no citizen should have to weigh his or her desire to express an opinion, or join a group, against the risk of having lawful speech or association used against him.

Persons most intimidated may well not be those at the extremes of the political spectrum, but rather those nearer the middle. Yet voices of moderation are vital to balance public debate and avoid polarization of our society. The federal government has recently been looked to for answers to nearly every problem. The result has been a vast centralization of power. Such power can be turned against the rights of the people. Many of the restraints imposed by the Constitution were designed to guard against such use of power by the government.

Since the end of World War II, governmental power has been increasingly exercised through a proliferation of federal intelligence programs. The very size of this intelligence system, multiplies the opportunities for misuse.

Exposure of the excesses of this huge structure has been necessary. Americans are now aware of the capability and proven willingness of their Government to collect intelligence about their lawful activities and associations. What some suspected and others feared has turned out to be largely true — vigorous expression of unpopular views, association with dissenting groups, participation in peaceful protest activities, have provoked both government surveillance and retaliation.

Over twenty years ago, Supreme Court Justice Robert Jackson, previously an Attorney General, warned against growth of a centralized power of investigation. Without clear limits, a federal investigative agency would "have enough on enough people" so that "even if it does not elect to prosecute them" the Government would, he wrote, still "find no opposition to its policies". Jackson added, "Even those who are supposed to supervise [intelligence agencies] are likely to fear [them]." His advice speaks directly to our responsibilities today:

I believe that the safeguard of our liberty lies in limiting any national police or investigative organization, first of all to a small number of strictly federal offenses, and secondly to nonpolitical ones. The fact that we may have confidence in the administration of a federal investigative agency under its existing head does not mean that it may not revert again to the days when the Department of Justice was headed by men to whom the investigative power was a weapon to be used for their own purposes.

Failure to Apply Checks and Balances—The natural tendency of Government is toward abuse of power. Men entrusted with power, even those aware of its dangers, tend, particularly when pressured, to slight liberty.

Our constitutional system guards against this tendency. It establishes many different checks upon power. It is those wise restraints which keep men free. In the field of intelligence those restraints have too often been ignored.

The three main departures in the intelligence field from the constitutional plan for controlling abuse of power have been:

(a) Excessive Executive Power—In a sense the growth of domestic intelligence activities mirrored the growth of presidential power generally. But more than any other activity, more even than exercise of the war power, intelligence activities have been left to the control of the Executive.

For decades Congress and the courts as well as the press and the public have accepted the notion that the control of intelligence activities was the exclusive prerogative of the Chief Executive and his surrogates. The exercise of this power was not questioned or even inquired into by outsiders. Indeed, at times the power was seen as flowing not from the law, but as inherent, in the Presidency. Whatever the theory, the fact was that intelligence activities were essentially exempted from the normal system of checks and balances.

Such Executive power, not founded in law or checked by Congress or the courts, contained the seeds of abuse and its growth was to be expected.

(b) Excessive Secrecy—Abuse thrives on secrecy. Obviously, public disclosure, of matters such as the names of intelligence agents or the technological details of collection methods is inappropriate. But in the field of intelligence, secrecy has been extended to inhibit review of the basic programs and practices themselves.

Those within the Executive branch and the Congress who would exercise their responsibilities wisely must be fully informed. The American public, as well, should know enough about intelligence activities to be able to apply its good sense to the underlying issues of policy and morality.

Knowledge is the key to control. Secrecy should no longer be allowed to shield the existence of constitutional, legal and moral problems from the scrutiny of all three branches of government or from the American people themselves.

(c.) Avoidance of the Rule of Law—Lawlessness by Government breeds corrosive cynicism among the people and erodes the trust upon which government depends.

Here, there is no sovereign who stands above the law. Each of us, from presidents to the most disadvantaged citizen, must obey the law.

As intelligence operations developed, however, rationalizations were fashioned to immunize them from the restraints of the Bill of Rights and the specific prohibitions of the criminal code. The experience of our investigation leads us to conclude that such rationalizations are a dangerous delusion.

B. Principles Applied in Framing Recommedations and The Scope of the Recommendations.

Although our recommendations are numerous and detailed, they flow naturally from our basic conclusion. Excessive intelligence activity which undermines individual rights must end. The system for controlling intelligence must be brought back within the constitutional scheme.

Some of our proposals are stark and simple. Because certain domestic intelligence activities were clearly wrong, the obvious solution is to prohibit them altogether. Thus, we would ban tactics such as those used in the FBI's COINTELPRO. But other activities present more complex problems. We see a clear need to safeguard the constitutional rights of speech, assembly, and privacy. At the same time, we do not want to prohibit or unduly restrict necessary and proper intelligence activity.

In seeking to accommodate those sometimes conflicting interests we have been guided by the earlier efforts of those who originally shaped our nation as a republic under law.

The Constitutional amendments protecting speech and assembly and individual privacy seek to preserve values at the core of our heritage, and vital to our future. The Bill of Rights, and the Supreme Court's decisions interpreting it suggest three principles which we have followed:

(1) Governmental action which directly infringes the rights of free speech and association must be prohibited. The First Amendment recognizes that even if useful to a proper end, certain governmental actions are simply too dangerous to permit at all. It commands that "Congress shall make no law" abridging freedom of speech or assembly.

(2) The Supreme Court, in interpreting that command, has required that any governmental action which has a collateral (rather than direct) impact upon the rights of speech and assembly is permissible only if it meets two tests. First, the action must be undertaken only to fulfill a compelling governmental need, and second, the government must use the least restrictive means to meet that need. The effect upon protected interests must be minimized.

(3) Procedural safeguards — "auxiliary precautions" as they were characterized in the Federalist Papers — must be adopted along with substantive restraints. For example, while the Fourth Amendment prohibits only "unreasonable" searches and seizures, it requires a procedural check for reasonableness-the obtaining of a judicial warrant upon probable cause from a neutral magistrate. Our proposed procedural checks range from judicial review of intelligence activity before or after the fact, to formal and high level Executive branch approval, to greater disclosure and more effective Congressional oversight.

The Committee believes that its recommendations should be embodied in a comprehensive legislative charter defining and controlling the domestic security activities of the Federal Government. Accordingly, Part i of the, recommendations provides that intelligence agencies must be made subject to the rule of law. In addition, Part i makes clear that no theory, of "inherent constitutional authority" or otherwise, can justify the violation of any statute. Starting from the conclusion, based upon our record, that the Constitution and our fundamental values require a substantial curtailment of the scope of domestic surveillance, we deal after Part i with five basic questions:

1. Which agencies should conduct domestic security investigations?

The FBI should be primarily responsible for such investigations. Under the minimization principle, and to facilitate the control of domestic intelligence operations, only one agency should be involved in investigative activities which, even when limited as we propose, could give rise to abuse. Accordingly, Part ii of these recommendations reflects the Committee's position that foreign intelligence agencies (the CIA, NSA, and the military agencies) should be precluded from domestic security activity in the United States. Moreover, they should only become involved in matters involving the rights of Americans abroad where it is impractical to use the FBI, or where in the course of their lawful foreign intelligence operations they inadvertently collect information relevant to domestic security investigations. In Part iii the Committee recommends that non-intelligence agencies such as the Internal Revenue Service and the Post Office be required, in the course of any incidental involvement in domestic security investigations, to protect the privacy which citizens expect of first class mail and tax records entrusted to those agencies.

2. When should an American be the subject of an investigation at all; and when can particularly intrusive covert techniques, such as electronic surveillance or informants, be used?

In Part iv, which deals with the FBI, the Committee's recommendations seek to prevent the excessively broad, ill defined and open ended investigations shown to have been conducted over the past four decades. We attempt to change the focus of investigations from constitutionally protected advocacy and association to dangerous conduct. Part iv also sets forth specific substantive standards for, and procedural controls on, particular intrusive techniques.

3. Who should be accountable within the Executive branch for ensuring that intelligence agencies comply with the law and for the investigation of alleged abuses by employees of those agencies?

In Parts v and vi, the Committee recommends that these responsibilities fall initially upon the agency heads, their general counsel and inspectors general, but ultimately upon the Attorney General. The information necessary for control must be made available to those responsible for control, oversight and review; and their responsibilities must be made clear, formal, and fixed.

4. What is the appropriate role of the courts?

In Part vii, the Committee recommends the enactment of a comprehensive, civil remedy providing the courts with jurisdiction to entertain legitimate complaints by citizens injured by unconstitutional or illegal activities of intelligence agencies. Part viii suggests that criminal penalties should attach in cases of gross abuse. In addition, Part iv provides for judicial warrants before certain intrusive techniques can be used.

5. What is the appropriate role of Congress:

In Part xii the Committee reiterates its position that the Senate create a permanent intelligence oversight committee. The recommendations deal with numerous other issues such as the proposed repeal or amendment of the Smith Act, the proposed modernization of the Espionage Act to cover modern forms of espionage seriously detrimental to the national interest, the use of the GAO to assist Congressional oversight of the intelligence community, and remedial measures for past victims of improper intelligence activity.

Scope of Recommendations. — The scope of our recommendations coincides with the scope of our investigation. We examined the FBI, which has been responsible for most domestic security investigations, as well as foreign and military intelligence agencies, the IRS, and the Post Office, to the extent they became involved incidentally in domestic intelligence functions. While there are undoubtedly activities of other agencies which might legitimately be addressed in these recommendations, the Committee simply did not have the time or resources to conduct a broader investigation. Furthermore, the mandate of Senate Resolution 21 required that the Committee exclude from the coverage of its recommendations those activities of the federal government which are directed at organized crime and narcotics.

The Committee believes that American citizens should not lose their constitutional rights to be free from improper intrusion by their Government when they travel overseas. Accordingly, the Committee proposes recommendations which apply to protect the rights of Americans abroad as well as at home.

1. Activities Covered

The Domestic Intelligence Recommendations pertain to: the domestic security activities of the federal government; and any activities of military or foreign intelligence agencies which affect the rights of Americans and any intelligence activities of any non-intelligence agency working in concert with intelligence agencies, which affect those rights.

2. Activities Not Covered

The recommendations are not designed to control federal investigative activities directed at organized crime, narcotics, or other law enforcement investigations unrelated to domestic security activities.

3. Agencies Covered

The agencies whose activities are specifically covered by the recommendations are:

(i) the Federal Bureau of Investigation; (ii) the Central Intelligence Agency; (iii) the, National Security Agency and other intelligence agencies of the Department of Defense; (iv) the Internal Revenue Service; and (v) the United States Postal Service.

While it might be appropriate to provide similar detailed treatment to the activities of other agencies, such as the Secret Service, Customs Service, and Alcohol, Tobacco and Firearms Division (Treasury Department), the Committee did not study these agencies intensively. A permanent oversight committee should investigate and study the intelligence functions of those agencies and the effect of their activities on the rights of Americans.

4. Indirect Prohibitions

Except as specifically provided herein, these Recommendations are intended to prohibit any agency from doing indirectly that which it would be prohibited from doing directly. Specifically, no agency covered by these Recommendations should request or induce any other agency, or any person, whether the agency or person is American or foreign, to engage in any activity which the requesting or inducing agency is prohibited from doing itself.

5. Individuals and Groups Not Covered

Except as specifically provided herein, these Recommendations do not apply to investigation of foreigners who are officers or employees of a foreign power, or foreigners who, pursuant to the direction of a foreign power, are engaged in or about to engage in "hostile foreign intelligence activity" or "terrorist activity".

6. Geographic Scope

These Recommendations apply to intelligence activities which affect the rights of Americans whether at home or abroad, including all domestic security activities within the United States.

7. Legislative Enactment of Recommendations

Most of these Recommendations are designed to be implemented in the form of legislation and others in the form of regulations pursuant to statute. (Recommendations 85 and 90 are not proposed to be implemented by statute.

C. Recommendations

Pursuant to the requirement of Senate Resolution 21, these recommendations set forth the new congressional legislation [the Committee] deems necessary to "safeguard the rights of American citizens." We believe these recommendations are the appropriate conclusion to a traumatic year of disclosures of abuses. We hope they will prevent such abuses in the future.

i. Intelligence Agencies Are Subject to the Rule of Law

Establishing a legal framework for agencies engaged in domestic security investigation is the most fundamental reform needed to end the long history of violating and ignoring the law set forth in Finding A. The legal framework can be created by a two-stage process of enabling legislation and administrative regulations promulgated to implement the legislation.

However, the Committee proposes that the Congress, in developing this mix of legislative and administrative charters, make clear to the Executive branch that it will not condone, and does not accept, any theory of inherent or implied authority to violate the Constitution, the proposed new charters, or any other statutes. We do not believe the Executive has, or should have, the inherent constitutional authority to violate the law or infringe the legal rights of Americans, whether it be a warrantless break-in into the home or office of an American, warrantless electronic surveillance, or a President's authorization to the FBI to create a massive domestic security program based upon secret oral directives. Certainly, there would be no such authority after Congress has, as we propose it should, covered the field by enactment of a comprehensive legislative charter. Therefore statutes enacted pursuant to these recommendations should provide the exclusive legal authority for domestic security activities.

Recommendation 1.—There is no inherent constitutional authority for the President or any intelligence agency to violate the law.

Recommendation 2. — It is the intent of the Committee that statutes implementing these recommendations provide the exclusive legal authority for federal domestic security activities.

(a) No intelligence agency may engage in such activities unless authorized by statute, nor may it permit its employees, informants, or other covert human sources to engage in such activities on its behalf.

(b) No executive directive or order may be issued which would conflict with such statutes.

Recommendation 3.—In authorizing intelligence agencies to engage in certain activities, it is not intended that such authority empower agencies, their informants, or covert human sources to violate any prohibition enacted pursuant to these Recomendations or contained in the Constitution or in any other law.

ii. United States Foreign and Military Agencies Should Be Precluded from Domestic Security Activities

Part iv of these Recommendations centralizes domestic security investigations within the FBI. Past abuses also make it necessary that the Central Intelligence Agency, the National Security Agency, the Defense Intelligence Agency, and the military departments be preeluded expressly, except as specifically provided herein, from investigative activity which is conducted within the United States. Their activities abroad should also be controlled as provided herein to minimize their impact on the rights of Americans.

a. Central Intelligence Agency The CIA is responsible, for foreign intelligence and counterintelligence. These recommendations minimize the impact of CIA operations on Americans. They do not affect CIA investigations of foreigners outside of the United States. The, main thrust is to prohibit past actions revealed as excessive, and to transfer to the FBI other activities which might involve the CIA in internal security or law enforcement matters. Those limited activities which the CIA retains are placed under tighter controls.

The Committee's recommendations on CIA domestic activities are similar to Executive Order 11905. They go beyond the Executive Order, however, in that they recommend that the main safeguards be made law. And, in addition, the Committee proposes tighter standards to preclude repetition of some past abuses.

General Provisions The first two Recommendations pertaining to the CIA provide the context for more specific proposals. In Recommendation 4, the Committee endorses the prohibitions of the 1947 Act upon exercise by the CIA of subpoena, police or law enforcement powers or internal security functions. The Committee intends that Congress supplement, rather than supplant or derogate from the more general restrictions of the 1947 Act.

Recommendation 5 clarifies the role of the Director of Central Intelligence, in the protection of intelligence sources and methods. He should be charged with "coordinating" the protection of sources and methods—that is, the development of procedures for the protection of sources and methods. (Primary responsibility for investigations of security leaks should reside in the FBI.) Recommendation 5 also makes clear that the Director's responsibility for protecting sources and methods does not permit violations of law. The effect of the new Executive Order is substantially the same as Recommendation 5.

Recommendation 4 -- To supplement the prohibitions in the 1947 National Security Act against the CIA exercising "police, subpoena, law enforcement powers or internal security functions," the CIA should be prohibited from conducting domestic security activities within the United States, except as specifically permitted by these recommendations.

Recommendation 5 -- The Director of Central Intelligence should be made responsible for "coordinating" the protection of sources and methods of the intelligence community. As head of the CIA, the Director should also be responsible in the first instance for the security of CIA facilities, personnel, operations, and information. Neither function, however, authorizes the Director of Central Intelligence to violate any federal or state law, or to take any action which is otherwise inconsistent with statutes implementing these recommendations.

CIA Activities Within the United States 1. Wiretapping, Mail Opening and Unauthorized Entry.—The Committee's recommendations on CIA domestic activities apply primarily to actions directed at Americans. However, in Recommendation 6 the Committee recommends that the most intrusive and dangerous investigative techniques (electronic surveillance; mail opening; or unauthorized entry) should be used in the United States only by the FBI and only pursuant to the judicial warrant procedures described in Recommendations 53, 54 and 55.

This approach is similar to the Executive order except that the Order permits the CIA to open mail in the United States pursuant to applicable statutes and regulations (i.e., with a warrant). The Committee's recommendations (see Parts iii and iv), places all three techniques—mail opening, electronic surveillance and unauthorized entry— under judicial warrant procedures and centralizes their use within the FBI under Attorney General supervision. The Committee sees no justification for distinguishing among these techniques, all of which represent an exercise of domestic police powers which is inappropriate for a U.S. foreign intelligence agency within the United States and which inherently involve special dangers to civil liberties and personal privacy.

2. Other Covert Techniques—The use of other covert techniques by the CIA within the United States is sharply restricted by Recommendation 7 to specific situations.

The Committee would permit the CIA to conduct physical surveillance of persons on the premises of its own installations and facilities. Outside of its premises, the Committee would permit the CIA to conduct limited physical surveillance and confidential inquiries of its own employees as part of a preliminary security investigation.

Although the Committee generally centralizes such investigations within the FBI, it would be too burdensome to require the Bureau to investigate every allegation that an employee has personal difficulties, which could make him a security risk, or allegations of suspicious behavior suggesting the disclosure of information. Before involving the FBI, the CIA could conduct a preliminary inquiry, which usually consists of nothing more than interviews with the subject's office colleagues, or his family, neighbors or associates, and perhaps confrontation of the subject himself. In some situations, however, limited physical surveillance might enable the CIA to resolve the allegation or to determine that there was a serious security breach involved.

Unlike the Executive Order, however, the Committee recommendations limit this authority to present CIA employees who are subject to summary dismissal. The only remedy available to the Government for security problems with past employees is criminal prosecution or other legal action. All security leak investigations for proposed criminal prosecution should be centralized in the FBI. Authorizing the use of any covert technique against contractors and their employees, let alone former employees of CIA contractors, as the Executive Order does, would authorize CIA surveillance of too large a number of Americans. The CIA can withdraw security clearances until satisfied by the contractor that a security risk has been remedied and, in serious cases, any investigations could be handled by the FBI.

The recommendation on the use of covert techniques within the United States also precludes the use of covert human sources such as undercover agents and informants," with one exception expressly stated to be limited to "exceptional" cases. The Committee would authorize the CIA to place an agent in a domestic group, but only for the purpose of establishing credible cover to be used in a foreign intelligence mission abroad and only when the Director of Central Intelligence finds it to be "essential" to collection of information "vital" to the United States and the Attorney General finds that the operation will be conducted tinder procedures designed to prevent misuse.

Apart from this limited exception, the CIA could not infiltrate groups within the United States for any purpose, including, as was done in the, past, the purported protection of intelligence sources and methods or the general security of the CIA's facilities and personnel. (The Executive Order prohibits infiltration of groups within the United States "for purposes of reporting on or influencing its activities or members," but does not explicitly prohibit infiltration to protect intelligence sources and methods or the physical security of the agency.)

3. Collection of Information—In addition to limiting the use of particular covert techniques, the Committee limits, in Recommendation 8, the situations in which the CIA may intentionally collect, by any means, information within the United States concerning Americans. The recommendation permits the CIA to collect information within the United States about Americans only with-respect to persons working for the CIA or having some other significant affiliation or contact, with CIA. The CIA should not be in the business of investigating Americans as intelligence or counterintelligence targets within the United States—a responsibility which should be centralized in the FBI and performed only under the circumstances proposed as lawful in Part iv.

The Executive Order only restricts CIA collection of information about Americans if the information concerns "the domestic activities of United States citizens." Unlike the Committee, the Order does not restrict CIA collection of information about foreign travel or wholly lawful international contacts and communication of Americans. As the Committee has learned from its study of the CIA's CHAOS operation, in the process of gathering information about the international travel and contacts of Americans, the CIA acquired within the United States a great deal of additional information about the domestic activities of Americans.

The Executive Order also permits collection within the United States of information about the domestic activities of Americans in several other instances not permitted under the Committee recommendations:

(a) Collection of "foreign intelligence or counterintelligence" about the domestic activity of commercial organizations. (The Committee's restrictions on the collection of information apply to investigations of organizations as well as individuals.) ;

(b) Collection of information concerning the identity of persons in contact with CIA employees or with foreigners who are subjects of a counterintelligence inquiry. (Within the United States, the Committee would require any investigations to collect such information to be conducted by the FBI, and only if authorized under Part iv, and subject to its procedural controls.) ;

(c.) Collection of "foreign intelligence" from a cooperating source within the United States about the domestic activities of Americans. "Foreign intelligence," is an exceedingly broad and vague standard. The use of such a standard raises the prospect of another Project CHAOS. (The Committee would prohibit such collection by the CIA within the United States, except with respect to persons presently or prospectively affiliated with CIA.) ;

(d) Collection of information about Americans "reasonably believed" to be acting on behalf of a foreign power or engaging in international terrorist or narcotic activities. (The Committee would require investigations to collect,such information within the United States, to be conducted by the FBI, and only if authorized under Part iv.) ;

(e) Collection of information concerning persons considered by the CIA to pose a clear threat to intelligence agency facilities or personnel, provided such information is retained only by the "threatened" agency and that proper coordination is established with the FBI. (This was the basis for the Office of Security's RESISTANCE program investigating dissent throughout the country.) (The Committee would require any such "threat" collection outside the CIA be conducted by the FBI, and only if authorized by Part iv, or by local law enforcement.)

Recommendation 6—The CIA should not conduct electronic surveillance, unauthorized entry, or mail opening within the United States for any purpose.

Recommendation 7—The CIA should not employ physical surveillance, infiltration of groups or any other covert techniques against Americans within the United States except:

(a) Physical surveillance of persons on the grounds of CIA installations;

(b) Physical surveillance during a preliminary investigation of allegations an employee is a security risk for a limited period outside of CIA installations. Such surveillance should be conducted only upon written authorization of the Director of Central Intelligence and should be limited to the subject of the investigation and, only to the extent necessary to identify them, to persons with whom the subject has contact;

(c.) Confidential inquiries, during a preliminary investigation of allegations an employee is a security risk, of outside sources concerning medical or financial information about the subject which is relevant to those allegations;

(d) The use of identification which does not reveal CIA or government affiliation, in background and other security investigations permitted the CIA by these recommendations, and the conduct of checks, which do not reveal CIA or government affiliation for the purpose of judging the effectiveness of cover operations, upon the written authorization of the Director of Central Intelligence;

(e) In exceptional cases, the placement or recruitment of agents within an unwitting domestic group solely for the purpose of preparing them for assignments abroad and only for as long as is necessary to accomplish that purpose. This should take place only if the Director of Central Intelligence makes a written finding that it is essential for foreign intelligence collection of vital importance to the United States, and the Attorney General makes a written finding that the operation will be conducted under procedures designed to prevent misuse of the undisclosed participation or of any information obtained therefrom. In the case of any such action, no information received by CIA from the agent as a result of his position in the group should be disseminated outside the CIA unless it indicates felonious criminal conduct or threat of death or serious bodily harm, in which case dissemination should be permitted to an appropriate official agency if approved by the Attorney General.

Recommendation 8.—The CIA should not collect information within the United States concerning Americans except:

(a) Information concerning CIA employees, CIA contractors and their employees, or applicants for such employment or contracting;

(b) Information concerning individuals or organizations providing, or offering to provide, assistance to the CIA;

(c.) Information concerning individuals or organizations being considered by the CIA as potential sources of information or assistance;

(d) Visitors to CIA facilities;

(e) Persons otherwise in the immediate vicinity of sensitive CIA sites; or

(f) Persons who give their informed written consent to such collection.

In (a), (b) and (c) above, information should be collected only if necessary for the purpose of determining the person's fitness for employment, contracting or assistance. If, in the course of such collection, information is obtained which indicates criminal activity, it should be transmitted to the FBI or other appropriate agency. When an American's relationship with the CIA is prospective, information should only be collected if there is a bona fide expectation the person might be used by the CIA.

CIA Activities Outside of the United States The Committee would permit a wider range of CIA activities against Americans abroad than it would permit the CIA to undertake within the United States, but it would not permit the CIA to investigate abroad the lawful activities of Americans to any greater degree than the FBI could investigate such activities at home.

Abroad, the FBI is not in-a position to protect the CIA from serious threats to its facilities or personnel, or to investigate all serious security violations. To the extent it is impractical to rely on local law enforcement authorities, the CIA should be free to preserve its security by specified appropriate investigations which may involve Americans, including surveillance, of persons other than its own employees.

The Committee gives to the FBI the sole responsibility within the United States for authorized domestic security investigations of Americans. However, when such an investigation has overseas aspects, the FBI looks to the CIA as the overseas operational arm of the intelligence community. The recommendations would authorize the CIA to target Americans abroad as part of an authorized investigation initiated by the FBI.

The Committee does not recommend permitting the CIA itself to initiate such investigations of Americans overseas. Present communications permit rapid consultation with the Department of Justice. Moreover, the lesson of CHAOS is that an American's activities abroad may be ambiguous, such as contact with persons who may be acting on behalf of hostile foreign powers at an international conference on disarmament. The question is who shall determine there is sufficient information to justify making an American citizen a target of his government's intelligence apparatus?

The limitations contained in Recommendation 9 only pertain to the CIA initiating investigations or otherwise intentionally collecting information on Americans abroad. The CIA would not be prohibited from accepting and passing on information on the illegal activities of Americans which the CIA acquires incidentally in the course of its other activities abroad.

The Committee believes that judgments should be centralized within the Justice Department to promote consistent, carefully controlled application of the appropriate standards and protection of Constitutional rights. This is the same position taken by Director Colby in setting current CIA policy for mounting operations against Americans abroad. In March 1974, Director Colby formally terminated the CHAOS program and promulgated new guidelines for future activity abroad involving Americans, which, in effect, transferred such responsibilities to the Department of Justice.

The Committee is somewhat more restrictive than the Executive Order with respect to collection of information on Americans. As mentioned earlier, the Order only restricts CIA collection of information about the "domestic activities" of Americans and does not prohibit the collection of information regarding the lawful travel or international contacts of American citizens. This creates a particularly significant problem with respect to CIA activities directed against Americans abroad.

The Order permits the CIA wider latitude abroad than do the Committee's Recommendations in two other important respects. The Order permits collection of information if the American is reasonably believed to be acting on behalf of a foreign power. That exemption on its face would include Americans working for a foreign country on business or legal matters or otherwise engaged in wholly lawful activities in compliance with applicable registration or other regulatory statutes. More importantly, the Order permits the CIA to collect "foreign intelligence" or "counterintelligence" information abroad about the domestic activities of Americans. The Order then broadly defines "foreign intelligence" as information about the intentions or activities of a foreign country or person, or information about areas outside the United States. This would authorize the CIA to collect, abroad, for example, information about the domestic activities of American businessmen which provided intelligence about business transactions of foreign persons.

The CIA does not at present specifically collect intelligence on the economic activities of Americans overseas. The Committee suggests that appropriate oversight committees examine the question of the overseas collection of economic intelligence.

Use of Covert Techniques Against Americans Abroad Recommendation 11 requires the use of all covert techniques be governed by the same standards, procedures, and approvals required for their use by the Justice Department against Americans within the United States. Thus, in the case of electronic surveillance, unauthorized entry, or mail opening, a judicial warrant would be required. As a matter of sound Constitutional principle, the Fourth Amendment protections enjoyed by Americans at home should also apply to protect them against their Government abroad. It would be just as offensive to have a CIA agent burglarize an American's apartment in Rome as it would be for the FBI to do so in New York.

Requirements that a warrant be obtained in the United States would not present an excessive burden. Electronic surveillance and unauthorized entries are not presently conducted against Americans abroad without prior consultation and approval from CIA Headquarters in Langley, Virginia. Moreover, the, present Deputy Director of CIA for Operations has testified that bona fide counterintelligence investigations are lengthy and time consuming and prior review within the United States, including consultation with the Justice Department, would not be a serious problem. Indeed electronic surveillance of Americans abroad under present administration policy also requires approval by the Attorney General.

The Committee reinforces the general restrictions upon overseas targeting of Americans by recommending that the CIA be prohibited from requesting a friendly foreign intelligence service or other person from undertaking activities against Americans which the CIA itself may not do. This would not require that a foreign government's use of covert techniques be conducted under the same procedures, e.g., warrants, required by those Recommendations for the CIA and the FBI. It would mean that the CIA cannot ask a foreign intelligence service to bug the apartment of an American unless the circumstances would permit the United States Government to obtain a judicial warrant from a Federal Court in this country to conduct such surveillance of the American abroad.

The Committee places greater restrictions upon the CIA's use of covert techniques against Americans abroad than does the Executive Order. For example, the Order permits the CIA to conduct electronic surveillance and unauthorized entries under "procedures approved by the Attorney General consistent with the law." No judicial warrant procedure is required. In addition, the Order's restriction on CIA's opening mail of Americans is limited to mail "in the United States postal channels." In other words, under the Order the CIA is not prevented from intercepting abroad and opening a letter mailed by an American to his family, or sent to him from the United States.

The Order also contains no restrictions on the CIA infiltrating a group abroad, even if it were one composed entirely of Americans engaged in wholly lawful activities such as a political club of American students in Paris. Furthermore, the Order permits the CIA to conduct physical surveillance abroad of any American "reasonably believed to be" engaged in "activities threatening to the national security." On its face this language appears overly permissive and might be read to authorize a repetition of the CHAOS program in which Americans were targeted for surveillance because of their participation in international conferences critical of the U.S. role in Vietnam.

Recommendation 9. — The CIA should not collect information abroad concerning Americans except:

(a) Information concerning Americans which it is permitted to collect within the United States;

(b) At the request of the Justice Department as part of criminal investigations or an investigation of an American for suspected terrorist, or hostile foreign intelligence activities or security leak or security risk investigations which the FBI has opened pursuant to Part iv of those recommendations and which is conducted consistently with recommendations contained in Part iv.

Recommendation 10. — The CIA should be able to transmit to the FBI or other appropriate agencies information concerning Americans acquired as the incidental byproduct of otherwise permissible foreign intelligence and counterintelligence operations, whenever such information indicates any activity in violation of American law.

Recommendation 11. — The CIA may employ covert techniques abroad against Americans:

(a) Under circumstances in which the CIA could use such covert techniques against Americans within the United States; or

(b) When collecting information as part of Justice Department investigation, in which case the CIA may use a particular covert techniques under the standards and procedures and approvals applicable to its use against Americans within the United States by the FBI (See Part iv); or

(c.) To the extent necessary to identify persons known or suspected to be Americans who come in contact with foreigners the CIA is investigating.

CIA Human Experiments and Drug Use Recommendation 12 tracks similar restrictions in the Executive Order but proposes an additional safeguard — giving the National Commission on Biomedical Ethics and Human Standards jurisdiction to review any testing on Americans.

Recommendation 12 -- The CIA should not use in experimentation on human subjects, any drug, device or procedure which is designed or intended to harm, or is reasonably likely to harm, the physical or mental health of the human subject, except with the informed written consent, witnessed by a disinterested third party, of each human subject, and in accordance with the guidelines issued by the National Cornmission for the Protection of Human Subjects for Biomedical and Behavioral

Research. The jurisdiction of the Commission should be amended to include the Central Intelligence Agency and other intelligence agencies of the United States Government.

Review and Certification Recommendation 13 ensures careful monitoring of those CIA activities authorized in the recommendations which are directed at Americans.

Recommendation 13 -- Any CIA activity engaged in pursuant to Recommendations 7, 8, 9, 10, or 11 should be subject to periodic review and certification of compliance with the Constitution, applicable statutes, agency regulations and executive orders by:

(a) The Inspector General of the CIA;

(b) The General Counsel of the CIA in coordination with the Director of Central Intelligence;

(c.) The Attorney General; and

(d) The oversight committee recommended in Part xii.

All such certifications should be available for review by congressional oversight committees.

b. National Security Agency

The recommendations contained in this section suggest controls on the electronic surveillance activities of the National Security Agency insofar as they involve, or could involve, Americans. There is no statute which either authorizes or specifically restricts such activities. NSA was created by executive order in 1952, and its functions are described in directives of the National Security Council.

While, in practice, NSA's collection activities are complex and sophisticated, the process by which it produces foreign intelligence can be reduced to a few easily understood principles. NSA intercepts messages passing over international lines of communication, some of which have one terminal within the United States. Traveling over these lines of communication, especially those with one terminal in the United States, are the messages of Americans, most of which are irrelevant to NSA's foreign intelligence mission. NSA often has no means of excluding such messages, however, from others it intercepts which might be of foreign intelligence value. It does have, however, the capability to select particular messages from those it intercepts which are of foreign intelligence value. Most international communications of Americans are not selected, since they do not meet foreign intelligence criteria. Having selected messages of possible intelligence value, NSA monitors (reads) them, and uses the information it obtains as the basis for reports which it furnishes the intelligence agencies.

Having this process in mind, one will more readily understand the recommendations of the Committee insofar as NSA's handling of the messages of Americans is concerned. The Committee recommends first that NSA monitor only foreign communications. It should not monitor domestic communications, even for foreign intelligence purposes. Second, the Committee recommends that NSA should not select messages for monitoring, from those foreign communications it has intercepted, because the message is to or from or refers to a particular American, unless the Department of Justice has first obtained a search warrant, or the particular American has consented. Third, the Committee recommends that NSA be required to make every practicable effort to eliminate or minimize the extent to which the communications of Americans are intercepted, selected, or monitored. Fourth, for those communications of Americans which are nevertheless incidentally selected and monitored, the Committee recommends that NSA be prohibited from disseminating such communication, or information derived therefrom, which identifies an American, unless the communication indicates evidence of hostile foreign intelligence or terrorist activity, or felonious criminal conduct, or contains a threat of death or serious bodily harm. In these cases, the Committee recommends that the Attorney General approve any such dissemination as being consistent with these policies.

In summary, the Committee's recommendations reflect its belief that NSA should have no greater latitude to monitor the communications of Americans than any other intelligence agency. To the extent that other agencies are required to obtain a warrant before monitoring the communications of Americans, NSA should be required to obtain a warrant.

Recommendation 14 — NSA should not engage in domestic security activities. Its functions should be limited in a precisely drawn legislative charter to the collection of foreign intelligence from foreign communications.

Recommendation 15 — NSA should take all practicable measures consistent with its foreign intelligence mission to eliminate or minimize the interception, selection, and monitoring of communications of Americans from the foreign communications.

Recommendation 16 — NSA should not be permitted to select for monitoring any communication to, from, or about an American without his consent, except for the purpose of obtaining information about hostile foreign intelligence or terrorist activities, and then only if a warrant approving such monitoring is obtained in accordance with procedures similar 37 to those contained in Title III of the Omnibus Crime Control and Safe Streets Act of 1968.

(This recommendation would eliminate the possibility that NSA would re-establish its "watch lists" of the late 1960s and early 1970s. In that case, the names of Americans were submitted to NSA by other federal agencies and were used as a basis for selecting and monitoring, without a warrant, the international communications of those Americans.)

Recommendation 17 — Any personally identifiable information about an American which NSA incidentally acquires, other than pursuant to a warrant, should not be disseminated without the consent of the American, but should be destroyed as promptly as possible, unless it indicates:

(a) Hostile foreign intelligence or terrorist activities; or

(b) Felonious criminal conduct for which a warrant might be obtained pursuant to Title III of the Omnibus Crime Control and Safe Streets Act of 1968; or

(c.) A threat of death or serious bodily harm.

If dissemination is permitted, by (a), (b) and (c) above, it must only be made to an appropriate official and after approval by the Attorney General.

(This recommendation is consistent with NSA's policy prior to the Executive Order. 38 NSA's practice prior to the Executive Order was not to disseminate material containing personally identifiable information about Americans.)

Recommendation 18 — NSA should not request from any commercial carrier any communication which it could not otherwise obtain pursuant to these recommendations.

(This recommendation is to ensure that NSA will not resume an operation such as SHAMROCK, disclosed during the Committee's hearings, whereby NSA received for almost 30 years copies of most international telegrams transmitted by certain international telegraph companies in the United States.)

Recommendation 19—The Office of Security at NSA should be permitted to collect background information on present or prospective employees or contractors of NSA, solely for the purpose of determining their fitness for employment. With respect to security risks or the security of its installations, NSA should be permitted to conduct physical surveillances, consistent with such surveillances as the CIA is permitted to conduct, in similar circumstances, by these recommendations.

c. Military Service and Defense Department Investigative Agencies This section of the Committee's recommendations pertains to the controls upon the intelligence activities of the military services and Department of Defense insofar as they involve Americans who are not members of or affiliated with the armed forces.

In general, the restrictions seek to limit military investigations to activities in the civilian community which are necessary and pertinent to the military mission, and which cannot feasibly be accomplished by civilian agencies. In overseas locations where civilian agencies do not perform investigative activities to assist the military mission, military intelligence is given more latitude. Specifically, the Committee recommends that military intelligence be limited within the United States to conducting investigations of violations of the Uniform Code of Military Justice; investigations for security clearances of Department of Defense employees and contractors; and investigations immediately before and during the deployment of armed forces in connection with civil disturbances. None of these investigations should involve the use of any covert technique employed against American civilians. In overseas locations, the Committee recommends that military intelligence have additional authority to conduct investigations of terrorist activity and hostile foreign intelligence activity. In these cases, covert techniques directed at Americans may be employed if consistent with the Committee's restrictions upon the use of such techniques in the United States in Part iv.

Recommendation 20—Except as specifically provided herein, the Department of Defense should not engage in domestic security activities. Its functions, as they relate to the activities of the foreign intelligence community, should be limited in a precisely drawn legislative charter to the conduct of foreign intelligence and foreign counterintelligence activities and tactical military intelligence activities abroad, and production, analysis, and dissemination of departmental intelligence.

Recommendation 21—In addition to its foreign intelligence responsibility, the Department of Defense has a responsibility to investigate its personnel in order to protect the security of its installations and property, to ensure order and discipline within its ranks, and to conduct other limited investigations once dispatched by the President to suppress a civil disorder. A legislative charter should define precisely—in a manner which is not inconsistent with these recommendations—the authorized scope and purpose of any investigations undertaken by the Department of Defense to satisfy these responsibilities.

Recommendation 22—No agency of the Department of Defense should conduct investigations of violations of criminal law or otherwise perform any law enforcement or domestic security functions within the United States, except on military bases or concerning military personnel, to enforce the Uniform Code of Military Justice.

Control of Civil Disturbance Intelligence The Department of the Army has executive responsibility for rendering assistance in connection with civil disturbances. In the late 1960s, it instituted a nationwide collection program in which Army investigators were dispatched to collect information on the political activities of Americans. This was done on the theory that such information was necessary to prepare the Army in the event that its troops were sent to the scene of civil disturbances. The Committee believes that the Army's potential role in civil disturbances does not justify such an intelligence effort directed against American civilians.

Recommendation 23—The Department of Defense should not be permitted to conduct investigations of Americans on the theory that the information derived therefrom might be useful in potential civil disorders. The Army should be permitted to gather information about geography, logistical matters, or the identity of local officials which is necessary to the positioning, support, and use of troops in an area where troops are likely to be deployed by the President in connection with a civil disturbance. The Army should be permitted to investigate Americans involved in such disturbances after troops have been deployed to the site of a civil disorder, (i) to the extent necessary to fulfill the military mission, and (ii) to the extent the information cannot be obtained from the FBI. (The FBI's responsibility in connection with civil disorders and its assistance to the Army is described in Part IV.)

Recommendation 24—Appropriate agencies of the Department of Defense should be permitted to collect background information on their present or prospective employees or contractors. With respect to security risks or the security of its installations, the Department of Defense should be permitted to conduct physical surveillance consistent with such surveillances as the CIA is permitted to conduct, in similar circumstances, by these recommendations.

Prohibitions and Limitations of Covert Techniques During the Army's civil disturbance collection program of the late 1960s, Army intelligence agents employed a variety of covert techniques to gather information about civilian political activities. These included covert penetrations of private meetings and organizations, use of informants, monitoring amateur radio broadcasts, and posing as newsmen. This provision is designed to prevent the use of such covert techniques against American civilians. The Committee believes that none of the legitimate investigative tasks of the military within the United States justified the use of such techniques against unaffiliated Americans.

Recommendation 25—Except as provided in 27 below, the Department of Defense should not direct any covert technique (e.g., electronic surveillance, informants, etc.) at American civilians.

Limited investigations Abroad The military services currently conduct preventive intelligence investigations within the United States where members of their respective services are agents of, or are collaborating with, a hostile foreign intelligence service. These investigations are coordinated with, and under the ultimate control of, the FBI. The Committee's recommendations are not intended to prevent the military services from continuing to assist the FBI with such investigations involving members of the armed forces. They are intended, however, to place responsibility for these investigations, insofar as they take place within the United States, in the FBI, and not in the military services themselves. The military services, on the other band, are given additional responsibility to conduct investigations of Americans who are suspected of engaging in terrorist activity or hostile foreign intelligence activity in overseas locations.

Recommendation 26—The Department of Defense should be permitted to conduct abroad preventive intelligence investigations of unaffiliated Americans as described in Part iv below, provided 'Such investigations are first approved by the

FBI. Such investigations by the Department of Defense, including the use of covert techniques, should ordinarily be conducted in a manner consistent with the recommendations pertaining to the FBI, contained in Part iv; however, overseas locations, where U.S. military forces constitute the governing power, or where U.S. military forces are engaged in hostilities, circumstances may require greater latitude to conduct such investigations.

iii. Non-Intelligence Agencies Should Be Barred From Domestic Security Activity

a. Internal Revenue Service

The Committee's review of intelligence collection and investigative activity by IRS' Intelligence Division and of the practice of furnishing information in IRS files to the intelligence agencies demonstrates that reforms are necessary and appropriate. The primary objective of reform is to prevent IRS from becoming an instrumentality of the intelligence agencies, beyond the scope of what IRS, as the Federal tax collector, should be doing. Recommendations 27 through 29 are designed to achieve this objective by providing that IRS collection of intelligence and its conduct of investigations are to be confined strictly to tax matters. Moreover, programs of tax investigation, in which targets are selected partly because of indications of tax violations and partly because of reasons relating to domestic security, are prohibited where they would erode constitutional rights. Where otherwise appropriate, such programs must be conducted under special safeguards to prevent any adverse effect on the exercise of those rights.

These recommendations should prevent a recurrence of the excesses associated with the Special Services Staff and the Intelligence Gathering and Retrieval System.

Targeting of Persons or Groups for Investigations or Intelligence-Gathering by IRS 39

Recommendation 27 — The IRS should not, on behalf of any intelligence agency or for its own use, collect any information about the activities of Americans except for the purposes of enforcing the tax laws.

Recommendation 28 — IRS should not select any person or group for tax investigation on the basis of political activity or for any other reason not relevant to enforcement of the tax laws.

Recommendation 29 — Any program of intelligence investigation relating to domestic security in which targets are selected by both tax and non-tax criteria should only be initiated:

(a) Upon the written request of the Attorney General or the Secretary of the Treasury, specifying the nature of the requested program and the need therefore; and

(b) After the written certification by the Commissioner of the IRS that procedures have been developed which are sufficient to prevent the infringement of the constitutional rights of Americans; and

(c.) With congressional oversight committees being kept continually advised of the nature and extent of such programs.

Disclosure Procedures The Committee's review of disclosure of tax information by IRS to the FBI and the CIA showed three principal abuses by those intelligence agencies: (1) the by-passing of disclosure procedures mandated by law, resulting in the agencies obtaining access to tax returns and tax-related information through improper channels, and, sometimes, without a proper basis; (2) the failure to state the reasons justifying the need for the information and the uses contemplated so that IRS could determine if the request met the applicable criteria for disclosure; and (3) the improper use of tax returns and information, particularly by the FBI in

COINTELPRO. Recommendations 30 through 35 are designed to prevent these abuses from occurring again.

While general problems of disclosure are being studied by several different congressional committees with jurisdiction over IRS, these recommendations reflect this Committee's focus on disclosure problems seen in the interaction between IRS and the intelligence agencies.

Recommendation 30—No intelligence agency should request 40 from the Internal Revenue Service tax returns or tax related information except under the statutes and regulations controlling such disclosures. In addition, the existing procedures under which tax returns and tax-related information are released by the IRS should be strengthened, as suggested in the following five recommendations.

Recommendation 31—All requests from an intelligence agency to the IRS for tax returns and tax-related information should be in writing, and signed by the bead of the intelligence agency making the request, or his designee. Copies of such requests should be filed with the Attorney General. Each request should include a clear statement of:

(a) The purpose for which disclosure is sought;

(b) Facts sufficient to establish that the requested information is needed by the requesting agency for the performance of an authorized and lawful function;

(c.) The uses which the requesting agency intends to make of the information;

(d) The extent of the disclosures sought;

(e) Agreement by the requesting agency not to use the documents or information for any purpose other than that stated in the request; and

(f) Agreement by the requesting agency that the information will not be disclosed to any other agency or person except in accordance with the law.

Recommendation 32—IRS should not release tax returns or tax-related information to any intelligence agency unless it has received a request satisfying the requirements of Recommendation 31, and the Commissioner of Internal Revenue has approved the request in writing.

Recommendation 33—IRS should maintain a record of all such requests and responses thereto for a period of twenty years.

Recommendation 34—No intelligence agency should use the information supplied to it by the IRS pursuant to a request of the agency except as stated in a proper request for disclosure.

Recommendation 35—All requests for information sought by the FBI should be filed by the Department of Justice. Such requests should be signed by the Attorney General or his designee, following a determination by the Department that the request is proper under the applicable statutes and regulations.

b. Post Office (U.S. Postal Service)

These recommendations are designed to tighten the existing restrictions regarding requests by intelligence agencies for both inspection of the exteriors of mail ("mail cover") and inspection of the contents of first class mail ("mail opening"). As to mail cover, the Committee's recommendation is to centralize the review and approval of all requests by requiring that only the Attorney General may authorize mail cover, and to eliminate unjustified mail covers by requiring that the mail cover be found "necessary" to a domestic security investigation. With respect to mail opening, the recommendations provide that it can only be done pursuant to court warrant.

Recommendation 36—The Post Office should not Permit the FBI or any intelligence agency to inspect markings or addresses on first class mail, nor should the Post Office itself inspect markings or addresses on behalf of the FBI or any intelligence agency, on first class mail, except upon the written approval of the Attorney General or his designee. Where one of the correspondents is an American, the Attorney General or his designee should only approve such inspection for domestic security purposes upon a written finding that it is necessary to a criminal investigation or a preventive intelligence investigation of terrorist activity or hostile foreign intelligence activity.

Upon such a request, the Post Office may temporarily remove from circulation such correspondence for the purpose of such inspection of its exterior as is related to the investigation.

Recommendation 37—The Post Office should not transfer the custody of any first class mail to any agency except the Department of Justice. Such mail should not be transferred or opened except upon a judicial search warrant.

(a) In the case of mail where one of the correspondents is an American, the judge must find that there is probable cause to believe that the mail contains evidence, of a crime. 41

(b) In the case of mail where both parties are foreigners:

(1) The judge must find that there is probable cause to believe that both parties to such correspondence are foreigners, and one of the correspondents is an officer, employee or conscious agent of a foreign power; and

(2) The Attorney General must certify that the mail opening is likely to reveal information necessary either (i) to the protection of the nation against actual or potential attack or other hostile acts of force of a foreign power; (ii) to obtain foreign intelligence information deemed essential to the security of the United States; or (iii) to protect national security information against hostile foreign intelligence activity.

iv. Federal Domestic Security Activities Should Be Limited and Controlled to Prevent Abuses Without Hampering Criminal Investigations or Investigations of Foreign Espionage

The recommendations contained in this part are designed to accomplish two principal objectives: (1) prohibit improper intelligence activities and (2) define the limited domestic security investigations which should be permitted. As suggested earlier, the ultimate goal is a statutory mandate for the federal government's domestic security function that will ensure that the FBI, as the primary domestic security investigative agency, concentrates upon criminal conduct as opposed to political rhetoric or association. Our recommendations would vastly curtail the scope of domestic security investigations as they have been conducted, by prohibiting inquiries initiated because the Bureau regards a group as falling within a vaguely defined category such as "subversive," "New Left," "Black Nationalist Hate Groups," or "White Hate Groups." The recommendations also ban investigations based merely upon the fact that a person or group is associating with others who are being investigated (e.g., the Bureau's investigation of the Southern Christian Leadership Conference because of alleged "Communist infiltration").

The simplest way to eliminate investigations of peaceful speech and association would be to limit the FBI to traditional investigations of crimes which have been committed (including the crimes of attempt and conspiracy). The Committee found, however, that there are circumstances where the FBI should have authority to conduct limited "intelligence investigations" of threatened conduct (terrorism and foreign espionage) which is generally covered by the criminal law, where the conduct has not yet reached the stage of a prosecuteable act.

The Committee, however, found that abuses were frequently associated even with such intelligence investigations. This led us also to recommend: precise limitations upon the use of covert techniques (Recommendations 51 to 60); restrictions upon maintenance and dissemination of information gathered in such investigations (Recommendations 64 to 68); and a statutory requirement that the Attorney General monitor these investigations and terminate them as soon as practical (Recommendation 69).

a. Centralize Supervision, Investigative Responsibility, and the Use of Covert Techniques

Investigations should be centralized within the Department of Justice. It is the Committee's judgment that if former Attorneys General had been held accountable by the Congress for ensuring compliance by the FBI and the intelligence agencies with laws designed to protect the rights of Americans, the Department of Justice would have been more likely to discover and enjoin improper activities. Furthermore, centralizing domestic security investigations within the FBI will facilitate the Attorney General's supervision of them.

Recommendation 38 — All domestic security investigative activity, including the use of covert techniques, should be centralized within the Federal Bureau of Investigation, except those investigations by the Secret Service designed to protect the life of the President or other Secret Service protectees. Such investigations and the use of covert techniques in those investigations should be centralized within the Secret Service.

Recommendation 39. — All domestic security activities of the federal government and all other intelligence agency activities covered by the Domestic Intelligence Recommendations should be subject to Justice Department oversight to assure compliance with the Constitution and laws of the United States.

b. Prohibitions

The Committee recommends a set of prohibitions, in addition to its later recommendations limiting the scope of and procedural controls for domestic security investigations.

The following prohibitions cover abuses ranging from the political use of the sensitive information maintained by the Bureau to the excesses of COINTELPRO. They are intended to cover activities engaged in, by, or on behalf of, the FBI. For example, in prohibiting Bureau interference in lawful speech, publication, assembly, organization, or association of Americans, the Committee intends to prohibit a Bureau agent from mailing fake letters to factionalize a group as well as to prohibit an informant from manipulating or influencing the peaceful activities of a group on behalf of the FBI.

Subsequent recommendations limit the kinds of investigations which can be opened and provide controls for those investigations. Specifically, the Committee limits FBI authority to collect information on Americans to enumerated circumstances; limits authority to maintain information on political beliefs, political assocations, or private lives of Americans; requires judicial warrants for the most intrusive covert collection techniques (electronic surveillance, mail opening, and surreptitious entry); and proposes new restrictions upon the use of other covert techniques, particularly informants.

Recommendation 41 — The FBI should be prohibited from engaging on its own or through informants or others, in any of the following activities directed at Americans:

(a) Disseminating any information to the White House, any other federal official, the news media, or any other person for a political or other improper purpose, such as discrediting an opponent of the administration or a critic of an intelligence or investigative agency.

(b) Interfering with lawful speech, publication, assembly, organizational activity, or association of Americans.

(c.) Harassing individuals through unnecessary overt investigative techniques 42 such as interviews or obvious physical surveillance for the purpose of intimidation.

Recommendation 41 — The Bureau should be prohibited from maintaining information on the political beliefs, political associations, or private lives of Americans except that which is clearly necessary for domestic security investigations as described in Part c. 43

c. Authorized Scope of Domestic Security Investigations

The Committee sought three objectives in defining the appropriate jurisdiction of the FBI. First, we sought to carefully limit any investigations other than traditional criminal investigations to five defined areas: preventive intelligence investigations (in two areas closely related to serious criminal activity — terrorist and hostile foreign intelligence activities), civil disorders assistance, background investigations, security risk investigations, and security leak investigations.

Second, we sought substantially to narrow, and to impose special restrictions on the conduct of, those investigations which involved the most flagrant abuses in the past: preventive intelligence investigations and civil disorders assistance. Third, we sought to provide a clear statutory foundation for those investigations which the Committee believes are appropriate to fill the vacuum in FBI legal authority.

Achieving the first and second objectives will have the most significant impact upon the FBI's domestic intelligence program and indeed, could eliminate almost half its workload. Recommendations 44 through 46 impose two types of restrictions upon the conduct of intelligence investigations and civil disorders assistance. First, the scope of intelligence investigations is limited to terrorist activities or espionage, and the scope of civil disorders assistance is limited to civil disorders which may require federal troops. Second, the Committee suggests that the threshold for initiation of a full intelligence investigation be "reasonable Suspicion." Preliminary intelligence investigations — limited in scope, duration, and investigative technique — could be opened upon a "specific allegation or specific or substantiated information." A written finding by the Attorney General of a likely need for federal troops is required for civil disorders assistance.

The Committee's approach to FBI domestic security investigations is basically the same as that adopted by the Attorney General's guidelines for domestic security investigations. Both are cautious about any departures from former Attorney General Stone's maxim that the FBI should only conduct criminal investigations. For example, neither the Committee nor the Attorney General would condone investigations which are totally unrelated to criminal statutes (e.g., the FBI's 1970 investigation of all black student unions).

However, the Committee views its recommendations as a somewhat more limited departure from former Attorney General Stone's line than the present Attorney General's guidelines. First, the Committee would only permit intelligence investigations with respect to hostile foreign intelligence activity and terrorism. The

Attorney General's guidelines have been read by FBI officials as authorizing intelligence investigations of "subversives" (individuals who may attempt to overthrow the government in the indefinite future). While the Justice Department, under its current leadership, might not adopt such an interpretation, a different Attorney General might. Second, the guidelines on their face appear to permit investigating essentially local civil disobedience (e.g., "use of force" to interfere with state or local government which could be construed too broadly).

There are two reasons why the Committee would prohibit intelligence investigations of "subversives" or local civil disobedience. First, those investigations inherently risk abuse because they inevitably require surveillance of lawful speech and association rather than criminal conduct. The Committee's examination of forty years of investigations into "subversion" has found the term to be so vague as to constitute a license to investigate almost any activity of practically any group that actively opposes the policies of the administration in power.

A second reason for prohibiting intelligence investigations of "subversion" and local civil disobedience is that both can be adequately handled by less intrusive methods without unnecessarily straining limited Bureau resources. Any real threats to our form of government can be best identified through intelligence investigations focused on persons who may soon commit illegal violent acts. Local civil disobedience can be best handled by local police. Indeed, recent studies by the General Accounting Office suggest that FBI investigations in these areas result in very few prosecutions and little information of help to authorities in preventing violence.

The FBI now expends more money in its domestic security program than it does in its organized crime program, and, indeed, twice the amount on "internal security" informant operations as on organized crime informant coverage. "Subversive investigations" and "civil disorders assistance" represent almost half the caseload of the FBI domestic security program. The national interest would be better served if Bureau resources were directed at terrorism, hostile foreign intelligence activity, or organized crime, all more serious and pressing threats to the nation than "subversives" or local civil disobedience.

For similar reasons, the Committee, like the Attorney General's guidelines, requires "reasonable suspicion" for preventive intelligence investigations which extend beyond a preliminary stage. Investigations of terrorism and hostile foreign intelligence activity which are not limited in time and scope could lead to the same abuses found in intelligence investigations of subversion or local civil disobedience. However, an equally important reason for this standard is that it should increase the efficiency of Bureau investigations. The General Accounting Office found that when the FBI initiated its investigations on "soft evidence" — evidence which probably would not meet this "reasonable suspicion" standard — it usually wasted its time on an innocent target. When it initiated its investigation on harder evidence, its ability to detect imminent violence improved significantly.

The Committee's recommendations limit preventive intelligence investigations to situations where information indicates that the prohibited activity will "soon" occur, whereas the guidelines do not require that the activity be imminent. This limit is essential to prevent a return to sweeping, endless investigations of remote and speculative "threats." The Committee's intent is that, to open or continue a full investigation, there should be a substantial indication of terrorism or hostile foreign intelligence activity in the near future.

The Committee's restrictions are intended to eliminate unnecessary investigations and to provide additional protections for constitutional rights. Shifting the focus of Bureau manpower in domestic security investigations from lawful speech and association to criminal conduct by terrorists and foreign spies provides further protection for constitutional rights of Americans as well as serving the nation's interest in security.

1. Investigations of Committed or Imminent Offenses

Recommendation 42—The FBI should be permitted to investigate a committed act which may violate a federal criminal statute pertaining to the domestic security to determine the identity of the perpetrator or to determine whether the act violates such a statute.

Recommendation 43—The FBI should be permitted to investigate an American or foreigner to obtain evidence of criminal activity where there is "reasonable suspicion" that the American or foreigner has committed, is committing, or is about to commit a specific act which violates a federal statute pertaining to the domestic security.

2. Preventive Intelligence Investigations

Recommendation 44—The FBI should be permitted to conduct a preliminary preventive intelligence investigation of an American or foreigner where it has a specific allegation or specific or substantiated information that the American or foreigner will soon engage in terrorist activity or hostile foreign intelligence activity. Such a preliminary investigation should not continue longer than thirty days from receipt of the information unless the Attorney General or his designee finds that the information and any corroboration which has been obtained warrants investigation for an additional period which may not exceed sixty days. If, at the outset or at any time during the course of a preliminary investigation the Bureau establishes "reasonable suspicion" that an American or foreigner will soon engage in terrorist activity or hostile foreign intelligence activity, it may conduct a full preventive intelligence investigation. Such full investigation should not continue longer than one year except upon a finding of compelling circumstances by the Attorney General or his designee.

In no event should the FBI open a preliminary or full preventive intelligence investigation based upon information that an American is advocating political ideas or engaging in lawful political activities or is associating with others for the purpose of petitioning the government for redress of grievances or other such constitutionally protected purpose.

The second paragraph of Recommendation 44 will serve as an important safeguard if enacted into any statute authorizing preventive intelligence investigations. It would supplement the protection that would be afforded by limiting the FBI's intelligence investigations to terrorist and hostile foreign intelligence activities. It re-emphasizes the Committee's intent that the investigations of peaceful protest groups and other lawful associations should not recur. It serves as a further reminder that advocacy of political ideas is not to be the basis for governmental surveillance. At the same time Recommendation 44 permits the initiation of investigations where the Bureau possesses information consisting of a "specific allegation or specific or substantiated information that [an] American or foreigner will soon engage in terrorist activity or hostile foreign intelligence activity."

This recommendation has been among the most difficult of the domestic intelligence recommendations to draft. It was difficult because it represents the

Committee's effort to draw the fine line between legitimate investigations of conduct and illegitimate investigations of advocacy and association. Originally the Committee was of the view that a threshold of "reasonable suspicion" should apply to initiating even limited preliminary intelligence investigations of terrorist or hostile foreign intelligence activities. However, the Committee was persuaded by the Department of Justice that, having narrowly defined terrorist and hostile foreign intelligence activities, a "reasonable suspicion" threshold might be unworkable at the preliminary stage. Such a threshold might prohibit the FBI from investigating an allegation of extremely dangerous activity made by an anonymous source or a source of unknown reliability. The "reasonable suspicion" standard requires that the investigator have confidence in the reliability of the individual providing the information and some corroboration of the information.

However, the Committee is cautious in proposing a standard of "specific allegation or specific or substantiated information" because it permits initiation of a preliminary investigation which includes the use of physical surveillance and a survey of, but not targeting of, existing confidential human sources. The Committee encourages the Attorney General to work with the Congress to improve upon the language we recommend in Recommendation 44 before including it in any legislative charter. If adopted, both the Attorney General and the appropriate oversight committees should periodically conduct a careful review of the application of the standard by the FBI.

The ultimate goal which Congress should seek in enacting such legislation is the development of a standard for the initiation of intelligence investigations which permits investigations of credible allegations of conduct which if uninterrupted will soon result in terrorist activities or hostile foreign intelligence activities as we define them. It must not permit investigations of constitutionally protected activities as the Committee described them in the last paragraph of Recommendation 44. The following are examples of the Committee's intent.

Recommendation 44 would prohibit the initiation of an investigation based upon "mere advocacy:"

-An investigation could not be initiated, for example, when the Bureau receives an allegation that a member of a dissident group has made statements at the group's meeting that "America needs a Marxist-Leninist government and needs to get rid of the fat cat capitalist pigs."

The Committee has found serious abuses in past FBI investigations of groups. In the conduct of these investigations, the FBI often failed to distinguish between members who were engaged in criminal activity and those who were exercising their constitutional rights of association. The Committee's recommendations would only permit investigation of a group in two situations: first, where the FBI receives information that the avowed purpose of the group is "soon to engage in terrorist activity or hostile foreign intelligence activity"; or second, where the FBI has information that unidentified members of a group are "soon to engage in terrorist activity or hostile foreign intelligence activity". In both cases the FBI may focus on the group to determine the identity of those members who plan soon to engage in such activity. However, in both cases the FBI should minimize the collection of information about law-abiding members of the group or any lawful activities of the group.

-Where the FBI has information that certain chapters of a political organization had "action squads," the purpose of which was to commit terrrorist acts, the FBI could investigate all members of a particular "action squad" where it had an allegation that this "action squad" planned to assassinate, for example, Members of Congress.

-An investigation could be initiated based upon specific information obtained by the FBI that unidentified members of a Washington, D.C., group are planning to assassinate Members of Congress.

The Committee's recommendations would not permit investigation of mere association:

-The FBI could not investigate an allegation that a member of the Klan has lunch regularly with the mayor of a southern community.

-The FBI could not investigate the allegation that a U.S. Senator attended a cocktail party at a foreign embassy where a foreign intelligence agent was present.

However, when additional facts are added indicating conduct which might constitute terrorist activity or hostile foreign intelligence activity, investigation might be authorized:

-The FBI could initiate an investigation of a dynamite dealer who met with a member of the "action squad" described above.

-Likewise, the FBI could initiate an investigation of a member of the National Security Council staff who met clandestinely with a known foreign intelligence agent in an obscure Paris restaurant.

Investigations of contacts can become quite troublesome when the contact takes place within the context of political activities or association for the purpose of petitioning the government. Law-abiding American protest groups may share common goals with groups in other countries. The obvious example was the widespread opposition in the late 1960's, at home and abroad, to America's role in Vietnam.

Furthermore, Americans should be free to communicate about such issues with persons in other countries, to attend international conferences and to exchange views or information about planned protest activities with like-minded foreign groups. Such activity, in itself, would not be the basis for a preliminary investigation under these recommendations:

-The FBI could not open an investigation of an anti-war group because "known communists" were also in attendance at a group meeting even if it had reason to believe that the communists' instructions were to influence the group or that the group shared the goals of the Soviet Union on ending the war in Vietnam.

-The FBI could not open an investigation of an anti-war activist who attends an international peace conference in Oslo where foreign intelligence agents would be in attendance even if the FBI had reason to believe that they might attempt to recruit the activist. Of course, the CIA would riot he prevented from surveillance of the foreign agent's activities.

However, if the Bureau had additional information suggesting that the activities of the Americans in the above hypothetical cases were more than mere association to petition for redress of grievances, an investigation would be legitimate.

-Where the FBI had received information that the anti-war activist traveling to Oslo intended to meet with a person he knew to be a foreign intelligence agent to receive instructions to conduct espionage on behalf of a hostile foreign country, the FBI could open a preliminary investigation of the activist.

The Committee cautions the Department of Justice and FBI that in opening investigations of conduct occurring in the context of political activities, it should endeavor to ensure that the allegation prompting the investigation is from a reliable source.

Certainly, however, where the FBI has received a specific allegation or specific or substantiated information that an American or foreigner will soon engage in hostile foreign intelligence activity or terrorist activity, it may conduct an investigation. For example, it could do so:

-Where the FBI receives information that an American has been recruited by a hostile intelligence service;

-Where the FBI receives information that an atomic scientist has had a number of clandestine meetings with a hostile foreign intelligence agent.

Recommendation 45—The FBI should be permitted to collect information to assist federal, state, and local officials in connection with a civil disorder either

(i) After the Attorney General finds in writing that there is a clear and immediate threat of domestic violence or rioting which is likely to require implementation of 10 U.S.C. 332 or 333 (the use of federal troops for the enforcement of federal law or federal court orders), or likely to result in a request by the governor or legislature of a state pursuant to 140 U.S.C. 331 for the use of federal militia or other federal armed forces as a countermeasure; or

(ii) After such troops have been introduced.

Recommendation 46—FBI assistance to federal, state, and local officials in connection with a civil disorder should be limited to collecting information necessary for

(1) the President in making decisions concerning the introduction of federal troops;

(2) military officials in positioning and supporting such troops; and

(3) state and local officials in coordinating their activities with such military officials.

4. Background Investigations

Recommendation 47 -- The FBI should be permitted to participate in the federal government's program of background investigations of federal employees or employees of federal contractors. The authority to conduct such investigations should not, however, be used as the basis for conducting investigations of other persons. In addition, Congress should examine the standards of Executive Order 10450, which serves as the current authority for FBI background investigations, to determine whether additional legislation is necessary to:

(a) modify criteria based on political beliefs and associations unrelated to suitability for employment; such modification should make those criteria consistent with judicial decisions regarding privacy of political association, and

(b) restrict the dissemination of information from name checks of information related to suitability for employment.

5. Security Risk Investigations

Recommendation 48—Under regulations to be formulated by the Attorney General, the FBI should be permitted to investigate a specific allegation that an individual within the Executive branch with access to classified information is a security risk as described in Executive Order 10450. Such investigation should not continue longer than thirty days except upon written approval of the Attorney General or his designee.

6. Security Leak Investigations

Recommendation 49—Under regulations to be formulated by the Attorney General, the FBI should be permitted to investigate a specific allegation of the improper disclosure of classified information by employees or contractors of the Executive branch. Such investigation should not continue longer than thirty days except upon written approval of the Attorney General or his designee.

d. Authorized Investigative Techniques

The following recommendations contain the Committee's proposed controls on the use of investigative techniques in domestic security investigations which would be authorized herein. There are three types of investigative techniques: (1) overt techniques (e.g., interviews), (2) name checks (review of existing government files), and (3) covert techniques (which range, for example, from electronic surveillance and informants to the review of credit records).

The objective of these recommendations, like the Attorney General's domestic security guidelines, is to ensure that the more intrusive the technique, the more stringent the procedural checks that will be applied to it. Therefore, the recommendation would permit overt techniques and name checks in any of the investigative areas described above.

With respect to covert technique, the Committee decided upon procedures to apply to the use of a particular covert technique based upon three considerations: (1) its potential for abuse, (2) the practicability of applying the procedure to the technique, and (3) the facts and circumstances giving rise to the request for use of the technique (whether the facts warrant a full investigation or only a preliminary investigation). The most intrusive covert techniques (electronic surveillance, mail opening, and surreptitious entry) would be permissible only if a judicial warrant were obtained as required in Recommendations 51 through 54. FBI requests to target paid or controlled informants, to review tax returns, to use mail covers, or to use any other covert techniques in domestic security investigations would be subject to review and in some cases to prior approval by the Attorney General's office, as described in Recommendations 55 through 62.

The judicial warrant requirement the Committee recommends for electronic surveillance is similar in many respects to the Administration's bill, which is a welcome departure from past practice. The Committee, like the Administration, believes that there should be no electronic surveillance within the United States which is not subject to a judicial warrant procedure. Both would also authorize warrants for electronic surveillance of foreigners who are officers, agents, or employees of foreign powers, even though the government could not point to probable cause of criminal activity.

However, while the constitutional issue has not been resolved, the Committee does not believe that the President has inherent power to authorize the targeting of an American for electronic surveillance without a warrant, as suggested by the Administration bill. Certainly, if Congress requires a warrant for the targeting of an American for traditional electronic surveillance or for the most sophisticated NSA techniques, at home or abroad, then the dangerous doctrine of inherent Executive power to target an American for electronic surveillance can be put to rest at last. 49a The Committee also would require that no American be targeted for electronic surveillance except upon a judicial finding of probable criminal activity. The Administration bill would permit electronic surveillance in the absence of probable crime if the American is engaged in (or aiding or abetting a person engaged in) "clandestine intelligence activity" (an undefined term) under the direction of a foreign power. Targeting an American for electronic surveillance in the absence of probable cause to believe he might commit a crime is unwise and unnecessary.

In Part X, the Committee recommends that Congress consider amending the Espionage Act to cover modern forms of industrial, technological, or economic espionage not now prohibited. At the same time, electronic surveillance targeted at an American should be authorized where there is probable cause to believe he is engaged in such activity. Thus, the Committee agrees with the Attorney General that such activity may subject an American to electronic surveillance. But, as a matter of principle, the Committee believes that an American ought not to be targeted for surveillance unless there is probable cause to believe he may violate the law. The Committee's record suggests that use Of undefined terms, not tied to matters sufficiently serious to be the subject of criminal statutes, is a dangerous basis for intrusive investigations.

The paid and directed informant was a principal source of excesses revealed in our record. However, we do not propose the application of a judicial warrant procedure to informants. Instead, we propose a requirement of approval by the Attorney General based upon a probable cause standard. Because of the potential for abuse, however, we believe the warrant issue should be thoroughly reviewed after two years' experience.

There are some differences between the Attorney General and the Committee on the use of informants. The Attorney General would permit the FBI to make unrestricted use of existing informants in a preliminary intelligence investigation. The Committee recognizes the legitimacy of using existing informants for certain purposes — for example, to identify a new subject who has come to the attention of the Bureau. However, the Committee believes there should be certain restrictions for existing informants. Indeed, almost all of the informant abuses — overly broad reporting, the ghetto informant program, agents provocateur, etc. — involved existing informants.

The real issue is not the development of new informants, but the sustained direction of informants, new or old, at a new target. Therefore, the restrictions suggested in Recommendations 55 through 57 are designed to impose standards for the sustained targeting of informants against Americans.

The Committee requires that before an informant can be targeted in an intelligence investigation the Attorney General or his designee must make a finding that he has considered and rejected less intrusive techniques and that targeting the informant is necessary to the investigation. Furthermore, the Committee would require that the informant cannot be targeted for more than ninety days in the intelligence investigation unless the Attorney General finds that there is "probable cause" that the American will soon engage in terrorist or hostile foreign intelligence activity, except that if the Attorney General finds compelling circumstances he may permit an additional sixty days.

Other than the restrictions upon the use of informants, the Committee would permit basically the same techniques in preliminary and full investigations as the Attorney General's guidelines, although the Committee would require somewhat closer supervision by the Attorney General or his designee. Interviews (including interviews of existing informant's), name checks (including checks of local police intelligence files), and physical surveillance and review of credit and telephone records would be permitted during the preliminary investigation. The Attorney General or his designee would have to review that investigation within one month.

Under the guidelines, preliminary investigations do not require approval by the Attorney General or his designee and can continue for as long as ninety days with an additional ninety-day extension. The remainder of the covert techniques would be permitted in full intelligence investigations. Under the Attorney General's guidelines, the Attorney General or his designee only become involved in the termination of such investigations (at the end of one year), while the Committee's recommendations would require the Attorney General or his designee to authorize the initiation of the full investigation and the use of covert techniques in the investigation.

1. Overt Techniques and Name Checks

Recommendation 50.—Overt techniques and name checks should be permitted in all of the authorized domestic security investigations described above, including preliminary and full preventive intelligence investigations.

2. Covert Techniques

a. Covert Techniques Covered

This section covers the standards and procedures for the use of the following covert techniques in authorized domestic security investigations:

(i) electronic surveillance,

(ii) search and seizure or surreptitious entry;

(iii) mail opening;

(iv) informants and other covert human sources;

(v) mail surveillance;

(vi) review of tax returns and tax-related information;

(vii) other covert techniques—including physical surveillance, photographic surveillance, use of body recorders and other consensual electronic surveillance, and use of sensitive records of state and local government, and other institutional records systems pertaining to credit, medical history, social welfare history, or telephone calls.

b. Judicial Warrant Procedures (Electronic Surveillance, Mail Opening, Search and Seizure, and Surreptitious Entry)

The requirements for judicial warrants, set forth below, are not intended to cover NSA communication intercepts. Recommendations 14 through 18 contain the Committee's recommendations pertaining to NSA intercepts, the circumstances in which a judicial warrant is required and the standards applicable for the issuance of such a warrant.

Recommendation 51—All non-consensual electronic surveillance, mail-opening, and unauthorized entries should be conducted only upon authority of a judicial warrant.

Recommendation 52—All non-consensual electronic surveillance should be conducted pursuant to judicial warrants issued under authority of Title III of the Omnibus Crime Control and Safe Streets Act of 1968.

The Act should be amended to provide, with respect to electronic surveillance of foreigners in the United States, that a warrant may issue if

(a) There is probable cause that the target is an officer, employee, or conscious agent of a foreign power.

(b) The Attorney General has certified that the surveillance is likely to reveal information necessary to the protection of the nation against actual or potential attack or other hostile acts of force of a foreign power; to obtain foreign intelligence information deemed essential to the security of the United States; or to protect national security information against hostile foreign intelligence activity.

(c.) With respect to any such electronic surveillance, the judge should adopt procedures to minimize the acquisition and retention of non-foreign intelligence information about Americans.

(d) Such electronic surveillance should be exempt from the disclosure requirements of Title III of the 1968 Act as to foreigners generally and as to Americans if they are involved in hostile foreign intelligence activity.

As noted earlier, the Committee believes that the espionage laws should be amended to include industrial espionage and other modern forms of espionage not presently covered and Title III should incorporate any such amendment. The Committee's recomendation is that both that change and the amendment of Title III to require warrants for all electronic surveillance be promptly made.

Recommendation 53 — Mail opening should be conducted only pursuant to a judicial warrant issued upon probable cause of criminal activity as described in Recommendation 37.

Recommendation 54 — Unauthorized entry should be conducted only upon judicial warrant issued on probable cause to believe that the place to be searched contains evidence of a crime, except unauthorized entry, including surreptitious entry, against foreigners who are officers, employees, or conscious agents of a foreign power should be permitted upon judicial warrant under the standards which apply to electronic surveillance described in Recommendation 52.

c. Administrative Procedures (Covert Human Sources, Mail Surveillance, Review of Tax Returns and Tax-Related Information, and Other Covert Techniques)

Recommendation 55 — Covert human sources may not be directed at an American except:

(1) In the course of a criminal investigation if necessary to the investigation provided that covert human sources should not be directed at an American as a part of an investigation of a committed act unless there is reasonable suspicion to believe that the American is responsible for the act and then only for the purpose of identifying the perpetrators of the act.

(2) If the American is the target of a full preventive intelligence investigation and the Attorney General or his designee makes a written finding that (i) he has considered and rejected less intrusive techniques; and (ii) he believes that covert human sources are necessary to obtain information for the investigation.

Recommendation 56 — Covert human sources which have been directed at an American in a full preventive intelligence Investigation should not be used to collect information on the activities of the American for more than 90 days after the source is in place and capable of reporting, unless the Attorney General or his designee finds in writing either that there are "compelling circumstances" in which case they may be used for an additional 60 days, or that there is probable cause that the American will soon engage in terrorist activities or hostile foreign intelligence activities.

Recommendation 57 — All covert human sources used by the FBI should be reviewed by the Attorney General or his designee as soon as practicable, and should be terminated unless the covert human source could be directed against an American in a criminal investigation or a full preventive intelligence investigation under these recommendations.

Recommendation 58 — Mail surveillance and the review of tax returns and tax-related information should be conducted consistently with the recommendations contained in Part iii. In addition to restrictions contained in Part iii, the review of tax returns and tax-related information, as well as review of medical or social history records, confidential records of private institutions and confidential records of Federal, state, and local government agencies other than intelligence or law enforcement agencies may not be used against an American except:

(1) In the course of a criminal investigation if necessary to the investigation;

(2) If the American is the target of a full preventive intelligence investigation and the Attorney General or his designee makes a written finding that (i) he has considered and rejected less intrusive techniques; and (ii) he believes that the covert technique requested by the Bureau is necessary to obtain information necessary to the investigation.

Recommendation 59—The use of physical surveillance and review of credit and telephone records and any records of governmental or private institutions other than those covered in Recommendation 58 should be permitted to be used against an American, if necessary, in the course of either a criminal investigation or a preliminary or full preventive intelligence investigation.

Recommendation 60—Covert techniques should be permitted at the scene of a potential civil disorder in the course of preventive criminal intelligence and criminal investigations as described above. Non-warrant covert techniques may also be directed at an American during a civil disorder in which extensive acts of violence are occurring and Federal troops have been introduced. This additional authority to direct such covert techniques at Americans during a civil disorder should be limited to circumstances where Federal troops are actually in use and the technique is used only for the purpose of preventing further violence.

Recommendation 61—Covert techniques should not be directed at an American in the course of a background investigation without the informed written consent of the American.

Recommendation 62—If Congress enacts a statute attaching criminal sanctions to security leaks, covert techniques should be directed at Americans in the course of security leak investigations only if such techniques are consistent with Recommendation 55 (1), 58 (1) or 59. With respect to security risks, Congress might consider authorizing covert techniques, other than those requiring a judicial warrant, to be directed at Americans in the course of security risk investigations, but only upon a written finding of the Attorney General that (1) there is reasonable suspicion to believe that the individual is a security risk, (ii) he has considered and rejected less intrusive techniques, and (iii) he believes the technique requested is necessary to the investigation.

(d) Incidental Overhears

Recommendation 63—Except as limited elsewhere in these recommendations or in Title III of the Omnibus Crime Control and Safe Streets Act of 1968, information obtained incidentally through an authorized covert technique about an American or a foreigner who is not the target of the covert technique can be used as the basis for any authorized domestic security investigation.

e. Maintenance and Dissemination of Information

The following limitations should apply to the maintenance and dissemination Information collected as a result of domestic security investigations.

1. Relevance

Recommendation 64—Information should not be maintained except where relevant to the purpose of an investigation.

2. Sealing or Purging

Recommendation 65 — Personally identifiable information on Americans obtained in the following kinds of investigations should be sealed or purged as follows (unless it appears on its face to be necessary for another authorized investigation):

(a) Preventive intelligence investigations of terrorist or hostile foreign intelligence activities — as soon as the investigation is terminated by the Attorney General or his designee pursuant to Recommendation 45 or 69.

(b) Civil disorder assistance — as soon as the assistance is terminated by the Attorney General or his designee pursuant to Recommendation 69, provided that where troops have been introduced such information need be sealed or purged only within a reasonable period after their withdrawal.

Recommendation 66 — Information previously gained by the FBI or any other intelligence agency through illegal techniques should be sealed or purged as soon as practicable.

3. Dissemination

Recommendation 67 — Personally identifiable information on Americans from domestic security investigations may be disseminated outside the Department of Justice as follows:

(a) Preventive intelligence investigations of terrorist activities — personally identifiable information on Americans from preventive criminal intelligence investigations of terrorist activities may be disseminated only to:

(1) A foreign or domestic law enforcement agency which has jurisdiction over the criminal activity to which the information relates; or

(2) To a foreign intelligence or military agency of the United States, if necessary for an activity permitted by these recommendations; or

(3) To an appropriate federal official with authority to make personnel decisions about the subject of the information; or

(4) To a foreign intelligence or military agency of a cooperating foreign power if necessary for an activity permitted by these recommendations to similar agencies of the United States; or

(5) Where necessary to warn state or local officials of terrorist activity likely to occur within their jurisdiction; or

(6) Where necessary to warn any person of a threat to life or property from terrorist activity.

(b) Preventive intelligence investigations of hostile foreign intelligence activities — personally identifiable information on Americans from preventive criminal intelligence investigations of hostile intelligence activities may be disseminated only:

(1) To an appropriate federal official with authority to make personnel decisions about the subject of the information; or

(2) To the National Security Council or the Department of State upon request or where appropriate to their administration of U.S. foreign policy; or

(3) To a foreign intelligence or military agency of the United States, if relevant to an activity permitted by these recommendations; or

(4) To a foreign intelligence or military agency of a cooperating foreign power if relevant to an activity permitted by these recommendations to similar agencies of the United States.

© Civil disorders assistance — personally identifiable information on Americans involved in an actual or potential disorder, collected in the course of civil disorders assistance, should not be disseminated outside the Department of Justice except to military officials and appropriate state and local officials at the scene of a civil disorder where federal troops are present.

(d) Background investigations—to the maximum extent feasible, the results of background investigations should be segregated within the FBI and only disseminated to officials outside the Department of Justice authorized to make personnel decisions with respect to the subject.

(e) All other authorized domestic security investigations—to governmental officials who are authorized to take action consistent with the purpose of an investigation or who have statutory duties which require the information.

4. Oversight Access

Recommendation 68—Officers of the Executive branch, who are made responsible by these recommendations for overseeing intelligence activities, and appropriate congressional committees should have access to all information necessary for their functions. The committees should adopt procedures to protect the privacy of subjects of files maintained by the FBI and other agencies affected by the domestie intelligence recommendations.

f. Attorney General Oversight of the FBI, Including Termination of Investigations and Covert Techniques

Recommendation 69—The Attorney General should:

(a) Establish a program of routine and periodic review of FBI domestic security investigations to ensure that the FBI is complying with all of the foregoing recommendations; and

(b) Assure, with respect to the following investigations of Americans that:

(1) Preventive intelligence investigations of terrorist activity or hostile foreign intelligence activity are terminated within one year, except that the Attorney General or his designee may grant extensions upon a written finding of "compelling circumstances";

(2) Covert techniques are used in preventive intelligence investigations of terrorist activity or hostile foreign intelligence activity only so long as necessary and not beyond time limits established by the Attorney General except that the Attorney General or his designee may grant extensions upon a written finding of "compelling circumstances";

(3) Civil disorders assistance is terminated upon withdrawal of federal troops or, if troops were not introduced. within a reasonable time after the finding by the Attorney General that troops are likely to be requested, except that the Attorney General or his designee may grant extensions upon a written finding of "compelling circurnstances;"

v. The Responsibility and Authority of the Attorney General for Oversight of Federal Domestic Security Activities Must Be Clarified and General Counsels and Inspectors General of Intelligence Agencies Strengthened

The Committee's Recommendations give the Attorney General broad oversight responsibility for federal domestic security activities. As the chief legal officer of the United States, the Attorney General is the most appropriate official to be charged with ensuring that the intelligence agencies of the United States conduct their activities in accordance with the law. The Executive Order, however, places primary responsibility for oversight of the intelligence agencies with the newly created Oversight Board.

Both the Recommendations and the Order recognize the Attorney General's primary responsibility to detect, or prevent, violations of law by any employee of intelligence agencies. Both charge the head of intelligence agencies with the duty to report to the Attorney General information which relates to possible violations of law by any employee of the respective intelligence agencies. The Order also requires the Oversight Board to report periodically, at least quarterly, to the Attorney General on its findings and to report, in a timely manner, to the Attorney General, any activities that raise serious questions about legality.

a. Attorney General Responsibility and Relationship With Other Intelligence Agencies

These recommendations are intended to implement the Attorney General's responsibility to control and supervise all of the domestic security activities of the federal government and to oversee activities of any agency affected by the Domestic Intelligence Recommendations:

Recommendation 70—The Attorney General should review the internal regulations of the FBI and other intelligence agencies engaging in domestic security activities to ensure that such internal regulations are proper and adequate to protect the constitutional rights of Americans.

Recommendation 71—The Attorney General or his designee (such as the Office of Legal Counsel of the Department of Justice) should advise the General Counsels of intelligence agencies on interpretations of statutes and regulations adopted pursuant to these recommendations and on such other legal questions as are described in b. below.

Recommendation 72—The Attorney General should have ultimate responsibility for the investigation of alleged violations of law relating to the Domestic Intelligence Recommendations.

Recommendation 73—The Attorney General should be notified of possible alleged violations of law through the Office of Professional Responsibility (described in c. below) by agency heads, General Counsel, or Inspectors General of intelligence agencies as provided in B. below.

Recommendation 74—The heads of all intelligence agencies affected by these recommendations are responsible for the prevention and detection of alleged violations of the law by, or on behalf of, their respective agencies and for the reporting to the Attorney General of all such alleged violations. Each such agency head should also assure his agency's cooperation with the Attorney General in investigations of alleged violations.

b. General Counsel and Inspectors General of Intelligence

The Committee recommends that the FBI and each other intelligence agency should have a general counsel nominated by the President and confirmed by the Senate. There is no provision in the Executive Order making General Counsels of intelligence agencies subject to Senate confirmation. The Committee believes that the extraordinary responsibilities exercised by the General Counsel of these agencies make it very important that these officials are subject to examination by the Senate prior to their confirmation. The Committee further believes that making such positions subject to Presidential appointment and senatorial confirmation will increase the stature of the office and will protect the independence of judgment of the General Counsel.

The Committee Recommendations differ from the Executive Order in two other important respects. The Recommendations provide that the General Counsel should review all significant proposed agency activities to determine their legality. They also provide a mechanism whereby the Inspector General or General Counsel of an intelligence agency can, in extraordinary circumstances, and if requested by an employee of the Agency, provide information directly to the Attorney General or appropriate congressional oversight committees without informing the head of the agency.

The Committee Recommendations also go beyond the Executive Order in requiring agency heads to report to appropriate committees of the Congress and the Attorney General on the activities of the Office of the General Counsel and the Office of the Inspector General. The Committee believes that the reporting requirements will facilitate oversight of the intelligence agencies and of those important offices within them.

Recommendation 75 — To assist the Attorney General and the agency heads in the functions described in a. above, the FBI and each other intelligence agency should have a General Counsel, nominated by the President and confirmed by the Senate, and an Inspector General appointed by the agency bead.

Recommendation 76 — Any individual having information on past, current, or proposed activities which appear to be illegal, improper, or in violation of agency policy should be required to report the matter immediately to the Agency head, General Counsel, or Inspector General. If the matter is not initially reported to the General Counsel, he should be notified by the Agency head or Inspector General. Each agency should regularly remind employees of their obligation to report such information.

Recommendation 77 — As provided in Recommendation 74, the heads of the FBI and of other intelligence agencies are responsible for reporting to the Attorney General alleged violations of law. When such reports are made, the appropriate congressional committees should be notified.

Recommendation 78 — The General Counsel and Inspector General of the FBI and of each other intelligence agency should have unrestricted access to all information in the possession of the agency and should have the authority to review all of the agency's activities. The Attorney General, or the Office of Professional Responsibility on his behalf, should have access to all information in the possession of an agency which, in the opinion of the Attorney General, is necessary for an investigation of illegal activity.

Recommendation 79 — The General Counsel of the FBI and of each other intelligence agency should review all significant proposed agency activities to determine their legality and constitutionality.

Recommendation 80 — The Director of the FBI and the heads of each other intelligence agency should be required to report, at least annually, to the appropriate committee of the Congress, on the activities of the General Counsel and the Office of the Inspector General.

Recommendation 81 — The Director of the FBI and the heads of each other intelligence agency should be required to report, at least annually, to the Attorney General on all reports of activities which appear illegal, improper, outside the legislative charter, or in violation of agency regulations. Such reports should include the General Counsel's findings concerning these activities, a summary of the Inspector General's investigations of these activities, and the practices and procedures developed to discover activities that raise questions of legality or propriety.

c. Office of Professional Responsibility

Recommendation 82—The Office of Professional Responsibility created by Attorney General Levi should be recognized in statute. The director of the office, appointed by the Attorney General, should report directly to the Attorney General or the Deputy Attorney General. The functions of the office should include:

(a) Serving as a central repository of reports and notifications provided the Attorney General; and

(b) Investigation, if requested by the Attorney General of alleged violations by intelligence agencies of statutes enacted or regulations promulgated pursuant to these recommendations.

d. Director of the FBI and Assistant Directors of the FBI

Recommendation 83—The Attorney General is responsible for all of the activities of the FBI, and the Director of the FBI is responsible to, and should be under the supervision and control of, the Attorney General.

Recommendation 84—The Director of the FBI should be nominated by the President and confirmed by the Senate to serve at the pleasure of the President for a single term of not more than eight years.

Recommendation 85—The Attorney General should consider exercising his power to appoint Assistant Directors of the FBI. A maximum term of years should be imposed on the tenure of the Assistant Director for the Intelligence Division.

vi. Administrative Rulemaking and Increased Disclosure Should Be Required

a. Administrative Rulemaking

Recommendation 86—The Attorney General should approve all administrative regulations required to implement statutes created pursuant to these recommendations.

Recommendation 87—Such regulations, except for regulations concerning investigations of hostile foreign intelligence activity or other matters which are properly classified, should he issued pursuant to the Administrative Procedures Act and should be subject to the approval of the Attorney General.

Recommendation 88—The effective date of regulations pertaining to the following matters should be delayed ninety days, during which time Congress would have the opportunity to review such regulations:

(a) Any CIA activities against Americans, as permitted in ii.a. above;

(b) Military activities at the time of a civil disorder;

(c.) The authorized scope of domestic security investigations, authorized investigative techniques, maintenance and dissemination of information by the FBI; and

(d) The termination of investigations and covert techniques as described in Part iv.

b. Disclosure

Recommendation 89—Each year the FBI and other intelligence agencies affected by these recommendations should be required to seek annual statutory authorization for their programs.

Recommendation 90.—The Freedom of Information Act (5 U.S.C. 552 (b)) and the Federal Privacy Act, (5 U.S.C. 552 (a)) provide important mechanisms by which individuals can gain access to information on intelligence activity directed against them. The Domestic Intelligence Recommendations assume that these statutes will continue to be vigorously enforced. In addition, the Department of Justice should notify all readily identifiable targets of past illegal surveillance techniques, and all

COINTELPRO victims, and third parties who had received anonymous COINTELPRO communications, of the nature of the activities directed against them, or the source of the anonymous communication to them.

vii. Civil Remedies Should Be Expanded

Recommendation 91 expresses the Committee's concern for establishing a legislative scheme which will afford effective redress to people who are injured by improper federal intelligence activity. The recommended provisions for civil remedies are also intended to deter improper intelligence activity without restricting the sound exercise of discretion by intelligence officers at headquarters or in the field.

As the Committee's investigation has shown, many Americans have suffered injuries from domestic intelligence activity, ranging front deprivation of constitutional rights of privacy and free speech to the loss of a job or professional standing, break-up of a marriage, and impairment of physical or mental health. But the extent, if any, to which an injured citizen can seek relief either monetary or injunctive—from the government or from an individual intelligence officer is far front clear under the present state of the law.

One major disparity in the current state of the law is that, under the Reconstruction era Civil Rights Act of 1871, the deprivation of constitutional rights by an officer or agent of a state government provides the basis for a suit to redress the injury incurred; but there is no statute which extends the same remedies for identical injuries when they are caused by a federal officer.

In the landmark Bivens case, the Supreme Court held that a federal officer could be sued for money damages for violating a citizen's Fourth Amendment rights. Whether monetary damages can be obtained for violation of other constitutional rights by federal officers remains unclear.

While we believe that any citizen with a substantial and specific claim to injury from intelligence activity should have standing to sue, the Committee is aware of the need for judicial protection against legal claims which amount to harassment or distraction of government officials, disruption of legitimate investigations, and wasteful expenditure of government resources. We also seek to ensure that the creation of a civil remedy for aggrieved persons does not impinge upon the proper exercise of discretion by federal officials.

Therefore, we recommend that where a government official—as opposed to the government itself—acted in good faith and with the reasonable belief that his conduct was lawful, he should have an affirmative defense to a suit for damages brought under the proposed statute. To tighten the system of accountability and control of domestic intelligence activity, the Committee proposes that this defense be structured to encourage intelligence officers to obtain written authorization for questionable activities and to seek legal advice about them.

To avoid penalizing federal officers and agents for the exercise of discretion, the Committee believes that the government should indemnify their attorney fees and reasonable litigation costs when they are held not to be liable. To avoid burdening the taxpayers for the deliberate misconduct of intelligence officers and agents, we believe the government should be able to seek reimbursement from those who willfully and knowingly violate statutory charters or the Constitution.

Furthermore, we believe that the courts will be able to fashion discovery procedures, including inspection of material in chambers, and to issue orders as the interests of justice require, to allow plaintiffs with substantial claims to uncover enough factual material to argue their case, while protecting the secrecy of governmental information in which there is a legitimate security interest.

The Committee recommends that a legislative scheme of civil remedies for the victims of intelligence activity be established along the following lines to clarify the state of the law, to encourage the responsible execution of duties created by the statutes recommended herein to regulate intelligence agencies, and to provide relief for the victims of illegal intelligence activity.

Recommendation 91 — Congress should enact a comprehensive civil remedies statute which would accomplish the following:

(a) Any American with a substantial and specific claim to an actual or threatened injury by a violation of the Constitution by federal intelligence officers or agents acting under color of law should have a federal cause of action against the government and the individual federal intelligence officer or agent responsible for the violation, without regard to the monetary amount in controversy. If actual injury is proven in court, the Committee believes that the injured person should be entitled to equitable relief, actual, general, and punitive damages, and recovery of the costs of litigation. If threatened injury is proven in court, the Committee believes that equitable relief and recovery of the costs of litigation should be available.

(b) Any American with a substantial and specific claim to actual or threatened injury by violation of the statutory charter for intelligence activity (as proposed by these Domestic Intelligence Recommendations) should have a cause of action for relief as in (a) above.

(c.) Because of the secrecy that surrounds intelligence programs, the Committee believes that a plaintiff should have two years from the date upon which he discovers, or reasonably should have discovered, the facts which give rise to a cause of action for relief from a constitutional or statutory violation.

(d) Whatever statutory provision may be made to permit an individual defendant to raise an affirmative defense that he acted within the scope of his official duties, in good faith, and with a reasonable belief that the action he took was lawful, the Committee believes that to ensure relief to persons injured by governmental intelligence activity, this defense should be available solely to individual defendants and should not extend to the government. Moreover, the defense should not be available to bar injunctions against individual defendants.

viii. Criminal Penalties Should Be Enacted

Recommendation 92 — The Committee believes that criminal penalties should apply, where appropriate, to willful and knowing violations of statutes enacted pursuant to the Domestic Intelligence Recommendations.

ix. The Smith Act and the Voorhis Act Should Either Be Repealed or Amended

Recommendation 93 — Congress should either repeal the Smith Act (18 U.S.C. 2385) and the Voorhis Act (18 U.S.C. 2386), which on their face appear to authorize investigation of "mere advocacy" of a political ideology, or amend those statutes so that domestic security investigations are only directed at conduct which might serve as the basis for a constitutional criminal prosecution, under Supreme Court decisions interpreting these and related statutes.

x. The Espionage Statute Should be Modernized

As suggested in its definition of "hostile foreign intelligence activity" and its recommendations on warrants for electronic surveillance, the Committee agrees with the Attorney General that there may be serious deficiencies in the Federal Espionage Statute (18 U.S.C. 792 et seq.). The basic prohibitions of that statute have not been amended since 1917 and do not encompass certain forms of industrial, technological, or economic espionage. The Attorney General in a recent letter to Senator Kennedy (Reprinted on p. S3889 of the Congressional Record of March 23, 1976) describes some of the problem areas of the statute, including industrial espionage (e.g., a spy obtaining information on computer technology for a foreign power). The Committee took no testimony on this subject and, therefore, makes no specific proposal other than that the appropriate committees of the Congress explore the necessity for amendments to the statute.

Recommendation 94—The appropriate committees of the Congress should review the Espionage Act of 1917 to determine whether it should be amended to cover modern forms of foreign espionage, including industrial, technological or economic espionage.

xi. Broader Access to Intelligence Agency Files Should be Provided to GAO, as an Investigative Arm of the Congress

Recommendation 95—The appropriate congressional oversight committees of the Congress should, from time to time, request the Comptroller General of the United States to conduct audits and reviews of the intelligence activities of any department or agency of the United States affected by the Domestic Intelligence Recommendations. For such purpose, the Comptroller General, or any of his duly authorized representatives, should have access to, and the right to examine, all necessary materials of any such department or agency.

xii. Congressional Oversight Should Be Intensified

Recommendation 96—The Committee reendorses the concept of vigorous Senate oversight to review the conduct of domestic security activities through a new permanent intelligence oversight committee.

xiii. Definitions For the purposes of these recommendations:

A. "Americans" means U.S. citizens, resident aliens and unincorporated associations, composed primarily of U.S. citizens or resident aliens; and corporations, incorporated or having their principal place of business in the United States or having majority ownership by U.S. citizens, or resident aliens, including foreign subsidiaries of such corporations provided, however, "Americans" does not include corporations directed by foreign governments or organizations.

B. "Collect" means to gather or initiate the acquisition of information, or to request it from another agency.

C. A "covert human source" means undercover agents or informants who are paid or otherwise controlled by an agency.

D. "Covert techniques" means the collection of information, including collection from record sources not readily available to a private person (except state or local law enforcement files), in such a manner as not to be detected by the subject.

E. "Domestic security activities" means governmental activities against Americans or conducted within the United States or its territories, including enforcement of the criminal laws, intended to:

1. protect the United States from hostile foreign intelligence activity including espionage;

2. protect the federal, state, and local governments from domestic violence or rioting; and

3. protect Americans and their government from terrorists.

F. "Foreign communications," refers to a communication between, or among, two or more parties in which at least one party is outside the United States, or a communication transmitted between points within the United States if transmitted over a facility which is under the control of, or exclusively used by, a foreign government.

G. "Foreigners" means persons and organizations who are not Americans as defined above.

H. "Hostile foreign intelligence activities" means acts, or conspiracies, by Americans or foreigners, who are officers, employees, or conscious agents of a foreign power, or who, pursuant to the direction of a foreign power, engage in clandestine intelligence activity, or engage in espionage, sabotage or similar conduct in violation of federal criminal statutes.

I. "Name checks" means the retrieval by an agency of information already in the possession of the federal government or in the possession of state or local law enforcement agencies.

J. "Overt investigative techniques" means the collection of information readily available from public sources, or available to a private person, including interviews of the subject or his friends or associates.

K. "Purged" means to destroy or transfer to the National Archives all personally identifiable information (including references in any general name index).

L. "Sealed" means to retain personally identifiable information and to retain entries in a general name index but to restrict access to the information and entries to circumstances of "compelling necessity."

M. "Reasonable suspicion" is based upon the Supreme Court's decision in the case of Terry v. Ohio, 392 U.S. 1 (1968), and means specific and articulable facts which taken together with rational inferences from those facts, give rise to a reasonable suspicion that specified activity has occurred, is occurring, or is about to occur.

N. "Terrorist activities" means acts, or conspiracies, which: (a) are violent or dangerous to human life; and (b) violate federal or state criminal statutes concerning assassination, murder, arson, bombing, hijacking, or kidnapping; and (c) appear intended to, or are likely to have the effect of:

(1) Substantially disrupting federal, state or local government; or

(2) Substantially disrupting interstate or foreign commerce between the United States and another country; or

(3) Directly interfering with the exercise by Americans, of Constitutional rights protected by the Civil Rights Act of 1968, or by foreigners, of their rights under the laws or treaties of the United States.

0. "Unauthorized entry" means entry unauthorized by the target.

Supplementary Detailed Staff Reports On Intelligence Activities And The Rights Of Americans

Warrantless FBI Electronic Surveillance

I. Introduction

Technological developments in this century have rendered the most private conversations of American citizens vulnerable to interception and monitoring by government agents. The electronic means by which the Government can extend its "antennae" are varied: microphones may be secretly planted in private locations or on mobile informants; so-called "spike mikes" may be inserted into the wall of an adjoining room; and parabolic microphones may be directed at speakers far away to register the sound waves they emit. Telephone conversations may be overheard without the necessity of attaching electronic devices to the telephone itself or to the lines connecting the telephone with the telephone company. An ordinary telephone may also be turned into an open microphone—a "miketel" capable of intercepting all conversations within hearing range even when the telephone is not in use.

Even more sophisticated technology permits the Government to intercept any telephone, telegram, or telex communication which is transmitted at least partially through the air, as most such communications now are. This type of interception is virtually undetectable and does not require the cooperation of private communications companies.

Techniques such as these have been used, and continue to be used, by intelligence agencies in their intelligence operations. Since the early part of this century the FBI has utilized wiretapping and "bugging" techniques in both criminal and intelligence investigations. In a single year alone (1945), the Bureau conducted 519 wiretaps and 186 microphone surveillances (excluding those conducted by means of microphones planted on informants). Until 1972, the Bureau used wiretaps and bugs against both American citizens and foreigners within the United States—without judicial warrant—to collect foreign intelligence, intelligence and counterintelligence information, to monitor "subversive" and violent activity, and to determine the sources of leaks of classified information. The FBI still uses these techniques without a warrant in foreign intelligence and counterintelligence investigations.

The CIA and NSA have similarly used electronic surveillance techniques for intelligence purposes. The CIA's Office of Security, for example, records a total of fifty-seven individuals who were targeted by telephone wiretaps or microphones within the United States between the years 1947 and 1968. Of these, thirty were employees or former employees of the CIA or of another federal agency who were presumably targeted for security reasons; four were United States citizens unconnected with the CIA or any federal agency.

One of the primary responsibilities of the National Security Agency (NSA) is to collect foreign "communications intelligence." To fulfill this responsibility, it has electronically intercepted an enormous number of international telephone, telegram, and telex communications since its inception in the early 1950's.

Electronic surveillance techniques have understandably enabled these agencies to obtain valuable information relevant to their legitimate intelligence missions. Use of these techniques has provided the Government with vital intelligence, which would be difficult to acquire through other means, about the activities and intentions of foreign powers, and has provided important leads in counterespionage cases.

By their very nature, however, electronic surveillance techniques also provide the means by which the Government can collect vast amounts of information, unrelated to any legitimate governmental interest, about large numbers of American citizens. Because electronic monitoring is surreptitious, it allows Government agents to eavesdrop on the conversations of individuals in unguarded moments, when they believe they are speaking in confidence. Once in operation, electronic surveillance techniques record not merely conversations about criminal, treasonable, or espionage-related activities, but all conversations about the full range of human events. Neither the most mundane nor the most personal nor the most political expressions of the speakers are immune from interception. Nor are these techniques sufficiently precise to limit the conversations overheard to those of the intended subject of the surveillance: anyone who speaks in a bugged room and anyone who talks over a tapped telephone is also overheard and recorded.

The very intrusiveness of these techniques implies the need for strict controls on their use, and the Fourth Amendment protection against unreasonable searches and seizures demands no less. Without such controls, they may be directed against entirely innocent American citizens, and the Government may use the vast range of information exposed by electronic means for partisan political and other improper purposes. Yet in the past the controls on these techniques have not been effective; improper targets have been selected and politically useful information obtained through electronic surveillance has been provided to senior administration officials.

Until recent years, Congress and the Supreme Court set few limits on the use of electronic surveillance. When the Supreme, Court first considered the legal issues raised by wiretapping, it held that the warrantless use of this technique was not unconstitutional because the Fourth Amendment's warrant requirement did not extend to the seizure of conversations. This decision, the 1928 case of Olmstead v. United States, 217 U.S. 438, arose in the context of a criminal prosecution, and it left agencies such as the Bureau of Prohibition and the Bureau of Investigation (the former name of the FBI) free to engage in the unrestricted use of wiretapping in both criminal and intelligence investigations.

Six years later, Congress imposed the first restrictions on wiretapping in the Federal Communications Act of 1934 which made it a crime for "any person" to intercept and divulge or publish the contents of wire and radio communications. The Supreme Court subsequently construed this section to apply to federal agents as well as ordinary citizens, and held that evidence obtained directly or indirectly from the interception of wire and radio communications was inadmissible in court. But Congress acquiesced in the Justice Department's interpretation that these cases did not prohibit wiretapping per se, only the divulgence of the contents of wire communications outside the federal establishment, and government wiretapping for purposes other than prosecution continued.

The Supreme Court reversed its holding in the Olmstead case, in 1967, holding in Katz v. United States, 389 U.S. 347 (1967), that the Fourth Amendment's warrant requirement did apply to electronic surveillances. But it expressly declined to extend this holding to cases "involving the national security." Congress followed suit the next year in the Omnibus Crime Control Act of 1968, which established a warrant procedure for electronic surveillance in criminal cases but included a provision that neither it nor the Federal Communications Act of 1934 "shall limit the constitutional power of the President" — a provision which has been relied upon by the Executive Branch as permitting "national security" electronic surveillances.

In 1972, the Supreme Court again addressed the issue of warrantless electronic surveillance. It held in United States v. United States District Court, 407 U.S. 297 (1972), that the constitutional power of the President did not extend to authorizing warrantless electronic surveillance in cases involving threats to the "domestic security." The Court distinguished — but remained silent on — the question of warrantless electronic surveillance where there was a "significant connection with a foreign power, its agents or agencies."

Without effective guidance by the Supreme Court or Congress, executive branch officials developed broad and ill-defined standards for the use of warrantless electronic surveillance. Vague terms such as "subversive activities," "national interest," "domestic security," and "national security" were relied upon to electronically monitor many individuals who engaged in no criminal activity and who, by any objective standard, represented no genuine threat to the security of the United States.

The secrecy which has enshrouded the warrantless use of this technique moreover, facilitated the occasional violation of the generally meager procedural requirements for warrantless electronic surveillance. Since the early 1940's, for example, Justice Department policy has required the approval of the Attorney General prior to the institution of wiretaps; such approval has been required prior to the institution of microphone surveillances since 1965. This requirement has often been ignored for wiretaps and bugs, and it was not even applied to NSA's electronic monitoring system and its program for "Watch Listing" American citizens. From the early 1960's until 1973, NSA compiled a list of individuals and organizations, including more than one thousand American citizens and domestic groups, whose communications were segregated from the mass of communications intercepted by the Agency, transcribed, and frequently disseminated to other agencies for intelligence purposes. The Americans on the list, many of whom were active in the anti-war and civil rights movements, were placed there by the FBI, CIA, Secret Service, Defense Department, and the Bureau of Narcotics and Dangerous Drugs without judicial warrant, without prior approval by the Attorney General, and without a determination that they satisfied the executive branch standards for warrantless electronic surveillance. For many years in fact, no Attorney General even knew of this project's existence.

Electronic monitoring by the National Security Agency and the CIA, however, is outside the scope of this Report. This Report focuses exclusively on the FBI's use of electronic surveillance; NSA's monitoring system is described at length in the Committee's Report on NSA. Because the legal issues and the FBI's policy and practice regarding consensual monitoring devices such as "body recorders" are distinct from those of nonconsensual wiretaps and microphone installations, the Report is also confined to the latter forms of electronic surveillance.

II. Presidential And Attorney General Authorization For Warrantless Wiretapping

FBI use of warrantless wiretapping for limited purposes has received the approval of Presidents and Attorneys General consistently — with only one three month exception in 1940 -- from 1931 to the present day. The legal theories advanced to justify the use of this technique, however, have been developed almost entirely by the executive branch itself, and have been "legitimized" largely by the reluctance of Congress and the Supreme Court to confront directly the arguments presented by executive officers.

The evolution of executive branch wiretapping policies from 1924 to 1975, and of the legislative and judicial reaction to these policies, is summarized below.

A. Pre-1940

Justice Department records indicate that the first time an Attorney General formally considered the propriety of warrantless wiretapping for either law enforcement or intelligence purposes, he found it to be "unethical:" in 1924, Attorney General Harlan Fiske Stone ordered a prohibition on the, use of this technique by Justice Department personnel, including those of the Bureau of Investigation (the original name of the Federal Bureau of Investigation). To implement this policy, the Director of the Bureau of Investigation, with the approval of Stone's successor, Attorney General John G. Sargent, included the following section in the Bureau's Manual of Rules and Regulations:

Unethical tactics: Wiretapping, entrapment, or the use of any other improper, illegal, or unethical tactics in procuring information in connection with investigative activity will not be tolerated by the Bureau.

This prohibition only applied to the Justice Department. During the 1920's, wiretapping was extensively used by the Bureau of Prohibition, then a part of the Department of the Treasury, in its investigations of violations of the National Prohibition Act. In Olmstead v. United States, 277 U.S. 438 (1928), criminal defendants charged with violating this Act challenged the Bureau of Prohibition's use of this technique, but the challenge was unsuccessful. In that case, the Court held that evidence obtained from wiretapping which did not involve a physical intrusion or trespass was admissible and that wiretapping was not unconstitutional because the Fourth Amendment's protections did not apply to the seizure of conversations. The Bureau of Prohibition continued thereafter to employ this technique in its investigations, but the restrictive policy of the Justice Department remained unchanged for the next three years.

In 1930, the Bureau of Prohibition was transferred from the Treasury Department to the Justice Department, and the differing policies regarding wiretapping posed a problem for Attorney General William B. Mitchell. "[T]he present condition in the Department cannot continue," he wrote. "We cannot have one Bureau in which wiretapping is allowed and another in which it is prohibited." He ultimately resolved his dilemma by permitting both the Bureau of Investigation and the Bureau of Prohibition to engage in wiretapping with senior level approval for limited purposes.

On February 19, 1931, instructions were issued at the direction of Attorney General Mitchell stating that no wiretap should be instituted without the written approval of the Assistant Attorney General in charge of the particular case, and that such approval would only be given in cases "involving the safety of victims of kidnappings, the location and apprehension of desperate criminals, and in espionage and sabotage and other cases considered to be of major law enforcement importance." The Manual provision relating to wiretapping was consequently altered to read as follows:

Wiretapping: Telephone or telegraph wires shall not be tapped unless prior authorization of the Director of the Bureau has been secured.

Three years later, Congress' first pronouncement on wiretapping threatened to invalidate the policy enunciated by Mitchell: in June 1934, Congress enacted Section 605 of the Federal Communications Act, 47 U.S.C. 605, which made it a crime for "any person" to intercept and divulge or publish the contents of wire and radio communications. The Supreme Court construed this section in 1937 to apply to Federal agents and held that evidence obtained from the interception of wire and radio communications was inadmissible in court. The Court elaborated on this decision two years later, holding that not only was evidence obtained from such interceptions inadmissible, but that evidence indirectly derived from such interceptions was equally inadmissible.

The Justice Department did not interpret these decisions as prohibiting the interception of wire communications per se, however; only the interception and divulgence of their contents outside the federal establishment was considered by the Department to be unlawful. Even after the Nardone decisions, the Department continued to authorize warrantless wiretapping, albeit with the recognition that evidence obtained through the use of this technique would be inadmissible in court.

B. 1940 to 1968

1. The Roosevelt Administration

Shortly after taking office in 1940, Attorney General Robert H. Jackson reversed the existing Justice Department policy concerning wiretapping. By Order No. 3343, issued March 15, 1940, he prohibited all wiretapping by the Federal Bureau of Investigation, and the previously operative Manual section, which described wiretapping as an unethical practice, was reinstated at his direction.

Jackson's prohibition proved to be short-lived, however, for less than three months later President Franklin D. Roosevelt informed the Attorney General that he did not believe the Supreme Court intended the 1939 Nardone decision to prohibit wiretapping in "matters involving the defense of the nation." The President sent the following memorandum to Attorney General Jackson, granting him authority to approve wiretaps on "persons suspected of subversive activities against the Government of the United States:"

> I have agreed with the broad purpose of the Supreme Court decision relating to wiretapping in investigations. The Court is undoubtedly sound both in regard to the use of evidence secured over tapped wires in the prosecution of citizens in criminal cases; and it is also right in its opinion that under ordinary and normal circumstances wiretapping by Government agents should not be carried on for the excellent reason that it is almost bound to lead to abuse of civil rights.

> However, I am convinced that the Supreme Court never intended any dictum in the particular case which it decided to apply to grave matters involving the defense of the nation.

> It is, of course, well known that certain other nations have been engaged in the organization of propaganda of so called "fifth column" in other countries and in preparation for sabotage, as well as in actual sabotage.

> It is too late to do anything about it after sabotage, assassinations and "fifth column" activities are completed.

> You are, therefore, authorized and directed in such cases as you may approve, after investigation of the need in each case, to authorize the necessary investigating agents that they are at liberty to secure information by listening devices directed to the conversation or other communications of persons suspected of subversive activities against the Government of the United States, including suspected spies. You are requested furthermore to limit these investigations so conducted to a minimum and to limit them insofar as possible to aliens.

In 1940 and 1941, several bills were introduced in Congress to authorize electronic surveillance for the purpose Roosevelt articulated in his letter to Jackson and for other purposes as well. One of these was a joint resolution introduced by Representative Emmanuel Celler authorizing the FBI "to conduct investigations, subject to the direction of the Attorney General, to ascertain, prevent, and frustrate any interference with the national defense by sabotage, treason, seditious conspiracy, espionage, violations of neutrality laws, or in any other manner." This resolution would have lifted Section 605's ban on wiretapping for such investigations.

Both President Roosevelt and Attorney General Jackson endorsed such legislation. Roosevelt wrote to Representative Thomas Eliot on February 21, 1941, "I have no compunction in saying that wire tapping should be used against those persons, not citizens of the United States, and those few citizens who are traitors to their country, who today are engaged in espionage or sabotage against the United States . . ."

The Justice Department also informed Congress about the theory that had been developed to rationalize ongoing electronic surveillance under Section 605. Attorney

General Robert Jackson advised Representative Hatton Summers on March 19, 1941, "The only offense under the present law is to intercept any communication and divulge or publish the same . . . Any person, with no risk of penalty, may tap telephone wires . . . and act upon what he hears or make any use of it that does not involve divulging or publication."

The import of these two statements was undoubtedly clear to the members of the House Judiciary Committee to whom they were addressed. The FBI would use wiretaps in the investigation of espionage and sabotage, despite the Federal Communications Act, since the results of the wiretaps would not be "divulged" outside the government. Legislation was needed only in order to use wiretap-obtained evidence or the fruits thereof in criminal prosecutions; a new statute was not necessary if the purpose of wiretapping was to gather intelligence that would not be used in court."

This policy was explicitly acknowledged several months later. After an incident where labor leader Harry Bridges discovered he was under surveillance, Attorney General Francis Biddle announced that FBI agents were, in fact, authorized to tap wires in cases involving espionage, sabotage, and serious crimes such as kidnapping after first securing the permission of the FBI Director and the Attorney General. At the same time Attorney General Biddle advised FBI Director Hoover:

A good deal of my press conference yesterday was consumed in questions about wiretapping. I refused to comment on the Bridges incident, on the ground that it would be improper for me to comment on a case now pending before me.

I indicated that the stand of the Department would be, as indeed it had been for some time, to authorize wiretapping in espionage, sabotage, and kidnaping cases, where the circumstances warranted. I described Section 605 of the Communications Act, pointing out that under the Statute interception alone was not illegal; that there must be both interception and divulgence or publication; that the Courts had held only that evidence could not be used which resulted from wiretapping; that the Courts had never defined what divulgence and publication was; that I would continue to construe the Act, until the Courts decided otherwise, not to prohibit interception of communications by an agent, and his reporting the result to his superior officer, as infraction of the law; that although this could be said of all crimes, as a matter of policy wiretapping would be used sparingly, and under express authorization of the Attorney General.

2. The Truman Administration

The permissible scope of wiretapping was expanded after World War II by President Truman to include "cases vitally affecting the domestic security, or where human life is in jeopardy." The documentary evidence suggests, however, that this expansion was inadvertent on Truman's part and that he actually intended simply to continue in force the policies articulated by President Roosevelt in 1940.

By memorandum of July 17, 1946, Attorney General Tom Clark asked President Truman to renew Roosevelt's authorization for warrantless wiretapping issued six years earlier. Attorney General Clark quoted from that authorization but omitted the portion of Roosevelt's letter which read: "You are requested furthermore to limit these investigations so conducted to a minimum and to limit them insofar as possible to aliens." He then stated to President Truman:

It seems to me that in the present troubled period in international affairs, accompanied as it is by an increase in subversive activity here at home, it is as necessary as it was in 1940 to take the investigative measures referred to in President Roosevelt's memorandum. At the same time, the country is threatened by a very substantial increase in crime. While I am reluctant to suggest any use whatever of these special investigative measures in domestic cases, it seems to me imperative to use them in cases vitally affecting the domestic security, or where human life is in jeopardy.

As so modified, I believe the outstanding directive should be continued in force ... In my opinion the measures proposed are within the authority of law, and I have in the files of the Department materials indicating to me that my two most recent predecessors as Attorney General would concur in this view.

Truman approved the Attorney General's 1946 memorandum, but four years later aides to President Truman discovered Clark's incomplete quotation and the President considered returning to the terms of the original 1940 authorization. A February 2, 1950, memorandum located in the Truman Presidential Library reflects that discovery: George M. Elsey, the Assistant Counsel to the President, wrote Truman that

Not only did Clark fail to inform the President that Mr. Roosevelt had directed the F.B.I. to hold its wiretapping to a minimum, and to limit it insofar as possible to aliens, he requested the President to approve very broad language which would permit wiretapping in any case 'vitally affecting the domestic security, or where human life is in jeopardy.' This language is obviously a very far cry from the 1940 directive.

Elsey recommended in this memorandum that "the President consider rescinding his 1046 directive." An order was drafted which closely paralleled Roosevelt's 1940 directive, but for reasons that are unclear it was never issued.

The wiretapping standards that were expressed in Clark's 1946 memorandum and approved by President Truman were continued under Attorney General J. Howard McGrath. In a 1952 memorandum to J. Edgar Hoover, McGrath also made explicit the requirement of prior approval by the Attorney General, which had been informally instituted by Attorney General Biddle in 1941:

There is pending, as you know, before the Congress legislation that I have recommended which would permit wiretapping under appropriate safeguards and make evidence thus obtained admissible. As you state, the use of wiretapping is indispensable in intelligence coverage of matters relating to espionage, sabotage, and related security fields. Consequently, I do not intend to alter the existing policy that wiretapping surveillance should be used under the present high restrictive basis and when specifically authorized by me.

3. The Eisenhower Administration

The Government's perceived inability to prosecute in espionage and sabotage cases where electronic surveillance had been used, which stemmed from the Nardone decisions in the late 1930's, led Attorney General Herbert Brownell to press strongly in 1954 for legislation to authorize "national security" wiretapping without judicial warrant. Rejecting arguments for a warrant requirement, Brownell contended that responsibility should be centralized in the hands of the Attorney General. He also saw a "strong danger of leaks if application is made to a court, because in addition to the judge, you have the clerk, the stenographer and some other officer like a law assistant or bailiff who may be apprised of the nature of the application." Discussing the objectives of "national security" wiretapping, Brownell observed:

> We might just as well face up to the fact that the communists are subversives and conspirators working fanatically in the interests of a hostile foreign power ...
>
> It is almost impossible to "spot" them since they no longer use membership cards or other written documents which will identify them for what they are. As a matter of necessity, they turn to the telephone to carry on their intrigue. The success of their plans frequently rests upon piecing together shreds of information received from many sources and many nests. The participants in the conspiracy are often dispersed and stationed in various strategic positions in government and industry throughout the country. Their operations are not only internal. They are also of an international and intercontinental character ...
>
> It is therefore neither reasonable, nor realistic that Communists should be allowed to have the free use of every modern communication device to carry out their unlawful conspiracies, but that law enforcement agencies should be barred from confronting these persons with what they have said over them.

The House Judiciary Committee accepted Brownell's reasoning and reported out warrantless wiretapping legislation in 1954. The full House, however, rejected the arguments in support of warrantless wiretapping and amended the bill on the floor to require a prior judicial warrant. Without the support of the Justice Department, the House bill received no formal consideration in the Senate and no serious attempt was again made to enact electronic surveillance legislation until the 1960s.

Because of Congressional deliberations regarding wiretapping, J. Edgar Hoover wrote a memorandum to Attorney General Brownell on March 8, 1955, in which he outlined the current FBI policy in that area and stated that this policy was based on the May 21, 1940, letter from President Roosevelt and the July 17, 1946, memorandum from Attorney General Clark, which was signed by President Truman. Specifically, he noted that the current policy permitted wiretapping, with the prior written approval of the Attorney General, in "cases vitally affecting the domestic security or where human life is in jeopardy."

Hoover also asked Brownell if he believed the Roosevelt and Truman statements constituted sufficient legal authority for wiretapping at the present time, and suggested that if Brownell did not believe they did, he "may want to present this matter to President Eisenhower to determine whether he holds the same view with respect to the policies of the Department of Justice with respect to wiretapping." Brownell responded that he did not believe it necessary to obtain further approval of the existing practice from President Eisenhower as he was of the opinion that President Roosevelt's approval was sufficient. The Attorney General wrote, in part:

In view of the fact that I personally explained to the President, the Cabinet, the National Security Council and the Senate and House Judiciary Committees during 1954 the present policy and procedure on wiretaps, at which time I referred specifically to the authorization letter to the Attorney General from President F. D.

Roosevelt, I do not think it necessary to reopen the matter at this time. . . . You will also remember that I made several public speeches during 1954 on the legal basis for the Department of Justice policy and procedure on wiretaps.

4. The Kennedy Administration

The existing policy and procedures for wiretapping continued in force through the Kennedy administration. On March 13, 1962, Attorney General Robert F. Kennedy issued Order No. 263-62, which finally rescinded Attorney General Jackson's March 15, 1940, order prohibiting wiretapping, and noted that this rescission was necessary "in order to reflect the practice which has been in effect since May 21, 1940." This order also changed the Manual provisions relating to wiretapping to formally permit use of this technique and reaffirmed the vitality of "[e]xisting instructions to the Federal Bureau of Investigation with respect to obtaining the approval of the Attorney General for wiretapping ...."

5. The Johnson Administration

During the Johnson administration, the procedures for conducting wiretaps were tightened and the criteria for use of this technique were altered. Until March 1965, no requirement had existed for the periodic re-authorization of wiretaps by the Attorney General: some surveillances consequently remained in operation for years without review. On March 30, 1965, Attorney General Katzenbach therefore suggested to J. Edgar Hoover that authorizations for individual telephone taps should be limited to six months, after which time a new request should be submitted for the Attorney General's reauthorization. This suggestion was immediately implemented by the FBI.

One week later, on April 8,1965, Katzenbach sent to the White House a proposed Presidential directive to all federal agencies on wiretapping. This directive, formally issued by President Lyndon Johnson in slightly modified form on June 30, 1965, revoked Attorney General Tom Clark's wiretapping standard of "cases vitally affecting the domestic security or where human life is in jeopardy." The new directive forbade the nonconsensual interception of telephone communications by federal personnel within the United States "except in connection with investigations related to the national security," and then only after first obtaining the written approval of the Attorney General. The President stated, in part:

> I am strongly opposed to the interception of telephone conversations as a general investigative technique. I recognize that mechanical and electronic devices may sometimes be essential in protecting our national security. Nevertheless, it is clear that indiscriminate use of these investigative devices to overhear telephone conversations, without the knowledge, or consent of any of the persons involved, could result in serious abuses and invasions of privacy. In my view, the invasion of privacy of communications is a highly offensive practice which should be engaged in only where the national security is at stake. To avoid any misunderstanding on this subject in the Federal Government, I am establishing the following basic guidelines to be followed by all government agencies:
>
> (1) No federal personnel is to intercept telephone conversations within the United States by any mechanical or electronic device, without the consent of one of the parties involved (except in connection with investigations related to the national security.)

(2) No interception shall be undertaken or continued without first obtaining the approval of the Attorney General.

(3) All federal agencies shall immediately conform their practices and procedures to the provisions of this order.

Despite this Presidential approval of "national security" wiretapping, Director Hoover informed Katzenbach on September 14, 1965, that he was restricting or eliminating the use of a number of investigative techniques by the Bureau

in view of the present atmosphere, brought about by the unrestrained and injudicious use of special investigative techniques by other agencies and departments, resulting in congressional and public alarm and opposition to any activities which could in any way be termed an invasion of privacy.

With regard to wiretapping, Hoover wrote that

[w]hile we have traditionally restricted wiretaps to internal security cases and an occasional investigation involving possible loss of life, such as kidnapping, I have further cut down on wiretaps and I am not requesting authority for any additional wiretaps..

Katzenbach responded on September 27, with a memorandum setting forth what he believed to be appropriate guidelines for the use of the techniques Hoover had restricted or eliminated. He noted that "[t]he use of wiretaps and microphones involving trespass present more difficult problems because of the inadmissibility of any evidence obtained in court cases and because of current judicial and public attitudes regarding their use." He continued:

It is my understanding that such devices will not be used without my authorization, although in emergency circumstances they may be used subject to my later ratification. At this time I believe it is desirable that all such techniques be confined to the gathering of intelligence in national security matters, and I will continue to approve all such requests in the future as I have in the past. I see no need to curtail any such activities in the national security field.

It is also my belief that there are occasions outside of the strict definition of national security (for example, organized crime) when it would be appropriate to use such techniques for intelligence purposes. However, in light of the present atmosphere, I believe that efforts in the immediate future should be confined to national security. I realize that this restriction will hamper our efforts against organized crime and will require a redoubled effort on the part of the Bureau to develop intelligence through other means.

While suggesting the possibility that warrantless wiretapping might appropriately be used at some future time in cases involving organized crime, in short, Katzenbach endorsed its use only in "the national security field."

On November 3, 1966, Attorney General Ramsey Clark circulated a memorandum to all United States Attorneys in which he reiterated the "national security" limitation on wiretapping contained in President Johnson's June 30, 1965, directive and in Katzenbach's September 27, 1965, letter to Hoover. He quoted as follows from the 1966 Supplemental Memorandum to the Supreme Court that had been filed in Black v. United States, a criminal case which involved a microphone installation:

> Present practice, adopted in July 1965 in conformity with the policies declared by President Johnson on June 30, 1965, for the entire Federal establishment, prohibits the installation of listening devices in private areas (as well as the interception of telephone and other wire communications) in all instances other than those involving the collection of intelligence affecting the national security. The specific authorization of the Attorney General must be obtained in each instance when this exception is invoked. Intelligence data so collected will not be available for investigative or litigative purposes.

Clark's subsequent guidelines for the use of wiretapping and electronic eavesdropping, issued in June 1967 to the heads of executive agencies and departments, reaffirmed the prohibition of wiretapping in all but "national security" cases.

C. The Omnibus Crime Control Act of 1968

Although Justice Department policy regarding wiretapping remained essentially constant from 1965 to 1968, two Supreme Court decisions during this period significantly altered the constitutional framework for electronic surveillance generally. In Berger v. New York, 388 U.S. 41 (1967), and Katz v. United States, 389 U.S. 347 (1967), the Supreme Court overruled Olmstead and held that the Fourth Amendment did apply to searches and seizures of conversations and protected all conversations of an individual as to which he had a reasonable expectation of privacy. Katz explicitly left open the question, however, whether or not a judicial warrant was required in cases "involving the national security."

In part as a response to the Berger and Katz decisions, Congress enacted Title III of the Omnibus Crime Control and Safe Streets Act of 1968, 18 U.S.C. 2510-20. This Act established procedures for obtaining judicial warrants permitting wiretapping by government officials, but the issue of "national security" wiretaps, which was left open in Katz, was similarly avoided. Section 2511 (3) of the Act stated that nothing in the Omnibus Crime Control Act or the Federal Communications Act of 1934 shall limit the constitutional power of the President in certain vaguely defined areas. The text of this subsection reads as follows:

(3) Nothing contained in this chapter or in section 605 of the Communications Act of 1934 (48 Stat. 1143, 47 U.S.C. 605) shall limit the constitutional powers of the President to take such measures as he deems necessary to protect the Nation against actual or potential attack or other hostile acts of a foreign power, to obtain foreign intelligence information deemed essential to the security of the United States, or to protect national security information against foreign intelligence activities. Nor shall anything contained in this chapter be deemed to limit the constitutional power of the President to take such measures as he deems necessary to protect the United States against the overthrow of the Government by force or other unlawful means, or against any other clear and present danger to the structure or existence of the Government. The contents of any wire or oral communication intercepted by authority of the President in the exercise of the foregoing powers may be received in evidence in any trial hearing or other proceeding only where such interception was

reasonable, and shall not be otherwise used or disclosed except as is necessary to implement that power.

Significantly, this subsection dose not define the scope of the President's constitutional power in the national security area. As the Supreme Court noted in the Keith case, it is merely a statement that to the extent such powers exist, if they exist at all they override the procedural requirements for electronic surveillance that are outlined in this statute and in the 1934 Act.

D. Justice Department Criteria for Warrantless Wiretaps: 1968-1975

1. 1968-1972

In fields other than national security, the Justice Department was obligated to conform with the warrant procedures of the 1968 statute. But in national security cases, Justice Department policy permitted — and the Act did not forbid — warrantless wiretapping if the proposed surveillance satisfied one or more of the following criteria (which paralleled the standards enunciated in Section 2511 (3)) :

(1) That it is necessary to protect the nation against actual or potential attack or any other hostile action of a foreign power;

(2) That it is necessary to obtain foreign intelligence information deemed essential to the security of the United States;

(3) That it is necessary to protect national security information against foreign intelligence activities;

(4) That it is necessary to protect the United States against the overthrow of the Government by force or other unlawful means; or

(5) That it is necessary to protect the United States against a clear or present danger to the structure or the existence of its Government.

Existing procedures for warrantless wiretaps requiring the prior written authorization of the Attorney General and subsequent reauthorization after 90 days remained in effect after the passage of the 1968 Act.

2. The Keith Case: 1972

On June 19, 1972, the Supreme Court decided the so-called Keith case, United States v. United States District Court, 407 U.S. 297 (1972), which held that the Fourth Amendment required prior judicial approval for "domestic security" electronic surveillance. The Court acknowledged the constitutional power of the President to "protect our Government against those who would subvert or overthrow it by unlawful means," but it held that this power did not extend to the authorization of warrantless electronic surveillance directed at a domestic organization which was neither directly nor indirectly connected with a foreign power.

To conform with the Keith decision, the Justice Department thereafter limited warrantless wiretapping to cases involving a "significant connection with a foreign power, its agents or agencies." A spokesman for the Department stated that such a connection might be shown by "the presence of such factors as substantial financing, control by or active collaboration with a foreign government and agencies thereof in unlawful activities directed against the Government of the United States."

3. 1972-1975

The Justice Department's criteria for warrantless electronic surveillance were next modified in 1975. On June 24, 1975, Attorney General Edward H. Levi wrote Senators Frank Church and Edward Kennedy a letter in which he set forth his standards for warrantless wiretaps. He wrote, in part:

Under the standards and procedures established by the President, the personal approval of the Attorney General is required before any nonconsensual electronic surveillance may be instituted within the United States without a judicial warrant. All requests for surveillance must be made in writing by the Director of the Federal Bureau of Investigation and must set forth the relevant factual circumstances that justify the proposed surveillance. Both the agency and the Presidential appointee initiating the request must be identified. Requests from the Director are examined by a special review group which I have established within the Office of the Attorney General. Authorization will not be granted unless the Attorney General has satisfied himself that the requested electronic surveillance is necessary for national security or foreign intelligence purposes important to national security.

In addition, the Attorney General must be satisfied that the subject of the surveillance is either assisting a foreign power or foreign-based political group, or plans unlawful activity directed against a foreign power or foreign-based political group. Finally, he must be satisfied that the minimum physical intrusion necessary to obtain the information will be used.

All authorizations are for a period of ninety days or less, and the specific approval of the Attorney General is again required for continuation of the surveillance beyond that period. The Attorney General has also been directed to review all electronic surveillance on a regular basis to ensure that the aforementioned criteria are satisfied. Pursuant to the mandate of United States v. United States District Court, electronic surveillance without a judicial warrant is not conducted where there is no foreign involvement.

In his public testimony before the Senate Select Committee on Intelligence Activities on November 6, 1975, Attorney General Levi again articulated current Department of Justice criteria for the approval of warrantless electronic surveillance. His formulation on that date returned to the three foreign-related categories which were based on Section 2511(3) of the 1968 Act, between 1972 and 1975, and a fourth category was also added. He stated:

Requests are only authorized when the requested electronic surveillance is necessary to protect the nation against actual or potential attack or other hostile acts of a foreign power; to obtain foreign intelligence deemed essential to the security of the nation; to protect national security information against foreign intelligence activities; or to obtain information certified as necessary for the conduct of foreign affairs matters important to the national security of the United States.

In his November 1975 testimony, the Attorney General also omitted the phrase in his June 24 letter which would have permitted warrantless electronic surveillance to be directed against American citizens or domestic groups which "plan[ned] unlawful activity directed against a foreign power or a foreign-based political group." Warrantless electronic surveillance, he said, would only be authorized when the subject of the proposed surveillance is "consciously assisting a foreign power or a foreign-based political group." The elimination of this category was apparently due to the decision of the Court of Appeals for the District of Columbia in Zweibon v. Mitchell, 516 F.2d 594 (D.C. Cir., 1975) (en banc), which held unconstitutional warrantless electronic surveillance of a domestic organization that was neither the agent of nor collaborator with a foreign power.

To date, neither Congress nor the Supreme Court has ever squarely faced the issue of whether the President may legitimately authorize warrantless electronic surveillance in "national security" cases involving the activities of foreign powers or their agents. As noted above, Section 2511(3) of the 1968 Omnibus Crime Control Act does not represent an affirmative grant of power to the President; it is simply an acknowledgement that Congress does not intend to limit or restrict whatever constitutional power the President may have in connection with "national security" cases. And the Supreme Court in Keith explicitly wrote that it only reached the question of the constitutionality of "national security" electronic surveillance in cases that involved "domestic security." While two federal circuit courts have determined that the President may constitutionally authorize warrantless electronic surveillance directed against foreign agents or collaborators, the Supreme Court denied certiorari in both cases and has yet to decide the issue. In the absence of a mandate from Congress or the Supreme Court, the Justice Department has relied on these circuit court cases to support its current standards for warrantless electronic surveillance.

Legislation has recently been introduced, with the support of Attorney General Levi, to require a prior judicial warrant for electronic surveillance of an "agent of a foreign power." One of seven specially designated federal judges would be authorized to issue a warrant upon a finding that there is "probable cause to believe that the target of the electronic surveillance is a foreign power or an agent of a foreign power." The term "agent of a foreign power" is defined as

(i) a person who is not a permanent resident alien or citizen of the United States and who is an officer or employee of a foreign power; or

(ii) a person who, pursuant to the direction of a foreign power, is engaged in clandestine intelligence activities, sabotage, or terrorist activities, or who conspires with, assists or aids and abets such a person in engaging in such activities.

Thus, the legislation would not define the activities which could subject an American to electronic surveillance in terms of the federal criminal laws.

The new legislation also would not reach electronic surveillance of Americans abroad or other "facts and circumstances ... beyond the scope" of its provisions. Authority for such surveillance would continue to be based on whatever may be "the constitutional power of the President." In other respects, however, the proposed statute is a significant step towards effective regulation of FBI electronic surveillance.

III. Presidential And Attorney General Authorization For Warrantless Microphone Surveillance

Warrantless microphone surveillance, while perhaps the most intrusive type of electronic surveillance, has received significantly less attention from Presidents and Attorneys General than has warrantless wiretapping. The first documentary indication that microphone surveillance was separately considered by any Attorney General is not found until 1952, when Attorney General McGrath prohibited its use in cases involving trespass. Two years later, Attorney General Brownell issued a sweeping authorization for microphone surveillance, even when it involved physical trespass, in cases where the Bureau determined such surveillance was in the national interest; no prior approval by the Attorney General was required. This policy continued until 1965, when microphone surveillance was placed on an equal footing with telephone surveillance, and since that time the policies for both these forms of electronic surveillance have remained identical.

A. Pre-1952

1. 1931 to 1942

The legal status of microphone, as opposed to telephone, surveillance was not addressed by the Supreme Court until 1942, and it was not addressed by Congress until 1968. It is perhaps for this reason that the Justice Department developed no distinct policy on microphone surveillance during the first half of the century.

The Olmstead case in 1928 involved a wiretap rather than a microphone surveillance. Similarly, the Federal Communications Act of 1934 was addressed only to the interception of wire and radio communications; microphone surveillance was not within its ambit. Neither Attorney General Mitchell's nor Attorney General Jackson's instructions on wiretapping in 1931 and 1940, respectively, encompassed microphone surveillance, and President Roosevelt's 1940 authorization and President Truman's 1946 authorization were also limited to wiretapping.

An internal Justice Department memorandum from William Olson, former Assistant Attorney General for Internal Security, to Attorney General Elliot Richardson notes that "[d]uring the period 1931-1940, it appears safe to assume that microphone surveillances were utilized under the same standards as telephone surveillances — 'in those cases involving the safety of the victims of kidnapping, the location and apprehension of desperate criminals, and in espionage, sabotage, and other cases considered to be of major law enforcement importance.'"

2. 1942-1952

In 1942, the Supreme Court decided Goldman v. United States, 316 U.S. 129, which held in the context of a criminal case that a microphone surveillance was constitutional when it did not involve physical trespass. Thereafter, the test for the validity of a microphone surveillance appeared to be whether or not it involved a trespass. There is no evidence, however, that an Attorney General gave any firm guidance to the FBI in this area until 1952. Although there did not appear to be any distinct articulated Justice Department policy on microphone surveillance for a decade after Goldman, J. Edgar Hoover summarized FBI practice since Goldman in a 1951 memorandum to Attorney General McGrath:

> As you are aware, this Bureau has also employed the use of microphone installations on a highly restrictive basis, chiefly to obtain intelligence information. The information obtained from microphones, as in the case of wiretaps, is not admissible in evidence. In certain instances, it has been possible to install microphones without trespass, as reflected by opinions rendered in the past by the Department on this subject matter. In these instances, the information obtained, of course, is treated as evidence and therefore is not regarded as purely intelligence information.
>
> As you know, in a number of instances it has not been possible to install microphones without trespass. In such instances the information received therefrom is of an intelligence nature only. Here again, as in the use of wiretaps, experience has shown us that intelligence information highly pertinent to the defense and welfare of this nation is derived through the use of microphones.

B. 1952 to 1965

The first clear instruction to the FBI from an Attorney General regarding microphone surveillance was issued in 1952. On February 26, 1952, Attorney General McGrath wrote to Mr. Hoover as follows:

> The use of microphone surveillance which does not involve a trespass would seem to be permissible under the present state of the law, United States v. Goldman, 316 U.S. 129. Such surveillances as involve trespass are in the area of the Fourth Amendment, and evidence so obtained and from leads so obtained is inadmissible.
>
> The records do not indicate that this question dealing with microphones has ever been presented before; therefore, please be advised that I cannot authorize the installation of a microphone involving a trespass under existing law.

As a result of this instruction, Hoover declared in a March 4, 1952, internal FBI memorandum that he would similarly not approve any request for a microphone surveillance in a case involving trespass.

The FBI evidently considered this policy on microphone surveillance to be too restrictive, however, especially in the area of internal security. 79 Under pressure from the FBI — and despite the 1954 Supreme Court decision in Irvine v. California 80 -- Attorney General Brownell reversed his predecessor's position. On May 22, 1954, he wrote Director Hoover:

> The recent decision of the Supreme Court entitled Irvine v. California, 347 U.S. 128, denouncing the use of microphone surveillances by city police in a gambling case, makes appropriate a reappraisal of the use which may be made in the future by the Federal Bureau of Investigation of microphone surveillance in connection with matters relating to the internal security of the country.
>
> It is clear that in some instances the use of microphone surveillance is the only possible way of uncovering the activities of espionage agents, possible saboteurs, and subversive persons. In such instances I am of the opinion that the national interest requires that microphone surveillance be utilized by the Federal Bureau of Investigation. This use need not be limited to the development of evidence for prosecution. The FBI has an intelligence function in connection with internal security matters equally as important as the duty of developing evidence for presentation to the courts and the national security requires that the FBI be able to use microphone surveillance for the proper discharge of both such functions. The Department of Justice approves the use of microphone surveillance by the FBI under these circumstances and for these purposes.
>
> I do not consider that the decision of the Supreme Court in Irvine v. California, supra, requires a different course. That case is readily distinguishable on its facts. The language of the Court, however, indicates certain uses of microphones which it would be well to avoid, if possible, even in internal security investigations. It is quite clear that in the Irvine

case the Justices of the Supreme Court were outraged by what they regarded as the indecency of installing a microphone in a bedroom. They denounced the utilization of such methods of investigation in a gambling case as shocking. The Court's action is a clear indication of the need for discretion and intelligent restraint in the use of microphones by the FBI in all cases, including internal security matters. Obviously, the installation of a microphone in a bedroom or in some comparably intimate location should be avoided wherever possible. It may appear, however, that important intelligence or evidence relating to matters connected with the national security can only be obtained by the installation of a microphone in such a location. It is my opinion that under such circumstances the installation is proper and not prohibited by the Supreme Court's decision in the Irvine case.

... It is realized that not infrequently the question of trespass arises in connection with the installation of a microphone.

The question of whether a trespass is actually involved and the second question of the effect of such a trespass upon the admissibility in court of the evidence thus obtained, must necessarily be resolved according to the circumstances of each case. The Department in resolving the problems which may arise in connection with the use of microphone surveillance will review the circumstances in each case in light of the practical necessities of investigation and of the national interest which must be protected. It is my opinion that the Department should adopt that interpretation which will permit microphone coverage by the FBI in a manner most conducive to our national interest. I recognize that for the FBI to fulfill its important intelligence function, consideration of internal security and the national safety are paramount and, therefore, may compel the unrestricted use of this technique in the national interest.

Brownell cited no legal support for this sweeping authorization. By not requiring prior approval by the Attorney General for specific microphone installations, moreover, he largely undercut the policy which had developed for wiretapping. The FBI in many cases could obtain equivalent coverage by utilizing bugs rather than taps and would not be burdened with the necessity of a formal request to the Attorney General.

On May 4, 1961, Director Hoover wrote a memorandum to Deputy Attorney General Byron R. White, in which he informed the Department that the FBI's policy with regard to microphone surveillance was based on the 1954 Brownell memorandum quoted above. Hoover stated that Brownell had "approved the use of microphone surveillances with or without trespass," and noted that "in the internal security field we are utilizing microphone surveillances on a restricted basis even though trespass is necessary to assist in uncovering the activities of [foreign] intelligence agents and Communist Party leaders." He continued: "In the interests of national safety, microphone surveillances are also utilized on a restricted basis, even though trespass is necessary, in uncovering major criminal activities. We are using such coverage in connection with our investigations of clandestine activities of top hoodlums and organized crime." This memorandum apparently did not lead to further reconsideration of microphone surveillance policy by Justice Department officials, and the practice articulated by Hoover continued without change until 1965.

The Department later summarized the policy during these years in the Supplemental Memorandum to the Supreme Court in the case of Black v. United States, referred to above.

The memorandum read, in part: "Under Department practice in effect for a period of years prior to 1963, and continuing until 1965, the Director of the Federal Bureau of Investigation was given authority to approve the installation of devices such as that in question [a microphone] for intelligence (and not evidentiary) purposes when required in the interest of internal security or national safety, including organized crime, kidnappings, and matters wherein human life may be at stake. Acting on the basis of the aforementioned Departmental authorization, the Director approved installation of the device involved in the instant case."

C. 1965 to the Present

On March 30, 1965, when Attorney General Katzenbach instituted the six month limitation on telephone taps, he also expressed the view that proposals for microphone surveillances should be submitted for the Attorney General's prior approval and that this type of surveillance should also be limited to six month periods. While Attorneys General since the 1950s had sporadically given their prior approval to microphone surveillances, the requirement of such approval had never been a consistent policy of the Justice Department, as it had been with respect to wiretapping for more than two decades. With the immediate implementation of Katzenbach's suggestions, therefore, the Justice Department procedures with regard to both wiretapping and microphone surveillance became identical.

President Johnson's June 30, 1965, directive to all federal agencies, which formally prohibited all wiretapping except in connection with "national security" investigations and then only with the prior approval of the Attorney General, referred to the issue of microphone surveillances only tangentially. It read:

> Utilization of mechanical or electronic devices to overhear nontelephone conversations is an even more difficult problem, which raises substantial and unresolved questions of constitutional interpretation. I desire that each agency conducting such investigations consult with the Attorney General to ascertain whether the agency's practices are fully in accord with the law and with a decent regard for the rights of others.

Apparently, J. Edgar Hoover did not find his "consultations" with the Attorney General to be encouraging. It is noted above that on September 14, 1965, the Director informed Katzenbach that, "[i]n accordance with the wishes you have expressed during various recent conversations with me" and because of public alarm at alleged invasions of privacy by Federal agencies, he was severely restricting or eliminating the use of a number of investigative techniques. Specifically with regard to microphone surveillance, he wrote that "we have discontinued completely the use of" this technique—despite Katzenbach's approval of the limited use of microphone surveillance in March of that year and despite the absence of a prohibition oil the use of the technique in the President's June directive.

It is also noted above in Section II that Katzenbach responded about two weeks later with a memorandum setting forth what he believed to be appropriate guidelines for the use of the techniques Hoover had restricted or eliminated. He gave virtually unrestricted authorization to the FBI to conduct microphone surveillances not involving trespass, writing, "[w]here such questions [i.e., of trespass] are not raised, I believe the Bureau should continue to use these techniques in cases where you believe it appropriate without further authorization from me." With regard to microphone surveillances that did involve trespass, he again treated the use of this technique in a fashion identical to warrantless wiretapping: for both he required his prior approval (except in "emergency circumstances") and for both the legitimate purposes were limited to the gathering of intelligence in "national security matters." While he expressed the belief that both wiretaps and microphone surveillances involving trespass might at some future time be appropriate to use in the area of organized crime, he gave no authority for such use at that time.

The policy set out in Katzenbach's September 27 letter to Hoover was reaffirmed by the Justice Department at least three times prior to the 1967 Katz decision and the passage of the Omnibus Crime Control Act of 1968.

In the July 1966 Supplemental Memorandum filed in the Black case, the Justice Department stated that "[p]resent Departmental practice, adopted in July 1965, prohibits the use of such listening devices in all instances other than those involving the collection of intelligence affecting the national security. The specific authorization of the Attorney General must be obtained in each instance when this exception is involved." This language was quoted by Attorney General Ramsey Clark in his November 3, 1966 memorandum to all United States Attorneys and reaffirmed in Clark's 1967 memorandum to heads of executive departments.

The Katz decision, in December 1967, held that a warrantless microphone installation on the side of a public telephone booth was unconstitutional in the context of a criminal case. Thus, Justice Department policy prohibiting microphone surveillances in non-"national security" cases became a constitutional requirement as well—regardless of whether or not the installation involved trespass. 90a As noted above, however, the issue of electronic surveillance in "national security" cases was not addressed by the Supreme Court in Katz.

The 1968 Omnibus Crime Control Act, unlike the Federal Communications Act of 1934, applies to both telephone wiretaps and microphone surveillances. Because of this, and because the Justice Department policy regarding both techniques became virtually identical in 1965, the description of the evolution of wiretapping policy over the past decade applies equally to the technique of microphone surveillance. In recent years, for all practical purposes, there has been but a single policy for both forms of electronic surveillance.

IV. An Overview Of FBI Electronic Surveillance Practices

The preceding two sections have dealt with the legal framework and Justice Department policy regarding warrantless wiretapping and bugging. This section attempts to provide an overview of FBI electronic surveillance practices. Without purporting to explore the full range of FBI electronic surveillance practices, a limited number of key areas are highlighted in order to suggest the manner in which electronic surveillances are conducted. More specifically, this section discusses the frequency of FBI use of this technique since 1940; internal FBI restrictions on the maximum number of simultaneous electronic surveillances; the method by which requests have been initiated and approved; the manner in which wiretaps and bugs have been installed; the means by which the FBI has responded to the legal obligation to produce electronic surveillance records in criminal trials; and the traditional reluctance of the FBI to permit outside scrutiny of its electronic surveillance practices. A discussion of the application of the Justice Department's standards for wiretapping and bugging to particular cases is reserved for Section VII below.

A. Extent of FBI Electronic Surveillance: 1940-1975

While FBI use of warrantless electronic surveillance has not been as pervasive as many other investigative techniques such as informants, both wiretaps and bugs have been strategically utilized in a large number of intelligence investigations. The Bureau's reliance on these techniques was greatest during World War II and the immediate postwar period. During the 1960s and early 1970s, internal FBI policy placed a ceiling on the number of simultaneous electronic surveillances conducted by the Bureau. This self -restriction did not act to curtail all use of this technique, but it apparently frustrated intelligence officials in the FBI and other agencies who sought—unsuccessfully—a change in this policy through the Huston Plan in 1970. In recent years, Judicial decisions have severely restricted the use of warrantless electronic surveillance against domestic targets, although wiretaps and bugs still continue to be commonly used in the area of foreign intelligence and counterintelligence.

1. Annual Totals for Wiretaps and Microphone Installations

According to Justice Department records, the annual totals of warrantless FBI wiretaps and microphones in operation between 1940 and 1974 were as follows:

Year	Telephone wiretaps	Microphones
1940	6	6
1941	67	25
1942	304	88
1943	475	193
1944	517	198
1945	519	186
1946	364	85
1947	374	81
1948	416	67
1949	471	75
1950	270	61
1951	285	75
1952	285	63
1953	300	52
1954	322	99
1955	214	102
1956	164	71
1957	173	73
1958	166	70
1959	120	75
1960	115	74
1961	140	85
1962	198	100
1963	244	83
1964	260	106
1965	233	67

1966	174	10
1967	113	0
1968	82	9
1969	123	14
1970	102	19
1971	101	16
1972	108	32
1973	123	40
1974	190	42

The statistics before 1968 encompass electronic surveillances for both intelligence and law enforcement purposes. Those after 1968, when the Omnibus rime Control Act was enacted, include surveillances for intelligence purposes only; electronic surveillances for law enforcement purposes were thereafter subject to the warrant procedures required by the Act.

Comparable figures for the year 1975, through October 29, are: 121 telephone wiretaps and 24 microphone installations.

It should be noted that these figures are cumulative for each year; that is, a wiretap on an individual in one year which continued into a second year is recorded in both years. The figures are also duplicative to some extent, since a telephone wiretap or microphone which was installed, then discontinued, and later reinstated is counted as a new surveillance upon reinstatement.

2. FBI Policy on the Maximum Number of Simultaneous Electronic Surveillances

From at least the early 1960s, J. Edgar Hoover placed a ceiling on the number of warrantless electronic surveillances that could be in operation at any one time. As expressed by Charles D. Brennan, who became Assistant Director in charge of the FBI's Domestic Intelligence Division in 1970, ". . . there was always a maximum figure which you were not allowed to exceed, and if you recommended an additional wiretap, it had to be done with the recognition that in another area you would take one off."

Until the mid-1960s, the maximum figure was approximately eighty. In response to the 1965 and 1966 investigation by the Senate Subcommittee on Administrative Practice, and Procedure into the use of electronic surveillance and other techniques by federal agencies, however, Hoover instructed Bureau officials to reduce by one half the number of warrantless electronic surveillances then in effect. According to Brennan, the ceiling was lowered out of a concern that this subcommittee's "inquiry might get into the use of that technique by the FBI . . . ." The number of warrantless wiretaps in the "security field" was subsequently reduced from 76 to 38, and remained close to the latter figure for several years thereafter.

Intelligence officials both within the FBI itself and in other intelligence agencies clearly felt constrained by Hoover's policy, and through the Huston Plan in 1970 they attempted to raise or eliminate the internal limitations on the number of simultaneous electronic surveillances. The Report that was presented to President Nixon in June of 1970 noted: "The limited number of electronic surveillances and penetrations substantially restricts the collection of valuable intelligence information of material important to the entire intelligence community," and it presented the President with the option of modifying "present procedures" to "permit intensification of coverage of individuals and groups in the United States who pose a major threat to the internal security." This option was specifically recommended to the President by Tom Charles Huston.

Director Hoover nonetheless remained strongly opposed to lifting restraints on the FBI's use of warrantless electronic surveillance. He added a footnote to the electronic surveillance section of the Huston Report which read:

The FBI does not wish to change its present procedure of selective coverage of major internal security threats as it believes this coverage is adequate at this time. The FBI would not oppose other agencies seeking authority of the Attorney General for coverage required by them and thereafter instituting such coverage themselves.

In part because of Hoover's opposition to the Huston Plan, President Nixon, who had originally endorsed the recommendations, withdrew his approval and the maximum number of electronic surveillance stayed essentially constant until 1972.

The policy of placing an arbitrary ceiling on simultaneous warrantless electronic surveillances was apparently terminated after J. Edgar Hoover's death in 1972. With the apparent lifting of this self-restriction, the number of foreign related surveillances increased—a fact which is reflected in the annual totals listed above.

B. Requests, Approvals, and Implementation

1. The Request and Approval Process

Recommendations for the use of electronic surveillance in particular cases are typically initiated at the field level of the Bureau, although at times they have originated with the Attorney General, the White House, and the head of another agency. If Headquarters approves a field request, the appropriate field office then conducts a feasibility study to determine whether or not the surveillance can be conducted with complete security. Upon a favorable security finding, the Director personally sends the Attorney General a formal request for coverage, setting forth the name and address of the person or persons to be monitored as well as pertinent facts about the case.

According to former Attorney General William Saxbe, the "request must contain very detailed information." In numerous cases in the past, however, the information supplied in the request has been minimal at best. For example, several of the so-called "17 wiretaps" during the Nixon administration were approved by Attorney General John Mitchell despite the lack of any data in the formal requests to support the need for the technique's use. It is possible that these and similarly defective requests submitted to other Attorneys General were supplemented by information imparted orally, but, as the District of Columbia Court of Appeals stated in Zweibon v. Mitchell:

> . . . we nevertheless note the possibility of abuse when there are no written records of the justifications for instituting a surveillance. Such lack of records allows a search to be justified on information subsequently obtained from the surveillance and permits the assertion that more information was relied on than was in fact the case. Prior judicial approval for wiretapping, among other benefits, of course freezes the record as to the data upon which the surveillance was based.

2. Implementation of Wiretaps and Bugs

If the Director receives the written approval of the Attorney General for a particular surveillance, the field office is instructed to implement it. In the case of wiretapping, an agent from the field office generally contacts a representative of the local telephone company who acts as Government liaison. One such telephone company representative in Washington, D.C., testified that he was simply orally advised by an agent of the FBI's Washington Field Office that authority had been granted to tap a particular telephone number.

According to the Washington Field Office supervisor in charge of the employees who implemented and monitored "national security" wiretaps, the telephone company representative would then assign "pair numbers" in the cable connecting the FBI's Washington, D.C. Field Office with the company's central office in the city, and the recording and monitoring devices would be attached to the assigned cable pair at the field office, where the Bureau monitoring agents were located. After the supervisor verified the wiretap by determining that the intercepted line was the correct one, he would give the tap a symbol number to be used in lieu of the words "telephone surveillance" in any later communication.

Generally, two agents would conduct the monitoring operation in eight-hour shifts. These monitors typically tape recorded all calls on the line and added supplementary notes concerning such items as the identity of the caller and the subject of the conversation if unclear from the tape. Each day, they typed up log summaries, which included anything they believed was consequential. Because the monitors were not told specifically what to look for, however, the summaries tended to be over-inclusive rather than under-inclusive: the supervising agent noted, for instance, that any information obtained about the subject's sex life or drug use would usually be included in the log summaries. He also stated that he disliked having empty summaries for any day, and so issued a general instruction to his monitors that an attempt should be made to include at least one item in the log each day. Even if there was no activity, a monitor would still have to file a log summary stating "no activity" or "no pertinent activity."

A special squad within the Washington Field Office was responsible for implementing microphone installations. According to one Bureau agent who served on this squad for a number of years, the authorizing document (which, he said, invariably bore J. Edgar Hoover's initials) would be transmitted to the field office and shown to him and the other members of the squad prior to the installation. This agent stated that in the majority of cases he was able to obtain a key to the target's premises, either from a landlord, hotel manager, or neighbor. In other cases, he simply entered through unlocked doors. He stated that only in a small proportion of the cases to which he was assigned was it necessary to pick a lock. Once the bug was planted, it was generally necessary for Bureau agents to monitor the conversations from a location close to the targeted premises.

C. The ELSUR Index

In the mid-1960s, the Justice Department established a policy of filing disclosures in the courts in cases where criminal defendants had been monitored by electronic surveillance. As a result, it became necessary to establish a general index of the names of all persons overheard on such surveillances. In September 1966, the Assistant Attorney General of the Criminal Division informed Director Hoover that:

> In recent months the Department has been confronted with serious problems concerning the prospective or continued prosecution of individuals who have been the subject of prior electronic surveillance. These problems have sometimes arisen comparatively late in the investigative or prosecutive process. For example, we recently were forced to close an important investigation involving major gambling figures in

Miami because we were advised that the evidence necessary to obtain a conviction was tainted....

In view of these experiences, it appears necessary and desirable that the Department have full knowledge of the extent of any device problem at as early a stage of preparation for prosecution as possible in order to determine whether a particular case may or may not be tainted or what responses will be necessary with respect to a motion under Rule 16 to produce statements.

Accordingly, I feel it is imperative for us to establish between the Bureau and the Department . . . some sort of "early warning" system. This may require the Bureau to set up and maintain appropriate indices with respect to electronic surveillance and the materials derived therefrom.

I have discussed this suggestion with the Attorney General and the Deputy Attorney General. Both feel that the establishment of such indices is necessary. . .

In fact, for a number of years prior to this suggestion the Bureau had maintained rudimentary indices within each field office, although there was no central index and those which existed on the field level were believed to be inadequate by Justice Department officials. Because Hoover believed the existing system was adequate, he reacted defensively when Assistant Attorney General Fred Vinson requested a conference between the Department and the Bureau to discuss the details of the Justice Department's proposal. The Director penned the following notation on the Vinson memorandum: "Since [an indexing system] is already operating, I see no need for such a conference.... Tell him it is already done and see that it is meticulously operated."

About one week later, however, Hoover directed officials at Headquarters to send a teletype to all field offices which had conducted electronic surveillances since January 1960. These offices were instructed to transmit to Headquarters the names of all individuals whose voices were were monitored through electronic surveillance any time within the previous six years, as well as the initial date of the monitoring and the identity of the subject against whom the installation was directed. Each office was also informed that it had a continuing obligation to submit to Headquarters on a weekly basis the names of any additional individuals monitored in the future.

The Bureau has since maintained a central index at Headquarters, referred to as the ELSUR Index, which contains the names of all individuals overheard, even incidentally, on both court-ordered and warrantless electronic surveillances. Additional information such as the initial date of the monitoring and the identity of the target of the surveillance is also included in the index. The method by which this index has been compiled, however, raises some questions as to its accuracy and completeness.

Although the ELSUR Index covers the period January 1, 1960, to the present, for example, the FBI's response to a request by the Senate Select Committee for the date and location of all electronic overhears of Martin Luther King, Jr., conceded that retrieval of some of the overhears of King may be impossible. Three factors contributing to this difficulty were set forth by the Bureau:

1. Prior to issuing instructions to field offices in October, 1966, directing them to submit the names of all individuals whose voices have been monitored through a microphone installed or a telephone surveillance operated by the offices anytime since 1/1/60, additional surveillances on which King was monitored are unaccountable for as these surveillance logs may have been destroyed.

2. Prior to the instructions, personnel handling logs may have felt that overhears were of no substance or significance and consequently were not recorded.

3. The setting up of the ELSUR indices was a fieldwide project of large proportions and the instructions going to the field 10/5/66, were subject to broad interpretation, thus leading to possible misinterpretation of these instructions. Also, the factor of human error might be involved, thereby causing incomplete indices until the mechanics of the procedure were ironed out.

In fact, several surveillances of King himself which were known to personnel at FBI headquarters were apparently not reflected in the ELSUR Index.

One Special Agent's description of the preparation of ELSUR Index cards by FBI monitors suggests that the Index may be incomplete even for the post-1966 period. According to this agent, the FBI monitors are under instructions to prepare ELSUR Index cards for each identifiable person who speaks over the intercepted line. Since the cards must contain the proper names of these individuals rather than phonetic spellings, and since this information is often difficult to obtain from an overhear alone, the monitors maintain a separate index of phonetic spellings prior to their determination of the proper spelling and its entry into the ELSUR Index. The monitors then attempt to confirm the identity of the persons overheard from various research aids kept at their disposal, such as telephone books and Congressional and federal agency directories, and from discussions with the Bureau agents assigned to the substantive cases. In most cases, it is possible to make an accurate identification, but when this proves to be impossible, the names of unidentified individuals never get entered into the ELSUR Index. Sometimes no entry has been made in the ELSUR Index even though positive identification was subsequently obtained. Thus, a person could be overheard and this fact would not be revealed by a check of the ELSUR Index.

D. Congressional Investigation of FBI Electronic Surveillance Practices: The Long Subcommittee

The Bureau has traditionally been reluctant to permit Congressional investigation into its electronic surveillance practices. During the 1965 and 1966 inquiry by the Senate Subcommittee on Administrative Practice and Procedure into the use of electronic surveillance and other techniques by federal agencies, the FBI took affirmative steps to avoid substantial exposure of such practices to the subcommittee. The Bureau's attempt to thwart this subcommittee's investigation into the use of mail covers in February and March of 1965 is described in the Senate Select Committee's Report on CIA and FBI Mail Opening; a similar attempt, apparently acquiesced in by the Subcommittee, was made in the area of electronic surveillance.

The Bureau's wary attitude toward this investigation is reflected in an internal memorandum dated August 2, 1965:

Senator [Edward V.] Long [of Missouri] is Chairman of the Senate Subcommittee on Administrative, Practice and Procedure. He has been taking testimony in connection with mail covers, wiretapping, and various snooping devices on the part of Federal agencies. He cannot be trusted and although the FBI has not become involved in these bearings, our name has been mentioned quite prominently on several occasions . . . .

When the Subcommittee's investigation began to touch on the Bureau's electronic surveillance practices in connection with organized crime several months later, Assistant Director Cartha DeLoach and another ranking Bureau official personally visited the Subcommittee's chairman, Senator Edward Long of Missouri, to explain to him the FBI's practices in the area of electronic surveillance. This meeting lasted approximately one and one-half hours, and there is no indication in the documentary record that any other briefing occurred prior to this visit. Nonetheless, an FBI memorandum notes that after the Senator "stated that unfortunately a number of people were bringing pressure on him to look into the FBI's activities in connection with usage of electronic devices," DeLoach suggested to him:

> that perhaps he might desire to issue a statement reflecting that he had held lengthy conferences with top FBI officials and was now completely satisfied, after looking into FBI operations, that the FBI had never participated in uncontrolled usage of wiretaps or microphones and that FBI usage of such devices had been completely justified in all instances.

According to this memorandum, Senator Long agreed, and when he "stated that he frankly did not know how to word such a release," DeLoach "told him that we would be glad to prepare the release for him on a strictly confidential basis."

The next day, Bureau agents prepared such a statement for Senator Long, noting that "it is written from the viewpoint of the Senator and his Committee in that it indicates they have taken a long, hard look at the FBI and have found nothing out of order — but that they will continue looking over our procedures and techniques from time to time in the future. Such an approach," it was stated, "is felt to be essential if the statement is to have the desired effect. A statement reflecting a stronger pro-FBI position might not only prove ineffective in thwarting those persons who are exerting pressure on the Subcommittee for a probe of our operations, but it could also bring criticism and additional pressure on Senator Long." The statement written by the Bureau for Senator Long reads in full:

> As Chairman of the Subcommittee on Administrative Practice and Procedure of the Senate Judiciary Committee, I instructed my staff at the outset of our activities to include the FBI, together with all other Federal agencies, among the organizations to be dealt with to ascertain if there had been invasion of privacy or other improper tactics in their operations. Toward this end, my staff and I have not only conferred at length with top officials of the FBI, but we have conducted exhaustive research into the activities, procedures, and techniques of this agency.
>
> While my Staff and I fully intend to carefully review FBI operations from time to time in the future, I am at the present time prepared to state, based upon careful study, that we are fully satisfied that the FBI has not

participated in highhanded or uncontrolled usage of wiretaps, microphones, or other electronic equipment.

The FBI's operations have been under strict Justice Department control at all times. In keeping with a rigid system of checks and balances, FBI installation of wiretaps and microphones has been strictly limited, and such electronic devices have been used only in the most important and serious of crimes either affecting the internal security of our Nation or involving heinous threats to human life. Included among these are major cases of murder, kidnapping, and sadism perpetrated at the specific instruction of leaders of La Cosa Nostra or other top echelons of the extralegal empire of organized crime.

Investigation made by my staff has reflected no independent or unauthorized installation of electronic devices by individual FBI Agents or FBI offices in the field. We have carefully examined Mr. J. Edgar Hoover's rules in this regard and have found no instances of violation.

As noted above, there is no indication in the record that any briefing about electronic surveillance by the FBI occurred prior to the preparation of this statement by Bureau agents other than the ninety-minute briefing given by DeLoach. No Bureau agents had been called to testify before the Subcommittee. It does not appear that any Senator or staff members reviewed FBI files on electronic surveillances. Nor is there any indication in the record that the Subcommittee ever learned of the bugging of a Congressman's hotel room, the bugging and wiretapping of Martin Luther King, Jr., or the wiretapping of a Congressional staff member, two newsmen, an editor of a political newsletter, and a former Bureau agent — all of which had occurred within the previous five years.

Ten days after the statement was prepared for Senator Long, DeLoach again visited him and "asked him point blank whether or not he intended to hold hearings concerning the FBI at any time in the future." According to DeLoach's memorandum:

He stated he did not. I asked him if he would be willing to give us a commitment that he would in no way embarrass the FBI. He said he would agree to do this.

When the Subcommittee's Chief Counsel asked DeLoach at this meeting "if it would be possible for [DeLoach] or Mr. Gale [another FBI Assistant Director] to appear before the Long Subcommittee ... and make a simple statement to the effect that the FBI used wiretaps only in cases involving national security and kidnapping and extortion, where human life is involved, and used microphones only in those cases involving heinous crimes and Cosa Nostra matters," DeLoach refused. He wrote that he informed the Chief Counsel:

that to put an FBI witness on the stand would be an attempt to open a Pandora's box, in so far as our enemies in the press were concerned [and] that such an appearance as only a token witness would cause more criticism than the release of the statement in question would ever cause.

DeLoach noted that Senator Long then stated "he had no plans whatsoever for calling FBI witnesses," but that the Chief Counsel indicated that he would like to call one former FBI agent who was known to DeLoach. According to DeLoach's memorandum regarding this meeting, he told the Chief Counsel that this agent "was a first class s.o.b., a liar, and a man who had volunteered as a witness only to get a public forum," and that the Chief Counsel then reconsidered. The memorandum concludes with the observation:

> While we have neutralized the threat of being embarrassed by the Long Subcommittee, we have not yet eliminated certain dangers which might be created as a result of newspaper pressure on Long. We therefore must keep on top of this situation at all times.

Partly as a result of the Subcommittee's apparently willing "neutralization" by the Bureau, the FBI's electronic surveillance practices were protected from intensive Congressional and public scrutiny until the 1970s.

V. Warrantless FBI Electronic Surveillance Of Foreign Intelligence And Counterintelligence Targets Within The United States

Foreign agents and foreign establishments within the United States have often been, and continue to be, the targets of warrantless FBI electronic surveillance. In general, the Fourth Amendment questions raised by electronic surveillance of foreigners are not as serious as those raised by the targeting of American citizens; and surveillance of foreign targets may be less susceptible to the types of abuses that have often been associated with wiretapping and bugging of American citizens. Because Americans are often overheard on "foreign" taps and bugs, however, and because American citizens may also be the indirect targets of "foreign" surveillances, the rights of Americans may nonetheless be affected even by surveillance of foreign targets.

Apparently, most warrantless electronic surveillances conducted by the FBI in the past fifteen years have fallen into this broad category. Foreign establishments and foreigners living within the United States have been the subject of wiretaps and bugs far more frequently than have American citizens connected with domestic organizations, for purposes ranging from the collection of foreign intelligence and counterintelligence information to the detection of terrorist activity. 138 Since the 1972 Keith decision, which invalidated "domestic security" warrantless electronic surveillances, the proportion of foreign targets has been even greater. As of November 1975, for example, all existing warrantless electronic surveillances were directed against foreigners.

The purpose and value of electronic surveillance against foreign targets, as well as "domestic" abuse questions which have arisen in this context, are discussed below.

A. Purpose and Value as an Investigative Technique

Electronic surveillance of foreign targets has been used extensively by the FBI for the purpose of collecting foreign counterintelligence information. Within the past fifteen years, both wiretaps and bugs designed to collect such information have been directed against targets in the following categories: "Foreign Establishments," "Foreign Commercial Establishments," "Foreign Officials," "Foreign Intelligence Agents," "Foreign Intelligence Contacts," "Foreign Intelligence Agents Suspect," "Foreign Officials' Contact," and "Foreign Intelligence Agents Business Office." Wiretaps alone have been used against "Foreign Intelligence Contact Suspect" and "a [foreign] Exile Group;" bugs alone have been used against the "wife of a foreign intelligence contact," a "relative of a foreign intelligence agent suspect," a "foreign intelligence agent contact," another "[foreign] exile group," and for "coverage of foreign officials."

Electronic surveillance of targets such as these is clearly considered by FBI officials to be one of the most valuable techniques for the collection of counterintelligence information. According to W. Raymond Wannall, the former Assistant Director in charge of the Bureau's Domestic Intelligence Division, wiretaps and bugs directed against foreign targets:

> give us a base line from which to operate.... Having the benefit of electronic surveillance, we are in a position to make evaluations, to make assessments, to make decisions as to [the conduct of counterintelligence operations].... It gives us leads as to persons . . . hostile intelligence services are trying to subvert or utilize in the United States, so certainly it is a valuable technique.

Some of the surveillances in the categories listed above have also been conducted for the primary purpose of collecting "positive" foreign intelligence (which may include economic intelligence) rather than counterintelligence information. While the collection of "Positive" foreign intelligence is outside the FBI's intelligence mandate, such surveillances have been responsive to specific requests of the Attorney General by the State Department and the CIA, both of which have a responsibility for "positive" intelligence.

In addition, the Bureau has electronically monitored foreign targets for the purpose of detecting and preventing violent and terrorist activities by foreigners within the United States. Wiretaps have been used for such purposes against a "Foreign Militant Group," a "Foreign Revolutionary Group," a "Foreign Militant Group Official," and a "Propaganda Outlet of the League of Arab States." Microphone surveillances in the last two of these categories and of an "Arab Terrorist Activist," and an "Arab Terrorist Activist Meeting" have been used for similar purposes.

B. Foreign Surveillance Abuse Questions

Even properly authorized electronic surveillances directed against foreign targets for the purposes noted above may result in possible abuses involving American citizens. Because wiretaps and bugs are capable of intercepting all conversations on a particular telephone or in a particular area, American citizens with whom the foreign targets communicate are also overheard, and information irrelevant to the purpose of the surveillance may be collected and disseminated to senior administration officials.

It is also possible to institute electronic surveillance of a foreigner for the primary purpose of intercepting the communications of a particular American citizen with that target; since the "foreign" surveillance in this situation can accomplish indirectly what a surveillance of the American could accomplish directly, the former may be used to circumvent the generally more stringent requirements for surveillances of Americans.

Both of these practices, which clearly affect the rights of the Americans involved, have occurred in the past and are discussed below.

1. Dissemination of Domestic Intelligence from Incidental Overhears

Essentially political information—unrelated to the authorized purpose of the surveillance—has occasionally been obtained as a by-product of electronic surveillance of foreign targets and disseminated to the highest levels of government. In the early 1960s, for example, Attorney General Robert Kennedy authorized the FBI to institute electronic surveillances of certain foreign targets in Washington, D.C., in connection with the possibly unlawful attempts of a foreign government to influence

Congressional deliberations over sugar quota legislation. From these surveillances, the Attorney General was provided with significant information not merely about possible foreign influence but about the reaction of key members of the House Agriculture Committee to the administration's sugar quota proposal as well.

Through the Bureau's coverage of certain foreign establishments in Washington, it was also able to supply two President's with reports of the contacts between members of Congress and foreign officials. According to a 1975 F BI memorandum:

> On March 14, 1966, then President Lyndon B. Johnson informed Mr. DeLoach [Cartha DeLoach, former Assistant Director of the FBI] ... that the FBI should constantly keep abreast of the actions of representatives of these [foreign countries] in making contacts with Senators and Congressmen and any citizens of a prominent nature. The President stated he strongly felt that much of the protest concerning his Vietnam policy, particularly the hearings in the Senate, had been generated by [certain foreign officials].

As a result of the President's request, the FBI prepared a chronological summary — based in part on existing electronic surveillances — of the contacts of each Senator, Representative, or staff member who communicated with selected foreign establishments during the period July 1, 1964, to March 17, 1966. This summary — which comprised 67 pages — was transmitted to the White House on March 21, 1966. The cover letter noted that: "based upon our coverage, it appears that" certain foreign officials "are making more contacts with" four named United States Senators "than with other United States legislators."

A second summary was prepared on further contacts between Congressmen and foreign officials and was transmitted to the White House on May 13, 1966. From that date until January 1969, when the Johnson administration left office biweekly additions to the second summary were regularly prepared and disseminated to the White House.

This practice was reinstituted during the Nixon administration. On July 27, 1970, Larry Higby, Assistant to H. R. Haldeman, informed the Bureau that Mr. Haldeman "wanted any information possessed by the FBI relating to contacts between [certain foreign officials] and Members of Congress and its staff." Two days later, the Bureau provided the White House with a statistical compilation of such contacts from January 1, 1967 to July 29, 1970. As in the case of the information provided to the Johnson White House, no members of Congress were targeted directly but many had been overheard on existing electronic surveillances of foreign officials in Washington, D.C.

2. Indirect Targeting of American Citizens Through Electronic Surveillance of Foreign Targets

There is also evidence that in at least one instance the FBI, at the request of the President, instituted an electronic surveillance of a foreign target for the purpose of intercepting telephone conversations of a particular American citizen. An FBI memorandum states that about one week before the 1968 Presidential election, President Johnson became suspicious that South Vietnamese Government might sabotage his peace negotiations in the hope that Presidential candidate Richard Nixon would win the election and take a "harder line" towards North Vietnam. More specifically, the President believed that Mrs. Anna Chennault, widow of General Clair Chennault and a prominent Republican leader, was attempting to [dis]suade

South Vietnamese officials "from attending the Paris peace negotiations until after the election since it would devolve to the credit of the Republican Party."

In order to determine the validity of this suspicion, the White House instructed the FBI to institute a physical coverage of Mrs. Chennault, as well as physical and electronic surveillance of the South Vietnamese Embassy. The electronic surveillance of the Embassy was authorized by Attorney General Ramsey Clark on October 29, 1968, installed the same day, and continued until January 6, 1969.

Significantly, a Bureau memorandum indicates that FBI officials were ill-disposed toward direct surveillance of Anna Chennault because "it was widely known that she was involved in Republican political circles and, if it became known that the FBI was surveilling her this would put us in a most untenable and embarrassing position." Thus, a "foreign" electronic surveillance was instituted to indirectly target an American citizen, who, it was apparently believed, should not be surveilled directly.

VI. Warrantless FBI Electronic Surveillance Of American Citizens

American citizens and domestic organizations have also been the direct targets of FBI wiretaps and bugs for intelligence purposes. Indeed, the use of these techniques against Americans for such purposes has a long history. In 1941, for example, Attorney General Francis Biddle approved a wiretap on the Los Angeles Chamber of Commerce under the standard of "persons suspected of subversive activities." Four years later, a high official in the Truman administration and a former aide to President Roosevelt were both the subject of warrantless electronic surveillance.

Between 1960 and 1972 numerous American citizens and domestic organizations were targeted for electronic surveillance. Most of these warrantless wiretaps and bugs were predicated on the need to protect the country against "subversive" and/or violent activities; many were based on the perceived need to discover the source of leaks of classified information; and an undetermined number of American citizens were wiretapped for other reasons such as the desire to obtain foreign intelligence or counterintelligence information.

The Keith decision in 1972 sharply restricted the grounds for wiretapping and bugging which had been asserted previously, although it did not prohibit warrantless electronic surveillance of American citizens for foreign intelligence or counterintelligence purposes when a substantial connection is shown to exist between the American individual or group and a foreign power. No Americans were the subjects of this technique as of November 1975, but a small number of Americans have been electronically monitored since the Keith case on the basis of such a foreign connection.

This section focuses on warrantless electronic surveillance of American citizens during the 1960 to 1972 period. It contains a general description of surveillances which were instituted because of the perceived "subversive" or violent nature of the targets, because of leaks of classified information, and on various other grounds. In Section VII, this Report elaborates on three types of abuse questions which have arisen in connection with warrantless electronic surveillance of American citizens.

A. Electronic Surveillance Predicated on Subversive Activity

Numerous American citizens and domestic organizations have been wiretapped and bugged because their activities, while not necessarily violent, were regarded as sufficiently "subversive" to constitute a threat to the security of the United States. In many of these cases, it was believed that the individuals or groups were controlled or financed by, or otherwise connected with, a hostile foreign power. In other cases, the surveillances were based only on the possibility that the targets, whether consciously or not, were being influenced by persons believed to be acting under the direction of a foreign power; such surveillance typically occurred in the context of COMINFIL (Communist infiltration) investigations.

The Communist Party, USA, provides the clearest example of a group that was selected for electronic surveillance on the ground of foreign-connected "subversive" activities. In addition to a wiretap on the Headquarters of the Communist Party, the FBI conducted wiretaps in the following target categories:

Communist Party Functionaries
Communist Party Propaganda Outlet
Communist Party Front Group
Communist Party Member
Communist Party Affiliate
Communist Party Publication

Microphone surveillances are recorded in these categories:

Communist Party Functionaries
Communist Party Front Groups
Communist Party Propaganda Outlets
Communist Party Front Groups Organizer
Communist Party Function
Communist Party Members
Communist Party Publications
Coverage of Communist Party Meeting
Communist Party Youth Activist
Communist Party Labor Group
Communist Party Youth Group
Communist Party Affiliate
Coverage of Communist Party Conference
Communist Party Apologist

Other groups adhering to a communist ideology have also been electronically monitored for similar reasons. According to FBI records, wiretaps were used in cases involving a "Marxist-Leninist Group Affiliate," a "Marxist Leninist Group Leader," and a "Marxist-Leninist Group Functionary." Microphone surveillances were also conducted against a "Basic Revolutionary Group Founder," a "Marxist-Oriented Youth Group," a "Trotskyite Organization," a "Basic Revolutionary Group," an "Organizer of a Basic Revolutionary Group," "Marxist-Leninist Groups," a "Basic Revolutionary Front Group," a "Basic Revolutionary Front Functionary," a "Marxist-Leninist Front Group," and a "Marxist-Oriented Racial Organization." One "Trotskyite Organization Meeting" was also bugged.

Several groups which were believed to have a connection with the Communist Party in Cuba and China have been targeted as well. Into this category fell wiretaps which were directed against a "Pro-Castro Organization," a "Pro Castro Movement Leader," a "Pro-Castro Group Functionary," and a "Pro-Chicom [Chinese

Communist] Propaganda Outlet;" and microphones directed against "Pro-Castro Organizations," a "Pro-Chicom Group," and a "Pro Cuban American Group which travelled to Cuba."

The "subversive activities" predicate was stretched furthest when used to support electronic surveillance of American citizens and domestic organizations not primarily because their own activities were considered to be subversive but because they were believed to be adversely influenced, whether consciously or not, by persons acting under the direction of a foreign power. One example of reliance on such a rationale is seen in the wiretapping and bug of Dr. Martin Luther King, Jr., and several of his associates. In October 1963, Attorney General Robert Kennedy authorized wiretaps on the residence and two office telephones of Dr. King on the ground of possible Communist infiltration into the Southern Christian Leadership Conference, of which Dr. King was President. The possibility that two of Dr. King's advisors may have been associated with the Communist Party, USA, led to four additional wiretaps on King and a total of fifteen microphone installations in his hotel rooms during 1964 and 1965. Apparently as part of this COMINFIL (Communist infiltration) investigation, several of King's associates were also wiretapped and bugged.

At least three other organizations have been targeted for electronic surveillance primarily on the ground of possible Communist infiltration. One such organization, believed to have been influenced by the Communist Party, USA, was wiretapped in 1962. In 1965, Attorney General Nicholas Katzenbach approved wiretaps on both the Student Non-Violent Coordinating Committee (SNCC) and the Students for a Democratic Society (SDS) for similar reasons; the former group had also been the subject of a microphone surveillance in 1964.

B. Electronic Surveillance Predicated on Violent Activity

Allegations of violent activity, or the threat of violent activity, have also served as the predicate for numerous warrantless electronic surveillance of Americans.

Most of the wiretaps and bugs which were instituted for this reason have been directed against "black extremists" and "black extremist organizations." In 1957, for example, Attorney General Herbert Brownell authorized a wiretap on Elijah Muhammad, a leader of the Nation of Islam, because of the organization's alleged "violent nature." This tap, which was never re-authorized until 1964, was finally terminated in 1966. A wiretap was also placed on Malcolm X, another Nation of Islam leader, in 1964 for essentially the same reason. Similarly, Attorney General Katzenbach approved a wiretap on a "black extremist leader" of the Revolutionary Action Movement in 1965. During the first half of the 1960's, microphone surveillances were also directed against a "black separatist group" (one surveillance in 1960 and 1961; two separate surveillances each year from 1962 until 1965) and a "black separatist group functionary"(from 1961 until 1965).

The possibility of violent activity also led to wiretaps on the Black Panther Party and one of its leaders in 1969. Both of these taps continued into 1970, when wiretaps on a "black extremist group affiliate" and two (non-white) "racial extremist groups" were added to the list. 1971 apparently represented the high point of wiretapping "black extremists:" in that year, there were wiretaps on the Black Panther Party (six separate taps as of March 29, 1971), two (nonwhite) "racial extremist groups," two individuals described as "militant black extremist group members" (one of whom was a member of SNCC), two individuals described as "militant black extremist group functionaries," and a "racial group member." A wiretap was also authorized to cover a "meeting of a militant [black] group." In 1972, wiretaps continued to be used against the Black Panther Party and one of its leaders, a (non-white) "racial extremist group," a "militant black extremist group member," and a "militant black extremist group functionary." Microphone surveillances during the Nixon Administration years were directed against the Black Panther Party in 1970 and a "Black Extremist Group Functionary" (Huey Newton, a leader of the Black Panther Party) from 1970 to 1972.

Electronic surveillance based on a "violent activity" predicate was certainly not confined to "black extremists," however. In the early and mid-1960's, wiretaps were placed on Ku Klux Klan members for similar reasons. Two "leaders of a racist organization," one of whom was a Klan member suspected of involvement in the bombing of a black church in Birmingham, Alabama, were wiretapped in 1963 and 1964. Another Ku Klux Klan member was wiretapped in 1964 and 1965. FBI records also disclose the bugging of The National States Rights Party in 1962.

White radical organizations were also the subjects of electronic surveillance in the late 1960's and early 1970's on the grounds of violent or potentially violent activity. A "New Left Campus Group" was both wiretapped and bugged in 1969, and the wiretap continued into 1970. Three anti-war organizations which were involved in planning the November 1969 "March on Washington" were also wiretapped in 1969. In 1970, the Headquarters of the Worker Student Alliance (an affiliate of SDS) and an individual who was a contact for the Weatherman organization were wiretapped. The tap on the Worker Student Alliance continued into 1971 and was supplemented in that year by wiretaps on a "New Left Activist", a "domestic protest group," and a "violence prone faction of a domestic protest group" (two separate wiretaps). Additional wiretaps and microphone surveillances during the years 1969 to 1972 fall into the categories: "Investigation of Clandestine Underground Group Dedicated to Strategic Sabotage;" "Weatherman Organization Publication;" "Publication of Clandestine Underground Group Dedicated to Strategic Sabotage;" "Leader of Revolutionary Group;" and "Weather Underground Support Apparatus."

For several years during the 1960's, Puerto Rican nationalist groups and their members were also electronically monitored because of their alleged proclivity towards violence. FBI records reveal wiretaps on a "Puerto Rican Independence Group" in 1960 and 1962; and on a "Puerto Rican Independence Group Member" in 1965. Microphone surveillances were placed on a "Contact of Puerto Rican Nationalist Party" in 1960; a "Puerto Rican Independence Group Office" in 1963, 1964, and 1965; a "Puerto Rican Revolutionary" in 1968; and "Pro-Puerto Rican Independence Group Activists" in 1964 and 1965.

Other organizations were the subject of electronic surveillance because they were seen as violent advocates of the interests of a foreign power or group. (To the extent an actual connection with a hostile foreign power was perceived, they would also be considered "subversive.") These organizations, which were, or may have been, composed at least in part of American citizens, are described by the following categories: "Pro-Arab Group," "Arab Terrorist Affiliate," "Pro-Palestine Group," "Militant Pro-Chicom [Chinese Communist] Group," "West Coast Fundraising Front for Arab Terrorist Groups," "Arab Terrorist Activist Affiliates," and "Co-Conspirators in Plot to Kidnap a Prominent Anti-Castro Cuban Exile."

C. Electronic Surveillance Predicated on Leaks of Classified Information

Another purpose of warrantless electronic surveillance of American citizens during the period 1960 to 1972 was to determine the source of perceived leaks of classified information. At least eight separate investigations into perceived leaks resulted in the wiretapping or bugging of nearly thirty American citizens, yet Bureau memoranda reveal no case in which the source of any leak was discovered by means of electronic surveillance. These investigations are described below.

Lloyd Norman: 1961. -- On June 27, 1961, Attorney General Robert Kennedy informed FBI Director Hoover that the most recent issue of Newsweek magazine contained an article about American military plans in Germany, which, the administration believed, was based on classified information. According to an FBI memorandum, Kennedy stated that the President had called him to see if it would be possible to determine who was responsible for the apparent leak. On the same day, and without specific authorization from the Attorney General, the FBI placed a wiretap on the residence of Lloyd Norman, the Newsweek reporter who wrote the article. Kennedy was informed about the tap on June 28, and formally approved it on June 30. It was discontinued on July 3, 1961, when "Norman left Washington, D.C., for the west coast on a month's vacation [and) the only person left at Norman's residence [was] his son."

Hanson Baldwin: 1962 — A July 1962 New York Times article about Soviet missile systems by Hanson Baldwin, which the administration also believed was based on classified information, led to the installation of wiretaps on the residences of both Baldwin and a New York Times secretary. According to contemporaneous Bureau memoranda, these wiretaps were instituted without the prior written approval of the Attorney General, and one of them — the tap on the secretary — was instituted without the Attorney General's prior knowledge. Formal written approval for these wiretaps was obtained on July 31, 1962, however, three days after the tap on Baldwin was installed and four days after the tap on his secretary was installed. The wiretap on the secretary continued until August 15, 1962; that on Baldwin until August 29,1962.

Former FBI Special Agent: 1962 — Warrantless electronic surveillance predicated on classified information leaks continued with the wiretapping of a former Bureau agent who "disclosed information of a confidential nature concerning investigations conducted by [the] Bureau" in a public forum on October 18, 1962. According to an internal memorandum, the coverage lasted from October 18, 1962, until October 26, 1962, and was repeated in January 1963. On October 19, 1962, Attorney General Kennedy was advised that the Bureau desired to place coverage on this agent; he was apparently not informed that coverage had already been effected the day before. Kennedy's written approval was granted on October 26, the day the surveillance was terminated. The surveillance was reinstituted in January: a Bureau memorandum dated January 9, 1963, simply states:

> Mr. Belmont called to say [FBI Assistant Director Courtney] Evans spoke to the Attorney General re placing the tech on [ ] again, and the Attorney General said by all means do this. Mr. Belmont has instructed New York to do so.

The authorization for the second surveillance therefore appears to have been oral. Coverage of this agent was permanently suspended on September 9, 1963.

High Executive Official: 1963 — Because of the possibility that a high-ranking executive official may have provided classified information not to the press but to a foreign intelligence officer, the FBI requested the Attorney General in February 1963 to authorize a wiretap on the residence telephone of this official. 205b According to the request which was sent to Attorney General Kennedy, "The President expressed personal interest in receiving information concerning the current relationship between [the official] and representatives of [a foreign country]."

The Attorney General approved the request, and it was instituted three days later. It was discontinued on June 14, 1963, when the target travelled abroad, reinstituted on July 14, 1963; and permanently discontinued on November 6, 1963, "because of lack of productivity."

Editor of an Anti-Communist Newsletter. 1965 — The publication in an anti-Communist newsletter of information believed to be classified led to the wiretapping of both the editor of the newsletter and an attorney in the Washington, D.C. area with whom the editor was in frequent contact. These surveillances were approved in writing by Attorney General Nicholas Katzenbach in April and June of 1965, respectively, and each began about three weeks after approval.

In November 1965, the FBI recommended discontinuance of the taps because "[w]e have not developed any data since outset of investigation which would show that [the targets] are currently receiving information from individuals in the Executive Branch of the Government. In fact, we now believe that it is highly unlikely that our technical coverage will develop such information in the future."

According to a memorandum sent to the Attorney General, the tap on the lawyer was discontinued on November 2, 1965, and that on the editor on November 10, 1965.

Joseph Kraft: 1969. -- The basic facts surrounding the wiretapping and microphone surveillance of columnist Joseph Kraft are a matter of public record. In June 1969, possibly in response to a leak from the National Security Council, John Ehrlichman instructed John Caulfield and John Ragan, two individuals associated with the White House "Plumbers" and unconnected with the FBI, to place a wiretap on the Washington, D.C. residence of Mr. Kraft. This tap was removed one week later, when the columnist left Washington on an extended trip to Europe. W. C. Sullivan, then Assistant Director of the FBI, subsequently followed Mr. Kraft abroad, apparently on instructions from Mr. Hoover and Mr. Ehrlichman. Overseas, Sullivan arranged with a foreign security agency to conduct electronic surveillance of Kraft in his hotel room: when the installation of a telephone tap proved to be impossible because of the "elaborate switchboard" of the hotel," a microphone was placed in his room instead. The results of this coverage, which lasted from July 3 to July 7, 1969, were transmitted back to Mr. Hoover personally through the FBI's Legal Attache at the American Embassy.

In November and December of that year, Mr. Kraft was again the target of FBI surveillance: the Washington Field Office conducted physical surveillance of the columnist from November 5 until December 12. In addition, Director Hoover requested approval from Attorney General Mitchell for a wiretap on Mr. Kraft on November 5, but approval was never granted and the wiretap never installed.

The "Seventeen Wiretaps:" 1969-1971. -- The wiretaps which were directed against seventeen government employees and newsmen between May 1969 and February 1971 have been the subject of civil litigation and extensive Congressional inquiries. In view of the pending civil litigation, the Committee has not attempted to duplicate the depositions which bear on the authorization of these wiretaps. The basic facts as recorded in FBI documents and public record testimony, however, may be summarized as follows:

On May 9, 1969, a story by William Beecher concerning American bombing raids in Cambodia appeared in the New York Times. According to a contemporaneous internal memorandum from J. Edgar Hoover to senior FBI officials, Henry Kissinger telephoned him that morning requesting the Bureau to "make a major effort to find out where [the story] came from." Kissinger called Mr. Hoover twice more that day, once to request that additional articles by Beecher be included in the inquiry and once to request that the investigation be handled discreetly "so no stories will get out." Before 5:00 p.m. on May 9, Hoover telephoned Kissinger to inform him that initial FBI inquiries suggested that Morton Halperin, a staff member of the National Security Council, could have been in a position to leak the information upon which Beecher was believed to have based his article: Hoover noted that Halperin "knew Beecher and that he [Hoover] considered [Halperin] a part of the Harvard clique, and, of course, of the Kennedy era."

According to Hoover, "Dr. Kissinger said he appreciated this very much and he hoped I would follow it up as far as we can take it and they will destroy whoever did this if we can find him, no matter where he is.

Dr. Kissinger has testified that he had been asked at a White House meeting, which, he believed, may have occurred in late April 1969 and which was attended by the President, the Attorney General, and J. Edgar Hoover, "to supply the names of key individuals having access to sensitive information which had leaked [even before the Cambodia story]." He noted that at this meeting "Director Hoover identified four persons as security risks and suggested that these four be put under surveillance initially." Among the persons so identified was Morton Halperin. Kissinger said that when the Cambodia story was published on May 9, "I called Mr. Hoover at President Nixon's request to express the President's and my concern about the seriousness of the leak appearing that date and to request an immediate investigation. He also stated that in these telephone conversations, "I do not recall any discussion of wiretapping. At that time, my understanding was that the wiretapping program had been authorized and that, therefore, Mr. Hoover or his staff had the right to use wiretapping in their investigations. I do not recall any discussions as to when the program would actually be put into effect." He further testified that "[i]n view of the President's authorization, Mr. Hoover evidently chose to institute the wiretaps after my calls to him on May 9, regarding the national security significance of the Beecher story in the New York Times of the same date."

The wiretap on Halperin was installed without the written approval of the Attorney General, in late afternoon on May 9, 1969. The next morning, Alexander Haig personally visited William Sullivan at FBI Headquarters. According to a memorandum from Sullivan to Cartha DeLoach, Haig requested that wiretaps be placed on four individuals, including Halperin, who were members of the National Security Council staff and Defense Department employees. Haig stated that this request "was being made on the highest authority" and "stressed that it is so sensitive it demands handling on a need-to-know basis, with no record maintained." According to Sullivan, Haig said that "if possible, it would be even more desirable to have the matter handled without going to the [Justice] Department."

Alexander Haig testified that Dr. Kissinger had instructed him to see Mr. Sullivan and to act as the "so-called liaison as this program was instituted, I believe, authorized by the President, the Director, and the Attorney General." He further stated that Dr. Kissinger provided him with the names to take to Sullivan and that he had the "impression" that the names were "cleared and concurred in by" the President or his representative, the Director, and the Attorney General. Haig denied that he requested the Bureau not to maintain a record of the surveillances, noting that "the point I would recall making very clearly was the extreme sensitivity of this thing, and the avoidance of unnecessary paperwork, which would make this program subject to compromise." He also testified that he does not recall urging Sullivan to avoid going to the Justice Department.

On May 12, a formal request was sent by the Director to Attorney General Mitchell for wiretaps on all four individuals (one of which had been in operation for three days); Mitchell approved; and the additional taps were subsequently instituted.

Over the course of the next one and one-half years, thirteen more individuals became the subjects of wiretaps in this same program. Bureau documents reflects the following authorizations from Attorney General Mitchell:

-- May 20, 1969: Two members of the staff of the National Security Council — May 29, 1969: A reporter for the London Sunday Times — June 4, 1969: A reporter for the New York Times — July 23, 1969: A White House domestic affairs adviser — August 4, 1969: A White House speech writer — September 10, 1969: A correspondent for CBS News — May 4, 1970: A Deputy Assistant Secretary of State; a State Department official of "Ambassador" rank; and a Brigadier General with the Defense Department — May 13 1970: Two additional staff members of the National Security Council — December 14,1970: A second White House domestic affairs adviser.

The longest of these wiretaps was the one on Halperin: it continued for twenty-one months, until February 10, 1971, and was apparently terminated at the insistence of Director Hoover, who was about to testify before the House Appropriations Committee. Other wiretaps lasted for periods of time varying from six weeks to twenty months.

Charles Radford: 1971-1979 — The December 1971 publication of an article by Jack Anderson which described private conversations between President Nixon and Henry Kissinger led to a total of four wiretaps on American citizens to determine the source of this apparent leak. According to an internal Bureau memorandum, Attorney General Mitchell personally contacted Deputy Associate FBI Director W. Mark Felt on December 22, 1971, and orally instructed him to institute a wiretap on Charles E. Radford II. Radford, a Navy Yeoman who was assigned to the Joint Chiefs of Staff, was apparently a primary suspect because he had frequent contact with the White House and the National Security Council and belonged to the same church as Jack Anderson. Mitchell informed Felt that this request originated with the President and noted that no prosecution was contemplated. The FBI was not requested to conduct a full investigation of the leak, only to wiretap Radford. After obtaining approval from J. Edgar Hoover, Felt secured the institution of the wiretap on Radford's residence on December 23.

On the basis of certain telephone contacts Radford subsequently made, additional wiretaps were placed on the residences of two of Radford's friends, one a former Defense Attache, the other a State Department employee. These wiretaps were instituted on January 5 and January 14, respectively, and both continued until February 17. When Radford was transferred to the Naval Reserve Training Center near Portland, Oregon, the Attorney General requested a wiretap on the home of Radford's step-father, 230a with whom he was to stay until he could locate a home of his own. This coverage was instituted immediately, and although Radford moved into his own residence by February 15, when another wiretap was installed on his new home, the tap on his step-father was not terminated until April 11, 1972. Coverage was also instituted on the training center where Radford worked on February 7, 1972, and like the tap on his step-father it continued until April 11.

The tap on Radford's Oregon residence was not terminated until June 20, 1972 -- one day after the Supreme Court's decision in the Keith case. One Bureau official wrote that "it was not discontinued on 6/19/72, as others falling under the Keith rule had been, since we were awaiting a decision from the White House."

In violation of Justice Department procedures, none of these Radford wiretaps was ever authorized by the Attorney General in writing. Two of the wiretaps apparently did not even receive the explicit oral approval of the Attorney General. An internal Bureau memorandum states that the surveillance of the State Department employee and the wiretap on the Naval Reserve Training Center were both requested by David Young, an assistant to John Ehrlichman, who merely informed the Bureau that the requests originated with Ehrlichman and had the Attorney General's concurrence.

Thus, between 1960 and 1972, nearly thirty American citizens ostensibly suspected of leaking classified information were wiretapped by the FBI without a warrant in the United States; another was the subject of an FBI microphone surveillance abroad. No fewer than seven of these targets were journalists or newsmen. At least ten of the wiretaps were instituted without the prior written approval of the Attorney General, which was required in every case. Although the taps generated a significant amount of both personal and political information — much of which was disseminated to the highest levels in the White House — Bureau memoranda do not reveal that the wiretaps succeeded in identifying a single person who had leaked national security information.

D. Electronic Surveillance Predicated on Other Grounds

In the course of at least three separate investigations between 1960 and 1972, Americans were the targets of FBI electronic surveillance for purposes which cannot easily be categorized as collecting information about subversive or violent activities or about leaks of classified material. Two of these cases — the "Sugar Lobby" and the Jewish Defense League surveillances, described below — related to foreign concerns. The Sugar Lobby investigation was apparently instituted to gather foreign intelligence information seen as necessary for the conduct of foreign affairs and to detect alleged attempts of foreign representatives to influence American officials. A wiretap on the Jewish Defense League (JDL) and one of its members, while requested primarily on the ground of "violent activities," was defended in a subsequent civil action as similarly necessary to gather information important to United States foreign relations.

The third case occurred in connection with the Warren Commission's review of events surrounding President John F. Kennedy's assassination. In 1964, the FBI installed one wiretap (with the approval of the Attorney General) and two microphone surveillances at the specific request of this Commission in order to obtain information about the assassination.

The "Sugar Lobby" Wiretaps: 1961-1962. 239 -- On February 9,1961, Attorney General Robert Kennedy requested the FBI to initiate an investigation for the purpose of:

> develop[ing] intelligence data which would provide President Kennedy a picture of what was behind pressures exerted on behalf of [a foreign country] regarding sugar quota deliberations in Congress ... in connection with pending sugar legislation.

This investigation lasted for approximately nine weeks, and was reinstituted for a three-month period in mid-1962. At its height, the investigation involved a total of twelve telephone wiretaps, three microphone surveillances, and physical surveillances of eleven separate individuals. Six of the wiretaps were directed against American citizens, who included three executive branch employees, a Congressional staff member, and two registered lobbying agents for foreign interests, one of whom was an attorney whose office telephone was wiretapped. One of the microphone surveillances was directed at a United States Congressman.

The expiration of existing import quotas for sugar in 1961 provided the backdrop against which these events were set. In early 1961, the intelligence community had learned that officials of a foreign government "intensely desired passage of a sugar bill by the U.S. Congress which would contain quotas favorable to [that government]." This fact had significant ramifications on American foreign policy. According to a CIA memorandum addressed to the President's national security advisor:

> It is thought by some informed observers that the outcome of the sugar legislation which comes up for renewal in the U.S. Congress in March 1961 will be all-important to the future of U.S. -- [foreign country] relations.

There was also a possibility that unlawful influence was involved. In early February, the FBI discovered that representatives of the foreign government might have made monetary payments or given gifts to influence certain Congressmen, Senators, and executive branch officials.

Because of the foreign intelligence interest involved, and on the ground that "the administration has to act if money or gifts are being passed by the [foreign representatives]," Robert Kennedy authorized a number of wiretaps on foreign targets and domestic citizens who were believed to be involved in the situation. Specifically, he approved wiretaps on the following American citizens: three officials of the Agriculture Department (residence telephones only) ; the clerk of the House Agriculture Committee (residence telephone only) ; and a registered agent of the foreign country (both residence and business telephones).

In the course of this investigation, the Bureau determined that Congressman Harold D. Cooley, the Chairman of the House Agriculture Committee, planned to meet with representatives of the foreign country in a hotel room in New York City, in mid-February 1961. At the instruction of Director Hoover, the New York Field Office installed a microphone in Cooley's hotel room to record this meeting, and the results were disseminated to the Attorney General.

Under the Justice Department policy that was in effect at this time, the Bureau was not required to obtain the prior written approval of the Attorney General for microphone surveillance, and none was obtained in this case. It is not certain, moreover, that Attorney General Kennedy was ever specifically informed that Congressman Cooley was the target of a microphone surveillance: a review of this case by Bureau agents in 1966 concluded that "our files contain no clear indication that the Attorney General was specifically advised that a microphone surveillance was being utilized . . . . It was noted, however, that on the morning of February 17, 1961 -- after the microphone was in place but an hour or two before the meeting actually occurred-the Director spoke with the Attorney General and, according to Hoover's contemporaneous memorandum, advised him that the Cooley meeting was to take place that day and that "we are trying to cover it." Hoover also wrote that he "stated [to the Attorney General] this New York situation is interesting and if we can get it covered we will have a full record of it," and that "the Attorney General asked that he be kept advised . . . ." As noted above, Kennedy did receive a summary of the results of the meeting, although no specific reference was made to the technique employed.

The 1961 "Sugar Lobby" investigation did discover that possibly unlawful influence was being exerted by representatives of the foreign country involved, but it did not reveal that money was actually being passed to any executive or legislative branch official. All of the electronic surveillances but two (both of which were on foreign targets) were discontinued in April 1961, about two weeks after the administration's own sugar bill passed the Senate.

The investigation was reinstituted in June 1962, however, when the Bureau learned that representatives of the same foreign country might be influencing Congressional deliberations concerning an amendment to the sugar quota legislation. On June 26, 1962, the Bureau requested authority for wiretaps on five foreign establishments plus the office telephones of an attorney who was believed to be an agent for the foreign country and, again, the residence telephone of the Clerk of the House Agriculture Committee. Robert Kennedy approved all of these taps on July 9, and they were instituted about one week later.

After one month of operation, the wiretaps on one foreign establishment and the Clerk of the House Agriculture Committee had "produced no information of value" and were consequently discontinued. While there is no indication that the other wiretaps produced evidence of actual payoffs, they did reveal that possibly unlawful influence was again being exerted by the foreign government and internal Bureau permission was obtained to continue them for another sixty days, after which time they were presumably terminated.

Jewish Defense League: 1970 and 1971—On September 14, 1970, the FBI requested a wiretap on six telephone lines of the New York Headquarters of the Jewish Defense League, an organization composed of American citizens who opposed, through both peaceful and violent means, the Soviet Union's treatment of Jewish citizens. Attorney General John Mitchell approved the wiretap on September 15; it was instituted on October 1 and continued for one month. It was re-authorized for two three-month periods on January 4, 1971, and March 31, 1971. Coverage was terminated July 3, 1971.

According to Attorney General Mitchell, the JDL wiretap was "deemed essential to protect this nation and its citizens against hostile acts of a foreign power and to obtain foreign intelligence information deemed essential to the security of the United States." More specifically, he contended that the activities of the Jewish Defense League toward official representatives of the Soviet Union, which had allegedly included acts of violence such as bombing the offices of a Soviet trade organization and the Soviet airlines, risked "the possibility of international embarrassment or Soviet retaliation against American citizens in Moscow," especially in light of vigorous protests by the Soviet Union. The wiretap was approved in order to obtain "advance knowledge of any activities of the JDL" which might have such repercussions; its re-authorization was sought and obtained on the ground that it had "furnished otherwise unobtainable information, well in advance of public statements by the JDL, thereby allowing for adequate countermeasures to be taken by appropriate police and security forces."

Criminal indictments were returned against several JDL members in May 1971, and shortly thereafter the prosecution revealed the existence of the wiretap to the defendants. In the context of the criminal case, the Government characterized the JDL wiretap as a "domestic security wiretap" and conceded that it was unlawful. The "foreign intelligence" predicate, however, was raised by Attorney General Mitchell and other civil defendants in the civil action—Zweiban v. Mitchell—subsequently filed by sixteen members of JDL who were oveheard on the wiretap.

The District Court in the Zweibon case agreed with Attorney General Mitchell that the JDL wiretap was in fact related to United States foreign affairs and held that its authorization by the Attorney General was a proper exercise of the constitutional power of the President and his designees. On appeal, the Court of Appeals did not reexamine the District Court's finding that the wiretap was originally predicated on foreign affairs needs because it held that even if one accepts the foreign relationship predicate, the wiretapping of American citizens who are neither the agents of nor collaborators with a foreign power is unconstitutional under the Fourth Amendment.

VII. Domestic Surveillance Abuse Questions

The possibilities for abuse of warrantless electronic surveillance have clearly been greatest when this technique is directed against American citizens and domestic organizations. The application of vague and elastic standards for wiretapping and bugging has resulted in electronic surveillances which, by any objective measure, were improper and seriously infringed the Fourth Amendment rights of both the targets and those with whom the targets communicated. Americans who violated no criminal law and represented no genuine threat to the "national security" have been targeted, regardless of the stated predicate. In many cases, the implementation of wiretaps and bugs has also been fraught with procedural violations, even when the required procedures were meager, thus compounding the abuse. The inherently intrusive nature of electronic surveillance, moreover, has enabled the Government to generate vast amounts of information—unrelated to any legitimate governmental interest—about the personal and political lives of American citizens. The collection of this type of information has, in turn, raised the danger of its use for partisan political and other improper ends by senior administration officials.

A. Questionable and Improper Selection of Targets

Judged against the principles established in the 1972 Keith case, nearly all of the Americans, unconnected with a foreign power, who were targets of warrantless electronic surveillance were improperly selected. Even without retrospective Fourth Amendment analysis of pre-Keith electronic surveillances, however, a close review of some of the particular cases 269a outlined above suggests that (regardless of whether the ostensible predicate was violence, "subversion," or any other basis) the standards for approval of electronic surveillances were far too broad to restrict the use of this technique to cases which involved a substantial threat to the nation. Moreover, the use of warrantless electronic surveillance against certain categories of individuals, such as attorneys, Congressmen and Congressional staff members, and journalists, has revealed an insensitivity to the values inherent in the Sixth Amendment and in the doctrines of "separation of powers" and "freedom of the press."

1. Wiretaps Under the "Domestic Security" Standard

In 1940, President Roosevelt approved the use of wiretapping against "persons suspected of subversive activities against the Government of the United States." As discussed in Section II, this formulation was supplemented by President Truman in

1946 to include "cases vitally affecting the domestic security, or where human life is in jeopardy." Several cases from the period 1960 to 1965 (when the "domestic security" standard was replaced by President Johnson's "national security" standard) suggest the ease with which the term "domestic security" was stretched to cover the targeting of Americans who posed no substantial threat to the internal security of the country.

Prior to the institution of the 1961 and 1962 "Sugar Lobby" wiretaps, for example, the Government did possess some evidence of possibly unlawful influence by foreign officials and some evidence of the importance of the sugar quota legislation to the foreign nation involved. But there was clearly no evidence that "human life" was in jeopardy, and neither the possibility of unlawful influence nor the desire to gain information relevant to our relations with the foreign country had a significant impact on the domestic security. The documentary record of the investigation, moreover, contains no suggestion that the three Agriculture Department employees, one Congressional staff aide, and two lobbyists who were tapped represented any internal security threat.

In the case of the 1961 wiretap on Lloyd Norman, the FBI apparently had no information beyond the fact of his authorship of the "suspect" article that Norman had obtained any classified material or that a leak had actually occurred. Norman himself told Bureau agents when interviewed that "he based his article on speculation and conjecture . . ." and a Pentagon source indicated that he "had no factual information as to who leaked the information or that Norman was actually the person who obtained the information." The wiretap subsequently produced no information which suggested that Norman had received any classified information. According to an internal summary of the final FBI report on the "leak": "The majority of those interviewed thought a competent, well informed reporter could have written the article without having reviewed or received classified data." This wiretap, in short, was approved by Robert Kennedy without any apparent evidence that the target had actually obtained classified information: the wiretap results, Norman's personal interview with the FBI, and the entire investigation all suggested, in fact, that he had not.

In April 1964, Kennedy approved "technical coverage" (electronic surveillance) on Malcolm X after the FBI advised him that the Nation of Islam leader was "forming a new group" which would be "more aggressive" and would "participate in racial demonstrations and civil rights activities." The only indication of possible danger reflected in the wiretap request, however, was that Malcolm X had "recommended the possession of firearms by members for their self-protection."

The wiretaps, discussed above, which were placed between 1962 and 1965 as part of COMINFIL investigations, also show the lengths to which the "domestic security" standard could be stretched. Most of these wiretaps were based not on specific actions of the targets that threatened the domestic security but on the possibility that the targets, consciously or even unwittingly encouraged by communists, would engage in such activities in the future. While the Attorney General and the FBI may properly have been concerned about certain advisors to Dr. Martin Luther King, Jr., for example, no serious argument can be made that Dr. King himself jeopardized the nation's security. Yet King was the target of no fewer than five wiretaps between 1963 and 1965, and an associate of his (who was not one of his suspected advisors) was also wiretapped in 1964.

In the case of the Student Non-Violent Coordinating Committee, even potential communist infiltration was apparently seen as sufficient to justify a wiretap under the "domestic security" standard. The request for a wiretap on SNCC which was sent to Attorney General Katzenbach in 1965 noted that "confidential informants" described SNCC as "the principal target for Communist Party infiltration among the various civil rights organizations" and stated that some of its leaders had "made public appearances with leaders of Communist-front organizations" and had "subversive backgrounds." The FBI presented no substantial evidence, however, that SNCC was in fact infiltrated by Communists—only that the organization was allegedly a target for such infiltration in the future.

2. Microphone Surveillances Under the "National Interest" Standard

Between 1954 and 1965, the prevailing standard for the approval of microphone surveillances was that established by Attorney General Brownell in 1954. "Considerations of internal security and the national safety are paramount," he then wrote, "and, therefore, may compel the unrestricted use of this technique in the national interest."

Under this standard, J. Edgar Hoover approved the bugging of Congressman Cooley's hotel room in February 1961, in connection with the "Sugar Lobby" investigation. Law enforcement purposes or the need to gather foreign intelligence information may arguably have supported this surveillance, but the documentary record of the Sugar Lobby investigation reveals no genuine "internal security" or "national safety" justification for the Cooley bug.

This standard was also used to justify the fifteen microphone surveillances of Dr. Martin Luther King, Jr., between January 1964 and October 1965. Significantly, FBI internal memoranda with respect to some of these installations, make clear that they were planted in Dr. King's hotel rooms for the express purpose of obtaining personal information about him rather than for internal security purposes. The validity of the "national interest" rationale for the other bugs—and for the microphone surveillances of certain associates of Dr. King—is also open to serious question.

At the 1964 Democratic National Convention in Atlantic City, New Jersey, the FBI also planted a microphone in the joint headquarters of the Student Non-Violent Coordinating Committee and the Congress on Racial Equality. The only reason for the SNCC bug expressed in contemporaneous FBI documents was the following:

> Sixty members of the SNCC from Jackson, Mississippi, plan to attend the Convention to assist in seating the Mississippi Freedom Democratic Party delegation. This group also reportedly will utilize walkie-talkies in connection with their planned demonstrations.

A 1975 Inspection Report on the FBIs activities at the 1964 Convention speculated that the bug may have been installed because the Bureau had information at that time that "an apparent member of the Communist Party, USA, was engaging in considerable activity, much in a leadership capacity in the Student Non-Violent Coordinating Committee." CORE appears to have been an incidental target of the SNCC bug, since the two groups shared offices in Atlantic City.

3. Wiretaps and Microphone Surveillances Under the Five Criteria Based on Section 2511 (3)

Improper and questionable selection of targets continued after the Justice Department altered the criteria under which wiretaps and bugs could be authorized to conform with the five categories set forth by Congress in Section 2511(3) of the 1968 Omnibus Crime Control Act. (These categories are discussed at p. 288-290.)

There does not appear to have been any genuine national security justification, for example, supporting the "Plumbers" wiretap on Joseph Kraft's Washington residence or the FBI's bug in his hotel room abroad. John Ehrlichman testified before the Senate Watergate Committee that the "national security" was involved, but did not elaborate further. According to the transcript of the White House tapes, President Nixon stated to John Dean, on April 16, 1973 that

> ... What I mean is I think in the case of the Kraft's stuff what the FBI did, they were both fine. I have checked the facts. There were some done through private sources. Most of it was done through the Bureau after we got—Hoover didn't want to do Kraft. What it involved apparently, John, was this: the leaks from the NSC [National Security Council]. They were in Kraft and others' columns and we were trying to plug the leaks and we had to get it done and finally we turned it over to Hoover. And then when the hullabaloo developed we just knocked it off altogether . . .

Beyond these claims, there is little evidence that any national security issue was involved in the case. Former Deputy Attorney General and Acting FBI Director William Ruckelshaus testified: "I did review the information on which the effort was made from one of the operations out of the White House to put a tap on Mr. Kraft and, frankly, I could never see any national security justification for doing so." Of the hotel room bug, Mr. Ruckelshaus stated: "The justification would have been that he was discussing with some—asking questions of some members of the North Vietnamese Government, representatives of that government. My own feeling is that this just is not an adequate national security justification for placing any kind of surveillance on an American citizen or newsman. It just is not an adequate justification . . ." Mr. Kraft stated in a 1974 Congressional hearing that he was in contact with North Vietnamese officials while he was overseas in 1969, but he noted that this was a common practice among journalists and that he never knowingly published any classified information on the basis of these or any other contacts he made there. He further stated that Henry Kissinger, then the President's Special Adviser for National Security, informed him that he had no contemporaneous knowledge of either the wiretap or the hotel room bug, and that former Attorney General Elliot Richardson indicated to him that "there was no justification for these activities." Attorney General Edward Levi recently wrote Mr. Kraft that the FBI's 115-document file on the columnist "did not indicate that Mr. Kraft's activities posed any risk to the national interest."

There is also no evidence of a "national security" justification for the physical surveillance or the proposed electronic surveillance of Kraft in the fall of 1969. A Bureau memorandum suggests that the Attorney General did desire some type of coverage of Kraft, but the record reveals no purpose for this coverage.

Perhaps significantly, the physical surveillance was discontinued after five weeks because it had "not been productive." Apparently, the Attorney General himself was unconvinced that a genuine "national security" justification supported the Kraft surveillance: he refused to authorize the requested wiretap and it was consequently never implemented.

The "Seventeen Wiretaps" in 1969, 1970, and 1971 clearly reveal the relative ease with which improper targets can be selected for wiretapping. Shortly after these wiretaps were revealed publicly, President Nixon stated that they had been justified by the need to prevent leaks of classified information harmful to the "national security." In the cases of several of these taps, however, no "national security" claim was advanced in the supporting documents that went to the Attorney General requesting authorization. Two of the targets were domestic affairs advisers at the White House, who had no foreign affairs responsibilities and apparently had no access to classified foreign policy materials. According to Bureau memoranda, their coverage was not requested through the President's National Security Advisor or his assistant, as Bureau memoranda indicate others in this series were, but by the White House directly: John Mitchell approved the first of these two taps at the request of "higher authority;" the second of these two was requested by H. R. Haldeman.

A third target was a White House speech writer who had been overheard on an existing tap agreeing to provide a reporter with background information on a Presidential speech concerning not foreign policy but revenue sharing and welfare reform. This tap was also requested by the White House directly. The reinstatement of the tap on one National Security Council staff member was apparently requested by H. R. Haldeman simply because "they have some concern [about him]; they may have a bad apple and have to get him out of the basket." The last four requests which were sent to the Attorney General, including that for reinstatement of the tap on the NSC staff member, do not mention any national security justification to support the requests. While national security issues were at least arguably involved in some of the taps, in short, additional targets were selected with no national security basis at all. As William Ruckelshaus has testified:

> I think some of the individuals who were tapped, at least to the extent I have reviewed the record, had very little, if any, relationship to any claim of a national security tie ... I think that as the program proceeded and it became clear to those who could sign off on taps how easy it was to institute a wiretap under the present procedure that those kinds of considerations [i.e., genuine national security justifications] were considerably relaxed as the program went on.

As noted in Section VI above, wiretaps were -also placed on three antiwar organizations which were involved in planning the "March on Washington" in November 1969. The first of these three wiretaps, approved by Attorney General Mitchell on November 6, was directed against the New Mobilization Committee to End the War in Vietnam (NMC). The FBI's request for coverage of this group noted that the anticipated size of the demonstration was cause for "concern" should violence break out, but it made no claim that NMC members in particular engaged in or were likely to engage in violent activity. The entire "justification" portion of the memorandum sent to John Mitchell reads as follows:

> The New Mobilization Committee to End the War in Vietnam (NMC) is coordinating efforts for a massive antiwar manifestation to take place in Washington, D.C., November 12-16, 1969. This group maintains a Washington, D.C., office at 1029 Vermont Avenue, Northwest, where the planning takes place.
>
> This demonstration could possibly attract the largest number of demonstrators ever to assemble in Washington, D.C. The large number is cause for major concern should violence of any type break out. It is

necessary for this Bureau to keep abreast of events as they occur, and we feel that in this instance advance knowledge of plans and possible areas of confrontation would be most advantageous to our coverage and to the safety of individuals and property. Accordingly, we are requesting authorization to install a telephone surveillance on the Washington office of the NMC.

Five days after he approved the first tap, the Attorney General authorized wiretaps on the Vietnam Moratorium Committee and a third antiwar organization, both of which were "closely coordinating their efforts with NMC in organizing the demonstration." The only additional justification given for the wiretap on the Vietnam Moratorium Committee was that the group "has recently endorsed fully the activities of the NMC concerning the upcoming antiwar demonstrations."

In 1970, approval for a wiretap on a "New Left-oriented campus group" was granted by Attorney General Mitchell on the basis of an FBI request which included, among other factors deemed relevant to the necessity for the wiretap, evidence that the group was attempting "to develop strong ties with the cafeteria, maintenance and other workers on campus" and wanted to "go into industry and factories and ... take the radical politics they learned on the campus and spread them among factory workers."

This approval was renewed three months later despite the fact that the request for renewal made no mention of violent or illegal activity by the group. The value of the wiretap was shown, according to the FBI, by such results as obtaining "the identities of over 600 persons either in touch with the national headquarters or associated with" it during the prior three months. Six months after the original authorization the number of persons so identified had increased to 1,428; and approval was granted for a third three-month period.

4. Electronic Surveillance of Journalists, Attorneys and Persons Involved in the Domestic Political Process

As the preceding three subsections indicate, the elasticity of the standards for instituting electronic surveillance has permitted this technique to be directed against American citizens with little or no adequate justification in the particular case. In addition, the targeting of individuals in certain categories, such as journalists, attorneys, and persons involved in the domestic political process, is an inherently questionable practice because of the special concerns which affect these groups.

Between 1961 and 1972, at least six American journalists and newsmen were electronically surveilled by the FBI: Lloyd Norman in 1961; Hanson Baldwin in 1962 ; the editor of an anti-Communist newsletter in 1965; Joseph Kraft in 1969; and two American newsmen in connection with the "Seventeen Wiretaps" during the period 1969 to 1971. All of these surveillances were ostensibly conducted to determine the source of leaks of classified information.

The wiretapping of journalists in the investigation of "leaks," however has proven to be a fruitless enterprise. As former Secretary of State Dean Rusk stated:

Tapping newsmen will not stop leaks and for the most part is not even going to uncover leaks. There are so many different ways in which leaks can be made and from so many different quarters that there is no way to get at the business of leaks and on sheer practical grounds this is rather foolish policy to pursue.

Aside from matters of practicality, the Constitution gives special protection to "freedom of the press." The precedent set by wiretapping newsmen inevitably tends to undermine the Constitutional guarantee of a free and independent press.

During the 1960s there were also numerous wiretaps on the office telephones of attorneys. In the course of the Sugar Lobby investigation in 1962, ten telephone lines of a Washington, D.C., law firm were wiretapped in order to intercept the conversations of a single lawyer who was believed to be acting as a lobbyist for foreign interests. In that same year, the office telephone of an advisor to Dr. Martin Luther King, Jr.—also a lawyer—was wiretapped and his office was bugged ; his telephone was wiretapped again in 1965. A second attorney who advised Dr. King was wiretapped in 1963 ; and the office telephone of an attorney who was in frequent contact with the editor of an anti-Communist newsletter was wiretapped in 1965. Attorneys have also been frequently overheard on wiretaps not specifically directed at them. The wiretap on the headquarters of the Jewish Defense League in 1970 and 1971, for instance, intercepted the conversations between Bertram Zweibon, an attorney for several JDL members, and his clients.

Both direct and indirect electronic surveillances of attorneys, such as those listed above, inevitably jeopardize the Sixth Amendment-based attorney-client privilege, because this technique, by its intrusive nature, is capable of providing the means by which the FBI and the Justice Department can learn the legal strategy to be used by actual and potential defendants as well as other information given in confidence by clients to their attorneys. In order to minimize the possibility of violating the attorney-client privilege, FBI monitoring agents in court-ordered electronic surveillance cases are currently under instructions to shut off interception equipment upon the commencement of conversations between a client and his attorney concerning a "pending criminal case." This policy is also applied to warrantless electronic surveillances. As a practical matter, however, it is difficult, if not impossible, to comply fully with this requirement since the monitoring agent must listen to the beginning of such a conversation even to recognize it.

In the Jewish Defense League case, the wiretap continued for more than a month after federal criminal indictments were returned against several JDL members. In violation of a specific instruction from the Attorney General to suspend the overhearing and recording of conversations between "individuals who are or may be defendants or attorneys in pending Federal cases," Bureau agents overheard and recorded conversations between some of the indicted JDL members and their attorney, Mr. Zweibon. The District of Columbia Court of Appeals wrote in regard to this matter:

> When criminal indictments have already been returned against some subjects of a surveillance, as was true in this case.... surreptitious surveillance may ... deny those subjects effective assistance of counsel in derogation of their Sixth Amendment rights ... We do not mean to suggest that appellees [Attorney General Mitchell and other government officials] were even partially motivated by a desire to overhear privileged attorney-client communications concerning pending criminal trials ... However, we note that such motivations may prompt surveillance in other situations and thus constitute another abuse which prior judicial authorization may help to curb.

Electronic surveillance of persons involved in the domestic political process, such as Congressmen, lobbyists, and Congressional aides, also raises special problems. Information is often the key to power; and the ability of high executive officials to use electronic surveillance to obtain information about their political opponents can give the President and his aides enormous influence. Apart from violating the rights of the surveillance targets, wiretapping and bugging on behalf of the President's political interests destroys the Constitutional system of checks and balances designed to limit the exercise of arbitrary power.

Electronic surveillance has been used to serve the interests of Presidents in almost every political arena; it has been a resource for executive power that has tempted administrations of both political parties. Officials succumbed to the temptation with a consistency which demonstrates the immense danger of vesting authority over the use of such techniques solely within the Executive Branch.

B. Procedural Violations

Frequent violations of the internal procedural requirements for warrantless electronic surveillance have compounded the abuses to which this technique is prone. Wiretaps and bugs have often been installed without the prior authorization of the Attorney General and at times without prior authority from Bureau Headquarters, thus defeating one of the few checks on the unrestricted use of electronic surveillance. Certain very sensitive surveillances have also been intentionally excluded from the ELSUR Index, rendering impossible the retrieval of overhears and other information about the surveillances through a regular file search. In two cases, surveillance records were physically removed from FBI Headquarters and stored at the White House. The occurrence of procedural violations such as these have doubtlessly facilitated the improper use of electronic surveillance of American citizens.

The failure of the FBI to secure the necessary prior approval of the Attorney General in a number of wiretapping cases has been described above. Wiretaps directed against Lloyd Norman, Hanson Baldwin's secretary, a former FBI agent, and Morton Halperin were all instituted and continued for a period of days without any approval or in some cases, apparently even knowledge, on the part of Attorneys General. No explicit approval was ever secured from the Attorney General for two of the four wiretaps in the Charles Radford series and, also in violation of existing regulations, no written approval was granted for the other two. After the requirement of prior Attorney General approval for microphone surveillance was imposed in 1965, the FBI installed at least three bugs in hotel rooms occupied by Dr. Martin Luther King, Jr., without advising the Attorney General before the fact. 330 Nor was the Attorney General's approval ever sought for the FBI's bugging of columnist Joseph Kraft in 1969. Both the SNCC bug in 1964 and an attempted microphone surveillance of Dr. King in 1966, moreover, occurred without even the approval of FBI Director Hoover: a 1975 Inspection Report on the Bureau's activities at the 1964 Democratic National Convention states that "a thorough review of Bureau records fails to locate any memorandum containing authorization for [the bug planted at SNCC headquarters] ;" and on a January 1966 memorandum reflecting the New York Office installation of a microphone in Dr. King's room, Associate Director Clyde Tolson wrote, "No one here approved this. I have told [FBI Assistant Director William C.] Sullivan [who bad authorized the New York office to install the bug] again not to institute mike surveillance without the Director's approval."

Violations of the requirement of periodic re-authorization of electronic surveillances, imposed in 1965, have also magnified this technique's abuses in the domestic area. Despite the lack of any evidence of a "national security" leak obtained from any of the "Seventeen Wiretaps," for example, -- the President himself privately admitted that the taps were unproductive and useless in determining the source of leaks -- ten of them remained in operation for periods longer than ninety days and none was ever re-authorized. After the tap on Halperin had been in place for two months, William C. Sullivan wrote the Director that "Nothing has come to light [on this tap] that is of significance from the standpoint of the leak in question ;" yet that tap continued for another nineteen months without re-authorization. The Halperin tap, and that on another National Security Council staff member, moreover, remained in operation long after both of these targets left the employ of the National Security Council and became advisors to Senator Edmund Muskie, then the leading Democratic prospect for the Presidency. These targets no longer had access to classified information but they were clearly in a position to provide political intelligence to the White House unwittingly. The wiretap on Charles Radford was similarly never re-authorized, although it continued for nearly six months after it was instituted in December 1971.

Because of their perceived sensitivity, the records of some wiretaps and bugs were purposefully not contemporaneously integrated into the regular FBI files for warrantless electronic surveillance. When the Bureau was first advised of the "Seventeen Wiretaps," for example, it was told that their sensitivity precluded the maintenance of multiple records; consequently, only one copy of the records was retained and no entries were made in the ELSUR Index. According to a 1973 FBI memorandum regarding the Radford wiretaps, "Our records have been kept completely isolated from other FBI records, and there are no indices whatsoever relating to this project." And in the case of Joseph Kraft, most of the summaries which W. C. Sullivan sent to J. Edgar Hoover from abroad were marked "DO NOT FILE" to make their retrieval through a normal file search impossible. In both the "Seventeen Wiretaps" case and the Kraft case, moreover, the limited surveillance records that were maintained were physically removed from the FBI headquarters and taken by Assistant Attorney General Robert Mardian to John Ehrlichman at the White House, apparently at the instruction of President Nixon. On May 12, 1973, these files were discovered by Acting FBI Director William Ruckelshaus in a safe in Ehrlichinan's outer office and returned to Bureau Headquarters.

The circumvention of normal approval and filing requirements, in short, accompanied and facilitated the improper wiretapping and bugging of American citizens. The knowledge that these requirements could, in secrecy, be ignored inevitably increased the likelihood that wiretaps and bugs would be employed without substantial justification.

C. Collection and Dissemination of Information Irrelevant to Legitimate Governmental Objectives

Wiretaps and microphones, by their nature, inevitably intercept conversations which are totally unrelated to the authorized purpose of the surveillance. Virtually all conversations are overheard, no matter how trivial, personal, or political they might be. In addition, the techniques are incapable of a surgical precision which would permit the FBI to overhear only the target's conversations. Anyone using a tapped telephone or conversing in a bugged room can be overheard. These characteristics of electronic surveillance have directly resulted in another type of abuse: the collection of information, including purely personal and political information, for dissemination to the highest levels in the Government.

1. Personal Information

One extreme example of the collection and dissemination of personal information is found in the surveillance of an American citizen at the direct request of the White House. Among the items of interest that the FBI obtained from a wiretap on this individual — and delivered in utmost secrecy to a Presidential aide — were the following: that "meat was ordered [by the target's family] from a grocer"; that the target's daughter had a toothache; that the target needed grass clippings for a compost heap he was building; and that during a telephone conversation between the target's wife and a friend the "matters discussed were milk bills, hair, soap operas, and church." Even the FBI evidently realized that this type of information was unrelated to national security: for the last four months of the surveillance, most of the summaries that were disseminated to the White House began, "The following is a summary of non-pertinent information concerning captioned individual as of . . ."

From the bug planted in Joseph Kraft's hotel room, John Ehrlichman learned about this columnist's social contacts there and his views about the activities of an American politician.

The "Seventeen Wiretaps" supplied the White House with a wealth of information about the personal lives of the targets and the people with whom they communicated. In the private words of President Nixon, these wiretaps produced "just gobs and gobs of material: gossip and bull." The White House did not learn that any of them were responsible for any national security leaks, but it did learn about their social contacts, their vacation plans, their employment satisfactions and dissatisfactions, their marital problems, their drinking habits, and even their sex lives. The fact that an Associate Justice of the United States Supreme Court was overheard on one of these wiretaps and intended to review a manuscript written by one of the subjects was also disseminated to the White House.

The most blatant example of the collection of entirely personal information and its dissemination to high-ranking government officials occurred in connection with the FBI's investigation of Dr. Martin Luther King Jr. As noted above, the Bureau installed at least fifteen bugs in hotel rooms occupied by Dr. King, some of which were installed for the express purpose of collecting personal information. In December 1964, the FBI, with the approval of the White House, disseminated a monograph on alleged communist influence in the civil rights movement to the heads of intelligence agencies as well as the State Department, the Defense Department, and USIA. This monograph contained a section on the personal life of Dr. King that was apparently based in part on the information obtained from these bugs. Between 1965 and 1968, at least two updated versions of the monograph, including the section on King's personal life, were similarly distributed. Other FBI summaries about Dr. King which were based in part on microphone surveillance were also disseminated to executive branch officials outside the FBI.

2. Political Information

Political information useful to the administration in power has also been obtained from electronic surveillance of American citizens and disseminated to Attorneys General and Presidents. While the generation of this type of information was incidental, in most cases, to the purpose of the wiretap, its dissemination has armed key officials with knowledge of the strategies of their political opponents.

The "Sugar Lobby" Investigation. — The "Sugar Lobby" wiretaps and microphone bugging during the Kennedy administration serve as one example of the collection and dissemination of essentially political information. Beyond the Attorney

General's concern about American foreign policy and the possibility of bribery, it is clear that at the time the initial wiretaps were placed, the Kennedy administration opposed any sugar bill that provided for the favorable quotas sought by the foreign government in question. The administration wanted a bill that would give the "Executive Branch necessary flexibility in establishing country quotas, ostensibly for the purpose of denying quotas to countries (such as [this particular foreign country]) whose foreign policy was at odds with ours. Even if the 1961 and the 1962 series of wiretaps were arguably legitimate under electronic surveillance law of the early 1960s, they generated some information that was potentially useful to the Kennedy administration in terms of this legislative objective. Given the nature of the techniques used and the targets they were directed against, the collection of such information is not surprising.

One summary of an overhear that was disseminated to the Attorney General noted that a particular lobbyist "mentioned he is working on the Senate and has the Republicans all lined up ..." This same lobbyist was also reported to have said that "he had seen two additional representatives on the House Agriculture Committee, one of whom was 'dead set against us' and who may reconsider, and the other was neutral and 'may vote for us.'" Robert Kennedy further learned that the "friend" of one of the foreign officials "was under strong pressure from the present administration, and since the 'friend' is a Democrat, it would be very difficult for him to present a strong front to a Democratic administration." From the bug in Congressman Cooley's hotel room, the Attorney General was informed that among other matters Mr. Cooley believed he "had not accomplished anything" and that "he had been fighting over the Rules Committee and this had interferred with his attempt to organize.' "

In general, coverage of the entire situation was "intensified during the time preceding the passage of the sugar quota law," 'and was apparently terminated in 1961 when the bill desired by the administration passed the Senate. According to a memorandum of a meeting between Attorney General Kennedy and Courtney Evans, an Assistant Director of the FBI, Kennedy stated that "now [that] the law has passed he did not feel there was justification for continuing this extensive investigation." The Bureau's own evaluation of these wiretaps in 1966 reads in part: "Undoubtedly, data from our coverage contributed heavily to the administration's success in [passage of the bill it desired]."

The 1964 Democratic National Convention—The dissemination of political information from electronic surveillance was repeated during the Johnson administration. At the request of the White House, the FBI sent a special squad to the Democratic National Convention site, in Atlantic City, New Jersey, on August 22, 1964, ostensibly to assist the Secret Set-vice in protecting President Lyndon Johnson and to ensure that the convention itself would not be marred by civil disruption. Approximately thirty Special Agents, headed by Assistant Director Cartha DeLoach, "were able to keep the White House fully apprised of all major developments during the Convention's course" by means of "Informant coverage, by use of various confidential techniques, by infiltration of key groups through use of undercover agents, and through utilization of agents using appropriate cover as reporters ..." Among the "confidential techniques" were two electronic surveillances: a wiretap on the hotel room occupied by Martin Luther King, Jr., and a microphone surveillance of SNCC and CORE.

The White House apparently did not know of the existence of either of these electronic surveillances. Walter Jenkins, an Administrative Assistant to President Johnson who was present at the Convention and the recipient of information developed by the Bureau, stated that he was unaware that any of the intelligence was obtained by wiretapping or bugging. DeLoach has testified that he is uncertain whether he ever informed Jenkins of these sources. It is clear, however, that Jenkins, and presumably President Johnson, nonetheless, received a significant volume of information from the King tap and the SNCC bug—much of it purely political and only tangentially related to possible civil unrest.

One of the most important issues that might have disturbed President Johnson at the Atlantic City Convention was the seating challenge of the regular, all-white Mississippi delegation by the predominantly black Mississippi Freedom Democratic Party (MFDP). From the electronic surveillances of King and SNCC, the White House was able to obtain the most sensitive details of the plans and tactics of individuals supporting the MFDP's challenge. On August 24, 1964, for example, Cartha DeLoach, the FBI official who was in charge of the Bureau's special squad in Atlantic City, reported to Jenkins that:

> King and [an associate] were drafting a telegram to President Johnson . . . to register a mild protest. According to King, the President pledged complete neutrality regarding the selecting of the proper Mississippi delegation to be seated at the convention. King feels that the Credentials Committee will turn down the Mississippi Freedom Party and that they are doing this because the President exerted pressure on the committee along this line. The MFDP wanted to get the issue before the full convention but because of the President's actions, this will be impossible.

The next day another associate of King's contacted (on the telephone in King's room) a member of the MFDP who:

> said she thought King should see Governor Endicott Peabody of Massachusetts, Mayor Robert Wagner of New York City, Governor Edmund G. (Pat) Brown of California, Mayor Richard Daley of Chicago, and Governor John W. King of New Hampshire.

DeLoach noted that "the purpose of King's seeing these individuals is to urge them to call the White House directly and put pressure on the White House in behalf of the MFDP." Jenkins was also informed that:

> MFDP leaders have asked Reverend King to call Governor Egan of Alaska and Governor Burns of Hawaii in an attempt to enlist their support. According to the MFDP spokesman, the Negro Mississippi Party needs these two states plus California and New York for the roll call tonight.

Significantly, a 1975 FBI Inspection Report stated that "several Congressmen, Senators, and Governors of states ..." were overheard on this King tap.

DeLoach reported, too, that an SCLC staff member told a representative of the MFDP: "Off the record, of course, you know we will accept the Green compromise proposed;" and for Jenkins' benefit, added that "[t]his refers to the proposal of Congresswoman Edith Green of Oregon."

On August 26, 1964, King was overheard conferring with another civil rights leader on a number of matters relating to the convention. The report that was sent to Jenkins on this conversation included the following paragraph:

> Discussion of a Vice-Presidential nominee came up and King asked what [the other leader] thought of Hugh [sic] Humphrey, and [the other individual] said Hugh Humphrey is not going to get it, that Johnson needs a Catholic ... to go into the ghettos [sic] where Johnson will not journey and, therefore, the Vice-President will be Muskie of Maine ...

According to both Cartha DeLoach and Walter Jenkins, the Bureau's coverage in Atlantic City did not serve political ends. 369 From the examples cited above, however, it is clear that the FBI's electronic surveillance did generate a great deal of potentially useful political intelligence, as well as political commentary that was totally unrelated to the possibility of civil unrest. A document located at the Lyndon B. Johnson Presidential Library, moreover, suggests that at least one actual political use was made of the FBI reports. This unsigned memorandum, which Walter Jenkins said was clearly intended for the President (although he disclaimed authorship), disclosed Martin Luther King's strategy in connection with a meeting to be attended by President Johnson. Among other items, this memorandum reports that:

> Deac DeLoach called me this morning to say that his information was that King had been advised by Joe Rauh [an attorney for the MFDP] that in this morning's meeting you were not going to let the group discuss seating of the "freedom party" delegation, but would take the initiative. King was, last night, pondering on whether to refuse to come to the meeting on the grounds of short notice ...

> Deac's information was that if King did show ... he was instructed to "speak up to the President."

Although FBI and White House officials claimed it was implemented to prevent violence at the Convention site, in short, the Bureau's coverage in Atlantic City — including two electronic surveillances — undeniably provided useful political intelligence to the President as well.

The "Seventeen Wiretaps." — In more recent years, FBI wiretaps have supplied political information to the Nixon administration as well. Since many of the "Seventeen Wiretaps" targets were personally involved in the domestic political process — as White House aides, reporters, and Congressional consultants — this program inevitably collected large amounts of essentially political information, much of which was disseminated to the White House. Among the examples of such items are the following:

-- That one of the targets told a friend it "is clear the administration will win on the ABM by a two-vote margin." Two Senators who apparently supported the administration's position were named.

-- That one of the targets "recently stated that he was to spend an hour with [one Senator's] Vietnam man, as [that Senator] is giving a speech on the 15th."

-- That one of the targets said Congressional hearings on Vietnam were being postponed because a key Senator did not believe they would be popular at that time.

-- That a well-known television news correspondent "was very depressed over having been 'singled out' by the Vice President."

-- That a friend of one of the targets wanted to see if a particular Senator would "buy a new [antiwar] amendment" and stated that "'They are going to meet with [another influential Senator].'"

-- That a friend of one of the targets said the Washington Star planned to publish an article critical of Henry Kissinger.

-- That a friend of one of the targets described one Senator as marginal" on the Church-Cooper Amendment but noted that another Senator might be persuaded to support it.

-- That one of the targets helped a former Ambassador write a press release criticizing a recent speech by President Nixon in which the President "attacked" certain Congressmen.

-- That one of the targets said Senator Mondale was in a "dilemma" over the "trade bill."

-- That the friend of one of the targets said he had spoken to former President Johnson and "Johnson would not back Senator Muskie for the Presidency as he intended to stay out of politics."

At least one example of a political use which was made of information such as this has also been documented. After J. Edgar Hoover informed the President that former Secretary of Defense Clark Clifford planned to write a magazine article criticizing President Nixon's Vietnam policy, Jeb Stuart Magruder wrote John Ehrlichman and H. R. Haldeman that "We are in a position to counteract this article in any number of ways. . ." Ehrlichman then noted to Haldeman that "This is the kind of early warning we need more of—your game planners are now in an excellent position to map anticipatory action—"and Haldeman responded, "I agree with John's point. Let's get going."

Perhaps significantly, after May 1970, copies of the letters summarizing the results of these wiretaps were no longer sent to Henry Kissinger, the President's national security advisor, but to H.R. Haldeman, the President's political advisor.

In summary electronic surveillance has proven to be a valuable technique for the collection of foreign intelligence and counterintelligence information within the legitimate mandate of the FBI. But the history of the use of this technique by the Bureau also proves that its dangers are equally great: without precise standards and effective checks to restrain its use, innocent American citizens may be its victims; without rigid means of restricting the dissemination of information generated through electronic surveillance, Government officials may learn the most personal— and the most political—expressions and beliefs of its targets.

Domestic CIA And FBI Mail Opening Programs

Part I: Summary And Principal Conclusions

Between 1940 and 1973, two agencies of the federal government—the CIA and the FBI—covertly and illegally opened and photographed first class letter mail within the United States. These agencies conducted a total of twelve mail opening programs for lengths of time varying from three weeks to twenty-six years. In a single program alone, more than 215,000 communications were intercepted, opened, and photographed; the photographic copies of these letters, some dated as early as 1955, were indexed, filed, and are retained even today. Information from this and other mail opening programs—"sanitized" to disguise its true source—was disseminated within the federal establishment to other members of the intelligence community, the Attorney General, and to the President of the United States.

The stated objective of the CIA programs was the collection of foreign intelligence and counterintelligence information; that of the FBI programs was the collection of counterespionage information. In terms of their respective purposes, seven of the twelve mail opening programs were considered to have been successful by Agency and Bureau officials. One CIA project and three of the FBI programs concededly failed to obtain any significant relevant information. Another CIA operation—clearly the most massive of all the programs in terms of numbers of letters opened—was believed to have been of value to the Agency by some officials, but was criticized by many others as having produced only minimally useful foreign intelligence. Despite two unfavorable internal reviews, this program nonetheless continued unabated for twenty years.

While all of these programs responded to the felt intelligence needs of the CIA and the FBI during the "cold war" of the 1950's and early 1960's, once in place they could be—and sometimes were—directed against the citizens of this country for the collection of essentially domestic intelligence. In the 1960's and early 1970's, large numbers of American dissidents, including those who challenged the condition of racial minorities and those who opposed the war in Vietnam, were specifically targeted for mail opening by both agencies. In one program, selection of mail on the basis of "personal taste" by agents untrained in foreign intelligence objectives resulted in the interception and opening of the mail of Senators, Congressmen, journalists, businessmen, and even a Presidential candidate.

The first mail opening program began shortly before the United States entered World War II, when representatives of an allied country's censorship agency taught six FBI agents the techniques of "chamfering" (mail opening) for use against Axis diplomatic establishments in Washington, D.C. The program was suspended after the war but reinstituted during the "cold war" in the early 1950's; the method was similar but the targets new. Shortly after this program was reinstituted, the CIA entered the field with a mail opening project in New York designed to intercept mail to and from the Soviet Union. Between 1954 and 1957, the FBI and the CIA each developed second programs, in response to post-war events in Asia, to monitor mail entering the United States from that continent; and the CIA briefly conducted a third operation in New Orleans to intercept Latin and Central American mail as well. The technique of chamfering was most widely used by the FBI during the period 1959 to 1966: in these years the Bureau operated no fewer than six programs in a total of eight cities in the United States. In July 1966, J. Edgar Hoover ordered an end to all FBI programs, but the Bureau continued to cooperate with the CIA, which acted under no such self-restriction, in connection with the Agency's New York project. In 1969, a fourth CIA program was established in San Francisco and was conducted intermittently until 1971. The era of warrantless mail opening was not ended until 1973, when, in the changed political climate of the times, the political risk—"flap potential"—of continuing the CIA's New York project was seen to outweigh its avowed minimal benefit to the Agency.

All of these mail opening programs were initiated by agency officials acting without prior authorization from a President, Attorney General, or Postmaster General; some of them were initiated without prior authorization by the Directors or other senior officials within the agencies themselves. Once initiated, they were carefully guarded and protected from exposure. The record indicates that during the thirty-three years of mail opening, fewer than seven Cabinet level officers were briefed about even one of the projects; only one President may have been informed; and there is no conclusive evidence any Cabinet officer or any President had contemporaneous knowledge that this coverage involved the actual opening—as opposed to the exterior examination—of mail. The postal officials whose cooperation was necessary to implement these programs were purposefully not informed of the true nature of the programs; in some cases, it appears that they were deliberately misled. Congressional inquiry was perceived by both CIA and FBI officials as a threat to the security of their programs; during one period of active investigation both agencies contemplated additional security measures to mislead the investigators and protect their programs against disclosure to Congress. Only in rare cases did the CIA and the FBI even inform one another about their programs.

Many of the major participants in these mail opening programs, including senior officials in policy-making positions, believed that their activities were unlawful. Yet the projects were considered to be so sensitive that no definitive legal opinions were ever sought from either the CIA's General Counsel or the Attorney General. The record is clear, in fact, that the perceived illegality of mail opening was a primary reason for closely guarding knowledge of the programs from ranking officials in both the executive and legislative branches of the government.

The legal fears of CIA and FBI officials were firmly based, for sanctity of the mail has been a long-established principle in American jurisprudence. Fourth Amendment restrictions on first class mail opening were recognized as early as 1878, when the Supreme Court wrote in Ex Parte Jackson, 96 U.S. 727,733 (1878):

Letters and sealed packages of this kind in the mail are as fully guarded from examination and inspection, except as to their outward form and weight, as if they were retained by the parties forwarding them in their own domiciles. The constitutional guaranty of the right of the people to be secure in their papers against unreasonable searches and seizures extends to their papers, thus closed against inspection, wherever they may be. Whilst in the mail, they can only be opened and examined under like warrant, issued upon similar oath or affirmation, particularly describing the thing to be seized, as is required when papers are subjected to search in one's own household. No law of Congress can place in the hands of officials connected with the postal service any authority to invade the secrecy of letters and such sealed packages in the mail; and all regulations adopted as to mail matter of this kind must be in subordination to the great principle embodied in the fourth amendment of the Constitution.

This principle was re-affirmed as recently as 1970 in United States v. Van Leeuwen, 397 U.S. 249, 251 (1970) : "It has long been held," the Supreme Court there wrote, "that first-class mail such as letters and sealed packages subject to letter postage—as distinguished from newspapers, magazines, pamphlets and other printed matter—is free from inspection by postal authorities, except in the manner provided by the Fourth Amendment."

Not only the Fourth Amendment's prohibition against unreasonable searches and seizures, but First Amendment values of free speech are involved in the opening of first class mail. As Justice Holmes stated in 1921, in a dissent now embraced by prevailing legal opinion: "The use of the mails is almost as much a part of free speech as the right to use our tongues." Milwaukee Pub. Co. v. Burleson, 255 U.S. 407, 437 (1921). Justice William 0. Douglas quoted this passage with approval in a 1965 decision which invalidated a procedure whereby incoming third and fourth class propaganda could be indefinitely detained by Postal and Customs officials—a procedure, incidentally, which had provided cover for three CIA and FBI mail opening programs. 1 Lamont v. Postmaster General, 381 U.S. 301, 305 (1965). In 1974, in a case involving censorship of prisoner mail, the Supreme Court also noted that "the addressee as well as the sender of direct personal correspondence derives from the First and Fourteenth Amendments a protection against unjustified governmental interference with the intended communication." Procunier v. Martinez, 416 U.S. 396,408-409 (1974).

Statutory as well as constitutional protection has traditionally been accorded first class letter mail. Throughout the entire postwar period in which FBI and CIA mail opening programs were conducted, the statutory framework of legal prohibitions against the unauthorized opening of mail have remained essentially constant. The pertinent statutes, enacted in 1948 and substantially unchanged since then, are set forth below:

1. 18 U.S.C. Sec. 1701:

Whoever knowingly and willfully obstructs or retards the passage of the mail, or any carrier or conveyance carrying the mail, shall be fined not more than $100 or imprisoned not more than six months, or both. (June 25, 1948, ch. 645, 62 Stat. 778.)

2. 18 U.S.C. Sec. 1702:

Whoever takes any letter, postal card, or package out of any post office or any authorized depository for mail matter, or from any letter or mail carrier, or which has been in any post office or authorized depository, or in the custody of any letter or mail carrier, before it has been delivered to the person to whom it was directed, with design to obstruct the correspondence, or to pry into the business or secrets of another, or opens, secretes, embezzles, or destroys the same, shall be fined not more than $2,000 or imprisoned not more than five years, or both. (June 25, 1948, ch. 645, 62 Stat. 778.)

3. 18 U.S.C. Sec. 1703 (b) :

Whoever, without authority, opens, or destroys any mail or package of newspapers not directed to him, shall be fined not more than $100 or imprisoned not more than one year, or both. (June 25, 1948, ch. 645, 62 Stat. 778; May 24, 1949, ch. 139, Sec. 37, 63 Stat. 95; Aug. 12, 1970, Pub. L. 91-375, ? 6 (j) (16), 84 Stat. 778.)

The issue of proper authority for the opening of mail, which is raised by 18 U.S.C. Sec. 1703(b) above, was, until 1960, dealt with in 18 U.S.C. Sec. 1717(c) : "No person other than a duly authorized employee of the Dead Letter office, or other person upon a search warrant authorized by law, shall open any letter not addressed to himself." This section was repealed in 1960 and recodified in essentially similar form at 39 U.S.C. 4057. When the Postal Service was reorganized in 1970, Section 4057 was in turn repealed and substantially recodified at 39 U.S.C. 3623 (d), which provides in part:

> No letter of such a class [i.e., first class] of domestic origin shall be opened except under authority of a search warrant authorized by law, or by an officer or employee of the Postal Service for the sole purpose of determining an address at which the letter can be delivered, or pursuant to the authorization of the addressee.

The only persons who can lawfully open first class mail without a warrant, in short, are employees of the Postal Service for a very limited purpose — not agents of the CIA or FBI.

In the face of the Constitution and these statutes, mail was surreptitiously opened for more than three decades without warrant; without Congressional or clear Presidential authority; frequently without approval by senior agency officials; and, in the case of the most massive program, despite critical internal evaluations as well. Seasoned intelligence officers in both agencies genuinely believed that this activity was important to safeguard the country from foreign adversaries. But to defend the national security, they chose to employ a technique that was neither sanctioned by the laws nor authorized by the elected leaders of the country they sought to protect. And since they defined the nature of our enemies, this technique came to be directed against American dissidents as well as foreigners.

Part II: CIA Domestic Mail Opening

I. Introduction And Major Facts

The CIA conducted four mail opening programs within the United States, the longest of which lasted for twenty years. These programs resulted in the opening and photographing of nearly a quarter of a million items of correspondence, the vast majority of which were to or from American residents. While the programs were ostensibly conducted for foreign intelligence and counterintelligence purposes, one former high-ranking CIA official characterized the Agency's use of this technique as a "shotgun" approach to intelligence collection; neither Congressmen, journalists, nor businessmen were immune from mail interception. With cooperation from the FBI, domestic "dissidents" were directly targeted in one of the programs.

The major facts regarding CIA domestic mail opening may be summarized as follows:

a. The CIA conducted four mail opening programs in four cities within the United States for varying lengths of time between 1953 and 1973: New York (1953-1973) ; San Francisco (four separate occasions, each of one to three weeks duration, between 1969 and 1971) ; New Orleans (three weeks in 1957) ; and Hawaii (late 1954 -- late 1955). The mail of twelve individuals in the United States, some of whom were American citizens unconnected with the Agency, was also opened by the CIA in regard to particular cases.

b. The stated purpose of all of the mail opening programs was to obtain useful foreign intelligence and counterintelligence information. At least one of the programs produced no such information, however, and the continuing value of the major program in New York was discounted by many Agency officials.

c. Despite the stated purpose of the programs, numerous domestic dissidents, including peace and civil rights activists, were specifically targeted for mail opening.

d. The random selection of mail for opening, by CIA employees untrained in foreign intelligence objectives and without substantial guidance from their superiors, also resulted in the interception of communications to or from high-ranking United States government officials, as well as journalists, authors, educators, and businessmen.

e. All of the mail opening programs were initiated without the prior approval of any government official outside of the Agency.

f. Only five Cabinet level officials, and possibly one President, were briefed in varying degrees of detail about the New York program during the twenty years it continued, and there is no conclusive evidence that any of these officials ever authorized—or knew of—the mail opening aspect of the project. The evidence suggests that in the cases of some of these officials, their professed lack of knowledge about mail opening was due to a stated desire to remain ignorant of the details of the program.

g. No high-ranking government official was ever briefed about three of the four mail opening programs.

h. Postal officials whose cooperation was necessary to effect the programs were purposefully misled as to the purpose of the projects, the question of custody of the letters, and the fact of mail opening itself.

i. One President of the United States, whether through design or negligence, was given false and misleading information about the existence of CIA mail opening programs. In 1970, the Director of Central Intelligence signed a document for submission to the President which stated that all mail opening programs by federal agencies had been discontinued. This Director knew that at that time the most extensive CIA mail opening program continued to operate in New York.

j. Within the Agency itself, two former Directors of Central Intelligence did not authorize and apparently did not even know about any of the mail opening programs that were conducted during their tenure. Another former Director was unaware of at least one mail opening project during his term.

k. Some senior Agency officials whose approvals were sought in connection to one mail opening program were apparently deceived as to its true nature by middle-level officers. The senior officials were requested to authorize a mail cover operation only, but mail opening was both contemplated at the time of the requests and did in fact occur.

l. None of the programs was ever subjected to formal internal evaluation. Such review as did occur concluded that the largest of the programs were poorly administered and without substantial benefit to the CIA. These conclusions were ignored and the project continued.

m. Because of the extreme sensitivity of the projects and the internal pattern of compartmentation, many of those CIA components which could have derived the greatest foreign intelligence value from the product were not even aware of the mail opening programs.

n. Most of the major participants in the mail opening programs believed that the Agency's activities in this area were unlawful. No definitive legal opinion was ever sought from the CIA's General Counsel, and the evidence suggests that knowledge of the programs was purposefully withheld from him for security reasons.

o. The general reaction among Agency officials to the perceived illegality of mail opening was to fabricate "cover stories" for public consumption and to agree on a public denial of CIA domestic mail opening activity in the event such activity were exposed.

p. During periods of active Congressional investigation into invasions of privacy by federal agencies, and when persons knowledgeable of CIA mail openings were in a position to be called to testify before Congress, security precautions for mail opening programs were tightened to reduce the risk of exposure.

q. In part because of his "secrecy agreement" with the Agency, a former CIA employee who was in a position at the Postal Service to force the termination of a mail opening program was inhibited from doing so for several years. His loyalty to the CIA, even after he left its service, prevented him from informing the Postmaster General of its existence.

r. The largest of the mail opening projects was not terminated until 1973, when, in the charged political climate of the times, it was considered too great a "political risk" to continue. It was not terminated because it was perceived to be illegal per se.

II. New York City Mail Intercept Project

The CIA's New York mail intercept project, encrypted HTLINGUAL by the Counterintelligence Staff and SRPOINTER by the Office of Security, was the most extensive of all the CIA's mail intercept programs, both in terms of the volume of mail that was opened and in terms of duration. Over the twenty year course of mail openings, more than 215,000 letters to and from the Soviet Union were opened and photographed by CIA agents in New York. Copies of more than 57,000 of these letters were also disseminated to the FBI, which learned of this operation in 1958, levied requirements on it, and received the fruits of the coverage until the project was terminated.

Despite the absence of clear authorization outside the CIA, despite the generally unfavorable internal reviews of the project in 1960 and 1969, and despite the facts that it was generally seen as illegal and that its primary value was believed by many agency officials to accrue to the FBI in the area of domestic intelligence, the momentum generated by this project from its inception in the early 1950's continued unchecked until February of 1973.

A. Operation of the Program

1. The Initial Phase: Mail Covers

The Original Proposal—The New York mail project originated in the spring of 1952 with a proposal by the Soviet (SR) Division, supported by the Chief of the Operations Staff (now the Deputy Director for Operations) and the Office of Security, to scan exteriors of all letters to the Soviet Union and to record, by hand, the names and addresses of the correspondents. While the original plan did not contemplate the opening of mail immediately, it was recognized that "[o]nce our unit was in position, its activities and influence could be extended gradually, so as to secure from this source every drop of potential intelligence information available." Specifically, it was believed that such a project could:

-- "furnish much live ammunition for psychological warfare;

-- "produce subjects, who if proven loyal to the United States, might be good agent material because of their contacts within the Soviet Union;

-- "offer documentary material for reproduction and subsequent use by our own agents;

-- "produce intelligence information when read in the light of other known factors and events; and

-- "create a channel for sending communications to American agents inside the Soviet Union."

Feasibility Study—On July 1, 1952, the Chief of the Special Security Division recommended that "[a]s an initial step . . . we should make contact in the Post Office Department at a very high level, pleading relative ignorance of the situation and asking that we, with their cooperation, make a thorough study of the volume of such mail, the channels through which it passes and particularly, the bottle necks within the United States in which we might place our survey teams." He advised against informing Post Office officials about the ultimate purposes of the project, however, noting that "[a]t the outset . . . as far as the Post Office Department is concerned, our main target could be the securing of names and addresses for investigation and possible future contact."

Two CIA officers from the Office of Security and the SR Division met with a representative of the International Division of the Post Office on the very day the Chief of the Special Security Division submitted the above recommendation. At this meeting, the Post Office official agreed to provide the Agency with a complete statement of "U.S.-U.S.S.R. postal accounting."

Clifton C. Garner, then Postal Inspector of the Post Office Department, was subsequently contacted by Agency personnel in the Offices of Operations and Security. It had been determined that most mail between the United States and the Soviet Union passed through the Port of New York, and on November 6, 1952, Garner was requested in writing to make arrangements for "one or two designated employees of this organization [i.e., CIA] to work with an inspector of your Department, under conditions determined by you to examine a portion of this mail traffic." While Garner cannot recall receiving this letter," he apparently agreed to make the necessary arrangments: one month later, Henry Montague, then Postal Inspector in Charge of the New York Division, approved the implementation of such an examination.

Commencement of the Project—The results of the initial survey were felt to be positive, and the project commenced on a full-time basis in February 1953. Henry Montague recalls that shortly prior to the commencement of the project, he had received a telephone call from David Stephens, who replaced Garner as Chief Postal Inspector under President Eisenhower, informing him that CIA agents would come to his office within the next few days to request his cooperation. According to Montague, Stephens instructed him to assist the Agency but warned him that there was to be no tampering with the mail beyond the minimum handling necessary for an exterior examination. When the agents visited Montague shortly thereafter, he specifically told the agents—and, according to Montague, the agents agreed—that mail should not be opened. Montague then requested a subordinate in the New York

Division to make the necessary arrangements and the CIA representatives were installed in a room in the New York General Post Office.

Briefing the Postmaster General—By September 1953, after seven months of operation, the project was considered to be sufficiently productive to merit expansion beyond hand-copying information from the outside of envelopes. A CIA officer of the Soviet Division proposed "the complete photographic coverage of the cover information on all letters posted from the Soviet Union to the U.S. and vice versa." Plans were made within the Agency to effect this type of coverage, but the postal officials who had cooperated thus far balked. It was noted in a January 4, 1954 internal CIA memorandum that "[f]or understandable reasons, postal authorities, at the level of our present dealings, are reluctant to extend that degree of cooperation without orders from above." This memorandum recommended that the Director of Central Intelligence brief both Postmaster General Arthur E. Summerfield and President Eisenhower on the project, and secure the oral approval of the President for photographing the exteriors of letters.

Director Allen Dulles and Richard Helms, then Chief of Operations in the Plans Directorate, met with the Postmaster General and the Chief Postal Inspector, David Stephens, on May 17, 1954. Dulles told Summerfield that the New York project had proven to be very valuable and that the Agency now desired to photograph the exteriors of letter mail from the Soviet Union. No mention was apparently made of mail opening. According to Helms' notes of the meeting, the Postmaster General "did not comment specifically" on the project but seemed receptive. Helms continued: "When the conference broke up, I spoke to David Stevens [sic] privately and asked him if he now had all the authorization he felt he needed. He replied in the affirmative." The second phase of the New York operation—photographing the exteriors of letters between the United States and the Soviet Union—began shortly after the Dulles Summerfield meeting.

2. Subsequent Evolution of the Project

The CI Staff Take-Over: "More" Mail Opening.—In November 1955, James Angleton, the Chief of the Counterintelligence (CI) Staff, submitted a proposal to Richard Helms for the further expansion of the New York mail intercept project. Until then, the CIA was only receiving access to a portion of the United States-Soviet Union mail in its New York facility; Angleton recommended that "we gain access to all mail traffic to and from the U.S.S.R. which enters, departs, or transits the United States through the Port of New York." He also suggested that the "raw information acquired be recorded, indexed and analyzed and various components of the Agency furnished items of information which would appear to be helpful to their respective missions." Perhaps most significantly, he recommended a shift in the focus of the project from photographing the mail to opening it. Even prior to the date this proposal was submitted, some mail opening had occurred "without the knowledge of the Post Office Department on a completely surreptitious basis . . . [by] swiping a letter, processing it at night and returning it the next day." This method, however, permitted agents to open a very limited number of items. Angleton proposed that "more [letters] could be opened" if the Agency acquired a separate room which would be off limits to postal employees and which would house special processing equipment. Because he realized that the Office of Security, which had been running the program to date, did not have sufficient manpower for the proposed expansion, Angleton also recommended that primary responsibility for the project be transferred within the Plans Directorate from 0/S to the CI Staff.

This proposal was approved by Helms on December 7, and funds were authorized by the Acting Deputy Director for Plans on March 3, 1956. They were implemented later in 1956 when the intercept location was moved from the General Post Office in Manhattan to a secure room at LaGuardia Airport. While postal officials cooperated to the extent of providing the CIA with the room, their approval was apparently not sought for the opening of mail.

FBI "Discovery" of the Project—The next significant expansion of the program occurred in January 1958 when the Federal Bureau of Investigation learned of its existence and shortly thereafter began to share in the fruits of the coverage. As early as January 1954 the CIA had contemplated informing the FBI about the project, because it was recognized that "outside of its definite foreign intelligence value . . . there will be produced information affecting Internal Security." Possibly because relations between the CIA and the FBI were strained during the mid-1950's, however, the Bureau was not officially informed about the project until Bureau inquiries relative to a proposed mail intercept program of its own uncovered the existence of the CIA project. Although the FBI never contributed any resources, either human or financial, to the operation of HTLINGUAL, it did levy requirements on the project and received copies of intercepted letters on a regular basis until the project was terminated in 1973. This aspect of the New York mail intercept project is treated in greater detail in Part III below.

The TSD Laboratory.—The final stage in the evolution of the project occurred in 1960 and 1961. By memorandum of February 25, 1960, James Angleton advised Richard Helms, now Acting Deputy Director for Plans, that the project would benefit from the establishment of a laboratory to examine a selected portion of the opened letters. He noted that at the present time there is no capability for "searching for secret writing and/or microdots; determination as to whether items have been previously opened and technically examined . . . . [or] opening items sealed with the more difficult and sophisticated adhesives." A laboratory, he argued, would make these activities feasible as well as enable the project staff "to increase our production about 20 percent." Helms approved the establishment of the laboratory, and it opened, under the direction of the Technical Services Division (TSD), about one year later in March 1961.

3. Full Operation of the Program

Volume of Mail Intercepted.—According to CIA records, a total of 28,322,796 letters were made available to CIA agents in New York during the twenty year course of the project. Of these, the exteriors of 2,705,706 letters were photographed, and 215,820 letters were actually opened. Mail opening had begun on a relatively small scale. In 1956, for example, only 832 letters were opened. But momentum developed quickly: two years later more than 8,000 letters were opened and by 1961, when the TSD laboratory was established, in excess of 14,000 letters were being opened annually. The height of the project in terms of volume was 1967, when a total of 23,617 letters were opened and analyzed.

Mechanics—Mail was physically intercepted at LaGuardia Airport from 1956 until 1962, when the project moved to Idlewild (Kennedy) Airport. At both locations, the mechanics were essentially the same: mail to and from the Soviet Union was delivered each day by a postal clerk to a secure room in which the agents worked. Five days a week, a team of about four Office of Security personnel screened and photographed this mail. The clerk, who received an annual bonus of $500 from the Agency for his efforts, also helped to sort the mail according to region within the

Soviet Union, but he was never informed that selected items would be opened. According to one of the agents who processed the mail, approximately two to six bags, containing a total of 5,000 to 15,000 items of correspondence, would be delivered and sorted each day. The exteriors of as many of these items as possible were photographed with a Diebold machine, and from 35 to 75 letters would be selected for opening daily. 33a Prior to 1969, the agents "swiped" the letters that had been selected for opening from the room by placing them in their pockets or an attache case, and hand carried them to the Office of Security's Manhattan Field Office for opening and photographing. From 1969 to 1973, opening and photographing were conducted at the intercept location itself.

The agents who opened the mail all attended a one-week course called "flaps and seals" (mail opening techniques), which was run by TSD at CIA Headquarters. The basic method of opening the mail was extremely simple, however: the glue on the envelopes was softened by steam from a kettle, and with the aid of a narrow stick the flap was pried open and the letter removed. One of the agents who opened the mail testified that "[y]ou could do it with your own teapot at home." It took approximately five to fifteen seconds to open a single letter. At one point in the 1960's, the CIA developed a type of steam "oven" that was capable of handling about one hundred letters simultaneously, but its performance was judged inadequate and the agents soon returned to the kettle and stick method.

The TSD laboratory, which became operative in 1961, was originally located in the Office of Security's Manhattan Field Office and subsequently transferred to Kennedy Airport. The Office of Security personnel who opened the mail brought it to this laboratory where it was subjected to further chemical and other technical examination for secret writing and censorship techniques by the two or three TSD agents permanently assigned to the project. Because examination was time consuming, it was only possible to test a small portion of those letters which had been opened and photographed.

The original letters, which had been opened, photographed, and possibly subjected to the TSD examination, were re-sealed and returned the next morning to the airport, at which point they would be re-inserted into the mail stream. Total delay time, therefore, averaged one day. The photographic copies were then bundled and sent by registered mail or courier on a near daily basis from the Manhattan Field Office to the Office of Security at CIA Headquarters, which would forward them to CT Staff analysts. These analysts, whose number varied from a minimum of two to a maximum of six, reviewed the contents of the letters and, on the basis of their knowledge of the requirements levied by various CIA components and the FBI, either fully translated or summarized each item of correspondence. The copies of the letters were indexed and retained in the CI Staff project room at Headquarters (where they are still on file), and appropriate translations and summaries were disseminated within the Agency to the SR Division, the Office of Security, and the CI Staff itself, as well as to the FBI.

B. Nature and Value of the Product

1. Selection Criteria

Letters were selected for opening by two basic methods: (1) on the basis of a list of names known as the "Watch List," and (2) randomly. By one CIA estimate, the "Watch List" accounted for approximately 25% of the total volume of mail that was opened; random selection for 75%.

The Watch List. — The Watch List originated in the mid-1950's, at which time it consisted of only ten to twenty names. With the SR Division, the CI Staff, the Office of Security, and the FBI all contributing names to the list it grew rapidly, however: by the end of the project the Watch List totaled about 600 names. One reason for the growth of the Watch List is that the categories into which these individuals or organizations fell were progressively broadened over the years. In April 1957, for example, a CIA memorandum suggested five narrow categories of names:

(1) former agents or covert contract personnel who originally came from "the Denied Area" in Europe, were utilized by the Agency, and have now been resettled in the United States or Canada;

(2) defectors from "the Denied Area" in Europe who were under the control or auspices of the Agency and who have now been resettled in the United States or Canada;

(3) repatriates from the United States or Canada who were originally brought to the United States or Canada under the auspices of the Agency and who have now returned or will return to the USSR;

(4) suspected Soviet agents or other individuals either temporarily or permanently residing in the United States, who are known or suspected of being engaged in counterespionage or counterintelligence activities on behalf of the USSR; and

(5) foreign nationals, originally from the USSR and satellite countries, now residing in the United States and presently being utilized by the Agency in any capacity.

Within a short time, the Watch List had expanded far beyond these relatively narrow and well-defined categories. The names of individuals who were in contact with Watch Listed persons and organizations were frequently added to the list themselves, and, as an August 1961 memorandum points out, a very large percentage of the names on the list were placed there because of "leads which came about through the random selection."

The focus of the Watch List also changed as it grew. In the early years of the project the names on the list might reasonably have been expected to lead to genuine foreign intelligence or counterintelligence information, but as the project evolved many of the names that were added to the list were far more likely to generate essentially domestic, rather than foreign, intelligence information. In 1969, for example, Richard Ober of the CIA solicited the FBI for names of domestic political radicals and black militants to include on the list. An FBI memorandum states that he "suggested to the Liaison Agent that the Bureau should not overlook the utilization of the agency's Hunter [New York mail opening] project for the development of leads in the New Left and Black Nationalist fields. Ober admitted that traffic involving individuals in these areas might be light but that the Bureau might wish to give consideration to placing stops on certain key personalities." A handwritten notation at the bottom of this memorandum indicated that "stops . . . on black extremists" were not felt to be "Warranted ... at this time" by the Bureau, but the names of a significant number of anti-war activists and groups were submitted to the CIA, as were the names of several "black extremists" at a later date. From 1958 to 1973, in fact, the FBI alone contributed a total of 286 names to the Watch List.

While Bureau requirements clearly augmented the emerging "domestic intelligence" nature of the Watch List, CIA components also contributed generously to this trend. Among the individuals and organizations who came to be placed on the Watch List by the CIA were numerous domestic peace organizations, such as the American Friends Service Committee; political activists, scientists and scientific organizations, such as the Federation of American Scientists; academics with a special interest in the Soviet Union; authors, such as Edward Albee and John Steinbeck; businesses, such as Fred A. Praeger Publishers; and Americans who frequently travelled to or corresponded with the Soviet Union, including one member of the Rockefeller family.

The Watch List, in short, originated with a relatively few names which might reasonably be expected to lead to genuine foreign intelligence or counterintelligence information, but expanded well beyond the initial guidelines into the area of essentially domestic intelligence.

Random Selection—The documentary record of the CIA suggests that a very large percentage of the letters that were opened in the course of the New York project were to or from individuals who were not on the Watch List at all. One CIA memorandum points out that the "New York Security officers who opened the mail selected about 75 percent at random, and the remaining 25 percent was on the basis of a watchlist compiled by the CI Staff." While there is some evidence that the percentage of random openings may have decreased in the later years of the project, it always represented a significant proportion of the mail that was opened.

The CIA mail "interceptors" were not foreign intelligence or counterintelligence experts. One of the CIA agents who opened the mail in this project testified that other than memorizing the Watch List, he received no instruction at all as to what categories of mail to select. When asked the basis for opening mail to or from people who were not on the Watch List. this agent replied: "It might be according to individual taste, if you will, your own reading about current events. ... I personally used to like to do Central and South America items [that were missent by the Post Office]. ... [Y]ou never knew what you would hit." He added: "We would try to get a smattering of everything, maybe the academic field or travel agencies or something. I don't recall a specific instruction. I kind of place that under our individual tastes."

Indeed, this lack of instruction appears to have been a conscious policy of the Office of Security. A CIA memorandum states that the Inspector General's Office, in its review of the New York project in the early 1960's, "took the position that the security officers who were selecting the mail to be opened should have some understanding of headquarters requirements so that their selection could be halfway informed on the basis of areas of interest.... [But the Office of Security] had a paper by [a CIA officer] which said, in effect, that the present system of purely random selection was best and that it wasn't necessary to develop any sort of coordinated approach.... The Office of Security apparently sees no reason why they should have their personnel trained in intelligence objectives."

The large random element in the selection process and the lack of formal intelligence training on the part of the agents who opened the mail combined with the "domestic" evolution of the Watch List to push the project even further from the original foreign intelligence and counterintelligence goals articulated in 1952. Over the twenty-year course of mail opening, the mail that was intercepted included that of many prominent Americans, including at least three United States Senators and a Congressman, one Presidential candidate and numerous educational, business, and civil rights leaders.

The "Special Category Items" File. — The occasional random interception of politicians' mail created a situation for the CIA which was potentially very embarrassing. In August 1971, the selection and opening of a letter from United States Senator Frank Church so concerned a new chief of the CI Staff "Project" that he wrote the Deputy Chief of Counterintelligence, Raymond Rocca: "In order to avoid possible accusations that the CIA engages in the monitoring of the mail of members of the U.S. government, the C/CI may wish to consider the advisability of (a) purging such mail from the files and machine records of the Project and (b) authorizing the issuance of instructions to the 'collectors' to cease the acquisition of such materials." He added: "Instructions would have to define in specific terms what categories of elected or appointed personnel were to be encompassed, and whether they extended to private mail communications." Several months later, in December 1971, a new policy for the handling of such mail was confirmed. An internal CIA memorandum dated December 22, 1971, reads in part:

> In accordance with a new policy confirmed yesterday .... Project HTLINGUAL will handle henceforth as follows items originated by or addressed to Elected or Appointed Federal and Senior State Officials (e.g. Governor, Lt. Governor, etc) :
>
> a. No officials in above categories are to be watchlisted;
>
> b. No instructions to be issued to interceptors specifically requesting or forbidding the acquisition of items in cited categories; thus acquisition will be left entirely to chance;
>
> . . . . . .
>
> d. No special-category items shall be carded for inclusion in the HTLINGUAL Machine Records System;
>
> e. Dissemination of special-category items will be at the discretion of DC/CI (and/or C/CI) only,
>
> f. All special-category items will be filed in a separate file titled "SPECIAL-CATEGORY ITEMS", which will be kept in C/CI/Project's safe ...

The new policy, therefore, did not prohibit the opening of letters to or from political figures; it simply created a special filing system for their mail. By the end of the project in 1973, the "Special-Category Items" file contained approximately ten photographs or summaries of correspondence to or from Senators Church and Edward M. Kennedy, one Congressman, and one Governor of an American territory. Because the master index was on microfilm, the analysts were unable to purge all references to those politicians whose correspondence had been opened prior to December 1971.

2. Value of the Product

Foreign Intelligence and Counterintelligence.—There has been considerable debate among CIA officials over the value of the product from the New York operation to the Agency's foreign intelligence and counterintelligence mission. James Angleton, who as Chief of the CI Staff was in charge of the project, was one of its most vocal supporters. He has testified that the New York project "was probably the most important overview [of Soviet intelligence activities] that counterintelligence had." In a February 1973 memorandum for Director Schlesinger, Angleton, contending against termination, summarized some of the benefits to the CIA which resulted from the New York project as follows:

A. The mail intercept Project ... provides information about Soviet-American contacts and insight into Soviet realities and the scope of Soviet interests in the academic, economic, scientific and governmental fields unavailable from any other source. The Project adds a dimension and a perspective to Soviet interests and activities which cannot be obtained from the limited resources available to this Agency and the FBI.

B. The Project is particularly productive in supporting both the Agency and the FBI in pursuing investigative and operational leads to visiting Soviet students, exchange scientists, academicians and intellectuals, trade specialists and experts from organizations such as . . .

C. In many instances the Project provides the only means of detecting continuing contact between [Soviet] controlled exchange students and Americans.

D. The Project provides information otherwise unavailable about the Soviet contacts and travel of Americans to the Soviet Union. . . .

E. Project material recorded for 18 years gives basic information about Soviet individuals and institutions useful to the analyst looking for specific leads and in gauging trends in Soviet interests and policies.

This highly favorable assessment of the value of the product from HTLINGUAL contrasts sharply with the views of many other CIA officers. In a 1961 review of the project by the Inspector General's Office, for example it was written:

The SR (Soviet Union) Division is the project's largest customer in the Agency. Information from the CI Staff flows to the SR Support Branch and from there to the operational branches. It may include operational leads, such as the identities of individuals planning to work or reside in the USSR, or items of interest on conditions inside the country. In our interviews we received the impression that few of the operational leads have ever been converted into operations, and that no tangible operational benefits had accrued to SR Division as a result of this project. We have noted elsewhere that the project should be carefully evaluated, and the value of the product to SR Division should be one of the primary considerations.

A second internal review eight years later, in 1969, was no more enthusiastic. John Glennon, a former member of the Inspector General's staff which conducted this review, wrote:

. . . Although at one time this material was useful in Soviet legal travel operations and as positive information on Soviet internal economic and political matters, we find that the Clandestine Service has little interest in it now. Most of the officers we spoke to find it occasionally helpful, but there is no recent evidence of it having provided significant leads or information which have had positive operational results. The Office of Security has found the material to be of very little value. The positive intelligence from this source is meager.

In general, he noted that "the take from this program . . . is of little value to this Agency . . ." When Mr. Glennon was asked in recent public hearings whether he still agreed with this basic conclusion, he responded that, if anything, the product was probably even less valuable than he indicated in 1969. Howard Osborn, who was Director of Security from 1964 to 1974, and therefore responsible for the role played by the Office of Security during those years, agreed that his office received no value from the product. He publicly testified that "[w]e got no benefit from it at all.... The product was worthless."

Even Richard Helms, who was personally involved with the New York mail project on a decisional level from mid-1954 through the days immediately prior to the 1973 termination, was tepid in his evaluation of the project's value to the Agency. Of the product from 215,820 opened letters and nearly three million photographed envelopes, he said: I thought from time to time that the Agency got useful information out of it."

Domestic Intelligence. — Given the nature of the selection criteria, it is not surprising that a significant — perhaps the primary — portion of the product related to domestic, rather than foreign, intelligence concerns. The 1961 review of the project, for example, characterized the product as "largely domestic CI/CE [counterintelligence and counterespionage]." This representation was repeated in the 1969 Inspector General's report and, as developed more fully below, by numerous senior Agency officials in the early 1970's.

Only to the extent that the CIA's mission was perceived as encompassing "domestic CI/CE" matters could the Agency itself benefit from this type of information. Thus, Gordon Stewart, the Inspector General whose staff reviewed the New York project and found its positive intelligence value "meager," conceded that the project in 1969 may logically have been valuable in terms of the domestic surveillance activities the Agency was then conducting. He testified that in the late 1960's and early 1970's:

... we were involved in compiling files on subversives in this country, the youth, and so on. And there was an enormous amount of pressure being placed on the Agency by the White House to develop, if possible, a connection between subversive organizations in this country and some external groups, say the Communists or Moscow or something of that sort. It would seem to me to be logical that if that is what you were doing, maybe at one phase this project had been regarded as useful to the Agency.

But it is questionable whether analysis of foreign influence on domestic political activity is within the CIA's mandate at all. Such domestic counterintelligence concerns are an aspect of internal security, which is the responsibility of the FBI, not the CIA.

Value to the FBI—The Bureau did in fact receive a great deal of product from the New York operation: for all but three years between 1958 and 1973 the FBI actually received more copies or summaries of opened letters than did any single component of the CIA. In view of the large quantity of disseminations to the Bureau and the largely domestic nature of the product generally, it is understandable that CIA officials assumed that the Bureau benefited significantly from the Agency's coverage. Angleton stressed the importance of this project to the Bureau's operations when he summarized its value for Director Schlesinger in 1973; this point was noted in both of the Inspector General staff's reviews and in the testimony of Howard Osborn and Richard Helms. Several CIA officials, convinced that the project was more valuable to the FBI than to the Agency itself, even recommended that the Bureau should assume operational responsibility for it.

Ironically, however, the testimony of Bureau officials suggests that the CIA may have mistaken quantity of product for quality. It is undeniable that the FBI received some benefit from HTLINGUAL. 70a But one senior Bureau official declared that any benefit received by the FBI had to be evaluated in light of the fact that the product was received gratuitously, with the expenditure of neither money nor manpower. He stated that the project did not provide leads to the identification of a single foreign illegal agent and that much of the product received by the FBI was worthless.

In short, it is not clear that HTLINGUAL made any substantial contribution to the CIA's legitimate foreign intelligence and counterintelligence mission or even to its questionable domestic intelligence activities; and while Agency officials assumed that the FBI benefitted greatly from their coverage, this assumption probably overestimated the actual value to the Bureau.

C. Internal Authorization and Controls

Unlike the FBI mail opening programs, the CIA's New York project was extremely de-centralized. It germinated and evolved without the prior approval of the Director of Central Intelligence at critical stages. It continued through the tenure of at least two Directors who were apparently not even informed of its existence. Because it had been exempted from the usual approval system, many of the division heads who would normally have to approve any proposed project of this scope were also never briefed and consequently had no opportunity to challenge the necessity or wisdom of the project. It was reviewed by disinterested agency components only twice during its twenty year history, in neither case extensively, and although both these reviews concluded that the operation was seriously flawed it continued until 1973, when largely external events forced its continuance.

1. Authorizations by Directors of Central Intelligence

Allen Dulles.—The New York mail project was initiated, and the first contact with the Post Office made, without the apparent authorization—or even the knowledge—of Director Allen Dulles. As noted above, two CIA officers of the Office of Security and the SR Division met with a representative of the International Division of the Post Office in July 1952 to secure statistics on the mail flow between the United States and the Soviet Union. It was largely on the basis of this overview that the Office of Security and the SR Division determined that further contact with Postal officials were desirable. CIA documents relating to the early stages of the project, however, make no reference to informing Director Dulles until September 30 of that year. In a memorandum on that date, the Chief of the SR Division wrote the Deputy Director for Plans that "[i]t is requested . . . that DCI be informed of I&S and SR Division intention to initiate action looking toward the most expeditious accumulation of information on all letter envelopes or covers passing through the New York City Post Office originating in the Soviet Union or destined for the Soviet Union."

While subsequent documents reflect no explicit authorization from the DCI—nor even whether or not the DCI was informed of the mail cover operation as per the September 30 request of the Chief of the SR Division—further contacts were made with the Post Office and the first phase of the project became operational in February 1953.

The first unambiguous documentary indication that the DCI was advised of what was then referred to as SRPOINTER is not found until January 4, 1954. On that date Sheffield Edwards, the Director of Security, wrote to Director Dulles to summarize the anticipated value of the project, to explain the problem regarding the reluctance of postal officials to cooperate with the planned expansion of the project, and to request the Director to meet with the Postmaster General and the President to secure their approval for photographing the exteriors of the envelopes. At this stage, the project was essentially a mail cover operation. No reference was made in that or a subsequent January 1954 memorandum to Director Dulles to the possibility of actually opening the mail.

The only written approvals for the project as it subsequently developed during Dulles' tenure appear to be those of Richard Helms and the Acting Deputy Director for Plans. In December 1955, Helms approved the concept as outlined by James Angleton; in February 1960, he approved establishment of the TSD laboratory. The approval of the Acting Deputy Director for Plans was obtained for funding in March 1956.

While it is unclear whether Dulles was ever informed about the laboratory, he was apparently at least made aware of the fact that mail was being opened. In May 1956, he received a memorandum from James Angleton in which Angleton noted that "for some time selected openings have been conducted and the contents examined."

John McCone.—CIA documents do not show that Director John McCone was ever informed about the project. McCone himself testified that he was unaware of it, and his testimony is consistent with that of James Angleton and Howard Osborn.

Admiral Raborn.—There is no evidence that indicates Director Admiral Raborn was ever made aware of the New York project.

Richard Helms.—The next Director who clearly knew about the New York mail opening project was Richard Helms, who became Acting Director in 1965 and Director in 1966. Helms had been involved with the project since 1954, and, as noted above, had personally approved the expansion of the project to include larger scale mail openings in December 1955 and a laboratory in February 1960. Numerous CIA documents reflect his continuing knowledge of and concern about the project during his tenure as Director.

James Schlesinger.—James Schlesinger, who succeeded Helms as Director in 1973, also was aware of the project. It was his order in February 1973 that led to its termination after two decades of operation.

2. Exemption from Normal Approval System

The New York mail opening project was initially approved by Helms and the ADD/P outside and it remained outside the normal channels for approval and review of CIA projects. As stated in the 1961 Inspector General's report:

> The activity cannot be called a "project" in the usual sense, because it was never processed through the approval system and has no separate funds.

The various components involved have been carrying out their responsibilities as part of their normal staff functions. Specific DD/P approval was obtained for certain budgetary practices in 1956 and for the establishment of a TSD lab in 1960, but the normal programming procedures have not been followed for the project as a whole . . . .

When the first request for formal approval had been submitted to Helms in November 1955, a branch chief of the CI staff suggested to ,James Angleton that "in view of the sensitivity of this project, steps should be taken to have this proposed project approved by the Director without recourse to the normal channels for presentation of projects." The Director himself apparently never formally authorized the project, but the thrust of the branch chief's recommendation was followed. As Angleton later explained, when a typical project "is conceived, it might cut across many jurisdictions to begin with, . . . different geographic divisions and so on, so there would have to be a signoff by the various components, and then it would go before a project review board [whose] members would be drawn from many parts of the clandestine services, and . . . you would have this tremendous opening up of the activity to a great number of people. . . . That is the reason why I think it was excepted from [the usual approval system], and that way it short-circuited the normal project approval process."

Because of the perceived sensitivity of the project, in short, the CI Staff did not want those Agency components with no "need to know" to become aware of it. The security of the operation was enhanced by this exemption but the opportunity for critical evaluation by disinterested division heads was lost.

3. Administrative Controls

Internal Review and Evaluation. — In part because of its exemption from the normal approval system, administrative control over the New York project was lax. It was not a project at all in the formal sense, so there was no mechanism for periodic internal review to determine whether or not its goals were being achieved. During its twenty-year history, the project was reviewed by disinterested Agency components only twice — in 1961, and again in 1969. Both of these reviews were limited: the first review was part of an evaluation of Office of Security Operations, and so did not encompass the roles played by the CI Staff and TSD; the second review encompassed only the role of the CI Staff.

The Inspector General's staff, which conducted both reviews, concluded that if the project was to continue at all, a more complete evaluation or a mechanism for periodic evaluation of the project was crucial. Specifically, the 1961 study recommended that: "The DD/P and the DD/S direct a coordinated evaluation of this project, with particular emphasis on costs, potential and substantive contributions to the Agency's Mission." And in 1969 the Inspector General's staff wrote that "[f]inally — and most important — a schedule for regular re-examination and re-evaluation of the product of the project and of its management, especially with respect to its security, should be established and adhered to."

Neither of these recommendations was implemented. The only response to the 1961 recommendation was a five-page summary of the project's mechanics and results by the Director of Security. This summary was apparently felt to constitute a sufficient evaluation, although there is no evidence that the Soviet Division or the FBI — the entities that were the primary recipients of the project's product — were ever asked to contribute their respective evaluations. In the case of the 1969 review, the Inspector General did discuss the study's major findings with then-Director Richard

Helms, who, according to the Inspector General, "listened intently, as I recall, and that was it." The system of regular re-evaluation which had been recommended was not adopted.

Administrative Problems. — The primary reason that these two studies concluded that an improved system for evaluation of the project was so essential was their common finding that, in the words of the Inspector General's staff member who conducted the 1969 review, the project "was poorly handled ... administratively and operationally." The 1961 study determined, for example, that it was impossible to analyze the project in terms of costs versus benefits to the Agency because costs were unknown: "The annual cost of this activity cannot be estimated accurately because both administration and operations have always been decentralized. The costs are budgeted by the contributing components as a part of their regular operating programs." It therefore recommended "that exact cost figures be developed to permit the Agency management to evaluate the activity."

In addition, these studies found that the decentralization and limited knowledge of the project within the Agency inhibited maximum exploitation of the product that was generated. The 1961 study noted that "[t]here is no coordinated procedure for processing information received through the program; each component has its own system. ... The same material could thus be recorded in several different indices, but there is no assurance that specific items would be caught in ordinary name traces." In the 1969 review, it was suggested that the product might be useful to some Agency components that did not even know about the project.

Even among those components that did receive product from the New York project, there was no procedure for regular feedback to the CI Staff analysts as to what types of product were considered to be valuable. The CI Staff project chief has testified that he may have received a "chance comment" from people in consumer components, but he was not regularly informed about which kinds of material were or were not useful.

One of the most serious administrative problems was that no single person with a knowledge of the CIA's intelligence and counterintelligence requirements was in direct control of the project. As the Inspector General's staff wrote in 1961:

> Probably the most obvious characteristic of the project is the diffusion of authority. Each unit is responsible for its own interests and in some areas there is little coordination.
>
> ... There is no single point in the Agency to which one might look for policy and operational guidance on the project as a whole. Contributing to this situation is the fact that all of the units involved are basically staff rather than command units, and they are accustomed to working in environments somewhat detached from the operational front lines.
>
> ... The greatest disadvantages are (a) there can be no effective evaluation of the project if no officer is concerned with all its aspects, and (b) there is no central source of policy guidance in a potentially embarrassing situation.

This theme was reiterated in the 1969 report:

If it is decided that CIA should continue to operate the mail intercept project, we believe that several steps should be taken to improve the management of the program and its effectiveness. Among these is the eventual assignment of a chief to the project who has some depth of experience in operations, especially counterintelligence operations, in order to bring to bear on the analysis of the material more seasoned judgment of its intelligence and counterintelligence value.

Despite these recommendations for more centralized control over the project by more experienced personnel, the project remained diffuse and informed guidance was almost non-existent.

Mail was opened and the contents analyzed and disseminated, five days a week for nearly twenty years, without a structure for the systematic evaluation of the project, without its true cost being known, without the effective exploitation of potential intelligence and counterintelligence benefits, and without any centralized coordination or guidance by a single officer trained in intelligence and counterintelligence operations. It is at least reasonable to suggest that if prior approval — and periodic reapproval — at the highest level of the Agency had been required, its defects would have been recognized and its momentum checked before 1973.

D. External Authorizations

The New York project lacked a formal structure for authorization by government officials outside as well as inside the CIA: it was never authorized in writing by any such official and the pattern of oral approval is both capricious and obscure. Placed in the light most favorable to the Agency, the CIA obtained the prior oral approval of a Postmaster General for the photographing of envelope exteriors in 1954, and the implied, post facto permission of two Postmasters Genera], one Attorney General, and one President for both the mail opening and the mail cover aspects of the operation. But the Cabinet officers who were allegedly informed of the mail openings deny such knowledge — in one case because the official acknowledged that he did not want to know and did not believe that he could or should control Agency projects that affected his own Department. In the case of the President, no documentary record of the briefing exists and the CIA official who allegedly informed him concedes that there is only a "possibility" that he "mentioned" it.

Even by its own accounting, the CIA supplied no information about this project to four Postmasters General, seven Attorneys General, and three Presidents under whom it continued. In at least one instance, knowledge of the project was consciously withheld from a Postmaster General; in another instance, a President, whether knowingly or negligently, was misled about the Agency's mail opening activities, and his apparent refusal to authorize use of this technique went unheeded.

1. Postmasters General

Arthur E. Summerfield. — Arthur Summerfield, Postmaster General during the Eisenhower Administration, was informed of the New York mail project in 1954, and, according to CIA memoranda, assented to the photographing of mail by CIA agents in connection with this project. There is no indication, however, that he approved, or was even advised of, the actual opening of mail by the Agency after that became the primary objective of the project in 1955.

As discussed in the project summary above, the first phase of the mail opening program — hand-copying information from envelope exteriors — had begun in February 1953 with cooperation from two Chief Postal Inspectors, Clifton Garner and David Stephens. But when Agency officials recommended in late 1953 that the use of photography rather than hand-copying would enable a greater volume of mail to be covered, postal authorities refused to cooperate without the express approval of the Postmaster General. A January 1954 memorandum, from Director of Security

Sheffield Edwards to DCI Dulles, suggested that a meeting between Director Dulles and Summerfield was necessary to resolve the problem.

The meeting between Dulles and Postmaster General Summerfield finally occurred about five months later, on May 17, 1954. Richard Helms, then Chief of Operations in the Plans Directorate, as well as Chief Postal Inspector Stephens and two other postal officials, were also in attendance. The only record of this meeting, a contemporaneous memorandum to Sheffield Edwards from Helms, reads in part:

> ... As regards SRPOINTER, the Director told the group how valuable we had found efforts in this field. He then went on to say that we would like to photograph the backs and fronts of first-class mail from the Soviet and satellite areas.

> ... (When he had finished his exposition, the Postmaster General did not comment specifically but it was clear that he was in favor of giving us any assistance which he could) . . .

The Postmaster General's implied approval was apparently for photographing mail only. Richard Helms, moreover, has recently testified that: "It is my opinion today from reading the records that [Summerfield] was not told the mail was being opened or would be opened." Nor is there any documentary or testimonial evidence that suggests that Summerfield was ever advised of mail openings at any time after that became the primary objective of the project in late 1955.

J. Edward Day.—J. Edward Day, who was Postmaster General under President Kennedy, from January 1961 to August 1963, also met with Director Dulles and others in regard to the New York mail intercept project. The evidence as to whether or not he was informed that mail was actually opened, however, tends to be contradictory.

In January 1961 a new administration was installed in Washington. As Mr. Helms explained:

> President Kennedy had just been sworn in. It was also a new party. The Republicans had had the White House and the executive branch before, and now the Democratic Party had it, and I think Mr. Dulles felt under the circumstances that it was desirable to speak to the Postmaster General because if [the New York project] was to go forward, we needed some support for it.

On January 27, 1961, less than one week after Day assumed the position of Postmaster General, the Deputy Chief of the Counterintelligence Staff wrote to Richard Helms to give him general background information for a proposed briefing of the Postmaster General and to advise him that:

> There is no record in any conversation with any official of the Post Office Department that we have admitted opening mail. All conversations have involved examination of exteriors. It seems to us quite apparent that they must feel sure that we are opening mail. . . .

> It is suggested that if the new Postmaster General asks if we open any mail, we confirm that some mail is opened. He should be informed, however, that no other person in the Post Office Department has been so informed. The reasons for this suggestion are (a) Despite all of our care in the selection and clearance of personnel for a knowledge of this project, at

some point, someone is likely to blow it. (b) The Postmaster General will have a better understanding of the importance of the project in the event we desire to expand it ....

On February 15, 1961, Director Allen Dulles, Richard Helms, and Cornelius Roosevelt, then Chief of TSD, met with the new Postmaster General in his office. What transpired at that meeting is a subject of controversy. The only contemporaneous written record is a memorandum dated February 16, one day after the meeting, from Richard Helms back to the Deputy Chief of the Counterintelligence Staff. Helms wrote:

We gave him [Day] the background, development, and current status, withholding no relevant details.

After we had made our presentation, the Postmaster General requested that we be joined by the Chief Postal Inspector, Mr. Henry Montague. This gentleman confirmed what we had had to say about the project and assured the Postmaster General that the matter had been handled securely, quietly, and that there had been no "reverberations." The meeting ended with the Postmaster General expressing the opinion that the project should be allowed to continue and that he did not want to be informed in any greater detail on its handling. He agreed that the fewer people who knew about it, the better.

While Helms cannot specifically recall now whether Day was informed of the fact of mail openings, he strongly suggests that Day must have been so informed. Helms recently testified as follows:

As I say, "withholding no relevant details." I assume when I wrote that I meant what I wrote. . . . I cannot imagine what the point of holding it back from him would have been. We were going down to get his permission to continue the operation, and after all, it was his Post Office, if we had lied to him, and then he had discovered through his Chief Postal Inspector that something else was going on, that would not have been a very wise way to behave, it seems to me.

Day's version of these events differs from Helms. Apparently Day did not believe that it was entirely "his Post Office," for in regard to sensitive CIA operations, even those that touched on postal matters, be testified: "It wasn't my responsibility. The CIA had an entirely different kind of responsibility than I did. And what they had to do, they had to do. And I had no control over them." 103 Because of this perception of the role of the Postmaster General vis-a-vis the Agency, he did not wish to know the details of the New York project. According to his account of the meeting, he interrupted Mr. Dulles before being informed that the project involved the opening of mail. Day stated:

. . . Mr. Dulles, after some preliminary visiting and so on, said that he wanted to tell me something very secret, and I said, "do I have to know about it?" And he said, "No."

I said, "My experience is that where there is something that is very secret, it is likely to leak out, and anybody that knew about it is likely to be suspected of having been part of leaking it out, so I would rather not know anything about it."

What additional things were said in connection with him building up to that, I don't know. But I am sure ... that I was not told anything about opening mail.

Day's general recollection is given some support by an internal CIA memorandum written more than a decade later by the Chief of the CI Staff Project (HTLINGUAL). This memorandum, written in August 1971 and attached to Helms' February 16,1961 summary, reads:

> The wording of this memo leaves some doubt as to the degree to which Day was made witting. I tend to feel that he was briefed on the "mail surveillance" aspect and NOT the clandestine opening. I find some confirmation in the sentence in para. 2 "This gentleman (i.e. the Inspector Montague) confirmed what we had to say about the Project ..." Montague was NOTWITTING [sic] OF THE clandestine opening and therefore the subject of the briefing of Day must have been mail surveillance only.

Thus, it cannot be definitely said that Day knew—or did not know—of the mail openings. All that is clear is that an Agency memorandum suggests that the CIA was prepared to inform the Postmaster General of this activity, that Helms at the time believed Day had been provided with enough of the "relevant details" to interpret his reaction as generally approving the continuance of the project; and that Day's general belief was that the Postmaster General had no control over and should defer to the Agency's covert operations, even those which might involve the United States mails—he "would rather not know anything about it."

John A. Gronouski.—There is no claim by the CIA that Mr. Gronouski, who was Postmaster General from August 1963 until November 1965, was ever informed of the CIA's New York mail intercept project. According to one internal CIA document, consideration was given to the idea of informing him in 1965 at the time of the hearings of the Senate Judiciary Subcommittee on Administrative Practice and Procedure. This subcommittee, chaired by Senator Edward V. Long of Missouri, was investigating the use of mail covers and various other techniques by federal agencies, and CIA officials were seriously concerned about "the dangers inherent in Long's subcommittee activities to the security of the Project's operations . . ." The idea of informing Gronouski was quickly rejected, however, "in view of various statements by Gronouski before the Long subcommittee." Since Gronouski had agreed with the Subcommittee that tighter administrative controls on mail covers were necessary and generally supported the principle of the sanctity of the mail, it is reasonable to infer that CIA officials assumed he would not be sympathetic to the technique of mail opening. Such an inference is supported by the next sentence in the memorandum which reflects this conversation: "[Thomas] Karamessines agreed with this thought and suggested that, in his opinion, the President would be more inclined to go along with the idea of the operation."

Lawrence F. O'Brien.—There is no claim by the CIA that Mr. O'Brien, who was Postmaster General from 1965 to 1968, was ever informed of the project.

W. Marvin Watson.—Similarly, there is no suggestion that Mr. Watson, who held the office of Postmaster General in 1968 and 1969, was ever told of the project.

Richard Helms has testified that he "never felt any need or compulsion to talk to Gronouski or O'Brien or Watson."

Winton M. Blount. — The next Postmaster General briefed about the New York mail intercept project was Winton Blount, who served in that office from the first days of the Nixon Administration in 1969 until October 1971. As with the CIA's briefing of Edward Day, however, it is not clear whether Blount was specifically informed about the mail opening aspect of the operation.

At least two reasons appear to have motivated Richard Helms, now Director of Central Intelligence, to seek a meeting with Postmaster General Blount about the New York project. First, he was strongly urged to do so by William Cotter, a former CIA employee who had been appointed Chief Postal Inspector in April 1969. In Cotter's capacity as Assistant Special Agent in Charge of the Office of Security's Manhattan Field Office during the mid-1950's, he had become aware of the Agency's mail opening project, and although he had no direct connection with the project he knew it continued during the 1960's. As Chief Postal Inspector, he was the only postal official who was aware of the CIA's mail openings, and since his responsibilities included guaranteeing the sanctity of the mail, he was uncomfortable with his knowledge. Partly because Cotter felt bound by his secrecy agreement with the Agency, however, he did not inform the Postmaster General about HTLINGUAL, nor did he initially take any steps to terminate the project.

Cotter's discomfort increased in January 1971 when he received a letter from Dr. Jeremy Stone, Director of the Federation of American Scientists, in which Stone inquired whether the Post Office ever permitted any federal agency to open first class letter mail. Recognizing one of the names on the association's letterhead to be another former CIA employee who was also knowledgeable about the project, Cotter feared that Stone's inquiry may have been based on information supplied by this former agent. He forwarded a copy of the letter to Howard Osborn, then the CIA's Director of Security, and requested a meeting with Helms to discuss his concern about embarrassment to the Agency and to himself if the project were publicly revealed. Helms subsequently did meet with Cotter, who urged him to discuss the project with the Postmaster General. As Cotter later testified:

> I felt . . . by getting the Postmaster General briefed by the CIA, the most senior people in the project, appropriate legal guidance could be obtained from the chief law officer, the Attorney General, and by pushing up to that arena if the project were unlawful I presumed it would have been stopped. But my concern was to get the top people aware of the project.

In addition to pressure from Cotter, the imminent reorganization of the Post Office also motivated Helms to arrange a briefing of Postmaster General Blount. In mid-1971, the Post Office was to become the Postal Service, and he felt that the consequent organization changes might have an adverse effect on the security of the New York operation.

Before meeting with the Postmaster General, Helms first spoke with Attorney General Mitchell. At this meeting, which is discussed in greater detail below, Helms recalls that he requested Mitchell's advice "as to whether this thing should be taken up with Mr. Blount because of [the Post Office reorganization]." According to Helms, Mitchell encouraged him to brief the Postmaster General, and a meeting was set up between Mr. Blount and Mr. Helms for June 2, 1971.

The written record of the Blount-Helms meeting on June 2 consists of a "Memorandum for the Record" written by James Angleton which described Helms' comments to top level CIA officials, including Angleton, about his recent briefings of the Attorney General and the Postmaster General. In regard to the Blount briefing, this memorandum reads as follows:

The DCI then indicated that yesterday, 2 June 1971, he had seen Postmaster General Blount. Mr. Blount's reaction ... was entirely positive regarding the operation and its continuation. He opined that "nothing needed to be done," and rejected a momentarily held thought of his to have someone review the legality of the operation as such a review would, of necessity, widen the circle of witting persons. Mr. Helms explained to the PMG that Mr. Cotter, then Chief Postal Inspector, has been aware of the operation for a considerable period of time by virtue of having been on the staff of CIA's New York Field Office. Mr. Helms showed the Postmaster General a few selected examples of the operation's product, including an item relating to Eldridge Cleaver, which attracted the PM's special interest.

Helms' subsequent testimony generally supports the accuracy of this memorandum. On the question of whether or not Blount was informed that the New York project involved mail opening, he testified that "[i]t is my recollection that I told him we were opening mail in New York."

Blount recalls the meeting with Helms, but does not believe that he was informed about the mail opening aspects of the project. In public session, Mr. Blount testified:

Well, as I recall, Mr. Helms explained to me about a project that he told me had been going on for a great number of years. I don't know whether he said 15 years or what, but there was some indication in my mind that this had been going on for at least 15 years, that it was an ongoing project. It was a project of great sensitivity and great importance to the national security of this country and that he wanted to inform me about it.

... [M]y best recollection is, he told me this was a project in which the Post Office was cooperating with the CIA, that there were a couple of postal employees in New York City that I believe he told me were the only ones who really were involved or know about this project, that the way in which it operated was that the postal employee would remove from the mail stream letters going to the Soviet Union and give it to two or three CIA employees and whatever they did with it, it was reintroduced into the mail stream the next day. That's about the ending of my recollection.

He added that he did not recall either asking Helms what was done with the mail or being informed by him that the mail was opened by CIA agents. While he did recall that Eldridge Cleaver's name was "mentioned," he did not believe that he was shown samples of Cleaver's opened mail or that Helms indicated in any way that Cleaver's mail had been opened.

On the statement in Angleton's memorandum that he "rejected a momentarily held thought of his to have someone review the legality of the operation", Blount agreed that he considered asking the General Counsel of that Post Office for a legal opinion, but insisted that this consideration was not based on his knowledge or assumption that mail was being opened. Whatever doubts he had about the legality of the operation described by Helms were assuaged when Helms informed him that he had seen or was about to see the Attorney General on this matter. Blount does not recall, however, ever discussing the legality — or any other aspect of the project — with the Attorney General personally, he accepted Helms' statement that Mitchell was knowledgeable about the project and "decided to let the Attorney General handle the legality of it."

Blount does not recall taking any action on the basis of his briefing by Helms; he made no further inquiries of the CIA or within his own Department about the conduct of the mail project and did not raise the matter with any other Cabinet officer or the President. As he later testified, "[M]y attitude was that if it is legal, I wanted to do what we could do to cooperate with the Central Intelligence Agency on a matter they considered of highest priority to this country and that dealt with national security."

Elmer T. Klassen. — There is no evidence that Elmer Klassen, who succeeded Blount as Postmaster General in 1971 and remained in that position through the termination of the project in 1973, was ever briefed on any aspect of the New York project.

2. Chief Postal Inspectors

The various roles of the Chief Postal Inspectors in regard to the New York mail intercept operation have been alluded to above. It is sufficient here to note that while all of the men who held this office during the course of the project Clifton Garner (until 1953); David Stephens (1953 to 1961) ; Henry Montague (1961 to 1969) ; William Cotter (1969 to 1975) -- were apparently aware of the mail cover aspects, only one — William Cotter — clearly knew that mail was also being opened by the CIA.

Garner had initially been contacted in November 1952 by CIA officials in the Offices of Operations and Security and apparently consented to the first survey of mail between the United States and the Soviet Union in New York. Montague helped implement this survey and the early operation of the project in 1953 in his position as Postal Inspector in Charge of the New York Region. As Chief Postal Inspector in 1961, he also attended part of the briefing of Edward Day by Allen Dulles, Richard Helms, and Cornelius Roosevelt. Stephens instructed Montague to cooperate with the CIA in regard to the project in 1953 and was present at the Summerfield briefing in May 1954. There is no evidence (or claim by the CIA) that any of these three men knew that the CIA project involved the opening of mail, however. As noted above, Montague has also testified that Stephens instructed him, and he in turn instructed the CIA agents who visited him in 1953, that mail opening would not be permitted.

William Cotter was therefore the first Chief Postal Inspector who was clearly aware of all aspects of the mail project. Despite his initial reluctance to take any action on the basis of his knowledge, Cotter was instrumental in arranging the Helms-Blount briefing in 1971 and ultimately in the termination of the project in 1973. His role in the project's termination is discussed below.

3. Attorneys General

There is no evidence in the record that any Attorney General before or after John Mitchell was ever informed about the CIA's New York project. At a minimum, Mitchell was briefed about certain CIA mail covers by Richard Helms on June 1, 1971, but as with the Day and Blount briefings, the evidence about Mitchell's knowledge of mail opening and the New York project specifically, tends to be contradictory.

The background for the Mitchell briefing has been described above: William Cotter, concerned about the letter he had received from Jeremy Stone and uncomfortable with his knowledge of the mail openings in New York, urged Richard Helms to discuss the operation with the Postmaster General; in addition, the imminent reorganization of the Post Office cast the future security of the project in doubt. Rather than go to the Postmaster General directly, Helms chose to consult first with the Attorney General, in part to seek Mitchell's opinion as to whether or not Mr. Blount should be informed. As Mr. Helms publicly explained,

> ... it was quite clear that [Mitchell] had a particular role for the President in sort of keeping an eye on intelligence matters and on covert action matters.... He was sort of, I think, a watchdog for the President, so I have consulted with Mr. Mitchell on a variety of the problems affecting the Agency over time that I would not have gone to the normal Attorney General about, nor would the normal Attorney General have been necessarily privy to these things.

According to a CIA memorandum dated June 3, 1971, two days after the June 1 meeting between the Director and the Attorney General, Helms told a group of ranking CIA officials that he had briefed Mitchell about the operation and "Mr. Mitchell fully concurred in the value of the operation and had no 'hang-ups' concerning it." Helms elaborated on this meeting with Mitchell in his recent public testimony, stating that he

> told him [Mitchell] about this operation, what it was doing for us, that it had been producing some information on foreign connections, dissidents, and terrorists, a subject in which he was intensely interested, and that we might have a problem when the U.S. Postal Service was founded. And I asked if it wouldn't be a good idea that I go and see the Postmaster General, Mr. Blount, and talk with him about this and see how he felt about it and to get some advice from him. And, it was my recollection that Mr. Mitchell acquiesced in this and said, "Go ahead and talk to Mr. Blount."

When asked whether or not he told Mitchell that the project involved the opening of mail, Helms replied: "... I don't recall whether I said specifically we are opening X numbers of letters. But the burden of my discussion with him, I don't see how it could have left any alternative in his mind because how do you find out what somebody is saying to another correspondent unless you have opened the letter?"

John Mitchell has acknowledged meeting with Helms on June 1, 1971, and recalls a discussion of "mail covers," but on the basis of his recollection denies that Helms told him mail was opened. He does not remember being informed of any of the details of the New York operation, and believes that even the discussion of mail covers was in relation to an intelligence operation distinct from one that would fit the description of the New York project. The former Attorney General testified that, as he recalled, "the discussion of the mail was ancillary to another discussion that was not extensive, and . . . it had to do with mail covers, or at least I assumed it [did] ..." He added that he had no recollection of Helms' asking his advice as to whether or not the Postmaster General should be briefed on any CIA project, and that the first time he became aware that the CIA had opened mail in the United States was when these operations were publicly revealed in 1974 and 1975.

James Angelton testified that he also met with John Mitchell during Mitchell's tenure as Attorney General, described the New York project to him, and showed him some samples of the product, specifically, a copy of a letter from Kathy Boudin. Angelton does not recall the possible date of such a meeting, however.

Mitchell does not recall ever having met with Angelton, or even having heard his name until recently. 4. Presidents

There is no documentary evidence that any President ever authorized the CIA's New York mail opening project. With the possible exception of Lyndon Johnson in 1967 or 1968, there is no CIA claim that any President was even informed of it. While proposals were made by CIA officials in 1954 and again in 1965 to advise the President of the existence of HTLINGUAL, it does not appear that these proposals were implemented. In the context of the so called "Huston Plan" deliberations, moreover, CIA officials actually withheld knowledge of the ongoing New York project from the President's representative and from President Nixon himself. And despite President Nixon's eventual refusal to authorize the use of "covert mail coverage" (mail opening) as an intelligence collection technique (after a brief period of approval), the CIA project continued without interruption for another two years.

1954 Proposals to Seek the Approval of President Eisenhower. — In a January 4, 1954 memorandum from Sheffield Edwards, then Director of Security, to Allen Dulles, Director of Central Intelligence, it was recommended that the Director and the Postmaster General (after having been himself briefed) meet "and then seek oral approval of [the] President." This recommendation was reiterated in a second memorandum from Edwards to Dulles eight days later.

In later years, it was assumed by some CIA officers that Dulles had in fact briefed President Eisenhower on the program. The 1969 review of the project by the Inspector General's staff, simply states, without citation: "It is believed that Mr. Dulles briefed President Eisenhower on this subject." Richard Helms has also testified that "I always assumed that Mr. Dulles, before we went to see Mr. Summerfield, had checked this out with President Eisenhower. I do not recall his ever specifically saying [that] to me, that was sort of an assumption on my part, that something of this importance he would have checked out and he would have proceeded on to his appointed task of speaking to the Postmaster General."

Summerfield himself had only been informed of the mail cover aspects of the project in 1954, however; the Agency apparently never returned to inform him that mail opening later became the primary program objective. Helms added, moreover, that he had never seen any documentary confirmation of a meeting between Director Dulles and the President in regard to the project. Beyond the proposals themselves and the later undocumented assumptions by CIA officials, there is no evidence that President Eisenhower was ever informed about any aspect of the New York operation.

1965 Proposal to Inform President Johnson. — In 1965, the Long Subcommittee hearings on the use of mail covers and other investigative techniques by federal agencies caused the Agency serious concern about possible Congressional discovery and revelation of the project. It is noted above that in September 1965, as a result of this concern, CIA officials briefly considered informing Postmaster General Gronouski of the project. When this proposal was rejected, presumably because Gronouski had cooperated extensively with the Subcommittee, Thomas Karamessines, then Acting Deputy Director for Plans, "suggested that, in his opinion, the President would be more inclined to go along with the idea of the operation."

Karamessines "gave instructions that steps should be taken to arrange to pass through McGeorge Bundy to the President after the Subcommittee has completed its investigation." Apparently, however, this was not clone. Mr. Bundy does not recall ever having been informed of the project; neither Thomas Karamessines nor Richard Helms knew of any attempt to inform Bundy so that he could in turn inform the President; and there is no documentary record of such an attempt.

The Helms-Johnson Meeting: 1967-1968. — Although it does not appear that President Johnson was contemporaneously informed about the mail project after the 1965 recommendation to do so, Richard Helms claims that he may have advised him about it in 1967 or 1968. Toward the end of President Johnson's term in office, the President instructed Helms to prepare a report detailing the truth or falsity of columnist Drew Pearson's allegation about CIA assassination attempts. Helms recalls that the President also asked him whether the CIA was engaged in any other operations that "might be regarded as sensitive." It is Helms' belief that they then "discussed two or three items, ... [and] it was at that time that I think I mentioned [the New York project]." When asked whether or not he indicated to the President that mail was opened in connection with the project, Helms said that "[i]f I discussed this with President Johnson I would not have deluded him by using one terminology to convey something else. I would have said, 'We are getting into Russian mail,' or something. I was not that kind of fellow with people." There are no CIA documents relating to this discussion, however, and Helms himself is not positive that it in fact occurred, only that "there was a possibility that I discussed ... this letter opening thing on that occasion."

Huston Plan: 1970. — During the summer of 1970, the so-called "Huston Plan" meetings and report presented the CIA with a clear opportunity to inform the President of their mail opening project. But this opportunity was apparently never taken.

As a result of his perceived need for more effective domestic intelligence, Richard Nixon instructed representatives of the major federal intelligence agencies to meet under the guidance of Tom Charles Huston and to prepare a series of options designed to achieve this goal. One of the options subsequently discussed at the four meetings that summer was the use of "covert mail coverage" (i.e. mail opening) directed against both foreign and domestic targets. Although the CIA's New York project was ongoing at the time, the CIA representatives at these meetings, James Angleton and Richard Ober, did not advise this group of intelligence experts about its existence, and the final report — to which Angleton and Ober contributed and which Richard Helms signed — was submitted to the President containing the statement that "covert coverage has been discontinued." At no time was either Huston, the President's representative, or the President himself informed that the CIA was then opening mail.

According to Angleton, the New York project was not revealed to the group because it was considered to be compartmented knowledge and such a revelation would serve "no useful purpose," especially in light of the security considerations which had been articulated by the National Security Agency's representative. 148 But he also conceded that neither Huston nor the President himself were told about the project in private.

Of the statement in the final report that all covert mail coverage had been discontinued, Richard Helms said:

. . . the only explanation I have for it was that this applied entirely to the FBI and had nothing to do with the CIA, that we never advertised to this Committee or told this Committee that this mail operation was going on, and there was no intention of attesting to a lie . . .

And if I signed this thing, then maybe I didn't read it carefully enough.

There was no intention to mislead or lie to the President.

Helms agreed, however, that on the face of the report the President could not have known that covert mail coverage in fact continued, and he stated that at no time did he personally ever inform President Nixon about the CIA's use of this technique in the New York project. The President, in short, was given a report — signed by Helms — which explicitly said mail opening had been discontinued when it had not.

On July 23, 1970, Tom Charles Huston wrote Director Helms that the President had approved the relaxation of restrictions on a number of the investigative techniques discussed in the final report. For the first time in the history of the CIA's mail project, the Agency had what appeared to be Presidential authorization for "covert mail coverage," although not specifically for the New York program, about which the President remained ignorant. But five days after Huston informed Helms of the President's approval, the authorization was withdrawn and Helms was asked to return the memorandum reflecting the original approval. Now the situation was reversed: a President had addressed the issue of the use of mail opening as an investigative technique and ultimately refused to endorse it. Despite the withdrawal of Presidential approval, however, the CIA did not terminate the New York project. The project continued for nearly three years after these events, and the CIA continued to open mail within the United States in the face of an apparent Presidential prohibition of this technique.

President Nixon's "General Awareness" of CIA Mail Covers but Not of Mail Openings. — Former President Nixon recently stated that he was aware of the CIA's use of mail covers but not of its mail opening operations. He explained:

While President, I remember being generally aware of the fact that the Central Intelligence Agency, acting without a warrant, both during and prior to my Administration, conducted mail covers of mail sent from within the United States to:

A. The Soviet Union; or

B. The People's Republic of China

However, I do not remember being informed that such mail covers included unauthorized mail openings.

He also noted that he did "not recall receiving information, while President, that any agency or employee of the United States Government, acting without a warrant, opened mail" in any program that would fit the description of the CIA's New York mail opening project or any other CIA or FBI mail opening project.

There is no claim in the documentary record or in the testimony of any CIA official that the Agency ever informed President Nixon about any aspect of the New

York project. Nor is there any claim that the President ever indicated to the CIA his approval of any aspect of this particular project, even the use of mail covers. Richard Helms, for example, testified in 1975 that he "never recall[ed] discussing [the New York mail opening project] with President Nixon," and added (before the former President made the comments quoted above) that "What President Nixon knew about it, I don't know to this day."

Dissemination of Information to the White Home. — According to a March 1971 CIA memorandum, sanitized information generated by the New York mail opening project was disseminated to the White House even after the President's July 1970 rejection of the use of this technique. This memorandum lists the types of information accumulated through the project, including data about "peace activists, anti-government groups, black radicals and other militant dissidents." It continues: "In all the above, HTLINGUAL provides the White House ... coverage of overseas contacts and activity of persons within the United States who are of critical concern from the viewpoint of internal national security, including bombing and terrorism."

At least one former White House official — John D. Ehrlichman — has testified that from his reading of the intelligence reports provided to the White House he was able to determine that mail was being intercepted. When asked whether he knew of a program of intercepting mail between the United States and Communist countries, Ehrlichman replied: "I knew that was going on because I had seen reports that cited those kinds of sources in connection with this, the bombings, the dissident activities" 156 He stated that he "assumed," but was not positive, that this was a CIA operation: "Maybe the way the things is [sic] couched, it is always obscurely put as to what the sources are, but it could have been the FBI for all I know." He did not know whether the President was aware of this program, however, and could not recall ever personally discussing the matter with him.

Ehrlichman added that he did not know of any conversation within the White House about the legality or propriety of such a program nor of any inquiry made by the White House.

The lack of a formal approval structure for HTLINGUAL outside, as well as inside the CIA, is plain: Cabinet officers were sometimes briefed, but much more frequently ignored (sometimes consciously so) ; no documentary record reflects the one possible "mention" of the project to a President; another President was misled; and the closest resemblance to a Presidential policy directive prohibiting mail opening went unheeded.

It is difficult to generalize from an inconsistent record, but these are among the conclusions that may be tentatively offered in regard to external authorization for the project: the agency desired external authority but was reluctant to ask for it, either for fear of refusal, out of concern with security, or simply because it was less complicated to maintain the status quo. If Cabinet officers were informed of mail openings, it was done so circuitously; only the minimum knowledge necessary to secure their approval was imparted. The officers who were briefed, for their part, apparently did not want to know the details, did not want to be held accountable, and deferred to the Agency on national security matters.

E. Termination of the Project

1. Proposed Termination: The 1969 Inspector General's Report

Four years before the actual termination of the project, the Inspector General's staff formally recommended that consideration be given to discontinuance. Its 1969 survey of HTLINGUAL had revealed that:

The principal customer is and has been the FBI ... [which] several years ago initiated a similar program to cover mail to and from Bloc countries. It discontinued the program because of the inherent sensitivity, but would dislike having us discontinue a similar one. We are sympathetic to the Bureau's position, but question whether their interest is sufficient justification for our assuming risk of most serious embarrassment.

This finding, coupled with the conclusion that the project was "of little value to this Agency," led the Inspector General's staff to recommend that the Director should negotiate with the FBI to take over the project or, in the event that the FBI should decline to assume responsibility, he should discontinue it.

Informally, the author of the 1969 report, John Glennon, had already discussed the possibility of an FBI takeover of the project with Sam Papich, Bureau liaison to the FBI, and he knew that there was virtually no chance the FBI would assume responsibility for it. According to Glennon, Papich told him "that the Bureau would not run it . . . and he implied that they just would not want to be involved in opening mail. I suppose because of the flap potential." Glennon was not surprised by the Bureau's attitude. He testified:

[I]t was fine of the Bureau not to take it over because we should not be doing it in the first place. If somebody else is foolish enough to do it, I can see the Bureau wanting to take advantage of it . . . [and] if the Agency got egg on its face, the Bureau would not get egg on its face."

Because he knew the FBI would not take over the project, Glennon acknowledged that the recommendation in the 1969 report was, in effect, a straight recommendation to abandon HTLINGUAL.

When the 1969 report was presented to the Director, however, Helms did not attempt to engage the FBI in negotiations over responsibility for the project. Rather, he "asked to have the FBI contacted to find out their feeling about the value of this operation [and was] told that they thought it was valuable and would hate to see it terminated." In balancing the perceived value to the FBI on the one hand, and the stated lack of value to several Agency components on the other, Helms decided in favor of continuing the project.

2. Increasing Security Risks: 1971

The question of terminating or turning over the project to the FBI came to the fore again in the spring of 1971, after Chief Postal Inspector William Cotter had received the letter from Dr. Jeremy Stone on behalf of the Federation of American Scientists inquiring whether the Post Office permitted any federal agencies to open mail. For reasons described above, Cotter viewed the letter as a genuine threat to the security of the New York project and believed his own position as Chief Postal Inspector would be seriously compromised if knowledge of the project were publicized. When he communicated his concern to Director of Security Howard Osborn, Osborn relayed it to Helms. Prompted by this new security risk, and possibly by additional security problems inherent in the imminent reorganizatioin of the Post Office, Helms convened a meeting of top CIA officials on May 19, 1971, to discuss the future of HTLINGUAL.

On the agenda were such security problems as the Stone letter, the postal clerk who brought the mail to the CIA's "interceptors" at JFK Airport, and Cotter's inability to testify truthfully before a Congressional committee that he had no knowledge of CIA mail opening. The subject of FBI exploitation of the project was also discussed. Thomas Karamessines, the Deputy Director for Plans, forcefully argued that in light of these security risks CIA involvement in the project should cease, and the FBI should assume responsibility for it. According to the minutes of the meeting:

On the question of continuance, the DDP [Karamessines] stated that he is gravely concerned, for any flap would cause the CIA the worst possible publicity and embarrassment. He opined that the operation should be done by the FBI because they could better withstand such publicity, inasmuch as it is a type of domestic surveillance. The D/S [Howard Osborn] stated that he thought the operation served mainly a Bureau requirement.

James Angleton contended that the project should be continued by the Agency: "The C/CI [Angleton] countered that the Bureau would not take over the operation now, and could not serve essential CIA requirements as we have served theirs; that, moreover, CI Staff sees this operation as foreign surveillance." When Helms asked whether or not the project should be continued "in view of the known risks," Angleton replied "that we can and should continue to live with them."

Apparently Helms was not entirely convinced by Angleton's arguments. At one point during the meeting, according to Howard Osborn, he turned to Angleton and asked, "If this project is so . . . important to the FBI, why ... don't they take it over?" Osborn testified that Angleton responded by noting that the FBI could not do so under the stringent limitations on investigative techniques imposed by J. Edgar Hoover.

The course of action that Helms finally decided upon has been recited above: he met with Cotter personally and was urged to inform the Postmaster General; before informing Mr. Blount, he also called on Attorney General Mitchell. Since Helms believed that both of these Cabinet officers had assented to the mail opening operation, he again supported its continuance. When he reported the favorable results of these briefings to the same group of CIA officials at a subsequent meeting on June 3, the minutes of that meeting show that "all present were gratified". The only instruction Helms gave to those in charge of the project was to tighten security measures, and the project continued.

3. William Cotter's Continuing Concern

The Secrecy Agreement and Cotter's Dilemma. — After Helms briefed Blount on the Now York project, William Cotter recalls that he received a telephone call from Blount, who informed him that the briefing had occurred and instructed him, in effect, to "carry on with the project." He was informed that the Attorney General had been advised of the project as well. Cotter's anxiety decreased with the knowledge that Blount and Mitchell had been briefed and apparently supported the project, but his peace of mind proved to be shortlived: in the latter part of 1971, Blount resigned as Postmaster General, and Mitchell stepped down as Attorney General shortly thereafter. Cotter was again the highest ranking Government official outside of the CIA and FBI who knew of the CIA's mail opening project.

From the first days of his tenure as Chief Postal Inspector, Cotter had been concerned about the New York mail project. He testified:

I was aware that when I assumed the capacity of Chief Postal Inspector I became responsible for enforcing the Postal laws, [and I also] became aware of the high, high sensitivity of Postal Inspectors with regard to violations of Section 1702 [of Title 18 of the United States Code, which prohibits tampering with the mail]. We arrest people every day for ...

opening mail, stealing, and so forth, and so I was very, very uncomfortable with [knowledge of this] project.

Entrusted with this responsibility, Cotter had felt constrained by the letter and the spirit of the secrecy oath, which he had signed when he left the CIA in 1969, "attesting to the fact that I would not divulge secret information that came into my possession during the time that I was with the CIA." "After coming from eighteen years in the CIA," Cotter said, "I was hypersensitive, perhaps, to the protection of what I believed to be a most sensitive project . . ." For this reason, he had written a response to the Jeremy Stone letter that by his own admission was untrue, explaining later that, "If I responded . . . accurately to Mr. Stone, it would have blown the whole operation for the CIA . . . " For the same reason, he had never informed Postmaster General Blount about the project, although, as noted above, he encouraged Helms to do so after he had been Chief Postal Inspector for two years. The minutes of the May 19, 1971, meeting in Director Helms' office aptly summarized Cotter's situation: ". . . in an exchange between the DCI and the DDP it was observed that while Mr. Cotter's loyalty to the CIA could be assumed, his dilemma is that he owes loyalty now to the Postmaster General."

When Blount resigned, Cotter did not know whether the project had ever been described to Blount's former deputy and successor as Postmaster General, Elmer Klassen. He again chose not to raise the matter with the new Postmaster General directly, but began communicating his concern to Howard Osborn and Thomas Karamessines at the Agency.

Cotter's Ultimatum. — Although Osborn and Karamessines were sympathetic to his position and were themselves convinced that the project should be stopped, Cotter's periodic expressions of concern resulted in neither a briefing of Postmaster General Klassen nor a termination of HTLINGUAL. "Since I wasn't getting any action on the part of the CIA," Cotter testified, "I suggested to Mr. Osborn that unless I received some indication that this project had been approved at an exceedingly high level in the United States Government, I was going to withdraw the Postal Service support." 185 Osborn recalls that Cotter specifically referred to authorization at the Presidential level — he would no longer be satisfied by the Postmaster General's approval — and that he set a deadline of February 15, 1973.

Effect Of Watergate. — By the time Cotter presented the CIA with his ultimatum, the Watergate revelations had contributed to the creation of a national political climate vastly different from that during the project's infancy and growth. An increasing number of CIA officials connected with the Now York operation believed that the time was ripe for its termination and welcomed Cotter's position as an opportunity to force the reexamination of its relative advantages and disadvantages. Howard Osborn testified that he "shared [Cotter's] concern. I thought it was illegal and in the Watergate climate we had absolutely no business doing this." He discussed the matter with William Colby, newly appointed DDP, who, according to Osborn, agreed that the project was illegal and should not be continued, "particularly in a climate of that type."

4. Schlesinger's Decision to Suspend the Project

When James Schlesinger, who had succeeded Richard Helms as Director of Intelligence, learned of Cotter's ultimatum, he scheduled briefings by Colby and James Angleton about the future of HTLINGUAL. Colby argued that the "substantial ... political risk [of revelation was] not justified by the operation's contribution to foreign intelligence and counterintelligence collection." Angleton, a strong supporter of the project in the past, attempted to persuade the new Director that the operation was valuable and still merited continuance.

According to a contemporaneous memorandum by William Colby, Schlesinger was unconvinced that "the product to the CIA [was] worth the risk of CIA involvement." The Director decided on a two-pronged course of action. First, he "directed the DDCI [Deputy Director Vernon Walters] to discuss the activity with the Acting Director, FBI (L. Patrick Gray], with a view to offering the FBI the opportunity to take over the project, including the offer to detailing the CIA personnel involved to the FBI to implement it under FBI direction and responsibility." Second, Schlesinger agreed, in light of Cotter's ultimatum, to suspend the operation "unless Mr. Cotter would accept its continuance for the time being under our assurances that the matter is being prosecuted at a very high level."

Cotter refused to extend his deadline, and William Colby authorized the suspension of the project on February 15, 1973. Colby notified Howard Osborn of the suspension and Osborn instructed the Office of Security's Manhattan Field Office to shut down the operation that afternoon. There is no evidence that any attempt was subsequently made to secure Presidential approval, and when the FBI refused to assume operational responsibility (for reasons discussed below), the suspension proved to be permanent.

F. Legal Considerations and the "Flap Potential"

Within the Agency, the legality of the New York mail opening project was perceived to be dubious at best. Among those agents and officers connected with it who considered its legal implications at all, some believed that the project would have been illegal but for the 'internal and external approvals which they assumed — sometimes erroneously — had been granted. Most simply recognized HTLINGUAL to be illegal but rationalized it nonetheless. The general reaction to the questionable legality of the project was neither to stop it nor to seek a definitive opinion as to its legal status; it was to tighten security in order to reduce the risk of exposure to Congress and the general public. The evidence regarding its termination, moreover, suggests that it was finally discontinued not so much because it was thought to be illegal per se, as because the so-called "flap potential" — the risk of embarrassment to the CIA that stemmed from its dubious legality — was seen to outweigh its foreign intelligence and counterintelligence value to the Agency.

1. Perceptions of Legal Issues Within the Agency

Generally, those agents who served on the "front lines" of the New York project, the interceptors and the analysts, did not concern themselves with legal issues at all; they did not ask if what they were doing was within or outside the law, and they were not told. As one of the agents who opened the mail in the New York facility said, "We would speculate when an Attorney General or a Postmaster would change, or even a President, if they would be briefed, [but] this would be knowledge which would never concern us. We would never be told . , . [Our work] was something that one entered into and did."

Among those Agency officials in a policymaking position, a few have testified that while they knew the legality of the project to be questionable, they believed that prior approvals internally and externally made it at least arguably lawful. Thomas Karamessines, former Deputy Director for Plans, for example, stated that because he believed the project had been discussed with a Postmaster General and Chief Postal Inspector, both of whom, he understood, had approved of it, the project must have fallen within an exception of the general statutory prohibition against mail opening.

His belief was buttressed by the participation of the FBI, the chief law enforcement agency in the country, and by the fact that he was told—erroneously—that Post Office Department lawyers had participated in the briefings of Postal officials and that at least one President had approved it. Richard Helms also testified that he did not assume the project was necessarily illegal. Since Allen Dulles, a former Director and eminent lawyer, knew of the project and presumably had "made his legal peace with [it]," Helms said that he never seriously questioned its legal status while it continued under his own tenure. This testimony is partially contradicted, however, by the fact that in 1970 Helms signed the Huston Report, in which covert mail coverage (mail opening) was specifically described as illegal and without the "sanction of law." Helms and the other signers of the Report presented the President of the United States with the option of authorizing a technique which they themselves characterized as unlawful.

Most of the, Agency officials who have testified on this subject simply assumed that mail opening was illegal. Gordon Stewart, who was appointed Inspector General by Richard Helms in 1968 and reviewed the Staff's role in the project in 1969, said flatly, "[O]f course we knew that this was illegal." When he discussed the 1969 report with Helms, he believed it was "unnecessary" to raise the matter of its illegality "since everybody knew that it was [illegal] and it didn't seem to me that I would be telling Mr. Helms anything that he didn't know." Howard Osborn agreed with this characterization of the project's legal status. He testified that at one point in the early 1970's, he approached Karamessines and "said this thing is illegal as hell." Even James Angleton, the project's strongest supporter and, as Chief of the CI Staff, the official most directly responsible for its operation, testified that his understanding of its legality was simply: "That it was illegal." When asked how he could rationalize conducting a program he believed to be illegal, he answered that in his opinion, the project's benefit to the national security outweighed legal considerations.

The documentary record of the project supports the views of those officials who testified that within the Agency the project was perceived as illegal. References to the lack of legal authority for mail opening in peacetime are found in internal memoranda written as early as 1955 and 1962. An internal document dated September 26, 1963, explicitly states: "There is no legal basis for monitoring postal communications in the United States except during time of war or national emergency when the President creates an independent goverment agency called the Office of Censorship . . ." It notes that "for the purposes of the above statement, the, word monitoring is given the meaning of examining the contents of postal communications without necessarily notifying addressee or sender that this is being done."

During the course of the project, there was only one documented attempt to develop a legal theory on which mail opening could be predicated; paradoxically, it was presented in the context of an argument for terminating, not continuing, the project. In the paper which William Colby used to brief James Schlesinger about the project in its final days, Colby wrote:

> While the recording of the addresses and return address is totally legal, the opening of first-class mail is in conflict with 39 U.S. Code Section 4057. A contention can be made that the operation is nonetheless within the Constitutional powers of the President to obtain foreign intelligence information or to protect against foreign intelligence activities (powers

statutorily recognized in 18 U.S.C. Section 119 [sic], with respect to bugging and wiretapping).

Two Postmasters General who were briefed on at least some aspects of the New York project—Edward Day and Winton Blount—testified that such an argument may have merit; for this reason, neither was certain that the CIA's New York project was plainly illegal.

The United States Supreme Court held in United States v. United States District Court, 407 U.S. 297 (1972), however, that the statutory section to which Colby apparently referred does not represent an affirmative recognition by Congress of Presidential power with regard to foreign intelligence and counterintelligence; it is, in effect, a statement of Congressional neutrality and deference to the judiciary in defining the scope of the President's power if any in this area. This section, moreover, relates to electronic surveillance only; those statutes which prohibit warrantless mail opening contain no analogous "exception." Furthermore, even if the President may constitutionally authorize warrantless mail opening for national security reasons, no President ever clearly authorized this program specifically or (with one five-day exception in 1970) the use of mail opening as an investigative technique generally.

Regardless of its merits, this first attempt at developing a legal theory to justify HTLINGUAL was not even set forth until February 14, 1973 -- one day before the suspension of the project. For twenty years prior to this date, the New York project had continued without the benefit of any perceived legal support.

2. Role of the General Counsel

The CIA's General Counsel was not asked for a legal opinion on Colby's theory. At no time, in fact, was the General Counsel ever requested to evaluate the legal aspects of the New York project; all the evidence, including the statement of the holder of this office himself, suggests that the General Counsel was never even aware of the project's existence.

Thomas Abernathy, who, as a member of the Inspector General's staff in the early 1960s had been in charge of the first review of the New York project, conceded that his review did not include consultations with the General Counsel, because legal matters were a matter for "top management." The 1969 review, headed by Inspector General Gordon Stewart, also bypassed the Office of the General Counsel. Stewart testified to at least two reasons why the General Counsel had no input into the project evaluation. First, the Inspector General's line of authority ran only to the Director of Central Intelligence; he had no independent authority to consult the General Counsel directly. Second, he believed that the security of the project precluded his broadening the circle of witting persons, even when the person to be included would be the Agency's own General Counsel. He testified:

Well, I am sure that it was held back from him [the General Counsel] on purpose. An operation of this sort in the CIA is run-if it is closely held, it is run by those people immediately concerned, and to the extent that it is really possible, according to the practices that we had in the fifties and sixties, those persons not immediately concerned were supposed to be ignorant of it.

Richard Helms also testified that he never consulted the General Counsel with regard to the legality of the operation, nor did he know of any attempt by anyone else to do so. He stated that in general, "sometimes we did [consult the General Counsel for statutory interpretations] ; sometimes we did not. I think the record on that is rather spotty, quite frankly."

3. The "Flap Potential"

Because many Agency officials connected with the project viewed it as illegal, and because many of these officials also saw it as essentially domestic surveillance and therefore outside, the CIA's jurisdiction in any event, there was general concern over the project's so-called "flap potential." This term was used by Agency officials to describe the risk of embarrassment to the CIA that would result from the revelation of such a project to the general public and to Congress. It was this concern over the project's flap potential that led to a general tightening of security, to the creation of "cover stories," and other strategies in case of exposure, and, ultimately, to the termination of the project.

In the CI Staff's original proposal in November 1955 to expand the Now York project to include large-scale mail opening, James Angleton recognized that " [t]here is no overt, authorized or legal censorship or monitoring of first class mails which enter, depart or transit the United States at the present time." He noted, therefore, that "[i]n the event of compromise of the aspect of the project involving internal monitoring of the mails, serious public reaction in the United States would probably occur. Conceivably, pressures would be placed on Congress to inquire into such allegation ..." At this point, however, he was confident that such inquiries could be thwarted. He continued: "... but it is believed that any problems arising could be satisfactorily handled." He wrote that the "cover story" was that the CIA interceptors were in fact "doing certain research work on foreign mail ..."

The review of the Office of Security's role in the project in the early 1960s raised the "flap potential" problem again. The Inspector General's report formally recommended that: "An emergency plan and cover story be prepared for the possibility that the operation might be blown." In response to this recommendation, the Deputy Director of Security suggested that in case of a local compromise in New York, the "Office of Security would utilize its official cover to explain any difficulties," and noted that "high-level police contacts with the New York City Police Department are enjoyed, which would preclude any uncontrolled inquiry in the event police action was indicated." If citizens complained about lost mail, he suggested that the proper course should be "referral to the Post Office Department for a normal official inquiry into lost registered mail." Finally, if the project was revealed by a disgruntled Agency employee, the Deputy Director of Security wrote that the charge "may be answered by complete denial of the activity."

The Deputy Chief of the Counterintelligence Staff also responded to the Inspector General's recommendation for a cover story. He wrote that "a 'flap' will put us 'out of business' immediately and may give rise to grave charges of criminal misuse of the mails by government agencies," and argued:

> Since no good purpose can be served by an official admission of the violation, and existing Federal statutes preclude the concoction of any legal excuse for the violation, it must be recognized that no cover story is available to any Government Agency. Therefore, it is important that all Federal law enforcement and U.S. Intelligence Agencies vigorously deny any association, direct or indirect, with any such activity as charged ...
>
> ... Unless the charge is supported by the presentation of interior items from the Project, it should be relatively easy to "hush up" the entire affair, or to

explain that it consists of legal mail cover activities conducted by the Post Office at the request of authorized Federal agencies. Under the most unfavorable circumstances. . . . it might be necessary after the matter has cooled off during an extended period of investigation, to find a scapegoat to blame for unauthorized tampering with the mails. Such cases by their very nature do not have much appeal to the imagination of the public, and this would be an effective way to resolve the initial charge of censorship of the mails.

The views of the Deputy Chief of the CI Staff were adopted by the Director of Security Sheffield Edwards in February 1962.

Three years later, the Long Subcommittee's investigation was believed to increase the risk of project exposure. An internal CIA memorandum dated April 23, 1965, states:

Mr. Karamessines [Assistant Deputy Director for Plans] felt that the dangers inherent in Long's subcommittee activities to the security of the Project's operations in New York should be thoroughly studied in order that a determination can be made as to whether these operations should be partially or fully suspended until the subcommittee's investigations are completed.

When it was learned that Chief Postal Inspector Henry Montague bad been contacted about the Long investigation and believed that it would "soon cool off," however, it was decided to continue the operation. No security changes were made, but Karamessines recommended that the program should be brought to the attention of President Johnson.

Although the Long subcommittee investigation did indeed "cool off" in 1966, the elevation of William Cotter to the position of Chief Postal Inspector in 1969 again raised the specter of discovery by Congress. A CIA internal memorandum written on the day that Cotter was sworn in shows that both Agency officials and Cotter himself recognized that whereas Henry Montague did not know of the mail opening aspects of the project and, therefore, could "testify under oath on the Hill in such a way as to—in effect—protect HTLINGUAL[,] Cotter will not be in such a position and will be particularly vulnerable in the event of a flap in view of his own past affiliation with the Agency." The minutes of the meeting of top Agency officials in the Director's office on May 19, 1971, also make clear that their concern over the Jeremy Stone letter focused largely on the fact that Cotter "would be unable to [deny knowledge of mail opening] under oath" before a congressional committee, as Mr. Montague had been able to do, if the letter created adverse publicity.

The various recommendations for terminating the project before 1973 were predicated not on the perceived illegality of the operation per se; but, to the extent legal factors were present at all, they were based on the "flap potential" stemming from its questionable legal status. The 1969 Inspector General's report, for example, cited lack of value to the Agency and "the continued flap potential inherent in this program" as grounds for its formal recommendation to request the FBI to assume responsibility for the project or, if the Bureau refused, to consider its discontinuance. The report did not raise legal questions directly, even though the then-Inspector General testified that he believed the project to be illegal at the time. At the May 1971 meeting of Agency officials concerning the security of HTLINGUAL, Deputy Director for Plans Thomas Karamessines also recommended that CIA involvement be discontinued because "any flap would cause the CIA the worst possible publicity and embarrassment" -- not because of the illegality of the project itself.

When the project was finally terminated in 1973, the evidence suggests that the decision did not turn on a determination that it was illegal — indeed, for the first time it was suggested that it might be legal. Rather, Director James Schlesinger accepted William Colby's evaluation that "[t]he political risk of revelation of CIA's involvement in this project is in any case substantial ... [and] is not justified by the operation's contribution to foreign intelligence and counterintelligence collection."

In short, many of its major participants saw the New York project as illegal. While a few CIA officials believed that it was lawful, neither the General Counsel nor the Attorney General was ever consulted for a legal opinion. Agency officials reacted to the project's generally perceived illegality, especially when it was threatened by congressional investigations, by focusing even more closely on the security precautions necessary to prevent exposure. Cover stories signed to obscure the CIA's true activities were fabricated, and, in recognition of the absence of any "legal excuse," it was ultimately agreed that the project's very existence should be flatly denied in the event of a serious "flap." "Admission" was a strategy that apparently was never considered. The project was finally terminated when, in a new political climate created by Watergate, it was decided that the political risk inherent in conducting such an operation clearly outweighed the project's minimal value to the Agency.

III. Other CIA Domestic Mail Opening Projects

While the New York project was clearly the most massive one, the CIA also conducted at least three other domestic mail opening projects: in San Francisco, on four separate occasions between 1969 and 1971; in New Oreans, for three weeks in 1957; and in Hawaii, for approximately one year in 1954 and 1955. In addition, the domestic mail of twelve foreign nationals, CIA employees, and American citizens unconnected with the Agency was also opened during particular investigations.

These mail opening projects present many of the major themes of the New York project: the lack of authorization, both internal and external; the deception of postal officials; the random selection of mail for opening; the attention to the correspondence of American "dissidents", despite the stated foreign intelligence and counterintelligence purposes; and the lack of formal review and evaluation. Some of these other programs were more tightly administered than the New York projects, and others more successful in achieving their goals, but taken as a whole the same patterns emerge. In several cases — such as the San Francisco mail project, for which internal approvals were secured through misrepresentation of its true nature; and the Hawaiian project, which was initiated by a sole field agent without any authorization from Headquarters — these themes are even more clearly defined.

A. The San Francisco Mail Intercept Project

The San Francisco mail intercept project, known as WESTPOINTER by the Office of Security and MKSOURDOUGH within the Plans Directorate, involved the exterior examination and opening of mail from an East Asian country to the United States. It was conducted jointly by the Far East Division (FE) and TSD, with the Office of Security providing cover and support. While referred to as a single project, it actually involved four separate trips, each of one to three weeks duration, by CIA personnel from Headquarters to the San Francisco area, in September 1969, February and May 1970, and October 1971. Only envelope exteriors were inspected on the first trip, but mail was both opened and subjected to chemical tests on the latter three. Although authorizations were obtained from the Director and from the Deputy Director of Plans and the Director of Security, the record suggests that these authorizations were for a mail cover operation only — not for mail opening. There is no evidence that any approval by Cabinet level officials or the President was ever secured for this project.

1. Operation of the Project

The Initial Phase. — In mid-1969, TSD personnel requested the Asian operations unit to assist them in determining the validity of TSD's assumption that mail from an East Asian country to the United States was subjected to intensive censorship. Originally, the mail stream was to be intercepted abroad: the CIA's East Asian stations undertook a survey of mail from the Asian country to the United States and conducted "dry runs" of possibilities for its interception. Because of the inherent risk and expense of an operation in Asia, however, and in light of TSD's experience with the New York project, it was decided that the project should be conducted in the United States after the mail had arrived but prior to its sorting and delivery.

In late August 1969, two TSD officers met with James Conway, Deputy Chief Postal Inspector in Washington, for the dual purpose of requesting information on mail entering the United States from this Asian country and to secure his permission for the exterior examination of such mail by CIA agents. Conway's response was favorable, and, at a subsequent meeting in September, the mechanical details for the operation were arranged.

In late September, two agents from TSD traveled to California for a visual examination of incoming mail from this Asian country in the air mail facility at the San Francisco International Airport. In the company of a Postal Inspector, they received access to and examined approximately 1,600 letters in five days before returning to Washington. This trip constituted only a feasibility study to assess the potential of a full-scale operation prior to the commitment of Agency funds and personnel; no mail was opened.

The Second Trip. — The results of the first trip were apparently successful, and in early October the Chief of TSD approved a second, larger scale survey of mail for the purpose of examining it for censorship techniques. The Far East Division, recognizing the foreign intelligence potential of the project, also became involved in order to collect postal intelligence and positive intelligence. During the next two months, approvals for a joint TSD/FE operation in San Francisco were obtained from the Deputy Director for Plans, Thomas Karamessines; the Director of Security, Howard Osborn; and the Director, Richard Helms.

The Deputy Chief Postal Inspector was again contacted and, in January 1970, granted his permission for a second session of CIA access to incoming Asian mail. Two TSD and two FE officers then flew to San Francisco and met with the Regional Postal Inspector in Charge, who had been notified of their appearance by Conway, to arrange for the mechanical details. Mail processing on this trip commenced on February 5, 1970, and continued for one week only, until February 12. The mail was picked up by a Postal Inspector at the San Francisco airport and delivered — in the company of an armed Office of Security agent — to a second Postal Inspector and the four TSD and FE personnel at a local Post Office. It was screened and the exteriors photographed during non-working hours at the Post Office, in the presence of the Postal Inspector. From 5 to 80 letters per day were selected for opening by the CIA agents and "lifted" by surreptitiously placing them in their pockets while the Inspector was temporarily out of the room or had his back turned. These letters were taken, at the end of each day, to a TSD laboratory in a CIA facility nearby for opening and chemical testing. The opened letters would then be resealed and returned by the CIA agents to the mail stream within 48 hours. During the one week of operation, a total of 7,014 letters were screened and 133 opened. The majority of these letters were incoming from the Asian country to the United States, but a CIA memorandum indicates that at least one bag of outgoing mail to that country was also made available to the agents.

The Third Trip.—CIA records pertaining to the third trip to San Francisco are fragmentary. A handwritten "dairy" of a TSD officer, however, contains an entry on April 4, 1970, to the effect that a memorandum written (for planned destruction) about the second trip "justifies further such trips, both on FI [foreign intelligence] and CI [counterintelligence] grounds as well as TSD technical needs." On April 28, this officer noted that the "next phase will include re-run of phase two, presumably in the same format. . . ." He also noted that the random selection of a female TSD agent for the project was the "only significant flaw" of the planned trip, since some of the other agents felt that "the presence [of a female] on the team is inappropriate and that things of this sort have caused trouble in the past. . . . "

James Conway was contacted and approved the operation for a third time in early May 1970, 242 and TSD and FE representatives again traveled to San Francisco to process mail between May 4 and May 27. During these three weeks, a total of 2,800 letters were screened. While Agency memoranda show that a portion of these letters were surreptitiously removed "to the TSD laboratory for opening and testing (with the assistance of a large handbag of the female team member", who apparently did make the trip), there are no precise figures as to the number of letters opened. In addition to airmail, some surface mail was also made available to CIA agents on this trip.

The Fourth Trip.—A fourth trip was proposed in August 1971, in part "to take advantage of the impending visit of the President of the United States to Asia." In addition to examination for censorship techniques and the collection of positive intelligence, which had been the purpose of the last two trips, it was anticipated that this fourth operation could also determine the "attitudes of Asians toward the present discussion between Mao and Nixon as expressed to close friends and relatives." Internal authorizations were obtained in September from the Deputy Director for Plans, the Chief of the Far East Division, the Director of Security, and the Director, although Helms noted that the operation should be limited to two weeks. William Cotter, the Chief Postal Inspector, was contacted about the project but he referred the Agency to Conway, who was now the Regional Inspector in Charge in San Francisco. Conway approved the San Francisco operation for a fourth time and screening and opening commenced on October 1, 1971. Between October 1 and October 15, when the fourth trip was terminated, three FE and two TSD agents processed a total of 4,500 items.

Although Agency documents state that mail opening did occur, it cannot be determined how many of the processed letters were actually opened.

2. Nature and Value of the Product

Selection Criteria.—According to an internal CIA memorandum, letters were selected for opening and testing on the basis of indications of censorship or operational interest: "Some [letters] would be chosen by the TSD team chief based upon heavy censorship or indicators that the letter should be more thoroughly examined at the Lab. Some would be chosen by CIA officers based on certain locations of mailings or possibly the individual to whom the letter was addressed or the kind of stationery that had been used." As was the case in New York, there was a Watch List for the San Francisco project. While this list was destroyed after the fourth and final trip, it is possible to partially reconstruct the categories of persons of interest from the project justification sent to Thomas Karamessines in September 1971 and from the "Sourdough Capsule Summary" prepared after the last trip.

The former memorandum refers to the goal of intercepting mail from former residents of the United States who had been approached by the Agency while residing in the United States and who had since returned to Asia. The "Sourdough Capsule Summary" reveals that among the persons whose mail was intercepted were many Americans living in an Asian country, including expatriots and former missionaries. It was also stated that the agents "saw several items" from a member of the Southern Christian Leadership Conference, and noted, "Black Panthers — we saw nothing from this group."

Foreign Intelligence and Technical Value. — The documentary record suggests that the San Francisco project was considered to be successful in achieving its foreign intelligence and technical objectives. The 1971 project justification sent to Thomas Karamessines by FE, for example, noted that "[t]he primary purpose of previous . . . SOURDOUGH efforts was the collection of [the Asian country's] postal intelligence but each effort produced useful positive intelligence, [such as] background information used as a basis for recruitment attempts and risk assessment of using U.S. letter drops for [foreign-based] agents." The subsequent report on the fourth trip to San Francisco described it as a "highly successful mission" also.

According to the "Sourdough Capsule Summary," the positive intelligence collected during the final trip included information on such topics as the health and activities of the Asian country's leaders and its internal events. TSD also considered the technical results of their examination for censorship techniques to be valuable because, as stated in a 1970 memorandum, "this was the first time it was possible to exert some measure of scientific control" in testing for the presence of censorship techniques.

Domestic Intelligence Value. — In contrast to the New York project, the primary value of the San Francisco project does not appear to have been in the area of domestic intelligence or counterintelligence. Some essentially domestic intelligence information was nonetheless collected, however, as evidenced by the reference in the project summary to the "several items" of correspondence from a member of SCLC that the Agency personnel "saw." The project justification for the fourth trip also noted that the two SOURDOUGH operations in 1970 had provided "leads for domestic operations (Asian operations) and the FBI."

There is no evidence that the FBI levied any requests on — or even knew of — the San Francisco project. The Bureau apparently received sanitized domestic intelligence leads from Sourdough, but there was no formalized procedure for requesting or receiving such information from it. One of the agents involved in the project speculated that the strained relations between the FBI and the Agency during this period may have inhibited the CIA from advising the Bureau of SOURDOUGH's existence.

3. Termination of the Project

The fourth trip to San Francisco in October 1971 proved to be the final visit, but exactly how the project was formally terminated is unclear. A December 1974 memorandum reads in part: "There is no information in the Office of Security's file on Project WESTPOINTER concerning when or by whom the decision was made to terminate the project." No other memoranda regarding the project shed any light on this question.

The reason for the termination is more apparent, however. According to a June 1973 memorandum to the Chief, East Asia Division (formerly the Far East Division) :

The operation achieved the objectives of (a) determining the extent of fan Asian country's censorship of mail to the USA and (b) the nature of the mail itself. It was terminated since the risk factor outweighed continuing an activity which had already achieved its objectives.

Thus, the "risk factor" or "flap potential" was again a crucial factor in the decision to terminate a mail opening program.

4. Internal Authorizations and Controls

Authorizations. — The lax pattern of internal authorization that characterized the New York mail project was repeated in the San Francisco project. There is no documentary evidence of any authorization — even by the Chief of TSD — prior to the initial contact with the Post Office in August 1969 or the first San Francisco trip in September. On October 6, 1969, the TSD Chief gave his approval for the formalized institution of the project, but according to the handwritten "diary" of a TSD agent, the Chief of TSD insisted that at least Thomas Karamessines, and "possibly [the] Attorney General or even the President," must concur before the project could be fully implemented.

Superficially, the subsequent internal chain of oral approvals was complete, if somewhat complex. The TSD Chief personally contacted Karamessines, who "agreed in principle" but requested TSD to secure concurrences from the CI Staff and Howard Osborn (Director of Security) before he would approach the Director on this matter. The Deputy Chief of the CI Staff was briefed and concurred. (Despite a statement in the "dairy" that the Deputy Chief of the CI Staff "will clear with C/CI [the Chief of the CI Staff]," this apparently was never done: James Angleton cannot recall ever having been informed about this project.) On October 23, Osborn was also briefed by TSD and FE personnel; he approved, but conditioned his approval on clearance from the Director. Karamessines was told of Osborn's position on October 27, and together they briefed the Director. Helms reacted favorably and, on November 4, 1969, TSD was advised to proceed with the project.

The record does not reveal any specific authorization for the third trip, but a project justification memorandum for the fourth trip was signed by Thomas Karamessines on September 20, 1971. He recalled that this written authorization — unique for SOURDOUGH — was necessary to except the project from the suspension of certain types of Agency activities with respect to an Asian country during the President's Asian trip, which had been requested by the State Department to avoid possible embarrassment to the United States. According to an October 1971 memorandum written shortly after the final trip, approvals had also been secured from Howard Osborn and Richard Helms.

Although the authorization chain appears to be relatively complete, the testimonial evidence suggests that in 1969, when Karamessines, Osborn, and Helms approved phase two of the project, all three of these officials believed they were approving a mail cover — not a mail opening — operation. Osborn testified that the TSD and FE personnel who briefed him on the project presented it as an operation "whereby they could inspect the exterior of envelopes to and from [an Asian country]." He continued: "... I did not know that they were going to open it; I had no idea they opened the mail. And I found out socially and personally from one of the people involved about a year ago [i.e., 1974] that they opened the mail."

When asked whether or not he was misled in order to secure his approval, Osborn stated:

> Yes, indeed—I wasn't misled but perhaps it seemed when [they] got out there and found out how easy it was to get it but I don't know, I wasn't told that they were to open mail. That isn't the circumstances under which I briefed Mr. Helms.... [If I had known it involved mail opening] I would not have approved it. The Director might have approved it, but it wasn't the way I briefed it ....

Karamessines stated that the first time he can recall knowing that the project involved mail opening rather than a mail cover was in September 1971, when he signed the written authorization for the fourth San Francisco trip. He testified that when he approved the project in 1969 he, too, had been led to believe that it was simply a mail cover operation.

Richard Helms cannot recall whether he understood the project to involve mail opening or not, but stated that it is probable, in light of the testimony of Osborn and Karamessines, who were his only sources of information about SOURDOUGH, that he was unaware of its mail opening aspects.

Thus, after the initial phase of the operation was completed, approvals were secured from the Deputy Director of Plans, the Director of Security, and the Director, but it appears that these approvals, whether purposefully or inadvertently, were based on a fundamental misunderstanding about the nature of the project.

Administrative Controls.—The documentary record reveals that five justification or summary memoranda were written for the project, four of which pertained to the last trip only. It is possible that more would have been written but for Howard Osborn's October 1969 admonition, reflected in the TSD agent's "diary," "to avoid preparing or exchanging any formal communications in writing re project."

There is no indication in the record that the San Francisco project was ever evaluated by the Inspector General's office.

5. External Authorizations

The pattern of external authorizations, or, more accurately, of the relative absence of external authorizations, also parallels that of the New York project. Those postal officials whose cooperation was necessary to implement SOURDOUGH were briefed, but none was told the true nature of the project. Although there are some suggestions in the record that the Attorney General and the President should be informed, and that the Postmaster General had been informed, there is no direct evidence that any of these briefings ever occurred.

Postal Officials.—James Conway, Deputy Chief Postal Inspector during the first three trips and Regional Postal Inspector in Charge during the fourth trip, was contacted by CIA agents about, and subsequently approved, all four of these operations. His uncontradicted testimony, however, is that he was never informed that the project involved mail opening and, in fact, that he explicitly instructed the agents not to open mail or remove it from postal facilities.

At the first meeting between TSD personnel and Conway about the project on August 26, 1969, the Deputy Chief Postal Inspector was told that the CIA's "interest lay in the possible use of international mail channels from [an Asian, country] for private correspondence involving secret writing." According to an internal Agency memorandum prepared shortly after this meeting, however, it had been explained to him that "the survey we hoped to be able to conduct did not involve opening envelopes or photographing letters, but the possibility that this might become desirable in the future, though not mentioned, was not foreclosed." At the subsequent meeting in September between Conway and these officers, one of the officers "brought up the question of broadening the scope of the survey to be performed in San Francisco to include chemical testing of the mail . . ." The memorandum on this meeting reads in part: ". . . he [Conway] acquiesced after brief deliberation when [the CIA officer] asked whether we could include this testing as part of the survey without going out of bounds. It was clear that, the key factor in this decision was the fact that the envelopes would not be opened." Conway agrees with this characterization of the basis of his decision, and testified that he explicitly instructed these agents that no mail should be opened.

Conway approved the second stage of the project on January 13, 1970, after another meeting with Agency officials. In order to ensure his approval, these officials presented him with "an imaginative cover Story" to the effect that the project was necessary for certain scientific reasonS. Conway nonetheless conditioned his approval on total Post Office control of the operations. According to the January 13 entry in the TSD "diary," Conway "approved in principal 'processing' of material but on P.O. premises and under P.O. control ... Opening has not been mentioned." In fact, the cover story was inaccurate, letters were surreptitiously removed from postal premises, and mail was opened. While Conway's approval was sought and received for the final two operations as well, all of the evidence, including his own testimony, suggests that he never learned of the mail opening aspect of the project.

It is also the claim of the Regional Postal Inspector in Charge who worked out the local arrangements for the first three trips, that he was informed neither of the purpose of the project nor of the planned or actual mail openings. This claim is supported by the agency's own documents.

Chief Postal Inspector William Cotter, who played a central role in the story of the New York project, was also aware of SOURDOUGH, but, like Conway and the Regional Inspector, he has testified that he had no knowledge that it involved mail opening. In November 1969, Howard Osborn spoke to Cotter about the San Francisco project. Osborn, who stated that he did not know that mail opening was contemplated himself, assured the Chief Postal Inspector that for the Agency's purposes exterior testing and surveying was sufficient and that mail would not be opened. Cotter was not unreceptive but, according to an agency document explained that he wanted the project "to go slowly and develop gradually." Because of his past CIA affiliation, Cotter also insisted that his assistant, Conway, should ultimately determine the degree of Postal Service Cooperation. He testified that he did not alert Conway to the possibility that the CIA agents may attempt to open the mail because mail opening was not an aspect of the project as he understood it and because "one doesn't have to tell or admonish a seasoned Postal Inspector what his responsibilities are ..."

Cotter apparently had no further contact with the San Francisco project until the fall of 1971, when he was contacted about the planned fourth trip. According to an Office of Security trip report prepared in October 1971:

> The Assistant Postmaster General for Inspection [Cotter] was contacted for his approval. He firmly indicated he did not know anything about the project, nor did he want to know. He stated, however, that he would

advise James Conway, [now the] Regional Inspector in San Francisco, that I would be in touch with him on 27 September 1971, and that we should be guided by Conway's decision.

There is no evidence that Postmaster General Winton Blount, the only Postmaster General under whom the project was conducted, ever knew of or approved SOURDOUGH. A 1973 CIA document addressed to Howard Osborn stated that "TSD understands (but has no evidence) that Mr. Helms briefed Postmaster Blount. Is this so, do you know?" But Helms has made no claim that he did brief Mr. Blount about this project, and there is no testimonial or documentary indication that TSD's understanding on this matter was correct.

Attorney General and President. — As noted above, when the Chief of TSD approved the formal institution of Sourdough on October 6, 1969, he stated that concurrences from the Deputy Director for Plans and "possibly [the] Attorney General or even the President" would be necessary prior to implementation. There is no evidence, however, that either Attorney General Mitchell or President Nixon, the only holders of these offices during the course of the project, were briefed about the San Francisco mail openings either before or after they occurred. President Nixon did state that he was "generally aware" of CIA mail covers "of mail sent from within the United States to . . . the Soviet Union . . . or the People's Republic of China," but he disclaimed knowledge of any CIA mail opening program.

Sourdough's record on external authorizations, in short, is even less complete than that of the New York project. Those postal officials who learned of the project in general terms were misled on the subject of opening and deceived on the subject of custody, and no Cabinet level official — or the President of the United States — apparently knew of the project at all.

B. The New Orleans Mail Intercept Project

A third CIA mail intercept project, encrypted "Project SETTER," was conducted in New Orleans for two and one-half weeks during 1957. This project, which was conducted by the CI Staff with cover and support functions provided by the Office of Security, involved the screening and opening of first class international surface mail transiting New Orleans enroute to and from South and Central America. Unlike the New York and the San Francisco projects, SETTER was operated with the cooperation of the United States Customs Service. There is no record of any internal authorization above the level of Deputy Director of Security and Deputy Chief of the CI Staff, and the only apparent external approval was by a Division head in the Customs Service, who stated that he was unaware the project involved the opening of mail. According to Agency documents, the project generated no useful intelligence information.

1. Operation of the Project

At the time of the New Orleans project, the Customs Service had Congressional authority under the Foreign Agents Registration Act, as amended by the Cunningham Act, to intercept and examine third and fourth class incoming mail from abroad which was suspected to contain Communist propaganda. In the early 1950's, Customs had established its first "control unit" designed to accomplish that purpose; additional "control units" were subsequently set up in at least nine other cities in the United States. Under pressure from certain members of Congress who were outraged at the "venomous propaganda" passing through New Orleans, the Customs Service planned a feasibility survey in August 1957 to determine whether or not it would be possible to establish a "control unit" in that city as well.

The Agency learned of the planned survey and in mid-July a meeting, attended by the Deputy Chief of the CI Staff, the Deputy Director of Security, and Soviet Bloc Division personnel, was called to discuss its possible exploitation by the CIA. "Based on experience with SRPOINTER [the New York project]," an Agency document reads, "CI Staff and O/S personnel ... agreed that CIA personnel would participate in the survey at New Orleans."

Even prior to this meeting, Irving Fishman, the head of the Customs Service's Restricted Merchandise Division, which maintained the "control units", had apparently agreed in principle to CIA participation in the survey. He was contacted in New York by the Assistant Special Agent in Charge of the Office of Security's Manhattan field office on July 18 "to discuss details of the operation."

Fishman and two of his associates left New York for New Orleans at the end of July to work out the arrangements for the Customs survey with the local postmaster. They were joined by four CIA agents during the first week of August, and the operation began on August 6. Each working day for the next two and one-half weeks, one of the Customs personnel went to the New Orleans mail dock to select approximately 25 bags of surface mail from various Central and South American locations that had been unloaded in New Orleans for transshipment to other points in Central and South America. These bags were brought to an office in the Parcel Post Annex of the Federal Building each morning for Customs and CIA scrutiny. While Fishman and the other Customs Service employees searched for communist propaganda by opening third and fourth class mail in the office itself, the CIA agents screened, opened, and photographed first class mail in an adjacent, walk-in vault. The agents' CIA affiliation was known to at least two of the Customs officials; postal employees who worked in the building, however, were informed that they were Customs Service personnel. At the end of each day, the mail would be re-sealed, rebagged, and returned to the mail dock.

Between August 6 and August 23, when the project was terminated, a total of 700 items were photographed and 60 items, mainly first class letters, were opened for examination and photographic reproduction of the contents.

2. Nature and Value of the Product

Selection Criteria.—The agents who participated in the New Orleans project were furnished a "Watch List" of names by the CI Staff to aid in the selection of items for opening.

Beyond the Watch List itself, however, it appears that the members of the interception team were given little guidance by their superiors. One member of this group stated that at no time was he instructed what types of items to select.

According to a project summary prepared in October 1957, an effort (was) made to obtain a representative sampling from the various countries available. Both business and personal mail was examined . . . ."

Value of the Product.— Agency memoranda indicate that SETTER resulted in the collection of no useful intelligence information. The project summary, for example, states: "On-the-spot check of items examined against CI Staff Watch List, and subsequent CI Staff examination of the material processed to date has developed no 'hits' on Watch List names, and, other than propaganda, no material having an intelligence value."

3. Termination

The lack of any significant intelligence value, coupled with the stated impossibility of examining a representative sample of the 20,000 bags of mail that transited New Orleans weekly, apparently led to the termination of Project SETTER. No formal termination of the project is recorded, however.

4. Authorizations

Internal Authorizations. — Both the Deputy Director of Security and the Deputy Chief of the CI Staff attended the July 1957 meeting at which CIA participation in the New Orleans survey was agreed upon. There is no evidence, however, of any internal authorization above the level of these officials. Although the CI Staff had sole operational responsibility for the project, James Angleton, the Chief of the CI Staff at the time, testified that he had no contemporaneous knowledge of it.

External Authorizations. — The only documented approval by a government official outside the CIA was that of Irving Fishman, the head of the Restricted Merchandise Division of the Customs Service. Only through his cooperation, both before and during the period of activity, was the implementation of the project possible at all. According to the October 1957 project summary, Fishman and one of his two associates "were aware, prior to the inception of the operation, of the nature of the BANJO [mail opening] operation." Both Fishman and the associate referred to in the memorandum, however, have stated that they cannot recall any opening of first class mail by the CIA agents.

There is no evidence that the Postmaster of New Orleans, who arranged for the Customs survey, knew of any mail opening by the CIA in connection with the project. The Customs survey itself, of which he was evidently aware, was entirely legal at the time.

C. The Hawaiian Mail Intercept Project

A fourth CIA mail intercept project was conducted in the Territory of Hawaii for about one year during the mid-1950's. It was initiated, without prior authorization from Headquarters, by the Agency's sole representative in Honolulu. Like the New Orleans project, it involved the cooperation of the Customs Service.

According to the agent who conducted the Hawaiian project, local personnel of the Customs Service approached him in late 1954 to request his assistance in identifying incoming political propaganda from Asia that had been intercepted by Customs officials acting under the Cunningham Act. The CIA officer agreed and, after a short period of time, noticed the presence of censorship chemicals on a portion of the mail from one of the country's being covered. Less than a week after he began to assist the Customs personnel, he started surreptitiously removing packets of mail for further exterior examination. By early 1955, without the knowledge of Customs officials, the agent was both opening and photographing items he had removed from the Customs facility.

In March 1955, he sent a formal report of these activities to CIA headquarters, noting that he had photographed the contents of approximately six hundred communications and tested four hundred. Included in the report was an evaluation of the results to date; specifically, an analysis of the Asian country's censorship techniques and other postal and positive intelligence information he had collected. According to the CIA officer, his report was very favorably received and he was encouraged to continue.

The CIA officer stated that for approximately two months in early 1955, he was joined by an FBI agent as well. A local FBI agent in Honolulu, who had received instructions to concentrate on Asian counterintelligence matters, apparently learned from Customs officials that the CIA officer participated in their examination of incoming propaganda. He contacted the CIA officer, was informed of the project, and notified Bureau Headquarters. The CIA officer stated that with his concurrence, an FBI agent trained in mail opening techniques was assigned the task of assisting him in his interception effort. The Bureau can locate no documents pertaining to this operation, however.

The CIA officer continued the project on his own after FBI participation ceased. In November 1955, he was transferred to a station in the continental United States, and the Hawaiian project was terminated.

D. Isolated Instances of CIA Mail Opening

In addition to generalized mail intercept projects, the CIA has also targeted the mail of particular individuals within the United States. At least twelve such instances of mail opening, directed against foreign nationals, Agency employees, and American citizens unconnected with the CIA are recorded in Agency files.

Part III: Project Hunter

I. Introduction And Major Facts

"Project Hunter" was the cryptonym given by the FBI to the receipt of information from the CIA's New York mail intercept program. The FBI first became aware of this operation in January 1958, approximately three and one-half years after the CIA began opening mail between the Soviet Union and the United States. In February 1958, the Bureau began to levy requirements on the CIA's project and received product from it continually from that time until the discontinuance of the project. In total, copies or summaries of more than 57,000 items of intercepted correspondence were disseminated by the CIA to the FBI, either on the basis of general guidelines established by the Bureau or on the basis of particular names of individuals and organizations for which the Bureau desired coverage. While most of these names and categories could reasonably be expected to generate counterespionage information—which was the stated purpose of the FBI's collaboration on the project—Bureau targets also included peace organizations, antiwar leaders, black activists, and women's groups. When the New York mail intercept project was terminated in 1973 and the FBI declined the opportunity to assume responsibility for it, Project Hunter ceased after fifteen years of operation.

The most pertinent facts about Project Hunter may be summarized as follows:

(a) The FBI knew of and levied requirements on the CIA's New York mail intercept project from 1958 until the project was terminated in 1973.

(b) Although the collection of counterespionage information was the stated purpose of Project Hunter, the Bureau specifically requested information on numerous individuals and organizations in the antiwar, civil rights, and women's movements, and on such general categories as "government employees" and "protest organizations."

(c.) The FBI received copies or summaries of more than 57,000 intercepted communications between 1958 and 1973. At the height of the project in 1966, the CIA disseminated 5,984 of the 15,499 items that had been opened to the Bureau—more than were disseminated to any one customer component of the CIA itself.

(d) The product was moderately valuable in terms of the FBI's counterespionage mission, but much of the correspondence has been characterized as "junk" by FBI personnel familiar with the program. It provided no leads to the identification of foreign illegal agents.

(e) No consideration was given to terminating FBI involvement in the CIA's New York intercept program when the Bureau's own projects were terminated in 1966 because information from the project was received at no expense or risk to the FBI.

(f) FBI officials decided against assuming responsibility for the CIA's New York mail intercept project in 1958 and again in 1973 because of its complexity, expense, and the inherent security risks, not primarily because of legal considerations.

II. FBI "Discovery" Of The CIA's New York Mail Intercept Project: 1958

A. A Proposed FBI Mail Opening Program for United States-Soviet Union Mail

In 1957, FBI officials were extremely concerned about the presence of Soviet and other hostile illegal intelligence agents in the United States. 298 The FBI had recently uncovered Rudolph Abel and at least three other illegal agents, yet no effective methods of locating and identifying illegal agents generally were then known. Bureau officials did not feel that they had been entirely successful in their attempts in the past, and searched for a means by which the communication links between the illegal agents and their principals could be intercepted.

On January 10, 1958, an allied nation's counterintelligence agency informed the FBI that when Soviet illegal agents throughout the world wished to meet with their principals, they were under instructions to send a communication to a particular address in the Soviet Union. Against the background of the Bureau's concern for locating and identifying illegal agents, the significance of this information was readily apparent: if the FBI could screen mail between the United States and the Soviet Union, it would be possible to intercept communications bearing this particular address and, it was hoped, trace the letter back to the illegal agent.

In 1958, mail between the United States and the Soviet Union was routed through air mail facilities in New York City and Washington, D.C. On the basis of its newly-acquired information, therefore, FBI Headquarters immediately instructed the New York and Washington Field Offices "to institute confidential inquiries with appropriate Post Office officials to determine the feasibility of covering outgoing correspondence from the U.S. to the U.S.S.R., looking toward picking up a communication dispatched to the aforementioned address." On January 21, 1958, the Special Agent in Charge of the New York Field Office notified Headquarters that his preliminary inquiries indicated that covert mail coverage would be possible at LaGuardia airport.

This was not the FBI's first attempt to utilize mail opening as an investigative technique in the counterintelligence field: at the time these inquiries were being made, the Bureau was conducting two mail opening programs of its own in the cities of Washington, D.C. and San Francisco (see Part IV, p. 636), and in the case of the Washington, D.C. program, the cooperation of the Post Office Department had been enlisted in delivering mail to Bureau agents.

B. Referral to Post Office Headquarters in Washington, D.C.

After the SAC in New York had made his preliminary inquiries, which made the prospects for successful implementation of the project appear favorable, he received a telephone call from the Chief Postal Inspector, David Stephens, in Washington, D.C., who informed him that he could not authorize Post Office cooperation after all because "something had happened in Washington on a similar matter."

He advised that FBI Headquarters should discuss the matter further with his office in Washington.

C. James Angleton's Initial Contact with Sam Papich Regarding HTLINGUAL

The SAC in New York relayed the Chief Postal Inspector's advice to FBI Headquarters, but before Headquarters was able to initiate a meeting with Postal officials in Washington, James Angleton, then Chief of the Counterintelligence Staff of the CIA, contacted Sam J. Papich, FBI Liaison to the CIA, on the matter to which Stephens had apparently referred. Angleton stated that it had come to his attention, through the Post Office, that the FBI was making inquiries into the possibility of covering mail between the United States and the Soviet Union, and that the CIA expected to be contacted by the FBI concerning this possibility. He then informed Papich "on a personal basis" that the CIA was already conducting an extensive operation, based in New York, which involved the opening of mail to and from the Soviet Union. He stated that this project was one of the largest and most sensitive of all CIA covert operations, and that "the sole purpose for the coverage was to identify persons behind the Iron Curtain who might have some ties in the U.S. and who could be approached in their countries as contacts and sources for the CIA."

Alan Belmont, then Assistant Director for the Domestic Intelligence Division, was informed of this operation by Papich and noted in a memorandum to Mr. Boardman, then Assistant to the Director, that "[i]t would appear that our inquiries of the Post Office officials in New York have flushed out a most secret operation of the CIA."

D. Decision Not to Challenge CIA Jurisdiction

Papich testified that FBI officials were greatly concerned over what was viewed as a possible intrusion by the CIA into the counterintelligence jurisdiction of the FBI, and he stated that he "anticipated all hell was going to break loose." In fact, however, the jurisdictional dispute which Papich anticipated never occurred. Rather, the FBI decided to capitalize on the situation by receiving the benefits of the program without the expense and manpower requirements which would accompany a more active role in its operation. Belmont wrote to Boardman:

The question immediately arises as to whether CIA in effecting this coverage in New York has invaded our jurisdiction. In this regard, it is believed that they have a legitimate right in the objectives for which the coverage was set up, namely, the development of contacts and sources of information behind the Iron Curtain. At the same time, there is an internal security objective here in which, because of our responsibilities, we have a definite interest, namely, the identification of illegal espionage agents who may be in the United States. While recognizing this interest, it is not believed that the Bureau should assume this coverage because of the inherent dangers in the sensitive nature of it, its complexity, size, and expense. It is believed that we can capitalize on this coverage by pointing out to CIA our internal security objectives and holding them responsible to share their coverage with us.

This memorandum was routed to the Director, and Hoover's approval—the phrase "OK. H."—appears on the last page.

K. FBI Briefing at CIA

On January 24, 1958. Sam Papich met with Janies Angleton, Sheffield Edwards, and a third CIA officer at the Agency. Papich told the group that he had reason to believe, from the FBI inquiries of Post Office officials in New York (and without mentioning Angleton's admission two or three days earlier), that the CIA had a mail coverage project in New York. The CIA representatives then proceeded to give Papich a full briefing on the CIA's mail intercept program, and agreed to "handle leads" for the Bureau. Papich was also told that Postmaster General Summerfield had approved the photographing of mail by the CIA but that the CIA did not have permission of the Post Office Department to open mail. In addition, the address given the Bureau by the allied counterintelligence agency was supplied to the CIA for use in the New York project.

Neither Angleton nor anyone else in the CIA was told at this time of either of the FBI's own on-going mail opening programs. According to the testimony of William Branigan, former FBI Section Chief of a section dealing with espionage matters, there was no reason to inform CIA about the Bureau's own mail opening programs since both of the programs then involved "strictly a domestic situation involving persons in the United States . . . [and] solely within the jurisdiction of the FBI."

III. Requests Levied By The FBI On The CIA's New York Mail Intercept Project

A. The Procedure Established

The "Hunter" procedure for requesting and receiving information was established in early February 1958. On February 6, James Angleton wrote the FBI Director to advise the Bureau of the form in which requests should be made and information would be disseminated. Designating correspondence between the two agencies which related to the New York project as "Project Hunter", Angleton suggested that the Bureau number all requests for placing particular persons on the Watch List, in consecutive order as "Hunter Request Number --." Identifying data about the requested person should be placed on a three by five card, with instructions as to the duration of the person's name on the Watch List and the type of treatment desired ("e.g., photograph exterior only; open and photograph contents as well, etc."). General requirements based on letter content or the class of the sender or addressee, could also be accommodated by the CI Staff project analysts.

Correspondence from the CIA to the FBI which contained information derived from the project was to be labeled consecutively, "Hunter Report Number --.".

B. Categories of Correspondence for Requested Coverage

At least five sets of categories of correspondence for which the Bureau desired coverage were transmitted to the CIA between 1958 and 1973. The focus of the original categories was clearly counterespionage, but subsequent general requirements became progressively more domestic in their focus and progressively broader in their scope. By the end of the project, one requirement simply asked for the intercepted correspondence of "New Left activists, extremists and other subversives."

The first set of categories of correspondence for which the FBI desired coverage was set forth in a memorandum from Alan Belmont to Mr. Boardman dated February 6, 1958. 315 This memorandum was approved by Hoover, and Sam Papich advised the CIA of the Bureau's interest in these categories on February 11. They were:

(1) All correspondence of a suspicious nature, et cetera.

(2) All correspondence indicating that the Soviets may be utilizing a hostage situation, i.e., correspondence indicating pressure being exerted on Soviet citizens who have close relatives in the U.S. or pressure being exerted on individuals in U.S.

(3) Any information appearing in correspondence indicating weaknesses or dissatisfaction on the part of any Soviet presently in the United States so

that the Bureau might give consideration to feasibility of approaching such individuals for defection or double agent purposes.

(4) Any information appearing in correspondence indicating Soviet control of direction of the CPUSA. [Communist Party, USA.]

If the CIA Staff analysts were not certain whether a particular letter fit into one of these four categories, they clearly gave the Bureau the benefit of their doubt. In August 1961, these categories had to be refined because of the large percentage of valueless letters (95% by one informed estimate) which the CIA disseminated to the Bureau in the first three and one-half years of the Hunter operation. The FBI informed the CIA that it was not interested in correspondence involving general travel arrangements of Americans travelling to Russia, personal letters with no intelligence value, letters to and from exchange students, and "holiday greeting" traffic. The Bureau stated, however, that it was specifically interested in receiving any correspondence in the following categories:

(1) Any traffic in the above-mentioned non-desired categories wherein the translator feels there is some intelligence significance....

(2) Any traffic wherein it is revealed U.S. addressee or addressor is a U.S. Government employee or is employed in a sensitive industry, i.e., missile field.

(3) Any traffic wherein we have an obvious intelligence interest such as an open offer by an individual to assist Soviets, an indication an individual is going to Russia and wants to become a citizen or wherein an individual professes pro-Soviet or pro-communist sympathies.

Other categories relating to particular espionage cases were also set forth.

The reference to "U.S. Government employee[s]" in category (2) was intended to be limited to employees in sensitive positions, according to one of the Bureau officials who formulated these categories. 321 But such limitation is not evident on the face of the request. The Bureau literally requested all intercepted correspondence to or from all federal employees, from the lowest Civil Service level to, presumably, the level of the Cabinet, the Congress, and the President.

On February 13, 1962, an additional category was requested by the FBI. This request was for any correspondence from the United States to the Soviet Union which contained any of the "indicators" on the outside of the envelope which suggested that the correspondence was from an illegal agent to his principal. The Bureau had acquired knowledge of these indicators in 1959 and used this knowledge in connection with several of its own mail opening programs in the period 1959 through 1966. Dissemination by the CIA to the FBI of correspondence which was opened on the basis of these indicators was code-named "Hunter-Don."

The categories were enlarged again on October 31, 1962. Among the new categories of correspondence desired by the FBI were the following:

(1) All material emanating from Puerto Rico of an anti-U.S. nature and pro-Soviet.

(2) Data re U.S. peace groups going to Russia and while in Russia.

(3) Data indicating death of any U.S. Communist abroad.

(4) Any traffic from or to U.S. students in Moscow or to U.S. persons who were former students in Moscow.

(5) Any traffic between U.S. persons who are with a current exposition or a previous exposition in the USSR.

In addition, the CIA was informed that the FBI had no interest in the correspondence of Soviet-bloc immigrants desiring to repatriate to the Soviet Union, legitimate American tourists in the Soviet Union, and American professors in academic research who corresponded with their counterparts in the Soviet Union.

A final revision of the guidelines occurred in March 1972, when James Angleton was told that the following were among the types of traffic which continues to be of interest to the FBI:

1. Current and former Soviet exchange students, visitors, researchers and scientists.

2. Current and former Soviet official visitors.

. . . . .

4. U.S. exchange students, researchers, and persons who have been in the USSR with American exhibitions and delegations.

. . . . .

6. . . . [P]ersons on the Watch List; known communists, New Left activists, extremists and other subversives; suspected and known espionage agents; individuals known to be of interest to the Soviets because of their specialized knowledge or work on classified matters ...

7. Communist party and front organizations . . . extremist and New Left organizations.

8. Protest and peace organizations, such as People's Coalition for Peace and Justice, National Peace Action Committee, and Women's Strike for Peace.

9. Communists, Trotskyites and members of other Marxist-Leninist, subversive and extremist groups, such as the Black Panthers, White Panthers, Black Nationalists and Liberation groups, Venceremos Brigade, Venceremos organization, Weathermen, Progressive Labor Party, Worker's Student Alliance, Students for a Democratic Society, Resist, Revolutionary Union, and other New Left groups. This would include persons sympathetic to the Soviet Union, North Korea, North Vietnam and Red China.

10. Cubans and pro-Castro individuals in the U.S.

11. Traffic to and from Puerto Rico and the Virgin Islands showing anti-U.S. or subversive sympathies.

This final set of requirements clearly reflected the domestic turmoil of the late 1960's and early 1970's. The process that began fourteen years earlier as a means of discovering Soviet intelligence efforts in the United States had expanded to encompass detection of the activities of domestic dissidents of all types. Even those merely "sympatlietic" — in the opinion of CI Staff analysts — to selected communist nations fell within the scope of the requirements.

C. Individuals and Organizations Placed on the Watch List

In addition to the general categories set forth above for which the FBI desired CIA mail coverage, the Bureau also submitted the names of particular individuals and organizations for inclusion on the CIA's Watch List. According to existing FBI records, "Hunter Request" numbers reached 286 by 1973, that is, the names of 286 individuals and organizations were submitted by the Bureau during the course of the Hunter Project.

The majority of these names were clearly in the counterespionage, area, but the specific requests also included: The National Guardian, Student Non-Violent Coordinating Committee, National Mobilization Committee to End the War in Vietnam, Students for a Democratic Society, Ramparts, Clergy and Laymen Concerned about Vietnam, the Liberation News Service, Jeremy J. Stone (Director of the Federation of American Scientists), Center for the Study of Public Policy, Linus Pauling, and the Institute for Policy Studies.

Aside from the 286 "Hunter Request" names submitted by the FBI for inclusion on the Watch List, about 180 more names were provided to the CIA for use in the special Latin America mail screening operation, known as Hunter Vince, which was run in conjunction with Hunter and which lasted for approximately one month in 1963. 327 On December 12, 1962, Liaison Agent Sam Papich had been informed by the CIA that because mail from the United States to a Latin America country was temporarily discontinued, all such mail would be shipped to that country from New York City, and the CIA intended to expand their coverage to include the screening and opening of a portion of this mail. The FBI expressed an interest in sharing the benefits of this coverage and submitted approximately 180 names of American and foreign citizens who were on the Security Index.

This aspect of the program, which commenced on February 21,1963, was suspended on March 19, less than one month later.

IV. Product Received By The FBI From The CIA's New York Mail Intercept Project

A. Volume According to a CIA document dated January 23, 1975, a total of 57,846 separate items were disseminated to the FBI from the CIA project. The yearly figures, from 1958 when the first product was disseminated to the Bureau, until the termination of the project, are as follows:

Year	Total Items Opened	Items disseminated to FBI
1958	8,633	666
1959	13,299	1,964

1960	12,725	2,342
1961	14,025	3,520
1962	13,932	3,017
1963	16,748	4,167
1964	14,904	5,396
1965	13,309	4,503
1966	15,499	5,984
1967	23,617	5,863
1968	12,288	5,322
1969	9,821	5,384
1970	10,207	4,975
1971	9.018	2,701
1972	8.060	1,400
1973	2,273	642

B. Administrative Processing of the Product Received

After the FBI liaison agent picked up the Hunter reports at CIA Headquarters, he would bring them to a single desk within the Soviet Section of the Domestic Intelligence Division. The person in charge of this desk was responsible for reviewing all of the correspondence and routing it to interested supervisors in the Division. Copies of the correspondence would then be returned to the control desk and either destroyed, if deemed to be of no value, or filed in a secure area, separated from the rest of the FBI files. Due to the sensitivity of the project, copies of the correspondence never went into a case file directly, although a cross-reference in the case file allowed the retrieval of any relevant correspondence.

Knowledge of the project was limited to the operational sections within the Domestic Intelligence Division at Headquarters. Neither the Criminal Division nor any of the field officers were ever advised of the nature of the source. When significant information was developed from Hunter, it would be paraphrased to disguise the true source prior to dissemination to the field officers or other divisions: an informant symbol replaced the term "Project Hunter" on all such correspondence. Field offices would be informed that "[Informant symbol], a most sensitive and reliable source, advised that (individual or organization) of (address) was in contact with (individual or organization; address) during (month, year) .... According to the informant...." The field offices were also warned that information from this source should not be disseminated outside the Bureau nor set out in any investigative report, and that information from the informant should be utilized for lead purposes only.

C. Nature and Value of the Product Received

During the fifteen years of Hunter's operation, the Bureau received information which was considered valuable in both its counterintelligence and its domestic intelligence efforts; it also received a significant volume of material that was valueless. Project Hunter revealed, for example, the location and future plans of a large number of individuals of investigative interest to the FBI, and the "pro-communist sympathies" of numerous American citizens, but it did not lead to the identification of any foreign illegal agents.

Typical counterintelligence information generated from the program, as stated in the annual FBI evaluation reports, included: "travel plans to the USSR of numerous Communist Party subjects; ... data indicating pro-Soviet sympathies of U.S. individuals; ... data indicating a U.S. person may be serving as a Soviet courier; . . .

data indicating the existence of particular Russian social and art clubs in the U.S.; . . . data indicating a desire of U.S. students to study in USSR; . . . contacts in this country of Security Index (SI) subjects vacationing and studying abroad; . . . [d]ata regarding current and former U.S. exchange students show[ing] Soviet and U.S. contacts before and after return, romantic involvements, sympathies and difficulties encountered in Russia, . . . plans of seven individuals to repatriate to the USSR; ... U.S. contacts with current and former known and suspected Soviet agents now in the USSR . . ."

In addition, essentially domestic intelligence was received "regarding persons involved in the peace movements, anti-Vietnam demonstrations, women's organizations, 'teach-ins' . . ., racial matters, Progressive Labor Party, Students for a Democratic Society, DuBois Clubs, Students Non-Violent Coordinating Committee, and other organizations." The fact that an aide to a United States Senator requested a Moscow dance company to perform in the United States was discovered through Hunter and duly filed, as was the fact that the foreign-born wife of a man who would shortly become an aide to Secretary of Agriculture Orville Freeman expected to be in a position to become friendly with President Kennedy.

Information such as that listed above was considered to be valuable by the Bureau. A 1966 evaluation of Hunter by the FBI's Domestic Intelligence Division stated that "[t]he value of this material is shown by the fact that there was an increase of 53% in the number of new cases opened on the basis of information furnished by the source. . . . More than 260 new cases were opened and 96 cases were reopened. The majority of new cases were opened on the basis of travel to the USSR and contacts of U.S. citizens, Latin Americans, and Cubans in the U.S. with individuals in the USSR." A 1973 informational memorandum routed to Acting Director Patrick Gray noted that "[w]e have always considered the product from Project Hunter as valuable to our investigative interests."

As discussed in Part II above, however, this project was not as valuable to the FBI's counterespionage mission as CIA officials assumed it to be. Large numbers of intercepted communications were received from the Agency, but many of them -- 95 percent according to the FBI Special Agent who was in charge of the administrative aspects of Hunter for five years — were considered valueless, either because they contained nothing of counterintelligence value or because the information supplied merely duplicated information already in the Bureau case files. William A. Branigan agreed that much of the product could be characterized as "junk," and asserted that the relative value of this project must be evaluated in light of the fact that this source cost the Bureau nothing, either in terms of dollars or in terms of manpower.

V. TERMINATION OF THE PROJECT All of the FBI's own mail opening programs were discontinued in mid-1966, yet Bureau officials gave no thought at that time to terminating the Hunter Project. As explained by Mr. Branigan, Hunter was considered to be a CIA operation. It was operated at no cost or risk to the Bureau. There was therefore no reason to cut off this source when the Bureau's own programs were terminated. Thus, the FBI continued to receive the fruits of mail opening long after its own agents were prohibited from opening the mail themselves.

Project Hunter was also not terminated for approximately three years after J. Edgar Hoover wrote a footnote in the 1970 "Huston Report" which contained this language: "The FBI is opposed to implementing any covert mail coverage [i.e., mail opening] because it is clearly illegal and it is likely that, if done, information would leak out of the Post Office to the press and serious damage would be done to the intelligence community." The FBI Director, therefore, was apparently willing to allow the Bureau to receive information from a source that he himself described as "clearly illegal" and which he believed could seriously jeopardize the American intelligence community.

Project Hunter was only terminated when the CIA itself suspended the New York operation in mid-February 1973, for reasons which are discussed in Part II above. At that time, the FBI was approached by Agency representatives to determine whether or not the Bureau wished to assume responsibility for the project, since the Bureau had been the largest consumer of information developed from this source. 349 Lieutenant General Vernon A. Walters, Deputy Director of the CIA, scheduled a meeting with Acting FBI Director Gray on February 16, 1973 to discuss this possibility. The Bureau, however, declined to assume responsibility for the project, primarily because of the attendant expense, manpower requirements, and security problems. According to William Branigan, legal considerations were not a factor in this decision; it was simply thought to be too large and risky an operation to be undertaken by Bureau agents. The suspension of operations therefore proved to be permanent.

VI. Internal Authorization And Controls

A. Initial Approval by and Continuing Knowledge of the Director

It is clear that FBI Director Hoover personally approved Project Hunter from its inception. Hoover's initial and his written "OK" are signed on the first document in the Project Hunter policy file, the January 22, 1958, memorandum from A. H. Belmont to L. V. Boardman, which sets out the basic facts regarding CIA coverage and possible use of such coverage. He also personally approved the first (1958) and the final (1972) guidelines that went to the Agency, the initial policy memorandum dealing with the handling of Hunter material, and informational memoranda regarding the "Hunter-Vince" (Latin American mail) aspect of the program.

In March 1961, the FBI was informed by James Angleton that the CIA had developed a laboratory capability in New York City to test intercepted correspondence for microdots and other secret writing techniques. The CIA offered the use of this laboratory to the Bureau if Bureau agents should ever want to use it. (Apparently this was never used by the FBI.) Hoover was informed of the laboratory and the CIA offer in a March 10, 1961, memorandum, on which he penned the phrase "Another inroad!"

Acting Director L. Patrick Gray was also made aware of Project Hunter by at least February 16, 1973, the date he initialed the February 15, 1973, memorandum from W. A. Branigan to E. S. Miller and was scheduled to meet with Lt. General Walters regarding the possible take-over of the project by the FBI. This, however, was one day after the project was actually terminated.

B. Internal Controls

Several of the internal controls which were developed for Project Hunter have already been noted. Knowledge of the true nature of this source was closely held to those sections within the Domestic Intelligence Division which had a need-to-know; dissemination of information outside Headquarters was always disguised and Field Offices were cautioned that the information could be used for lead purposes only. In addition, the project was evaluated at least annually by the Project Supervisor. These evaluations, which summarized the information received from the project during the previous year, were passed up through channels and generally were reviewed by at least an Assistant to the Director.

VII. External Authorization

A. Attorneys General

There is no evidence that any Attorney General was ever informed by Bureau officials about the existence of Project Hunter. It was explained by one Bureau official that since the project was a CIA rather than an FBI project, there was no need to seek Justice Department approval or even to inform Justice Department officials about the fact that mail was being opened in the project.

B. Postmasters General

There is also no evidence that any FBI official ever informed any Postmaster General or Chief Postal Inspector about Project Hunter. The February 15,1973 memorandum from W. A. Branigan to E. S. Miller states that "[a]rrangements for the [CIA project] were obviously worked out between the Agency and Post Office officials and we are not privy to the details."

C. Presidents

There is similarly no evidence that any President was aware of Project Hunter.

Part IV: FBI Mail Opening

I. Introduction And Major Facts

The FBI, like the CIA, conducted several mail opening programs of its own within the United States. Eight programs were conducted in as many cities between the years 1940 and 1966; the longest was operated, with one period of suspension, throughout this entire twentysix year period; the shot-test ran for less than six weeks. FBI use of this technique was initially directed against the Axis powers immediately before and during World War II, but during the decade of the 1950's and the first half of the 1960's all of the programs responded to the Bureau's concern with communism.

At least three more limited instances of FBI mail opening also occurred in relation to particular espionage cases in the early 1960's.

Significant differences may be found between the FBI mail opening programs and those of the CIA. First, the stated purposes of the two sets of program generally reflects the agencies' differing intelligence jurisdiction: the FBI programs were, in the main, fairly narrowly directed at the detection and identification of foreign illegal agents rather than the collection of foreign positive intelligence. Thus, no premium was placed on the large-scale collection of foreign intelligence information per se; in theory (if not always in practice), only information that might reasonably be expected to provide leads in counterespionage cases was sought. Because of this, the total volume of mail opened in Bureau programs was less than that in the CIA programs. An equally important factor contributing to the smaller volume of opened mail lay in the selection criteria used in several of the FBI's programs. These criteria were more sophisticated than the random and Watch List methods used by the CIA; they enabled trained Bureau agents to make more reasoned determinations, on the basis of exterior examinations of the envelopes, as to whether or not the communications might be in some sense "suspect." Third, the FBI mail opening programs were much more centralized and tightly administered than the CIA programs. All but one (which resulted in a reprimand from the Director) received prior approval at the highest levels of the Bureau. They were evaluated and had to be reapproved at least annually. Several of them — unlike the CIA's New York project — were discontinued on the basis of unfavorable internal evaluations. This high degree of central control clearly mirrored the organizational differences between the FBI and the CIA, and is not limited to mail opening operations alone. Finally, there is less evidence that FBI officials considered their programs to be illegal or attempted to fabricate "cover stories" in the event of exposure. Bureau officials, for the most part, apparently did not focus on questions of legality or "flap potential" strategies; they did not necessarily consider them to be legal or without the potential for adverse public reaction, they simply did not dwell on legal issues or alternative strategies at all.

In some respects, the Bureau's mail opening programs were even more intrusive than the CIA's. At least three of them, for example, involved the interception and opening of entirely domestic mail — that is, mail sent from one point within the United States to another point within the United States. All of the CIA programs, by contrast, involved at least one foreign "terminal". The Bureau programs also highlight the problems inherent in combining criminal and intelligence functions within a single agency: the irony of the nation's chief law enforcement agency conducting systematic campaigns of mail opening is readily apparent.

Despite their differences, however, the FBI mail opening programs illustrate many of the same themes of the CIA programs. Like the CIA, the FBI did not secure the approval of any senior official outside its own organization prior to the implementation of its programs. While these programs, like the CIA's, involved the cooperation of the Post Office Department and the United States Customs Service, there is no evidence that any ranking official of either agency was ever aware that mail was actually opened by the FBI. Similarly, there is no substantial evidence that any President or Attorney General, under whose office the FBI operates, was contemporaneously informed of the programs' existence. As in the case of the CIA, efforts were also made to prevent word of the programs from reaching the ears of Congressmen investigating possible privacy violations by federal agencies. The record, therefore, again suggests that these programs were operated covertly, by virtue of deception, or, at a minimum, lack of candor on the part of intelligence officials.

Although the FBI relied on more sophisticated selection criteria in some of their programs, moreover, one again sees the same type of "overkill" which is inherent in any mail opening operation. These criteria, while more precise than the methods used by the CIA, were never sufficiently accurate to result in the opening of correspondence to or from illegal agents alone. Indeed, even by the Bureau's own accounting of its most successful program, the mail of hundreds of American citizens was opened for every one communication that led to an illegal agent. And several of the FBI programs did not employ these refined criteria: mail in these programs was opened on the basis of methods much more reminiscent of the CIA's random and Watch List criteria.

In the FBI programs one again sees the tendency of this technique, once in place, to be used for purposes outside the agency's institutional jurisdiction. While the Bureau has no mandate to collect foreign positive intelligence, for example, several of the programs did in fact result in the gathering of this type of information. More seriously, the record reveals for a second time the ease with which these programs can be directed inward against American citizens: the Bureau programs, despite their counterespionage purpose, generated at least some information of a strictly domestic nature, about criminal activity outside the national security area, and, significantly, about antiwar organizations and their leaders.

Perhaps the most fundamental theme illustrated by both the FBI's and the CIA's programs is this: that trained intelligence officers in both agencies, honestly perceiving a foreign and domestic threat to the security of the country, believed that this threat sanctioned—even necessitated—their use of a technique that was not authorized by any President and was contrary to law. They acted to protect a country whose laws and traditions gave every indication that it was not to be "protected" in such a fashion.

The most pertinent facts regarding FBI mail opening may be summarized as follows:

(a) The FBI conducted eight mail opening programs in a total of eight cities in the United States for varying lengths of time, between 1940 and 1966.

(b) The primary purpose of most of the FBI mail opening programs was the identification of foreign illegal agents; all of the programs were established to gather foreign counterintelligence information deemed by FBI officials to be important to the security of the United States.

(c.) Several of these programs were successful in the identification of illegal agents and were considered by FBI officials to be one of the most effective means of locating such agents. Several of the programs also generated other types of useful counterintelligence information.

(d) In general, the administrative controls were tight. The programs were all subject to review by Headquarters semiannually or annually and some of the programs were terminated because they were not achieving the desired results in the counterintelligence field.

(e) Despite the internal FBI policy which required prior approval by Headquarters for the institution of these programs, however, at least one of them was initiated by a field office without such approval.

(f) Some of the fruits of mail openings were used for other than legitimate foreign counterintelligence purposes. For example, information about individuals who received pornographic material and about drug addicts was forwarded to appropriate FBI field offices and possibly to other federal agencies.

(g) Although on the whole these programs did not stray far from their counterespionage goals, they also generated substantial positive foreign intelligence and some essentially domestic intelligence about United States citizens. For example, information was obtained regarding two domestic anti-war organizations and government employees and other American citizens who expressed "pro-communnist" sympathies.

(h) A significant proportion of the mail that was opened was entirely domestic mail, i.e., the points of origin and destination were both within the United States.

(i) Some of the mail that was intercepted was entirely foreign mail, i.e., it originated in a foreign country and was destined to a foreign country, and was simply routed through the United States.

(j) FBI agents opened mail in regard to particular espionage cases (as opposed to general programs) in at least three instances in the early 1960's.

(k) The legal issues raised by the use of mail opening as an investigative technique were apparently not seriously considered by FBI officials while the programs continued. In 1970, however, after the FBI mail opening programs had been terminated, J. Edgar Hoover wrote that mail opening was "clearly illegal".

(l) At least as recently as 1972, senior officials recommended the reinstitution of mail opening as an investigative technique.

(m) No attempt was made to inform any Postmaster General of the mail openings.

(n) The Post Office officials who were contacted about these programs, including the Chief Postal Inspector, were not informed of the true nature of the FBI mail surveys, i.e., they were not told that the Bureau contemplated the actual opening of mail.

(o) The FBI neither sought nor received the approval of the Attorney General or the President of the United States for its mail opening programs or for the use of this technique generally.

(p) Although FBI officials might have informed Justice Department attorneys that mail was opened in two or three particular espionage cases and might have informed an Attorney General of some mail screening operations by the Bureau, no attempt was made to inform the Justice Department, including the Attorney General, of the full extent or true nature of these operations.

(q) There is no evidence that any President of the United States ever knew of any ongoing FBI mail opening program.

II. DESCRIPTION OF FBI MAIL OPENING PROGRAMS The eight FBI mail opening programs are, summarized below.

A. Z-Coverage

Z-Coverage, the first and the longest-running FBI mail opening program, originally involved the opening of mail addressed to the diplomatic establishments of Axis powers in Washington, D.C.; in later years, mail coming to similar establishments of several communist nations was targeted. The stated purpose of the program was "to detect individuals in contact with these establishments who might be attempting to make contact for espionage reasons, for purposes of defecting or who might be illegal agents."

This program was initiated in 1940, before the United States entry into World War II, with FBI agents who had been trained in the technique of "chamfering" (mail opening by representatives of an allied country's censorship agency). It was suspended after the war but reinstituted in Washington, D.C. in the early or mid-1950's on the recommendation of the local FBI field Office. For more than a decade, mail from both foreign and domestic points of origin was intercepted at the Main Post Office, brought to the FBI Laboratory for opening and photographing, and returned to the Post Office prior to delivery. In 1959, Z-Coverage was extended to New York City as well. As implemented in New York, about 30 to 60 letters addressed to various diplomatic establishments in that city were intercepted at the Grand Central and Lenox Hill Post Offices each day for opening and photographing at the New York Field Office. Some registered mail sent to these establishments was opened as well.

Despite its perceived success at both locations, Z-Coverage was terminated in July 1966.

B. Survey No. 1

Survey No. 1 operated in a total of six cities for varying lengths of time between 1959 and 1966. It involved the opening of certain outgoing mail to selected cities in Europe, Asia, and the Americas, and was considered to be the most successful of all the FBI's mail opening programs. Its purposes, as summarized in a 1961 FBI memorandum, were two: "(1) to identify persons corresponding with known espionage mail drops in Europe, and (2) to identify persons in the United States who are directing letters to possible mail drops in Europe and whose letters appear to be the product of an illegal agent."

Survey No. I was first instituted in New York City on October 1, 1959, as a direct result of knowledge the FBI had recently acquired about the means by which foreign illegal agents communicated to their principals abroad. Once in operation, Bureau agents, in a secure room at Idlewild Airport's Airmail Facility screened more than 425,000 letters from the United States to points in Western Europe each week. Selected items — a total of 1,011 in seven years -- were returned to the New York Field Office for opening and photographing prior to reinsertion into the mailstream. In August 1961, after nearly two years of operation in New York, FBI officials believed that Survey No. 1 was so successful that it was extended to four additional cities — Boston, Los Angeles, Seattle, and Washington, D.C. -- where coverage included mail not only to European cities but to Asia and the Americas as well. Survey No. 1 was also extended to Detroit on a sixty-day trial basis in April 1962.

The expanded coverage in all cities but Washington did not prove to be as successful as the original effort in New York, however. After thirteen months of operation in Los Angeles, seventeen months in Seattle, one year in Boston, and four months in Detroit, a decision was made at Headquarters to terminate the program in these cities because of "unproductivity and manpower needs." After February 1963, therefore, Survey No. 1 operated only in New York and Washington. In these two cities the annual evaluations continued to praise the effectiveness of Survey No. 1 and it was continued to operate at both locations until all of the mail opening programs were terminated in mid-1966.

C. Survey No. 2

Survey No. 2 operated in New York City, Detroit, and San Francisco for varying lengths of time between March 1961 and March 1962; its purpose was again the location and identification of illegal agents. No. 2 was, in essence, an inverse No. 1: incoming mail to urban postal zones in which illegal agents were believed likely to reside was screened and opened, on the basis of the same criteria used in Survey No. 1, in an attempt to intercept the other half of the communication link between illegal agents and their principals. Since mail coming into these postal zones was screened irrespective of the point of origin, much of the mail that was opened was entirely domestic mail.

Survey No. 2 originated as an outgrowth of No. 1. It was first implemented on March 8, 1961, in postal zones 23, 24, and 25 in New York City, with Post Office employees rather than Bureau agents screening the in-coming mail. The Post Office personnel were briefed by the FBI as to the selection criteria but were not informed of the true nature of the program. When they discovered a suspect communication, it was turned over to the FBI and, without their knowledge, opened and photographed at the field office before being returned to the mailstream. On the basis of "test" letters sent by the Bureau, however, their performance was judged inadequate and, in September 1961, FBI agents replaced the postal workers in screening the mail.

In October 1961, the program was also extended to both Detroit (zone 31 and the Hamtramck area) and San Francisco (all mail sent to that city from New York and Washington) on a trial basis.

Survey No. 2 was considered unsuccessful in all of these cities and was consequently discontinued in Detroit and San Francisco in February 1962, and in New York—after a total of approximately 2,350 letters had been opened -- on March 9, 1962.

D. Survey No. 3

Survey No. 3 was conducted in New York City from June 1963 to June 1964, and involved the opening of mail (irrespective of point of origin) addressed to known or suspected intelligence agents employed at a diplomatic establishment. The purpose of Survey No. 3 was to detect contacts of an intelligence nature, with these agents, who, FBI officials believed, received such mail using the secure cover of their diplomatic employment.

This program was apparently an outgrowth of the Bureau's coverage of mail to various other diplomatic establishments in New York (Z-Coverage). Although its precise genesis is undocumented, one of the participants in the program recalled that the idea originated with another agent, then involved with Z-Coverage, who felt that existing coverage was inadequate and should be expanded. Headquarters subsequently approved the idea, and, on June 25, 1963, Survey No. 3 was instituted in New York.

Each working day for the next year, a single agent from the New York office went to the Grand Central Post Office where a postal clerk brought him all the mail that was addressed to the Post Office box of the targeted diplomatic establishment—approximately 200 letters per day, according to the agent who was assigned to this task. On the basis of a list of about thirty diplomatic officials, which was compiled from public source information, the agent segregated the mail addressed to these officials and carried the letters—estimated by him to average five or six per day -- to the New York office for opening and photographing.

Survey No. 3 was not considered to be successful by the Bureau and was discontinued on June 26, 1964.

E. Survey No. 4

Survey No. 4 was conducted in Miami, Florida, between January 1963 and July 1966. It involved the screening and opening of certain airmail from Miami and San Juan, Puerto Rico, to two Latin American countries for the purpose of locating clandestine communications in particular espionage cases.

Survey No. 4 developed from an espionage case in which the Bureau had learned that a Latin American intelligence agent who operated in the United States but whose true identity was unknown, was under instructions to transmit material to his country's intelligence service by mail. In order to intercept this agent's written communications, Bureau officials at Headquarters formulated a plan to screen and selectively open mail from San Juan and Miami to that country utilizing their knowledge of its intelligence correspondence, and on December 21, 1962, they authorized the Miami Field Office to implement the program.

While the program was initially instituted as a response to a single espionage case, it soon developed into a more generalized survey to detect clandestine communications from any suspected espionage agent working for the same country. Its scope was further broadened on December 9, 1963, when the Miami office was instructed to cover mail from that city to another Latin American country as well.

Bureau agents in Survey No. 4 screened between 12,000 and 20,000 letters per day at the Biscayne Annex Post Office in Miami. A total of 400 letters were opened, either in the Post Office itself, or, when secret writing or microdots were suspected, in the FBI Laboratory in Washington, to which they were flown for more sophisticated examination before reinsertion into the mailstream.

Survey No. 4 was considered to be successful but was terminated along with other FBI mail opening programs, in July 1966.

F. Survey No. 5

Survey No. 5 was the first of three FBI mail opening programs which were conducted in San Francisco and directed against Asian communists and their sympathizers. It began in September 1954 and continued until January 1966. This survey originally involved the physical inspection of third and fourth class propaganda from a Far East Asian country; after August 1956, incoming first class letter mail was selectively opened and photographed as well. The stated purpose of this program was to identify individuals in the United States who, because of the nature of their foreign contacts, were believed to constitute a threat to the internal security of the United States.

Like the CIA's New Orleans and Hawaiian mail intercept projects, Survey No. 5 was initially an extension of the Customs Service examination of propaganda material entering the United States from abroad. Customs Service cooperation ceased, however, on May 26, 1965, as a result of the Supreme Court's decision in Lamont v. Postmaster General of the United States, U.S. 301 (1965), which invalidated the statutory authority under which Customs conducted its propaganda inspection. Contact was subsequently made with officials of the Post Office and, with their assistance, No. 5 Survey recommenced at the Rincon Annex Post Office on July 7, 1965.

Approximately 13,500 items of mail were screened in two hour periods each day by Bureau agents who participated in this program. A daily average of 50 to 100 of these letters were returned to the San Francisco Field Office for opening and photographing prior to their reinsertion into the mainstream.

Survey No. 5 was terminated on January 24, 1966, "for security reasons involving local changes in postal personnel."

G. Survey No. 6

Survey No. 6 was also conducted in San Francisco, operating from January 1964 until January 1966. This program involved the screening and opening of outgoing mail from the United States to the same Far East Asian country; it was essentially an inverse Survey No. 5. The stated purposes of Survey No. 6 were to obtain foreign counterintelligence information concerning Americans residing in the Far East Asian country; to detect efforts to persuade scientists and other persons of Asian descent residing in the United States to return to that country; to develop information concerning economic and social conditions there; and to secure information concerning subjects in the United States of a security interest to the Bureau who were corresponding with individuals in that Asian country.

In June 1963, the New York Field Office had extended its Survey No. 1 coverage to include airmail destined for Asia, which was then handled at the same location where European mail was processed. When Post Office procedures changed a few months later, and the Asian mail was routed through San Francisco rather than New York, Headquarters instructed the San Francisco office to assume responsibility for this coverage. The program operated, with one period of suspension, for two years until January 24, 1966, when it was terminated for the same security reasons as the Survey No. 5. Figures as to the volume of mail screened and opened cannot be reconstructed.

H. Survey No. 7

Survey No. 7 was conducted in San Francisco from January to November 1961. It involved the screening and opening of mail between North Americans of Asian descent for the purpose of detecting Communist intelligence efforts directed against this country.

Survey No. 7 evolved from the Survey No. 5 and particular espionage cases handled by the San Francisco Field Office. Without instructions from Headquarters, that office initiated a survey of mail between North Americans of Asian descent in January 1961, and informed Headquarters of the program shortly after it was implemented. On February 28, 1961, Headquarters officials instructed San Francisco to terminate the program because the expected benefits were not believed to justify the additional manpower required by the FBI Laboratory to translate the intercepted letters. The San Francisco Field Office was permitted to use this source when it was deemed necessary in connection with particular espionage cases, but even this limited use proved unproductive. It was terminated on November 20, 1961, after a total of 83 letters had been opened.

I. Typical Operational Details

The specific operational details of the eight programs described above obviously varied from program to program. The New York Field Office's conduct of Survey No. 1 represented a pattern that typified these programs, however, in terms of mechanical aspects such as the physical handling of the mail itself. In August 1961, before the extension of Survey No. 1 to Boston, Los Angeles, Seattle, and Washington, D.C., the New York Office was instructed to describe the operational details of this Survey as implemented in that city for the benefit of field offices in the four additional cities. A memorandum was subsequently prepared for distribution to these cities, pertinent portions of which are reproduced below:

[Survey No. 1] in Now York is located in a secure room at the U.S. Post Office Airmail Facility, New York International Airport, Idlewild, New York. ... This room ... measures approximately 9 feet wide by 12 feet long and ... is locked at all times, whether or not the room is in use ... Postal employees have no access to this room which is known to them as the Inspector's Room.

Seven Special Agents are assigned to [Survey No. 1] on a full-time basis. The survey operates 7 days a week and personnel work on rotating 8-hour shifts ... Personnel assigned to the survey work under the guise of Postal Inspectors and are known to Post Office personnel as Postal Inspectors working on a special assignment. ...

... [B]y arrangement with the postal officials, [mail] pouches to destinations in which we have indicated interest are not sealed but are placed in front of the [Survey No. 1] room. The [Survey No. 1] personnel then take the bag into the room, open the pouch, untie the bundles, and review the mail. Any suspect letters are held aside and the rest are rebundled and returned to the pouch. The pouch is then closed and placed outside the door to the room on a mail skid. Postal employees then take that pouch, seal it with a lead seal and place it aside for, or turn it over to, the carrier. ...

It should be noted that the mail must be turned over by the the Post Office Department to the carrier one hour before departure time ...

... Each day, one of the Agents is selected as a courier, and when the opportunity presents itself, he returns to the Field Office with the suspected communications. At the Field Office, he or another Agent who has been trained by the Bureau in certain techniques opens the communications. The envelope and its contents are photographed ... There will be instances where the Field Office, upon opening the communication, may deem it advisable to immediately notify the Bureau and possibly fly it by courier to the Bureau for examination by the Laboratory. Before making any arrangements to fly the communication to the Bureau, the Field Office should consider the time the examination will take and the time the suspected communication may be placed back in the mail without arousing any suspicion on the part of the addressee.

After the communication has been photographed and resealed, the courier returns to the airport and places the suspected communication in the next appropriate outgoing pouch examined in the [Survey No. 1] Room. If time permits, the pouch is held in the room until the suspected communication is returned.

A device developed by the FBI Laboratory and maintained at participating field offices facilitated the opening process. While this device was relatively simple, it was not as primitive as the kettle and stick method utilized by the CIA agents who opened mail in the New York project and allowed for greater efficiency: the FBI's opening process was reported to take only a second or two for a single letter, in contrast to five to fifteen seconds for the CIA. According to one of the agents involved, special training in the use of this device was given at the field office rather than at Headquarters, and was only of one or two days duration, in contrast to the week-long training sessions required of CIA mail openers.

Filing and internal dissemination procedures also varied somewhat from program to program. In Z-Coverage, the negatives of the photographic copies were filed at the field offices in New York and Washington for approximately one year after interception, after which time they were destroyed. If the developed prints were believed to contain valuable counterintelligence information, they would be disseminated to appropriate supervisors within the field office for placement in a confidential central file or a particular case file. In the latter case, the true source would be disguised by an informant symbol, although, as one supervisor in the New York office noted, the nature of the source would be clear to those familiar with Bureau operations.

No index was maintained of the names of all senders and/or addressees whose mail was intercepted, as was maintained by the CIA in the New York project. In rare cases when a letter was considered to be of exceptional counterintelligence value, a photograph would be sent to Headquarters as well. As a general rule, however, there was no dissemination, either of the photographs themselves or of abstracts of the letters, to other field offices. These procedures generally applied to Survey No. 1 and

Survey No. 2 as well, but in these two surveys the photographs of intercepted letters were dated and numbered, and one copy or abstract was placed in a control file maintained by each participating field office.

In Surveys No. 5 and No. 6, the San Francisco Field Office was responsible for conducting "name checks" on all individuals sending or receiving mail that had been opened. If, on the basis of the name check or the text of the letter itself, it was determined that the intercepted letter had intelligence value, a copy of the letter (if written in English) or of the translation (if written in a foreign language) was placed in the main files of the San Francisco office. That office was also responsible for paraphrasing the contents of letters in which other field offices may have had an intelligence interest, and disseminating the information to them in a manner which would not reveal the true source of the information. Except for letters written in a foreign language, photographs of which were sent to Washington for translation, copies were not sent to Headquarters unless the letter was of particularly great intelligence value.

J. Other Instances of FBI Mail Opening

In addition to the eight mail surveys described in sections A through H above, it has also been alleged that a Bureau agent actively participated in the CIA's Hawaiian mail intercept project during the mid-1950s. The CIA representative in Honolulu who conducted this operation stated that an FBI agent assisted him in opening and photographing incoming mail from Asia for a period of two months in early 1955. No supporting Bureau documents could be located to confirm this participation, however.

Aside from generalized surveys of mail, several isolated instances of mail opening by FBI agents occurred in connection with particular espionage cases. It was, in fact, a standard practice to attempt to open the mail of any known illegal agent. As stated by one former Bureau intelligence officer: "... anytime ... we identified an illegal agent ... we would try to obtain their mail." FBI agents were successful in this endeavor in at least three cases, described below.

1. Washington, D.C. (1961)

One isolated instance of mail opening by FBI agents occurred in Washington, D.C., in 1961, preceding the local implementation of Survey No. 1. This case involved the opening of several items of correspondence from a known illegal agent residing in the Washington area to a mail drop in Europe. The letters, which were returned to the FBI Laboratory for opening, were intercepted over a period in excess of six months.

2. Washington, D.C. (1963-64)

A second mail opening project in regard to a particular espionage case occurred for approximately one and one-half years in Washington, D.C., in 1963 and 1964, in connection with the FBI's investigation of known Soviet illegal agents Robert and Joy Ann Baltch. This case was subsequently prosecuted, but the prosecution was ultimately dropped, in part, according to FBI officials, because some of the evidence was tainted by use of this technique.

3. Southern California

A third isolated instance of mail opening occurred in a southern California city for a one to two-month period in 1962. This project involved the opening of approximately one to six letters received each day by a suspected illegal agent who resided nearby. The suspected agent's mail was delivered on a daily basis to three FBI agents who worked out of the local resident FBI office, find was opened in a back room in that office.

III. Nature And Value Of The Product

A. Selection Criteria

Those FBI mail opening programs which were designed to cover mail to or from foreign illegal agents utilized selection criteria that were more refined than the "shotgun" method used by the CIA in the New York intercept project. Mail was opened on the basis of certain "indicators" on the outside of the envelopes that suggested that the communication might be to or from an illegal agent. The record reveals, however, that despite the claimed success of these "indicators" in locating such agents, they were not so precise as to eliminate individual discretion on the part of the agents who opened the mail, nor could they prevent the opening of significant volumes of mail to or from entirely innocent American citizens. Mail in those programs which were designed for purposes other than locating illegal agents, moreover, was generally opened on the basis of criteria far less narrow and even more intrusive than these "indicators."

1. The Programs Based on Indicators

Before 1959, the FBI had developed no effective means to intercept the communication link between illegal agents and their principals. In Z-Coverage, selection was originally left to the complete discretion of the agents who screened the mail based on their knowledge and training in the espionage field. The focus was apparently on mail from individuals rather than organizations, and typewritten letters were considered more likely to be from foreign agents than handwritten letters. In March 1959, however, the FBI was able to develop much more precise selection criteria through the identification and subsequent incommunicado interrogation of an illegal agent. During the course of his interrogation by Bureau agents, he informed the FBI of the instructions he and other illegal agents were given when corresponding with their principals. Particular characteristics on the outside of the envelope, he advised them, indicated that the letter may be from such an agent.

Armed with a knowledge of these "indicators," the FBI agents involved in Z-Coverage were capable of a more selective and accurate means of identifying suspect communications. Survey No. 1 and Survey No. 2 were expressly developed to exploit this knowledge. While Survey No. 1 also utilized a Watch List which consisted of the addresses of known or suspected mail drops abroad, as well as the (generally fictitious) names of known or suspected foreign intelligence agents, 417 the primary selection criteria in both Surveys No. 1 and No. 2 were the "Indicators" about which the Bureau learned in early 1959.

By means of the "indicators," the Bureau did, in fact, identify three illegal agents through these programs. 419 But even by the Bureau's own accounting of the number of letters that were opened in the programs, it is clear that the mail of hundreds of innocent American citizens was opened and read for every successful lead obtained. 420 The random element in the selection process was never eliminated: although FBI officials at Headquarters instructed agents in the field to select only letters with multiple "indicators" on their face, 421 the field agents frequently opened letters with but one "indicator", which could often be of such a common nature that it could be found on most letters mailed in the United States.

One of the FBI agents who opened mail stated that he was trained in counterespionage work generally, and in the identification of the indicators specifically, but he conceded that in the final analysis "it was strictly my own judgment" as to which items would be selected for opening. Perhaps as a result of such personal discretion on the part of participating agents, Survey No. 1 generated essentially domestic intelligence on at least two American antiwar organizations as well as genuine counterespionage information.

In short, knowledge of the indicators did enable the Bureau to be more precise in the selection of mail than was previously possible, but this knowledge was not so precise as to totally eliminate the discretion — or bias — of the agents involved.

2. The Latin American-Oriented Program

In Survey No. 4, which involved the interception of mail to two Latin American nations, letters were selected for opening on the basis of lists of (a) known fictitious names used by illegal agents to address correspondence to their principals, and (b) accommodation addresses used by a foreign intelligence service for receiving clandestine communications. The "indicators" discussed above were not utilized in this or the Asian-oriented mail opening programs.

3. The Asian-Oriented Programs

Survey No. 5 and Survey No. 6 both employed seven general categories as selection criteria:

(a) Letters to or from a university, scientific, or technical facility;

(b) Letters to or from a doctor;

(c.) Letters to or from selected Security Index subjects residing in the United States;

(d) Letters to or from an Asian country where certain scientific activities were reportedly taking place;

(e) Letters to or from individuals who were known to be "turncoats" from the Korean conflict;

(f) Letters believed to emanate from an Asian Communist intelligence service based on covers of which the FBI was aware; and

(g) Letters indicating illegal travel of Americans to denied areas in Asia.

Even if one assumes that these guidelines were strictly observed by the agents opening the mail, (which, given some of the results of these programs as set forth below, is not necessarily as accurate assumption) there was obviously ample room for the capture of large numbers of entirely personal communications with no counterintelligence value at all.

The selection criteria utilized in Survey No. 7 cannot be reconstructed.

B. Requests by Other Intelligence Agencies

No large-scale requirements were levied upon the FBI's mail opening programs by any other intelligence agency. Bureau officials, in fact, severely restricted knowledge of their programs within the intelligence community; only the CIA knew of any of the Bureau's programs, and officers of that agency were formally advised about the existence of only one of the eight, Survey No. 1.

In July 1960, Bureau Headquarters originally rejected the recommendation of the New York Field Office to inform the CIA of Survey No. 1 in order to obtain from it a list of known mail drops in Europe for use in the program. Headquarters then wrote: "Due to the extremely sensitive nature of the source ..., the Bureau is very reluctant to make any contacts which could possibly jeopardize that source. Therefore, the Bureau will not make any contact with CIA to request from it [such a] list ... The Bureau will, however, continue to exert every effort to obtain from CIA the identities of all such mail drops in the normal course of operations."

Within six months of this rejection, however, Headquarters officers changed their minds: Donald Moore, head of the Espionage Research Branch and Sam Papich, FBI liaison to the CIA, met with CIA representatives in January 1961 to inform them of

Survey No. 1 and to exchange lists of known or suspected mail drops. CIA provided the Bureau with a list of 16 mail drops and accommodation addresses and the name and address of one Communist Party member in Western Europe, all of which were subsequently furnished the New York office for inclusion in Survey No. 1 coverage. The exchange of this information did not evolve into a reverse Project Hunter, however. While the Agency may have contributed a small number of additional addresses or names during the next five years, no large scale levy of general categories or specific names was ever made by the CIA or solicited by the FBI. According to Donald Moore, the particularized nature and objectives of Survey No. 1, especially when contrasted with the CIA's New York project, precluded active CIA participation in the program.

While there is no other evidence that any members of the intelligence community knew of or ever levied requests on the Bureau's mail opening programs, they did receive sanitized information from these programs when deemed relevant to their respective needs by the Bureau.

C. Results of the Programs

In terms of their counterespionage and counterintelligence raison d'etre, several of the Bureau's programs were considered to be successful by FBI officials; others were concededly ineffective and were consequently discontinued before the termination of all remaining FBI surveys in 1966. Significantly, some of the surveys also generated large amounts of "positive" foreign intelligence—the collection of which is outside the Bureau's mandate—and information regarding the domestic activities and personal beliefs of American citizens, at least some of which was disseminated within and outside the FBI. The Bureau surveys did remain more focused on their original goal than did the CIA programs. But in them—whether because the selection criteria were overbroad, or because these criteria were not scrupulously adhered to, or both—one again sees the tendency of mail opening programs to produce information well beyond the type originally sought.

1. Counterintelligence Results

Five of the eight FBI mail openings programs—Z-Coverage, Surveys 1, 4, 5, and 6 -- were clearly seen to have contributed to the FBI's efforts in the area of counterintelligence. The relative success of these programs, in fact, led many Bureau officials to conclude that mail opening—despite its legal status—was one of the most effective counterespionage weapons in their arsenal. The primary value of these five programs to the Bureau is summarized below:

Z-Coverage.—A lack of pertinent documentary and testimonial evidence prevents a meaningful evaluation of Z-Coverage during World War II, but a 1951 memorandum reflecting the Washington Field Office's recommendation for its reinstitution noted that "while Z-Coverage was utilized valuable information of an intelligence nature was obtained ..."

In evaluating the program during the 1950s and 1960s, Bureau officials have rated it highly in terms of the counterintelligence results it produced. W. Raymond Wannall, former Assistant Director in charge of the Domestic Intelligence Division, testified about two specific examples of mail intercepted in Z-Coverage which revealed attempts on the part of individuals in this country to offer military secrets to foreign governments. In the first case, the FBI intercepted a letter in July 1964, which was sent by an employee of an American intelligence agency to a foreign diplomatic establishment in the United States. In the letter, the employee offered to sell information relating to weapons systems to the foreign government and also expressed an interest in defecting. The Defense Department was notified, conducted a potential damage evaluation, and concluded that the potential damage could represent a cost to the United States Government, of tens of millions of dollars. In the second case, which occurred in mid-1964, an individual on the West Coast Offered to sell a foreign government tactical military information for $60,000.

Survey No. 1.—Survey No. 1 was considered to be one of the most successful of all the Bureau mail opening programs. In New York and Washington, a total of three illegal agents—the identification of which has been described by one senior FBI official as the most difficult task in counterintelligence work -- were located through No. 1. In addition. numerous letters were discovered which contained secret writing and/or were addressed to mail drops in Western Europe. Survey No. 1 in Boston, Los Angeles, Seattle, and Detroit was not successful, however, and as noted above, was discontinued in those cities on the basis of "unproductivity and manpower needs."

Survey No. 4—Survey No. 4 resulted in the identification of the illegal agent whose presence in the United States had originally motivated development of tile survey. In addition, this program led to the detection of a second intelligence agent operating in this country and to the discovery of approximately 60 items of correspondence which contained secret writing either on the letter itself or on the envelope containing the letter.

Survey No. 5—FBI officials have testified that Survey No. 5 was a very valuable source of counterintelligence (and interrelated positive intelligence) information about an Asian country. W. Raymond Wannall stated that its "principal value probably related to the identification of U.S. trained scientists of [Asian] descent who were recalled or who went voluntarily back to [an Asian country]." Because of this, he continued, the FBI was able to learn vital information about the progress of weapons research abroad.

Survey No. 6—Survey No. 6 was also believed to be a valuable program from the perspective of counterintelligence, although it was suspended for a nine-month period because the manpower requirements were not considered to outweigh the benefits it produced. Through this survey the FBI identified numerous American subscribers to Asian communist publications; determined instances of the collection of scientific and technical information from the United States by a foreign country; and recorded contacts between approximately fifteen Security Index subjects in the United States and Communists abroad.

The Other Programs—Three of the FBI's programs were not believed to have produced any significant amount of counterintelligence information. Bureau officials testified that they "had very little success in connection with [Survey No. 3]," and it was consequently discontinued after one year of operation. Similarly, no positive results were obtained through Survey No. 2 in any of the three cities in which it operated. Although the San Francisco office, for example, opened approximately 85 new cases as a result of Survey No. 2, all of these cases were resolved without the identification of any illegal agents, which was the goal of the program. As one Bureau official stated in regard to Survey No. 2: "The indicators were good, but the results were not that good. It, too, was terminated after approximately one year of operation.

Finally, the results of Survey No. 7, which was initiated without prior approval by Headquarters, were also considered to be valueless. Of the 83 letters intercepted in the program, 79 were merely exchanges of personal news between North Americans of Asian descent. The other four were letters from individuals in Asia to individuals in the United States, routed through contacts in North America, but were solely devoted to personal information. As noted above, Headquarters did not believe that this coverage justified the additional manpower necessary to translate the items and the San Francisco Field Office was so advised.

2. "Positive" Foreign Intelligence Results

Although the FBI has no statutory mandate to gather positive foreign intelligence, a great deal of this type of intelligence was generated as a byproduct of several of the mail opening programs and disseminated in sanitized form to interested government agencies. In an annual evaluation of Survey No. 5, for example, it was written:

> This source furnishes a magnitude of vital information pertaining to activities within [an Asian country]; including its economical [sic] and industrial achievements . . . A true picture of life in that country today is also related by the information which this source furnishes reflecting life in general to be horrible due to the lack of proper food, housing, clothes, equipment, and the complete disregard for a human person's individual rights.

Another evaluation stated that this program had developed information about such matters as the "plans and progress made in construction in railways, locations of oil deposits, as well as the location of chemical plants and hydraulic works." It continued: "While this is of no interest to the Bureau, the information has been disseminated to interested agencies." Survey No. 6 even identified, through the interception of South American mail routed through San Francisco to an Asian country, numerous "[Asian] Communist sympathizers" in Latin America.

W. Raymond Wannall, former head of the Bureau's Domestic Intelligence Division, explained that "as a member of the intelligence community, the FBI [was aware] of the positive intelligence requirements [which were] secularized within the community in the form of what was known as a current requirements list, delineating specific areas with regard to such countries that were needed, or information concerning which was needed by the community. So we contributed to the overall community need." He conceded, however, that the FBI itself had no independent need for or requirement to collect such positive intelligence. Just as the CIA mail opening programs infringed on the intelligence jurisdiction of the FBI, therefore, so the FBI programs gathered information which was without value to the Bureau itself and of a variety that was properly within the CIA's mandate.

3. Domestic Intelligence Results

In addition to counterespionage information and positive foreign intelligence, the FBI mail opening programs also developed at least some information of an essentially domestic nature. The collection of this type of Information was on a smaller scale and less direct than was the case in the CIA's New York project, for none of the FBI programs involved the wholesale targeting of large numbers of domestic political activists or the purposefully indiscriminate interception of mail. Nonetheless, the Bureau programs did produce domestic intelligence. An April 1966 evaluation of Survey No. 1, for example, noted that "organizations in the United States concerning whom informant [the survey] has furnished information include ... [the] Lawyers Committee on American Policy towards Vietnam, Youth Against War and Fascism ... and others."

An evaluation of the Survey No. 5 stated that that program had developed "considerable data" about government employees and other American citizens who expressed pro-Communists sympathies, as well as information about individuals, including American citizens, who were specifically targeted as a consequence of their being on the FBI's Security Index. Examples of the latter type of information include their current residence and employment and "anti-U.S. statements which they have made."

Another evaluation of a Bureau program noted that that program had identified American recipients of pornographic material and an American citizen abroad who was a drug addict in correspondence with other addicts in the New York City area; it indicated that information about the recipients of pornographic material was transmitted to other field oflices and stated that "pertinent" information was also forwarded to other Federal agencies.

Given the ready access which Bureau agents had to the mail for a period of years, it is hardly surprising that some domestic intelligence was collected. Indeed, both logic and the evidence support the conclusion that if any intelligence agency undertakes a program of mail opening within the United States for whatever purpose, the gathering of such information cannot be avoided.

IV. Internal Authorization And Controls

While the FBI and the CIA mail opening programs were similar in many respects, the issues of authorization and control within these agencies highlight their differences. The pattern of internal approval for the CIA mail opening programs was inconsistent at best: the Now York project began without the approval of the Director of Central Intelligence; at least two Directors were apparently not even advised of its existence; and it is unclear whether any Director knew the details of the other mail opening programs. 459 Administrative controls in most of the CIA projects, especially the twenty-year-New York operation, were clearly lax: periodic reevaluation was non-existent and operational responsibility was diffused.

Probably as a function of the FBI's contrasting organizational structure, the mail opening programs conducted by the Bureau were far more centrally controlled by senior officials at Headquarters. With one significant exception, the FBI mail programs all received prior approval from the highest levels of the Bureau, up to and including J. Edgar Hoover, and the major aspects of their subsequent operation were strictly regulated by officials at or near the top of an integrated chain of command.

A. Internal Authorization

While the documentary record of FBI mail opening programs is incomplete, that evidence which does exist reveals J. Edgar Hoover's explicit authorization for the following surveys:

-- The extension of Survey No. 1 to Los Angeles, Boston, Seattle, and Washington, D.C., on August 4,1961;

-- The re-authorization of Survey No. 1 in New York, on December 22, 1961 ;

-- The re-authorization of Survey No. I in New York and Washington, D.C., on April 15,1966 ;

-- The extension of Survey No. 2 to three additional postal zones in New York and its implementation with FBI rather than Post Office employees, on August 31, 1961 ; and

-- The institution of Survey No. 6 in San Francisco, on November 20,1963.

The documentary evidence also reveals authorizations from former Associate Director Clyde Tolson and/or the former Assistant Director in charge of the Domestic Intelligence Division, William C. Sullivan, for the, following surveys:

-- The extension of Survey No. 1 to Detroit on April 13, 1962 ;

-- The extension of Survey No. 12 to Detroit on October 4, 1961 ;

-- The re-authorization of Survey No. 2 in New York on December 26, 1961 ; and

-- Administrative changes in the filing procedures for the Survey No. 5 on June 28, 1963.

Further, unsigned memoranda and airtels from Headquarters, "Director, FBI," authorized the extension of Survey No. 2 to San Francisco on October 18, 1961, and the institution of Survey No. 4 on December 21, 1962. Bureau procedures normally require that such memoranda and airtels must be seen and approved by at least an Assistant Director, and there is no reason to assume that this did not occur in these instances.

Despite the absence of some authorizing documents, witness testimony is consistent-and often emphatic—on the point that unwritten Bureau policy required J. Edgar Hoover's personal approval before the institution of a new mail opening program or even the initial use of mail opening as a technique in specific espionage cases. The approval of at least the Assistant Director for the Domestic Intelligence Division, moreover, was required for the periodic re-authorization or the extensions of existing mail surveys to additional cities, as well as for their termination, upon the recommendation of the field office involved. The only surveys for which this policy was apparently violated were Survey No. 7 and possibly—though this is unclear—Survey No. 1.

The testimony of senior FBI officials conflicts on whether Hoover actually authorized the formal institution of Survey No. 1 in New York in 1959, or whether he merely approved the general concept of a mail opening program utilizing the recently acquired knowledge of the "indicators," but not Survey No. 1 in particular. The former heads of the Espionage Research Branch at Headquarters and of the Espionage Division at the New York Field Office both believe the former to be the case; the Section Chief of the section at Headquarters out of which the program was run testified to the latter. Even if Hoover only approved the general concept of such a project, however, he was soon aware of the program, and, as noted above, authorized its extension to four additional cities in August 1961.

Survey No. 7 was initiated by the San Francisco Field Office on its own motion without prior approval from Washington. When Headquarters was advised of the implementation of this program, ranking FBI officials immediately demanded justification for it from the Field Offiee, subsequently determined the justification to be inadequate, and ordered its termination as a generalized survey. The last sentence of the instruction to end the program warns: "Do not initiate such general coverage without first obtaining specific Bureau authority."

Unlike most of their CIA counterparts, then, it appears that the Bureau's mail opening programs were—with one clear exception—personally approved by the Director before their implementation, and at the highest levels of the organization before major changes in their operation. In the one certain case where prior Headquarters approval was not secured, the field office which implemented the programs was reprimanded.

B. Administrative Controls by Headquarters

FBI Headquarters exerted tight, centralized control over the mail opening programs in other ways as well. One manifestation of this control was found in the periodic evaluations of each program required of every participating field office for the benefit of Headquarters. In general, written evaluations were submitted semiannually for the first few years of the operation of a program in a city; and annually thereafter. These evaluations frequently contained such headings as: "Origin;" "Purpose;" "Scope;" "Cost;" "Overall Value;" and "Operation of Source." Every field office was also obligated to determine whether the counterintelligence benefits from each program justified its continuation in light of manpower and security considerations; on the basis of this recommendation and other information supplied, Headquarters then decided whether to re-authorize the program until the next evaluation period or order its termination. The net effect of this system of periodic reexamination was that FBI officials were far better informed than were CIA officials of the true value of the programs to their organization. It was difficult for a program to continue unproductively without the knowledge of the highest ranking officials of the Bureau: as noted above, several programs—Surveys No. 2, 3, and 7 -- were in fact discontinued by Headquarters before 1966 because the results as set forth in the evaluations were felt to be outweighed by other factors.

Also in contrast to the CIA mail opening programs, the Bureau programs were conducted at the field level with Special Agents who were experienced in intelligence work and given detailed instructions regarding the "indicators" and other selection criteria. No control procedure could ever eliminate the individual discretion of these agents—ultimately, selection was based on their personal judgment. But Headquarters ensured through the training of these agents that their judgment was at least more informed than that of the Office of Security "interceptors" in the CIA's New York project, who were neither foreign intelligence experts nor given guidance beyond the Watch List itself as to which items to select. At both the Field Office and the Headquarters levels, moreover, responsibility for the operation of the programs was not diffused, as it was in the CIA's New York project but was centralized in the hands of experienced senior officials within a single chain of command.

C. Knowledge of the Mail Opening Programs Within the FBI

Officials of the Domestic Intelligence Division at Headquarters carefully controlled knowledge and dissemination procedures of their mail opening programs within the FBI itself. Knowledge of the operations was strictly limited to the Domestic Intelligence Division. The Criminal Division, for example, was never advised of the existence of (and so never levied requests on) any of these programs, but an internal memorandum indicates that it may have received information generated by the programs without being advised of the true source. Some FBI witnesses assigned to espionage squads which were engaged in mail opening even testified that they were unaware of other mail opening programs being conducted simultaneously by other espionage squads in the same field office.

The direct dissemination of the photographic copies of letters or abstracts between field offices was prohibited, but Headquarters avoided some of the problems caused by restricted knowledge in the CIA programs by requiring these offices to paraphrase the contents of letters in which other field offices might have an intelligence interest and disseminate the information to them in sanitized form.

Thus, control over the major aspects of the programs was concentrated at the top of the FBI hierarchy to a degree far greater than that which characterized the CIA programs. With few exceptions, senior officials at Headquarters initially authorized the programs, maximized central influence over their actual operation, restricted knowledge of their existence within the Bureau, and regulated the form in which information from them should be disseminated.

V. External Authorizations

Despite the differences between the FBI's and the CIA's mail opening programs with regard to internal authorization, the respective patterns of authorization outside the agencies were clearly parallel. There is no direct evidence that any President or Postmaster General was ever informed about any of the FBI mail opening programs until four years after they ceased. While two Attorneys General may have known about some aspect of the Bureau's mail interceptions — and the record is not even clear on this point — it does not appear that any Attorney General was ever briefed on the full scope of the programs. Thus, like the CIA mail opening programs, the Bureau programs were isolated even within the executive department. They were initiated and operated by Bureau officials alone, without the knowledge, approval, or control of the President or his cabinet.

A. Post Office Department

The FBI mail opening programs, like those of the CIA, necessitated the cooperation of the Post Office Department. But the record shows that the Bureau officials who secured this cooperation intended to and did in fact accomplish their task without revealing the FBI's true interest in obtaining access to the mail; no high ranking Postal official was apparently made aware that the FBI actually opened first class mail.

1. Postmasters General

There is no evidence that any Postmaster General was ever briefed about any of the FBI mail opening programs, either by the FBI directly or by a Chief Postal Inspector. Henry Montague, who as Chief Postal Inspector was aware of the mail cover (as opposed to the mail opening) aspect of several Bureau programs, stated that he never informed the Postmaster General because he "thought it was our duty to cooperate in this interest, and really, I did not see any reason to run to the Postmaster General with the problem. It was not through design that I kept it away from ... the Postmaster General. ... It was just that I did not see any reason to run to [him] because he had so many other problems."

2. Chief Postal Inspectors

It is certain that at least one and probably two Chief Postal Inspectors were aware of the fact that Bureau agents received direct access to mail, and in one case permission may have been given to physically remove letters from the mailstream as well, but there is no direct evidence that any Chief Postal Inspector was ever informed that FBI agents actually opened any mail.

Clifton Garner. — Clifton Garner was Chief Postal Inspector under the Truman administration during the period when Z-Coverage may have been reinstituted in Washington, D.C. No FBI testimony or documents, however, suggest that his approval was sought prior to this reinstitution, nor can he recall being contacted by Bureau officials about such a program.

David Stephens. — Henry Montague testified that prior to the 1959 implementation of Z-Coverage in New York, when he was Postal Inspector in Charge of that region, he was instructed by Chief Postal Inspector David Stephens to cooperate with Bureau agents in their proposed program of special "mail covers." As Montague recalls, Stephens approved the "mail cover" operation and left the mechanical arrangements up to him. Donald Moore has also testified that Stephens must have been contacted by Bureau officials in Washington prior to the implementation of Survey No. 1 in the same year, although he did not participate in any such meeting himself, and no other FBI official who testified could shed any light on who might have made such contact. There is no evidence, however, that Stephens was ever informed that mail would actually be opened by Bureau agents in either program.

Henry Montague. — As Postal Inspector in Charge of the New York Region, Montague followed David Stephens' instructions to cooperate with the FBI regarding Z-Coverage and made the necessary mechanical arrangements within his office. He stated, however, that he was told by the Bureau representatives who came to see him, including Donald Moore (whose testimony is consistent) that this was a mail cover rather than a mail opening operation. He was simply informed that the Bureau had an interest in obtaining direct access to particular mail for national security reasons and that his cooperation would be appreciated. While he realized that even this type of access was highly unusual, he agreed because "... they knew what they were looking for; we did not. ... [T]hey could not give any names to the Postal Service, as far as I knew, for mail to look for. ... [P]erhaps they knew who the agent might be, or something of this sort, which knowledge was not ours and which, at that time, I did not feel was in our province to question." Montague also acknowledged that during his tenure as Postal Inspector in Charge of the New York Region, he may have known of an FBI operation at Idlewild Airport (Survey No. 1) as well, but stated that he had no "positive recollection" of it.

As Chief Postal Inspector from 1961 to 1969, Montague personally authorized Postal Service cooperation with the Bureau's programs in at least two instances, and in one case possibly approved the removal of selected letters by Bureau agents to a point outside the postal facility in which they worked. According to a 1961 FBI memorandum, it was recommended by Bureau officials and approved by Director Hoover that Postal officials in Washington should be contacted "to explore the possibility of instituting" Survey No. 2. In February of that year, Donald Moore met with Montague about this matter, explaining only — according to both Moore and Montague — that the program would involve screening the mail and that it was vital to the security of the country. The fact that the FBI intended to open selected items was apparently not mentioned. Because he "felt it was our duty to cooperate with the Agency which was responsible for the national security in espionage cases," Montague agreed to assist the Bureau. On this occasion, however, he indicated that he would prefer to have postal employees rather than FBI agents conduct the "cover" since "it was our position that whenever possible ... the mail should remain in the possession of the Postal Service."

Less than two years later, Montague did allow Bureau agents to screen mail directly in Survey No. 4. A 1962 FBI memorandum noted that the FBI liaison to the Post Office approached him on December 19 to secure his approval for the Bureau's plan to cover mail from Miami to a Latin American country. According to this memorandum, Montague did approve and authorized the removal of selected letters to the FBI laboratory as well. The former Chief Postal Inspector remembers approving the screening aspects of the project and knowing that mail left the custody of postal employees, but cannot recall whether or not he specifically granted his permission for flying certain letters to Washington. He testified, in any event, that he was not informed that mail would be opened.

In June 1965, Montague reconsidered his original approval of the project, possibly in light of Senator Edward Long's investigation into the use of mail covers and other techniques by federal agencies. A June 2 1965. FBI airtel from the Miami office to Headquarters reads in part: "[The Assistant Postal Inspector in Charge of the

Atlanta Region] said that due to investigations by Senate and Congressional committees, Mr. Montague requested he be advised of the procedures used in this operation." Montague had appeared before the Long Subcommittee and had testified on the subject of mail covers several times earlier that year, but he recalls that his concern in detemining the procedures used in Survey No. 4 in June focused more on the new Postal regulations regarding mail covers that were issued about that time than on the Senate hearings. Regardless of his motivation, Montague asked the Assistant Postal Inspector in Charge to ascertain the details of the Miami operation; the procedures were described to this postal official by representatives of the Miami Field Office, apparently without mention of the fact that mail was actually opened; and the Assistant Postal Inspector reported back to Montague, who found them to be acceptable and did not withdraw his support for the survey.

Montague has stated that he was never informed that FBI agents in Survey No. 4 or in any of the other Bureau programs intended to or actually did open first class mail. This testimony is supported by that of Donald Moore, who on at least two occasions was the Bureau representative who sought Montague's cooperation for the programs. Moore does not believe that he ever told Montague that mail would be opened; he said, moreover, that it was "understood" within the Bureau that Postal officials should not be informed. Of his meeting with Montague about Z-Coverage, for example, Moore stated: "I am sure I didn't volunteer it to him and, in fact, would not volunteer it to him" because of the belief that such information should be closely held within the Bureau. He added that it was a general, though unwritten, policy that whenever Bureau agents contacted Postal officials concerning the mail programs "it was understood that they would not be told [that mail opening was contemplated]."

Montague, for his part, did not specifically warn FBI agents against tampering with the mail because they were Federal officers and he trusted them not to do so. He stated:

> I do not recall that I asked [if they intended to open mail], because I never thought that would be necessary. I knew that we never opened mail in connection with a mail cover. I knew that we could not approve it, that we would not approve any opening of any mail by anybody else. Both the CIA and the FBI were Government employees the same as we were, had taken the same oath of office, so that question was really not discussed by me....

> With regard to the CIA when they first started [in 1953], we did put more emphasis on that point that mail could not be tampered with, that it could not be delayed, because, according to my recollection, this was the first time that we had had any working relationship with the CIA at all. With the FBI, I just did not consider that it was necessary to emphasize that point. I trusted them the same as I would trust another Inspector. I would never feel that I would have to tell a Postal person that you cannot open mail. By the same token, I would not consider it necessary to emphasize it to any great degree with the FBI.

In short, it does not appear that any senior postal official knew that the FBI opened mail. Postal officials did cooperate extensively with the Bureau, but out of trust did not ask whether mail would be opened and because of a concern for security they were not told.

B. Department of Justice

The record presents no conclusive evidence that any Attorney General ever knew of any of the FBI mail opening programs. The evidence summarized below, does suggest that one and possibly two Attorneys General may have been informed of selected aspects of the Bureau's mail operations, but generally supports the view that no Attorney General was ever briefed on their full scope.

1. Robert F. Kennedy

New York Field Office Briefings. — On April 5, 1962, and again on November 4, 1963, Attorney General Robert F. Kennedy visited the FBI's New York field office was briefed in foreign espionage matters. The person who briefed him on these occasions, the Assistant Special Agent in Charge for the Espionage Division, testified that he may have mentioned the mail intercept projects then being conducted by the New York field office to the Attorney General, but has no definite recollection whether he did or not. Other participants at these briefings could not recall the technique of mail opening being discussed, nor do the internal FBI memoranda relating to the briefings indicate that the topic arose.

The Baltch Case. — It is also possible, though again the evidence is far from conclusive, that Robert Kennedy learned that mail opening was utilized in the Baltch investigation, which is described on page 648. On July 2, 1963, FBI agents arrested two alleged Soviet illegal agents who used the names Robert and Joy Ann Baltch; they were indicted for espionage on July 15. Several conferences were held between FBI representatives and Assistant Attorney General for Internal Security, J. Walter Yeagley, regarding this case and the possibility that some of the evidence was tainted. Yeagley subsequently briefed Kennedy on the problems involved in prosecuting the Baltchs. Donald E. Moore, who was one of the FBI representatives who discussed the Baltch case with Yeagley, testified that he believed, though he had no direct knowledge, that the fact of mail opening did come to the attention of the Attorney General in this context. Yeagley, however, cannot recall being specifically advised that mail was opened (although he knew that a "mail intercept or cover" had occurred) and stated that he did not inform Kennedy about any mail openings.

Other Espionage Cases. — Internal FBI memoranda concerning at least two other espionage cases that were considered for prosecution while Kennedy was Attorney General, also raise the possibility that Justice Department attorneys, including Yeagley, may have been advised of mail openings that occurred. Yeagley cannot recall being so advised, however, and, as noted above, stated that he never informed the Attorney General of any mail openings. There is no indication in the memoranda, moreover, that these matters were ever raised with Kennedy.

2. Nicholas deB. Katzenbach

The Baltch Case. — The Baltch case did not come to trial until early October 1964, when Nicholas deB. Katzenbach was Acting Attorney General. At the time the trial commenced, FBI representatives, including Donald Moore, conferred with Thomas K. Hall, a Justice Department attorney who was assigned to the case, again on the subject of tainted evidence. Hall then discussed the case with Katzenbach and, according to an FBI internal memorandum, "Katzenbach recognized the problems, but felt in view of the value of the case, an effort should be made to go ahead with the trial even if it might be necessary to drop the overt act where our tainted source is involved..." Because he subsequently determined that the case "could not be further prosecuted without revealing national security information," however, Katzenbach ordered the prosecution to be dropped entirely.

In fact, there were at least two sources of tainted evidence other than mail opening involved in the Baltch case—a surreptitious entry and a microphone installation—and it is only these which Katzenbach recalls. He testified that although he did discuss the taint issues with both Hall and Joseph Hoey, the United States Attorney who originally presented the government's case, neither of them brought to his attention the fact of mail opening. Hoey's recollection supports this contention: a Bureau memorandum suggests that Hoey may have learned of a "mail intercept" in the case, but he recalls neither being informed of an actual opening nor conferring with the Acting Attorney General about any issue related to mail. Assistant Attorney General Yeagley recalls discussing the case generally with Katzenbach also, and "may have informed him of the mail intercept or cover which had occurred," but Yeagley stated that he had no definite knowledge himself that the "intercept or cover" involved the actual opening of mail, and so would not have been in a position to advise him that it did.

Katzenbach has testified that he was never aware of the Bureau's use of mail opening in any espionage investigation. He added:

> Even if one were to conclude that the Bureau did in fact reveal that mail had been opened and that this fact was relayed by lawyers in the [Baltch] case to me, I am certain that that fact would have been revealed by the FBI—and I would have accepted it—as an unfortunate aberration, just then discovered in the context of a Soviet espionage investigation, not a massive mail-opening program. In that event, nothing would have led me to deduce that the Bureau was, as a matter of policy and practice, opening letters.

The Long Subcommittee Hearings. — According to Donald Moore, he and Assistant Director Alan H. Belmont did inform Mr. Katzenbach at the time of the 1965 Long Subcommittee hearings that Bureau agents screened mail both inside and outside postal facilities as a matter of practice, although he does not claim that the subject of actual opening arose.

In February of that year, the Long Subcommittee directed Chief Postal Inspector Montague to provide it with a list of all mail covers, including those in the areas of organized crime and national security, by federal agencies within the previous two years. As a restilt of this and other inquiries by the Subcommittee, especially regarding electronic surveillance practices, President Johnson requested Katzenbach to coordinate all executive department matters under his investigation.

In executing this responsibility, Katzenbach met with Moore, Belmont, and Courtney Evans, a former FBI Assistant Director who had retired from the Bureau but was then working as a special assistant to the Attorney General, on February 27, 1965, to discuss problems raised by the Subcommittee which affected the FBI. One of the subjects discussed at that meeting was the question of Bureau access to the mail. Four days earlier, the Chief Postal Inspector had testified before the Subcommittee that he had no knowledge of any case in which mail left the custody of Postal employees during the course of a mail cover. At the time, Montague did know that this practice had occurred -- indeed, as Chief Postal Inspector he had approved the direct screening of mail by FBI agents in Survey No. 4 -- but he believed that "there was an understanding ... that national security cases were not included within this particular part of the hearing." According to Moore, Katzenbach had been made aware of the possible inaccuracy of Montague's testimony, and the Bureau officials consequently "pointed out [to the Attorney General] that we do receive mail from the Post Office in certain sensitive areas . ..." Moore believes moreover, that they informed him that this custody was granted in on-going projects rather than isolated instances.

Katzenbach acknowledged that he was aware, while Attorney General, that "in some cases the outside of mail might have been examined or even photographed by persons other than Post Office employees," but he stated that he never knew the FBI gained custody to mail on a regular basis in large-scale operations. 537 He also testified that [at] the time of the February meeting he considered Montague's testimony to be "essentially truthful." While the record shows that he spoke to Senator Long less than a week after this meeting, Katzenbach stated that this was in regard to the requested list of all mail covers by federal agencies rather than the issue of mail custody. The testimony of Courtney Evans, who was also present at the February 27 meeting, supports that of Katzenbach: at no time, Evans said, was he personally ever made aware that FBI agents received direct access to mail on an ongoing basis.

Moore does not claim that he told Katzenbach that mail was actually opened by Bureau agents. According to him, this information was volunteered by neither Belmont nor himself and Katzenbach did not inquire whether opening was involved. When asked if he felt any need to hold back from Katzenbach the fact of mail openings as opposed to the fact that Bureau agents received direct access to the mail, Moore replied: "It is perhaps difficult to answer. Perhaps I could liken it to ... a defector in place in the KGB. You don't want to tell anybody his name, the location, the title, or anything like that. Not that you don't trust them completely, but the fact is that anytime one additional person becomes aware of it, there is a potential for the information to ... go further."

Probably the strongest suggestion in the documentary evidence that Katzenbach may have been made aware of actual FBI mail openings at the time of the Long Subcommittee hearings is found in a memorandum from Hoover to ranking Bureau officials, dated March 2, 1965. This memorandum reads, in part:

> The Attorney General called and advised that he had talked to Senator Long last night. Senator Long's committee is looking into mail covers, et cetera. The Attorney General stated he thought somebody had already spoken to Senator Long as he said he did not want to get into any national security area and was willing to take steps not to do this. The Attorney General stated that Mr. Fensterwald [Chief counsel to the Subcommittee] was present for part of the meeting and Fensterwald had said that he had some possible witnesses who are former Bureau agents and if they were asked if mail was opened, they would take the Fifth Amendment. The Attorney General stated that before they are called, he would like to know who they are and whether they were ever involved in any program touching on national security and if not, it is their own business, but if they were, we would want to know. The Attorney General stated the Senator promised that he would have a chance to look at the names if he wanted to, personally and confidentially, and the list would have any names involving national security deleted and he would tell the Senator how many but no more.

Katzenbach testified as follows concerning his passage:

[Even] assuming the accuracy of the memo, it is not consistent with my being aware of the Bureau's mail opening program. Had I been aware of that program, I naturally would have assumed that the agents had been involved in that program, and I would scarcely have been content to leave them to their own devices before Senator Long's committee. Moreover, it would have been extremely unusual for ex-FBI agents to be interviewed by the Senate committee staff without revealing that fact to the Bureau. In those circumstances both the Director and I would have been concerned as to the scope of their knowledge with respect to the very information about mail covers which the Senator was demanding and which we were refusing, as well as about any other matters of of a national security nature. If the witnesses in fact existed (which I doubted strongly), then both the Director and I wanted to know the extent of their knowledge about Bureau programs, and the extent of their hostility toward the FBI. That is a normal concern that we would have had anytime any ex-FBI agent testified before any Congressional committee on any subject.

The most that can reasonably be inferred from the record on possible knowledge of FBI mail opening by Attorneys General is this: one or two Attorneys General may have known that mail was opened in connection with particular espionage investigations, and one Attorney General may have learned that the FBI regularly received mail from the Post Office and that five former FBI agents possibly opened mail. Evidence exists which casts doubt on the reasonableness of even these inferences, however. More significantly, there is no indication in either the documents or the testimony that the approval of any Attorney General was ever sought prior to the institution of any Bureau program, and despite a clear opportunity to inform Attorney General Katzenbach of the full scope and true nature of these operations in 1965, he was intentionally not told. In the name of security, the Bureau neither sought the approval of nor even shared knowledge of its programs with the Cabinet officer who was charged with the responsibility of controlling and regulating the FBI's conduct.

The first uncontroverted evidence that any Attorney General knew of the FBI mail opening programs is not found until 1970, four years after the programs were terminated. John Mitchell, upon reading the 1970 "Huston Report", learned that the Bureau had engaged in "covert mail coverage" in the past, but that this practice had "been discontinued." While the report itself stated that mail opening was unlawful, however, Mitchell did not initiate any investigation, nor did he show much interest in the matter. He testified:

> I had no consideration of that subject matter at the time. I did not focus on it and I was very happy that the plan was thrown out the window, without pursuing any of its provisions further. ... I think if I had focused on it I might have considered [an investigation into these acts] more than I did.

C. Presidents

There is no evidence that any President was ever contemporaneously informed about any of the FBI mail opening programs. In 1970, Bureau officials who were involved in the preparation of the "Huston Report" apparently advised Tom Charles Huston that mail opening as an investigative technique had been utilized in the past, for this fact was reflected in the report which was sent to President Nixon.

VI. Termination Of The FBI Mail Opening Programs

A. Hoover's Decision to Terminate the Programs in 1966

1. Timing

By mid-1966 only three FBI mail opening programs continued to operate: Z-Coverage in New York and Washington, Survey No. 1 in those same cities, and Survey No. 4 in Miami. Three of the programs — No. 2, No. 3, and No. 7 -- and the extensions of Survey No. 1 to four cities other than New York and Washington had all been terminated prior to 1966 because they had produced no valuable counterintelligence information while tying up manpower needed in other areas. 551 Two of the programs — Surveys No. 5 and 6 -- had been suspended in January 1966 for security reasons involving changes in local postal personnel and never reinstituted. As the San Francisco Field office informed Headquarters in May of that year in regard to both programs: "While it is realized that these sources furnished valuable information to the Federal Government, it is not believed the value justifies the risk involved. It is not recommended that contact with sources be re-instituted."

The remaining three programs were all terminated in July 1966 at the direct instruction of J. Edgar Hoover. Apparently this instruction was delivered telephonically to the field offices; no memoranda explicitly reflect the order to terminate the programs. There is no evidence that the FBI has employed the technique of mail opening in any of its investigations since that time, although the FBI continued to receive the fruits of the CIA's mail opening program until 1973.

2. Reasons

Given the perceived success of these three programs the reasons for their termination are not entirely clear. While all FBI officials who testified on the subject were unanimous in their conclusion that the decision was Hoover's alone, none could testify as to the precise reasons for his decision.

At least three possible reasons are presented by the record. First, the Director may have believed that the benefits derived from mail opening were outweighed by the need to present espionage cases for prosecution which were untainted by use of this technique. Regardless of whether or not the mail opening in the Baltch case was actually a factor in Acting Attorney General Katzenbach's decision to drop the prosecution, for example, Bureau officials believed that their use of the technique in that case did in fact preclude prosecution. On a memorandum dealing with the evidentiary issues in the Baltch case, Hoover wrote the following notation: "We must immediately and materially reduce the use of techniques which 'taint' cases."

Second, Hoover may have believed that the Attorney General and other high government officials would not support him in the FBIs use of questionable investigative practices. It is known that Hoover cut back on a number of other techniques in the mid-1960's: the use of mail covers by the FBI was suspended in 1964, and in July 1966 -- the same month which saw the end of the mail opening programsHoover terminated the technique of surreptitious entries by Bureau agents. In a revealing comment on a 1965 memorandum regarding the Long Subcommittee's investigation of such techniques as mail covers and electronic surveillance, Hoover wrote:

I don't see what all the excitement is about. I would have no hesitance in discontinuing all techniques — technical coverage [i.e. wiretapping], microphones, trash covers, mail covers, etc. While it might handicap us I doubt they are as valuable as some believe and none warrant FBI being used to justify them.

His lack of support from above had been tentatively suggested by some witnesses as a reason for this general retrenchment. Donald Moore, for example, surmised that:

There had been several questions raised on various techniques, and some procedures had changed, and I feel that Mr. Hoover in conversation with other people, of which I am not aware, decided that he did not or would not receive backing in these procedures and he did not want them to continue until the policy question was decided at a higher level.

While former Attorney General Katzenbach testified that he was unaware of the FBI mail openings, his views on this subject tend to support Moore's. He speculated that the reason the programs were terminated in 1966 may have related to the then-strained relations between Mr. Hoover and the Justice Department stemming from the case of Black v. United States and the issue of warrantless electronic surveillance. Hoover had wanted the Justice Department to inform the Supreme Court, in response to an order by the Court that the type of warrantless microphone surveillance that occurred in that case had been authorized by every Attorney General since Herbert Brownell. Katzenbach, not believing this to be so, approved a Supplemental Memorandum to the Court which simply stated that microphone installations had been authorized by longstanding "practice." According to Katzenbach, "this infuriated Hoover. . . . He was very angry, [and] that may have caused him to stop everything of this kind."

A third, related reason was suggested by W. Raymond Wannall, former Assistant Director in charge of the FBIs Domestic Intelligence Division. Wannall believed that there was a genuine "question in [Hoover's] mind about the legality" of mail opening, and noted that by at least 1970, as expressed in one of the Director's footnotes in the Huston Report, Hoover clearly considered mail opening to be outside the framework of the law. This footnote also suggests that, like CIA officials, Hoover was concerned that the perceived illegality of the technique would lead to an adverse public reaction damaging to the FBI and other intelligence agencies if its use were made known. His note to President Nixon read:

The FBI is opposed to implementing any covert mail coverage [i.e., mail opening] because, it is clearly illegal and it is likely that, if done, information would leak out of the Post Office to the press and serious damage would be done to the intelligence community.

B. Recommended Reinstitution

1. Within the Bureau

Whatever the reasons for it, the FBI Director's decision to terminate all mail opening programs in 1966 was not favorably received by many of the participating agents in the field. As one official of the New York Field Office at the time of the termination testified:

... the inability of the government to pursue this type of investigative technique meant that we would no longer be able to achieve the results that I felt were necessary to protect the national security, and I did not feel that I wanted to continue in any job where you are unable to achieve the results that really your job calls for. ... That was a big influence on my taking retirement from the FBI.

Several recommendations came in from the field to consider the reinstitution of the mail opening programs between 1966 and the time of Hoover's death in 1972. None of them was successful. A 1970 internal FBI memorandum, for example, reflects the recommendation of the New York office that the programs be reinstituted, but Headquarters suggested that this course was "not advisable at this time." Underlining the words "not advisable," Hoover noted: "Absolutely right."

There is no evidence that any recommendation to reinstitute these programs ever reached the desk of an Acting Director or Director of the Bureau after Hoover's death.

2. Huston Plan

The only known attempt to recommend reinstitution of FBI mail by officials outside the FBI is found in the Huston Report in 1970. The Report itself stated that mail opening did not have the "sanction of law," but proceeded to note several advantages of relaxing restrictions on this technique, among them:

1. High-level postal authorities have, in the past, provided complete cooperation and have maintained full security of this program.

2. This technique involves negligible risk of compromise. Only high echelon postal authorities know of its existence, and personnel involved are highly trained, trustworthy, and under complete control of the intelligence agency.

3. This coverage has been extremely successful in producing hard-core and authentic intelligence which is not obtainable from any other source ...

Primarily because of the objections Hoover expressed in the footnote he added, which are discussed above, this aspect of the Huston Plan was never implemented, however.

VII. Legal And Security Considerations Within The FBI

During the years that the FBI mail opening programs operated, Bureau officials attempted only once, in 1951, to formulate a legal theory to justify warrantless mail opening, and the evidence suggests that they never relied upon even this theory. At the same time, there is little in the record (until Hoover's comment in the 1970 Huston Report) to indicate that Bureau officials perceived mail opening to be illegal, as many CIA officials did. The FBI officials who directed the programs apparently gave little consideration to factors of law at all; ironically, it appears that of the two agencies which opened first class mail without warrants, that agency with law enforcement responsibilities and which was a part of the Justice Department gave less thought to the legal ramifications of the technique. Despite its inattentive attitude toward legal issues, the Bureau was at least as concerned as the CIA that disclosure of their programs outside the FBI—even to its own overseer, the Attorney General, and especially to Congress—would, as Hoover wrote in 1970, "leak ... to the press and serious[ly] damage" the FBI. To avoid such exposure, the Bureau, like the CIA, took measures to prevent knowledge of their programs from reaching this country's elected leadership.

A. Consideration of Legal Factors by the FBI

1. Prior to the Commencement of Mail Opening Programs In the Post-War Period

In June 1951, when the Washington Field Office recommended to Headquarters that consideration should be given to the reinstitution of Z-Coverage, it was specifically suggested that Bureau officials determine whether or not Postal Inspectors have the authority to order the opening of first class mail in espionage cases. Headquarters conducted research on this possible legal predicate to the peacetime reinstitution of the program, and the results were summarized in a second memorandum on Z-Coverage in September 1951. The basic conclusion was that Postal Inspectors had no authority to open mail; only employees of the Dead Letter Office and other persons with legal search warrants had such power. It was argued, however, that Postal Inspectors may have sufficient legal authority to open even first class mail whose contents were legally non-mailable under 18 U.S.C. Section 1717. This class of non-mailable items included, and includes today, "[e]very letter ... in violation of sections ... 793, 794 [the espionage statutes] ... of this title ..." Since it was a crime to mail letters whose contents violated the espionage statutes, it was reasoned, it may not be unlawful to intercept and open such letters, despite the general prohibition against mail opening found in 18 U.S.C. Sections 1701, 1702, and 1703. The study concluded:

> ... it is believed that appropriate arrangements might be worked out on a high level between the Department and the Postmaster General or between the Bureau and the appropriate Post Office officials whereby the mail of interest to the Bureau could be checked for items in violation of the espionage and other security statutes which are itemized in Title 18, U.S. Code Section. ... It is respectfully suggested that appropriate discussions be held on this matter.

This theory ignores the fact that the warrant procedure itself responds to the problem of non-mailable items. If, on the basis of an exterior examination of the envelope or on the basis of facts surrounding its mailing, there exists probable cause for a court to believe that the espionage statutes have been violated, a warrant may be obtained to open the correspondence. If the evidence does not rise to the level of probable cause, the law does not permit the mail to be opened. There is no indication, in any event, that discussions were ever held with any Postmaster General or Attorney General in an attempt to either test or implement this theory. While Z-Coverage was in fact reinstituted after this study was made, it was conducted with FBI personnel rather than Postal Inspectors, and its mail opening aspect was apparently unknown to any high-ranking Postal officials. In regard to the recommendation that "appropriate discussions be held on this matter," Assistant to the Director Alan Belmont penned the notation, "No action at this time. File for future reference."

2. Post-1951

After the mail opening programs were underway, there was apparently no further consideration by FBI officials of the legal factors involved in the operations. Unlike that regarding CIA mail opening, the documentary record on the FBI programs does not contain references (until 1970, four years after the programs ceased) to the illegality of mail opening; nor does it suggest that mail opening was considered legal. At most, the record reveals the recognition by Bureau officials that evidence obtained from their surveys was tainted and, hence, inadmissible in court, but not the recognition that the technique was invalid per se. Indeed, after the Supreme Court decisions in Nardone v. United States, 302 U.S. 379 (1937) and 308 U.S. 338 (1939), this distinction was explicitly made in the area of electronic surveillance: while the Nardone decisions prohibited the admission in court of evidence obtained from wiretapping, the cases were not interpreted by the Bureau to preclude use of the technique itself, and the practice continued.

The testimonial record, moreover, clearly suggests that legal considerations were simply not raised in contemporaneous policy decisions affecting the various mail surveys: W. Raymond Wannall, William Branigan, and others have all so testified. None of these officials has any knowledge that any legal theory — either the one which was filed for "future reference" in 1951 or one based on a possible "national security" exception to the general prohibition against mail opening — was ever developed by Bureau officials after 1951 to justify their programs legally, or that a legal opinion from the Attorney General was ever sought. To these officials, such justification as existed stemmed not from legal reasoning but from the end they sought to achieve and an amorphous, albeit honestly held, concept of the "greater good." As William Branigan stated: "It was my assumption that what we were doing was justified by what we had to do." He added that he believed "the national security" impelled reliance on such techniques:

> The greater good, the national security, this is correct. This is what I believed in. Why I thought these programs were good, it was that the national security required this, this is correct.

At least some of the agents who participated in the mail opening program have testified that they believed the surveys were legal because they assumed (without being told) that the programs had been authorized by the President or Attorney General, or because they assumed (again without being told) that there was a "national security" exception to the laws prohibiting mail opening. Those officials in a policymaking position, however, apparently did not focus on the legal questions sufficiently to state an opinion regarding the legality or illegality of the programs, nor did they advise the field offices or participating agents about these matters.

Only in the 1970's, at least four years after the FBI mail opening programs ceased, is there any clear indication that Bureau officials, like those of the CIA, believed their programs to be illegal. As noted above, Hoover's footnote to the 1970 Huston Report described the technique as "clearly illegal;" and in the recent public hearings on FBI mail opening, W. Raymond Wannall testified that, as of 1975, "I cannot justify what happened. ..."

In light of the Bureau's major responsibilities in the area of law enforcement and the likelihood that some of the espionage cases in which mail opening was utilized would be prosecuted, it is ironic that FBI officials focused on these legal issues to a lesser degree than did their CIA counterparts. But the Bureau's Domestic Intelligence Division made a clear distinction between law enforcement and counterintelligence matters; what was appropriate in one area was not necessarily appropriate in the other. As William Branigan again testified:

> In consideration of prosecuting a case, quite obviously [legal factors] would be of vital concern. In discharging counterintelligence responsibilities, namely to identify agents in the United States to determine the extent of damage that they are causing to the United States ... we would not necessarily go into the legality or illegality. ... We were trying to identify agents and we were trying to find out how this country was being hurt, and [mail opening] was a means of doing it, and it was a successful means.

B. Concern with Exposure

Although Bureau officials apparently did not articulate the view prior to 1970 that mail opening was necessarily illegal, they did believe that their use of this technique was so sensitive that its exposure to other officials within the executive branch, the courts, Congress, and the American public generally should be effectively prevented. This fear of exposure may have resulted from a perceived though unexpressed sense that its legality was at least questionable; it was almost certainly a consequence of a very restricted, even arrogant, view of who had a "need to know" about the Bureau's operations. But whatever its source, this concern with security clearly paralleled the CIA's concern with the "flap potential" of their projects and resulted in similar efforts to block knowledge of their use of this technique from reaching the general public and its leaders.

The reluctance of FBI officials to disclose the details of their programs to other officials within the executive branch itself has been described above: there is no clear evidence that any Bureau official ever revealed the complete nature and scope of the mail surveys to any officer of the Post Office Department or Justice Department, or to any President of the United States. It was apparently a Bureau policy not to inform the Postal officials with whom they dealt of the actual intention of FBI agents in receiving the mail, and there is no indication that this policy was ever violated. 587 When Attorney General Katzenbach met with Donald Moore and Alan Belmont on the subject of Bureau custody of mail, Moore testified that he did not inform the Attorney General about the mail opening aspect of the projects because of security reasons: "anytime one additional person becomes aware of it, there is a potential for the information to ... go further." One Bureau agent at Headquarters who was familiar with the mail programs (but not in a policy-making position) also speculated that the questionable legal status of this technique may have been an additional reason for not seeking the Attorney General's legal advice. He testified as follows:

> Q. Do you know why the opinion of the Attorney General was apparently or probably not sought?
>
> A. Because of the security of the operation. I would imagine that would be the main reason. It was a program we were operating. We wanted to keep it within the Bureau itself—and the fact that it involved opening mail.
>
> Q. What do you mean by the last statement, "... the fact that it involved opening mail"?
>
> A. That was not legal, as far as I knew.

With respect to the Justice Department generally, only the minimum knowledge necessary to resolve a specific prosecutive problem was imparted. Donald Moore said of his meeting with Assistant Attorney General Yeagley about the Baltch case, for example, that he did not disclose to him the FBI's general use of this technique: "I am sure it was confined to the issue at hand, which was anything at all which involved the prosecution of Baltch." Even the term "mail opening" was avoided, and the more ambiguous term "mail intercept" was used: while susceptible of only one meaning within the FBI, the latter term was apparently misinterpreted by Yeagley and other Justice Department officials with different assumptions about Bureau operations.

The FBI's concern with exposure extended to the courts as well. In an internal memorandum regarding the Baltch case, it was written that "under no circumstances is the Bureau willing to admit [to the court] that a mail intercept was utilized. ..."

Similarly, FBI officials, like their counterparts in the CIA, did not want their use of this technique known to Congress. One senior Bureau official testified that the FBI feared that the Long Subcommittee's 1965 investigation could publicly expose the mail programs ; another that such Congressional exposure could "wrack up" the Bureau. Attorney General Katzenbach had been requested by the President to coordinate executive branch responses to inquiries by the Subcommittee, but the FBI was apparently not content with his efforts in preventing the disclosure of "national security" information generally. To ensure that their mail surveys, as well as certain practices in the area of electronic surveillance, remained unstudied, Bureau officials themselves directly attempted to steer the Subcommittee away from probing these subjects.

Alan Belmont's February 27, 1965, memorandum reflecting his meeting with the Attorney General about Henry Montague's testimony on mail custody, reads in part: "I told Mr. Katzenbach that I certainly agree that this matter should be controlled at the committee level but that I felt pressure would have to be applied so that the personal interest of Senator [Edward] Long became involved rather than on any ideological basis." The memorandum continues: "I called Mr. DeLoach [an Assistant Director of the FBI] and briefed him on this problem in order that he might contact Senator [James 0.] Eastland in an effort to warn the Long committee away from those areas which would be injurious to the national defense. (Of course, I made no mention of such a contact to the Attorney General.)" According to an FBI memorandum, J. Edgar Hoover himself subsequently contacted Senator Eastland, who, he reported, "is going to see Senator Long not later than Wednesday morning to caution him that [the chief counsel] must not go into the kind of questioning he made of Chief Inspector Montague of the Post Office Department."

The strategy worked. The Subcommittee never learned of the FBI's use of mail opening as an investigative technique. Despite the fact that in 1965 the FBI conducted a total of five mail opening programs in the United States—and despite the fact that in that year alone more than 13,300 letters were opened by CIA agents in New York—the Subcommittee, the general public, the Attorney General, and apparently even Henry Montague himself accepted as true Montague's testimony that year that:

> The seal on a first-class piece of mail is sacred. When a person puts first-class postage on a piece of mail and seals it, he can be sure that the contents of that piece of mail are secure against illegal search and seizure.

National Security Agency Surveillance Affecting Americans

1. Introduction And Summary

This report describes the Committee's investigation into certain questionable activities of the National Security Agency (NSA). The Committee's primary focus in this phase of its investigation was on NSA's electronic surveillance practices and capabilities, especially those involving American citizens, groups, and organizations.

NSA has intercepted and disseminated international communications of American citizens whose privacy ought to be protected under our Constitution. For example, from August 1945 to May 1975, NSA obtained copies of many international telegrams sent to, from, or through the United States from three telegraph companies. In addition, from the early 1960s until 1973, NSA targeted the international communications of certain American citizens by placing their names on a "watch list." Intercepted messages were disseminated to the FBI, CIA, Secret Service, Bureau of Narcotics and Dangerous Drugs (BNDD), and the Department of Defense. In neither program were warrants obtained.

With one exception, NSA contends that its interceptions of Americans' private messages were part of monitoring programs already being conducted against various international communications channels for "foreign intelligence" purposes. This contention is borne out by the record. Yet to those Americans who have had their communications sent with the expectation that they were private — intentionally intercepted and disseminated by their Government, the knowledge that NSA did not monitor specific communications channels solely to acquire their messages is of little comfort.

In general, NSA's surveillance of Americans was in response to requests from other Government agencies. Internal NSA directives now forbid the targeting of American citizens' communications. Nonetheless, NSA may still acquire communications of American citizens as part of its foreign intelligence mission, and information derived from these intercepted messages may be used to satisfy foreign intelligence requirements.

NSA's current surveillance capabilities and past surveillance practices were both examined in our investigation. The Committee recognizes that NSA's vast technological capability is a sensitive national asset which ought to be zealously protected for its value to our common defense. If not properly controlled, however, this same technological capability could be turned against the American people, at great cost to liberty. This concern is compounded by the knowledge that the proportion of telephone calls and telegrams being sent through the air is still increasing.

In addition to reviewing facts and issues relating to electronic surveillance, the Committee also examined certain questionable activities of the NSA's Office of Security. See pp. 777-783.

A. NSA's Origins and Official Responsibilities

NSA does not have a statutory charter; its operational responsibilities are set forth exclusively in executive directives first issued in the 1950s. One of the questions which the Senate asked the Committee to consider was the "need for specific legislative authority to govern the operations of ... the National Security Agency."

According to NSA's General Counsel, no existing statutes control, limit, or define the signals intelligence activities of NSA. Further, the General Counsel asserts that the Fourth Amendment does not apply to NSA's interception of Americans' international communications for foreign intelligence purposes.

1. Origins

NSA was established in 1952 by a Top Secret directive issued by President Truman. Under this directive, NSA assumed the responsibilities of the Armed Forces Security Agency, which had been created after World War II to integrate American cryptologic efforts. These efforts had expanded rapidly after World War II as a result of the demonstrated wartime value of breaking enemy codes, particularly those of the Japanese.

2. Responsibilities

(a) Subject Matter Responsibilities. — The executive branch expects NSA to collect political, economic, and military information as part of its "foreign intelligence" mission. "Foreign intelligence" is an ambiguous term. Its meaning changes, depending upon the prevailing needs and views of policymakers, and the current world situation. The internal politics of a nation also play a role in setting requirements for foreign intelligence; the domestic economic situation, an upcoming political campaign, and internal unrest can all affect the kind of foreign intelligence that a political leader desires. Thus, the definition constantly expands and contracts to satisfy the changing needs of American policymakers for information. This flexibility was illustrated in the late 1960s, when NSA and other intelligence agencies were asked to produce "foreign intelligence" on domestic activists in the wake of major civil disturbances and increasing antiwar activities.

NSA's authority to collect foreign intelligence is derived from a Top Secret National Security Council directive which is implemented by directives issued by the Director of Central Intelligence. These directives give NSA the responsibility for "Signals Intelligence" (SIGINT) and "Communications Security" (COMSEC). SIGINT is subdivided into "Communications Intelligence" (COMINT) and "Electronics Intelligence" (ELINT). COMINT entails the interception of foreign communications and ELINT involves the interception of electronic signals from radars, missiles, and the like. The COMSEC mission includes the protection of United States Government communications by providing the means for enciphering messages and by establishing procedures for maintaining the security of equipment used to transmit them.

NSA's interception of communications — the area on which the Committee focused — arises under the COMINT program. The controlling NSCID defines COMINT in broad terms as "technical and intelligence information derived from foreign communications by other than the intended recipients." The same NSC directive also states that COMINT "shall not include (a) any intercept and processing of unencrypted written communications, press and propaganda broadcasts, or censorship."

The specific exclusion of unencrypted written communications from NSA's mandate would appear to prohibit NSA's interception of telegrams. NSA contends that this exclusion is and always has been limited to mail and communications other than those sent electronically.

The same NSCID which discusses foreign communications also states that NSA is to produce intelligence "in accordance with objectives, requirements, and priorities established by the Director of Central Intelligence with the advice of the United States Intelligence Board." USIB was composed of representatives from the FBI, CIA, Treasury Department, Energy Research and Development Administration, State Department, and Defense Department. Since 1966, NSA annually received general requirements from USIB for the collection of foreign intelligence. These requirements ordinarily identified broad areas of interest, such as combating international terrorism, and were supplemented by more specific "amplifying requirements" periodically submitted to NSA by other USIB members.

(b) Geographic Responsibilities. — Although none of the applicable executive directives explicitly prohibit NSA from intercepting communications which occur wholly within the United States, internal NSA policy has always prohibited such interceptions. In practice, NSA limits itself to communications where at least one of the terminals is in a foreign country. This means that when Americans use a telephone or other communications link between this country and overseas, their words may be intercepted by NSA.

(c.) Jurisdiction with Respect to Nationality. — Although the controlling NSCID contains no limitation relating to the citizenship of persons whose "foreign communications" may be intercepted, the relevant DCID does exclude messages "exchanged among private organizations and nationals, acting in a private capacity, of the U.S." This restriction is designed to prevent NSA from processing communications between two Americans, regardless of their location.

In the late 1960s and early 1970s, however, NSA did intercept and disseminate some messages exchanged between two Americans where one of the terminals was foreign. NSA does not now knowingly process or disseminate messages where both the sender and recipient are American citizens, groups, or organizations.

B. Summary of Interception Programs

The Committee's hearings disclosed three NSA interception programs: the "watch lists" containing names of American citizens; "Operation SHAMROCK," whereby NSA received copies of millions of telegrams leaving or transiting the United States, and the monitoring of certain telephone links between the United States and South America at the request of the Bureau of Narcotics and Dangerous Drugs. In addition, the Committee's investigation revealed that although NSA no longer includes the names of specific citizens in its selection criteria, it still intercepts international communications of Americans as part of its foreign intelligence collection activity. Information derived from such communications is disseminated by NSA to other intelligence agencies to satisfy foreign intelligence requirements.

1. Watch Lists Containing Names of Americans

From the early 1960s until 1973, NSA intercepted and disseminated international communications of selected American citizens and groups on the basis of lists of names supplied by other Government agencies. In 1967, as part of a general concern within the intelligence community over civil disturbances and peace demonstrations, NSA responded to Defense Department requests by expanding its watch list program. Watch lists came to include the names of individuals, groups, and organizations involved in domestic antiwar and civil rights activities in an attempt to discover if there was "foreign influence" on them.

In 1969, NSA formalized the watch list program under the codename MINARET. The program applied not only to alleged foreign influence on domestic dissent, but also to American groups and individuals whose activities "may result in civil disturbances or otherwise subvert the national security of the U.S." At the same time, NSA instructed its personnel to "restrict the knowledge" that NSA was collecting such information and to keep its name off the disseminated "product."

Prior to 1973, NSA generally relied on the agencies requesting information to determine the propriety and legality of their actions in submitting names to NSA. NSA's new director, General Lew Allen, Jr., indicated some concern about Project MINARET in August 1973, and suspended the dissemination of messages under the program. In September 1973, Allen wrote the agencies involved in the watch lists, requesting a recertification of their requirements, particularly as to the appropriateness of their requests.

In October 1973, Assistant Attorney General Henry Petersen and Attorney General Elliot Richardson concluded that the watch lists were of "questionable legality" and so advised NSA. In response, NSA took the position that although specific names had been targeted, the communications of particular Americans included on the watch lists had been collected "as an incidental and unintended act in the conduct of the interception of foreign communications." Allen concluded:

[NSA's] current practice conforms with your guidance that "relevant information acquired [by NSA] in the routine pursuit of the collection of foreign intelligence information may continue to be furnished to appropriate government agencies.

2. Obtaining Copies of Messages from International Telegraph Companies: Operation SHAMROCK

From August 1945 until May 1975, NSA received copies of millions of international telegrams sent to, from, or transiting the United States. Codenamed Operation SHAMROCK, this was the largest governmental interception program affecting Americans, dwarfing CIA's mail opening program by comparison. Of the messages provided to NSA by the three major international telegraph companies, it is estimated that in later years approximately 150,000 per month were reviewed by NSA analysts.

NSA states that the original purpose of the program was to obtain the enciphered telegrams of certain foreign targets. Nevertheless, NSA had access to virtually all the international telegrams of Americans carried by RCA Global and ITT World Communications. Once obtained, these telegrams were available for analysis and dissemination according to NSA's selection criteria, which included the watch lists.

The SHAMROCK program began in August 1945, when representatives of the Army Signals Security Agency approached the commercial telegraph companies to seek post-war access to foreign governmental traffic passing over the facilities of the companies. Despite advice from their attorneys that the contemplated intercept operation would be illegal in peacetime, the companies agreed to participate, provided they received the personal assurance of the Attorney General of the United States that he would protect them from suit, and that efforts be immediately undertaken to legalize the intercept operation. Apparently these assurances were forthcoming, because the intercept program began shortly thereafter.

In 1947, representatives of the companies met with Secretary of Defense Forrestal to discuss their continued participation in SHAMROCK. Forrestal told them that the program was "in the highest interests of national security" and urged them to continue. The companies were told that President Truman and Attorney General Tom C. Clark approved and that they would not suffer criminal liability, at least while the current Administration was in office. Those assurances were renewed in 1949, when it was again emphasized that future administrations could not be bound. There is no evidence that the companies ever sought such assurances again.

Throughout the operation NSA never informed the companies that it was analyzing and disseminating telegrams of Americans. Yet the companies, who had feared in 1945 that their conduct might be illegal, apparently never sought assurances that NSA was limiting its use to the messages of the foreign targets once the intercept program had begun.

3. Monitoring of South American Links for Drug Traffic Control Purposes

From 1970 to 1973, at the request of the Bureau of Narcotics and Dangerous Drugs, NSA monitored selected telephone circuits between the United States and certain countries in South America to obtain information relating to drug trafficking.

The BNDD was initially concerned about drug deals that were being arranged in calls to a South American city from public telephone booths in New York City. The Bureau determined that it could not legally tap the public telephones and enlisted NSA's help to monitor international communications links that carried these telephone calls. Thus, instead of intercepting calls from a few telephone booths, as the BNDD would have done with a wiretap, NSA had access to international calls placed from, or received in, cities all over the United States that were switched through New York.

In addition, BNDD submitted the names of 450 Americans to NSA for a "drug" watch list. This list resulted in the dissemination of about 1,900 reports on drug traffickers to BNDD and CIA.

The CIA began to assist NSA's monitoring effort in late 1972, but later determined that the program served a law enforcement function and terminated its participation in February 1973. NSA was affected by the CIA decision, as it had come to view this program as possibly serving a law enforcement function and thus beyond the scope of its proper mission. NSA terminated this activity in June 1973, but continued to monitor some of the same United States South American links for foreign intelligence purposes until July 1975.

4. "Incidental" Intercepts of Americans' Communications

Although NSA does not now target communications of American citizens, groups, or organizations for interception by placing their names on watch lists, other selection criteria are used which result in NSA's reviewing many communications to, from, or about an American. The initial interception of a stream of communications is analogous to a vacuum cleaner: NSA picks up all communications carried over a specific link that it is monitoring. The combination of this technology and the use of words to select communications of interest results in NSA analysts reviewing the international messages of American citizens, groups, and organizations for foreign intelligence.

The interception and subsequent processing of communications are conducted in a manner that minimizes the number of unwanted messages. Only after an analyst determines that the content of a message meets a legitimate requirement will it be disseminated to the interested intelligence agencies. In practically all cases, the name of an American citizen, group, or organization is deleted by NSA before a message is disseminated.

Internal NSA guidelines ensure that the decision to disseminate an intercepted communication is now made on the basis of the importance of the foreign intelligence it contains, not because a United States citizen, group, or organization is involved. This procedure is, of course, subject to change by internal NSA directives.

In short, NSA's pursuit of international communications does result in the incidental interception and dissemination of communications which the American sender or receiver expected to be kept private. This issue of the latitude NSA should be given in disseminating incidental intercepts must be dealt with if we are to resolve the dilemma between the need for effective foreign intelligence and the need to protect the rights of American citizens.

C. Issues and Questions

Pursuant to its mandate, the Committee has studied whether NSA's jurisdiction and operations should be governed and controlled by a legislative charter. The facts discovered by the Committee with respect to NSA's programs and capabilities suggest that the following questions should be posed for legislative resolution:

1. Should NSA, which like the CIA has vast powers intended for "foreign" purposes, be barred from using those powers domestically?

2. Should NSA, like the CIA, be prohibited from exercising "law enforcement powers" or "internal security functions"?

3. Should NSA be permitted specifically to target the international communications of Americans? If so, for what purposes and should a warrant be required?

4. Should NSA be permitted to disseminate information derived from the "incidental" interception of Americans' messages obtained by monitoring an international communications link for foreign intelligence purposes? If so, to whom, for what use, and under what controls?

II. NSA's Monitoring Of International Communications

A. Summary of the Watch List Activity

Lists of words and phrases, including the names of individuals and groups, have long been used by the National Security Agency to select information of intelligence value from intercepted communications. These lists are referred to as "watch lists" by NSA and the agencies requesting intelligence information from them, such as the Federal Bureau of Investigation, Central Intelligence Agency, Bureau of Narcotics and Dangerous Drugs, Secret Service, and Department of Defense. The great majority of names on watch lists have always been foreign citizens and organizations.

The Committee examined two types of watch lists which included Americans. One focused on domestic civil disturbances, the other on drug trafficking. Messages selected on the basis of these watch lists were analyzed and forwarded to other Federal agencies, including the FBI, CIA, BNDD, and DOD. The Secret Service also received information from NSA regarding potential threats to persons under its protection.

Between 1967 and 1973, NSA received watch lists from these agencies which included the names of Americans as well as foreign citizens and organizations. These lists were used to select messages from intercepted traffic and to discover whether there was foreign influence on, or support of, domestic antiwar and civil rights activities. From 1970 until 1973, similar lists were used to gather intelligence on international drug traffic.

NSA itself added names to the watch lists to enhance the selection criteria used to support the requirements levied by other agencies. NSA's Office of Security also added names to the lists for counterintelligence and counterespionage purposes.

Between 1969 and 1973, NSA disseminated approximately 2,000 reports (e.g., the text or summaries of intercepted messages) to the various requesting agencies as a result of the inclusion of American names on the watch lists." No evidence was found, however, of any significant foreign support or control of domestic dissidents.

Information generated by the watch list activity was the product of collection conducted against channels of international communications ("links") with at least one terminal in a foreign country. Nevertheless, the messages NSA intercepted and disseminated were sometimes between two American citizens, one in the United

States and one abroad. With one exception, NSA intercepted messages only from "links" it was already monitoring as part of its foreign intelligence mission.

This exception occurred in 1970, when the Bureau of Narcotics and Dangerous Drugs asked NSA to provide intelligence on international drug trafficking. NSA began to monitor certain international communications links between the United States and South America to acquire intelligence on drugs entering the United States. The BNDD also supplied NSA with the names of Americans suspected of drug trafficking for inclusion on a watch list. Reports on drug-related activities of American citizens were disseminated to both the BNDD and CIA.

Both the drug and "nondrug" watch lists of United States citizens were discontinued in 1973 as a result of questions concerning their legality and propriety, raised by the Justice Department and by NSA itself.

B. History

1. Early Period: 1960-1967

The exact details of the origin of the watch list activity are unclear. Testimony from NSA employees indicates that the early 1960s marked the beginning of watch lists and the inclusion of names of American citizens. According to a senior NSA official, "the term watch list had to do with a list of names of people, places or events that a customer would ask us to have our analysts keep in mind as they scan large volumes of material."

Originally these lists were used for two purposes: (1) monitoring travel to Cuba and other communist countries; and (2) protecting the President and other high Government officials. According to NSA, neither of these tasks involved a regular program for including American names on the lists: requests from other agencies were infrequent and generally ad hoc. Prior to 1962, NSA did not have an office specifically in charge of interagency dealings, which also limited the number of requests for information from other agencies.

In the early 1960s requesting agencies, usually the FBI, submitted names of United States citizens and business firms having dealings with Cuba to NSA. In turn, NSA provided the FBI with intelligence on American commercial and personal communications with Cuba. A May 18, 1962, internal FBI memorandum from Raymond Wannall, Chief of the Nationalities Intelligence Section of the Domestic Intelligence Division, to Assistant Director William Sullivan reported on a meeting with NSA officials concerning Cuba. The purpose of the meeting was to devise a way for the FBI to make better use of NSA intercepts relating to "commercial and personal communications between persons in Cuba and in the United States." The memorandum stated:

> of the raw traffic now available, the material which would be most helpful to us would consist of periodic listing of firms in the U.S. which are doing business with individuals in Cuba and the Cuban government.... With regard to personal messages, we feel that those relating to individuals travelling between Cuba and the U.S. would be the most significant.... We will furnish NSA a list of persons in whom we have an investigative or an intelligence interest.

The second area of concern in the early 1960s was protection of the President. According to NSA, the Secret Service submitted the names of the Presidents and others under its protection, possibly as early as 1962. This activity, however, was not instituted for the purpose of acquiring the communications of the protectees, but to determine possible threats to their well-being. After President Kennedy was assassinated in November 1963, interest in presidential protection naturally intensified, and NSA's joint efforts with the Secret Service were expanded.

This early activity was not directed against American citizens; no intelligence program called for the systematic inclusion of American citizens on a watch list. The evidence indicates, however, that NSA did intentionally monitor certain international activities of some American citizens as early as 1962. These objectives, which began as legitimate concerns for the life of the President, expanded when the watch list activity intensified in 1967.

2. Systematic Inclusion of American Names: 1967

The major watch list effort against American citizens began in the fall of 1967. In response to pressures from the White House, FBI, and Attorney General, the Department of the Army established a civil disturbance unit. An area of special interest was possible foreign involvement in American civil rights and antiwar groups. General William Yarborough, the Army Assistant Chief of Staff for Intelligence (ACSI), directed the operations of this unit.

On October 20, 1967, Yarborough sent a message to the Director of NSA, General Marshall Carter, requesting that NSA provide any available information concerning possible foreign influence on civil disturbances in the United States. Yarborough specifically asked for "any information on a continuing basis" concerning:

A. Indications that foreign governments or individuals or organizations acting as agents of foreign governments are controlling or attempting to control or influence the activities of U.S. "peace" groups and "Black Power" organizations.

B. Identities of foreign agencies exerting control or influence on U.S. organizations.

C. Identities of individuals and organizations in U.S. in contact with agents of foreign governments.

D. Instructions or advice being given to U.S. groups by agents of foreign governments.

A senior NSA official knowledgeable in this area testified that such a request for information on civil disturbances or political activities was "unprecedented. . . . It is kind of a landmark in my memory; it stands out as a first." The initial request was also vague; it did not discuss the targeting of American citizens, or what specific organizations or groups were of interest. The Army was "interested in determining whether or not there is evidence of any foreign action to develop or control these anti-Vietnam and other domestic demonstrations."

The following day, Carter sent a cable to Yarborough, Director of Central Intelligence Richard Helms, and each member of the United States Intelligence Board, informing them that NSA was "concentrating additional and continuing effort to obtain SIGINT" in support of the Army request. Although USIB members were notified of this new requirement, there is no record of discussion at USIB meetings of the watch list, nor did USIB ever validate a requirement for monitoring in support of the civil disturbance unit.

Watch list names were submitted directly to NSA by the FBI, Secret Service, Defense Intelligence Agency, the military services, and the CIA. These same agencies received reports of intercepted communications pertaining to their areas of interest. The State Department also received some reports on international terrorism and drug activities, but it is unclear whether they submitted any American names.

Between 1967 and 1973, a cumulative total of about 1,200 American names appeared on the civil disturbance watch list. The FBI submitted the largest proportion, approximately 950. The Secret Service's list included about 180 American individuals and groups active in civil rights and antiwar activities. The DIA submitted the names of 20 American citizens who traveled to North Vietnam, and the CIA submitted approximately 30 names of alleged American radicals. The Air Force Office of Special Investigations, the Naval Investigative Service, and the Army Assistant Chief of Staff for Intelligence all submitted a small number of names to NSA. In addition, NSA contributed about 50-75 names to support the watch list activity.

At its height in early 1973, there were 600 American names and 6,000 foreign names on the watch lists. According to NSA, these lists produced about 2,000 reports that were disseminated to other agencies between 1967 and 1973. NSA estimates 10 percent of these reports were derived from communications between two American citizens.

3. Increasing Security and Concealment of Programs Involving American Citizens

The watch list activity was always a highly sensitive, compartmented operation. The secrecy was not due to the nature of the communications intercepted (most were personal and innocuous) but to the fact that American citizens were involved. NSA requested that some of the agencies receiving watch list product either destroy the material or return it within two weeks. This procedure was not followed with even the most sensitive of NSA's legitimate foreign intelligence product.

When NSA intercepts, analyzes, and disseminates a foreign communication, the regular procedure is for the communication to be classified, given a serial number, and filed. From 1967-1969, much of the watch list material was treated in this manner, and given the same classification as the most sensitive NSA intercepts. As a senior NSA official testified:

> During the 1967-1969 period, communications that had a U.S. citizen on one end and a foreigner on the other were given [a high level security classification] . . . and went out as serialized product, through a limited by name only distribution.

Other material was even more highly classified. Whenever communications between two Americans were intercepted, they were classified Top Secret, prepared with no mention of NSA as the source, and disseminated "For Background Use Only." No serial number was assigned to them, and they were not filed with regular communications intelligence intercepts. This effectively limited access to the material and prevented its use in any official study or report. As Benson Buffham, Deputy Director of NSA, testified:

> first it is true that we maintain permanent type records of all of our product. However, it is my understanding that this material was dealt with separately. It was not serialized and put out in regular distribution lists. These items were produced as display items, show-to items and thus the normal procedures that would be followed for our serialized product were not followed. So as best as I know, there would not be any record of this material held in other places within the Agency in the permanent files.

The project's sensitivity was due to a number of factors. The requirements — protection of the President, terrorism, civil disturbances, drug activities — involved sensitive subjects. NSA also wanted to ensure protection of the SIGINT source and of other intercept operations, which could be jeopardized by unauthorized release of the watch list material. Finally, American citizens, firms, and groups were involved, and this was "different from the normal mission of the National Security Agency."

The fact that NSA did not serialize and file the intercepted communications between Americans indicates they did not view this activity as part of their "normal" mission. Buffham stated that he believed the interception and dissemination of communications between American citizens to be outside NSA's mission, as defined in applicable executive directives.

4. Project MINARET: Further Expansion and Increased Secrecy

The civil disturbance watch list program became even more compartmented in July 1969, when NSA issued a charter to establish Project MINARET.

MINARET established more stringent controls over the information collected on American citizens and groups involved in civil disturbances. To enhance security, MINARET effectively classified all of this information as Top Secret, "For Background Use Only," and stipulated that the material was not to be serialized or identified with the National Security Agency. Prior to 1969, only communications between two Americans were classified in this manner; with the adoption of MINARET, communications to, from, or mentioning United States citizens were so classified.

The MINARET charter established tighter security procedures for intercepted messages which contained:

a. information on foreign governments, organizations, or individuals who are attempting to influence, coordinate or control U.S. organizations or individuals who may foment civil disturbance or otherwise undermine the national security of the U.S.;

b. information on U.S. organizations or individuals who are engaged in activities which may result in civil disturbances or otherwise subvert the national security of the U.S. An equally important aspect of MINARET will be to restrict the knowledge that such information is being collected and processed by the National Security Agency.

This charter was prepared within NSA and issued by an NSA Assistant Director. According to testimony given the Committee, the charter was discussed with NSA Deputy Director Louis Tordella and probably with the Director, but other agencies involved in the watch list activity were not informed of the new procedures until the charter had been adopted.

In addition to regulating the distribution and format of watch list product, MINARET also initiated a more formal procedure for submission of names. No longer were names accepted over the telephone or by word of mouth. According to NSA, the watch list "was handled less systematically prior to 1969 ... some watch lists entered NSA during that time via direct channels, including secure telephone." NSA maintains, however, that the regular procedure was for agencies submitting names by secure telephone, or in person to confirm them with written requests. A senior NSA official testified: "From 1969 on [the watch list] was handled in a very careful, reviewed and systematic way."

The MINARET charter was an effort both to restrict knowledge of the watch list program and to disguise NSA's participation in it. NSA maintains that its concern for the security of SIGINT sources, i.e., NSA's intercept operations, was the primary reason for initiating these measures. NSA further maintains that it was concerned with the privacy of U.S. communications and, by imposing the MINARET restrictions, sought to ensure that dissemination was made exclusively to those outside NSA who had a legitimate need for the information. It is apparent that the MINARET restrictions also protected NSA's role from exposure. Dissemination of foreign communications to domestic agencies was obviously a sensitive matter. It involved considerable risk of exposure which would increase if the number of people within the intelligence community who were aware of the activity grew. Therefore, NSA placed more restrictive security controls on MINARET material than it placed on other highly classified foreign intercepts in order to conceal its involvement in activities which were beyond its regular mission.

C. Types of Names on Watch Lists

The names of Americans submitted to NSA for the watch lists ranged from members of radical political groups, to celebrities, to ordinary citizens involved in protests against their Government. Names of organizations were also included; some were communist front groups, others were nonviolent and peaceful in nature.

The use of names, particularly those of groups and organizations, to select international communications results in NSA unnecessarily reviewing many messages. There is a multiplier effect: if an organization is targeted, all its member's communications may be intercepted; if an individual is on the watch list, all communications to, from, or mentioning that individual may be intercepted. These communications may also contain the names of other "innocent" parties. For example, a communication mentioning the wife of a U.S. Senator was intercepted by NSA, as were communications discussing a peace concert, a correspondent's report from Southeast Asia to his magazine in New York, and a pro-Vietnam war activist's invitations to speakers for a rally. According to testimony before the Committee, the material that resulted from the watch lists was not very valuable; most communications were of a private and personal nature, or involved rallies and demonstrations that were public knowledge.

D. Overlapping Nature of Intelligence Community Requests

As noted above, the primary purpose of the watch lists on Americans from 1967-1973 was to collect intelligence on civil disturbances. NSA also responded to a requirement from BNDD to monitor for illegal drug trafficking from 1970 1973. In addition, NSA supplied information to Federal agencies (FBI, CIA, Secret Service, and Department of Defense) on possible terrorist activity, and disseminated reports to the Secret Service which related to the protection of the President. The demarcations between these categories, however, was not always clear.

Secret Service officials, for example, have told the Committee that presidential and executive protection includes "providing a secure environment" for the White House for foreign embassies within the United States and in areas where high Government officials travel. According to the Secret Service, this requires "information regarding civil disturbances and anti-American or anti-U.S. Government demonstrations in the U.S. or overseas, as these demonstrations may affect the Secret Service's mission of protecting U.S. and foreign officials." After the October 20, 1967, Yarborough cable, the Secret Service began submitting names of individuals and organizations active in the antiwar and civil rights movements to

NSA. Although these individuals and groups were not considered a direct threat to protectees, it was believed they might participate in demonstrations against United States policy which would endanger the physical well-being of Government officials. Intercepted communications to, from, or mentioning these individuals and groups were always disseminated by NSA to the Secret Service and the CIA, and often to the FBI.

There was considerable overlap among various agencies in submissions for watch list coverage and requests for material. For example, the CIA was interested in:

The activities of U.S. individuals involved in either civil disorders, radical student or youth activities, racial militant activities, radical antiwar activities, draft evasion/deserter support activities, or in radical related media activities, where such individuals have some foreign connection by virtue of: foreign residence, foreign travel, attendance at international conferences or meetings and/or involvement or contact with foreign governments, organizations, political parties or individuals; or with Communist front organizations. [Emphasis added.]

The FBI was interested in similar kinds of information, as illustrated by excerpts of two memoranda from J. Edgar Hoover to the Director, NSA:

> This is to advise you that this Bureau has a continuing interest in receiving intelligence information obtained under MINARET regarding the targets previously furnished you. . . . Information derived from this coverage has been helpful in determining the extent of international cooperation among New Leftists and has been used for lead purposes.

The purpose of this communication is to advise of general areas of interest to this Bureau in connection with racial extremist matters and to request your assistance in such matters.

There are both white and black racial extremists in the United States advocating and participating in illegal and violent activities for the purpose of destroying our present form of government. Because of this goal, such racial extremists are natural allies of foreign enemies of the United States. Both material and propaganda support is being given to United States racial extremists by foreign elements. The Bureau is most interested in all information showing ties between United States racial extremists and such foreign elements. [Emphasis added.]

These requests reflect an underlying similarity of interests among agencies, despite the differing needs which are expressed in their requirements. To some extent the DIA, FBI, CIA, and the Secret Service received information on Black activists and groups, and on the antiwar movement. All were concerned with how civil disturbances and antiwar demonstration were affecting the internal security of the United States. Although their general area of concern was the same, each agency used the information for its own particular purposes. The DIA was interested in travel to North Vietnam; the CIA kept files on alleged antiwar radicals for its Project CHAOS; the FBI used the information to develop "leads" on new left activists, at the same time it was conducting COINTELPRO efforts against alleged radicals; and the Secret Service was concerned with protecting the President. Despite slight variations in focus, the different agencies' requests reflected the overriding fear that the nation was being undermined internally and externally. It was this perception which produced the watch list program directed against Americans.

E. Drug Watch Lists: United States—South American Intercepts

1. Initial Monitoring: 1970

An unofficial requirement to collect and disseminate international communications concerning drug trafficking was levied on NSA by the Bureau of Narcotics and Dangerous Drugs on April 10, 1970. BNDD Director John Ingersoll sent a memorandum to NSA Director Noel Gayler requesting "any and all COMINT information which reflects illicit traffic in narcotics and dangerous drugs." NSA initiated its monitoring in June 1970, but a general requirement to obtain foreign intelligence on drug trafficking was not validated by the United States Intelligence Board until August 1971.

The Ingersoll memorandum specified that BNDD was interested in individuals and organizations involved in illegal drug activities, information on production centers, and all violations of United States laws pertaining to narcotics and dangerous drugs. In order to assist NSA in fulfilling the requirement, BNDD stated that they would provide NSA lists of individuals and organizations which had a history of involvement with illegal drug activities. According to the Ingersoll memorandum, "this watch list will be updated on a monthly basis and and additions/deletions will be forwarded to NSA."

NSA implemented this request by monitoring international communications traffic. The first intercepts began in June 1970. Telephone traffic carried on circuits between the United States and certain South American cities was first monitored in September 1970. Unlike other watch list monitoring, the United States-South American effort required NSA to devote additional resources to intercepting communications over this specifically targeted link.

This link included the telephone circuits between New York City and a South American city. BNDD was initially concerned about drug deals that were being arranged in calls from public telephone booths in New York City to South America. According to a senior NSA official:

> BNDD had some information that led them to believe that arrangements were being made by telephone from New York City, a Grand Central Station telephone booth, to some individuals in [a South American city].

BNDD felt that it could not legally tap the public telephones and thus enlisted NSA's help to cover the international link that carried these telephone calls. At BNDD's request, NSA began to intercept telephone conversations carried over this link in September 1970. Additional United States-South American links were soon added. BNDD also supplied NSA with code names for drugs and names of individuals, including American citizens.

The telephone monitoring was conducted from one NSA site until December 1970, when that intercept station was closed. An NSA East Coast facility, operated by the military, began monitoring United States-South American links in March 1971. According to NSA, 19 United States-South American links were monitored for voice traffic at the two sites between 1970 and 1973. 67 Six South American cities were of primary interest, in addition to New York and Miami.

During this period, BNDD submitted 450 American names to NSA for inclusion on the drug watch list. At the high point, in early 1973, 250 Americans were on the active list.

Of the calls intercepted at the East Coast site, less than 10 percent were sent to NSA headquarters, and less than 10 percent of these were disseminated. Yet it is clear that many personal and business calls of Americans were reviewed during this operation. This results from the lack of an effective method for avoiding the incidental interception of calls involving American citizens when a link with one terminal in the United States in monitored.

2. CIA/NSA Drug Activity

In October 1972, NSA requested CIA assistance in monitoring United States-South American communication links to collect intelligence on illicit drug traffic. According to Buffham, NSA made this request

> because we felt that this was a sensitive matter, and that greater security would be achieved by utilizing the career intercept operators of the CIA to perform the activity, and, in addition, they could be more selective in providing items because we would be able to give the CIA operators the specific names on the watch list, and we did not feel that we could or should provide those names to the [East Coast military station].

NSA's concern about the security of American names being provided to the East Coast station stemmed from the fact that the operators were young military personnel on short tours of duty. They were not professional intelligence officers, and NSA felt that monitoring American citizens was too sensitive a task for them. The use of CIA career operators satisfied NSA that targeting of American citizens would not be disclosed.

The Rockefeller Commission also investigated this activity, but found no evidence that the CIA directly targeted American citizens. The Rockefeller Commission report stated:

> For a period of approximately six months, commencing in the fall of 1973 [sic], the Directorate monitored telephone conversations between the United States and Latin America in an effort to identify foreign drug traffickers. . . .

> A CIA intercept crew stationed at an East Coast site monitored calls to and from certain Latin American telephone numbers contained on a "watch list" provided by NSA. While the intercept was focused on foreign nationals, it is clear that American citizens were parties to many of the monitored calls. . . .

> The Commission's investigation disclosed that, from the outset of the Agency's involvement in the narcotics control program, the Director and other CIA officials instructed involved personnel to collect only foreign intelligence and to make no attempt—either within the United States or abroad—to gather information on American citizens allegedly trafficking in narcotics.

The evidence examined by the, Select Committee directly contradicts this finding. An internal CIA memorandum of November 17, 1972, to the Director of Communications from the Chief, Special Programs Division, reveals that the CIA was receiving the names of U.S. citizens.

> NSA had tasked [the East Coast site] with this requirement [to monitor for drug traffic] but were unwilling to provide the site with the specific names and U.S. telephone numbers of interest on security/sensitivity grounds ... to get around the problems mentioned above NSA requested the Agency undertake intercept of the long lines circuits of interest. They have

provided us with all information available (including the "sensitive") and the [CIA] facility is working on the requirement.

This memorandum and subsequent testimony by NSA officials revealed that the CIA was monitoring these circuits to intercept the calls of American citizens suspected of illegal drug trafficking. During this period, NSA continued to monitor the same circuits at its East Coast site, but that site did not have the specific BNDD "sensitive" watch lists of American names which were supplied to the CIA. Thus, the conclusion reached by the Rockefeller Commission that CIA intercepts were not undertaken for the purpose of gathering intelligence on American citizens – is not supported by the evidence.

3. Termination of Drug Activity

Three months after the CIA monitoring was initiated, CIA General Counsel Lawrence Houston issued an opinion which stated that the intercepts may violate Section 605 of the Communications Act of 1934. This law, as amended in 1968, prohibits the unauthorized disclosure of any private communication of an American citizen to another party, unless undertaken pursuant to the President's constitutional authority to collect foreign intelligence, which is crucial to the security of the United States. Since intercepted messages were provided to BNDD, Houston concluded that the activity was for law enforcement purposes, which is also outside the CIA's charter. As a result of this memorandum, the CIA suspended its collection. NSA, which has no charter, continued to monitor these links for drug information.

NSA officials have testified that they were told in early 1973 that the CIA was terminating collection because it was concerned about operating an intercept station within the United States. This concern is completely different from the one expressed in Houston's memorandum. NSA officials have told the Committee that questions concerning the legality of the activity were either not mentioned by the CIA, or else mentioned secondarily.

NSA Deputy Director Buffham testified that after the CIA decided to stop the United States-South American drug monitoring, NSA began to review the legality and appropriateness of its efforts in support of BNDD. Although NSA is not prohibited by statute or executive directive from disseminating information that may pertain to law enforcement, it has always viewed its sole mission as the collection and dissemination of foreign intelligence. A senior NSA official testified: "We do not understand our mission to be one of supporting an agency with a law enforcement responsibility."

Although BNDD clearly was a law enforcement agency, NSA initially held that the intelligence it was supplying BNDD was a part of a legitimate USIB-approved effort to prevent drugs from entering the United States. This international aspect of the requirement was interpreted by NSA as sufficient justification for classifying the activity as part of its "foreign intelligence" mission.

After discussions with the General Counsel's office at NSA and within the Office of the Secretary of Defense, the Director of NSA terminated the activity in June 1973. All of NSA's drug materials product, internal memoranda, and administrative documents – were destroyed in late August or early September 1973. Ordinarily, NSA keeps material for five years or more. According to a senior NSA official: "it wasn't thought we would get back into the narcotics effort anytime soon. There didn't seem to be any point in keeping them."

4. Continuation of NSA's United States-South American Monitoring

In June 1975 the Committee received information that NSA continued to monitor United States-South American telephone calls after the June 1973 termination of the drug watch list activity. NSA officials confirmed that the same links targeted for the purpose of curbing illegal drug traffic were monitored by NSA for foreign intelligence after June 1973. Certain of these links were monitored until July 9, 1975.

According to NSA, this activity was terminated when "it did not prove productive." While this effort was underway, NSA states that it did not collect or disseminate any information on narcotics traffic from the United States-South American links. A senior NSA official stated: "Nothing ever came. No by-product. The problem was dead."

5. Current Internal Policy Concerning Telephone Monitoring

No statute or executive directive prohibits NSA's monitoring a telephone circuit with one terminal in the United States. An internal NSA instruction was issued on August 7, 1975, that requires the personal approval of the chief of a major element within the Agency before monitoring of voice communications with a terminal in the United States is initiated. According to Deputy Director Buffham, "It is obvious that no such collection will be undertaken unless it is extremely important and is properly reviewed within the Agency."

F. Termination of the Civil Disturbance Watch List Activity

The watch list activity involving civil disturbances was officially terminated in the fall of 1973. This was due to a combination of factors: growing concern within NSA regarding the program's vulnerability and propriety; the fact that courts were beginning to require the Government to reveal electronic surveillance conducted against particular criminal defendants; and the questions, raised by the drug watch list activity, about NSA's authority to engage in monitoring for law enforcement purposes. What follows is a description of events leading to the termination of the watch lists.

The only Supreme Court case addressing the issue of electronic surveillance purportedly undertaken for national security purposes is United States v. United States District Court, commonly referred to as the Keith case. The Supreme Court's decision was handed down on June 19, 1972, over a year before the watch list activity was terminated.

The case involved warrantless wiretaps on three U.S. citizens who were subsequently indicted for conspiracy to destroy Government property. There was no evidence of foreign participation in the alleged conspiracy.

After examining logs of the wiretaps in camera, the District Court judge had held that the surveillance on the defendants was unlawful and required that the overheard conversations be disclosed. The Supreme Court affirmed the District Court's ruling.

While recognizing the President's constitutional duty to "protect our Government against those who would subvert or overthrow it by unlawful means," 85c the Court held that the power inherent in such a duty does not extend to the authorization of warrantless electronic surveillance deemed necessary to protect the nation from subversion by domestic organizations. The Court declared that the Fourth Amendment warrant requirement for electronic surveillance developed in two 1967 cases applied, and that the electronic surveillances employed in the instant case were found to be unlawful. The Court did not reach the issue of whether the Executive has the constitutional power to authorize electronic surveillance without a warrant in cases involving the activities of foreign powers or agents.

Although the Keith ruling involved wiretaps and did not apply specifically to NSA, it did have a bearing on NSA's activities. Operation MINARET did entail warrantless electronic surveillance against certain domestic organizations. If there was no evidence to show that these domestic organizations were acting in concert with a foreign power, the Keith case would seem to cast doubts upon the legality of intercepting their messages without a warrant.

The watch list activity was never disclosed in a court proceeding; thus its legality has never been judicially determined. A 1973 criminal case did result in the Government's disclosure that some of a defendant's communications had been subject to a "foreign intelligence intercept." Some of the defendants in this 1973 case were members of a group which had been included on an NSA watch list by the Secret Service and FBI in mid-1971, and NSA had distributed some of their international communications to these agencies. The propriety of these actions was never considered by the court, because the Government moved to dismiss the case rather than reveal the specifics of the watch list activity.

General Lew Allen, Jr. became the Director of NSA on August 15, 1973. In the course of familiarizing himself with his new responsibilities, he was fully briefed on the watch list activity.

According to Allen, the BNDD watch list activity had been terminated just prior to his arrival at NSA because the Agency feared "that it might not be possible to make a clear separation between requests for information submitted by BNDD as it pertained to legitimate foreign intelligence requirements and the law enforcement responsibility of BNDD." He also stated that the activity in support of the FBI, CIA, and Secret Service was suspended when NSA "stopped the distribution of information in the summer [August] of 1973." Deputy Director Buffham told the Committee this dissemination was terminated due to three concerns: (1) NSA could not be certain as to what uses were being made of the information it was providing other agencies; (2) it feared that broad judicial discovery procedures might lead to the disclosure of sensitive intelligence sources and methods; and (3) NSA wanted to be "absolutely certain that we are providing information only for lawful purposes and in accordance with our foreign intelligence charter."

During July and August 1973, meetings were held between NSA and Justice Department representatives. According to NSA, these discussions influenced the Agency's decision to suspend the dissemination of watch list material. As Buffham testified:

I believe although I am not positive, that Dr. Tordella, the Deputy Director, had discussions with people at Justice regarding the legality of our activities, and that these could have influenced then the determination in NSA to cease the activities in August, even though we had not yet received any formal statements from Justice.

At a meeting on August 28, 1973, NSA officials informed Assistant Attorney General Henry Petersen that communications involving the defendants in the 1973 criminal case had been intercepted and that NSA opposed "any disclosure of this technique and program." Petersen apprised Attorney General Richardson of these events in a memorandum of September 4, 1973. On September 7, 1973, Petersen sent a memorandum to FBI Director Clarence Kelley, requesting to be advised by September 10 of:

the extent of the FBI's practice of requesting information intercepted by the NSA concerning domestic organizations or persons for intelligence, prosecutorial, or any other purposes ... [and] any comments which you may desire to make concerning the impact of the Keith ease upon such interceptions. . . .

Kelley responded three days later that the FBI had requested intelligence from NSA "concerning organizations and individuals who are known to be involved in illegal and violent activities aimed at the destruction and overthrow of the United States Government." He continued that the FBI did not view the materials supplied it by NSA, or the watch list activity in general as inconsistent with the Keith decision: the information "cannot possibly be used for any prosecutive purpose" and "we do not consider the NSA information as electronic surveillance information in the sense that was the heart of the Keith decision." The FBI's position was that the information supplied by NSA did not result from specific targeting of an individual's communications in the same sense as a wiretap; therefore, it was not "electronic surveillance." Kelley maintained

> We do not believe that the NSA actually participated in any electronic surveillance, per se of the defendants for any other agency of the government, since under the procedures used by that agency they are unaware of the identity of any group or individual which might be included in the recovery of national security intelligence information.

This position is difficult to defend since intelligence agencies, including the FBI, submitted specific American names for watch lists which resulted in the interception of Americans' international communications.

On September 17, Allen wrote FBI Director Kelley and the heads of other agencies receiving information from NSA regarding continuation of the watch list activity. Noting that "the need for proper handling of the list and related information has intensified, along with ever-increasing pressures for disclosure of sources by the Congress, the courts, and the press," Allen requested, "at the earliest possible date," that Kelley and the other agency heads "review the current list your agency has filed with us in order to satisfy yourself regarding the appropriateness of its contents. . . ."

After receiving Kelley's September 10 memorandum, Petersen advised the Attorney General that the current number of individuals and organizations on NSA watch lists submitted by the FBI was "in excess of 600." Petersen pointed out many legal problems arising from this program and recommended that

> the FBI and Secret Service be immediately advised to cease and desist requesting NSA to disseminate to them information concerning individuals and organizations obtained through NSA electronic coverage and that NSA should be informed not to disclose voluntarily such information to Secret Service or the FBI unless NSA has picked up the information on its own initiative in pursuit of its foreign intelligence mission.

He also recommended that the standards and procedures which applied to "cases where the FBI seeks to acquire foreign intelligence or counterespionage information by means of its own listening devices" be extended to apply to the watch list activity. These procedures included obtaining prior written approval by the Attorney General.

On October 1, Richardson sent memoranda to FBI Director Kelley and the Director of the Secret Service, instructing them to cease requesting information obtained by NSA "by means of electronic surveillance." The Attorney General also requested that his approval be sought prior to either agency's renewing requests to NSA for foreign intelligence or counterespionage information.

On the same day, Richardson sent a letter to Allen, stating that he found the watch list activity to be of questionable legality in view of the Keith decision, and requesting that NSA "immediately curtail the further dissemination" of watch list information to the FBI and Secret Service. Although Richardson specified that NSA was not to respond to "a request from another agency to monitor in connection with a matter that can only be considered one of domestic intelligence," he stated that "relevant information acquired by you in the routine pursuit of the collection of foreign intelligence information may continue to be furnished to appropriate Government agencies."

Kelley responded to Richardson's memorandum on October 3 and agreed to comply with the Attorney General's "instructions to discontinue requests to NSA for electronic surveillance information and to obtain approval prior to any future inquires to NSA for such information." There was apparently some confusion at this point whether Richardson's instructions meant that NSA was prohibited from disseminating any information to FBI. After further consultations, it was determined that the caveats Richardson placed on dissemination applied only to information on American citizens and organizations, and not to foreign intelligence and counterespionage matters.

Allen replied to Richardson's letter on October 4, stating that he had "directed that no further information be disseminated to the FBI and Secret Service, pending advice on legal issues." Although Allen had agreed to suspend dissemination, NSA's position remained that these communications had always been collected "as an incidental and unintended act in the conduct of the interception of foreign communications." Allen thus asserted that NSA's "current practice conforms with your [Richardson's] guidance that, 'relevant information acquired [by NSA] in the routine pursuit of the collection of foreign intelligence information may continue to be furnished to appropriate government agencies.' "

As a result of these and other exchanges between officials at NSA and Justice, the Agency officially terminated its watch list activity involving American citizens and organizations in the fall of 1973. It would no longer accept such names from other agencies for the purpose of monitoring their international communications.

To a substantial degree, this decision was prompted by the legal implications of the Keith case and by NSA's fear that criminal prosecutions of persons on the watch lists would inevitably lead to disclosure of its intelligence sources and methods. Indeed, the 1973 criminal case referred to above posed the threat that the watch list activity might have to be disclosed for the first time in a public forum.

It is important to note that the decision to terminate the watch list was ultimately the administrative decision of an executive agency. There is no statute which expressly forbids such activity, and no court case where it has been squarely at issue. Without legislative controls, NSA could resume the watch list activity at any time upon order of the Executive.

G. Authorization

Authorization of the watch list activity must be viewed in the context of how NSA operates. It is a service agency which provides foreign intelligence information at the request of consumer agencies. Specific requirements are levied on NSA, although the Agency also engages in collection activities that are not responsive to specific tasking. For example, many USIB requirements—such as those aimed at terrorist activities, gathering economic intelligence, or discovering foreign links to civil disturbances—were so broad that NSA was given wide discretion for selecting not only the communications channels to be monitored, but also what information was disseminated. While this is often appropriate because only NSA has the knowledge and expertise to make these decisions, it also allows NSA considerable flexibility in carrying out its mission.

NSA also responds to specific requests from other Federal agencies. Indeed, it is no exaggeration to state that NSA's operations are undertaken almost entirely to satisfy the intelligence needs of other agencies. The watch list activity was no exception.

1. Knowledge and Authorization Outside NSA

In the case of the 1967-1973 watch list activity, NSA clearly received instructions from the Army in 1967 to look for possible foreign influence on, or control of, American peace and Black power activists. NSA subsequently received the names of American and foreign citizens and groups from other intelligence agencies.

This activity was not formally approved by USIB. Although NSA notified USIB members that it was responding to the Army's request, the inclusion of American names on an NSA watch list was never discussed at subsequent USIB meetings. Although there were official USIB requirements for information concerning international drug activity, presidential protection, and terrorism, there was no approval or discussion of targeting American citizens. NSA officials contend that the submission of American names by USIB members constituted approval.

The desire for tight security over the watch list program resulted in limiting participation to those "with a need to know." Therefore, it was not in NSAs best interests to have formal USIB approval of a requirement since knowledge would have been more widely spread.

According to documents supplied to the Committee and testimony of NSA officials, Defense Secretaries Melvin Laird and James Schlesinger, as well as Attorneys General John Mitchell and Richard Kleindienst, were informed that NSA was monitoring Americans. Former NSA Director, Admiral Noel Gayler sent a Top Secret "Eyes Only" memorandum to Laird and Mitchell on January 26, 1971, which outlined ground rules for "NSA's Contribution to Domestic Intelligence." In this memorandum, Gayler refers to a discussion he had earlier that day with both men on how NSA could assist them with "intelligence bearing on domestic problems." The memorandum mentioned the monitoring for drug trafficking and foreign support of subversive activities, but did not discuss "watch lists" specifically.

NSA Deputy Director Buffham supplied the Committee with a Memorandum for Record which indicated that he had personally shown the Gayler memorandum to Mitchell and had been told by the Military Assistant to Secretary of Defense Laird that the Secretary had read and agreed to the memorandum. In a handwritten note made available to the Committee, Gayler recalls that he personally showed the January 26, 1971, memorandum to Kleindienst on July 1, 1972.

Finally, former NSA Deputy Director Tordella testified that he accompanied General Samuel C. Phillips, Gayler's successor as Director of NSA, to brief Secretary of Defense Schlesinger on the watch list in the summer of 1973.

In summary, a number of Federal agencies were aware of NSA's watch lists and used them. It is clear that the United States Intelligence Board, which ordinarily set the intelligence requirements to which NSA responded, never gave its formal approval for the watch list activity. It also appears that at least two Attorneys General and two Secretaries of Defense were generally aware that NSA was monitoring the international communications of American citizens, but none took measures to halt the practice.

2. Knowledge and Approval Within NSA

There is a discrepancy in the testimony of knowledgeable NSA staff members and a former NSA Director with regard to his knowledge of the watch list activity. When asked whether NSA had included the names of American citizens or organizations on its watch lists, Admiral Noel Gayler (who was Director of NSA during the height of the activity) responded:

> I don't know that I even knew that in that specific way. I knew that communications of one foreign terminal sometimes concerned doings of interest of people, including American citizens, yes. And when I became aware of that, I can't tell you, I guess it was a year or so after I got there.

Gayler became NSA Director in August 1969. He maintains that he first became aware of the watch list activity about the time of the June 1970 Huston plan for domestic surveillance, ten months after his arrival and eleven months after the MINARET Charter was issued.

Gayler was one of the original participants in the Huston plan deliberations and in the Intelligence Evaluation Committee (early 1971). Both of these efforts were designed to use the resources of NSA and other intelligence agencies to gather information on internal security matters. In fact, part of the Huston plan called for the expansion of the watch list activity. Buffham told the Committee that if the plan had been implemented he assumed "other intelligence agencies would then increase the numbers of names on their lists" and NSA would possibly target specific communications channels to obtain the international traffic of American citizens. 110 NSA was particularly concerned that the executive branch directives would have had to be changed to permit such an expansion. The alternatives outlined in the Huston plan included the recommendation that the controling NSCID and the relevant DCID be changed to allow NSA to target international communications links carrying the messages of American citizens.

NSA was already engaged in watch list activity which although it did not involve targeting of specific communications links, did involve targeting Americans by name. The Huston Plan states:

> NSA is currently doing so on a restricted basis, and the information it has provided has been most helpful. Much of this information is particularly useful to the White House ....

As discussed earlier, the July 1, 1969, MINARET charter was designed to restrict knowledge of the watch list activity. It was released about a month before Gayler arrived at NSA and, according to a senior NSA official, Gayler "knew everything that was in it, what was going on, and endorsed it." Gayler recalls that his first knowledge of the watch list came during the Huston Plan deliberations, almost a year later. Another senior NSA official testified that Gayler "review every piece of MINARET product" and maintained that "the Director kept a close eye on this activity and reviewed the requirements." This employee also testified that Gayler was shown the product of the watch list activity and was kept fully informed.

H. Conclusions

NSA's monitoring of international communications comprises only a portion of its total mission, but the examination of this capability to intrude on the telephone calls and telegrams of Americans represents a major part of the Committee's work on NSA. The watch list activities and the sophisticated technological capabilities that they highlight present some of the most crucial privacy issues facing this nation. Space age technology has outpaced the law. The secrecy that has surrounded much of NSA's activities and the lack of Congressional oversight have prevented, in the past, bringing statutes in line with NSA's capabilities. Neither the courts nor Congress have dealt with the interception of communications using NSA's highly sensitive and complex technology.

The analysis presented here, of the deliberate targeting of American citizens and the associated incidental interception of their communications demonstrates the need for a legislative charter that will define, limit, and control the signals intelligence activities of the National Security Agency. This should be accomplished both to preserve and protect the Government's legitimate foreign intelligence operations, and to ensure that the constitutional rights of Americans are safeguarded.

The next section describes a recently terminated NSA collection program which also involved United States citizens—Operation SHAMROCK. This program did not require any special technology; international telegrams were simply turned over to NSA at the offices of three cable companies.

III. A Special NSA Collection Program: SHAMROCK

SHAMROCK is the codename for a special program in which NSA received copies of most international telegrams leaving the United States between August 1945 and May 1975. Two of the participating international telegraph companies—RCA Global and ITT World Communications—provided virtually all their international message traffic to NSA. The third, Western Union International, only provided copies of certain foreign traffic from 1945 until 1972. SHAMROCK was probably the largest governmental interception program affecting Americans ever undertaken. Although the total number of telegrams read during its course is not available, NSA estimates that in the last two or three years of SHAMROCK's existence, about 150,000 telegrams per month were reviewed by NSA analysts.

Initially, NSA received copies of international telegrams in the form of microfilm or paper tapes. These were sorted manually to obtain foreign messages. When RCA Global and ITT World Communications switched to magnetic tapes in the 1960s, NSA made copies of these tapes and subjected them to an electronic sorting process. This means that the international telegrams of American citizens on the "watch lists" could be selected out and disseminated.

A. Legal Restrictions

1. The Fourth Amendment to the Constitution of the United States

Obtaining the international telegrams of American citizens by NSA at the offices of the telegraph companies appears to violate the privacy of these citizens, as protected by the Fourth Amendment. That Amendment guarantees to the people the right to be "secure ... in their papers . . . against unreasonable searches and seizures." It also provides that "no Warrants shall issue, but upon probable cause." In no case did NSA obtain a search warrant prior to obtaining a telegram.

2. Section 605 of the Communications Act of 1934 (47 U.S.C. 605)

As enacted in 1934, eleven years before SHAMROCK began, section 605 of the Communications Act provided:

No person receiving, assisting in receiving, transmitting, or assisting in transmitting, any interstate or foreign communication by wire or radio shall divulge or publish the existence, contents, substance, purport, effect, or meaning thereof....

Section 605 was amended in 1968 by the addition of the phrase: "Except as authorized by chapter 119, Title 18, no person . . . " The import of this 1968 addition, however, is not clear, and the Supreme Court has yet to rule on the point.

The relevant provision in chapter 119, section 2511 (3), provides that "nothing contained in this chapter or in section 605 of the Communications Act of 1934. . . shall limit the constitutional power of the President ... to obtain foreign intelligence information deemed essential to the security of the United States. . . ." Yet the Supreme Court, in the Keith decision (1972), held that this section "confers no power" and "merely provides that the Act shall not be interpreted to limit or disturb such power as the President may have under the Constitution."

It is thus uncertain what the phrase in the 1968 amendment to section 605 -- "except as authorized by chapter 119, title 18" [Emphasis added.] -- means. The Supreme Court has held that the relevant section of chapter 119 does not authorize any activity. The applicability of section 605 to the interception of international telegrams for foreign intelligence purposes is therefore unclear. It would appear that where such telegrams are intercepted for other than foreign intelligence purposes (e.g., the watch list activity), section 605 would be violated.

3. The Controlling National Security Council Intelligence Directive

Since 1958, this executive directive has authorized NSA to conduct communications intelligence activities. 119 These have been defined as excluding "the intercept and processing of unencrypted written communications." It would appear that if copies of international telegrams are "written communications," NSA has exceeded its authority under the executive's own internal directives.

B. The Committee's Investigation

The SHAMROCK operation was alluded to in documents furnished to the Committee by the Rockefeller Commission in May 1975. They indicated that CIA had provided "cover" for an NSA operation in New York where international telegrams had been copied.

In early June 1975, an oral inquiry regarding the operation was made to NSA officials, but no confirmation of the project was forthcoming. In July, the Committee sent written interrogatories to NSA, and was told that this subject was so sensitive that it would be disclosed only to Senators Church and Tower. No such briefing was immediately arranged, however.

In July and August, news stories were published which appeared to reveal small parts of the SHAMROCK operation.

The Committee continued to press the matter with NSA, and in early September the agency gave the Committee its first detailed information. This briefing was followed by interviews with present and former NSA employees who had been responsible for the program and by examinations of documents at NSA and the Department of Defense. NSA assured the Committee at the time that it had examined all NSA documents which pertained to SHAMROCK. On September 23, the full Committee was briefed by an NSA official in executive session. Following this briefing, the Committee interviewed officials in the telegraph companies which had participated in the SHAMROCK program.

On the basis of this investigation, the Committee prepared a report which it submitted to NSA for review. NSA had no specific comments regarding the accuracy of the report, but expressed its general objection to public disclosure of the operation on the grounds that the report was based on classified information.

On November 6, 1975, in a public session of the Committee, Chairman Frank Church read the report on SHAMROCK into the record. Due to the refusal of the executive branch of provide witnesses in public session, no other public record was made.

At this point, the Committee's active investigation ceased. The Committee presumed that it had exhausted all sources of information about SHAMROCK.

On March 25, 1976 as the Committee was about to send this report to press, it was informed by the Department of Defense that NSA had "discovered" a file containing various documents and memoranda about SHAMROCK. An NSA official explained that the file had been held by a lower-level employee at NSA until around March 1, 1976, when he brought it to the attention of his superiors. Since this occurred several months after the Committee's public report, and, in the opinion of NSA, did not substantially alter the Committee's findings, it was not immediately reported to the Committee.

After examining the documents, the Committee decided that the final NSA report should incorporate this new information. Although it does not alter the basic findings reported in November 1975, it does change some of the details.

C. The Origins of SHAMROCK

During World War II, under the wartime censorship laws, all international message traffic was made available to military censors. Copies of pertinent foreign traffic were turned over to military intelligence. With the cessation of the War in 1945, this practice was to end.

In August 1945, the Army sought to continue that part of the wartime arrangement which had allowed military intelligence access to certain foreign traffic. At that time, most of this traffic was still conveyed via the facilities of three carriers.

On August 18, 1945, two representatives of the Army Signal Security Agency were sent to New York

> to make the necessary contacts with the heads of the Commercial Communications Companies in New York, secure their approval of the interception of all Governmental traffic entering the United States, leaving the United States, or transiting the United States, and make the necessary arrangements for this photographic intercept work.

They first approached an official at ITT, who "very definitely and finally refused" to agree to any of the Army proposals. The Army representatives then approached a vice president of Western Union Telegraph Company, who agreed to cooperate unless the Attorney General of the United States ruled that such intercepts were illegal.

Having succeeded with Western Union, the Army representatives returned to ITT on August 21, 1945, and suggested to an ITT vice president that "his company would not desire to be the only non-cooperative company on this project." The vice president decided to reconsider and broached the matter the same day with the president of the company. The ITT president agreed to cooperate with the Army, provided that the Attorney General decided that the program was not illegal.

These Army representatives also met with the president of RCA on August 21, 1945. The RCA president indicated his willingness to cooperate, but withheld final approval until he, too, had heard from the Attorney General.

After their trip, the Army representatives reported to their superiors that the companies were worried about the illegality of their participation in the program:

> Two very evident fears existed in the minds of the heads of each of these communications companies. One was the fear of the illegality of the procedure according to present FCC regulations. In spite of the fact that favorable opinions have been received from the Judge Advocate General of the Navy and the Judge Advocate General of the Army, it was feared that these opinions would not hold in civil court and, as a consequence, the companies would not be protected. If a favorable opinion is handed down by the Attorney General, this fear will be completely allayed, and cooperation may be expected for the complete intercept coverage of this material. The second fear uppermost in the minds of these executives is the fear of the ACA which is the communications union. This union has reported on many occasions minor infractions of FCC regulations and it is feared that a major infraction, such as the proposed intercept coverage, if disclosed by the Union, might cause severe repercussions.

Later memoranda by another Army representative who was present indicate that the companies had consulted their corporate attorneys during these three days of discussions, and that their attorneys uniformly advised against participation in the proposed intercept program. The company executives were apparently willing to ignore this advice if they received assurances from the Attorney General that he would protect them from any consequences.

The new documentary evidence made available to the Committee did not reveal that the Attorney General at that time, Tom C. Clark, actually made the assurances that the companies desired. It is clear, however, that the program began shortly after the August meetings: ITT and Western Union began their participation by September 1, and RCA by October 9, 1945.

In a letter from the Army Signals Security Agency to the Army Chief of Staff on March 19, 1946, the writer indicates that SHAMROCK was well underway, but that concerns about its legality had not vanished:

> It can be stated that both [Western Union and RCA] have placed themselves in precarious positions since the legality of such operations has not been established and has necessitated the utmost secrecy on their part in making these arrangements. Through their efforts, only two or three individuals in the respective companies are aware of the operation.

April 26, 1976, while this report was being printed, DOD informed the Committee that nine additional documents relating to SHAMROCK had been found in the National Archives. The documents revealed that the Office of Secretary of Defense James Forrestal attempted unsuccessfully in June 1948 to have Congress pass an amendment to relax the disclosure restrictions of Section 605 of the Federal Communications Act of 1934. Agencies designated by the President would have been allowed to obtain the radio and wire communications of foreign governments. If the amendment had passed, the SHAMROCK program, as it was originally conceived, would have been authorized by law.

The proposed amendment sought to allay concerns of the companies on the legality of their participation in SHAMROCK. The companies were demanding assurances in 1947 not only from the Secretary of Defense and the Attorney General, but also from the President that their participation was essential to the national interest and that they would not be subject to prosecution in the Federal Courts. Secretary Forrestal, who stated he was speaking for the President, gave ITT and RCA representatives these assurances at a December 16, 1947, meeting in Washington, D.C. 139 Forrestal warned, however, that the assurances he was making could not bind his successors in office.

Representatives of Western Union were not present at this meeting. Documents made available to the Committee indicate that the President and Operating Vice President of Western Union were briefed in January 1948 on the earlier meeting with RCA and ITT.

In early June 1948, the Chairmen of the Senate and House Judiciary Committees were informed of the Government's need for a relaxation of Section 605 and of its position with the telegraph companies. The delicacy of the problem and the top secret nature of the information were made clear to these two Chairmen. The amendment was considered in an executive session of the Senate Judiciary Committee on June 16, 1948, and approved. Since support for the bill was not unanimous, however, the Committee voted to leave it to the Chairman's discretion whether or not to release the bill to the Senate floor. The representative of the Secretary of Defense then told the Senate Judiciary Chairman that "we did not desire an airing of the whole matter on the Floor of the Senate at this late date in the session." The bill apparently was not reported out.

A Defense Department official expressed the view that he thought a great deal had already been accomplished and that the administration had sufficient ammunition to be able to effect a continuation of the present practices with the companies. Apparently no other statutory attempts were made to authorize the companies' participation in SHAMROCK.

The companies sought renewed assurances from Forrestal's successor, Louis Johnson, in 1949. Johnson told them that the President and Attorney General had been consulted and had given their approval. To the knowledge of those interviewed by the Committee, this was the last instance in which the companies such assurances from the Department of Defense.

Dr. Louis Tordella, who was NSA Deputy Director from 1958 until 1974 and the NSA official with chief administrative responsibility for SHAMROCK, testified that to the best of his knowledge, no President since Truman knew of the program. He "was not sure" whether any Attorney General since Tom Clark had been informed of it, or if succeeding Secretaries of Defense were aware of it. Tordella stated he briefed former Secretary of Defense Schlesinger about the SHAMROCK operation in the summer of 1973.

The Army Signals Security Agency controlled the collection program until 1949, when the Armed Forces Security Agency was formed. Responsibility for the program passed from AFSA to the National Security Agency when it was created in 1952.

D. The Participation of the Companies

None of the telegraph companies could find any record of an agreement with NSA or its predecessors wherein the companies would provide copies of telegrams to the Government, or which reflected anything about arrangements with NSA. No one interviewed by the Committee had any recollection or knowledge that the Government had given the companies specific assurances to ensure their cooperation in 1945, 1947, 1949, or at any time thereafter.

Apparently only a few people in each company—apart from those who physically turned over the materials—had any knowledge of the NSA arrangement. These were primarily mid-level executives charged with the operational aspects of the companies' business. All assumed that the arrangement was valid when it was made and thus continued it. No witness from the telegraph companies recalled that there had ever been a review of the arrangements at the executive levels of their respective companies.

Furthermore, none of the participating companies was apparently aware that information other than foreign traffic was extracted from the messages they were providing. Yet no official at any of the three companies could recall his company asking NSA what it was doing with the information it was furnished and, specifically, whether NSA was reading the telegrams of the companies' American customers.

Finally, both the telegraph companies and NSA deny that the companies ever received anything for their cooperation in SHAMROCK, whether in the form of compensation or favoritism from the Government. All claim they were motivated by purely patriotic considerations.

If there were similarities as to their involvement in SHAMROCK, the participation of each company varied in practice.

1. RCA Global According to a memorandum prepared by Army representatives, RCA (the parent company of RCA Global) agreed in August 1945 to allow Army personnel, who were to be dressed in civilian clothes, to photograph foreign traffic passing over its facilities in New York, Washington, and San Francisco. The memorandum further provided that "only the desired traffic will be filmed."

The company official at RCA Global who was charged with implementing the SHAMROCK program testified that several alternatives were discussed with Army representatives. He stated that the Army had first proposed tapping into the company's overseas lines, but the official rejected this idea as unfeasible. The Army representatives then proposed that company employees sort out pertinent traffic and turn it over to them; the official rejected this because he did not want company employees involved. The RCA official finally agreed to provide paper tapes of all international message traffic. It was understood that these messages would be sorted manually by persons from the Army Signals Security Agency on the company's premises, and that only certain foreign traffic would be selected. There was never a written agreement to this effect, however, according to the former official.

In New York, Army representatives were given office space in the area where the paper tapes of RCA Global's international message traffic were sorted manually for foreign traffic. Messages of interest were transmitted over teletype machines located in that office sSpace.

In Washington and San Francisco, Army agents were permitted to pick up copies of foreign messages, which they took to another office for microfilming. By 1950, a Recordak (microfilm) machine was placed in the New York office and was used to film messages of intelligence interest.

This arrangement continued without substantial disruption until 1963, when RCA Global began to store its message traffic on magnetic tapes. NSA made arrangements to obtain copies of these tapes from the RCA Global facilities in New York—they were taken "on loan," copied, and returned, the same day if possible. Gradually, magnetic tapes began to supercede paper tapes and microfilm as a means of storing messages. By 1966, the New York office was turning over only magnetic tapes to NSA. The offices in Washington and San Francisco, however, continued to furnish copies of international message traffic for microfilming by NSA. RCA Global employees in Washington, D.C. were under the impression they were providing information only to the FBI.

2. ITT World Communications

In August 1945, ITT agreed to allow the Army access to all incoming, outgoing, and transiting messages passing over the facilities of its subsidaries involved in international communications. It was agreed that "all traffic will be recorded on microfilm, that all Governmental traffic will be recorded on a second microfilm in addition to the original one, that these films will be developed by the SSA [Signals Security Agency], and the complete traffic will be returned to ITT."

It is not clear whether these arrangements, agreed to at the outset, were actually implemented in the manner described. The ITT official with the earliest recollections of the program could recall only that by the early 1950s, ITT World Communications was providing NSA representatives with copies of the company's international message traffic, which NSA then sorted and microfilmed.

When ITT World Communications began to use paper tapes to transmit its messages, these were turned over to NSA as well. It is not clear whether these tapes were transmitted from the premises of ITT World Communications to another location (as with RCA Global) or whether they were simply transported to NSA for sorting.

When ITT World Communications began to use magnetic tapes to store its incoming and outgoing messages—the best recollection of this change places it around 1965 -- the magnetic tapes were turned over to NSA for duplication. They were returned to the company on the same day. By 1968, ITT World Communications was turning over only its magnetic tapes to NSA.

The Washington and San Francisco offices of ITT World Communications participated in a similar fashion. In Washington, however, company officials believed that they were providing the telegrams to the FBI, rather than NSA. 166 It is clear from the information made available to the Committee that the Washington messages were sent to NSA.

3. Western Union International

At the August 1945 meeting between Army representatives and the Western Union Telegraph Company (the parent company of Western Union International), the company stated that it

> desired that Western Union personnel operate the [microfilm] camera and do all the actual handling of the messages. It was agreed that [the Army Signal Security Agency] would furnish the necessary cameras and film for the complete intercept coverage of Western Union traffic outlets. The film, after exposure, will be delivered [to the office of a company vice-president], at which place an officer from the Signal Security Agency, in civilian clothes, will pick it up.

The company agreed to implement this arrangement at its New York, San Francisco, Washington, and San Antonio facilities.

This arrangement was apparently implemented as originally agreed. In New York, at least, company employees segregated such messages and processed them through a microfilm machine on the transmission room floor. At approximately 4:00 each morning, an NSA courier would come to the floor to pick up the microfilm cartridge. In San Antonio, an Army signal officer from Ft. Sam Houston was tasked with picking up the microfilm each day.

It appears that Western Union turned over to NSA only its telegraph traffic to one foreign country. Approached in 1959 by persons who identified themselves as being from Ft. Holabird, Maryland (Army intelligence), Western Union agreed to allow them to duplicate the traffic going to a particular country. In 1970, the company also began to provide copies of messages going to a particular city within that country which were not being duplicated as part of the previous arrangement. These messages were apparently sorted by NSA personnel in space provided by Western Union at its New York offices.

Western Union International (which was formed in 1963) continued to microfilm certain foreign traffic for NSA until about 1965, when a company executive discovered the existence of the microfilm machine on the transmission room floor. After ascertaining its purpose, he demanded that NSA renew its request to have this information in writing. He recalled that instead of submitting such a request, NSA simply had the machine removed. This recollection, however, was not borne out by documents furnished by NSA. The documents showed that on February 2, 1968, a company vice president (not the one referred to above) had discovered the existence of NSA's Recordak (microfilm) machine in the Western Union transmission room. The machine was reported to the company president, who directed his employees to find out to whom the machine belonged and what the basis for the arrangement was. The NSA courier, when asked these questions by a Western Union International official on February 9, 1968, replied that he was from the Department of Defense and did not know what the basis for the arrangement was or what was being done with the microfilm being furnished. Yet the documents do not reflect whether the Recordak machine was removed, either in 1965 or in 1968.

It is clear that NSA continued to receive duplicates of all messages to the foreign country referred to above until 1972; when again as a result of "discovery" by company officials, this procedure was halted. Although the original request for this intercept procedure had been made by "Holabird people" (Army intelligence), when the company attempted to contact someone regarding its termination, it was ultimately referred to NSA.

Finally, Western Union International, unlike its competitors, never utilized magnetic tapes to store its message traffic. Accordingly, none was ever provided NSA.

In effect, Western Union International's participation in SHAMROCK ended by 1972. 179

E. NSA's Participation

1. Origins and Early Development

From 1952 (when NSA first inherited the SHAMROCK sources) until 1963, microfilm and paper tapes originating with the sources were brought to NSA's headquarters at Ft. Meade, Maryland several times a week. As noted above, some of these had undergone initial screening, either by NSA operatives or company employees. Even with this preliminary screening, however, the volume of messages which reached NSA daily was apparently quite large.

Several witnesses have told the Committee that during this period the sheer volume of traffic would have likely prohibited the selection of messages on the basis of content. Messages which were selected out were passed on to NSA analysts, who screened them further.

2. The Switch to Magnetic Tape

The character of the SHAMROCK operation changed markedly with the use of magnetic tape. RCA Global was the first company to begin using such tape in the early 1960s. NSA was notified of the changeover in early 1963 and, by 1964, was able to sort electronically the information provided by RCA Global against its selection criteria. This is significant because it meant that the telegrams of citizens whose names were on NSA's "watch list" could be selected for processing by NSA analysts.

From 1964 until 1966, magnetic tapes from RCA Global were brought to Ft. Meade daily and returned to New York the same day. By 1965, ITT World Communications had also begun its changeover to magnetic tapes and was beginning to provide traffic in this form to NSA messengers.

3. CIA Cover Support

To alleviate the administrative burden entailed by these daily roundtrips, NSA in 1966 sought to find a place in New York City where the tapes could be duplicated. NSA Deputy Director Tordella requested that the CIA provide "safe" space where this operation could be conducted. The CIA agreed to rent office space in lower Manhattan, under the guise of a television tape processing company, where the tape duplication process could be carried out. CIA designated this project "LPMEDLEY."

The cover support began in November 1966 and lasted until August 1973, when CIA terminated its part of the program. Tordella was told that the CIA General Counsel was "concerned about any kind of operation in which the CIA was engaged in the continental United States. Regardless of whether CIA was doing anything so small as renting an office, he said 'get out of it.'" NSA subsequently moved its duplicating operation to new office space in Manhattan, where it remained until SHAMROCK was terminated in 1975.

4. Control of the Program

Numerous NSA employees were aware of SHAMROCK, but responsibility for its conduct rested only with the Director, Deputy Director, and one lower-level managerial employee. Throughout the program's existence, only two individuals occupied this lower-level managerial position: the first between 1952-1970; the other from 1970-1975.

The manager was instructed to report directly to the Deputy Director of NSA regarding any problems with the companies. As a routine matter, this individual was in charge of the NSA couriers who traveled between New York and Ft. Meade; he usually received information regarding the SHAMROCK operation from these couriers rather than from the companies. The individual who held this position between 1952-1970 told the Committee that he met with company officials on only two occasions during this time, and both meetings were perfunctory.

Both of the NSA employees who acted as liaison with the companies confirmed to the Committee that the companies had never asked what NSA was extracting from the materials provided, and that NSA had never volunteered this information. Neither of the lower-level employees knew what NSA did with the materials; they stated that the messengers who worked under them also had no knowledge of what was sorted from the telegrams. It seems clear, therefore, that the companies never learned that NSA sorted anything except foreign traffic from the telegrams that the companies provided NSA.

Since none of the companies (treating them as separate from their parent corporations) engage in domestic communications, they could not have provided NSA with domestic traffic. The Committee has no evidence to show that NSA has ever received domestic telegrams from any source.

5. Consideration of SHAMROCK in Connection with the Huston Plan

Former NSA Deputy Director Tordella told the Committee that in 1970, in connection with the Huston plan, the principals involved in this project — Helms of CIA, Sullivan of the FBI Bennett of DIA, and Gayler of NSA — discussed the feasibility of the FBI's taking over the SHAMROCK program in order to obtain more information on internal unrest. The FBI did not want the responsibility, according to Tordella, and NSA did not want to jeopardize its own working relationship with the companies. The idea was therefore dropped.

F. Termination of SHAMROCK

Operation SHAMROCK terminated on May 15, 1975, by order of Secretary of Defense James Schlesinger. NSA claims that the program was terminated because (1) it was no longer a valuable source of foreign intelligence, and (2) the risk of its exposure had increased.

IV. NSA Personnel Security And Related Matters

The Committee investigated the NSA Office of Security to examine personnel security activities which may have been conducted in an overzealous and, possibly, unlawful manner. These activities are not part of NSA's two primary missions — the collection of signals intelligence and the protection of United States communications. Although this subject area is more narrow than others investigated by the Committee, there are similiarities involving the protection of both the rights of citizens and the national security.

A. Background

The NSA Office of Security is responsible for safeguarding the security of NSA facilities, operations, and personnel, and for protecting classified materials from unauthorized disclosure. This Office also administers NSA's security clearance program and investigates suspected breaches of security by NSA employees. The CIA's Office of Security performs the same functions for that Agency.

Personnel in the NSA Office of Security are quick to point out that substantial intangible differences exist between the role of the CIA and NSA Offices of Security. In recent years, the NSA Office has not enjoyed the same high status within NSA that the CIA Office has had within its own organization. At least two factors appear to contribute to this difference. First, the work of an Office of Security investigator bears no similarity to that performed by the professionals conducting signals intelligence and communications security activities, which comprise the heart of NSA. Second, during the 1950s and 1960s, personnel security programs at NSA suffered some widely publicized failures, resulting in both prosecutions for espionage and actual defections to the Soviet Union by NSA employees.

These factors have impelled the Office in conflicting directions. On the one hand, its personnel are not expected, and ordinarily do not tend to take actions on their own initiative that would exceed the normal bounds of keeping the Agency reasonably secure. On the other hand, failures in personnel security have occasionally generated intense public pressure (especially from the House Committee on Un-American Activities) to take extraordinary measures to protect that security.

A fair analysis of the incidents listed below, all of which are of dubious legality or propriety, requires an awareness of these dynamics. Like other Government officials, personnel in the Office of Security must be held responsible for their actions. Yet, like most people in the United States, they have been greatly sensitized by the Watergate scandal and the recent congressional investigations of the intelligence community to the need to protect civil liberties against dangerous encroachments in the name of "national security." In this section we disclose certain aberrations from that sensitivity, in the confidence that this disclosure will encourage its growth.

B. Questionable Activities

1. NSA Office of Security: Access to Files on American Citizens

From NSA's inception in 1952 until October 1974, a unit of the Agency outside the Office of Security maintained a large number of files on American citizens. At the time of the destruction of these records, approximately 75,000 United States citizens were included. Unlike CIA's Operations CHAOS, these files were not created for the purpose of monitoring the activities of Americans, but for carrying out NSA's legitimate foreign intelligence mission.

Many circumstances could contribute to the creation of such a file, perhaps the most frequent being the mere mention of an American citizen's name in a communication intercepted by NSA. The files also included reports from other intelligence agencies, such as the CIA and military intelligence units, which mentioned the name of the citizen and were routinely forwarded to NSA. Materials from open sources, such as newspapers, were also in the files.

Until the files were destroyed, the Office of Security was often supplied with information from them when it was conducting background investigations on applicants for employment at NSA or when other persons were being considered for clearances to receive intelligence gathered by NSA. In effect, this meant that the Office of Security was a beneficiary of the vast communications intelligence apparatus of the entire Agency, a resource which is on an entirely different order of sophistication than the wiretapping capability of any police or security force in the nation.

(a) CIA Access to NSA Files. — The NSA files contained entries on many prominent Americans in business, the performing arts, and politics, including members of Congress. Although the Committee has no reason to believe that any person at NSA used them improperly, it has learned that for at least 13 years, one or more employees of the CIA worked full-time in these files, retrieving information for the CIA without any supervision from NSA. One of these CIA employees recalled, with varying degrees of certainty, checking in these files for the names of various well-known civil rights, antiwar, and political leaders.

It is likely, although the Committee is not in a position to so state, that some of the information obtained from NSA found its way into Operation CHAOS.

NSA did not develop these files for any sinister reason. They were useful in many ways to conducting successfully NSA's legitimate communications intelligence functions. Nevertheless, the fact that CIA personnel used the files without NSA supervision to gather information on American citizens — during a period when the CIA was engaged in unlawful domestic activities aimed against many of those same citizens — illustrates the danger of maintaining such files. The massive centralization of this information creates a temptation to use it for improper purposes, threatens to "chill" the exercise of First Amendment rights, and is inimical to the privacy of citizens.

(b) Destruction of Files. — The Committee was informed by NSA that the files on American citizens were destroyed in 1974. At that time, a centralized information storage system for foreign names was set up in the intelligence community. This reorganization provided the impetus for a re-evaluation of the files on American citizens, and a consensus was reached that their usefulness did not justify the costs in time, money, and storage space.

2. Failure to Purge "Suitability Files"

Like other Federal agencies, NSA maintains "suitability files" conearning its employees. These files, which are held by the Office of Civilian Personnel, constitute an interface between that Office and the Office of Security. The latter provides information to these files and has access to them. These files contain highly personal information which might show the kind of unreliability or vulnerability of an employee which could lead to compromises of classified information. According to NSA, the purpose of these files is to aid the Agency in providing counseling and other forms of assistance to individuals with personal problems, not to threaten or damage such employees. The Committee has no reason to believe that the information in these files has been misused. During its investigation, the Committee reviewed 50 of these files, selected on a random basis, with the names of all individuals deleted.

Since the information stored in these files is so personal, it seems reasonable to expect that its retention would be kept to the minimum necessary for the purposes of these files. Unfortunately, this policy does not seem to have been observed in the past. Much of the information is either many years old or simply irrelevant to the suitability of an individual for employment.

If a systematic effort had been made periodically to review these files and purge them of inappropriate or dated information. such notations would probably have been eliminated long ago. The establishment of such a system has now been undertaken by NSA. Although persons in sensitive positions at agencies such as NSA may be expected to sacrifice some degree of privacy to the need to protect national security, that sacrifice must be kept within reasonable bounds.

A related question is the access of employees to their own files. NSA regulations provide: "In no instance will employees be given access to their own Suitability File." Nevertheless, with the recent implementation of the Privacy Act, employees may ask for, and be granted, access to their files. Since the Committee found that these files sometimes contain unsolicited and unsubstantiated statements from neighbors, spouses, and others, the Privacy Act should result in much of this information being purged.

3. Files on Nonaffiliates of NSA Who Publish Writings Concerning the Agency

The Office of Security maintained files on two individuals who have published materials describing the work of the National Security Agency. In one case, the relevant writings were published in the late 1960s; in the other case, much more recently.

By the time of the second case, NSA had gained some experience in dealing with publicity. The file on this person consisted mainly of checks with other Federal agencies to determine what information they possessed concerning the author, and the results of various internal NSA inquiries as to where the author might have obtained information. Nevertheless, the Office of Security did submit the author's name for inclusion on the NSA watch list. There is no evidence that this submission resulted in the dissemination of any international messages sent or received by the author.

In the earlier case, the Agency appears to have overreacted. NSA had learned of the author's forthcoming publication and spent innumerable hours attempting to find a strategy to prevent its release, or at least lessen its impact. These discussions extended to the highest levels of the Agency, including the Director, and resulted in the matter being brought to the attention of the United States Intelligence Board.

In the course of these discussions, possible measures to be taken against the author were considered with varying degrees of seriousness. The Director suggested planting disparaging reviews of the author's work in the press, and such a review was actually drafted. Also discussed were: purchasing the copyright of the writing; hiring the author into the Government so that certain criminal statutes would apply if the work were published; undertaking "clandestine service applications" against the author, which apparently meant anything from physical surveillance to surreptitious entry; and more explicit consideration of conducting a surreptitious entry at the home of the author. To the credit of those involved, none of these measures were carried out.

Other steps, however, were taken. The author's name was placed on the NSA watch list and various approaches were made to his publisher. The publisher submitted a manuscript of the work to the Department of Defense, apparently without the author's permission. Despite requests from NSA to halt publication or to make extensive deletions, publication took place with only minor changes, to which the author had agreed.

The most remarkable aspect of this entire episode is that the conclusion reached as a result of NSA's review of this manuscript was that it had been written almost entirely on the basis of materials already in the public domain. It is therefore accurate to describe the measures considered by NSA and USIB as an "overreaction."

4. Other Files Maintained by the Office of Security

Although the Office of Security does not maintain files today on persons not affiliated with the Agency, it has done so in the past. The Agency describes these files in the following terms:

> The maintenance of these files began in the late 1950s. In early 1974, approximately 2800 files concerning nonaffiliated organizations and personnel were destroyed in accordance with DOD Directive 5200.27. The files consisted of reports from the FBI and other intelligence, security and federal agencies as well as state and municipal agencies who maintained such records. Information was also obtained from the congressional records of the House Committee on Un-American Activities, and open source, commercial publications. These files were retained primarily as a reference source for security education purposes, as an aid to our personnel security process and to provide assessment regarding the vulnerability of this Agency to foreign intelligence activities and extremists activities which posed a threat to the NSA mission, functions and property.
>
> Of the 2800 files which were accumulated, the great majority concerned foreign controlled and subversive organizations cited by the Attorney General of the United States. These organizations were those advocating

the overthrow of the U.S. Government, and the violent disruption of the orderly process of government, etc. The small percentage of files maintained on individuals concerned suspected espionage agents, extremists, anarchists, etc. These persons were both U.S. and foreign citizens.

DOD Directive 5200.27 was first issued in March 1971, and it greatly restricted the discretion of Department of Defense units to retain such files. The Directive stated, however, that it was "not applicable to the acquisition of foreign intelligence information or to activities involved in ensuring communications security." 203 NSA's General Counsel interpreted this language as exempting NSA from the coverage of the Directive, and was supported in this opinion by a Deputy General Counsel in the Department of Defense. Only in 1973 was NSA informed by the Defense Investigative Review Council (DIRC) that some of its activities were subject to the Directive. Once this was established, NSA took steps to comply, which included destruction of of the 2800 files.

In April 1975, the DIRC conducted an unannounced inspection of the NSA Office of Security to ascertain its compliance with DOD Directive 5200.27. Although substantial compliance was found, the DIRC did note that the Office still maintained three files with some questionable entries. These files concerned "threats" to NSA functions and property; characterizations of organizations; and unsolicited inulries and "cranks." Since the time of the DIRC report, NSA has drastically reduced the amount of materials in these files.

The Committee did obtain from NSA copies of the files as they existed at the time of the DIRC inspection. As the DIRC report noted, the first two of these files contained some questionable entries. At the time of the inspection, the "threat" file still contained extensive information on a peaceful demonstration of less than 40 persons near NSA headquarters in 1974. Similarly, the "characterizations" file reflects the fact that in the past the Office of Security would prepare a characterization of almost any organization that an NSA employee wanted information about before joining it or otherwise becoming involved. The characterizations were prepared largely on the basis of NSA's own files and from information supplied by other agencies.

It appears that DOD Directive 5200.27 and its enforcement through the DIRC mechanism are functioning effectively at this time to prevent the excessive accumulation of files on American citizens.

5. Office of Security Participation in Watch List Activity.

In his testimony before the Committee, NSA Director, General Lew Allen, Jr., detailed the efforts made by the Agency to intercept communications to and from certain American citizens from the late 1960s until 1973. Not all of the names "watch listed" under this program were submitted to NSA from the outside. The Office of Security also submitted approximately 13 names for monitoring.

Of these names, 11 had some present or past affiliation with NSA. Each of these 11 individuals had either defected to the Soviet Union, been convicted of espionage, were suspected of some other connection to an unfriendly power, or had made threats against NSA or its Director. Two of the names were of American citizens not affiliated with NSA. As described earlier, these two persons had published writings in this country about the Agency's activities, causing the Office of Security concern about the possible compromise of classified information.

The Government does have a continuing legitimate interest in the communications of defectors and suspected enemy agents, and should be permitted to intercept such communications if the proper procedures (e.g., a warrant or approval of the Attorney General) are established. The danger in allowing the Office of Security to place names on a watch list is that the decision as to whether the activities of a particular individual are sufficiently suspicious to justify intrusion into the privacy of his communications is left in the hands of an interested party: the Office of Security itself. The inclusion of the names of two persons not affiliated with the Agency—neither of whom was seriously suspected of any intent to aid a foreign power and each of whom was directly exercising First Amendment freedoms—illustrates the tendency of limited infringements of privacy to be extended to an ever-widening scope. Only the involvement of a neutral third party can help safeguard against such extensions.

6. Conventional Electronic Surveillance and Surreptitious Entries

For many years, the Office of Security has scrupulously avoided the use of conventional electronic surveillance off NSA premises. It has neither tapped any telephones nor engaged in any bugging of rooms outside the Agency since 1958.

In the late 1950s, four instances of electronic surveillance without a court order did take place. Three of these incidents transpired at the residences of present or former NSA employees. The fourth occurred in a New York City hotel room occupied by one of those same persons. The subjects of surveillance ranged from persons convicted of espionage activities to persons friendly with diplomatic personnel of unfriendly foreign powers and/or homosexuals. The duration of the coverage varied from a few days to three months.

The technology of the bugging devices used by the Office of Security in the late 1950s was such that they could only be installed by trespassory means. Each of the above instances thus involved a surreptitious entry at the place being bugged. Moreover, the devices were battery operated; in the case of a surveillance lasting three months, periodic re-entries were necessary to charge the batteries powering the device.

In addition, the Office of Security conducted four surreptitious entries in the early 1960s which were unrelated to electronic surveillance and which did not involve warrants. The entries involved two defectors to the Soviet Union (Martin and Mitchell), an employee suspected of taking classified documents out of NSA, and an employee who had contact with an embassy of an unfriendly foreign power.

With the passage of many years since these relatively isolated incidents, it is difficult to ascertain the levels at which they were approved. Both past and present Directors of Security at NSA have stated that they would not have taken place without the approval of the person holding that position, and that at the time of these incidents the Director of Security enjoyed such a close working relationship with the Director of NSA that the surveillance would not likely have occurred without the Director's knowledge.

7. "External Collection Program"

In 1963, after a review of the Office of Security's counterintelligence program by the Office and the Director of NSA, several steps were taken to strengthen the program. Among these was the establishment in October 1963 of an "External Collection Program." It appears that this "program" was, from its beginning, highly informal. Office of Security personnel had only vague and conflicting recollections as to what it had consisted of or how long it had lasted.

Most did recall that the program included brief periodic visits to bars, restaurants, and other establishments in the vicinity of NSA headquarters by Office of Security personnel. These visits were made to determine where NSA employees gathered after hours, whether they discussed classified information, and whether agents of hostile intelligence services also frequented these locations. The program also involved an effort to encourage persons working in these establishments to report any suspicious incident to NSA and to make the local police aware of the sensitivity of NSA's mission.

Since the revelant documents were destroyed in 1973, the Committee has been unable to establish whether the External Collection Program was used to gather information on persons other than NSA employees and foreign agents. The Office of Security, in fact, soon discovered that it lacked the personnel to carry on such a program, and it died quietly "in approximately 1966-1967."